eurostat
Statistical books

European business

Facts and figures

CARDIFF
CAERDYDD

2007 edition

eurostat

EUROPEAN COMMISSION

Europe Direct is a service to help you find answers to your questions about the European Union

Freephone number (*):

00 800 6 7 8 9 10 11

(*) Certain mobile telephone operators do not allow access to 00 800 numbers or these calls may be billed.

More information on the European Union is available on the Internet (http://europa.eu).

Luxembourg: Office for Official Publications of the European Communities, 2007

ISBN 978-92-79-07024-2
ISSN 1830-8147
Cat. No. KS-BW-07-001-EN-C

Theme: Industry, trade and services
Collection: Statistical books

EUROSTAT

L-2920 Luxembourg — Tel. (352) 43 01-1 — website http://ec.europa.eu/eurostat

Eurostat is the Statistical Office of the European Communities. Its mission is to provide the European Union with high-quality statistical information. For that purpose, it gathers and analyses figures from the national statistical offices across Europe and provides comparable and harmonised data for the European Union to use in the definition, implementation and analysis of Community policies. Its statistical products and services are also of great value to Europe's business community, professional organisations, academics, librarians, NGOs, the media and citizens.

Eurostat's publications programme consists of several collections:
• **News releases** provide recent information on the Euro-Indicators and on social, economic, regional, agricultural or environmental topics.
• **Statistical books** are larger A4 publications with statistical data and analysis.
• **Pocketbooks** are free of charge publications aiming to give users a set of basic figures on a specific topic.
• **Statistics in focus** provides updated summaries of the main results of surveys, studies and statistical analysis.
• **Data in focus** present the most recent statistics with methodological notes.
• **Methodologies and working papers** are technical publications for statistical experts working in a particular field.
Eurostat publications can be ordered via the EU Bookshop at http://bookshop.europa.eu.

All publications are also downloadable free of charge in PDF format from the Eurostat website http://ec.europa.eu/eurostat. Furthermore, Eurostat's databases are freely available there, as are tables with the most frequently used and demanded short- and long-term indicators.

Eurostat has set up with the members of the 'European statistical system' (ESS) a network of user support centres which exist in nearly all Member States as well as in some EFTA countries. Their mission is to provide help and guidance to Internet users of European statistical data. Contact details for this support network can be found on Eurostat Internet site.

European business - Facts and figures

2007 edition

This publication has been produced by Eurostat unit G1 responsible for structural business statistics. The opinions expressed are those of the individual authors alone and do not necessarily reflect the position of the European Commission.

Editor and project co-ordinator	Mr Ulf Johansson
	Eurostat, the Statistical Office of the European Communities
	Unit G1 Structural business statistics
	Bâtiment Joseph Bech
	Rue Alphonse Weicker 5
	L-2721, Luxembourg
Production	Data processing, statistical analysis, design and desktop publishing
	INFORMA sarl
	Giovanni Albertone, Simon Allen, Edward Cook, Séverine Gautron, Andrew Redpath
Data extracted	The majority of data were extracted in May 2007, complemented by an extraction in June and July for certain specific data sources.
Contact details	
For individuals:	Eurostat provides a support network at a national and European level. More information including a full list of support centres may be obtained at http://epp.eurostat.ec.europa.eu/pls/portal/url/page/PGP_S3WD/PGE_S3WD_services.
For journalists:	Eurostat media support
	Tel: (352) 4301 33408
	Fax: (352) 4301 35349
	eurostat-mediasupport@ec.europa.eu
For more information	The European business 'dedicated section' on the Eurostat website provides access to a selection of publications, data and background information describing the European business economy. All the chapters of European business: facts and figures in PDF format and MS Excel files containing the data used in the tables and figures can be downloaded from here, free of charge. The European business dedicated section is located directly under the theme 'Industry, trade and services', which is available from the left frame of the Eurostat homepage, at http://ec.europa.eu/eurostat.

INTRODUCTION   1

OVERVIEW

1. Business economy overview   **5**
1.1   Macro-economic outlook   5
1.2   Structural profile of the business economy   10
1.3   Costs, productivity and profitability   19
1.4   Enterprise demography and size class analysis   25
1.5   Labour force characteristics   32
1.6   Evolution of production, employment and turnover   35
1.7   External trade   38
1.8   The business economies of Bulgaria and Romania   41

SECTORAL ANALYSIS OF MANUFACTURING ACTIVITIES (EXCLUDING FUEL PROCESSING AND RECYCLING)

2.   Food, beverages and tobacco   **47**
2.1   Meat   54
2.2   Fish   56
2.3   Dairy products   57
2.4   Bread, sugar, confectionery and other food products   59
2.5   Miscellaneous food products   62
2.6   Beverages   64
2.7   Tobacco   67

3.   Textiles, clothing, leather and footwear   **71**
3.1   Textiles   77
3.2   Clothing   80
3.3   Leather and footwear   83

4.   Wood and paper   **87**
4.1   Wood and wood products   93
4.2   Pulp, paper and paper products   95

5.   Chemicals, rubber and plastics   **99**
5.1   Basic industrial chemicals (including petrochemicals), pesticides and agrochemicals   106
5.2   Pharmaceuticals   109
5.3   Miscellaneous chemical products   111
5.4   Man-made fibres   114
5.5   Rubber   115
5.6   Plastics   118

6.   Other non-metallic mineral products   **123**
6.1   Glass   128
6.2   Ceramic and clay products   130
6.3   Cement and concrete   132
6.4   Stone and miscellaneous non-metallic mineral products   134

7.   Metals and metal products   **137**
7.1   First processing of ferrous metals   143
7.2   Basic precious and non-ferrous metals   145
7.3   Casting   147
7.4   Structural metal products   148
7.5   Boilers, metal containers and steam generators   150
7.6   Other metal processing   152
7.7   Miscellaneous fabricated metal products   153

Table of contents

8. Machinery and equipment — 157

8.1 Power machinery — 163
8.2 Industrial processing machinery — 165
8.3 Agricultural and forestry machinery — 168
8.4 Arms and ammunition — 170
8.5 Domestic appliances — 171

9. Electrical machinery and optical equipment — 175

9.1 Instrument engineering — 181
9.2 Computers and office equipment — 184
9.3 Electrical machinery and equipment — 187
9.4 Radio, television and communication equipment — 190

10. Transport equipment — 195

10.1 Motor vehicles, trailers and semi-trailers — 202
10.2 Aerospace equipment — 205
10.3 Ships and boats — 207
10.4 Railway equipment — 208
10.5 Miscellaneous transport equipment — 210

11. Furniture and other manufacturing activities — 213

11.1 Furniture — 218
11.2 Musical instruments, sports goods, toys and games, jewellery — 220

SECTORAL ANALYSIS OF MINING, ENERGY, WATER AND RECYCLING

12. Non-energy mining and quarrying — 223

13. Energy — 229

13.1 Mining and quarrying of energy producing materials — 236
13.2 Fuel processing — 239
13.3 Network supply of electricity, gas and heat — 240

14 Recycling and water supply — 247

14.1 Recycling — 251
14.2 Water supply — 253

SECTORAL ANALYSIS OF CONSTRUCTION

15. Construction — 257

15.1 Site preparation — 262
15.2 General construction — 263
15.3 Building installation activities — 265
15.4 Building completion activities — 266
15.5 Renting of construction equipment — 268

SECTORAL ANALYSIS OF NON-FINANCIAL SERVICES

16. Motor trades — 271

16.1 Motor vehicles and motorcycles distribution — 276
16.2 Retail sale of automotive fuel — 279

17.   Wholesale trade   **283**
   17.1   Wholesale on a fee or contract basis   289
   17.2   Agricultural wholesaling   291
   17.3   Wholesaling of consumer goods   292
   17.4   Wholesaling of intermediate goods   294
   17.5   Wholesaling of machinery and equipment   296
   17.6   Other wholesale trade   298

18.   Retail trade and repair   **301**
   18.1   Non-specialised in-store retailing   308
   18.2   Specialised in-store food retailing   310
   18.3   Specialised in-store new goods retailing other than food   312
   18.4   Second-hand goods retailing in stores   315
   18.5   Retail sales not in stores   315
   18.6   Repair of personal and household goods   317

19.   Hotels and restaurants   **319**
   19.1   Accommodation services   325
   19.2   Restaurants, bars and catering   328

20.   Transport services   **331**
   20.1   Rail transport   339
   20.2   Road and other land transport   340
   20.3   Water transport   342
   20.4   Air transport   344
   20.5   Pipelines   346
   20.6   Auxiliary transport activities   347
   20.7   Travel agencies   350

21.   Communications and media   **353**
   21.1   Postal and courier services   358
   21.2   Telecommunication services   361
   21.3   Publishing, printing and reproduction of recorded media   365

22.   Business services   **371**
   22.1   Computer services   379
   22.2   Legal, accounting and management services   381
   22.3   Architectural and engineering activities; technical testing and analysis   383
   22.4   Advertising and direct marketing   386
   22.5   Labour recruitment and temporary work services   387
   22.6   Other business services   389

23.   Real estate, renting and R&D   **393**
   23.1   Real estate services   398
   23.2   Renting and leasing   399
   23.3   Research and development   401

SECTORAL ANALYSIS OF FINANCIAL SERVICE ACTIVITIES

24.   Financial services   **405**
   24.1   Financial intermediation   408
   24.2   Insurance and pension funds   412
   24.3   Financial auxiliaries   416

BACKGROUND INFORMATION   **421**
   Notes on data sources   422
   Abbreviations   430

Introduction

OBJECTIVES, SCOPE AND STRUCTURE OF THE PUBLICATION

This publication gives a comprehensive picture of the structure, development and characteristics of European business and its different activities: from the manufacture of food, beverages and tobacco to real estate, renting and research and development services. It presents the latest available statistics from a wide selection of statistical sources describing for each activity: output and employment; country specialisation and regional distribution; gross operating and tangible investment expenditure, productivity and profitability; the importance of small and medium sized enterprises (SMEs); labour force characteristics; external trade etc.

The publication covers what is referred to as the business economy, which here is the sum of industry, construction and services (NACE Sections C to K). It does not cover agriculture, forestry and fishing, nor the public administration and largely non-market services such as education and health. Note that because of the lack of standard business statistics, financial services is kept separate from the other sectors, and comparisons are made throughout the publication against a benchmark called the non-financial business economy (as defined by NACE Sections C to I and K).

In this publication the business economy is divided into 23 main sectors. The first chapter provides a general overview of the EU-27's business economy, with comparisons made across the main sectors. In addition, some information of a cross-sectoral nature is presented, such as research and development, business demography, the importance of foreign controlled enterprises, etc.

The overview chapter is followed by 23 sectoral chapters, consisting of an overview of the activity in question, followed by a number of subchapters that analyse its component activities. The chapters and subchapters present a standard set of information complemented by sector specific information that highlights aspects of specific concern and distinguishing features. Each chapter concludes with a statistical annex presenting a selection of the most important indicators. The analyses focus on the EU-27, but available data for Norway are included in the statistical annex at the end of each chapter.

DATA SOURCES

The main part of the analysis contained within European business is derived from structural business statistics (SBS), including the core business statistics which are disseminated regularly, as well as information compiled on a multi-yearly basis and the latest results from development projects on topics of specific interest. EU-27 aggregates include estimates that are rounded, which means that there may be a difference between totals and sub-components. Note that a combination of available rounded and non-rounded estimates (for example to fill gaps in data availability) could generate estimates which are not a good proxy of the true value.

Other data sources which are used extensively throughout the publication include short-term statistics (STS), the labour force survey (LFS), PRODCOM (statistics by product) and external trade (the last two are only used for industrial chapters). In addition, use has also been made of specialist sources for particular areas, notably transport, energy, research and development, environment, tourism and information society statistics, as well as national accounts.

This edition of European business has also benefited from the co-operation of a wide variety of professional trade associations (representative organisations for various activities) and other non-official bodies. Tables and figures based on data from these non-official sources are presented in shaded boxes.

TIME FRAME

The majority of the data presented within this edition of European business was extracted from Eurostat databases during May 2007, complemented by an extraction in June and July for certain specific data sources. The text was written during the second and third quarters of 2007. Data are generally available up to the 2004 reference year for structural business statistics, and up to 2006 for the other official sources.

CHANGES COMPARED WITH THE PREVIOUS EDITION

Following the accession of Bulgaria and Romania, data for the 27 Member States are now consistently being presented, with the EU-27 total as a benchmark.

This edition of European business continues the efforts made in recent years to focus increasingly on official statistics, and to broaden and deepen the analysis as the European statistical system continues to make advances. A particular effort has been made in this edition to include, where available, data at the most detailed activity level (NACE four digit or class level) and to facilitate further comparisons across the different activities of the business economy (chapters and subchapters) covered by SBS.

A number of changes in the structure and organisation of the chapters have been made when compared with the 2006 edition, essentially to try to follow more closely the NACE classification and to re-align chapter definitions with those activities covered by the SBS Regulation.

1. Chapter 10 (transport equipment): two subchapters on motor vehicles and motor vehicle parts and accessories have been merged into a single subchapter; the two larger miscellaneous other transport equipment activities, namely ships and boats, and railway equipment, have been separated as two new subchapters, with a miscellaneous subchapter retained for the remaining other transport equipment manufacturing activities;

3. Chapter 14 (recycling and water supply): this chapter has been renamed as waste management and sewerage have been removed;

4. Chapter 20 (transport services): one subchapter has been split in two, separating pipelines from road and other land transport;

5. Chapter 21 (communications and media): the subchapter on audiovisual services has been removed from the publication.

DEDICATED WEBSITE

Within Eurostat's website several dedicated sections are available which provide more information on selected topics. The 'European business' dedicated section provides access to a selection of publications, data and background information describing European business, compiled by Eurostat's structural business statistics unit. It includes a presentation of the statistics by topic (including special topics such as globalisation, SMEs, foreign controlled enterprises, etc), with specific links to publications, data, methodology, policy documents, etc. All the chapters of European business: facts and figures in PDF format and MS Excel files containing the data used in the tables and figures can be downloaded from here, free of charge. The structural business statistics dedicated section is located directly under the theme 'Industry, trade and services' on the Eurostat website or by using the following link:

http://epp.eurostat.ec.europa.eu/pls/portal/url/page/PGP_DS_EUROBUS/PGE_DS_EUROBUS_01.

There are also dedicated sections available for:

Short-term business statistics:
http://epp.eurostat.ec.europa.eu/pls/portal/url/page/PGP_DS_QPEB/PGE_DS_QPEB_01;

Statistics by product:
http://epp.eurostat.ec.europa.eu/pls/portal/url/page/PGP_DS_PRODCOM/PGE_DS_PRODCOM;

External trade:
http://epp.eurostat.ec.europa.eu/pls/portal/url/page/PGP_DS_COMEXT/TAB1.

MORE STATISTICS AVAILABLE ON-LINE

The publication presents only a selection of the most important data available. Readers who are interested in knowing more about a certain topic or sector, or accessing a longer time-series, or downloading the freshest data are encouraged to consult the data available on Eurostat's website. These data are available free of charge at: http://epp.eurostat.ec.europa.eu.

Pre-defined tables

There are a number of ways for users to access/extract data. The most simple is to use what are referred to as pre-defined (automatically updated) tables, presenting selected indicators. Pre-defined tables are available for practically the full range of subjects for which Eurostat has data, not just business statistics. For structural business statistics there are a set of pre-defined tables which provide an overview of business structures in the countries and/or for the EU as a whole, as well as tables which provide selected data for specific sectors: industry and construction, distributive trades, services and financial services. Most tables contain data by country and years; these are only available with a limited activity breakdown. They are complemented by some tables which show a more detailed activity breakdown only for the EU-27 aggregate.

http://epp.eurostat.ec.europa.eu/pls/portal/url/page/PGP_QUEEN/PGE_QUEEN_TREE?screen=welcomeref&open=/basic/YEARLIES_NEW/D&language=en&product=EU_MAIN_TREE&root=EU_MAIN_TREE

Complete database

Open table access allows users to access the complete database with the most recent data available for the different topics, and based on that define their own specific data extraction. This option should be used by those who wish to make their own selection of statistics. The data that is returned when querying the database may be extracted in a variety of formats:

i. as an HTML page for an Internet browser;
ii. as a tab delimited file for a spreadsheet application, or;
iii. a flat text file for a database application.

Structural business statistics (SBS)

Structural business statistics are available as part of the industry, trade and services domain (theme 4) of the Eurostat data tree (available on the Eurostat website). The following description of the SBS data set concentrates on access through what is termed the horizontal view, within which one branch presents Structural Business Statistics. The first heading of this branch concerns Annual enterprise statistics, the first table (European business) presents the majority of the important indicators used in the publication across a full range of NACE divisions. Thereafter the tables are structured by activity, again these include the main structural variables (such as value added and employment), as well as derived indicators (including apparent labour productivity, average personnel costs and wage adjusted labour productivity). However, the list of indicators is considerably longer than the main indicators that are used within European business and the NACE breakdown is often more detailed. As the data are split according to activity, users who wish to obtain data across all NACE will need to make a number of extractions. Note that the data under the heading annual enterprise statistics do not include much information for financial intermediation (NACE Section J), as specific tables are provided for credit institutions, insurance services, and pension funds.

The next entry in the SBS data tree is for annual enterprise statistics broken down by size class. As with the annual series, the first table is a summary table of size class information that covers all NACE divisions. Thereafter, the tables present information structured by activity and reference year with the additional breakdown according to enterprise size classes based on the number of persons employed per enterprise. Again, if users wish to obtain data across all NACE, or for a lengthy time-series, then a number of extractions may have to be made.

The next heading in the SBS data tree contains the information that was used to construct maps that are presented in the overview of each chapter, in other words annual regional statistics.

The link below takes the user into the Eurostat database at the point where the SBS data tree can be expanded, from where tailor-made extractions can be made, specifying all of the dimensions of the data request, including the countries, time periods, indicators, and units.

http://epp.eurostat.ec.europa.eu/pls/portal/url/ page/PGP_QUEEN/PGE_QUEEN_TREE?screen= welcomeref&open=/intrse/sbs&product= EU_MASTER_industry_trade_services_horizontal &depth=2

Special topics of structural business statistics
In addition to those tables which are documented above, there is also more specific SBS information on a collection of particular topics, such as:

- Business demography
- Business services
- Demand for services
- Distributive trades: breakdown of turnover by product
- Factors of business success
- Foreign control of enterprises
- Intangible investment and subcontracting
- Inter-enterprise relations
- Iron and steel
- Purchases of energy products
- Statistics on environmental protection
- Trade: other multi-yearly statistics

http://epp.eurostat.ec.europa.eu/pls/portal/url/ page/PGP_QUEEN/PGE_QUEEN_TREE?screen= welcomeref&open=/intrse/sbs_spec&product= EU_MASTER_industry_trade_services_horizonta l&depth=2

Short-term business statistics
The information on short-term business statistics (STS) is also available as part of the industry, trade and services domain within the Eurostat website. The data are structured under three main headings: industry; construction; and trade and other services.

Within the industry domain the data is broken down according to the indicators specified in the STS Regulation. There are tables presented for indices of production, turnover, new orders, labour input (number of persons employed; volume of work done/hours worked, gross wages and salaries), and producer prices (output prices). A number of tables exist for each of these indices, with monthly, quarterly and annual frequencies often available, while there may be different presentations for certain indices (gross or working day adjusted, seasonally adjusted, trend cycle).

The structure of the tables presented for construction follows very closely the structure used for industry, with separate tables for indices of production, new orders, labour input, construction costs for new residential buildings, and building permits (number of dwellings and area).

The structure of the tables for distributive trades and other services is somewhat different, as the information is initially divided according to the activity under analysis, with separate tables for motor trade, wholesale trade, retail trade and other services.

http://epp.eurostat.ec.europa.eu/pls/portal/url/ page/PGP_QUEEN/PGE_QUEEN_TREE?screen=w elcomeref&open=/intrse/ebt&product= EU_MASTER_industry_trade_services_horizontal &depth=2.

PRODCOM
Information on product statistics (PRODCOM) is also available as part of the industry, trade and services domain, under a separate heading called Statistics by product. This set of data is quite particular insofar as the link presented takes the user to an MS Access application rather than the standard interface used for most Eurostat data. The application presents the user with the choice of extracting external trade or PRODCOM data (annual or monthly). The interface permits the selection of the country, PRODCOM code (PRCCODE), volume or value data (measurement unit), period, and indicator (production, imports or exports). The application also allows for exports and imports to be extracted at the same time.

http://fd.comext.eurostat.cec.eu.int/xtweb/.

The data can also be downloaded in MS Excel format from the PRODCOM dedicated section:

http://epp.eurostat.ec.europa.eu/pls/portal/url/ page/PGP_DS_PRODCOM/PGE_DS_PRODCOM/ PGE_DS_PRODCOM_01.

Business economy overview

The re-launched Lisbon strategy for growth and jobs was presented on 25 January 2006 [1]. It distinguishes between macro-economic, micro-economic and employment challenges when analysing how to make Europe the world's most dynamic, competitive, knowledge-based economy, while keeping unemployment as low as possible.

1.1: MACRO-ECONOMIC OUTLOOK

GROSS DOMESTIC PRODUCT (GDP)
The most common indicator for measuring a nation's economic activity is gross domestic product (GDP). This indicator covers the production activity of resident producers, calculated as the sum of gross value added from all activities/industries within an economy (the so-called output approach).

Figure 1.1 shows the evolution of constant price GDP (at fixed 2000 exchange rates) between 1995 and 2008 in the three Triad economies of the EU-27, Japan and the United States (forecasts are made for 2007 and 2008). For the whole of this period, GDP rose on average by 2.4 % per annum in the EU-27, which was below the average rate of 3.1 % per annum for the United States, but above the 1.4 % per annum growth rate recorded in Japan.

[1] 'Time to move up a gear - the new partnership for growth and jobs', COM(2006) 30.

Figure 1.1

**GDP at market prices in constant prices
(EUR billion, chain-linked volumes, at 2000 exchange rates) (1)**

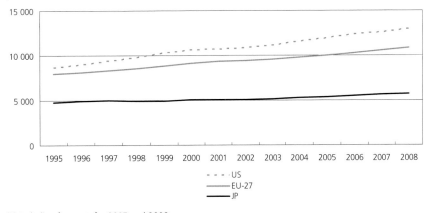

(1) Including forecasts for 2007 and 2008.
Source: Eurostat (Economy and finance)

GDP growth in the EU-27 rose at a relatively fast pace during the period 1997 to 2000, with annual rates of growth ranging from 2.7 % (1997) to 3.9 % (2000), after which there was a slowdown in the pace at which economic activity expanded, with 2.0 % growth in 2001 followed by increases of just over 1 % in both 2002 and 2003. The rate of GDP growth for the EU-27 returned to a somewhat higher level in 2004 (2.5 %), before slowing again in 2005 (1.7 %), although there was a faster expansion in 2006 (3.0 %) – the highest growth rate for six years. In 2006, some of the highest rates of GDP growth were recorded among the 12 Member States that recently joined the EU. This distribution of growth follows what is often referred to as the 'convergence hypothesis', according to which countries with relatively low levels of per capita GDP grow more rapidly.

It is important to bear in mind these cyclical changes in GDP that are observed for EU-27 economic output when reading the sectoral chapters that follow in this publication, as the evolution of output or sales in many activities follows closely the economic cycle of the whole economy.

The level of GDP, per se, says little about the economic performance of a country, as large countries will tend to have higher levels of GDP. In order to normalise GDP, one of the most common approaches is to use the measure of GDP per capita, obtained by dividing GDP by the number of inhabitants in a country (or region). This indicator is frequently used as a measure of living standards, and is also used as an overall measure of competitiveness. For international comparisons ideally, GDP per capita should be calculated in terms of purchasing power standards (PPS) (2).

Luxembourg stood out as having by far the highest GDP per capita in 2006, almost 2.7 times the EU-27 average (see Figure 1.2), while the next Member State in the ranking was Ireland, where GDP per capita was slightly less than 46 % above the EU-27 average. At the other end of the range, Greece and Portugal and all 12 of the Member States that joined the EU in 2004 or 2007 reported GDP per capita below the EU-27 average.

The growth of GDP per capita in the EU is almost entirely driven by additional value added being generated, as most of the Member States have relatively stable levels of population. GDP per capita has, nevertheless, grown at a slower pace in the EU-27 over the past decade than in the United States. This may, in part, be explained by productivity gains in the EU slowing, while technological gains stimulated GDP growth in the United States (3). These trends have structural features, which became the focus of the Lisbon strategy and its subsequent re-launch. Indeed, the main focus of policies for improving European competitiveness are concerned with boosting productivity growth through investment in research and development (R&D), improving European infrastructure, enhancing human capital, and promoting competition.

---

(2) A purchasing power parity is a currency conversion rate that allows indicators expressed in national currency to be converted to an artificial common currency while adjusting for different price levels between countries; this artificial common currency is called the purchasing power standard (note that EU-27 values are unchanged in euro and PPS terms).
(3) Communication from the Commission, 'Economic reforms and competitiveness: key messages from the European Competitiveness Report 2006', COM(2006) 697 final.

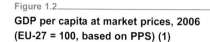

Figure 1.2

GDP per capita at market prices, 2006 (EU-27 = 100, based on PPS) (1)

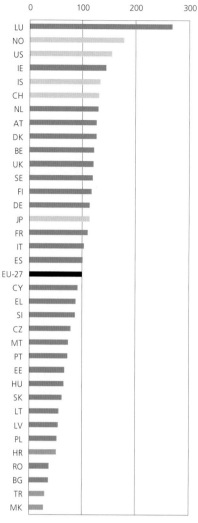

(1) Forecasts.
Source: Eurostat (Economy and finance)

Figure 1.3

Total intramural research and development expenditure (GERD), 2005 (% of GDP)

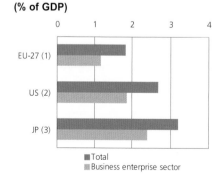

■ Total
■ Business enterprise sector

(1) Estimates.
(2) Provisional, 2004.
(3) 2003.
Source: Eurostat (Research and development)

RESEARCH AND DEVELOPMENT (R&D)
The revamping of the Lisbon strategy in 2005 is, as noted above, partly based on a decision to encourage more innovation and research, with the hope that this will stimulate technologically-driven productivity gains. This policy also depends, to some degree, on creating a business environment that provides sufficient incentives to enterprises so they will commit resources to innovation. It also relies on a capital market in which it is possible to raise the necessary finance for funding research.

In economic terms, the allocation of resources to research efforts suffers from what are often referred to as 'market failures'. It is often difficult for an enterprise to protect their intellectual assets, and as a result, their private returns may fall short of potential social returns: for example, consider a pharmaceuticals enterprise that might spend decades looking for a cure to an illness, only to find imitators copying their new drug as soon as it is available to the general public. Another example of market failure is a poorly functioning capital market, which may result from problems associated with asymmetric information: for example, a banker may well have less information about the value of a certain project than the entrepreneur, who is unwilling to reveal certain aspects of their research for fear of this becoming public knowledge.

The latest round of the Community Innovation Survey (CIS4) sheds some light on these problems. When asked about factors hampering innovation, 23.6 % of all enterprises (4) cited innovation costs as being too high, while 15.4 % complained about a lack of appropriate sources of finance, and 10.6 % that a lack of qualified personnel was hampering their innovation efforts. For all three of these factors, a higher proportion of small enterprises (with between 10 and 49 persons employed) faced difficulties that hampered their innovation efforts, while large enterprises (with 250 or more persons employed) faced the least difficulties.

---

(4) Eurostat, CIS4: the survey only covers NACE Sections C, D, E, I and J, NACE Divisions 51 and 72, and NACE Groups 74.2 and 74.3; EU averages based on available information (innovation costs too high: excluding Denmark, Malta and Sweden; lack of appropriate sources of finance: excluding Cyprus, Malta, Sweden and the United Kingdom; lack of qualified personnel: excluding Denmark, Luxembourg, Malta and Romania).

A low level of business enterprise expenditure is often given as a reason for the relatively low levels of R&D expenditure in the EU-27 (compared with Japan or the United States). R&D expenditure made by the business enterprise sector stood at 1.17 % of GDP in 2005 in the EU-27, compared with a provisional value of 1.87 % in the United States for 2004 and 2.40 % in Japan in 2003 (see Figure 1.3). While the business enterprise sector contributed approximately 64 % of total R&D expenditure in the EU-27, this proportion rose to 70 % in the United States and 75 % in Japan.

HUMAN RESOURCES IN SCIENCE AND TECHNOLOGY (HRST)

Education and training initiatives are also central to the revised Lisbon objectives. There are many policies within the Member States that aim to raise the proportion of higher education graduates, with the belief that if Europe is to remain competitive in the knowledge-driven economy, it will need a higher number of graduates with qualifications suitably adapted to increasingly demanding labour market requirements. Education and in particular tertiary education, not only renews stocks of human capital but also promotes economic growth. Therefore, investment in education can be seen as an investment in future economic well-being as well as an investment in individual success.

Table 1.1 shows that EU-27 human resources in science and technology (HRST) totalled 75.3 million persons in 2006 (note that there is some overlap as regards the breakdown of this total figure as some persons have a science or technology education and work in a science or technology occupation). Almost 53 % of the HRST workforce were employed within business economy activities (as defined by NACE Sections D to K), with a relatively high proportion working in predominantly public sector activities (NACE Sections L to Q).

EXCHANGE RATES

The competitiveness of an economy can be radically changed as a result of movements in currency exchange rates, as the price of exports and imports is directly affected. Euro exchange rates were fixed for eleven Member States in 1999; Greece subsequently joined the euro area in 2001 and was followed by Slovenia at the start of 2007. Entry into the single currency of the euro area is conditional upon Member States meeting a set of convergence criteria. While Denmark and the United Kingdom have a special opt-out, the remaining twelve Member States have derogations, and are expected to adopt the euro once the necessary conditions are fulfilled. By fixing their exchange rates, enterprises within the euro area face a

Table 1.1 ————————————————————————

Human resources in science and technology (HRST), EU-27, 2006 (thousands, 25-64 years old)

	NACE Sections	Total HRST	Core (1)	Education (2)	Occupation (3)	Scientists/ engineers (4)
Total	**A to Q**	75 320	33 990	51 022	58 288	10 116
Manufacturing	**D**	10 317	3 516	6 386	7 447	1 806
Elec., gas, water supply & construction	**E and F**	3 422	1 020	2 307	2 135	704
Distributive trades	**G**	7 230	1 580	4 167	4 644	542
Hotels and restaurants	**H**	897	90	749	238	11
Transport, storage and communication	**I**	3 156	915	2 024	2 047	355
Financial intermediation	**J**	3 661	1 179	2 280	2 561	229
Real estate, renting & business activities	**K**	11 111	5 731	7 736	9 106	2 599
Others		35 526	19 959	25 373	30 110	3 870

(1) Successfully completed the third level of a science and technology field of study and employed in a science and technology occupation.
(2) Successfully completed the third level of a science and technology field of study.
(3) Employed in a science and technology occupation.
(4) Employed in physical, mathematical and engineering occupations or in life science and health occupations.
Source: Eurostat (Human resources in science & technology)

more stable business environment, in particular because the majority of exports made by Member States are destined for other Member States. For those enterprises that operate outside of the euro area there is sometimes a higher degree of uncertainty when dealing with suppliers or customers abroad.

Exchange rate movements are inherent within all the monetary indicators that are presented in this publication, as data are consistently shown in the euro (EUR) denomination. As such, exchange rate fluctuations should be born in mind when analysing the evolution of series over time, especially between euro area and non-euro area countries. As an example of currency exchange rate effects, the value of the euro fell by 29.5 % overall against the American dollar between 1996 and 2001, leading to more expensive imports, but lower prices for those trying to export to the United States. Between 2001 and 2004 this trend was reversed as the euro appreciated by 38.9 % overall against the dollar, while the exchange rate was almost unchanged in 2005 and 2006. The first table presented within the background information found at the end of this publication shows exchange rates against the euro for the period 1996 to 2006.

STRUCTURE OF THE EU ECONOMY – AN OVERVIEW

The following chapters within European business cover the business economy as defined by NACE Sections C to K. According to national accounts, this group of activities together accounted for 75.7 % of the total value added generated in the EU-27 in 2006 (see Figure 1.4). Financial, real estate, renting and business activities (NACE Sections J and K) accounted for 27.6 %, while distribution; hotels, restaurants and catering (HORECA); communications and transport services (NACE Sections G to I), as well as industry (NACE Sections C to E) accounted for more than one fifth of the EU-27's economic output each; construction (NACE Section F) registered a 6.4 % share. Of the activities not covered in European business, the lion's share of the remaining added value (22.4 %) was generated by public administration, health, education, other services, and households (NACE Sections L to P), while the remaining 1.9 % was attributed to agriculture, hunting, forestry and fishing (NACE Sections A and B).

There has been a shift in the structure of economic output within the EU-27 resulting from an outsourcing phenomenon, as supporting and ancillary operations which were previously done in-house are awarded to outside contractors (for example, transport and logistics, information technology, accounts, industrial cleaning), while organisation, know-how, innovation, brand creation/management and customised services have been increasingly important as sources of competitive advantage. At the same time, relatively high wages, and increased global trade have driven out price sensitive segments of production to lower labour cost regions of the world. Finally, the demand for manufactured goods is affected by physiological limits to further consumption (for example, food) and many mature EU markets for manufactured goods are saturated, presenting little opportunity for rapid growth. On the other hand, the income elasticity of demand for immaterial sources of well-being is thought to be much higher and so as disposable income rises, consumers tend to devote an increasing share of their expenditure to services.

These changes may, at least in part, explain why the share of industry in EU-27 total value added declined by 3 percentage points between 1996 and 2006, and that of agriculture, hunting, forestry and fishing by 1 percentage point (from an already low starting point of 2.9 % in 1996). The largest relative gains in economic activity between 1996 and 2006 were concentrated within the services sector, in particular financial, real estate, renting and business activities (which reported a 3 percentage point increase in its share of EU-27 total value added).

In employment terms (see Figure 1.5) the situation was quite different, as the business economy accounted for just under two thirds (64.6 %) of the EU-27's workforce in 2006, some 11.1 percentage points lower than its corresponding share of value added. The largest employer in 2006 was public administration, health, education, other services, and households, where almost three out of ten (29.1 %) persons in the workforce were employed, while just under one in four (24.9 %) worked within the activities of distribution, hotels, restaurants and catering (HORECA), communications and transport services, 17.9 % in industrial activities and 14.7 % in financial, real estate, renting and business activities, the latter contrasting starkly with its 27.6 % share of value added. It is interesting to note that with the accession of Bulgaria and Romania, the proportion of the EU-27's workforce working in agriculture, hunting, forestry and fishing activities reached 6.4 %.

These differences between the relative shares of total value added and employment provide a measure of labour productivity: industry and financial, real estate, renting and business activities were the most productive (or capital intensive) activities within the EU economy using this measure (Figure 1.14 later in this chapter presents a much more detailed sectoral breakdown of labour productivity). All of the remaining activities were relatively labour intensive; this was particularly the case for public administration, health, education, other services, and households.

Figure 1.4 _____

Breakdown of value added in current prices, EU-27 (% of total value added)

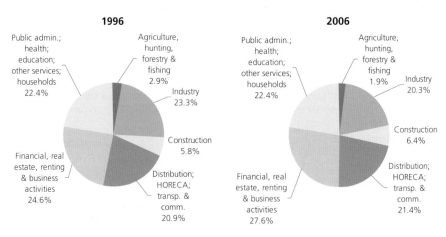

Source: Eurostat (Economy and finance)

Figure 1.5 _____

Breakdown of employment, EU-27 (% of total employment)

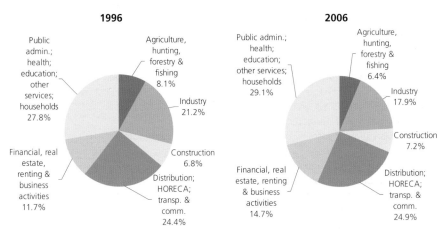

Source: Eurostat (Economy and finance)

Looking at the evolution of value added over time (in real terms), EU-27 output grew, on average, by 2.4 % per annum between 1996 and 2006. The slowest growth rates were recorded for agriculture, hunting, forestry and fishing (on average, 0.6 % per annum). The highest growth rates were registered for financial, real estate, renting and business activities (3.2 % per annum), while the only other activity to report above average growth was distribution; hotels, restaurants and catering (HORECA); communications and transport services (3.1 % per annum).

The number of persons working in the EU-27 rose by 19.2 million persons between 1996 and 2006. The largest relative and overall gains were recorded for financial, real estate, renting and business activities, where employment rose by an average of 3.3 % per annum, or some 8.7 million persons overall. The rate of EU-27 employment growth averaged 1.4 % per annum for construction (an overall gain of 2.1 million persons employed), a rate that was repeated for public administration, health, education, other services, and households (8.1 million persons), while average employment growth equated to 1.1 % per annum for distribution, hotels, restaurants and catering (HORECA), communications and transport services (5.8 million persons). Two activities reported a net reduction in EU-27 employment between 1996 and 2006, with the agriculture, hunting, forestry and fishing workforce reduced by an average of 1.4 % per annum (2.2 million fewer persons overall), and that for industry contracting by 0.8 % per annum (3.3 million).

As such, the two activities with the highest levels of labour productivity had diverging employment trends: as industry registered the largest absolute decline in employment between 1996 and 2006, while financial, real estate, renting and business activities recorded the largest increase (in relative and absolute terms). These contrasting developments may, in part, be related to changes in the business paradigm, as many industrial enterprises have made cost-motivated investments in production facilities in eastern Europe, China or India. Such moves may well be driven by the benefits associated with relatively low unit labour costs, as well as market entry into untapped regions with potentially high future sales. This trend has led to the re-location of labour, with European enterprises focusing their home production increasingly on knowledge-intensive, innovative activities.

STRUCTURAL DIFFERENCES BETWEEN THE MEMBER STATES

Figure 1.6 shows the relative contribution of the six national accounts activity aggregates to total value added in 2006. The structural differences observed should be borne in mind when reading the sectoral chapters that follow. It is also important to bear in mind the relative importance of those sectors that are not included within the business economy, as these sometimes account for an important proportion of total economic activity. Shares and ratios which will later be presented in relation to the non-financial business economy (used as the denominator) will, to some degree, depend on the relative importance/performance of the non-financial business economy in relation to the total economy.

Agriculture, hunting, forestry and fishing accounted for a relatively high share of national value added in Romania and Bulgaria (9.6 % and 8.5 %) in 2006, while Lithuania, Greece (2005), Poland, Hungary and Slovakia reported these activities generating at least 4 % of their value added. Upwards of 25 % of total value added was generated by public administration, health, education, other services, and households in Malta, Sweden, Denmark, Portugal and France (2005), compared with an EU-27 average of 22.4 %. In contrast, less than 16 % of national value added was derived from these activities in Estonia, Lithuania, Slovakia, Bulgaria and Romania.

Among the activities which are covered by this publication, Luxembourg, France (2005), the United Kingdom (2005), Germany and Belgium were all relatively specialised in financial, real estate, renting and business activities, to such a degree that no other Member State could report that these activities had a share of total

Figure 1.6

Breakdown of gross value added at basic prices, 2006

(% share of total gross value added)

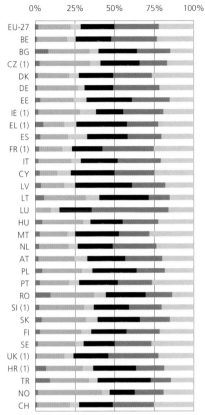

■ Agriculture, hunting, forestry & fishing
▨ Industry
▨ Construction
■ Distribution; HORECA; transp. & comm.
■ Financial, real estate, renting & business activities
▨ Public admin.; health; education etc.

(1) 2005.
Source: Eurostat (Economy and finance)

value added that was above the EU-27 average. In Luxembourg, financial, real estate, renting and business activities accounted for almost half (48.6 %) of the total value added generated in 2006.

While just over one fifth (20.3 %) of the EU-27's value added was generated in industrial activities, the share rose to 27 % or higher in the Czech Republic (2005), Slovenia (2005), Slovakia and Romania. The tourism-rich economies of Cyprus and Malta, as well as the Baltic States and Greece (2005) all reported relatively high shares of value added being generated in distribution, hotels, restaurants and catering (HORECA), communications and transport services, while the most specialised Member States within the construction sector were Spain (12.2 % of total value added) and Ireland (10.0 %, 2005).

Figure 1.7

Breakdown of employment, 2006

(% share of total employment)

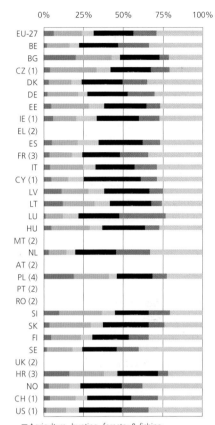

■ Agriculture, hunting, forestry & fishing
▨ Industry
▨ Construction
■ Distribution; HORECA; transp. & comm.
■ Financial, real estate, renting & business activities
▨ Public admin.; health; education etc.J72

(1) 2005.
(2) Not available.
(3) 2004.
(4) Estimates.
Source: Eurostat (Economy and finance)

Figure 1.7 shows a similar breakdown to the previous graph, but this time for employment instead of value added. One of the most noticeable aspects is the relatively high proportion of the workforce occupied in agriculture, hunting, forestry and fishing activities, which rose to double-digits in Bulgaria, Poland (2005), Lithuania and Latvia. The relative importance of public administration, health, education, other services, and households was also usually much higher for employment than for value added, with as many as 40.2 % of the Swedish workforce occupied in these activities in 2006.

1.2: STRUCTURAL PROFILE OF THE BUSINESS ECONOMY

In the face of globalisation and international competition, and in keeping with the revised Lisbon objectives, the European Commission launched a new industrial policy in October 2005 [5]. It included initiatives on: competitiveness, energy and the environment; intellectual property rights; better regulation; industrial research and innovation; market access; skills, and managing structural change; as well as sector-specific policies for: pharmaceuticals; life sciences and biotechnology; chemicals; defence; the European space programme; information and communication technologies; mechanical engineering; food; fashion and design industries. The policy is designed to improve Europe's economic standing by allowing businesses to compete openly and fairly, and by

[5] Communication from the Commission, 'Implementing the Community Lisbon Programme: A policy framework to strengthen EU manufacturing - towards a more integrated approach for industrial policy', COM(2005) 474 final.

making Europe an attractive place to invest and work in, and provides the policy framework for many of the business economy activities covered by this publication.

Structural business statistics (SBS) constitute the principal source of information used in this publication. The main SBS aggregates, often referred to during the course of this publication, include:

- the non-financial business economy (NACE Sections C to I and K);
- industry (NACE Sections C to E);
- construction (NACE Section F), and;
- non-financial services (NACE Sections G to I and K).

Note that financial services (NACE Section J) are kept separate (see Chapter 24) because of their specific nature and the limited availability of most standard business statistics in this area. Note also that the industrial activity of printing,

although included in the industry SBS aggregate, is covered in Chapter 21, within the non-financial services section of this publication.

STRUCTURAL PROFILE OF THE EU-27'S NON-FINANCIAL BUSINESS ECONOMY

There were 18.9 million active enterprises within the EU-27's non-financial business economy in 2004 (see Table 1.2). The vast majority of these (73.9 %) were operating within non-financial services, while a higher proportion of enterprises were active in the construction sector (14.3 % of the total) than within industry (12.1 %).

On the basis of the activity aggregates used for the sectoral chapters that follow in the remainder of this publication, the largest numbers of enterprises were usually found within activities that are, to some degree, characterised as having relatively low barriers to entry, and large, proximity markets. Business services (see Chapter 22), retail trade and repair

Table 1.2

Main indicators for the non-financial business economy, EU-27, 2004

Chapter		Enterprises		Turnover		Value added		Persons employed	
		(thousands)	(% of non-financial business economy)	(EUR billion)	(% of non-financial business economy)	(EUR billion)	(% of non-financial business economy)	(thousands)	(% of non-financial business economy)
1	Non-financial business economy (1)	18 900	100.0	19 000	100.0	5 100	100.0	125 000	100.0
	Industry (2)	2 280	12.1	6 930	36.5	1 800	35.3	37 500	30.0
2	Food, beverages & tobacco	296	1.6	928	4.9	200	3.9	4 772	3.8
3	Textiles, clothing, leather & footwear (1)	266	1.4	242	1.3	68	1.3	3 410	2.7
4	Wood & paper (1)	217	1.1	278	1.5	77	1.5	2 060	1.6
5	Chemicals, rubber & plastics (1)	100	0.5	870	4.6	250	4.9	3 700	3.0
6	Other non-metallic mineral products (3)	102	0.5	211	1.1	73	1.4	1 600	1.3
7	Metals & metal products	399	2.1	699	3.7	213	4.2	4 991	4.0
8	Machinery & equipment	164	0.9	532	2.8	172	3.4	3 661	2.9
9	Electrical machinery & optical equipment (3)	196	1.0	631	3.3	190	3.7	3 600	2.9
10	Transport equipment (3)	43	0.2	862	4.5	177	3.5	3 200	2.6
11	Furniture & other manufacturing (4)	227	1.2	164	0.9	51	1.0	1 900	1.5
12	Non-energy mining & quarrying	17	0.1	40	0.2	15	0.3	291	0.2
13	Energy (1)	21	0.1	1 147	6.0	240	4.7	1 980	1.6
14	Recycling & water supply (1)	23	0.1	70	0.4	27	0.5	500	0.4
15	Construction	2 695	14.3	1 289	6.8	434	8.5	13 153	10.5
	Non-financial services (5)	13 962	73.9	11 131	58.6	2 817	55.2	73 833	59.1
16	Motor trades	782	4.1	1 185	6.2	151	3.0	4 067	3.3
17	Wholesale trade	1 682	8.9	3 916	20.6	463	9.1	9 554	7.6
18	Retail trade & repair	3 735	19.8	2 038	10.7	384	7.5	16 970	13.6
19	Hotels & restaurants	1 605	8.5	386	2.0	163	3.2	8 652	6.9
20	Transport services (1)	1 120	5.9	1 030	5.4	360	7.1	8 600	6.9
21	Communications & media (4)	270	1.4	743	3.9	340	6.7	4 900	3.9
22	Business services	3 901	20.6	1 450	7.6	740	14.5	19 433	15.5
23	Real estate, renting & R&D (4)	1 072	5.7	620	3.3	304	6.0	3 500	2.8

(1) Rounded estimates based on non-confidential data.
(2) This aggregate does not match the sum of the activities covered in Chapters 2 to 14, as the industrial activity of publishing is covered in Chapter 21; rounded estimates based on non-confidential data.
(3) Rounded estimates based on non-confidential data for number of persons employed and related shares.
(4) Rounded estimates based on non-confidential data, except for number of enterprises and related share.
(5) This aggregate does not include the activity of industrial printing, which is covered in chapter 21.
Source: Eurostat (SBS)

(see Chapter 18) and construction (see Chapter 15) together accounted for almost 55 % of all enterprises active in the EU-27's non-financial business economy in 2004. At the other end of the scale, there were relatively few enterprises operating within activities characterised by high barriers to entry (such as, those with considerable start-up costs to reach a minimum efficient scale of production). These included capital-intensive activities such as transport equipment manufacturing (see Chapter 10), recycling and water supply (see Chapter 14), energy (see Chapter 13) and non-energy mining and quarrying (see Chapter 12); none of these sectors accounted for more than 0.2 % of the total number of enterprises active in the EU-27's non-financial business economy.

The distribution of enterprises across the European economy provides little information when analysing the relative economic importance of the different sectors. Economic weight is more generally measured in terms of value added. Non-financial services contributed a 55.2 % share of the total added value in the EU-27's non-financial business economy in 2004. The proportion accounted for by industrial activities, 35.3 %, was 23.2 percentage points higher than the share of industry in terms of enterprises; construction accounted for the remaining 8.5 % of added value. Looking in more detail, using the activity aggregates used for each sectoral chapter in this publication, the three largest sectors together contributed 32.1 % of the value added generated in the EU-27's non-financial business economy; they were business services, wholesale trade (see Chapter 17) and construction.

Comparing two output measures, namely value added and turnover, the most noticeable difference between the distribution of value added and turnover across the EU-27's non-financial business economy was within distributive trades activities (especially for wholesale trade); the relatively high proportion of sales occurring within these activities is a direct consequence of the nature of these activities, whereby large volumes of products are purchased and resold, normally with a relatively small margin.

In employment terms, the importance of the relatively labour-intensive construction and non-financial services sectors rose (when compared with shares recorded for output variables such as turnover or value added). Non-financial services accounted for 59.1 % of the EU-27's non-financial business economy workforce, while 30 % were employed in industrial activities and 10.5 % in construction. At a sectoral level, none of the industrial activities represented more than 4 % of the employment total; the highest share being recorded for metals and metal products (Chapter 7). Among the services, the largest

Figure 1.8

Number of enterprises, EU-27, 2004 (thousands)

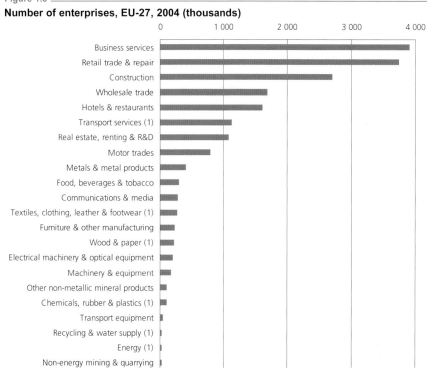

(1) Rounded estimates based on non-confidential data.
Source: Eurostat (SBS)

Figure 1.9

Value added and employment, EU-27, 2004 (% share of total)

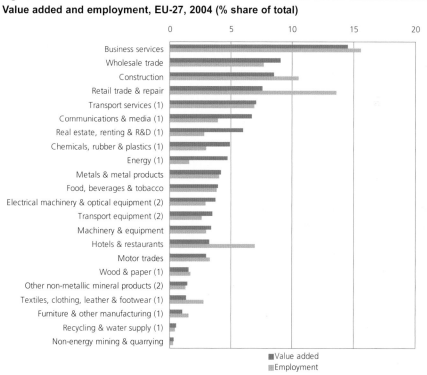

(1) Rounded estimates based on non-confidential data.
(2) Rounded estimates based on non-confidential data for number of persons employed and related shares.
Source: Eurostat (SBS)

workforces were found within the activities of business services (15.5 %) and retail trade and repair (13.6 %), the latter in particular using a lot of part-time employment.

Table 1.3

Main indicators for the non-financial business economy, 2004

	Enterprises		Turnover		Value added		Persons employed	
	(thousands)	(% of EU-27)	(EUR million)	(% of EU-27)	(EUR million)	(% of EU-27)	(thousands)	(% of EU-27)
BE	395	2.1	681 170	3.6	139 118	2.7	2 383	1.9
BG	240	1.3	52 119	0.3	8 288	0.2	1 771	1.4
CZ	880	4.7	239 128	1.3	52 495	1.0	3 573	2.9
DK	192	1.0	360 370	1.9	102 168	2.0	1 660	1.3
DE	1 695	9.0	3 776 609	19.9	1 068 460	21.0	20 687	16.5
EE	36	0.2	25 412	0.1	5 076	0.1	384	0.3
IE (1)	:	0.5	:	1.4	:	1.6	:	0.8
EL	:	:	:	:	:	:	:	:
ES	2 455	13.0	1 718 799	9.0	458 712	9.0	12 839	10.3
FR	2 227	11.8	2 901 660	15.3	718 122	14.1	14 287	11.4
IT	3 740	19.8	2 422 608	12.8	567 204	11.1	14 687	11.7
CY (2)	:	0.2	:	0.1	:	0.1	:	0.2
LV	58	0.3	23 981	0.1	5 339	0.1	593	0.5
LT	53	0.3	32 346	0.2	6 973	0.1	794	0.6
LU (3)	22	0.1	49 496	0.3	11 321	0.2	199	0.2
HU	564	3.0	197 264	1.0	36 103	0.7	2 573	2.1
MT	:	:	:	:	:	:	:	:
NL	485	2.6	986 469	5.2	234 001	4.6	4 609	3.7
AT	265	1.4	426 428	2.2	122 795	2.4	2 354	1.9
PL	1 457	7.7	440 387	2.3	104 778	2.1	7 484	6.0
PT	584	3.1	288 410	1.5	64 481	1.3	2 944	2.4
RO	377	2.0	110 107	0.6	21 583	0.4	4 001	3.2
SI	89	0.5	55 108	0.3	13 511	0.3	568	0.5
SK	36	0.2	63 669	0.3	13 195	0.3	895	0.7
FI	186	1.0	286 892	1.5	72 762	1.4	1 213	1.0
SE	504	2.7	531 045	2.8	148 043	2.9	2 579	2.1
UK	1 530	8.1	3 153 178	16.6	965 093	18.9	17 993	14.4

(1) Excluding mining and quarrying of energy producing materials (NACE Subsection CA) and electricity, gas and water supply (NACE Section E).
(2) Excluding real estate activities (NACE Division 70) and research and development (NACE Division 73).
(3) 2003.
Source: Eurostat (SBS)

SPECIALISATION AND CONCENTRATION WITHIN THE MEMBER STATES

Table 1.3 shows that together the economies of Germany, Spain, France, Italy and the United Kingdom generated about three quarters (74.1 %) of the added value within the EU-27's non-financial business economy in 2004, making 73.5 % of all sales, and employing nearly two thirds (64.4 %) of the EU-27's workforce within 61.6 % of all enterprises. These figures hide considerable differences, as Italy and Spain had a larger population of enterprises (in relative and absolute terms), while Germany, France and the United Kingdom had relatively high shares of value added and turnover.

Table 1.4

Largest and most specialised Member States (on the basis of value added for sectoral chapter headings and value added specialisation ratios relative to the EU-27 for sectoral chapter headings), 2004 (1)

Chapter		Largest	Second largest	Most specialised	Second most specialised
2	Food, beverages & tobacco (2)	Germany	United Kingdom	Poland	Lithuania
3	Textiles, clothing, leather & footwear (3)	Italy	Germany	Bulgaria	Lithuania
4	Wood & paper (4)	Germany	Italy	Finland	Latvia
5	Chemicals, rubber & plastics (5)	Germany	France	Slovenia	Belgium
6	Other non-metallic mineral products	Germany	Italy	Czech Republic	Portugal
7	Metals & metal products	Germany	Italy	Slovakia	Slovenia
8	Machinery & equipment	Germany	Italy	Germany	Italy
9	Electrical machinery & optical equipment	Germany	France	Hungary	Finland
10	Transport equipment	Germany	France	Germany	Czech Republic
11	Furniture & other manufacturing (6)	Germany	Italy	Lithuania	Estonia
12	Non-energy mining & quarrying (7)	United Kingdom	Germany	Bulgaria	Poland
13	Energy (8)	United Kingdom	Germany	Poland	Lithuania
14	Recycling & water supply (9)	Germany	United Kingdom	Bulgaria	Slovakia
15	Construction	United Kingdom	Spain	Spain	Luxembourg
16	Motor trades	Germany	United Kingdom	Slovenia	Portugal
17	Wholesale trade	United Kingdom	Germany	Latvia	Estonia
18	Retail trade & repair	United Kingdom	Germany	France	United Kingdom
19	Hotels & restaurants	United Kingdom	France	Spain	Austria
20	Transport services	Germany	United Kingdom	Lithuania	Latvia
21	Communications & media (4)	Germany	United Kingdom	Bulgaria	Latvia
22	Business services	United Kingdom	Germany	United Kingdom	Luxembourg
23	Real estate, renting & R&D (10)	Germany	United Kingdom	Denmark	Sweden

(1) Greece and Malta, not available; Ireland and Cyprus, not available for specialisation ratio; Luxembourg, 2003.
(2) Latvia, 2003.
(3) Denmark, Latvia, Austria, Romania and Slovakia, not available; Portugal, 2003 for value added and not available for specialisation ratio.
(4) Luxembourg, not available.
(5) Portugal, 2003.
(6) Denmark and Ireland, not available; Bulgaria, 2003.
(7) Portugal, not available.
(8) Bulgaria, Denmark, Ireland, Cyprus, Latvia, Austria, Portugal, Romania and Slovakia, not available; Luxembourg, not available for specialisation ratio.
(9) Denmark and Cyprus, not available; Bulgaria, 2003.
(10) Cyprus and Luxembourg, not available.
Source: Eurostat (SBS)

Table 1.4 presents, for the activity aggregates used in the sectoral chapters of this publication, information on the two countries with the highest levels of value added. It shows that Germany was ranked either first or second for the vast majority of activities, with the only exceptions being construction and hotels and restaurants (Chapter 19). Italy was among the two largest producers for six of the industrial activities, while the United Kingdom was one of the two principal generators of added value for each of the service sector chapters.

Relative specialisation ratios are calculated for each Member State as the share of a particular activity in non-financial business economy value added. This share is divided by the same ratio for the EU-27 to create a final indicator that is expressed as a ratio in percentage terms (values above 100 % indicating a relative specialisation in relation to the EU-27 average): Table 1.4 also shows the most specialised Member States for each activity. Some of the larger Member States also appeared as the most specialised countries within a range of activities, including Germany for the manufacture of machinery and equipment (Chapter 8) and transport equipment, Spain for the construction sector and hotels and restaurants (Chapter 19), and the United Kingdom for business services. Nevertheless, particularly in industrial activities, several of the Member States that joined the EU in 2004 or 2007 are among the most specialised, with Lithuania, Bulgaria and Latvia frequently appearing as the most or second most specialised country.

Table 1.5

Largest and most specialised activities (on the basis of value added for sectoral chapter headings and value added specialisation ratios relative to the EU-27 for sectoral chapter headings), 2004

	Largest	Second largest	Most specialised	Second most specialised
BE	Business services	Wholesale trade	Chemicals, rubber & plastics	Recycling & water supply
BG (1)	Communications & media	Transport services	Non-energy mining & quarrying	Textiles, clothing, leather & footwear
CZ	Business services	Wholesale trade	Other non-metallic mineral products	Metals & metal products
DK (2)	Business services	Wholesale trade	Real estate, renting & R&D	Transport services
DE	Business services	Wholesale trade	Transport equipment	Machinery & equipment
EE	Wholesale trade	Transport services	Wood & paper	Textiles, clothing, leather & footwear
IE (3)	Chemicals, rubber & plastics	Business services	:	:
EL	:	:	:	:
ES	Construction	Business services	Construction	Other non-metallic mineral products
FR	Business services	Retail trade & repair	Retail trade & repair	Business services
IT	Business services	Construction	Textiles, clothing, leather & footwear	Furniture & other manufacturing
CY (4)	Construction	Hotels & restaurants	:	:
LV (5)	Wholesale trade	Transport services	Wood & paper	Wholesale trade
LT	Energy	Wholesale trade	Textiles, clothing, leather & footwear	Energy
LU (6)	Business services	Construction	Transport services	Metals & metal products
HU	Electrical machinery & optical equipment	Business services	Electrical machinery & optical equipment	Energy
MT	:	:	:	:
NL	Business services	Wholesale trade	Wholesale trade	Transport services
AT (7)	Business services	Wholesale trade	Wood & paper	Hotels & restaurants
PL	Energy	Wholesale trade	Non-energy mining & quarrying	Energy
PT (8)	Wholesale trade	Construction	Other non-metallic mineral products	Recycling & water supply
RO (7)	Wholesale trade	Transport services	Non-energy mining & quarrying	Recycling & water supply
SI	Wholesale trade	Chemicals, rubber & plastics	Recycling & water supply	Textiles, clothing, leather & footwear
SK (7)	Wholesale trade	Metals & metal products	Recycling & water supply	Metals & metal products
FI	Business services	Electrical machinery & optical equipment	Wood & paper	Electrical machinery & optical equipment
SE	Business services	Wholesale trade	Wood & paper	Non-energy mining & quarrying
UK	Business services	Wholesale trade	Business services	Hotels & restaurants

(1) Energy, not available; furniture & other manufacturing and recycling & water supply, 2003.
(2) Textiles, clothing, leather & footwear, furniture & other manufacturing, energy and recycling & water supply, not available.
(3) Furniture & other manufacturing and energy, not available for value added.
(4) Energy, recycling & water supply and real estate, renting & R&D, not available for value added.
(5) Textiles, clothing, leather & footwear and energy, not available; food, beverages & tobacco, 2003.
(6) Wood & paper, energy, communications & media and real estate, renting & R&D, not available; textiles, clothing, leather & footwear and energy, not available for specialisation ratio; all data, 2003.
(7) Textiles, clothing, leather & footwear and energy, not available.
(8) Non-energy mining & quarrying and energy, not available; textiles, clothing, leather & footwear, 2003 for value added and not available for specialisation ratio; chemicals, rubber & plastics, 2003.
Source: Eurostat (SBS)

Table 1.5 also presents information on the largest activities and those with the highest specialisation ratios, this time structured by Member State instead of activity aggregate. This information confirms some regional patterns: for example, several Baltic, Scandinavian and alpine Member States were relatively specialised in the manufacture of wood and paper products (see Chapter 4), while mining (of energy and non-energy products) was relatively important in several central and eastern European countries (Bulgaria, Lithuania, Poland and Romania). The specialisation trends cited above are to a large degree related to endowments of natural resources. However, there are other factors that may play a role, such as the availability of skills, the breakdown of costs, access to infrastructure, or impediments to doing

business created by legislation. These may explain, for example, why the textiles, clothing, leather and footwear manufacturing sector (see Chapter 3) is no longer an activity dominated by the Mediterranean Member States of Italy, Portugal and Spain, as production is increasingly moved to eastern Europe (and beyond) in search of lower labour costs.

SPECIALISATION AT A REGIONAL LEVEL
Regional structural business statistics provide data with a detailed sectoral breakdown which can be used to study the nature, characteristics and evolution of the regional business economy for example in relation to the European Union's economic and regional policies.

The maps on pages 15 and 16 show the proportion of the non-financial business economy workforce occupied within the industrial and non-financial services sectors in 2004 (note that a similar map for the construction sector is presented within Chapter 15). There is a clear pattern of industrial employment being concentrated within parts of Germany, central and eastern Europe. There were a few regions where industrial employment accounted for more than 50 % of the regional workforce in 2004; these were exclusively located in Bulgaria, Romania and Slovakia.

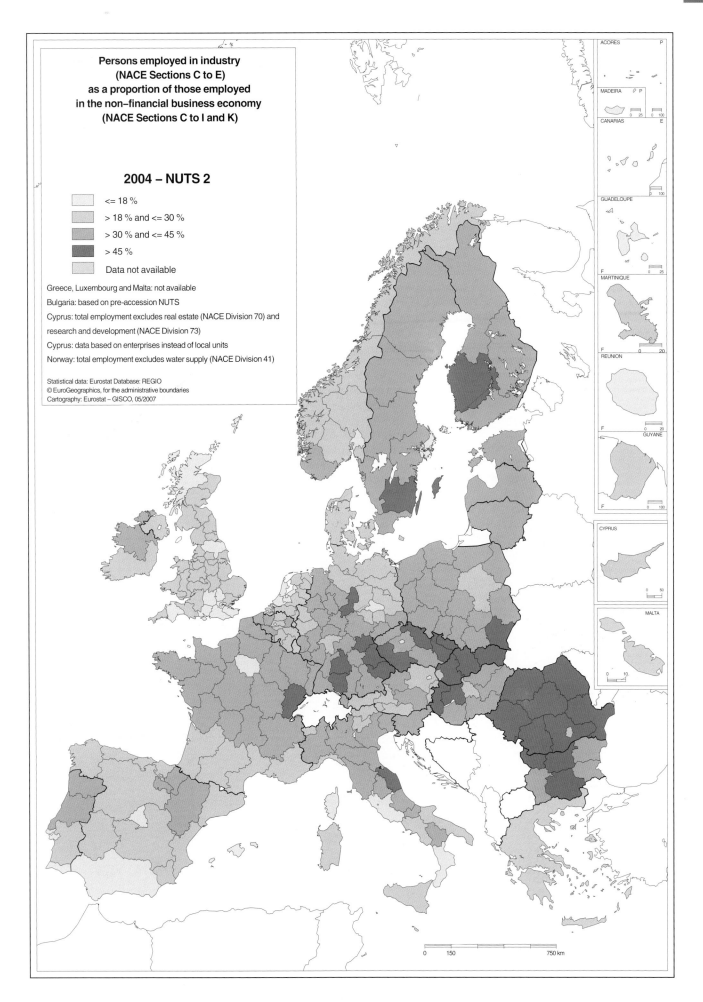

Persons employed in industry
(NACE Sections C to E)
as a proportion of those employed
in the non–financial business economy
(NACE Sections C to I and K)

2004 – NUTS 2

<= 18 %

> 18 % and <= 30 %

> 30 % and <= 45 %

> 45 %

Data not available

Greece, Luxembourg and Malta: not available

Bulgaria: based on pre-accession NUTS

Cyprus: total employment excludes real estate (NACE Division 70) and

research and development (NACE Division 73)

Cyprus: data based on enterprises instead of local units

Norway: total employment excludes water supply (NACE Division 41)

Statistical data: Eurostat Database: REGIO
© EuroGeographics, for the administrative boundaries
Cartography: Eurostat – GISCO, 05/2007

ACORES P

MADEIRA P

CANARIAS E

GUADELOUPE

MARTINIQUE

REUNION

GUYANE

CYPRUS

MALTA

0   150   750 km

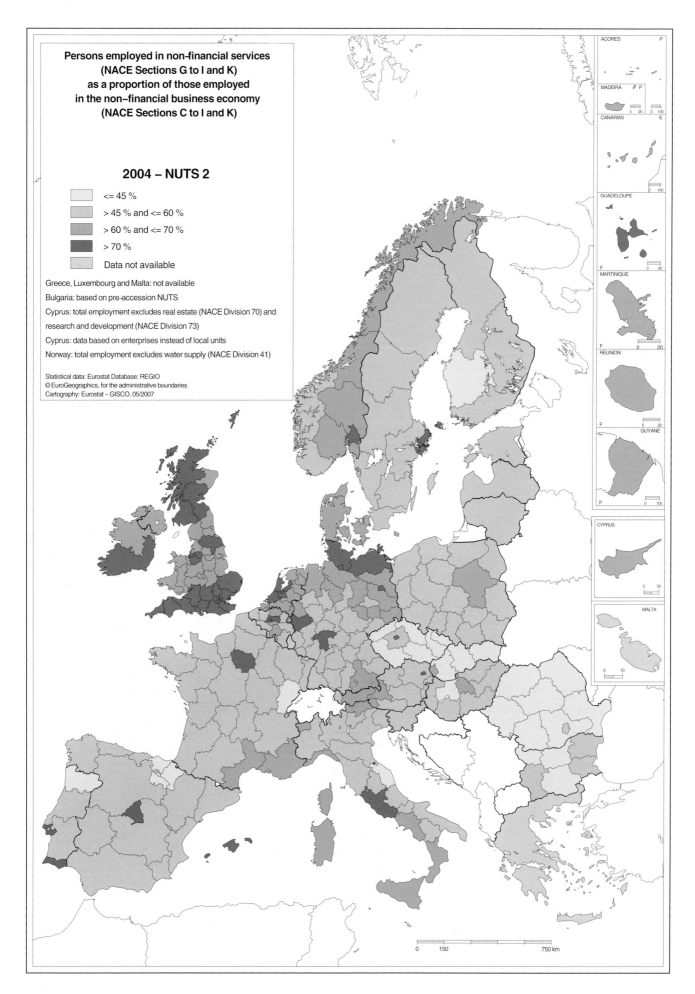

Persons employed in non-financial services
(NACE Sections G to I and K)
as a proportion of those employed
in the non-financial business economy
(NACE Sections C to I and K)

2004 – NUTS 2

- <= 45 %
- > 45 % and <= 60 %
- > 60 % and <= 70 %
- > 70 %
- Data not available

Greece, Luxembourg and Malta: not available

Bulgaria: based on pre-accession NUTS

Cyprus: total employment excludes real estate (NACE Division 70) and
research and development (NACE Division 73)

Cyprus: data based on enterprises instead of local units

Norway: total employment excludes water supply (NACE Division 41)

Statistical data: Eurostat Database: REGIO
© EuroGeographics, for the administrative boundaries
Cartography: Eurostat – GISCO, 05/2007

ACORES P

MADEIRA P

CANARIAS E

GUADELOUPE

MARTINIQUE

REUNION

GUYANE

CYPRUS

MALTA

Table 1.6 _____

**Three most specialised regions (NUTS 2 for sectoral chapter headings), EU-27 and Norway, 2004
(% share of non-financial business economy employment) (1)**

Chapter	Most	Second	Third
2 Food, beverages & tobacco	Bretagne (FR)	Podlaskie (PL)	La Rioja (ES)
3 Textiles, clothing, leather & footwear	Norte (PT)	Nord-Est (RO)	Nord-Vest (RO)
4 Wood & paper	Itä-Suomi (FI)	Norra Mellansverige (SE)	Mellersta Norrland (SE)
5 Chemicals, rubber & plastics	Rheinhessen-Pfalz (DE)	Alsace (FR)	Auvergne (FR)
6 Other non-metallic mineral products	Centro (PT)	Swietokrzyskie (PL)	Prov. Namur (BE)
7 Metals & metal products	Vychodne Slovensko (SK)	Arnsberg (DE)	Norra Mellansverige (SE)
8 Machinery & equipment	Tübingen (DE)	Unterfranken (DE)	Stuttgart (DE)
9 Electrical machinery & optical equipment	Zapadne Slovensko (SK)	Oberpfalz (DE)	Mittelfranken (DE)
10 Transport equipment	Braunschweig (DE)	Stuttgart (DE)	Niederbayern (DE)
11 Furniture & other manufacturing	Warminsko-Mazurskie (PL)	Friuli-Venezia Giulia (IT)	Nord-Vest (RO)
12 Non-energy mining & quarrying	Övre Norrland (SE)	Dolnoslaskie (PL)	Guyane (FR)
13 Energy	Slaskie (PL)	Sud-Vest Oltenia (RO)	Sud - Muntenia (RO)
14 Recycling & water supply	Stredne Slovensko (SK)	Vychodne Slovensko (SK)	Sud-Vest Oltenia (RO)
15 Construction	País Vasco (ES)	Canarias (ES)	Andalucía (ES)
16 Motor trades	Brandenburg - Südwest (DE)	Réunion (FR)	Guyane (FR)
17 Wholesale trade	Flevoland (NL)	Región de Murcia (ES)	Prov. Vlaams-Brabant (BE)
18 Retail trade & repair	Ciudad Autónoma de Ceuta (ES)	Ciudad Autónoma de Melilla (ES)	Merseyside (UK)
19 Hotels & restaurants	Illes Balears (ES)	Algarve (PT)	Provincia Autonoma Bolzano/Bozen (IT)
20 Transport services	Åland (FI)	Bratislavsky kraj (SK)	Mazowieckie (PL)
21 Communications & media	Köln (DE)	Lazio (IT)	Île de France (FR)
22 Business services	Inner London (UK)	Utrecht (NL)	Berkshire, Buckinghamshire & Oxfordshire (UK)
23 Real estate, renting & R&D	Inner London (UK)	Latvia (LV)	Berkshire, Buckinghamshire & Oxfordshire (UK)

(1) Greece, Luxembourg and Malta, not available; Bulgaria is based on pre-accession NUTS; Cyprus, not available for real estate, renting and R&D; Norway, not available for recycling and water supply; Cyprus, based on enterprises and not local units.
Source: Eurostat (SBS)

In contrast, employment within the non-financial services sector (see Map 1.2) was often concentrated in the capital city, for example, some 88.9 % of the total in Inner London in 2004, while upwards of 75 % of the workforce were employed in non-financial services in a number of other regions which include the capital, such as Noord-Holland (the Netherlands), Berlin (Germany), Région de Bruxelles-Capitale/Brussels Hoofdstedelijk Gewest (Belgium), Île de France (France), Comunidad de Madrid (Spain) and Wien (Austria).

Table 1.6 shows, for each of the activity aggregates used for the sectoral chapters, the three most specialised NUTS 2 level regions – on the basis of employment specialisation. As mentioned above, geographical and geological factors may help explain why some regions are particularly specialised in activities like mining and quarrying, energy, or forest-based activities. For example, Slaskie (Poland), Sud-Vest Oltenia and Sud - Muntenia (both Romania) are centres for mining and energy activities, while over 70 % of Norra Mellansverige (Sweden) and Itä-Suomi (Finland) are covered by forests, around which much of the local economy has developed. In a similar vein, it is not surprising that Bretagne (France) is the most specialised region for food and beverage manufacturing, as it is a largely rural area with a high proportion of agricultural land. Another factor that can play a key role in driving relative specialisation is weather, landscape and location: the most specialised regions for hotels and restaurants included the Illes Balears (Spain), the Algarve (Portugal) and

the Provincia Autonoma Bolzano/Bozen (northern Italy), all of which are popular destinations for tourists. A critical mass of clients (other enterprises or households/consumers) within close proximity, or a supply of highly skilled labour can also be drivers of specialisation, for example, research parks developing near to universities, or computer services, communications and media, and other business services being concentrated around capital cities and other densely populated regions. Sometimes the concentration of enterprises within a particular activity results in strategic clusters emerging to provide products and services designed specifically for a particular activity. For example, manufacturers of motor vehicle parts and accessories are clustered around Stuttgart and Wolfsburg in the Braunschweig region, while communication and media related enterprises are concentrated around Köln (all Germany), and many aerospace suppliers are located around Toulouse in the Midi-Pyrénées (France).

Table 1.7

Selected top/main manufacturing products sold in value terms, EU-27, 2006 (1)

	Prodcom code	Value (EUR million)
Motor vehicles with a petrol engine > 1500 cm³ (including motor caravans of a capacity > 3000 cm³)	34.10.22.30	119 405
Motor vehicles with a diesel or semi-diesel engine > 1500 cm³ but <= 2500 cm³	34.10.23.30	96 646
Beer made from malt (excluding non-alcoholic beer, beer containing <= 0.5% by volume of alcohol, alcohol duty)	15.96.10.00	29 320
Radio transmission apparatus with reception apparatus	32.20.11.70	26 906
Fresh bread containing by weight in the dry matter state <= 5% of sugars and <= 5% of fat	15.81.11.00	23 219
Ready-mixed concrete	26.63.10.00	22 686
Grated; powdered; blue-veined and other non-processed cheese (excluding fresh cheese; whey cheese and curd)	15.51.40.50	21 623
Cartons; boxes and cases of corrugated paper or paperboard	21.21.13.00	18 809
Cake and pastry products; other baker's wares with added sweetening matter	15.81.12.00	18 201
Sausages not of liver	15.13.12.15	17 686
Goods vehicles with a diesel or semi-diesel engine, of a gross vehicle weight <= 5 tonnes (excluding dumpers for off-highway use)	34.10.41.10	16 850
Motor vehicles with a diesel or semi-diesel engine <= 1500 cm³	34.10.23.10	16 241
Grey Portland cement (including blended cement)	26.51.12.30	15 226
Hot rolled flat products in coil (wide strip) of a width of 600 mm or more (of steel other than of stainless steel or of high speed steel)	27.10.60.20	14 801
Vehicle compression-ignition internal combustion piston engines (diesel or semi-diesel) (excluding for railway or tramway rolling stock)	34.10.13.00	14 712
Prefabricated structural components for building of cement	26.61.12.00	13 448
Cigarettes containing tobacco or mixtures of tobacco and tobacco substitutes (excluding tobacco duty)	16.00.11.50	13 198
Vehicle reciprocating piston engines of a cylinder capacity > 1000 cm³	34.10.12.00	12 581
Motor vehicles with a diesel or semi-diesel engine > 2500 cm³	34.10.23.40	12 489
Fresh or chilled cuts of beef and veal	15.11.11.90	12 442

(1) Excluding products of a generic nature (other), sales of services such as repair, maintenance and installation; estimates.
Source: Eurostat (PRODCOM)

Table 1.8

Selected manufacturing products sold in volume and value terms, EU-27, 2006 (1)

	Prodcom code	Volume (millions)	Unit	Value (EUR million)
Grey Portland cement (including blended cement)	26.51.12.30	216 165	kg	15 225
Flat semi-finished products (slabs) (of stainless steel)	27.10.32.10	600	kg	1 215
Champagne (important: excluding alcohol duty)	15.93.11.30	244	litres	4 189
Perfumes	24.52.11.50	35	litres	471
Coniferous wood; sawn or chipped lengthwise; sliced or peeled; of a thickness > 6mm; planed (excluding end-jointed or sanded)	20.10.10.34	19	m³	3 670
Oxygen	24.11.11.70	27 393	m³	2 063
Cigarettes containing tobacco or mixtures of tobacco and tobacco substitutes (excluding tobacco duty)	16.00.11.50	795 205	units	13 190
Flat panel colour TV receivers, LCD/plasma, etc. excluding television projection equipment, apparatus with video recorder/player, video monitors, television receivers with integral tube	32.30.20.60	13	units	8 178

(1) Excluding products of a generic nature (other), sales of services such as repair, maintenance and installation; estimates.
Source: Eurostat (PRODCOM)

MOST PRODUCED PRODUCTS

PRODCOM is a system for the collection and dissemination of statistics on the production of goods in the EU-27. Information provided in PRODCOM includes data for the value and volume of production in the Member States that has been sold by their producers in a particular reference year. Commodities are specified in the PRODCOM list, which includes around 4 500 products, updated on an annual basis. The products are listed according to an eight-digit code, of which the first six are directly aligned with the statistical classification of products by activity in the European Community, the CPA.

Table 1.7 shows a selection of the 20 products with the highest values of production sold in the EU-27 in 2006, excluding a few products: those of a generic nature, sales of services (such as repair, maintenance and installation), and confidential values. As can be seen, transport equipment products (CPA 34) dominated, occupying the first two places, with a further five products among the top twenty. Table 1.8 illustrates the information that is available in volume terms, where the measurement unit used varies depending on the nature of the product.

1.3: COSTS, PRODUCTIVITY AND PROFITABILITY

Competitiveness at the sectoral and micro-economic level is often defined as the ability of a particular activity or enterprise to improve its position in (global) markets. A high degree of prominence is often given to productivity gains when trying to explain how particular activities or enterprises become more competitive. This section looks in more detail at cost profiles (in particular the cost of energy and labour), productivity and profitability issues.

Labour market reforms enacted across many Member States have recently been accompanied by a tendency towards higher employment rates (in other words, a greater proportion of the population being in work). These increases (which at the same time swell tax revenues and reduce social protection expenditure) are seen as an integral part of the 'strategy for jobs and growth'. The parallel goal of raising productivity levels (or the added value generated by each person employed) is likely to stem from areas such as the re-organisation and re-allocation of production, improved labour skills, or the introduction of new products and processes (in particular through information and communication technologies).

TOTAL EXPENDITURE

A breakdown of total expenditure sheds some light on the different cost structures that exist across activities in terms of operating and capital expenditure. These statistics provide an insight into the capital/labour intensities of different sectors and the extent to which they convert or distribute products. Figure 1.10 shows the cost structures of different activities, with a breakdown of total expenditure into its three components, namely, purchases of goods and services, personnel costs, and gross tangible investment. On average, some 78.7 % of all EU-27 total expenditure in the non-financial business economy was allocated to purchases of goods and services in 2004, while 16.4 % was accounted for by personnel costs and the remaining 4.9 % by gross tangible investment. The breakdowns for industry and non-financial services were both similar to the overall figures for the whole of the non-financial business economy. However, there was a distinct split within non-financial service activities, as the three distributive trades activities recorded the highest proportions of purchases of goods and services within total expenditure (upwards of 90 % for both wholesale and motor trades); perhaps no surprise, given that these activities are characterised by purchases for resale without transformation. With the exception of distributive trades, the other non-financial

Figure 1.10

Structure of total expenditure, EU-27, 2004 (%)

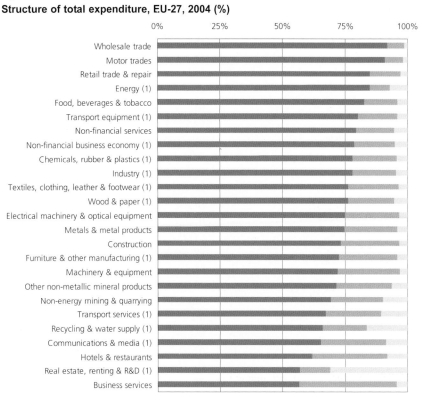

(1) Rounded estimates based on non-confidential data.
Source: Eurostat (SBS)

services were all relatively labour-intensive, with personnel costs accounting for a high proportion of total expenditure in 2004; this ratio rose as high as 39.3 % for business services for the EU-27.

Given the extremely high share of purchases of goods and services, unsurprisingly distributive trades recorded the lowest rate of investment intensity (as defined by the share of gross tangible investment in total expenditure) in 2004, while rates were also relatively low for construction, where the vast majority of enterprises are relatively small and specialised in activities such as plastering, plumbing, electrical installations. By the same measure, investment intensity was low within a number of manufacturing activities, such as machinery and equipment manufacturing, electrical machinery and optical equipment manufacturing, the manufacture of textiles, clothing, leather and footwear, or furniture and other manufacturing industries. The most investment-intensive activity (as measured by a relatively high share of gross tangible investment in total expenditure) was real estate, renting and R&D.

This is perhaps not surprising as many enterprises within these activities are owners of the capital goods that they sell, rent and lease. In a similar vein, the investment intensity of hotels and restaurants was also relatively high, due to the relatively high degree of investment required in buildings, both in terms of initial purchase or construction, and for major renovations. Other activities that were relatively investment-intensive included those requiring specialist machinery and equipment or investment in infrastructure networks (for example, water, energy and telecommunications). It should be noted that the level of investments in a given year could be volatile, in particular on a detailed level (activity/country), with a year with large investments followed by a period with little or no investments.

Most EU-15 Member States reported personnel costs accounting for a relatively high share of total expenditure in 2004, with the highest proportion (19.2 %) recorded for Germany, while shares of 18 % or more were also recorded in Sweden, Austria, France and the United Kingdom – see Table 1.9 [6]. However, it was Cyprus that registered the highest proportion of total costs being devoted to personnel (21.1 %). Slovenia reported a cost structure that was similar to the EU-27 average (16.4 %), with personnel costs accounting for 15.7 % of total expenditure, while the relative importance of personnel costs was considerably lower for the remaining 11 Member States that joined the EU since 2004, ranging from 11.3 % in Lithuania down to 7.1 % in Bulgaria. In contrast many of these Member States recorded a particularly high level of investment intensity. Romania recorded a 12.9 % ratio for investment intensity in 2004 that was almost three times as high as the EU-27 average (4.9 %). Poland was the only one of the 12 Member States that joined the EU since 2004 to report a level of investment intensity that was below the EU-27 average. Among the EU-15 Member States, the share of gross tangible investment in total expenditure was relatively high in Denmark, Austria and Portugal (7 % or above), while the lowest shares (4 % or lower) were recorded for Germany and the Benelux countries.

ENERGY AND RAW MATERIAL COSTS

One particular aspect of purchases of goods and services that has come under close scrutiny in the past couple of years is the price of energy and mineral products. There are considerable challenges in ensuring a security of supply with respect to both energy products and a range of other important inputs, including metals and minerals. Reliable supplies are often considered to be one of the key elements for the competitiveness of an economy, as many products are not available within the Member States (or they exist in such small volumes that it is not economic to mine/extract them). This reliance on imports is often quite striking, as 37 % of the world's copper was mined in Chile in 2004, while 40 % of the world's bauxite was from Australia, 53 % of its chromium from South Africa, and 87 % of its tungsten from China, while most EU-27 oil and gas imports originated from Russia, Norway and Saudi Arabia [7].

[6] Ireland, excluding mining and quarrying of energy producing materials (NACE Subsection CA) and electricity, gas and water supply (NACE Section E); Cyprus, excluding real estate activities (NACE Division 70) and research and development (NACE Division 73); Luxembourg, 2003; Greece and Malta, not available.
[7] Securing raw material supply for EU industries, press release by European Commission Vice President Günter Verheugen, 5 June 2007, based on World mining data (2006).

Table 1.9

Total expenditure, non-financial business economy, 2004 (%)

	Value (EUR million)				Share (% of total expenditure)		
	Total expenditure	Purchases of goods & services	Personnel costs	Gross tangible investment	Purchases of goods & services	Personnel costs	Gross tangible investment
EU-27	18 160 000	14 300 000	2 970 000	890 000	78.7	16.4	4.9
BE	652 351	544 864	82 817	24 670	83.5	12.7	3.8
BG	52 432	44 516	3 726	4 190	84.9	7.1	8.0
CZ	228 808	191 297	25 204	12 307	83.6	11.0	5.4
DK	333 444	245 017	58 360	30 067	73.5	17.5	9.0
DE	3 495 062	2 684 098	670 154	140 810	76.8	19.2	4.0
EE	25 335	20 832	2 623	1 880	82.2	10.4	7.4
IE (1)	:	:	:	:	82.2	12.9	4.9
EL	:	:	:	:	:	:	:
ES	1 673 619	1 326 424	256 754	90 442	79.3	15.3	5.4
FR	2 812 442	2 166 296	515 014	131 132	77.0	18.3	4.7
IT	2 266 202	1 873 011	291 628	101 562	82.6	12.9	4.5
CY (2)	:	:	:	:	73.3	21.1	5.7
LV	23 808	19 227	2 217	2 364	80.8	9.3	9.9
LT	31 855	26 034	3 587	2 234	81.7	11.3	7.0
LU (3)	46 586	38 166	6 989	1 431	81.9	15.0	3.1
HU	190 784	159 263	18 776	12 745	83.5	9.8	6.7
MT	:	:	:	:	:	:	:
NL	890 498	720 259	138 295	31 944	80.9	15.5	3.6
AT	414 218	308 077	75 858	30 283	74.4	18.3	7.3
PL	401 115	343 530	38 722	18 864	85.6	9.7	4.7
PT	289 582	230 587	38 734	20 261	79.6	13.4	7.0
RO	118 661	92 496	10 862	15 302	78.0	9.2	12.9
SI	53 295	42 111	8 368	2 815	79.0	15.7	5.3
SK	61 932	51 174	6 321	4 437	82.6	10.2	7.2
FI	275 858	220 707	42 977	12 175	80.0	15.6	4.4
SE	518 723	390 587	97 050	31 087	75.3	18.7	6.0
UK	2 792 378	2 136 307	509 843	146 228	76.5	18.3	5.2

(1) Excluding mining and quarrying of energy producing materials (NACE Subsection CA) and electricity, gas and water supply (NACE Section E).
(2) Excluding real estate activities (NACE Division 70) and research and development (NACE Division 73).
(3) 2003.
Source: Eurostat (SBS)

Figure 1.11

Purchases of energy products, average for available Member States, 2004 (% share of total expenditure) (1)

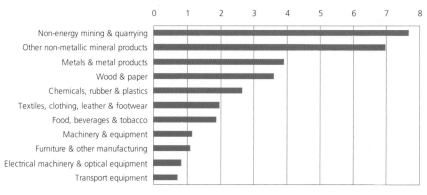

(1) Average for Belgium, Czech Republic, Germany, Estonia, Spain, France, Italy, Cyprus, Lithuania, Hungary, Netherlands, Finland and United Kingdom; NACE Sections C to E, excluding energy, recycling and water supply (NACE Subsection CA and Divisions 23, 37, 40 and 41).
Source: Eurostat (SBS)

Rising global demand for many of these raw materials has been driven by the unprecedented expansion of output in several emerging economies, such as China, India and Brazil. Increased demand on the one hand, as well as political instability in producing countries on the other, can, to some degree, be used to explain the rapidly spiralling price increases that were observed for oil and gas between 2002 and 2006. For more information concerning the evolution of crude oil prices see Chapter 13.

The rising price of oil had an impact on the price of substitutes, and also translated into price increases in other downstream activities. For example, rising oil prices have been used to explain gas price increases, as the price of gas is often set in long-term contracts that are linked to the price of oil. Oil price increases were also passed down the production chain in the form of higher electricity prices, thus affecting a wide range of downstream activities, in particular, activities which are energy-intensive (such as the manufacture of iron and steel, aluminium, concrete or ceramics), or those industries that use oil and its derivatives as inputs in their own manufacturing processes (for example, the manufacture of chemicals, rubber and plastics).

A breakdown of industrial purchases of energy gives an indication of their importance in the cost structures of different activities. The data shown are based on averages constructed on the basis of available data [8] for 2004. Across industrial activities, the chemicals, rubber and plastics (22.9 %) and metals and metal products (20.8 %) manufacturing sectors accounted for the highest proportions of industrial energy purchases. When viewed in terms of the relative importance of energy costs in total expenditure – see Figure 1.11 – the most energy-intensive activities included non-energy mining and quarrying and the manufacture of other non-metallic mineral products, where energy costs accounted for upwards of 7 % of expenditure. These ratios were almost double those recorded in the next most energy-intensive activities, namely, the production of metals and metal products, and the manufacture of wood and paper, where energy accounted for just less than 4 % of expenditure.

[8] Averages based on Belgium, Czech Republic, Germany, Estonia, Spain, France, Italy, Cyprus, Lithuania, Hungary, the Netherlands, Finland and the United Kingdom; data cover total industry (NACE Sections C to E), excluding energy, recycling and water supply (NACE Subsection CA and Divisions 23, 37, 40 and 41).

Figure 1.12

Average personnel costs per employee, EU-27, 2004 (EUR thousand per employee) (1)

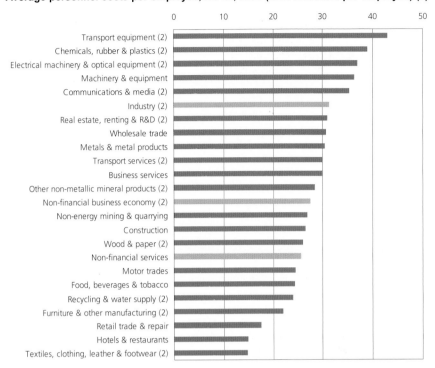

(1) Energy, not available.
(2) Rounded estimate based on non-confidential data.
Source: Eurostat (SBS)

PERSONNEL COSTS

In recent years, many governments have reformed their labour market policy, in the face of competition from countries with lower labour costs, and with the goal of avoiding a pensions' crisis through encouraging higher employment rates.

Personnel costs are defined as the total remuneration, in cash or in kind, payable by an employer to an employee (permanent and temporary employees as well as home workers) in return for work done by the latter, including taxes and employees' social security contributions that are retained by the unit, and employer's compulsory and voluntary social contributions. Note that there may be costs associated with employing staff that are not covered by personnel costs, for example, training, recruitment costs, or the provision of working clothes.

As has been shown, personnel costs accounted for 16.4 % of the total expenditure in the EU-27's non-financial business economy in 2004. In relation to the number of paid workers, personnel costs averaged EUR 27 600 per employee in the EU-27's non-financial business economy. Average personnel costs for industrial activities were somewhat higher, at EUR 31 300 per employee, than those for construction (EUR 26 600) or non-financial services (EUR 25 700).

Across the activity aggregates used for the sectoral chapters in this publication [9], personnel costs per employee were highest for the manufacture of transport equipment at EUR 43 000, falling to just one third of this level (EUR 14 800 per employee) for the manufacture of textiles, clothing, leather and footwear – see Figure 1.12. The ratio of average personnel costs per employee is calculated on the basis of headcounts for employees (as opposed to full-time equivalents), which is particularly important for several service sectors, where the propensity to employ persons on a part-time basis is often high – for example, hotels and restaurants and retail trade and repair. Indeed, these two sectors which reported the highest proportion of part-time employment also recorded the second and third lowest levels of average personnel costs per employee (across the activity aggregates used for the sectoral chapters).

Wages and salaries represented more than three quarters (78.0 %) of total personnel costs in the EU-27's non-financial business economy in 2004, leaving 22.0 % of personnel costs committed to social security costs – see Figure 1.13. These social costs correspond to the value of costs incurred by employers in order to secure for their

[9] Energy, not available.

employees entitlements to social benefits, including schemes for pensions, sickness, maternity, disability, unemployment, occupational accidents and diseases, and family allowances, regardless of whether these are statutory, collectively agreed, contractual or voluntary in nature. Social security costs accounted for a relatively low share of total personnel costs in Denmark (8.0 %), Cyprus, Ireland, the United Kingdom and Luxembourg (2003) – between 11.9 % and 12.8 % [10], while their relative importance rose to upwards of 30.0 % in France and Sweden. The proportion of total personnel costs that is accounted for by social security costs tends to be relatively uniform across activities within each Member State, as employers' contributions are often set on a statutory basis for the whole economy.

PRODUCTIVITY

Productivity is a key measure of economic efficiency, showing how effectively economic inputs are converted into output. Apparent labour productivity is defined as the value added generated by each person employed (measured by headcounts): this measure is therefore limited insofar as it does not consider differences in the extent of part-time work across activities. Part-time workers are most frequent in several non-financial services, such as hotels and restaurants, retail trade, and certain business services (see Chapter 1.5).

Figure 1.14 shows that on average each person employed in the EU-27's non-financial business economy generated EUR 40 900 of value added in 2004; with apparent labour productivity higher for industrial activities (EUR 49 000) than for non-financial services (EUR 38 200) or for construction (EUR 33 000). Labour productivity tended to be highest among those sectors that are characterised as being capital-intensive or high-tech, for example, energy, real estate, renting and R&D, communications and media, or the manufacture of chemicals, rubber and plastics. It was lowest among labour-intensive activities, such as the manufacture of textiles, clothing, leather and footwear, or hotels and restaurants, where labour productivity levels were less than half the non-financial business economy average.

Another measure of productivity is the wage adjusted labour productivity ratio, defined as value added divided by personnel costs and subsequently adjusted by the share of paid employees in the total number of persons employed, or more simply: apparent labour

Figure 1.13

Breakdown of personnel costs, non-financial business economy, 2004 (% share of total personnel costs) (1)

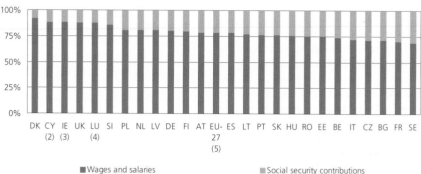

■ Wages and salaries   ■ Social security contributions

(1) Greece and Malta, not available.
(2) Excluding real estate activities (NACE Division 70) and research and development (NACE Division 73).
(3) Excluding mining and quarrying of energy producing materials (NACE Subsection CA) and electricity, gas and water supply (NACE Section E).
(4) 2003.
(5) Rounded estimates based on non-confidential data.
Source: Eurostat (SBS)

Figure 1.14

Apparent labour productivity, EU-27, 2004 (EUR thousand per person employed)

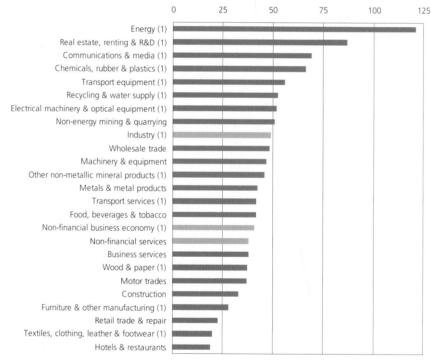

(1) Rounded estimate based on non-confidential data.
Source: Eurostat (SBS)

productivity divided by average personnel costs (expressed as a ratio in percentage terms). Given that this indicator is based on expenditure for labour input rather than a headcount of labour input, it is more relevant for comparisons across activities (or countries) with very different incidences of part-time employment or self-employment.

The wage adjusted labour productivity ratio for the EU-27's non-financial business economy stood at 148.0 % in 2004 (see Figure 1.15). Among the activity aggregates used for the sectoral chapters [11], the highest ratio was recorded for real estate, renting and R&D, followed by several other capital-intensive activities, such as recycling and water supply, communications and media, and non-energy

_____

[10] Ireland, excluding mining and quarrying of energy producing materials (NACE Subsection CA) and electricity, gas and water supply (NACE Section E); Cyprus, excluding real estate activities (NACE Division 70) and research and development (NACE Division 73); Luxembourg, 2003; Greece and Malta, not available.

_____

[11] Energy, not available.

mining and quarrying. At the other end of the range, value added per person employed covered average personnel costs by less than 130 % for the machinery and equipment, transport equipment, retail trade and repair, furniture and other manufacturing, hotels and restaurants, and business services sectors, falling to a low of 123.7 % for construction.

The ranking of the sectoral chapters was similar whether based on apparent labour productivity or wage adjusted labour productivity. However, transport equipment manufacturing moved from fifth most productive to sixth least productive, once apparent labour productivity was adjusted for the average personnel costs (highest among all of the activity aggregates used for the sectoral chapters). On the other hand, motor trades, and textiles, clothing, leather and footwear manufacturing moved up in the ranking, the latter having recorded the lowest average personnel costs.

Across the Member States [12] (see Table 1.10) there were wide ranging differences in apparent productivity levels and average personnel costs; both tended to be higher among the EU-15 Member States. When average personnel costs were used to adjust apparent labour productivity, many of the EU-15 Member States reported relatively low wage adjusted productivity ratios; this was particularly notable for Italy, France, Sweden and Belgium.

PROFITABILITY:
THE GROSS OPERATING RATE
The gross operating rate is defined as the gross operating surplus (value added at factor cost less personnel costs) divided by turnover; it is expressed as a percentage. The gross operating surplus measures the operating revenue that is left to compensate the capital factor input, after the labour factor input has been recompensed. The surplus is used to recompense the providers of own funds and debt, to pay taxes, and eventually for self-financing all or a part of investment. Although not always the case, the gross operating surplus will therefore generally be higher for capital-intensive activities and lower for those activities which have a relatively high proportion of their costs accounted for by personnel costs. The gross operating rate can be considered as one measure of profitability and is a key indicator for measuring competitiveness and enterprise success.

---

[12] Ireland, excluding mining and quarrying of energy producing materials (NACE Subsection CA) and electricity, gas and water supply (NACE Section E); Cyprus, excluding real estate activities (NACE Division 70) and research and development (NACE Division 73); Luxembourg, 2003; Greece and Malta, not available.

Figure 1.15 _____

Wage adjusted labour productivity ratio, EU-27, 2004 (%) (1)

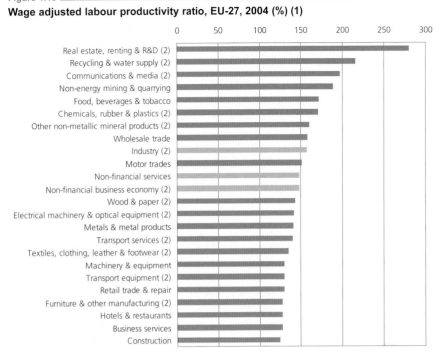

(1) Energy, not available.
(2) Rounded estimate based on non-confidential data.
Source: Eurostat (SBS)

Figure 1.16 _____

Gross operating rate, EU-27, 2004 (%)

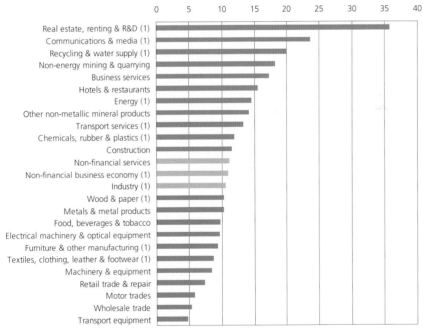

(1) Rounded estimate based on non-confidential data.
Source: Eurostat (SBS)

The EU-27's gross operating rate for the non-financial business economy was 11.0 % in 2004 (see Figure 1.16), while the rates for industry (10.6 %), construction (11.6 %) and non-financial services (11.2 %) were all closely grouped. In terms of the activity aggregates used for the sectoral chapters, the real estate, renting and R&D sector reported by far the highest gross operating rate (35.8 %), more than 50 % higher than the second highest rate (23.6 %) for the communications and media sector. The lowest EU-27 gross operating rate in 2004 was recorded for the manufacture of transport equipment, where relatively high average personnel costs weigh heavily on the gross operating surplus.

Table 1.10

Productivity and profitability, non-financial business economy, 2004

	Apparent labour productivity (EUR thousand per person employed)	Average personnel costs (EUR thousand per employee)	Wage adjusted labour productivity ratio (%)	Gross operating ratio (%)
EU-27 (1)	40.9	27.6	148.0	11.0
BE	58.4	42.0	138.8	8.3
BG	4.7	2.5	189.9	8.8
CZ	14.7	9.1	161.6	11.4
DK	61.6	37.7	163.1	12.2
DE	51.6	35.3	146.3	10.5
EE	13.2	7.0	188.6	9.7
IE (2)	81.7	32.8	249.1	19.1
EL	:	:	:	:
ES	35.7	24.2	147.5	11.7
FR	50.3	38.0	132.3	7.0
IT	38.6	29.7	129.9	11.4
CY (3)	30.7	20.4	150.1	13.6
LV	9.0	3.9	230.1	13.0
LT	8.8	4.7	187.8	10.5
LU (4)	56.9	37.4	152.3	8.7
HU	14.0	8.4	166.1	8.8
MT	:	:	:	:
NL	50.8	33.5	151.6	9.7
AT	52.2	35.7	146.1	11.0
PL	14.0	6.7	208.0	15.0
PT	21.9	14.4	151.7	8.9
RO	5.4	2.8	194.2	9.7
SI	23.8	16.3	145.7	9.3
SK	14.7	7.1	207.0	10.8
FI	60.0	37.5	159.8	10.4
SE	57.4	43.2	132.8	9.6
UK	53.6	30.7	175.0	14.4

(1) Rounded estimates based on non-confidential data.
(2) Excluding mining and quarrying of energy producing materials (NACE Subsection CA) and electricity, gas and water supply (NACE Section E).
(3) Excluding real estate activities (NACE Division 70) and research and development (NACE Division 73).
(4) 2003.
Source: Eurostat (SBS)

1.4: ENTERPRISE DEMOGRAPHY AND SIZE CLASS ANALYSIS

BUSINESS DEMOGRAPHY

In the form of a new product/service (innovation), the entrepreneur disturbs market equilibrium. For this reason, entrepreneurship is often cited as a key driver of competitiveness, as it forces enterprises that already exist to improve their efficiency, while driving inefficient enterprises out of business. The European Commission encourages entrepreneurship as part of its revised Lisbon process, re-launched as the growth and jobs strategy [13]. Access to markets, competition policy and employment creation are other important aspects in relation to entrepreneurship, although newly born enterprises in their initial start-up stage often actually have no paid employees, but operate with a working owner and/or unpaid family and friends.

SBS business demography statistics focus on so-called real enterprise births and deaths. Under the definitions employed, births do not include entries into the business enterprise population due to mergers, break-ups, splits or the restructuring of enterprises, nor do they include changes resulting from a change in the enterprise's principal (main) activity.

It is often quite difficult, statistically, to determine the exact date of cessation with respect to enterprise deaths. Therefore, the convention is to consider an enterprise as dead if it has not had any turnover and employment for at least two years; as such, information presented on enterprise deaths is often provisional in nature.

There were 1.3 million newly born enterprises in the business economy of 18 countries for which data are available for 2004 [14]: to put this in perspective newly born enterprises accounted for 9.9 % of the total stock of enterprises, while the average death rate was 8.3 % [15].

---

[13] For more details see http://ec.europa.eu/enterprise/entrepreneurship/index_en.htm.
[14] Bulgaria, the Czech Republic, Estonia, Spain, Italy, Cyprus, Latvia, Lithuania (2003), Luxembourg, Hungary, the Netherlands, Portugal, Romania, Slovenia (2003), Slovakia, Finland, Sweden and the United Kingdom; data cover the business economy (NACE Sections C to K, excluding Class 74.15).
[15] The Czech Republic (2003), Estonia, Spain, Italy (2003), Latvia, Luxembourg (2003), Hungary (2003), the Netherlands (2003), Portugal (2003), Romania, Slovakia, Finland (2003), Sweden and the United Kingdom; provisional data.

Figure 1.17

Enterprise birth and death rates, average for available Member States, 2004 (% share of active enterprises)

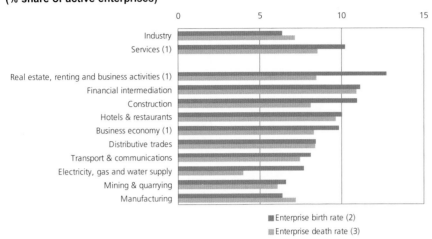

(1) Excluding management activities of holding companies (NACE Class 74.15).
(2) Weighted average based on Bulgaria, Czech Republic, Estonia, Spain, Italy, Cyprus, Latvia, Lithuania (2003), Luxembourg, Hungary, Netherlands, Portugal, Romania, Slovenia (2003), Slovakia, Finland, Sweden and United Kingdom.
(3) Weighted average based on Czech Republic (2003), Estonia, Spain, Italy (2003), Latvia, Luxembourg (2003), Hungary (2003), Netherlands (2003), Portugal (2003), Romania, Slovakia, Finland (2003), Sweden and United Kingdom.
Source: Eurostat (SBS)

Economic theory suggests that relatively low numbers of enterprise births are likely to be recorded for those activities where higher barriers to entry exist, perhaps because a greater level of initial investment in production factors is required to reach a minimum efficient scale of production. Consequently, where barriers to entry (and exit) are lower, as is the case for many services and construction activities, there are generally higher levels of enterprise birth and deaths.

Figure 1.17 shows enterprise birth rates and preliminary death rates for 2004 across a range of NACE sections based on averages for those Member States for which data are available (see footnote 13 for details of the country coverage for birth rates and footnote 14 for details of the coverage for death rates). Real estate, renting and business activities (NACE Section K, excluding Class 74.15), financial intermediation (NACE Section J) and construction (NACE Section F) reported the highest enterprise birth rates (12.7 %, 11.2 % and 11.0 % respectively), with hotels and restaurants (NACE Section H) the only other sector (at the NACE section level of detail) to report a birth rate above the business economy average (9.9 %). All four of these sectors reported a positive difference between their birth and death rates, suggesting a net increase in the number of enterprises in these activities. However, the highest difference (3.7 percentage

points) between birth and death rates was recorded for electricity, gas and water supply (NACE Section E), where the provisional death rate was only 4.0 %. This relatively large difference might, among other reasons, be explained by a recent period of liberalisation measures within these activities in a number of countries, resulting in the creation of energy and water distribution companies that enter the market to compete with established, formerly monopoly suppliers. At the other end of the range, there were more deaths within the population of manufacturing (NACE Section D) enterprises than births (7.2 % compared with 6.4 %). It should however be noted that the difference between the two demographic rates of births and deaths is not the only factor that affects the number of enterprises within a particular sub-population, as the number of enterprises may also change as a function of mergers, take-overs, split-offs and break-ups.

Some 77.0 % of all enterprises born in the industrial economy (NACE Sections C to E) in 2002 survived to 2004 among the 16 countries for which data are available [16]. Two-year survival rates were slightly lower for construction (75.3 %) and services (NACE Sections G to K, excluding Class 74.15, 75.2 %).

---

[16] The Czech Republic, Estonia, Spain, Italy, Latvia, Lithuania (2003), Luxembourg, Hungary, the Netherlands, Portugal, Romania, Slovenia (2003), Slovakia, Finland, Sweden and the United Kingdom.

Among 18 of the Member States for which data are available (see Table 1.11), countries with relatively low/high overall birth rates also tended to report relatively low/high death rates. Italy, the Netherlands, Portugal, Slovenia, Finland and Sweden were among those countries with the lowest levels of renewing their enterprise populations, while Estonia, Romania and the United Kingdom reported some of the highest rates (in particular for services).

FACTORS OF BUSINESS SUCCESS

In a bid to encourage more entrepreneurs, a European Council meeting in 2006 agreed that all Member States should establish (by the end of 2007) one-stop shops for entrepreneurs to undertake all procedures involved in starting a new business (for example, tax and VAT, social security, as well as the actual creation of the company), while reducing the time needed to no more than a week. This was followed on 11 July 2007 by the European Parliament accepting a Commission proposal for removing unnecessary burdens on small businesses [17].

Based on the business demography data collection exercise, a special SBS survey was launched with respect to factors of business success. The objective was to profile successful entrepreneurs by studying enterprises that were born in 2002 and had survived through to 2005, analysing differences in relation to gender, age-group, education and previous experience. Table 1.12 presents an overview of the results based on averages constructed from available information for a subset of Member States [18]; it is important to note that the information presented only describes the characteristics of the sub-population of successful entrepreneurs. As such, while 72.0 % of all surviving enterprises were in the hands of men, this statistic says nothing about whether a higher proportion of unsuccessful entrepreneurs were men or women.

The most popular motivation for starting an enterprise, among successful entrepreneurs, was a desire to be one's own boss, as selected by 75.0 % of respondents (multiple responses were allowed); this criterion was particularly important (80.8 %) within the construction sector. The next most important motivation was the prospect of making more money (72.6 %), while more than two thirds (67.8 %) of successful entrepreneurs also cited a desire for new challenges.

Table 1.11 _____

Enterprise birth and death rates, 2004, and two-year survival rates for enterprises born in 2002 (%) (1)

	Industry			Construction			Services (2)		
	Birth rate	2-year survival rate	Death rate	Birth rate	2-year survival rate	Death rate	Birth rate	2-year survival rate	Death rate
BG	8.1	:	:	9.8	:	:	10.9	:	:
CZ	7.9	69.9	10.7	10.3	66.9	11.0	10.5	63.4	13.3
EE	11.4	78.2	10.0	22.4	78.0	15.9	16.4	72.0	12.5
ES	6.0	79.7	5.2	12.1	73.2	6.4	9.7	75.9	6.3
IT	4.6	77.9	6.4	9.8	75.0	8.3	7.9	74.4	7.5
CY	2.6	:	:	11.1	:	:	5.4	:	:
LV	8.6	57.9	6.8	11.7	63.5	8.4	10.8	62.0	7.9
LT (3)	8.8	87.1	:	11.1	81.8	:	9.2	80.3	:
LU	6.4	72.9	5.4	8.4	81.4	7.4	10.8	81.7	9.1
HU	5.8	75.3	8.6	10.8	75.2	10.4	10.6	68.8	11.1
NL	5.9	75.8	6.7	8.0	76.4	6.8	9.2	70.7	9.5
PT	5.7	96.1	4.8	7.8	96.7	3.4	6.8	95.8	5.7
RO	15.2	78.4	7.9	24.2	78.5	6.9	19.2	76.5	8.4
SI (3)	3.8	87.4	:	6.7	89.5	:	7.4	83.1	:
SK	8.4	64.1	6.3	10.9	62.3	5.6	11.0	68.0	8.1
FI	5.0	70.8	5.8	9.5	72.6	6.6	8.7	66.9	7.5
SE	4.9	88.2	4.5	6.8	89.6	4.8	6.7	87.5	5.5
UK	8.6	83.0	10.4	13.4	83.2	10.2	15.2	81.7	11.9
Avg. (4)	6.4	77.0	7.2	11.0	75.3	8.1	10.2	75.2	8.6
CH	2.2	:	3.0	3.2	:	3.0	4.0	:	3.8

(1) Enterprise death rates are preliminary.
(2) Excluding management activities of holding companies (NACE Class 74.15).
(3) 2003 for birth and death rates; enterprises born in 2001 and surviving to 2003 for survival rate..
(4) Birth rates - weighted average based on Bulgaria, Czech Republic, Estonia, Spain, Italy, Cyprus, Latvia, Lithuania (2003), Luxembourg, Hungary, Netherlands, Portugal, Romania, Slovenia (2003), Slovakia, Finland, Sweden and United Kingdom; 2-year survival rates - weighted average based on Czech Republic, Estonia, Spain, Italy, Latvia, Lithuania (2003), Luxembourg, Hungary, Netherlands, Portugal, Romania, Slovenia (2003), Slovakia, Finland, Sweden and United Kingdom; death rates - weighted average based on Czech Republic (2003), Estonia, Spain, Italy (2003), Latvia, Luxembourg (2003), Hungary (2003), Netherlands (2003), Portugal (2003), Romania, Slovakia, Finland (2003), Sweden and United Kingdom.
Source: Eurostat (SBS)

Table 1.12 _____

Factors of business success among entrepreneurs who started an enterprise in 2002 which had survived to 2005, average for available Member States (1)

	Business economy (2)	Industry	Construction	Services (2)
Start-up motivation:				
Desire to be one's own boss	75.0	76.7	80.8	73.5
Prospect of making more money	72.6	72.2	74.0	72.4
Desire for new challenges	67.8	67.8	64.2	68.5
Start-up financing:				
Own funds or savings	85.4	85.1	90.5	84.3
Financial assistance from family or friends	26.5	30.9	17.2	27.8
Bank loan with collateral	11.2	12.9	12.1	10.8
Start-up difficulties:				
Deal with legal / governmental / administrative matters	63.2	68.4	64.8	62.0
To establish contacts with customers	61.1	63.3	64.5	60.0
To get financing	55.0	65.8	59.9	52.2
Impediments to selling products or services:				
Competition too vigorous	82.3	81.3	86.6	81.6
Too little demand	55.3	57.4	48.8	56.3
Difficult pricing	43.1	46.6	53.6	40.2
Impediments to developing the business activity:				
Regulatory and administrative burden	69.2	71.3	75.6	67.4
Profitability	67.1	69.2	66.5	66.9
Non or late paying customers	51.5	57.8	74.9	45.5

(1) Average based on data for Bulgaria, Czech Republic, Denmark, Italy, Lithuania, Luxembourg, Austria, Romania, Slovakia and Sweden; only the three most popular replies are shown; multiple answers permitted.
(2) Excluding management activities of holding companies (NACE Class 74.15).
Source: Eurostat (SBS)

_____
[17] See http://ec.europa.eu/enterprise/newsroom/cf/itemshortdetail.cfm?item_id=734 for more details.
[18] Average based on data for Bulgaria, the Czech Republic, Denmark, Italy, Lithuania, Luxembourg, Austria, Romania, Slovakia and Sweden; data cover the business economy (NACE Sections C to K, excluding Class 74.15).

The survey also provides information on difficulties faced when starting an enterprise. The most often cited start-up difficulties included dealing with legal/governmental/administrative matters (63.2 %), closely followed by establishing contacts with customers (61.1 %), and getting finance (55.0 %) – this latter category was a preoccupation for a considerably higher proportion of successful, industrial entrepreneurs (65.8 %) where start-up costs are often higher than within construction or service sectors. Regulatory and administrative burdens were also the most often cited impediment to developing a business activity (69.2 %), followed by profitability (67.1 %), and problems of non or late paying customers (51.5 %) – the importance of this final burden was particularly high among successful entrepreneurs within the construction sector, as cited by 74.9 %.

INTER-ENTERPRISE RELATIONS

The challenges of globalisation and increased competition, coupled with the possibilities offered by information and communications technologies, has led many enterprises to re-assess how they do business. One of the main changes in the behaviour of enterprises in recent years has been an increase in the establishment of long-term relations with other enterprises, through outsourcing or networking, in relation to both core activities and supportive functions. This process may well have been stimulated by the possibilities and advantages offered by ICT developments.

Inter-enterprise relations are defined as relations between enterprises, excluding legal ownership and relations arising from the normal purchase or sale of goods and services for immediate consumption. They cover outsourcing, franchising, networking, licensing, joint ventures, as well as non-permanent co-operation, but exclude relations between holding companies and their subsidiaries. An ad hoc survey on these types of relationships was carried out in 2003 in six Member States (Denmark, Germany, France, Portugal, Finland and Sweden) across the activities of manufacturing (NACE Sections D), construction (NACE Section F) and non-financial services (NACE Sections G to I and K).

Figure 1.18

Share of value added and employment generated by foreign-controlled enterprises, average for available Member States, 2004 (%) (1)

(1) Weighted average based on data available for Bulgaria, the Czech Republic, Estonia, Spain, Cyprus, Latvia, Lithuania, Hungary, Austria (2003), Portugal, Romania and Slovakia.
Source: Eurostat (SBS)

In five Member States that took part in the survey (excluding France), between 60 % and 70 % of enterprises answered favourably when questioned about the perceived impact of relations with other enterprises on their own competitiveness during the previous three year period. A higher proportion of large enterprises were found to engage in long-term relations with other enterprises, a feature that was particularly pronounced in Denmark and Portugal. The propensity of enterprises to engage in long-term relations also varied between economic activities, as witnessed by half of all German fuel processing (NACE Subsection DF) enterprises being engaged in long-term relations; this particularly high proportion probably reflects the need for strategic partnerships in this activity in order to secure energy supplies.

Of the seven different types of long-term relation that were surveyed, outsourcing was the most prevalent, while networking was generally the next most important type of relation (in particular in the Scandinavian countries), while other types were usually of minor importance, except for joint ventures in France and licensing in Germany.

Some of the most commonly cited reasons for engaging in relations with other enterprises included increased flexibility, resources or expertise, and cost reduction or economies of scale. Increased flexibility was cited as either very or somewhat important by an average of 70 % of respondents, suggesting that enterprises sought relations to protect themselves from rapidly changing markets, through product diversification, supply chain management, vertical integration, or more cost-effective locations for plant and distribution networks.

FOREIGN-CONTROLLED ENTERPRISES (INWARD FATS)

Globalisation has had a considerable impact on the location of production. Many enterprises have extended their operations beyond national borders in an attempt to (amongst other things) increase proximity to customers, circumvent trade barriers, reduce costs (labour, transportation or material inputs), guarantee the supply of material inputs or avoid regulation. Groups of (predominantly large) enterprises are at the core of the globalisation process and may be seen as agents of cross-border transactions, as they control decisions, information flows and strategies across a range of countries. The qualitative nature of information required to define a group's perimeter can often make it difficult to obtain reliable statistical information on these economic actors. One of the main constraints when trying to measure their activities is that global enterprises make their decisions against a worldwide backdrop, while their decisions continue to be analysed using national data collections.

Aside from exports or enterprise creation, there are a number of alternatives for an enterprise wishing to diversify into new markets, among which is to control an enterprise in another country. Information on foreign-controlled enterprises is covered by inward foreign affiliates statistics (inward FATS). For the purpose of the inward FATS data collection, the concept of control is defined as the ability to determine general corporate policy; however in practice, a share of ownership is often used as a proxy.

These inward FATS statistics show that the number of foreign affiliates tends to be generally low. However, given their relatively large average size, these enterprises can often exercise a significant economic impact. Figure 1.18 shows that foreign-controlled enterprises generated 30 % of the manufacturing sector's (NACE Section D) total value added in 2004 in the ten Member States for which data are available [19]. In contrast less than 8 % of the value added within the construction (NACE Section F) and the hotels and restaurants (NACE Section H) sector was created by foreign-controlled enterprises.

More detailed country information is provided in Table 1.13, supporting the view that foreign-controlled enterprises had a relatively large average size and higher levels of apparent labour productivity when compared with nationally-controlled enterprises. Across those countries for which data are available, the share of foreign-controlled enterprises in the total enterprise population was (with the exception of Estonia) always below 6 %, and more generally less than 2 %. Nevertheless, foreign-controlled enterprises contributed a double-digit share of the non-financial business economy workforce in each country (except Portugal and Cyprus), with almost a third of the workforce in Estonia working for a foreign-controlled enterprise. The labour productivity of foreign-controlled enterprises was relatively high, as in Hungary, Bulgaria, Lithuania and Portugal, the share of foreign-controlled enterprises in value added was at least twice as high as the corresponding share of foreign-controlled enterprises in the number of persons employed; while in the remaining countries for which data are available foreign-controlled enterprises accounted for a higher proportion of total value added than their share of total employment. Note that the difference in productivity levels may at least in part be due to the larger, average size of foreign-controlled enterprises (as productivity generally increase by enterprise size, see next section), rather than any inherent difference in productivity levels between nationally-controlled and foreign-controlled enterprises.

---

[19] Bulgaria, the Czech Republic, Estonia, Spain, Latvia, Lithuania, Hungary, Austria (2003), Portugal and Slovakia.

Table 1.13

Impact of foreign-controlled enterprises, non-financial business economy, 2004 (% share of total)

	Number of enterprises	Value added	Number of persons employed
BG	2.3	31.1	13.5
CZ	1.7	35.1	20.8
EE	19.6	41.2	31.6
ES	0.2	15.3	10.1
CY	0.7	4.2	3.1
LV	4.1	26.1	13.8
LT	3.4	25.1	11.0
HU	0.3	40.3	16.5
AT (1)	1.1	16.4	11.8
PT	0.3	15.6	7.5
RO	0.9	34.7	17.6
SK	5.7	44.8	26.6

(1) 2003.
Source: Eurostat (SBS)

SIZE CLASS ANALYSIS: THE ROLE OF SMALL AND MEDIUM-SIZED ENTERPRISES (SMES)

The European Commission has placed SMEs at the centre of industrial policy-making [20], realising that 'if SMEs are to have a significant impact on Europe's economy, they need to grow bigger – take on more employees, and expand their product ranges, markets and turnover'. Innovation is often seen as the most important driver of growth, whether it leads to new products and services or more efficient ways of delivering existing ones (through the introduction of new technology, know-how, additional staff with new skills, or access to new markets).

Commission Recommendation 2003/361/EC regarding the definition of SMEs has been in effect since 1 January 2005. It applies to all Community policies in favour of SMEs and covers the whole of the European Economic Area. It was revised to ensure that enterprises which were part of larger groups could no longer benefit from SME support schemes, and that help was targeted specifically at genuine SMEs. Under the recommendation, enterprises are classified as SMEs when they have fewer than 250 employees and remain independent of larger companies. Furthermore, their annual turnover should not exceed EUR 50 million, or their annual balance sheet total should not exceed EUR 43 million. This definition is critical in establishing which SMEs may benefit from EU programmes, policies and competition rules.

---

[20] More details can be found on the web-site for the Directorate-General for Enterprise and Industry, available at http://ec.europa.eu/enterprise/entrepreneurship/index_en.htm.

Figure 1.19

Density of SMEs: number of SMEs per 1 000 inhabitants, non-financial business economy, 2004 (1)

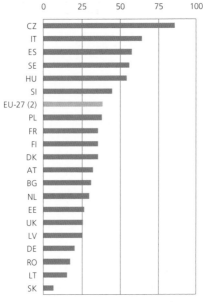

(1) Belgium, Ireland, Greece, Cyprus, Luxembourg, Malta and Portugal, not available.
(2) Rounded estimate based on non-confidential data.
Source: Eurostat (SBS, DEMO)

Figure 1.20

Density of large enterprises: number of large enterprises per 100 000 inhabitants, non-financial business economy, 2004 (1)

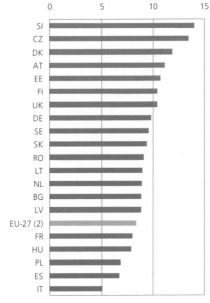

(1) Belgium, Ireland, Greece, Cyprus, Luxembourg, Malta and Portugal, not available.
(2) Rounded estimate based on non-confidential data.
Source: Eurostat (SBS, DEMO)

Table 1.14

Breakdown of activity within the non-financial business economy by size-class, EU-27, 2004 (% share of total) (1)

Chapter	No. of enterprises					Value added					No. of persons employed				
	SMEs	Micro	Small	Med.	Large	SMEs	Micro	Small	Med.	Large	SMEs	Micro	Small	Med.	Large
1 Non-financial business economy	99.8	91.8	7.0	1.1	0.2	57.0	20.2	18.8	17.9	43.0	67.1	29.6	21.0	16.9	33.1
Industry	99.0	79.5	15.7	3.8	0.9	41.8	7.0	14.2	21.2	59.8	56.7	13.0	19.6	24.1	44.5
2 Food, beverages & tobacco	99.0	77.7	17.5	3.7	0.9	44.1	7.7	14.7	21.7	55.9	62.0	15.9	21.3	24.8	38.0
3 Textiles, clothing, leather & footwear	99.2	78.9	15.8	3.8	1.5	74.6	13.8	28.5	31.3	26.9	72.7	16.8	27.3	30.3	27.3
4 Wood & paper	99.5	82.9	12.0	2.4	0.5	57.0	11.0	19.8	25.9	43.0	72.8	21.4	25.2	25.2	27.2
5 Chemicals, rubber & plastics	95.7	61.0	25.0	9.5	2.5	33.6	2.5	9.4	21.8	64.8	47.9	5.5	14.9	27.5	52.3
6 Other non-metallic mineral products	99.0	78.7	16.2	4.1	1.0	52.0	6.9	18.4	26.8	48.0	62.5	14.2	21.3	27.1	37.8
7 Metals & metal products	99.3	78.8	17.2	3.3	0.5	61.6	11.4	24.3	26.0	38.4	71.2	17.6	27.8	25.9	28.8
8 Machinery & equipment	98.8	72.9	19.8	6.1	1.3	50.5	6.2	16.7	27.6	49.5	56.2	9.1	19.0	28.1	43.8
9 Electrical machinery & optical equipment	98.8	81.0	14.1	3.7	1.1	36.0	5.8	11.6	18.7	64.0	47.2	10.5	15.6	21.6	53.8
10 Transport equipment	96.0	69.6	18.6	7.9	3.8	12.7	:	3.9	8.9	87.3	19.7	2.5	5.6	11.9	78.1
11 Furniture & other manufacturing	99.6	86.7	10.9	2.0	0.4	72.5	17.9	26.1	28.0	27.5	73.7	24.7	26.3	24.8	24.1
12 Non-energy mining & quarrying	99.4	70.5	24.6	4.2	0.6	65.2	10.0	30.8	24.3	34.8	66.4	12.8	29.3	24.3	33.6
13 Energy	95.2	:	13.3	:	4.6	20.4	:	:	:	80.2	13.5	1.5	3.3	8.8	85.0
14 Recycling & water supply	98.7	77.8	15.7	5.2	1.4	46.2	9.2	16.2	21.0	54.2	48.0	8.9	15.5	24.9	50.0
15 Construction	99.9	91.9	7.8	0.8	0.1	82.5	33.1	31.9	17.6	17.5	88.2	42.6	30.4	15.4	11.8
Non-financial services	99.9	93.7	5.4	0.7	0.1	62.7	26.9	19.9	16.0	37.4	68.3	35.6	19.3	13.4	31.7
16 Motor trades	99.9	91.1	8.0	0.9	0.1	79.7	27.9	29.9	21.9	20.4	88.5	44.3	28.5	16.0	11.6
17 Wholesale trade	99.9	90.3	8.4	1.2	0.1	77.2	23.8	30.3	23.8	22.8	83.7	33.5	28.8	19.6	17.8
18 Retail trade & repair	99.9	95.9	3.7	0.3	0.1	57.3	32.8	16.0	8.3	42.7	65.3	43.7	14.5	7.1	34.7
19 Hotels & restaurants	99.9	91.2	8.1	0.6	0.1	75.8	36.5	26.2	13.5	24.2	82.3	45.4	26.3	10.5	17.7
20 Transport services	97.3	91.2	7.1	1.2	0.2	50.8	16.6	18.2	16.0	50.0	58.1	24.2	18.6	15.6	41.9
21 Communications & media	99.5	85.5	10.4	2.1	0.5	22.1	5.1	7.6	9.3	78.0	34.3	10.9	12.2	11.8	65.6
22 Business services	99.7	94.7	4.4	0.8	0.2	66.4	28.4	20.0	17.9	33.6	64.9	31.2	16.9	16.8	35.1
23 Real estate, renting & R&D	99.9	96.5	2.9	0.5	0.1	83.1	47.7	17.1	18.5	16.8	80.0	47.4	17.1	15.7	18.6

(1) Rounded estimates based on non-confidential data; note that estimates may result in the sum of the size classes not being equal to 100 %.
Source: Eurostat (SBS)

However, for reasons of feasibility, the collection of structural business statistics on SMEs only uses the criteria based on employment. As such, for the purpose of the statistics presented hereafter, SMEs are defined as having fewer than 250 persons employed; and subsequently large enterprises are defined as employing 250 or more persons. The sub-population of SMEs (1 to 249 persons employed) may be further divided into:

- micro enterprises (with 1 to 9 persons employed);
- small enterprises (with 10 to 49 persons employed), and;
- medium-sized enterprises (with 50 to 249 persons employed).

According to SBS, there are considerable differences between Member States in the number of enterprises that make-up the non-financial business economy. On average there were 38.6 SMEs (with less than 250 persons employed) in the EU-27's non-financial business economy for each 1 000 inhabitants in 2004. This ratio more than doubled in the Czech Republic to 86 SMEs per 1 000 inhabitants,

while at the other end of the range there were just 6.5 SMEs per 1 000 inhabitants in neighbouring Slovakia (see Figure 1.19).

There was an average of 8.4 large enterprises (with 250 or more persons employed) in the EU-27's non-financial business economy per 100 000 inhabitants (for comparison with the SME figures this is 0.08 large enterprises per 1 000 inhabitants) in 2004. A relatively high ratio of large enterprises to inhabitants was recorded in Slovenia and in the Czech Republic, while only France, Hungary, Poland, Spain and Italy reported ratios below the EU average (see Figure 1.20).

In total, there were almost 19 million enterprises in the EU-27's non-financial business economy in 2004. Of these, 99.8 % were SMEs, the majority of which were micro enterprises (employing fewer than 10 persons). However, on average large enterprises in the EU-27's non-financial business economy in 2004 employed just over 1 000 persons, compared with an average 4.4 persons employed by SMEs. As such, the relative weight of a single large enterprise in employment terms was, on average, equivalent to that of 227 SMEs.

Just over two thirds (67.1 %) of the EU-27's non-financial business economy workforce was employed within SMEs in 2004. Enterprise structures vary considerably between activities – see Table 1.14 – with, for example, large enterprises accounting for 85.0 % of those employed in the energy sector, 78.1 % of those employed in the transport equipment manufacturing sector, or 65.6 % of those employed in the communications and media sector. In contrast, SMEs employed 88.5 % of motor trades workforce, or 88.2 % of those employed in the construction sector. The relative importance of SMEs in terms of their contribution to labour markets also varies considerably across countries, as SMEs employed 81.2 % of the non-financial business economy workforce in Italy in 2004, a share that fell close to 50 % in Slovakia and the United Kingdom (see Table 1.15).

Table 1.15

Breakdown of the non-financial business economy by size-class, 2004 (% share of total)

	No. of enterprises					Value added					No. of persons employed				
	SMEs	Micro	Small	Med.	Large	SMEs	Micro	Small	Med.	Large	SMEs	Micro	Small	Med.	Large
EU-27 (1)	99.8	91.8	7.0	1.1	0.2	57.0	20.2	18.8	17.9	43.0	67.1	29.6	21.0	16.9	33.1
BE	:	:	:	0.9	:	:	:	:	18.9	:	:	:	:	15.5	:
BG	99.7	90.2	8.0	1.6	0.3	49.5	14.3	15.8	19.3	50.5	71.7	29.3	21.3	21.0	28.3
CZ	99.8	95.3	3.8	0.8	0.2	56.7	19.8	16.7	20.2	43.3	68.9	31.8	18.4	18.7	31.1
DK	99.7	86.9	10.9	1.9	0.3	:	:	:	20.9	:	:	:	:	21.1	:
DE	99.5	82.8	14.4	2.3	0.5	:	:	17.7	:	:	60.1	19.2	21.9	19.0	39.9
EE	99.6	81.5	15.1	3.0	0.4	:	:	23.7	:	:	:	:	27.7	:	:
IE	:	:	:	:	:	:	:	:	:	:	:	:	:	:	:
EL	:	:	:	:	:	:	:	:	:	:	:	:	:	:	:
ES	99.9	92.3	6.8	0.8	0.1	68.1	27.3	23.6	17.2	31.9	79.1	38.9	25.5	14.7	20.9
FR	99.8	92.3	6.4	1.0	0.2	53.7	19.4	18.3	16.0	46.3	60.9	23.6	20.6	16.7	39.1
IT	99.9	94.6	4.8	0.5	0.1	70.3	30.8	23.3	16.3	29.7	81.2	46.9	21.9	12.4	18.8
CY	:	:	:	:	:	:	:	:	:	:	:	:	:	:	:
LV	99.7	83.1	13.9	2.7	0.3	:	:	:	:	:	75.0	22.6	26.2	26.3	25.0
LT	99.4	75.5	19.7	4.3	0.6	56.7	9.3	21.7	25.7	43.3	71.3	17.0	26.4	27.9	28.7
LU	:	:	:	:	:	:	:	:	:	:	:	:	:	:	:
HU	99.9	:	:	:	0.1	51.9	:	:	:	48.1	72.2	:	:	:	27.8
MT	:	:	:	:	:	:	:	:	:	:	:	:	:	:	:
NL	99.7	89.0	9.1	1.6	0.3	60.4	:	:	21.3	39.6	67.4	29.2	20.9	17.3	32.6
AT	99.7	86.9	11.1	1.7	0.3	:	:	20.5	:	:	:	:	23.4	:	:
PL	99.8	96.2	2.7	0.9	0.2	47.8	16.5	10.7	20.6	52.2	70.3	40.1	11.7	18.5	29.7
PT (2)	:	:	6.6	:	:	:	:	21.0	:	:	:	:	23.6	:	:
RO	99.5	88.1	9.0	2.3	0.5	44.5	12.3	13.1	19.1	55.5	58.2	18.5	17.2	22.5	41.8
SI	99.7	92.9	5.5	1.3	0.3	:	:	:	21.6	:	:	:	:	:	:
SK	98.6	:	:	5.5	1.4	42.4	:	:	17.3	57.6	51.2	:	:	22.5	48.8
FI	99.7	92.4	6.1	1.2	0.3	:	:	:	:	:	:	:	:	:	:
SE	99.8	94.7	4.3	0.8	0.2	56.5	21.1	17.5	17.9	43.5	64.2	26.3	20.3	17.7	35.8
UK	99.6	86.4	11.4	1.8	0.4	50.7	17.8	16.1	16.8	49.3	53.9	21.1	18.0	14.8	46.1

(1) Rounded estimates based on non-confidential data.
(2) 2003.
Source: Eurostat (SBS)

Table 1.16

Apparent labour productivity by size-class, EU-27, 2004 (EUR thousand per person employed)

	Chapter	SMEs	Micro	Small	Med.	Large
1	Non-financial business economy	34.9	28.1	36.9	43.4	53.4
	Industry (1)	36.7	26.0	35.7	43.0	64.2
2	Food, beverages & tobacco	29.7	20.3	28.8	36.6	61.6
3	Textiles, clothing, leather & footwear (1)	20.0	16.7	22.0	21.0	20.0
4	Wood & paper (1)	29.0	19.0	29.5	38.0	60.0
5	Chemicals, rubber & plastics (1)	47.5	30.3	42.7	53.6	83.7
6	Other non-metallic mineral products	37.9	22.0	39.4	45.0	57.8
7	Metals & metal products	36.8	27.6	37.2	42.8	56.8
8	Machinery & equipment	42.1	31.7	41.2	46.2	53.0
9	Electrical machinery & optical equipment	40.2	29.0	39.3	45.6	62.7
10	Transport equipment	35.6	-0.4	37.9	41.0	61.7
11	Furniture & other manufacturing	26.4	19.4	26.6	30.3	30.5
12	Non-energy mining & quarrying	49.9	39.9	53.5	50.9	52.8
13	Energy (1)	181.5	:	:	150.0	113.2
14	Recycling & water supply (1)	49.0	53.0	54.2	43.8	57.0
15	Construction	30.8	25.6	34.6	37.6	48.6
	Non-financial services	35.0	28.9	39.3	45.5	45.0
16	Motor trades	33.3	23.3	38.8	50.8	65.3
17	Wholesale trade	44.7	34.4	50.9	58.8	62.0
18	Retail trade & repair	19.9	17.1	25.0	26.7	27.9
19	Hotels & restaurants	17.4	15.1	18.8	24.2	25.7
20	Transport services (1)	36.4	28.7	41.1	43.0	50.0
21	Communications & media (1)	44.5	32.5	46.0	54.3	82.6
22	Business services (1)	39.0	35.0	45.2	40.6	36.4
23	Real estate, renting & R&D (1)	90.0	87.1	86.0	100.0	80.0

(1) Rounded estimates based on non-confidential data.
Source: Eurostat (SBS)

The economic importance of SMEs was lower in terms of their contribution to total value added, as they generated 57.0 % of the EU-27's non-financial business economy value added in 2004. When combined with information on employment shares this suggests that the apparent labour productivity of SMEs was generally lower than that of larger enterprises. This view is supported by economic theory that suggests economies of scale may lead to larger enterprises generating more value added per person employed. This was the case for most of the activity aggregates used for the sectoral chapters covered in Table 1.16. Indeed, the manufacture of textiles, clothing, leather and footwear; energy; business services; and real estate, renting and R&D were the only four exceptions where apparent labour productivity was similar or higher among SMEs than large enterprises.

On average, apparent labour productivity in large enterprises was 53.2 % higher than in SMEs across the whole of the EU-27's non-financial business economy. These differentials in the apparent labour productivity ratios between SMEs and large enterprises were generally more marked for industrial activities, where persons employed in large enterprises were on average 74.9 % more productive than SMEs, while among non-financial services the same differential was reduced to 28.6 %. Apparent labour productivity differentials were particularly marked when the apparent labour productivity ratio of large enterprises was compared with that of micro enterprises within the food, beverages and tobacco, and wood and paper manufacturing sectors, as large enterprises reported ratios that were at least three times as high as those recorded for micro enterprises.

Despite considerable differences in the levels of labour productivity between Member States, there was a general pattern of labour productivity rising as a function of average enterprise size. This pattern was particularly apparent for industrial activities in the majority of countries. Exceptions to this rule included Bulgaria and Romania where the biggest difference in productivity ratios between large enterprises and SMEs was reported for non-financial services, and in the Czech Republic, Italy, Latvia and Hungary where construction activities reported the biggest differences.

Table 1.17

Apparent labour productivity by size-class, 2004 (EUR thousand per person employed)

	Industry (1)		Construction (2)		Non-financial services	
	SMEs	Large	SMEs	Large	SMEs	Large
EU-27 (3)	36.7	64.2	30.8	48.6	35.0	45.0
BE	:	:	38.5	61.2	49.7	56.3
BG	3.3	8.2	3.4	4.4	3.2	9.2
CZ	12.3	22.8	9.1	19.9	12.8	16.4
DK	:	:	44.2	55.8	59.2	57.7
DE	45.0	71.0	33.8	48.6	45.5	49.9
EE	:	:	10.0	19.0	14.4	15.2
IE	:	:	107.2	117.7	52.4	59.7
EL	:	:	20.1	67.3	:	:
ES	36.9	83.8	28.2	58.7	29.7	42.0
FR	43.0	72.2	37.6	46.9	46.5	52.6
IT	39.5	74.3	29.4	59.1	31.1	51.4
CY	:	:	28.0	34.2	:	:
LV	7.1	11.3	6.7	10.8	:	:
LT	6.3	14.8	6.4	9.7	7.5	11.9
LU	:	:	39.6	43.2	:	:
HU	10.4	25.7	7.1	27.5	10.2	18.4
MT	:	:	:	:	:	:
NL	58.1	120.9	45.6	61.9	42.4	46.1
AT	:	:	43.5	59.3	44.9	47.6
PL	10.7	29.8	8.3	16.3	9.1	17.8
PT	:	:	13.6	37.2	18.7	33.2
RO	3.5	7.0	4.2	1.3	4.5	9.5
SI	:	:		23.1	22.5	27.8
SK	9.3	16.3	9.1	10.9	13.9	12.8
FI	:	:	46.5	47.3	53.9	46.6
SE	50.7	87.2	41.1	49.5	52.0	56.4
UK	55.7	96.0	57.2	73.1	47.9	46.3

(1) Germany, Latvia, Hungary and Slovakia, 2003.
(2) Luxembourg, 2003
(3) Rounded estimates based on non-confidential data.
Source: Eurostat (SBS)

1.5: LABOUR FORCE CHARACTERISTICS

The European Union has developed its employment strategy over a number of years following the Luxembourg jobs summit in 1997. Realignments of this strategy to fit with the Lisbon objectives and the Stockholm Council meeting of 2001 have resulted in a more significant use of labour force statistics to study not only changes in the absolute numbers of people in work or unemployed, but also a wide range of labour force characteristics, such as age, gender, working time, educational and skills profiles, as well as activity and employment rates. The information that is presented within this section is largely derived from the Labour Force Survey (LFS) which collects information from individual households (rather than from enterprises) – note that the data pertain to the second quarter of each reference year and not to annual averages.

According to SBS data, across the EU-27's non-financial business economy the average share of paid employees in the total number of persons employed was 86.2 % in 2004. This ratio was generally highest within industrial activities (94.5 % for industry), falling to 83.0 % for non-financial services and 81.0 % for construction where a higher proportion of working proprietors and unpaid family workers contributed to the workforce. As has been mentioned, SBS employment data refer to headcounts and as such make no distinction between full-time and part-time, or in the number of hours worked. However, data from the LFS shed some light on these differences – as while the majority of the workforce tends to work a regular five day week, from Monday to Friday, there are some activities within the non-financial business economy that lend themselves to different working time profiles.

Across the whole of the business economy (NACE Sections C to K), an average of 14.4 % of the EU-27's labour force worked on a part-time basis. This ratio rose to as high as 29.0 % of those employed within the retail trade and repair sector in 2006 (see Table 1.18), while the corresponding ratio for hotels and restaurants was 28.2 %. In contrast, there was very little part-time work within traditional, industrial activities, and in particular non-energy mining and quarrying (2.9 % of the workforce) or the energy sector (3.9 %).

The EU-27's labour force is also characterised by considerable differences in terms of its gender profile. Across the whole of the business economy, almost two thirds (64.2 %) of those employed in the EU-27 in 2006 were male. This imbalance tended to be repeated for most activities, with men outnumbering women by

Table 1.18

Employment characteristics, EU-27, 2006 (% share of total number of persons employed)

Chapter	Share of employees in persons employed, 2004	Gender		Time at work		Age		
		Male	Female	Full-time	Part-time	15-29	30-49	50+
Business economy	:	64.2	35.8	85.6	14.4	24.1	54.3	21.6
1 Non-financial business economy	86.2	65.0	35.0	85.6	14.4	24.2	54.2	21.6
Industry	94.5	70.1	29.9	92.4	7.6	20.9	56.6	22.4
2 Food, beverages & tobacco	93.9	59.2	40.8	88.6	11.4	24.1	56.0	19.9
3 Textiles, clothing, leather & footwear	92.1	30.9	69.1	91.8	8.2	19.8	59.3	20.9
4 Wood & paper	90.0	79.0	21.0	93.5	6.5	21.3	57.2	21.5
5 Chemicals, rubber & plastics	97.8	67.5	32.5	93.4	6.6	20.1	58.2	21.7
6 Other non-metallic mineral products	94.3	76.4	23.6	94.7	5.3	19.1	58.6	22.3
7 Metals & metal products	92.5	84.4	15.6	94.8	5.2	21.0	54.5	24.4
8 Machinery & equipment	95.7	81.5	18.5	94.6	5.4	19.4	55.7	24.9
9 Electrical machinery & optical equipment	95.4	66.8	33.2	93.2	6.8	22.8	56.9	20.3
10 Transport equipment	98.9	82.1	17.9	94.6	5.4	21.2	56.7	22.1
11 Furniture & other manufacturing	88.7	71.4	28.6	90.1	9.9	22.9	56.8	20.3
12 Non-energy mining & quarrying	96.0	89.4	10.6	97.1	2.9	16.8	56.0	27.2
13 Energy	:	80.0	20.0	96.1	3.9	14.3	58.6	27.2
14 Recycling & water supply	97.5	79.0	21.0	93.7	6.3	14.9	58.1	27.1
15 Construction	81.0	91.9	8.1	94.1	5.9	24.6	53.8	21.6
Non-financial services	83.0	55.7	44.3	79.6	20.4	26.0	52.9	21.1
16 Motor trades	81.7	82.0	18.0	90.4	9.6	29.4	50.3	20.4
17 Wholesale trade	85.9	66.2	33.8	89.3	10.7	22.6	56.7	20.8
18 Retail trade & repair	78.5	38.3	61.7	71.0	29.0	30.4	49.5	20.1
19 Hotels & restaurants	80.6	44.3	55.7	71.8	28.2	35.8	47.3	17.0
20 Transport services	88.0	79.2	20.8	90.7	9.3	17.6	57.3	25.1
21 Communications & media	95.4	59.9	40.1	82.3	17.7	21.9	56.0	22.1
22 Business services	84.0	55.4	44.6	78.7	21.3	23.6	55.5	20.8
23 Real estate, renting & R&D	74.3	54.4	45.6	81.1	18.9	19.6	50.6	29.8
24 Financial services	:	48.1	51.9	85.9	14.1	21.7	57.1	21.2

Source: Eurostat (SBS, LFS)

approximately nine to one within non-energy mining and quarrying and construction activities. There are some activities, however, such as textiles, clothing, leather and footwear manufacturing; retail trade and repair; hotels and restaurants; and financial services, where the majority of the EU-27 workforce were women in 2006.

The age profile of the EU-27 workforce also varies between the different sectors of the business economy, in part reflecting education/skills levels and experience requirements. The hotels and restaurants sector reported a relatively large proportion (35.8 %) of young workers, as defined by those aged between 15 and 29 years old, while much lower proportions of young persons were employed within the energy and the recycling and water supply sectors (less than 15 %).

Differences in the labour characteristics of the workforce across the Member States can often be explained by structural factors, insofar as they are repeated across most activities. As such, the proportion of females working within the business economy was generally high in the Baltic Member States, Bulgaria and Romania, where women accounted for more than four out of ten persons employed in 2006. In contrast, the proportion of women within the workforce was generally low in most Mediterranean Member States, in particular in Spain, Italy, and Malta (where the lowest rate was recorded, 24.8 %) – see Figure 1.21. The proportion of women in the workforce probably reflects, to some degree, socio-economic policies regarding family allowances, the availability of crèches and after school care, the propensity to employ on a part-time basis, and cultural differences with respect to interdependence/independence of (extended) family units. It should be noted, though, that traditionally women account for a relatively large part of the workforce of the 'public sector' in many countries, activities outside of the business economy as presented here. That probably explains to a large degree the low figures reported for Sweden for example, where public administration, health and education account for a relatively large part of the total economy.

As regards part-time employment, the Netherlands stood out as having by far the highest part-time employment rate in 2006 (38.0 %), largely due to three out of every four women within the Dutch workforce being employed on a part-time basis. This situation contrasted vividly with the situation in Slovakia, Romania and Bulgaria where no more than 1 in 50 of the workforce was working on a part-time basis in 2006 (see Figure 1.22).

Figure 1.21

Employment breakdown by gender, business economy, 2006 (% share of total number of persons employed)

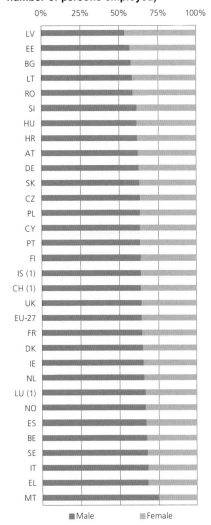

(1) 2005.
Source: Eurostat (LFS)

Figure 1.22

Employment breakdown by time at work, business economy, 2006 (% share of total number of persons employed) (1)

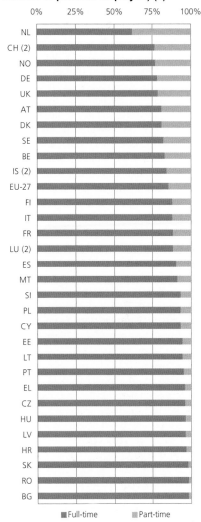

(1) Ireland, not available.
(2) 2005.
Source: Eurostat (LFS)

Age profiles within the respective workforces of the Member States also reflect socio-economic characteristics and policies, including demographic trends such as an ageing population or a baby-boom cohort. The proportion of young workers in the business economy may reflect factors such as differences in higher education rates and the average length of higher education courses, as well as the availability of work and job placements. Nevertheless, the age profile of the business economy workforce tends to be relatively similar across the Member States at an aggregate level (see Figure 1.23). While some activities, for example, information, technology and communication-related sectors may favour younger workers that are more up-to-date with recent technological developments, at the other end of the age range, the proportion of older workers may be influenced, among many other factors, by pension rights, age-related wage schemes, and life-long learning programmes in particular activities. Between countries, there was a relatively high proportion of the Irish (35.7 %) and Maltese (34.7 %) business economy workforces composed of persons aged between 15 and 29 years old. In contrast, Luxembourg (19.3 %) and Italy (19.9 %) recorded the lowest proportion of young workers. The lowest proportion of the workforce aged over 50 years was reported in Romania (16.1 %), with relatively low shares also recorded in Luxembourg (16.7 %) and Ireland (17.3 %). Older workers made-up at least one quarter of the workforce in 2006 in Sweden, Finland, Estonia, the Czech Republic, the United Kingdom and Denmark.

Figure 1.23_____

Employment breakdown by age, business economy, 2006 (% share of total number of persons employed)

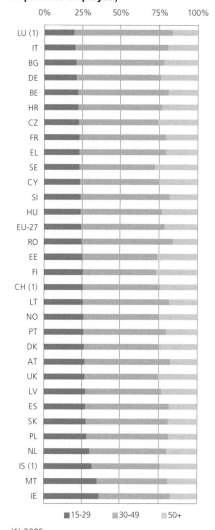

(1) 2005.
Source: Eurostat (LFS)

1.6: EVOLUTION OF PRODUCTION, EMPLOYMENT AND TURNOVER

The index of production for industrial activities and that for construction shows the development of value added at constant prices. This indicator provides information on the speed and direction of structural change, in particular showing the cyclical evolution of activity (which is often related to the general economic developments within the whole economy). As no production index exists within short-term business statistics for service sectors an index of turnover is used instead to analyse the evolution of output. Note that the index of turnover for services is generally based on a current price series (and as a result includes the effects of price increases) – the retail trade sector is the only exception, as an index is available for measuring the volume of retail sales.

The EU-27 index of production for total industry (NACE Sections C to E) rose strongly between 1996 and 2000 (on average by 3.4 % per annum) during a period of rapid, global, economic expansion (see Figure 1.24). Thereafter, the production index stabilised, with little change between 2000 and 2003 (rising on average by 0.1 % per annum), since when there has been renewed vigour in the pace at which industrial output rose, with average growth of 2.4 % between 2003 and 2006. Growth quickened during this period, as industrial output in the EU-27 rose by 3.7 % in 2006 when compared with the year before.

The output of construction activities followed a somewhat different path, as there was a small contraction in the level of production in 1996 and 1997, after which there were successive year-on-year expansions through to 2004, although average growth was modest at 1.6 % per annum. After a year of stagnation in 2005, the EU-27's index of production for construction posted its highest year on year growth rate in 2006, as output rose by 5.6 %.

Among the service sectors, the EU-27 index of turnover for business services (NACE Divisions 72 and 74) rose particularly strongly in the period between 2000 and 2006, on average by 6.3 % per annum, as did the turnover index for transport, storage and communication services (NACE Section I), where growth averaged 6.0 % per annum – see Figure 1.25. The remaining four services that are presented in Figure 1.25 also reported a positive evolution to the development of sales, averaging between 3.5 % and 4.7 % per annum.

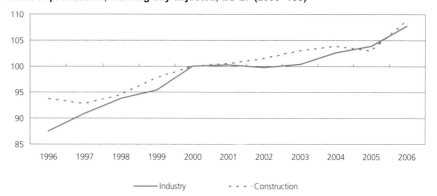

Figure 1.24

Index of production, working day adjusted, EU-27 (2000=100)

Industry — Construction

Source: Eurostat (STS)

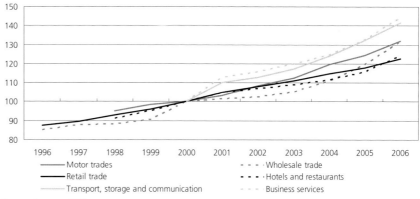

Figure 1.25

Index of turnover, working day adjusted, EU-27 (2000=100)

Motor trades — Wholesale trade
Retail trade — Hotels and restaurants
Transport, storage and communication — Business services

Source: Eurostat (STS)

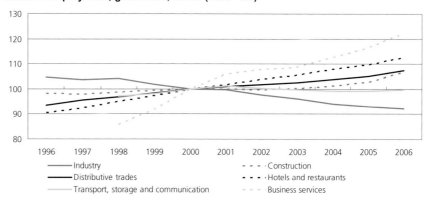

Figure 1.26

Index of employment, gross data, EU-27 (2000=100)

Industry — Construction
Distributive trades — Hotels and restaurants
Transport, storage and communication — Business services

Source: Eurostat (STS)

Annualised short-term business statistics are also available to analyse the evolution of employment. The EU-27 index of employment for industrial activities showed a steady decline during the period 1996 to 2006, with reductions averaging 1.3 % per annum. In contrast, there was employment growth within construction, as well as the four non-financial services that are presented in Figure 1.26. There were relatively fast rates of employment growth for business services (4.5 % per annum between 1998 and 2006), as well as for hotels and restaurants (2.2 % per annum between 1996 and 2006).

EVOLUTION WITHIN INDUSTRIAL ACTIVITIES

EU-27 production indices for the majority of the NACE subsections within the industrial economy increased during the period between 1996 and 2006 (see Figure 1.27), with only two exceptions, the extraction of energy producing materials and the manufacture of textiles, clothing, leather and footwear.

In contrast, the three activities (at the NACE subsection level of detail) within the EU-27's industrial economy that recorded the highest growth rates were electrical machinery and optical equipment (NACE Subsection DL), where output rose by an average of 4.2 % per year, transport equipment manufacturing (NACE Subsection DM), where output rose on average by 4.1 % per annum, and the manufacture of chemicals, rubber and plastics (NACE Subsections DG and DH), where production increased by 3.3 % per annum. Expansions in EU-27 industrial production were achieved, for the most part, with a reduced workforce – see Figure 1.28 – reinforcing the notion of productivity improvements. The only industrial subsection that reported an increase in its workforce was rubber and plastic products manufacturing, while there were also gains reported for construction. In both of these cases, average gains in output were in excess of the additional labour input (suggesting that productivity gains were also apparent in these two activities).

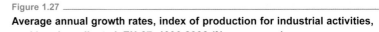

Figure 1.27

Average annual growth rates, index of production for industrial activities, working day adjusted, EU-27, 1996-2006 (% per annum)

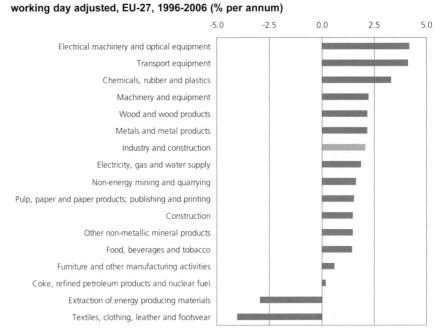

Source: Eurostat (STS)

Figure 1.28

Average annual growth rates, index of employment for industrial activities, gross data, EU-27, 1996-2006 (% per annum)

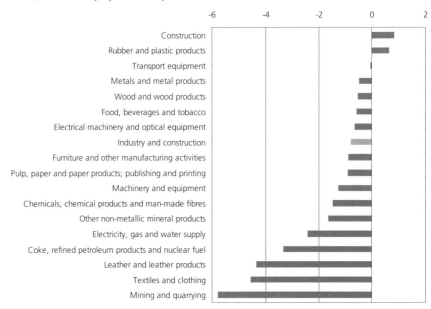

Source: Eurostat (STS)

EVOLUTION WITHIN SERVICE SECTORS

During the five-year period from 2001 to 2006, the EU-27 index of turnover increased for each of the NACE divisions within the non-financial services sector for which data are available – see Figure 1.29. The highest rates of sales growth tended to be reported for transport services, with average growth of 5.8 % per annum for land transport and transport via pipelines (NACE Division 60), 5.6 % per annum for air transport (NACE Division 62), and 5.4 % per annum for water transport services (NACE Division 61). The slowest rates of turnover growth across the NACE divisions for non-financial services were registered for hotels and restaurants (3.5 % per annum) and for retail trade (3.1 % per annum).

In contrast to the industrial economy, the evolution of employment within services sectors tended to show the number of persons employed rising for the majority of activities across the EU-27. The sharpest rate of increase between 2001 and 2006 was registered for one part of the business services sector, other business activities (NACE Division 74), where there was an average increase of 3.2 % in the number of persons employed. There were two service activities – air transport and post and telecommunications – that reported reductions in their respective workforces between 2001 and 2006 (see Figure 1.30).

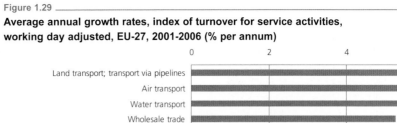

Figure 1.29

Average annual growth rates, index of turnover for service activities, working day adjusted, EU-27, 2001-2006 (% per annum)

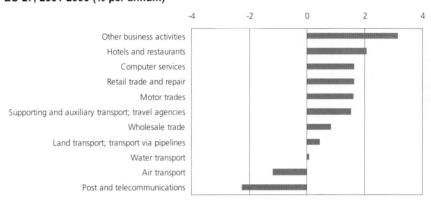

Source: Eurostat (STS)

Figure 1.30

Average annual growth rates, index of employment for service activities, gross data, EU-27, 2001-2006 (% per annum)

Source: Eurostat (STS)

1.7: EXTERNAL TRADE

The world economy is increasingly inter-related, with foreign-controlled enterprises and globalisation making the distinction between domestic and non-domestic production less clear. With the successive removal of trade barriers (particularly those under the auspices of the World Trade Organisation's multilateral discussions) there has been a notable increase in world trade, which flourished initially with respect to the freeing-up of international trade in goods, and more recently some services.

There have been rapid changes in trade patterns in recent years, associated with emerging economies such as China and India accounting for a growing share of world trade across many different product areas (in particular those that are price-sensitive). There have also been structural changes in the origin of imports within particular product groupings, for example, the rapid growth in energy imports originating from the Russian Federation (an important global supplier of energy).

EU exports are mainly concentrated among medium-high technology products that are produced with low to intermediate labour skills. This means that the EU is exposed to competition from producers in emerging economies, resulting in some EU producers trying to shift their output to higher value, specialist products.

EU-27 external trade data shows (see Figure 1.31) that after having almost stagnated during the period 2001 to 2003 during a period of global slowdown, there was subsequently growth in the level of EU exports and imports through to 2006 as global economic fortunes improved. The EU-27 trade balance (the value of exports minus imports) for industrial goods resulted in a progressively larger deficit through to 2006, reflecting to some degree buoyant demand, changes in exchange rates, and the relative price of imports (in particular, higher prices for oil and gas which accounted for an increasing proportion of the EU-27's imports). The widening trade deficit for goods grew to EUR 169.5 billion by 2006.

Figure 1.31

Evolution of external trade for industrial products, EU-27 (EUR billion)

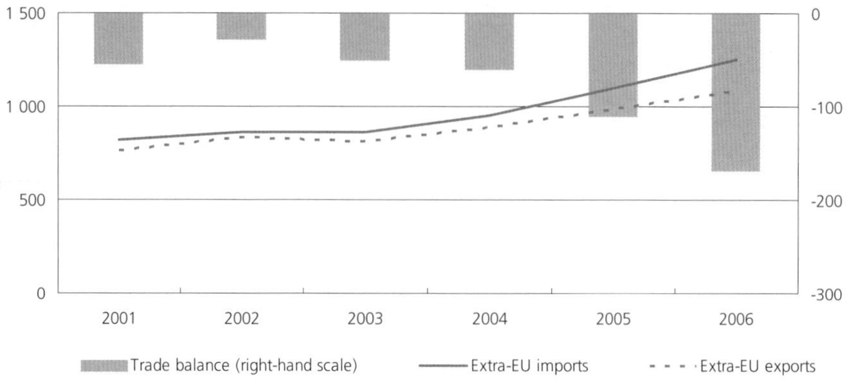

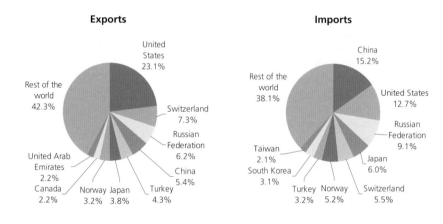

Trade balance (right-hand scale) —— Extra-EU imports - - - Extra-EU exports

Source: Eurostat (Comext)

Figure 1.32

Main trading partners, industrial products, EU-27, 2006 (% share of total)

Exports

United States 23.1%
Rest of the world 42.3%
Switzerland 7.3%
Russian Federation 6.2%
China 5.4%
United Arab Emirates 2.2%
Canada 2.2%
Norway 3.2%
Japan 3.8%
Turkey 4.3%

Imports

China 15.2%
Rest of the world 38.1%
United States 12.7%
Russian Federation 9.1%
Taiwan 2.1%
South Korea 3.1%
Japan 6.0%
Turkey 3.2%
Norway 5.2%
Switzerland 5.5%

Source: Eurostat (Comext)

EU-27 TRADE PARTNERS

The most important destination for EU-27 industrial exports in 2006 was the United States which accounted for a little less than a quarter (23.1 %) of the total (see Figure 1.32). The proportion of exports that were destined for the United States fell gradually in recent years, while a similar pattern was observed for the second largest market for EU-27 exports of industrial goods, namely Switzerland, which accounted for a 7.3 % share of total exports in 2006. The declining share of EU-27 exports to established, industrialised trading partners was offset by the growing importance of trade with Russia and China, whose combined market share rose to 11.6 % by 2006.

The relatively slow change in the structure of EU-27 exports by partner was in contrast to more rapid developments as regards the origin of EU-27 imports. The relative importance of the United States diminished considerably in recent years, as American imports accounted for 12.7 % of the total in 2006 (approximately half their share of a decade before). There was also a considerable reduction in relative share of Japanese imports, declining to 6.0 % of EU-27 imports in 2006. In contrast, the share of EU-27 imports that originated from China and Russia increased rapidly to reach 15.2 % and 9.1 % respectively by 2006.

EVOLUTION OF PRODUCTION

The past decade has seen greater amplitude to changes in the index of production for industry and construction in Bulgaria and Romania, than for the EU-27.

A considerable downturn in industrial and construction activity was recorded in Romania from the middle to the end of the 1990s, as output declined to a low point in 1999 (no data are available for this period for Bulgaria). Short-term business statistics show that the evolution of industrial and construction activity within Bulgaria and Romania thereafter grew at a considerably faster pace than in the EU-27 (see Figure 1.34).

Figure 1.35 shows that the EU-27 index of production for industry and construction rose, on average, by 1.5 % per annum between 2001 and 2006, while the corresponding rate for Romania was 5.0 % and that for Bulgaria averaged 10.4 %. Subject to data availability and according to a breakdown of aggregates at the NACE subsection level of detail, the highest growth rates within industry in Bulgaria were recorded for furniture and other manufacturing activities; metals and metal products; other non-metallic mineral products; and wood and wood products – all of which registered average gains of around 20 % per annum over the period considered. Growth rates for industrial output were less rapid in Romania, although they were generally higher than for the EU-27, the highest being recorded for transport equipment manufacturing (14.6 %).

Figure 1.34

Index of production, working day adjusted, industry and construction (2000=100)

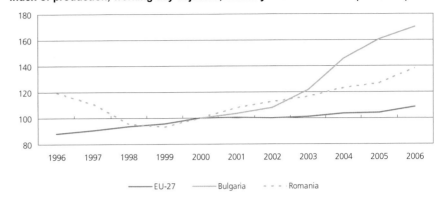

Source: Eurostat (STS)

Figure 1.35

Average annual growth rates, index of production, working day adjusted, 2001-2006 (% per annum)

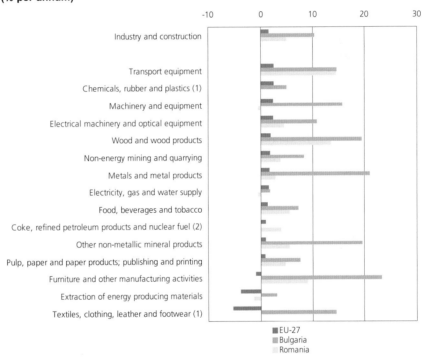

(1) Romania, not available.
(2) Bulgaria, not available.
Source: Eurostat (STS)

EXTERNAL TRADE

A breakdown of the structure of external trade for 2006 according to the breakdown of aggregates used for the sectoral chapters in this publication shows that more than two thirds (68.3 %) of EU-27 industrial exports were concentrated among four product groups – namely: transport equipment; electrical machinery and optical equipment; chemicals, rubber and plastics; and machinery and equipment.

Bulgarian industrial exports were concentrated among energy products, steam and hot water (29.0 %) and metals and metal products (27.0 %), a pattern that was repeated in Romania, where shares of 24.0 % and 25.0 % were recorded for the same product groups – see Table 1.26. The main difference in the composition of exports was the relatively high share of Romanian exports from transport equipment products (14.5 % of the industrial total) when compared with a 2.3 % share in Bulgaria – which resulted from a high degree of exports of motor vehicles and associated parts and accessories.

The two largest product groups for EU-27 imports in 2006 were energy products, steam and hot water (25.7 % of the industrial total) and electrical machinery and optical equipment (21.3 %). This pattern was to some degree repeated in Romania, as more than a third (35.2 %) of Romanian industrial imports was composed of energy products, steam and hot water. On the other hand, some 18.1 % of industrial imports in Bulgaria were composed of metals and metal products, while non-energy mining and quarrying products accounted for 15.6 % of Bulgarian imports (in contrast to shares of 3 % or less in Romania and the EU-27).

Table 1.26

Structure of external trade, 2006 (% of industrial products)

Chapter		Exports			Imports		
		EU-27	BG	RO	EU-27	BG	RO
2	Food, beverages and tobacco	5.0	6.2	1.3	3.8	5.4	5.5
3	Textiles, clothing, leather and footwear	4.2	4.1	3.2	7.8	8.0	6.7
4	Wood and paper	2.7	2.3	6.2	1.7	1.9	0.8
5	Chemicals, rubber and plastics	18.0	11.7	12.9	10.3	9.4	8.7
6	Other non-metallic mineral products	1.6	2.7	0.9	0.8	2.4	1.3
7	Metals and metal products	8.3	27.0	25.0	8.3	18.1	8.2
8	Machinery and equipment	15.8	5.4	6.7	6.0	7.9	5.9
9	Electrical machinery and optical equipment	18.3	4.5	3.3	21.3	15.2	16.3
10	Transport equipment	16.3	2.3	14.5	8.1	7.7	6.9
11	Furniture; other manufactured goods n.e.c.	2.7	1.0	1.8	3.3	1.4	1.1
12	Non-energy mining and quarrying	1.3	3.5	0.3	2.5	15.6	3.0
13	Energy products, steam and hot water	5.2	29.0	24.0	25.7	6.7	35.2

Source: Eurostat (Comext)

Food, beverages and tobacco

Enterprises within food, beverages and tobacco processing activities not only generate products for final consumption (many of which are essential daily products) but also intermediate products for other manufacturing activities (such as oils, fats and sugars).

The food, beverages and tobacco manufacturing sector is fragmented; there are a small number of large enterprises/groups that have a global market presence (see Table 2.1) and a large number of much smaller enterprises/groups that serve more local and national markets. There has been continued consolidation, with a number of the larger enterprises/groups growing through acquisitions and partnerships.

Although this manufacturing sector does not cover agricultural activities these are clearly linked; the Confederation of Food and Drink Industries (CIAA) of the EU estimated in February 2007 that "70 % of EU agricultural production is processed by EU food and drink companies". Therefore, the sector is not only affected by legislation such as food hygiene (the EU's new Hygiene Package came into force at the start of 2006) and labelling, but also aspects of the Common Agricultural Policy (CAP) that may have implications for processes and costs (such as the European Commission's Communication on a Community Action Plan on Animal Welfare [1] and improved competitiveness (such as the European Commission's simpler framework for the CAP [2].

[1] COM(2006) 13.
[2] COM(2006) 822.

This chapter refers to the processing of food, beverages and tobacco products (NACE Divisions 15 and 16). Importantly, it excludes the agricultural activities of growing, farming, rearing and hunting and also fishing (NACE Divisions 01 and 05, which are not covered in this publication). Given that a number of products, such as wine, olive oil, eggs and cheese are also sold directly by agricultural holdings and recorded in part, therefore, as an agricultural activity when own-produced, this distinction is important to bear in mind.

NACE
15: manufacture of food products and beverages;
15.1: production, processing and preserving of meat and meat products;
15.2: processing and preserving of fish and fish products;
15.3: processing and preserving of fruit and vegetables;
15.4: manufacture of vegetable and animal oils and fats;
15.5: manufacture of dairy products;
15.6: manufacture of grain mill products, starches and starch products;
15.7: manufacture of prepared animal feeds;
15.8: manufacture of other food products;
15.9: manufacture of beverages;
16: manufacture of tobacco products.

Table 2.1

Largest agro-food enterprises/groups in Europe ranked by world sales in food products, 2005

	Country	Main products	Food sales (EUR billion)
Nestlé	CH	Multi-product	58.8
Unilever	NL/UK	Multi-product	39.7
Diageo	UK	Alcoholic beverages	14.2
Danone	FR	Multi-product	13.0
InBev	BE	Beer	11.7
Heineken	NL	Beer	10.8
Cadbury Schweppes	UK	Beverages, confectionery	9.5
Associated British Foods	UK	Sugar, starches, prepared foods	8.8

Source: CIAA, http://www.ciaa.be

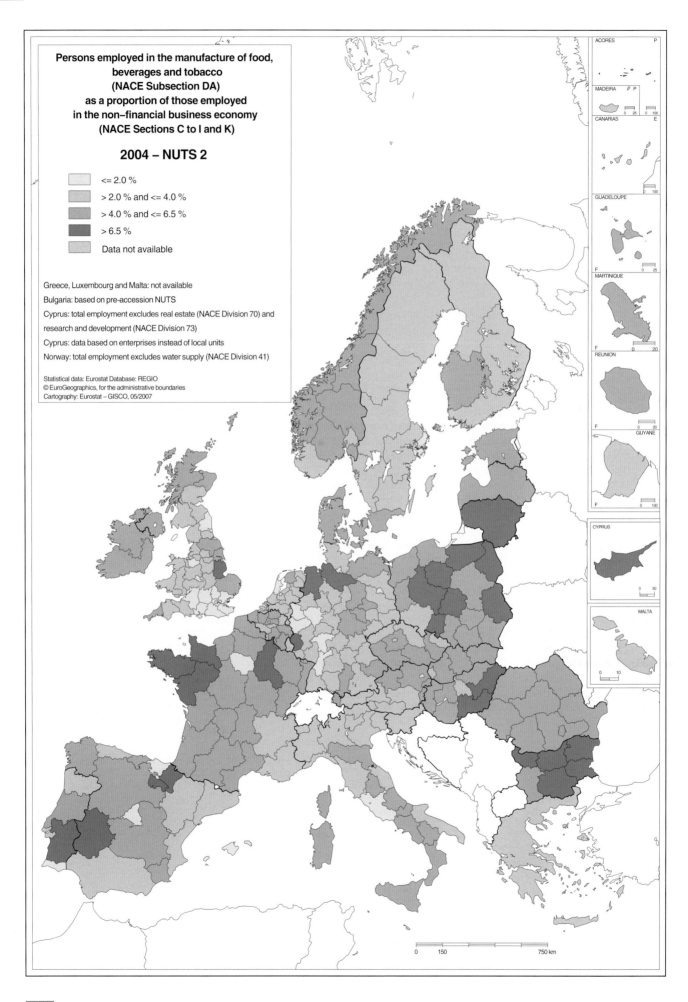

Persons employed in the manufacture of food,
beverages and tobacco
(NACE Subsection DA)
as a proportion of those employed
in the non–financial business economy
(NACE Sections C to I and K)

2004 – NUTS 2

- <= 2.0 %
- > 2.0 % and <= 4.0 %
- > 4.0 % and <= 6.5 %
- > 6.5 %
- Data not available

Greece, Luxembourg and Malta: not available

Bulgaria: based on pre-accession NUTS

Cyprus: total employment excludes real estate (NACE Division 70) and

research and development (NACE Division 73)

Cyprus: data based on enterprises instead of local units

Norway: total employment excludes water supply (NACE Division 41)

Statistical data: Eurostat Database: REGIO
© EuroGeographics, for the administrative boundaries
Cartography: Eurostat – GISCO, 05/2007

ACORES   P
MADEIRA   P
CANARIAS   E
GUADELOUPE
F
MARTINIQUE
F
REUNION
F
GUYANE
F
CYPRUS
MALTA

Table 2.5

Manufacture of food products, beverages and tobacco (NACE Subsection DA)
Productivity and profitability, EU-27, 2004

	Apparent labour productivity (EUR thousand)	Average personnel costs (EUR thousand)	Wage adjusted labour productivity (%)	Gross operating rate (%)
Food products, beverages and tobacco	41.8	24.4	171.7	9.8
Meat and meat products	30.1	21.4	140.6	5.4
Processing and preserving of fish and fish products	29.4	19.6	150.0	6.7
Dairy products (1)	44.0	28.0	160.0	5.8
Bread, sugar, confectionery and other food products	35.0	21.4	163.3	14.4
Miscellaneous food products (1)	48.0	27.0	180.0	7.4
Beverages (1)	70.0	33.0	210.0	15.4
Tobacco products	162.2	47.8	339.4	10.2

(1) Rounded estimates based on non-confidential data.
Source: Eurostat (SBS)

The gross operating rate for the food, beverages and tobacco sector in the EU-27 was 9.8 % in 2004, below the average of the non-financial business economy (11.0 %). According to this measure of profitability, there were particularly high rates in the manufacture of bread, sugar, confectionery and other food products (14.4 %) and beverages (15.4 %). In contrast, the gross operating rate for the production, processing and preserving of meat and meat products was about half the average for the non-financial business economy. Among the Member States for which data are available [7], the rates were highest in Ireland (22.7 %) and Poland (21.5 %) and lowest in Slovakia, Slovenia and Estonia (between 4.9 % and 5.9 %).

EXTERNAL TRADE
The EU-27 had a positive trade balance of EUR 5.9 billion with the rest of the world in food products, beverages and tobacco (CPA Subsection DA) in 2006. This surplus resulted from EU-27 exports of EUR 54.0 billion (a

[7] Latvia and Luxembourg, 2003; Greece and Malta, not available.

5.0 % share of total industrial exports) and imports of food products, beverages and tobacco to the value of EUR 48.2 billion (a 3.8 % share of total industrial imports) – see Table 2.6.

This trade surplus comprised a large trade surplus mainly in beverages (CPA Group 15.9), bread, sugar, confectionary and other food products (CPA Group 15.8) and dairy products (CPA Group 15.5), outweighing the large deficits in fish products (CPA Group 15.2) and miscellaneous food products (the grouping of CPA Groups 15.3, 15.4, 15.6 and 15.7).

Exports and imports of food, beverages and tobacco products both grew strongly in 2006 (each up 10 %), maintaining the upturn in growth since 2003 and sustaining the level of trade surplus noted since 2001. Nevertheless, there was some change in the composition of exports and imports of food, beverages and tobacco products in the period between 2001 and 2006; within EU-27 exports, the shares of beverages and of other food products rose to 31.1 % and 26.1 % respectively in 2006 at the

expense, principally, of dairy products (down from 12.3 % to 9.5%) and within EU-27 imports, the share of miscellaneous food products rose to 34.5 %, principally at the expense of meat and meat products (CPA Group 15.1, down from 13.3 % to 12.1 %) and dairy products (down from 2.9 % to 1.7 %).

Almost three-quarters (74.6 %) of the value of exports of food, beverages and tobacco products by EU-27 Member States were to other EU Member States, the highest proportion among any of the chapters in this publication. As a proportion of industrial exports, the export of food, beverage and tobacco products was particularly important for Denmark (accounting for 17.9 % in 2006) and Greece (14.8 %). In terms of industrial imports, these products were also important in Denmark (10.2 %) and Malta (10.1 %). The United States was the EU-27's largest export market for food products, beverages and tobacco as a whole (a 21.2 % share of EU-27 exports), followed by Russia (9.2 %).

Table 2.6

Food products, beverages and tobacco (CPA Subsection DA)
External trade, EU-27, 2006

	Extra-EU exports		Extra-EU imports		Trade balance (EUR million)	Cover ratio (%)
	(EUR million)	(% share of industrial exports)	(EUR million)	(% share of industrial imports)		
Food products, beverages and tobacco	54 044	5.0	48 169	3.8	5 875	112.2
Meat	5 227	0.5	5 805	0.5	-578	90.0
Fish	2 053	0.2	13 509	1.1	-11 456	15.2
Dairy products and ice cream	5 129	0.5	823	0.1	4 307	623.4
Bread, sugar, confectionery and other food products	14 108	1.3	6 605	0.5	7 503	213.6
Miscellaneous food products	8 937	0.8	16 594	1.3	-7 658	53.9
Beverages	16 803	1.6	4 480	0.4	12 323	375.1
Tobacco products	1 788	0.2	354	0.0	1 434	504.7

Source: Eurostat (Comext)

2.1: MEAT

This subchapter covers all meat processing stages that follow on from animal rearing; in other words, the activities of slaughtering through to the preparation of meat for final consumption (NACE Group 15.1), including fresh, chilled, frozen, processed, dried, salted and smoked meats. The data presented also include the treatment of hides and skins, the rendering of fats and the processing of animal offal.

With various animal sanitary health crises in recent years, the European Commission and Council have been active in revising and strengthening legislation in the areas of animal health and welfare. In January 2006, the European Commission launched a Community Action Plan on the Protection and Welfare of animals 2006-2010 [8]. This is expected to be complemented by a Commission Communication on animal health policy. Furthermore, the Regulation on the Protection of Animals during Transport came into effect [9] in January 2007. The European Commission also requested in February 2007 that the European Food Agency give it advice on the implications of the commercial use of meat from cloned animals.

STRUCTURAL PROFILE

The production, processing and preserving of meat and meat products (NACE Group 15.1, hereafter termed the meat processing sector) was the main activity of 46 000 enterprises in the EU-27 in 2004, which generated EUR 31.3 billion in value added in 2004, representing 15.7 % of the total generated by food, beverages and tobacco manufacturing as a whole (NACE Subsection DA). There were just over one million workers in the meat processing

[8] COM(2006) 13.
[9] Council Regulation (EC) No 1/2005.

sector of the EU-27 in 2004, representing over one in five (21.8 %) of all those working in food, beverages and tobacco manufacturing. Within the meat processing sector, the production of meat and poultry products (NACE Class 15.13) was the largest, both in terms of value added and employment; it generated 60 % of the EU-27's meat processing sector value added in 2004 and employed a little over half (54.9 %) of all those working in the sector. A little less than one third (30.8 %) of the sectoral workforce were also employed in the EU 27's production and preserving of meat (NACE Class 15.11) subsector, almost double the level of those employed in the production and preserving of poultrymeat products (NACE Class 15.12) subsector.

More than half (57.0 %) of the value added in the meat processing sector of the EU-27 came from Germany, France and the United Kingdom (see Table 2.7). These three Member States also

had about one half (48.2 %) of the EU-27's meat processing workforce, Poland accounting for a further 11.8 % of workers. Denmark was the only country, however, that showed notable specialisation in the activities of meat processing in terms of value added; its contribution to the value added of the non-financial business economy being more than twice the EU-27 average in 2004. Employment specialisation (within the non-financial business economy) in meat processing was highest in Poland (almost double the EU-27 average) but also relatively high in Hungary, Denmark, Lithuania and France.

Over the decade between 1996 and 2006, the output price index for meat processing included some downturns, notably in 1998, 1999 and 2002 when it is likely that food health scares had an impact on demand, with some corresponding adjustment to production levels (see Figure 2.6).

Figure 2.6

Production, processing, preserving of meat, meat products (NACE Group 15.1)
Evolution of main indicators, EU-27 (2000=100)

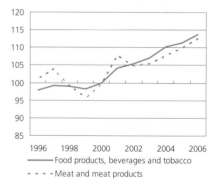

Source: Eurostat (STS)

Table 2.7

Production, processing, preserving of meat, meat products (NACE Group 15.1)
Structural profile: ranking of top five Member States, 2004

Rank	Share of EU-27 value added (%) (1)	Share of EU-27 employment (%) (1)	Value added specialisation ratio (EU-27=100) (2)	Employment specialisation ratio (EU-27=100) (2)
1	Germany (23.2)	Germany (20.8)	Denmark (214.9)	Poland (196.5)
2	France (18.6)	France (16.2)	Hungary (135.4)	Hungary (167.6)
3	United Kingdom (15.2)	Poland (11.8)	France (132.0)	Denmark (151.9)
4	Spain (9.0)	United Kingdom (11.3)	Finland (114.4)	Lithuania (150.2)
5	Italy (8.5)	Spain (7.6)	Germany (110.8)	France (141.4)

(1) Greece and Malta, not available; Luxembourg, 2003.
(2) Ireland, Greece, Cyprus and Malta, not available; Luxembourg, 2003.
Source: Eurostat (SBS)

Table 2.8

Production, processing, preserving of meat, meat products (NACE Group 15.1)
Productivity and profitability, EU-27, 2004

	Apparent labour productivity (EUR thousand)	Average personnel costs (EUR thousand)	Wage adjusted labour productivity (%)	Gross operating rate (%)
Meat and meat products	30.1	21.4	140.6	5.4
Meat (1)	:	21.0	:	:
Poultrymeat (1)	23.0	20.0	120.0	3.1
Meat and poultrymeat products (1)	33.2	22.0	148.0	7.2

(1) Rounded estimates based on non-confidential data.
Source: Eurostat (SBS)

Table 2.9

Production, processing, preserving of meat, meat products (NACE Group 15.1)
External trade, EU-27, 2006

	Extra-EU exports		Extra-EU imports		Trade balance (EUR million)	Cover ratio (%)
	(EUR million)	(% share of chapter)	(EUR million)	(% share of chapter)		
Meat	5 227	9.7	5 805	12.1	-578	90.0
Fresh and preserved meat, except poultry	3 650	6.8	3 956	8.2	-306	92.3
Fresh and preserved poultry meat	781	1.4	586	1.2	195	133.2
Meat and poultry meat products	796	1.5	1 262	2.6	-466	63.1

Source: Eurostat (Comext)

COSTS, PRODUCTIVITY AND PROFITABILITY

The cost structure of the meat processing sector of the EU-27 was broadly similar to the food, beverages and tobacco manufacturing sector as a whole. Among the Member States, the proportion of gross investment in tangible goods within total expenditure (gross operating and tangible investment expenditure) was highest in Latvia (17.4 %), Slovenia (10.9 %) and Lithuania (10.6 %).

The apparent labour productivity of the EU-27 meat processing sector was EUR 30 100 per person employed in 2004 (see Table 2.8), considerably lower than the average level for the food, beverages and tobacco manufacturing sector as a whole (EUR 41 800 per employee) and the non-financial business economy (EUR 40 900 per employee). Although average personnel costs in the meat processing sector of the EU-27 (EUR 21 400 per employee) were almost one-quarter (22.5 %) less than the average across the non-financial business economy in 2004, wage adjusted labour productivity ratio for the meat processing sector (140.6 %) in the EU-27 remained 5 % below that of the non-financial business economy and significantly less than the ratio for the food, beverages and tobacco sector (171.7 %).

For the majority of Member States, the wage adjusted labour productivity of their meat processing sectors was significantly lower than the ratio for their respective non-financial business economies; the most notable exception was Bulgaria, where the wage adjusted labour productivity of the meat processing sector was 34.7 % higher than the ratio for the non-financial business economy.

The profitability of the meat processing sector, as indicated by the gross operating rate, was the lowest of all the food, beverages and tobacco manufacturing sectors in 2004 at 5.4 %, just under half the rate of profitability of the non-financial business economy (11.0 %). Indeed, profitability was particularly low in the production of meat and poultry meat products (3.1 %). The characteristic of relatively low profitability in the sector was common to all of the Member States for which data are available [10].

[10] Luxembourg, 2003; Ireland, Greece, Cyprus and Malta, not available.

EXTERNAL TRADE

Extra EU-27 exports of meat and meat products (CPA Group 15.1) in 2006 were valued at EUR 5.2 billion, representing 9.7 % of all exports of food products, beverages and tobacco products (CPA Subsection DA) – see Table 2.9. Combined with imports of EUR 5.8 billion, this lead to a trade deficit of EUR 578 million. There was a moderate trade surplus of EUR 195 million in fresh and preserved poultrymeat (CPA Class 15.12) in 2006, but this was outweighed by the trade deficits of EUR 466 million for meat and poultrymeat products (CPA Class 15.13) and EUR 306 million for fresh and preserved meat, except poultry (CPA Class 15.11).

Exports of meat and meat products by EU-27 Member States were mainly intra-EU-27 based (85.3 %). The main external markets for EU-27 exports were Russia (22.9 %) and Japan (16.7 %). Almost two-thirds of the value of EU-27 imports came from Brazil (34.0 %), New Zealand (18.5 %) and Argentina (9.2 %).

Among the Member States, Denmark, the Netherlands, Ireland and Belgium recorded the largest trade surpluses (intra and extra-EU) in 2006. In contrast, the United Kingdom and Italy were the Member States that were most reliant on imports of meat and meat products in 2005 (recording trade deficits of EUR 4.6 billion and EUR 3.5 billion respectively).

2.2: FISH

> This subchapter includes information on the preparation and preservation of fish, crustaceans and molluscs (be they fresh, frozen, smoked, salted or canned) and the manufacture of prepared fish and seafood dishes, all included within NACE Group 15.2.

The activity of this sector is linked to the fishing sector, and the issues relating to fish stocks and quotas. In May 2006, the European Commission published a Communication [11] titled "Halting the loss of biodiversity by 2010" that aims to clarify the responsibilities concerning the implementation of existing policies, and this underlined the damaging impact current practices have on commercially harvested fish stocks as well as on non-target species and habitats. Conservation policies have dominated recent legislative developments; there have been Council Regulation proposals for new multi-annual (recovery) plans for cod stocks [12], bluefin tuna stocks [13], conservation and enforcement measures in the North Atlantic Fisheries Organisation [14] and the use of drift nets [15].

STRUCTURAL PROFILE

The fish processing sector (NACE Group 15.2) of the EU-27 consisted of 4 000 enterprises which generated a value added of EUR 3.8 billion in 2004, representing only 1.9 % of the value added generated by food, beverages and tobacco manufacturing (NACE Subsection DA). The 128 700 people employed in fish processing in the EU-27 in 2004 represented 2.7 % of the food, beverages and tobacco workforce. A little more than half (53.1 %) of the value added generated by the fish

[11] COM(2006) 216.
[12] COM(2006) 411.
[13] COM(2007) 169.
[14] COM(2006) 609.
[15] COM(2006) 511.

processing sectors of the EU-27 came from France, Spain and the United Kingdom. These three Member States also had the largest workforces in fish processing (a combined 43.7 %), with Poland also having a sizeable workforce (10.2 %) – see Table 2.10. In relative terms, the fish processing sectors in the Baltic Member States and Denmark were, by far, the most specialised. In Latvia and Lithuania, the contribution of the value added of fish processing activities to the value added of the non-financial business economy was between six and seven times the EU-27 average.

The output of EU-27 fish processing grew every year since a relative trough in 1997 (see Figure 2.7), despite concerns about the EU's own fish stocks. Indeed, growth in output (an average 2.0 % per annum) was among the highest of the food, beverages and tobacco manufacturing sectors and accelerated in the period between 2001 and 2005 (an average 4.3 % per annum).

COSTS, PRODUCTIVITY AND PROFITABILITY

The apparent labour productivity of fish processing activities in the EU-27 was EUR 29 400 per person employed, the lowest among the food, beverages and tobacco manufacturing sectors. However, average personnel costs in the fish processing sector were EUR 19 600 per employee and resulted in a wage adjusted labour productivity ratio (150.0 %) for fish processing close to the non-financial business economy (148.0 %), but considerably less , than the average ratio for food, beverages and tobacco (171.7 %). In Hungary and Estonia, the wage adjusted productivity level of the fish processing sector was about half (51.3 % and 54.4 % respectively) that of the non-financial business economy.

The gross operating rate of 6.7 % for the fish processing sector was also low, both compared to the wider food, beverages and tobacco manufacturing sector (9.8 %) and the non-financial business economy average (11.0 %).

Figure 2.7

Processing and preserving of fish and fish products (NACE Group 15.2)
Evolution of main indicators, EU-27 (2000=100)

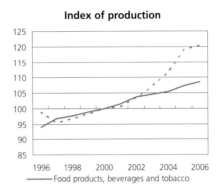
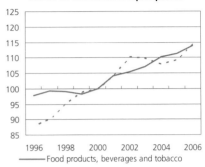

Source: Eurostat (STS)

Table 2.10

Processing and preserving of fish and fish products (NACE Group 15.2)
Structural profile: ranking of top five Member States, 2004

Rank	Share of EU-27 value added (%) (1)	Share of EU-27 employment (%) (2)	Value added specialisation ratio (EU-27=100) (3)	Employment specialisation ratio (EU-27=100) (4)
1	United Kingdom (18.4)	Spain (17.6)	Latvia (675.4)	Latvia (1 180.1)
2	Spain (18.3)	United Kingdom (14.1)	Lithuania (600.1)	Estonia (867.8)
3	France (16.4)	France (12.0)	Estonia (485.1)	Lithuania (587.4)
4	Germany (11.1)	Poland (10.2)	Denmark (371.4)	Denmark (342.1)
5	Denmark (7.4)	Germany (7.7)	Portugal (246.7)	Portugal (184.8)

(1) Czech Republic, Greece, Italy, Cyprus, Malta, Netherlands, Austria, Slovenia and Sweden, not available; Luxembourg and Finland, 2003.
(2) Czech Republic, Greece, Italy, Cyprus, Malta, Austria, Slovenia and Sweden, not available; Luxembourg and Finland, 2003.
(3) Czech Republic, Ireland, Greece, Italy, Cyprus, Malta, Netherlands, Austria, Slovenia and Sweden, not available; Luxembourg and Finland, 2003.
(4) Czech Republic, Ireland, Greece, Italy, Cyprus, Malta, Austria, Slovenia and Sweden, not available; Luxembourg and Finland, 2003.
Source: Eurostat (SBS)

EXTERNAL TRADE

Strong demand for fish and fish products in the EU-27, coupled with low fish stocks in EU waters, is leading to an increasing reliance on imports of fish and fish products from a spread of non-member countries. Imports of fish and fish products (CPA Group 15.2) were valued at EUR 13.5 billion in 2006, accounting for 28 % of all imports of food products, beverages and tobacco (CPA Subsection DA). A quarter of the value of EU-27 imports came from Norway (9.0 %), China (8.6 %) and Iceland (7.2 %) combined. Although the value of EU-27 exports of fish and fish products increased to EUR 2.1 billion in 2006, the trade deficit grew to EUR 11.5 billion, the largest deficit recorded among the ten CPA groups that make up food, beverages and tobacco products.

2.3: DAIRY PRODUCTS

> This subchapter includes the production of fresh milk, cream, butter, yoghurt, cheese, whey, ice creams and sorbets which are all classified within NACE Group 15.5. The data presented do not cover activities within the confines of farms themselves.

There are three main policy areas of relevance to the dairy products manufacturing sector. The first concerns changes in the current framework conditions for dairy products in the EU; in April 2007, there was an increase of 0.5 % in milk quotas that came into force in 11 Member States, and in July 2007 there was a further cut in the intervention price of butter. The second concerns the so-called "Dairy-Mini Package" that is part of the European Commission's "Action Plan on the Simplification of the CAP", which was published in October 2006, and has important proposals on protein standardisation (important for powder manufacturers and milk processors), and the liberalisation of fat content of drinking milk, which may give manufacturers greater flexibility to respond to consumer trends towards low-fat milks. The third area of policy concerns the World Trade Organisation negotiations, suspended in July 2006, which included proposals for the possible phasing out of export subsidies, without volume restrictions, and a proposal on market access for dairy products from third countries.

STRUCTURAL PROFILE

There were 400 000 persons employed in the 12 500 enterprises with the manufacture of dairy products (NACE Group 15.5) as their main activity in the EU-27 in 2004, representing 8.4 % of the workforce in the food, beverages and tobacco manufacturing sector. The majority of these workers (87.5 %) were engaged in the operation of dairies and cheese making (NACE Class 15.51). The manufacture of dairy products in the EU-27 generated EUR 18.1 billion of value added in 2003, representing 9.4 % of the total recorded for food, beverages and tobacco manufacturing (NACE Subsection DA).

The main Member States for dairy products manufacturing in terms of value added in 2004 were France (EUR 3.2 billion), Germany (EUR 3.1 billion), Italy (EUR 2.8 billion), the United Kingdom and Spain (both EUR 1.7 billion). However, Germany and the United Kingdom were among the least specialised Member States in dairy products manufacturing. In contrast, the dairy products sector in Latvia accounted for a little over twice the EU-27 average share of the non-financial business economy value added in 2003 (see Table 2.11).

Figure 2.8

Manufacture of dairy products (NACE Group 15.5)
Evolution of main indicators, EU-27 (2000=100)

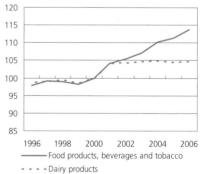

Source: Eurostat (STS)

Table 2.11

Manufacture of dairy products (NACE Group 15.5)
Structural profile: ranking of top five Member States, 2004

Rank	Share of EU-27 value added (%) (1)	Share of EU-27 employment (%) (2)	Value added specialisation ratio (EU-27=100) (3)	Employment specialisation ratio (EU-27=100) (4)
1	France (17.4)	France (15.8)	Latvia (222.8)	Lithuania (430.1)
2	Italy (17.3)	Italy (13.0)	Estonia (190.8)	Latvia (222.1)
3	Germany (16.5)	Poland (11.5)	Poland (177.8)	Estonia (221.4)
4	United Kingdom (11.1)	Germany (10.5)	Italy (155.6)	Poland (192.8)
5	Spain (8.2)	United Kingdom (7.5)	Hungary (152.7)	Bulgaria (147.7)

(1) 2003; Denmark, Greece, Luxembourg, Malta and Sweden, not available.
(2) Denmark, Greece, Luxembourg and Malta, not available.
(3) 2003; Denmark, Ireland, Greece, Cyprus, Lithuania, Luxembourg, Malta and Sweden, not available.
(4) Denmark, Ireland, Greece, Cyprus, Luxembourg and Malta, not available.
Source: Eurostat (SBS)

There was relatively steady growth in the production index of dairy products in the EU-27 between 1996 and 2006. Over the period as a whole, there was an average rate of growth of 1.0 % per annum despite small declines in 2002 and 2004. In contrast, the domestic price index for dairy products was largely stagnant except for a 4.2 % jump in prices in 2001 – see Figure 2.8.

COSTS, PRODUCTIVITY AND PROFITABILITY

Average personnel costs in the dairy products manufacturing sector were EUR 28 000 per employee in the EU-27 in 2004, a little higher (1.4 %) than the average across the non-financial business economy and more significantly above the average (14.8 % higher) within the food, beverages and tobacco manufacturing sector. The apparent labour productivity of EUR 44 000 per person employed in the dairy products sector was 7.6 % higher than the average rate for the non-financial business economy in 2004. This situation in 2004 resulted in a wage adjusted labour productivity ratio of 160.0 % for the dairy products sector, which was moderately higher than the average ratio for the non-financial business economy (148.0 %). In Spain and Portugal, the wage adjusted labour productivity ratio of the dairy products sector was significantly higher (37.8 % and 45.2 % respectively) than the average ratio for their non-financial business economies in 2004 (see Figure 2.9), despite the fact that average personnel costs in the dairy sector were also sharply higher (27.4 % and 20.5 %). In contrast, the wage adjusted labour productivity ratio of dairy products was half (50 %) that of the non-financial business economy in Slovenia, the lowest relative level among the Member States.

The profitability of the EU-27 dairy products manufacturing sector, as measured by the gross operating rate was only 5.8 % in 2004, about half (52.7 %) of the rate of profitability of the non-financial business economy. This characteristic was common across the majority of the Member States; only in Hungary and Portugal were the gross operating rates of the dairy products sector slightly higher than the average rates for their respective non-financial business economies. Indeed, in the Netherlands and Slovenia the gross operating rate of the dairy products sector was negative in 2004 (-1.0 and -2.8 % respectively), due to a negative gross operating surplus as personnel costs were higher than value added.

Figure 2.9

Manufacture of dairy products (NACE Group 15.5)
Productivity and profitability characteristics relative to national averages, 2004
(non-financial business economy=100) (1)

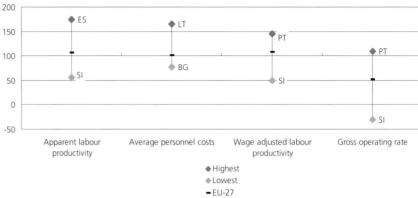

(1) Denmark, Ireland, Greece, Cyprus, Luxembourg and Malta, not available.
Source: Eurostat (SBS)

EXTERNAL TRADE

The EU-27 exported EUR 5.1 billion of dairy products and ice cream (CPA Group 15.5) in 2006, representing 9.5 % of food, beverages and tobacco product (CPA Subsection DA) exports. Dairy products accounted for almost all (97.2 %) of these exports. During the period 2001 to 2005, there was a trend of falling imports of dairy products and ice cream and an uneven rise in exports, which had resulted in a growing trade surplus. However, this pattern of trade was not continued in 2006 with the value of imports rising (3.1 % higher), the value of exports falling (down 4.5 %) and the trade surplus shrinking 5.8 % to EUR 4.3 billion.

Extra-EU exports accounted for nearly one-fifth (19.6 %) of the value of all exports (intra- and extra-EU) of dairy products and ice cream by the EU-27 Member States in 2004. The principal external export markets for these products were the United States and Russia (13.6 % and 11.7 % respectively of EU exports). A little over two-thirds of dairy product imports to the EU-27 came from Switzerland (37.0 %) and New Zealand (32.0 %).

Among the Member States, France recorded the largest trade surplus in dairy products in 2006 (a total of EUR 2.4 billion, of which EUR 0.9 billion was extra-EU trade). The Netherlands, Germany, Denmark and Ireland also registered (extra and intra-EU) trade surpluses for dairy products at or above EUR 1.0 billion. In contrast, Italy and the United Kingdom recorded trade deficits of EUR 1.4 billion and EUR 1.6 billion respectively in dairy products in 2006.

Table 2.17

Manufacture of vegetable and animal oils and fats (NACE Group 15.4)
Structural profile: ranking of top five Member States, 2004

Rank	Share of EU-27 value added (%) (1)	Share of EU-27 employment (%) (2)	Value added specialisation ratio (EU-27=100) (3)	Employment specialisation ratio (EU-27=100) (4)
1	Spain (20.7)	Spain (20.0)	Hungary (392.2)	Bulgaria (273.6)
2	Italy (20.5)	Italy (18.9)	Romania (237.9)	Romania (259.7)
3	Germany (20.0)	Germany (11.5)	Spain (230.1)	Slovakia (212.3)
4	United Kingdom (5.4)	Romania (8.3)	Bulgaria (191.3)	Spain (198.9)
5	Sweden (3.1)	Czech Republic (4.8)	Italy (184.2)	Czech Republic (165.2)

(1) Estonia, Greece, France, Latvia, Luxembourg, Malta, Netherlands, Slovenia and Finland, not available.
(2) All Member States, 2003, except Denmark, Estonia, Greece, Luxembourg, Malta and Sweden, not available.
(3) Estonia, Ireland, Greece, France, Cyprus, Latvia, Luxembourg, Malta, Netherlands, Slovenia and Finland, not available.
(4) All Member States, 2003, except Denmark, Estonia, Ireland, Greece, Cyprus, Lithuania, Luxembourg, Malta and Sweden, not available.
Source: Eurostat (SBS)

VEGETABLE AND ANIMAL OILS AND FATS

Vegetable and animal oils and fats manufacturing was the main activity of 7 200 enterprises in the EU-27 and generated EUR 3.9 billion of value added in 2004, representing 2.0 % of the food, beverages and tobacco manufacturing (NACE Subsection DA) total. Despite average personnel costs in the sector (EUR 30 400 per employee) that were relatively high in the EU-27 in 2004, the wage adjusted productivity ratio (200.0 %) of this sector was a little over one third higher (35.1 %) than the ratio for the non-financial business economy.

The majority of the value added (61.2 %) generated by the manufacture of vegetable and animal oils and fats in the EU-27 came from production in Germany, Spain and Italy. However, among the Member States for which data are available [23], Hungary was by far the most specialised in the production of vegetable and animal oils and fats, as it contributed almost four times as much to the value added of its non-financial business economy as the EU-27 average (see Table 2.17), with Spain and Romania also being relatively specialised with contributions that were more than twice the average.

[23] Estonia, Ireland, Greece, France, Cyprus, Latvia, Luxembourg, Malta, Netherlands, Slovenia and Finland.

The EU-27 had a trade deficit in vegetable and animal oils and fats (CPA Group 15.4) to the value of EUR 6.8 billion in 2004. This was the second largest deficit among the CPA groups of the food, beverages and tobacco products (CPA Subsection DA). Imports of these oils and fats accounted for almost one-fifth (19.5 %) of all EU-27 imports of food, beverages and tobacco products and were valued at EUR 9.4 billion in 2004. One-half (49.5 %) of these imports came from Argentina and Brazil. The vast majority of imports (85 %) were of crude oils and fats, the largest part of which was soya for animal compound feed.

GRAIN MILL AND STARCH PRODUCTS

The manufacture of grain mill and starch products was the principal activity of 8 500 enterprises across the EU-27 in 2004, which generated EUR 6.8 billion of value added, representing 3.4 % of the total value added for the food, beverages and tobacco sector (NACE Subsection DA). A little over one quarter (26.4 %) of the value added was generated in the United Kingdom. These activities employed 127 900 people across the EU-27, representing 2.7 % of the workforce in the food, beverages and tobacco sector. Hungary and Romania were relatively specialised in the manufacture of grain mill and starch products; this activity contributed over twice as much of the value added of the respective national non-financial business economies than the EU-27 average in 2004 (see Table 2.18).

Personnel costs in the grain mill and starch products manufacturing sector of the EU-27 accounted for a relatively low proportion (10.6 %) of total expenditure (gross operating and tangible investment expenditure) compared to the non-financial business economy (16.4 %). However, average personnel costs in the sector were almost one-tenth (8.7 %) higher than the non-financial business economy average, at EUR 30 000 per employee in 2004. The apparent labour productivity of those working in the sector (EUR 53 400 per person employed) was almost one-third (30.6 %) higher than the non-financial business economy average. The higher personnel costs, however, narrowed the difference between the respective wage adjusted labour productivity ratios to 23 % (a ratio of 182.0 % for the sector compared with 148.0 % for the non-financial business economy as a whole).

EU-27 exports of grain mill and starch products (CPA Group 15.6) were valued at EUR 1.7 billion in 2006, accounting for only 3.2 % of the value of EU-27 exports of food, beverages and tobacco products (CPA Subsection DA).

Table 2.18

Manufacture of grain mill products, starches and starch products (NACE Group 15.6)
Structural profile: ranking of top five Member States, 2004

Rank	Share of EU-27 value added (%) (1)	Share of EU-27 employment (%) (2)	Value added specialisation ratio (EU-27=100) (3)	Employment specialisation ratio (EU-27=100) (4)
1	United Kingdom (26.4)	Germany (12.3)	Hungary (234.6)	Romania (383.7)
2	France (15.4)	Romania (12.3)	Romania (203.9)	Bulgaria (264.8)
3	Germany (14.8)	United Kingdom (11.7)	Bulgaria (190.2)	Hungary (207.6)
4	Italy (11.1)	France (11.4)	Slovakia (186.8)	Slovakia (194.9)
5	Spain (6.0)	Poland (10.0)	Poland (156.6)	Poland (167.4)

(1) Estonia, Greece, Lithuania, Luxembourg and Malta, not available.
(2) Estonia, Greece, Lithuania, Luxembourg and Malta, not available; Slovenia, 2003.
(3) Estonia, Ireland, Greece, Cyprus, Lithuania, Luxembourg and Malta, not available.
(4) Estonia, Ireland, Greece, Cyprus, Lithuania, Luxembourg and Malta, not available; Slovenia, 2003.
Source: Eurostat (SBS)

Table 2.19

Manufacture of prepared animal feeds (NACE Group 15.7)
Structural profile: ranking of top five Member States, 2004

Rank	Share of EU-27 value added (%) (1)	Share of EU-27 employment (%) (2)	Value added specialisation ratio (EU-27=100) (3)	Employment specialisation ratio (EU-27=100) (4)
1	France (19.6)	France (16.3)	Hungary (240.2)	Slovakia (194.8)
2	Germany (14.7)	Spain (11.3)	Poland (218.3)	Hungary (194.8)
3	United Kingdom (13.8)	Germany (11.0)	Netherlands (210.4)	Czech Republic (183.0)
4	Spain (10.5)	United Kingdom (10.0)	Czech Republic (190.4)	Netherlands (159.4)
5	Netherlands (9.7)	Poland (8.2)	Portugal (156.9)	Portugal (145.9)

(1) Denmark, Greece and Malta, not available; Cyprus, Latvia, Lithuania and Luxembourg, 2003.
(2) Denmark, Greece and Malta, not available; Cyprus, Lithuania, Luxembourg and Slovenia, 2003.
(3) Denmark, Ireland, Greece, Cyprus, Lithuania and Malta, not available; Latvia and Luxembourg, 2003.
(4) Denmark, Ireland, Greece, Cyprus, Lithuania and Malta, not available; Luxembourg and Slovenia, 2003.
Source: Eurostat (SBS)

PREPARED ANIMAL FEED

There were 5 100 enterprises in the EU-27 with the manufacture of animal feed as their main activity in 2004, employing 132 700 people and generating EUR 7.2 billion of value added. The major producers of animal feed in the EU-27 were France, Germany, the United Kingdom and Spain. Among the Member States for which data are available [24], however, Hungary, Poland and the Netherlands were the most specialised, as these activities' contribution to the non-financial business economy value added was a little more than double the EU-27 average (see Table 2.19).

Personnel costs in the animal feed manufacturing sector of the EU-27 accounted for a low proportion (7.7 %) of total expenditure (gross operating and tangible investment expenditure), although compared to the non-financial business economy, average personnel costs in the sector (EUR 32 000 per employee) were relatively high (15.9 % more). Although the apparent labour productivity of those employed in the animal feed sector was relatively high (at EUR 54 100 per person employed), the relatively high personnel costs kept the wage adjusted labour productivity ratio down to 169.1 % in 2004.

[24] Denmark, Greece, Cyprus, Lithuania, Luxembourg and Malta, not available.

2.6: BEVERAGES

NACE Group 15.9 covers both alcoholic and non-alcoholic beverages. As such, the data presented in this subchapter include mineral waters, soft drinks, beer, wine and spirits. However, they do not include fruit and vegetable juices (NACE Class 15.32) or the processing of tea and coffee (NACE Class 15.86).

In September 2006, the European Commission adopted a proposal on revised excise duties on alcohol and alcoholic beverages [25] that would increase the minimum rates of excise duty applied to alcohol and alcoholic beverages by 31 % (beer and spirits only, as the excise rate for wine would remain at zero) and this proposal is currently under discussion. In October 2006, the European Commission also adopted a Communication [26] on reducing alcohol-related health and social harm that set out priorities to fight alcohol abuse.

[25] COM(2006) 486.
[26] COM(2006) 625.

Figure 2.11

Manufacture of beverages (NACE Group 15.9)
Value added, EU-27, 2004 (EUR million)

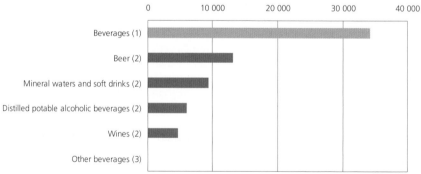

(1) Value added, 2003.
(2) Rounded estimate based on non-confidential data.
(3) Not available; share of value added is approximately 3 %.
Source: Eurostat (SBS)

Table 2.20 _____

Manufacture of beverages (NACE Group 15.9)

Structural profile: ranking of top five Member States, 2004

Rank	Share of EU-27 value added (%) (1)	Share of EU-27 employment (%) (2)	Value added specialisation ratio (EU-27=100) (3)	Employment specialisation ratio (EU-27=100) (4)
1	Germany (16.6)	Germany (16.7)	Poland (400.1)	Bulgaria (265.4)
2	United Kingdom (15.9)	Spain (10.8)	Romania (270.1)	Slovakia (215.5)
3	France (14.3)	United Kingdom (10.8)	Latvia (265.9)	Romania (198.1)
4	Spain (11.8)	France (9.7)	Bulgaria (186.4)	Lithuania (181.5)
5	Poland (7.5)	Italy (7.8)	Czech Republic (181.6)	Hungary (169.4)

(1) All Member States, 2003, except Greece, Malta and Sweden, not available.
(2) Greece and Malta, not available; Ireland, Luxembourg and Slovenia, 2003.
(3) All Member States, 2003, except Ireland, Greece, Cyprus, Lithuania, Malta and Sweden, not available.
(4) Ireland, Greece, Cyprus and Malta, not available; Luxembourg and Slovenia, 2003.
Source: Eurostat (SBS)

STRUCTURAL PROFILE

The beverages sector (NACE Group 15.9) of the EU-27 consisted of about 22 000 enterprises, which generated EUR 34.2 billion of value added in 2003. Within food, beverages and tobacco manufacturing (NACE Subsection DA) as a whole, this represented the second largest share (17.7 %) at the NACE group level. Within the EU-27's beverages sector, the manufacture of beer (NACE Class 15.96) generated EUR 13.2 billion of value added in 2004, the largest amount at the NACE class level (see Figure 2.11). The manufacture of mineral water and soft drinks (NACE Class 15.98) generated a further EUR 9.4 billion, the manufacture of distilled potable alcohol beverages (NACE Class 15.91) EUR 6.0 billion, and wines (NACE Class 15.93) another EUR 4.6 billion of value added. The beverages sector was also a major employer, engaging 479 600 people throughout the EU-27, corresponding to almost one in every ten people (10.1 %) working within food, beverages and tobacco manufacturing as a whole in 2004.

The beverages sector in the United Kingdom generated EUR 5.9 billion of value added in 2004, a little more than in Germany (EUR 5.3 billion) and France (EUR 5.1 billion). Together, these three Member States accounted for almost half of the value (46.7 %) added generated by the beverages sector in the EU-27 in 2003 (note that EU-27 data are not available for 2004). Poland, Romania and Latvia were the Member States that were the most relatively specialised in the manufacture of beverages, generating between two and a half and four times as high a share of the non-financial business economy's value added in this sector as the EU-27 average (see Table 2.20).

Figure 2.12 _____

Manufacture of beverages (NACE Group 15.9)

Evolution of main indicators, EU-27 (2000=100)

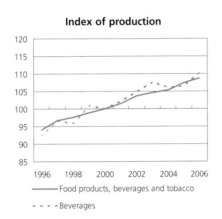

Index of production

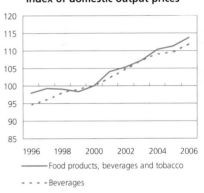

Index of domestic output prices

Source: Eurostat (STS)

Over the period between 1996 and 2006, there was an upward trend in the production index of beverages in the EU-27 that was similar to that of food, beverages and tobacco as a whole (see Figure 2.12). The index for beverages was somewhat more volatile, however, with relatively strong increases in output in 1997 (up 4.4 %), 1999 (up 5.3 %) and 2003 (up 2.8 %), followed in each case by relatively small declines (all between 0.8 % and 1.4 %). The production index for beverages rose by 3.5 % in 2006, to its highest level over the decade. At the NACE class level the strongest expansion in output over the reference period was noted for mineral waters and soft drinks (average annual growth of 3.3 %). In the case of wine, output has stabilised at relatively high levels since 2002. In the case of beer, annual output has been relatively stable since 2000.

Table 2.21

Manufacture of beverages (NACE Group 15.9)
Productivity and profitability, EU-27, 2004 (1)

	Apparent labour productivity (EUR thousand)	Average personnel costs (EUR thousand)	Wage adjusted labour productivity (%)	Gross operating rate (%)
Beverages	70.0	33.0	210.0	15.4
Wines	55.0	26.0	210.0	11.6
Beer	88.0	40.0	220.0	16.8
Malt	70.0	37.0	200.0	:
Mineral waters and soft drinks	60.0	33.0	180.0	11.5

(1) Rounded estimates based on non-confidential data; distilled potable alcoholic beverages, production of ethyl alcohol from fermented materials, cider and other fruit wines and other non-distilled fermented beverages, not available.
Source: Eurostat (SBS)

Table 2.22

Beverages (CPA Group 15.9)
External trade, EU-27, 2006

	Extra-EU exports (EUR million)	(% share of chapter)	Extra-EU imports (EUR million)	(% share of chapter)	Trade balance (EUR million)	Cover ratio (%)
Beverages	16 803	31.1	4 480	9.3	12 323	375.1
Distilled alcoholic beverages	6 374	11.8	950	2.0	5 424	671.2
Ethyl alcohol	53	0.1	295	0.6	-242	18.0
Wines	5 541	10.3	2 414	5.0	3 127	229.5
Cider and other fruit wines	59	0.1	20	0.0	38	286.7
Other non-distilled fermented beverages	137	0.3	3	0.0	134	5 095.1
Beer	1 938	3.6	258	0.5	1 681	752.4
Malt	599	1.1	7	0.0	593	8 800.7
Mineral waters and soft drinks	2 101	3.9	534	1.1	1 568	393.8

Source: Eurostat (Comext)

COSTS, PRODUCTIVITY AND PROFITABILITY

Average personnel costs in the beverages sector of the EU 27 were EUR 33 000 per employee (see Table 2.21), relatively high compared to the average across non-financial business economy (19.6 % higher) and particularly when compared to the average cost across food, beverages and tobacco manufacturing activities as a whole (35.2 % higher). Despite these relatively high average personnel costs, the wage adjusted labour productivity ratio of the beverages sector (210.0 %) in 2004 was the second highest behind tobacco manufacturing among the ten NACE groups that comprise food, beverages and tobacco manufacturing, much higher than the average for the non-financial business economy as a whole (148.0 %). This was due to the high apparent labour productivity ratio of EUR 70 000 per person employed in the beverages sector.

As a measure of profitability, the gross operating rate of 15.4 % for the beverages sector in 2004 was the highest among the ten NACE groups of food, beverages and tobacco manufacturing and almost 40 % higher than the average for the non-financial business economy.

EXTERNAL TRADE

Exports to non-member Community countries accounted for a much higher share (44.6 %) of all exports of beverages (intra- and extra-EU) than other food and tobacco products (an average share of 21.2 %). The value of EU-27 exports of beverages (CPA Group 15.9) was EUR 16.8 billion in 2006 (see Table 2.22), representing a little less than one third (31.1 %) of the value of EU-27 exports of all food, beverages and tobacco (CPA Subsection DA). The key export market for EU beverages in 2006 was the United States (41.7 % in value terms), which dwarfed the next largest market, Japan (6.8 %). Exports of distilled alcoholic beverages (CPA Class 15.91) and wines (CPA Class 15.93) accounted for more than two-thirds (70.9 %) of the value of EU-27 exports of beverages.

The value of EU-27 imports of beverages was EUR 4.5 billion in 2006, and as such the trade surplus was EUR 12.3 billion. A little over half (53.9 %) of all EU-27 imports of beverages were wines (valued at EUR 2.4 billion in 2006), of which the largest shares came from Australia (35.9 %), Chile (18.1 %) and South Africa (15.7 %). The largest part of the trade surplus for beverages in 2006 came from distilled alcoholic beverages (EUR 5.4 billion), with the other significant contribution coming from wine (EUR 3.1 billion).

Among the Member States, France recorded the largest trade surplus (intra- and extra-EU) in beverages in 2006 (EUR 8.6 billion), followed by Italy (EUR 3.1 billion) both with large surpluses in wine, and Austria (EUR 1.2 billion) with a large surplus from mineral water and soft drinks.

2.7: TOBACCO

NACE Division 16 covers the manufacture of all tobacco products, namely, cigarettes, cigarette tobacco, cigars, pipe tobacco, chewing tobacco and snuff.

In January 2007, the European Commission issued a Green Paper [27] titled "towards a Europe free from tobacco smoke" looking at policy options ranging from binding legislation to voluntary measures and from self-regulation to co-ordinated convergence. The European Commission also launched a review of the structure and rates of excise duty applied on cigarettes and other manufactured tobacco. It is intended that a legislative proposal will be put forward by the European Commission at the end of 2007.

_____

[27] COM(2007) 27.

STRUCTURAL PROFILE

The tobacco manufacturing sector (NACE Division 16) consisted of only 300 enterprises across the EU-27, although they generated EUR 10.8 billion of value added in 2004, contributing 5.4 % to the total value added for food, beverages and tobacco manufacturing (NACE Subsection DA). The tobacco manufacturing sector of the EU-27 is concentrated in a few Member States; a little over two-thirds (68.4 %) of the value added of the EU-27 tobacco sector in 2004 came from Poland (21.0 %), the United Kingdom (17.2 %), the Netherlands (15.7 %) and Germany (14.5 %) – see Table 2.23. The tobacco sector was relatively small in terms of numbers of people employed (66 900 in 2004), with about two in every four workers (41.8 %) employed in the four aforementioned Member States. In relative terms, Poland, Bulgaria and the Netherlands were highly specialised in tobacco manufacturing activities, with the proportion of value added from this sector in their respective national non-financial business economies significantly higher than the EU-27 average.

Between 1998 and 2006, there were consecutive annual reductions in the production index of tobacco products (NACE Division 16), at an average rate of decline of 4.5 % per annum (see Figure 2.13). In contrast, there was a steep increase in prices over the period from 1996 to 2006. Prices increased every year during this period, at an average rate of 6.0 % per annum.

Table 2.23 _____

Manufacture of tobacco products (NACE Division 16)
Structural profile: ranking of top five Member States, 2004

Rank	Share of EU-27 value added (%) (1)	Share of EU-27 employment (%) (2)	Value added specialisation ratio (EU-27=100) (3)	Employment specialisation ratio (EU-27=100) (4)
1	Poland (21.0)	Germany (17.3)	Poland (1 022.4)	Bulgaria (899.9)
2	United Kingdom (17.2)	Bulgaria (12.7)	Bulgaria (452.6)	Netherlands (191.7)
3	Netherlands (15.7)	Poland (9.8)	Netherlands (341.4)	Poland (163.4)
4	Germany (14.5)	Spain (9.2)	Portugal (128.3)	Belgium (158.6)
5	France (6.2)	United Kingdom (7.6)	Romania (104.5)	Romania (148.6)

(1) Czech Republic, Denmark, Greece, Italy, Latvia, Lithuania, Luxembourg, Malta, Austria, Slovenia, Slovakia and Sweden, not available; Ireland, France and Finland, 2003.
(2) Czech Republic, Denmark, Ireland, Greece, France, Italy, Lithuania, Luxembourg, Malta, Austria, Slovenia, Slovakia, Finland and Sweden, not available.
(3) Czech Republic, Denmark, Ireland, Greece, Italy, Cyprus, Latvia, Lithuania, Luxembourg, Malta, Austria, Slovenia, Slovakia and Sweden, not available; France and Finland, 2003.
(4) Czech Republic, Denmark, Ireland, Greece, France, Italy, Cyprus, Lithuania, Luxembourg, Malta, Austria, Slovenia, Slovakia, Finland and Sweden, not available.
Source: Eurostat (SBS)

Table 2.24 _____

Production of selected products - tobacco products (CPA Division 16), EU-27, 2006 (1)

	Prodcom code	Production value (EUR million)	Volume of sold production (thousands)	Unit of volume
Cigarettes containing tobacco or mixtures of tobacco and tobacco substitutes (excluding tobacco duty)	16.00.11.50	13 190	795 204 656	units
Cigars, cheroots and cigarillos containing tobacco or mixtures of tobacco and tobacco substitutes (excluding tobacco duty)	16.00.11.30	1 283	11 741 885	units
Smoking tobacco (excluding tobacco duty)	16.00.12.30	1 249	97 987	kg

(1) Estimated.
Source: Eurostat (PRODCOM)

Figure 2.13 _____

Manufacture of tobacco products (NACE Division 16)
Evolution of main indicators, EU-27 (2000=100)

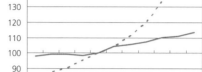
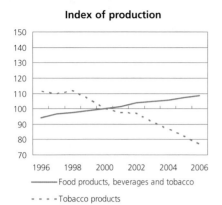

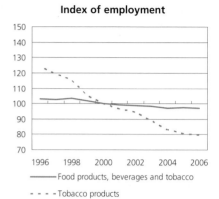

Source: Eurostat (STS)

COSTS, PRODUCTIVITY AND PROFITABILITY

Average personnel costs in the tobacco manufacturing sector of EUR 47 800 per employee were the highest among the ten NACE groups within the food, beverages and tobacco manufacturing sector and almost three-quarters (73.2 %) more than the average across the non-financial business economy. Nevertheless, as a proportion of gross operating and intangible investment expenditure, personnel costs only accounted for 12.1 %, significantly less than the 16.4 % average for the non-financial business economy. Despite the high average personnel costs, the wage adjusted labour productivity ratio in the tobacco manufacturing sector was 339.4 %, more than double the average ratio of the non-financial business economy, thanks to a very high level of apparent labour productivity (EUR 162 200 per person).

The gross operating rate for the EU-27's tobacco manufacturing sector was 10.2 % in 2004, suggesting that whilst profitability was similar to the level across the food, beverages and tobacco sector as a whole (9.8 %), it remained a little lower than the average across the non-financial business economy (11.0 %). There were considerable differences in this measure of profitability, however, between Member States; the gross operating rate of the tobacco manufacturing sector was substantially lower than the average rate of the non-financial business economy in some countries in 2004 (particularly in Hungary, Germany and Romania) but more than double it in the Netherlands and Spain, triple it in Portugal, or five times the non-financial business economy rate of profitability in Poland.

EXTERNAL TRADE

EU-27 trade in tobacco products (CPA Division 16) was relatively small; exports of tobacco products were sustained at EUR 1.8 billion in 2006, representing 3.3 % of the value of EU-27 exports of food, beverages and tobacco products (CPA Subsection DA), and imports of tobacco products remained at EUR 350 million, accounting for only 0.7 % of the value of EU-27 imports of food, beverages and tobacco products. The main non-member countries for tobacco products exports in 2006 were Turkey (9.3 % of the total value of EU-27 exports), the United Arab Emirates (8.4 %) and Japan (7.1 %).

Table 2.25

Manufacture of food products and beverages (NACE Division 15)

Main indicators, 2004

	EU-27	BE	BG	CZ	DK	DE	EE	IE (1)	EL	ES	FR	IT (1)	CY	LV	LT
No. of enterprises (thousands)	295.8	8.2	6.3	6.1	1.8	32.6	0.4	0.7	:	29.8	68.1	70.0	1.0	0.8	:
Turnover (EUR million) (2)	852 109	29 790	2 492	:	:	161 684	1 013	21 884	:	82 607	142 794	:	1 174	1 219	:
Production (EUR million) (2)	780 416	28 339	2 175	:	:	148 335	899	19 476	:	78 494	128 923	:	1 077	1 132	:
Value added (EUR million) (2)	188 780	5 866	376	:	:	34 904	176	7 150	:	16 959	28 824	:	335	272	:
Gross operating surplus (EUR million) (2)	82 854	2 447	191	:	:	12 302	60	5 308	:	7 804	9 893	:	126	130	:
Purchases of goods & services (EUR million) (2)	659 112	23 685	2 195	:	:	123 979	857	14 308	:	68 086	112 520	:	826	915	:
Personnel costs (EUR million) (2)	105 926	3 419	185	1 041	:	22 602	116	1 842	:	9 155	18 931	:	210	141	:
Investment in tangible goods (EUR million) (2)	32 667	1 103	269	610	:	4 670	52	456	:	3 918	4 966	:	61	146	:
Employment (thousands) (2)	4 705	99	104	:	:	847	18	49	:	378	649	:	13	36	:
Apparent labour prod. (EUR thousand) (2)	40.1	59.3	3.6	:	:	41.2	9.8	144.6	:	44.8	44.4	:	24.9	7.6	:
Average personnel costs (EUR thousand) (2)	24.0	38.1	1.9	:	:	27.8	6.5	37.5	:	25.6	31.0	:	15.9	4.0	:
Wage adjusted labour productivity (%) (2)	167.1	155.5	190.0	:	:	148.2	150.4	385.9	:	175.0	143.5	:	156.6	191.4	:
Gross operating rate (%) (2)	9.7	8.2	7.7	:	:	7.6	5.9	24.3	:	9.4	6.9	:	10.7	10.7	:
Investment / employment (EUR thousand) (2)	6.9	11.1	2.6	:	:	5.5	2.9	9.2	:	10.4	7.6	:	4.5	4.1	:

	LU (1)	HU	MT	NL	AT	PL	PT	RO	SI	SK	FI	SE	UK	NO
No. of enterprises (thousands)	0.2	7.0	:	4.5	4.3	18.3	8.5	10.9	0.8	:	1.9	3.2	7.1	2.0
Turnover (EUR million) (3)	:	9 916	:	48 708	:	29 341	11 501	5 974	:	:	8 989	:	108 796	:
Production (EUR million) (3)	:	8 667	:	43 590	:	26 480	10 775	5 508	:	:	8 132	:	97 863	:
Value added (EUR million) (3)	:	1 859	:	8 990	:	7 202	2 455	963	:	:	2 146	:	31 180	:
Gross operating surplus (EUR million) (3)	:	808	:	3 956	:	4 718	1 113	502	:	:	800	:	15 799	:
Purchases of goods & services (EUR million) (3)	:	7 828	:	39 726	:	23 138	9 234	5 668	:	:	6 999	:	73 216	:
Personnel costs (EUR million) (3)	:	1 051	:	5 035	:	2 484	1 343	461	:	:	1 390	:	15 382	:
Investment in tangible goods (EUR million) (4)	:	544	:	1 381	:	1 628	704	637	:	:	424	:	:	:
Employment (thousands) (3)	:	130	:	128	:	443	103	203	:	:	40	:	471	53
Apparent labour prod. (EUR thousand) (3)	:	14.3	:	70.3	:	16.3	23.8	4.7	:	:	53.7	:	66.1	:
Average personnel costs (EUR thousand) (3)	:	8.3	:	41.1	:	6.0	13.5	2.3	:	:	35.3	:	33.0	:
Wage adjusted labour productivity (%) (3)	:	172.2	:	171.1	:	273.2	176.6	205.9	:	:	152.3	:	200.3	:
Gross operating rate (%) (3)	:	8.1	:	8.1	:	16.1	9.7	8.4	:	:	8.9	:	14.5	:
Investment / employment (EUR thousand) (4)	:	4.2	:	10.6	:	3.7	6.8	3.1	:	:	10.6	:	:	:

(1) 2003. (2) France, 2003. (3) Finland, 2003. (4) Netherlands and Finland, 2003.
Source: Eurostat (SBS)

Table 2.26

Manufacture of tobacco products (NACE Division 16)

Main indicators, 2004

	EU-27	BE	BG	CZ	DK	DE	EE	IE (1)	EL	ES	FR	IT (1)	CY	LV	LT
No. of enterprises (thousands)	0.3	0.0	0.0	0.0	0.0	0.0	0.0	0.0	:	0.1	0.0	0.0	0.0	0.0	:
Turnover (EUR million) (2)	75 472	1 594	632	:	:	18 694	0	1 748	:	1 374	12 352	:	162	:	:
Production (EUR million) (2)	64 790	1 549	604	:	:	13 549	0	1 632	:	1 372	9 948	:	147	:	:
Value added (EUR million) (2)	10 850	235	80	:	:	1 573	0	275	:	595	628	:	12	:	:
Gross operating surplus (EUR million) (2)	7 671	124	30	:	:	444	0	216	:	324	404	:	4	:	:
Purchases of goods & services (EUR million) (2)	22 333	1 336	212	:	:	7 834	0	275	:	796	3 033	:	41	:	:
Personnel costs (EUR million) (2)	3 179	112	50	36	:	1 129	0	59	:	271	223	:	8	:	:
Investment in tangible goods (EUR million) (2)	736	20	20	11	:	176	0	21	:	46	41	:	1	:	:
Employment (thousands) (2)	67	2	9	:	:	12	0	1	:	6	4	:	0	0	:
Apparent labour prod. (EUR thousand) (2)	162.2	116.2	9.4	:	:	135.9	:	346.0	:	96.8	153.0	:	32.8	:	:
Average personnel costs (EUR thousand) (2)	47.8	56.7	5.9	:	:	97.6	:	73.8	:	44.4	54.4	:	22.2	:	:
Wage adjusted labour productivity (%) (2)	339.4	204.9	158.3	:	:	139.2	:	468.8	:	218.0	281.3	:	147.6	:	:
Gross operating rate (%) (2)	10.2	7.7	4.7	:	:	2.4	:	12.4	:	23.6	3.3	:	2.5	:	:
Investment / employment (EUR thousand) (2)	11.0	9.9	2.4	:	:	15.2	:	26.7	:	7.5	10.0	:	2.8	:	:

	LU	HU	MT	NL	AT	PL	PT	RO	SI	SK	FI	SE	UK	NO
No. of enterprises (thousands)	0.0	0.0	:	0.0	0.0	0.0	0.0	0.0	0.0	:	0.0	0.0	0.0	0.0
Turnover (EUR million) (3)	:	1 042	:	5 608	:	2 768	420	694	:	:	108	:	13 550	:
Production (EUR million) (3)	:	936	:	5 348	:	2 816	418	713	:	:	91	:	13 136	:
Value added (EUR million) (3)	:	70	:	1 700	:	2 279	176	48	:	:	19	:	1 870	:
Gross operating surplus (EUR million) (3)	:	11	:	1 424	:	2 185	122	27	:	:	6	:	1 493	:
Purchases of goods & services (EUR million) (3)	:	271	:	1 905	:	529	224	279	:	:	88	:	1 549	:
Personnel costs (EUR million) (3)	:	60	:	276	:	94	54	21	:	:	17	:	377	:
Investment in tangible goods (EUR million) (4)	:	13	:	75	:	51	20	60	:	:	1	:	:	:
Employment (thousands) (3)	:	2	:	5	:	7	1	3	:	:	0	:	5	0
Apparent labour prod. (EUR thousand) (3)	:	41.0	:	359.4	:	348.3	131.7	15.1	:	:	48.9	:	367.1	:
Average personnel costs (EUR thousand) (3)	:	34.8	:	58.0	:	14.4	40.3	6.7	:	:	44.9	:	74.1	:
Wage adjusted labour productivity (%) (3)	:	117.9	:	619.3	:	2 426.4	326.9	225.2	:	:	108.9	:	495.6	:
Gross operating rate (%) (3)	:	1.0	:	25.4	:	79.0	29.1	3.9	:	:	5.4	:	11.0	:
Investment / employment (EUR thousand) (4)	:	7.5	:	16.2	:	7.8	14.9	18.7	:	:	3.6	:	:	:

(1) 2003. (2) France, 2003. (3) Finland, 2003. (4) Netherlands and Finland, 2003.
Source: Eurostat (SBS)

Textiles, clothing, leather and footwear

Under the auspices of the World Trade Organisation (WTO), the ten-year, transitional Agreement on Textiles and Clothing (ATC) closed on 31st December 2004 with the abolition of textile and clothing import quotas. Other trade practices and disputes, however, continue to be of issue for the European Union; divergent tariffs and the imposition of non-tariff barriers (such as import charges) by some countries remain obstacles to greater third country market access; intellectual property right infringements and counterfeiting erode market share and consumer confidence, and the "dumping" of goods through a system of hidden subsidies can distort market prices and market share. Against this background, a raft of new initiatives and actions that may help European textiles, clothing and leather goods enterprises have been launched. The European Commission adopted a Communication in April 2007 titled "Global Europe: A Stronger Partnership to deliver Market Access" as a framework strategy for breaking down trade barriers abroad and creating new export opportunities for all goods and services. EU Ministers agreed in May 2007 to reduce sharply the fees for registering trademarks and designs for goods and services as a way of extending the umbrella of copyright protection. In addition, the Council of the European Union agreed [1] in October 2006 to impose new, definitive anti-dumping duties on footwear with leather uppers originating from China and Vietnam for a period of two years from October 7th 2006. The duty on imports from China was fixed at 16.5 % and those from Vietnam at 10 %.

_____
[1] 12516/1/06.

Aside from trade developments, textile, clothing and leather manufacturing activities within the EU-27 continue to be redefined according to what to produce, where to produce it and how to produce it. Pressure has come from low labour cost manufacturing competitors, stricter environmental and safety legislation (see Chapter 5 for more details on the beginning of the REACH legislation in June 2007, by way of example), a shortage of qualified employees in textile manufacturing (according to the European Apparel and Textile Organisation) and technological developments for both product materials, product design and production processes.

STRUCTURAL PROFILE

The textiles, clothing and leather manufacturing sector of the EU-27 (NACE Subsections DB and DC) consisted of about 266 000 enterprises in 2004, which generated EUR 67.8 billion of value added, corresponding to 1.3 % of the value added generated by the non-financial business economy. In terms of employment, the textiles, clothing and leather manufacturing sector of the EU-27 was rather more significant, the 3.4 million workers in 2004 corresponding to 2.7 % of the non-financial business economy workforce.

This chapter covers the manufacture of textiles, clothing, fur and leather goods, as defined by NACE Subsections DB and DC, hereafter referred to as textiles, clothing and leather manufacturing. The manufacture of textiles (NACE Division 17) is dealt with in the first subchapter, while the manufacture of wearing apparel and the dressing and dyeing of fur (NACE Division 18), hereafter called the manufacture of clothing, is the subject of the second subchapter. The final subchapter concentrates on the manufacture of leather and leather products including that of footwear (as covered by NACE Subsection DC), hereafter referred to as leather manufacturing.

NACE

17: manufacture of textiles;
17.1: preparation and spinning of textile fibres;
17.2: textile weaving;
17.3: finishing of textiles;
17.4: manufacture of made-up textile articles, except apparel;
17.5: manufacture of other textiles;
17.6: manufacture of knitted and crocheted fabrics;
17.7: manufacture of knitted and crocheted articles;
18: manufacture of wearing apparel; dressing and dyeing of fur;
18.1: manufacture of leather clothes;
18.2: manufacture of other wearing apparel and accessories;
18.3: dressing and dyeing of fur; manufacture of articles of fur;
19: tanning and dressing of leather; manufacture of luggage, handbags, saddlery, harness and footwear;
19.1: tanning and dressing of leather;
19.2: manufacture of luggage, handbags and the like, saddlery and harness;
19.3: manufacture of footwear.

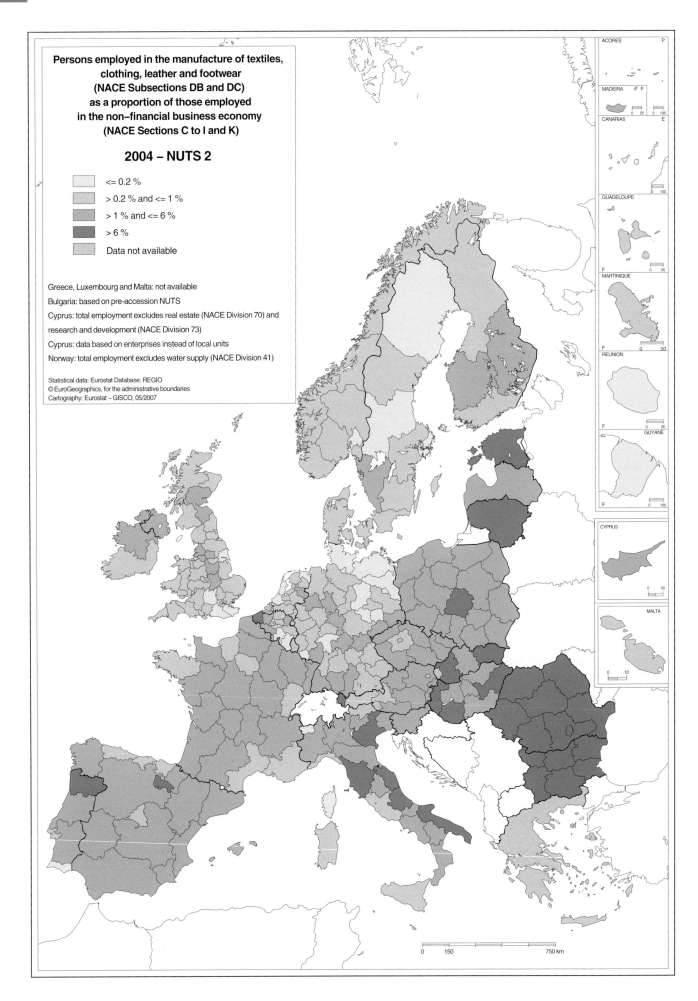

Persons employed in the manufacture of textiles, clothing, leather and footwear (NACE Subsections DB and DC) as a proportion of those employed in the non–financial business economy (NACE Sections C to I and K)

2004 – NUTS 2

- <= 0.2 %
- > 0.2 % and <= 1 %
- > 1 % and <= 6 %
- > 6 %
- Data not available

Greece, Luxembourg and Malta: not available

Bulgaria: based on pre-accession NUTS

Cyprus: total employment excludes real estate (NACE Division 70) and research and development (NACE Division 73)

Cyprus: data based on enterprises instead of local units

Norway: total employment excludes water supply (NACE Division 41)

Statistical data: Eurostat Database: REGIO
© EuroGeographics, for the administrative boundaries
Cartography: Eurostat – GISCO, 05/2007

ACORES   P

MADEIRA   P

CANARIAS   E

GUADELOUPE

MARTINIQUE

REUNION

GUYANE

CYPRUS

MALTA

Table 3.1 _____

**Manufacture of textiles and textile products; manufacture of leather and leather products (NACE Subsections DB and DC)
Structural profile, EU-27, 2004 (1)**

	No. of enterprises		Turnover		Value added		Employment	
	(thousands)	(% of total)	(EUR million)	(% of total)	(EUR million)	(% of total)	(thousands)	(% of total)
Textiles, clothing and leather products	266.1	100.0	241 961	100.0	67 762	100.0	3 409.9	100.0
Textiles	77.3	29.0	112 000	46.3	32 000	47.2	1 216.5	35.7
Clothing	141.8	53.3	84 500	34.9	23 500	34.7	1 583.4	46.4
Leather	47.0	17.7	45 000	18.6	12 000	17.7	610.0	17.9

(1) Rounded estimates based on non-confidential data.
Source: Eurostat (SBS)

Table 3.2 _____

**Manufacture of textiles and textile products; manufacture of leather and leather products (NACE Subsections DB and DC)
Structural profile: ranking of top five Member States, 2004**

Rank	Value added (EUR million) (1)	Employment (thousands) (2)	Share of non-financial business economy			
			No. of enterprises (3)	Turnover (4)	Value added (4)	Employment (5)
1	Italy (22 536)	Italy (705.5)	Portugal (3.6 %)	Italy (3.8 %)	Bulgaria (5.6 %)	Bulgaria (11.8 %)
2	Germany (7 924)	Poland (299.0)	Latvia (2.6 %)	Portugal (3.8 %)	Portugal (5.4 %)	Portugal (9.9 %)
3	France (7 901)	Portugal (284.9)	Lithuania (2.5 %)	Slovenia (3.2 %)	Lithuania (4.0 %)	Lithuania (7.6 %)
4	Spain (6 257)	Spain (253.1)	Bulgaria (2.5 %)	Bulgaria (2.6 %)	Italy (4.0 %)	Estonia (6.7 %)
5	United Kingdom (6 009)	France (209.5)	Italy (2.3 %)	Lithuania (2.3 %)	Estonia (3.5 %)	Slovenia (6.1 %)

(1) Denmark, Greece, Latvia, Malta, Austria, Romania and Slovakia, not available; Luxembourg and Portugal, 2003.
(2) Denmark, Greece, Malta, Austria, Romania and Slovakia, not available; Luxembourg, Portugal and Slovenia, 2003.
(3) Ireland, Greece, Cyprus, Malta, Romania and Slovakia, not available; Luxembourg and Portugal, 2003.
(4) Denmark, Ireland, Greece, Cyprus, Latvia, Malta, Austria, Romania and Slovakia, not available; Luxembourg and Portugal, 2003.
(5) Denmark, Ireland, Greece, Cyprus, Malta, Austria, Romania and Slovakia, not available; Luxembourg, Portugal and Slovenia, 2003.
Source: Eurostat (SBS)

Within the textiles, clothing and leather manufacturing sector, textile manufacturing (covering the activities within NACE Division 17) was the largest in terms of value added, accounting for a little under half (47.2 %) of the value added for the sector as a whole in 2004 (see Table 3.1), while the manufacture of clothing (as defined by the activities in NACE Division 18) was the second largest generating about one third (34.7 %) of the sectoral value added. In terms of employment, however, a significantly higher proportion of workers within the sector were engaged in the manufacture of clothing (46.4 %) than textiles (35.7 %) in 2004. By both measures, the manufacture of leather and leather products (NACE Subsection DC) was the smallest subsector within the textiles, clothing and leather manufacturing sector.

Italy was the principal textiles, clothing and leather manufacturing Member State, contributing EUR 22.5 billion of value added or one third (33.3 %) of the value added generated by this sector across the whole of the EU-27 in 2004. The other main textiles, clothing and leather manufacturing Member States within the EU-27 were Germany and France (each with an 11.7 % share of the EU-27 value added), Spain (9.2 %) and the United Kingdom (8.9 %). Of these five Member States, only Italy was relatively highly specialised in the manufacture of textiles, clothing and leather; the sector contributed 4.0 % of the value added generated by the non-financial business economy in Italy, considerably more than the average across the EU-27 (1.3 %). There were other Member States that were more highly specialised in this sector (see Table 3.2); the value added generated by the textiles, clothing and leather manufacturing sector in Bulgaria contributed 5.6 % of the overall value added generated by its non-financial business economy, with the proportion being 5.4 % in Portugal (2003) and 4.0 % in Lithuania. Despite incomplete data, Romania is also highly specialised in this sector, the value added created by the textiles and clothing subsectors (NACE Subsection DB) contributing 5.1 % of the value added of the non-financial business economy in 2004.

The map on page 72 shows the contribution of the textiles, clothing and leather manufacturing sector to employment within the non-financial business economy (NACE Sections C to I and K) of each region. The most specialised region (at the level of detail shown in the map) was Norte (Portugal), where one in every five people (21.0 %) employed in the non-financial business economy worked in the manufacture of textiles, clothing and leather manufacturing. The map also shows a high specialisation of textiles, clothing and leather manufacturing in many regions in Italy as well as across many Member States in central and eastern Europe, particularly Romania and Bulgaria, but also certain regions of Slovakia, Hungary as well as Estonia and Lithuania (which are each considered as a single region at the level of detail in the map).

There was a marked downward trend in the index of production for EU-27 textiles, clothing and leather manufacturing during the period 1996 to 2006 (with an average decline of 4.0 % per annum) – see Figure 3.1. The rate of decline in the production index was relatively moderate in 2006 (a fall of 1.4 %), following a five-year period of much stronger rates of decline (an average fall of 6.0 % per annum) in the period between 2000 and 2005. These developments were in sharp contrast to the generally upward trend for industry as a whole (NACE Sections C to E).

Between 1996 and 2003, the domestic output price index for textiles, clothing and leather manufacturing increased at a similar pace to the average for industry as a whole. However, the strength of global competition in the sector is probably the main reason why output prices for textiles, clothing and leather manufacturing have been relatively flat in the three years through until 2006, whilst the average domestic price for industrial output rose strongly on the back of sharply higher energy prices.

Small and medium-sized enterprises (SMEs) that employ less than 250 people dominated the textiles, clothing and leather manufacturing sector in the EU-27 (see Figure 3.2). Almost exactly three-quarters (74.6 %) of the value added generated by the textiles, clothing and leather manufacturing sector of the EU-27 came from its SMEs in 2004, a much larger contribution than SMEs made to the value added of the non-financial business economy (at 57.0 %). Small and medium sized enterprises (10-49 persons employed) within the textiles, clothing and leather manufacturing sector were particularly important, the proportion of value added generated by micro-enterprises (those employing less than ten persons) being much lower than the average across the non-financial business economy (13.8 % compared to 20.2 %). SMEs also accounted for the lion's share (72.7 %) of employment within the textiles, clothing and leather manufacturing sector of the EU-27, although this was only a little higher than the average across the non-financial business economy (67.1 %).

Figure 3.1

Manufacture of textiles and textile products; manufacture of leather and leather products (NACE Subsections DB and DC)
Evolution of main indicators, EU-27 (2000=100)

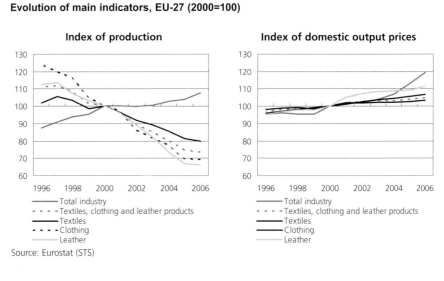

Source: Eurostat (STS)

Figure 3.2

Manufacture of textiles and textile products; manufacture of leather and leather products (NACE Subsections DB and DC)
Share of value added by enterprise size class, EU-27, 2004

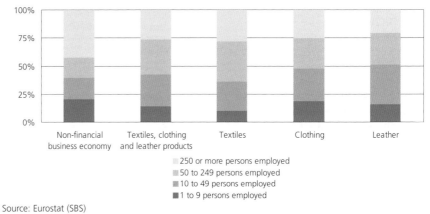

Source: Eurostat (SBS)

EMPLOYMENT CHARACTERISTICS
The textiles, clothing and leather manufacturing sector is the only industrial sector (among the NACE subsections within Sections C to E) that employs more women than men in the EU-27 as a whole; in 2006 a little more than two thirds (69.1 %) of the sector's workforce were women compared to an industrial average of 29.9 % and an average of about one third (35.0 %) for the non-financial business economy as a whole (see Figure 3.3). The prevalence of women workers within the sector was common to almost all of the Member States, but particularly distinctive in the Baltic Member States where about nine in every ten workers in 2006 were female.

Given the high proportion of women employed in the textiles, clothing and leather manufacturing sector of the EU-27, it is interesting to note that only a relatively small proportion of the workers in this sector were engaged on a part-time basis (8.2 %), particularly when compared to the average for the non-financial business economy (14.4 %) and the characteristic that many activities with a high proportion of women in the workforce also record high part-time rates.

Table 3.9
Textiles (CPA Division 17)
External trade, EU-27, 2006 (1)

	Extra-EU exports		Extra-EU imports			
	(EUR million)	(% share of chapter)	(EUR million)	(% share of chapter)	Trade balance (EUR million)	Cover ratio (%)
Textiles	18 060	39.5	27 891	28.6	-9 832	64.8
Textile yarn and thread	1 578	3.4	2 966	3.0	-1 387	53.2
Textile fabrics	6 597	14.4	5 000	5.1	1 596	131.9
Made-up textile articles, except apparel	1 672	3.7	6 787	7.0	-5 115	24.6
Other textiles	5 144	11.2	3 691	3.8	1 453	139.4
Knitted and crocheted fabrics	1 256	2.7	774	0.8	481	162.2
Knitted and crocheted articles	1 812	4.0	8 673	8.9	-6 861	20.9

(1) Textile finishing services, not available.
Source: Eurostat (Comext)

EXTERNAL TRADE
Trade in textiles (CPA Division 17) by the EU-27 Member States was largely Community based, as intra-EU trade accounted for a clear majority (71.6 %) of all (intra- and extra-EU) exports by EU-27 Member States. Nevertheless, there was a sharp rise (10.7 %) in imports to the EU-27 from non-member countries to EUR 27.9 billion in 2006. EU-27 imports of textiles represented a little more than one-quarter (28.6 %) of the value of imports of textiles, clothing and leather products (CPA Subsections DB and DC) in 2006, with a little more than half coming from China (26.4 %), Turkey (17.6 %) and India (8.8 %).

Although the value of EU-27 exports of textiles also rose in 2006 (to EUR 18.1 billion), there was a substantial widening (EUR 2.0 billion) in the trade deficit for textiles to EUR 9.8 billion (see Table 3.9). Much of the widening in this trade deficit can be attributed to knitted and crocheted articles (CPA Group 17.7), made-up textile articles, except apparel (CPA Group 17.4) and textile yarn and thread (CPA Group 17.1). The largest trade deficits among the seven CPA groups among textiles were for knitted and crocheted articles (EUR 6.9 billion) and made-up textile articles, except apparel (EUR 5.1 billion). Although there were trade surpluses for some textiles CPA groups, the surplus for textile fabrics (CPA Group 17.2) narrowed to EUR 1.6 billion in 2006 and that for other textiles (CPA Group 17.5) remained stable at EUR 1.5 billion.

Almost half of the exports (intra and extra-EU) by EU-27 Member States in textiles came from Italy (22.5 %), Germany (17.9 %) and Belgium (10.3 %) in 2006. The largest trade surplus in textiles in 2006 was recorded in Italy (EUR 6.5 billion), although this surplus narrowed steadily from the level of EUR 8.8 billion in 2001 as a result, principally, of falling exports within the EU-27 and rising imports from outside of the EU-27. Apart from small surpluses in Luxembourg, the Netherlands and Portugal, the only other notable trade surplus in textiles in 2006 was recorded in Belgium (EUR 2.4 billion). The absence of a trade surplus in textiles for the majority of Member States underlined the significance of imports from non-member countries. The largest trade deficit in textiles in 2006 was recorded in the United Kingdom (EUR 4.4 billion).

3.2: CLOTHING

This subchapter contains information on various clothing manufacturing activities (hereafter referred to as clothing manufacturing), as defined by NACE Division 18: the manufacture of leather clothes, work wear, outerwear, underwear, and articles of fur.

The manufacture of clothing comprises a number of stages; these cover the design (styling, prototyping and choice of collections), development (patterns, sourcing fabric) and manufacturing (cutting, sewing, pressing and finishing) processes. Innovations not only offer a broader choice in the manufacturing process but also improved customisation, distribution and clothing product ranges and applications. Among the wide range of new "intelligent" and "smart" product categories are entertainment clothing (interfacing with music products or gaming software), and biophysical clothing for health threat detection (such as respiration, heart rate, sugar level monitors). The clothing manufacturing sector in the EU-27 is characterised as having a large number of small and medium sized enterprises. One key challenge faced by many of these small producers who want to develop new products and applications is the ease and ability to secure additional capital, whether from public or private bodies.

Table 3.10

Manufacture of wearing apparel; dressing and dyeing of fur (NACE Division 18)
Structural profile, EU-27, 2004 (1)

	No. of enterprises (thousands)	Turnover (EUR million)	Value added (EUR million)	Employment (thousands)
Clothing	141.8	84 500	23 500	1 583.4
Leather clothes	3.5	982	289	21.1
Other wearing apparel and accessories	134.0	82 403	22 862	1 544.1
Workwear	:	3 640	1 120	:
Other outerwear	90.0	54 700	14 500	:
Underwear	:	11 200	3 300	:
Other wearing apparel and accessories n.e.c.	28.0	12 800	3 950	:
Dressing and dyeing of fur; articles of fur	4.7	1 100	300	18.2

(1) Rounded estimates based on non-confidential data.
Source: Eurostat (SBS)

STRUCTURAL PROFILE

The 142 000 enterprises in the EU-27 with clothing manufacturing (NACE Division 18) as their main activity in 2004 generated EUR 23.5 billion of value added (see Table 3.10), which represented just over one third (34.7 %) of the value added generated by the activities of textiles, clothing and leather manufacturing as a whole (NACE Subsections DB and DC). The manufacture of other wearing apparel and accessories (NACE Group 18.2) was the predominant activity in the sector, providing almost all (97.3 %) of the value added generated within the sector and almost all of the employment (97.5 %) for the 1.6 million people working in the clothing manufacturing sector across the EU-27. The remaining activities of the manufacture of leather clothes (NACE Group 18.1) and dressing and dyeing of fur; manufacture of articles of fur (NACE Group 18.3) were of similar, small size in terms of their respective workforces and value added. Within

the other wearing apparel and accessories subsector, the manufacture of other outerwear (NACE Class 18.22), such as coats, jackets and trousers, accounted for almost two thirds (63.4 %) of value added in 2004, with most of the rest coming from the manufacture of other wearing apparel and accessories not elsewhere classified (NACE Class 18.24) and the manufacture of underwear (NACE Class 18.23).

The clothing manufacturing sector in Italy was the largest within the EU-27, generating EUR 7.5 billion of value added in 2004, a little under one third (31.8 %) of the total for the EU-27 (see Table 3.11). The Italian clothing manufacturing sector was also a significant employer, with a workforce of a little over one quarter of a million people (accounting for 16.6 % of the EU-27 workforce in the sector). The clothing manufacturing workforce was largest in Romania (a little under one third of a million), accounting for 20.2 % of the EU-27

Table 3.11

Manufacture of wearing apparel; dressing and dyeing of fur (NACE Division 18)
Structural profile: ranking of top five Member States, 2004

Rank	Share of EU-27 value added (%) (1)	Share of EU-27 employment (%) (2)	Value added specialisation ratio (EU-27=100) (3)	Employment specialisation ratio (EU-27=100) (4)
1	Italy (31.8)	Romania (20.2)	Romania (823.8)	Bulgaria (679.2)
2	France (13.3)	Italy (16.6)	Bulgaria (765.2)	Romania (632.2)
3	Germany (10.6)	Poland (10.7)	Lithuania (501.4)	Lithuania (385.9)
4	Spain (10.0)	Bulgaria (9.6)	Portugal (460.1)	Portugal (340.8)
5	United Kingdom (8.5)	Portugal (8.0)	Estonia (308.3)	Estonia (256.2)

(1) Greece, Luxembourg and Malta, not available.
(2) Greece, Luxembourg and Malta, not available; Slovenia, 2003.
(3) Ireland, Greece, Cyprus, Luxembourg and Malta, not available.
(4) Ireland, Greece, Cyprus, Luxembourg and Malta, not available; Slovenia, 2003.
Source: Eurostat (SBS)

Table 3.12

Production of selected products - wearing apparel; furs (CPA Division 18), EU-27, 2006 (1)

	Prodcom code	Production value (EUR million)	Volume of sold production (thousands)	Unit of volume
Women's or girls' dresses (excluding knitted or crocheted)	18.22.34.70	c	49 715	units
Women's or girls' jackets and blazers (excluding knitted or crocheted)	18.22.33.30	1 791	53 476	units
Men's or boys' shirts (excluding knitted or crocheted)	18.23.21.00	1 398	101 873	units
Men's or boys' suits (excluding knitted or crocheted)	18.22.22.10	1 353	20 285	units
Women's or girls' trousers and breeches, of wool or fine animal hair or man-made fibres (excluding knitted or crocheted and for industrial and occupational wear)	18.22.35.49	1 322	111 934	units
Men's or boys' jackets and blazers (excluding knitted or crocheted)	18.22.23.00	1 122	25 880	units
Articles of apparel of leather or of composition leather (including coats and overcoats) (excluding clothing accessories, headgear, footwear)	18.10.10.00	1 112	12 904	units
Men's or boys' trousers and breeches, of denim (excluding for industrial or occupational wear)	18.22.24.42	954	55 148	units
Brassieres	18.23.25.30	952	200 220	units

(1) Estimated.
Source: Eurostat (PRODCOM)

workforce in the sector. In contrast to Italy, however, the value added generated by the clothing manufacturing sector in Romania was a little under EUR 1 billion, accounting for only 3.5 % of EU-27 total. In relative terms, however, the contribution made by the clothing manufacturing sector in Romania to the value added of its non-financial business economy was the highest in the EU-27, closely followed by Bulgaria, and was about eight times as high as the EU-27 average. Lithuania, Portugal and Estonia, were also relatively specialised (the value added generated by the sector relative to the value added generated by their respective non-financial business economies being between three and five times the average across the EU-27).

During the period from 1996 to 2006, there was a sharp and continuous decline in the production index of the EU-27's clothing manufacturing sector (an average decline in the production index of 5.7 % per annum). This was a faster rate of decline than that for textiles, clothing and leather manufacturing (NACE Subsections DB and DC) as a whole (down an average 5.0 % per annum). Within clothing manufacturing, the decline in the output of the relatively small activity of the dressing and dyeing of fur and the manufacture of articles of fur (NACE Group 18.3) between 1996 and 2006 was particularly strong (an average rate of decline of 8.1 % per annum). Despite the overall picture for the EU-27, there were contrasting developments among the Member States that demonstrate the broad shift in the location of clothing manufacturing from the West to the East; there were rapid and sustained declines in the production indices of the clothing manufacturing sectors of Belgium (an average 14.2 % per annum), Ireland (14.3 % per annum) and France (15.5 % per annum) between 1996 and 2006, but moderate rises in the Baltic Member States and Romania as well as a doubling of output in Bulgaria between 2000 and 2006.

COSTS, PRODUCTIVITY AND PROFITABILITY

The apparent labour productivity of the EU-27's clothing manufacturing sector (NACE Division 18) was EUR 15 000 per person employed in 2004, about one quarter (24.5 %) less than the average level for textiles, clothing and leather manufacturing (NACE Subsections DB and DC) as a whole. Indeed, it was the lowest level of apparent labour productivity within the non-financial business economy among the NACE divisions [5] and much less than half (36.7 %) of the average productivity level of EUR 40 900 per person employed across the non-financial business economy. Average personnel costs within the clothing manufacturing sector were also lowest (at EUR 11 000 per employee) among the NACE divisions [6] of the non-financial business economy and less than half (39.9 %) the average cost.

[5] Mining of uranium and thorium ores (NACE Division 12) and other mining and quarrying (NACE Division 14), not available.
[6] Mining of coal and lignite (NACE Division 10), mining of uranium and thorium ores (NACE Division 12), mining of metal ores (NACE Division 13), other mining and quarrying (NACE Division 14), the manufacture of coke, refined petroleum products and nuclear fuel (NACE Division 23), and water transport (NACE Division 61), not available.

Table 3.13

Manufacture of wearing apparel; dressing and dyeing of fur (NACE Division 18)
Productivity and profitability, EU-27, 2004

	Apparent labour productivity (EUR thousand)	Average personnel costs (EUR thousand)	Wage adjusted labour productivity (%)	Gross operating rate (%)
Clothing (1)	15.0	11.0	137.0	9.3
Leather clothes	13.7	10.5	130.0	10.9
Other wearing apparel and accessories	14.8	10.8	137.4	9.2
Dressing and dyeing of fur; articles of fur (1)	17.0	14.0	120.0	11.0

(1) Rounded estimates based on non-confidential data.
Source: Eurostat (SBS)

Note that the low value for average personnel costs in the EU-27 in Figure 3.4 is due to the particular dominance of low-wage Member States in the total number of employees in the clothing sector, in sharp contrast to the non-financial business economy as a whole.

The low average personnel costs just about recompensed the also quite low value added generated per person employed, so that the wage adjusted labour productivity ratio, 137 % in 2004 (see Table 3.13), was a little higher than the average across textiles, clothing and leather manufacturing and only about 7 % less than the average across the non-financial business economy. There were considerable differences, however, between the Member States; the wage adjusted labour productivity ratio for the clothing manufacturing sector was a little higher than the non-financial business economy average in Italy, Sweden and the United Kingdom but only about half the average in the Netherlands (56.2 %) and Slovakia (51.5 %) – see Figure 3.4.

The gross operating rate, a measure of profitability, for the EU-27's clothing manufacturing sector was 9.3 % in 2004, a little higher than the rate (8.7 %) recorded for textiles, clothing and leather manufacturing as a whole although about 15 % less than the average across the non-financial business economy. Among the Member States, the gross operating rate was between 20 % and 25 % higher than the average for the non-financial business economy in Bulgaria, the Czech Republic, Romania and the United Kingdom but almost 75 % lower in Slovakia and even slightly negative in Slovenia, indicating that value added failed to cover personnel costs.

Figure 3.4

Manufacture of wearing apparel; dressing and dyeing of fur (NACE Division 18)
Productivity and profitability characteristics relative to national averages, 2004
(non-financial business economy=100)

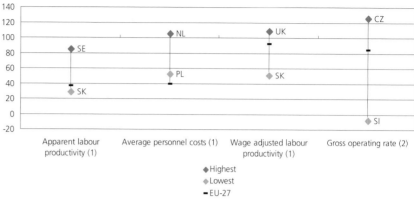

(1) Ireland, Greece, Cyprus, Luxembourg and Malta, not available; Slovenia, 2003.
(2) Ireland, Greece, Cyprus, Luxembourg and Malta, not available.
Source: Eurostat (SBS)

EXTERNAL TRADE

The value of imports of wearing apparel and furs (CPA Division 18, hereafter referred to as clothing) from non-member countries to the EU-27 reached EUR 49.2 billion in 2006. In comparison, EU-27 exports of clothing were valued at EUR 15.5 billion which resulted in a substantial trade deficit in clothing for the EU-27 valued at EUR 33.7 billion in 2006 (see Table 3.14).

At a more detailed level, the largest clothing trade deficits (at the CPA class level) in 2006 were recorded for outerwear (CPA Class 18.22) and underwear (CPA Class 18.23), where deficits for the EU-27 reached EUR 14.6 billion and EUR 14.5 billion respectively.

Despite the strong growth in EU-27 trade with non-member countries in clothing over recent years, total exports (intra- and extra-EU) of clothing from Member States are still focused on the internal market, with intra-EU exports accounting for nearly three-quarters (74.9 %) of all exports of clothing products by the EU-27 Member States. The largest trade surplus in clothing products in 2006 was recorded for Italy (EUR 3.5 billion), followed by Romania (EUR 2.7 billion), and there were also smaller surpluses in a number of other countries.

A little more than half (51.5 %) of all EU-27 clothing imports came from China and Turkey in 2006. Clothing imports to the EU-27 from China accounted for 37.3 % of the market in 2006, surpassing the share that the Chinese authorities and the European Commission had estimated in August 2005 would be reached by the end of the Shanghai Agreement in 2007.

Table 3.14

Wearing apparel; furs (CPA Division 18)
External trade, EU-27, 2006

	Extra-EU exports		Extra-EU imports		Trade balance	Cover ratio
	(EUR million)	(% share of chapter)	(EUR million)	(% share of chapter)	(EUR million)	(%)
Wearing apparel; furs	15 455	33.8	49 150	50.4	-33 695	31.4
Leather clothes	311	0.7	1 012	1.0	-701	30.7
Other wearing apparel and accessories	14 467	31.6	47 663	48.9	-33 196	30.4
Workwear	175	0.4	923	0.9	-749	18.9
Outerwear	6 649	14.5	21 246	21.8	-14 597	31.3
Underwear	2 956	6.5	17 484	17.9	-14 528	16.9
Other wearing apparel and accessories n.e.c.	4 687	10.2	8 010	8.2	-3 323	58.5
Furs; articles of fur	678	1.5	475	0.5	203	142.6

Source: Eurostat (Comext)

3.3: LEATHER AND FOOTWEAR

This subchapter covers the leather and leather products manufacturing sector of NACE Subsection DC, hereafter referred to as leather manufacturing. It includes tanning and dressing, as well as the manufacture of luggage, handbags and footwear.

In addition to concerns about trade distortions and environmental legislation, the availability of affordable raw hides and skins (bovine and ovine) is also an important issue. The Confederation of National Associations of Tanners and Dressers of the EU (COTANCE) has noted a continued upward trend in the price of raw hides and skins throughout 2006, and it expects that this higher cost will be passed on to consumers.

STRUCTURAL PROFILE

The leather manufacturing sector (NACE Subsection DC) comprised about 47 000 enterprises across the EU-27 in 2004 which generated EUR 12.0 billion of value added, representing 17.7 % of the total value added of the textiles, clothing and leather manufacturing (NACE Subsections DB and DC) sector. The manufacture of footwear was the largest activity within the sector, accounting for a little less than three quarters (72.2 %) of employment and a majority (59.8 %) of the value added created within the sector (see Table 3.15).

Table 3.15

Tanning and dressing of leather; manufacture of luggage, handbags, saddlery, harness and footwear (NACE Subsection DC)
Structural profile, EU-27, 2004 (1)

	No. of enterprises (thousands)	Turnover (EUR million)	Value added (EUR million)	Employment (thousands)
Leather (1)	47.0	45 000	12 000	610.0
Tanning and dressing of leather (1)	4.0	10 300	2 000	60.0
Luggage, handbags and the like, saddlery	15.1	8 979	2 581	108.9
Footwear	28.1	26 323	7 179	440.3

(1) Rounded estimates based on non-confidential data.
Source: Eurostat (SBS)

A little under half (46.6 %) of the value added of the leather manufacturing sector came from Italy (EUR 5.6 billion) - this was Italy's largest contribution to EU-27 value added of any industrial (NACE Sections C to E) NACE subsection. Italy, Portugal and Romania (although the data set is incomplete) were relatively specialised in leather manufacturing (see Table 3.16), across all parts of the sector in the case of Italy, but focused particularly on footwear (NACE Group 19.3) in Portugal and Romania; as a proportion of the value added of the non-financial business economy, the leather manufacturing sector of the EU-27 contributed only 0.1 % in 2004 but was considerably higher in Italy (1.0 %), Portugal (1.1 % in 2003) and Romania (1.2 % for footwear).

Apart from a small rise in output in 1997, the production index of leather manufacturing in the EU-27 declined steadily and sharply over the period between 1996 and 2006 (an average annual fall of 5.2 %). Between 2000 and 2005, the rate of decline in leather manufacturing output accelerated, principally as a result of falling output for footwear (an average decline of 9.4 % per annum). The rate of decline in the production index of footwear (NACE Group 19.3) as well as luggage, handbags and the like (NACE Group 19.2) slowed in 2006 and there was even a sharp upturn (7.2 %) in the production index of the tanning and dressing of leather (NACE Group 19.1).

Table 3.16

Tanning and dressing of leather; manufacture of luggage, handbags, saddlery, harness and footwear (NACE Subsection DC)
Structural profile: ranking of top five Member States, 2004

Rank	Share of EU-27 value added (%) (1)	Share of EU-27 employment (%) (2)	Value added specialisation ratio (EU-27=100) (3)	Employment specialisation ratio (EU-27=100) (4)
1	Italy (46.6)	Italy (29.3)	Italy (419.1)	Italy (249.4)
2	France (11.3)	Spain (9.5)	Slovenia (220.5)	Bulgaria (231.4)
3	Spain (10.4)	Poland (6.6)	Bulgaria (180.5)	Hungary (126.1)
4	Germany (7.6)	France (5.9)	Spain (115.5)	Estonia (114.3)
5	United Kingdom (3.8)	Germany (3.7)	Estonia (108.0)	Poland (110.6)

(1) Denmark, Greece, Latvia, Luxembourg, Malta, Austria, Portugal, Romania and Slovakia, not available.
(2) Denmark, Greece, Luxembourg, Malta, Austria, Portugal, Romania, Slovenia and Slovakia, not available.
(3) Denmark, Ireland, Greece, Cyprus, Latvia, Luxembourg, Malta, Austria, Portugal, Romania and Slovakia, not available.
(4) Denmark, Ireland, Greece, Cyprus, Luxembourg, Malta, Austria, Portugal, Romania, Slovenia and Slovakia, not available.
Source: Eurostat (SBS)

Table 3.17

Tanning and dressing of leather; manufacture of luggage, handbags, saddlery, harness and footwear (NACE Subsection DC)
Productivity and profitability, EU-27, 2004

	Apparent labour productivity (EUR thousand)	Average personnel costs (EUR thousand)	Wage adjusted labour productivity (%)	Gross operating rate (%)
Leather (1)	19.0	14.0	130.0	8.1
Tanning and dressing of leather (1)	36.0	26.0	140.0	6.7
Luggage, handbags and the like, saddlery	23.7	17.9	132.3	10.1
Footwear	16.3	12.3	132.1	8.0

(1) Rounded estimates based on non-confidential data.
Source: Eurostat (SBS)

COSTS, PRODUCTIVITY AND PROFITABILITY

Both average personnel costs (EUR 14 000 per employee) and apparent labour productivity (EUR 19 000 per person employed) within the EU-27's leather manufacturing sector (see Table 3.17) were a little below the respective averages for textiles, clothing and leather manufacturing in 2006 and about half (50.7 % and 46.5 % respectively) the averages for the non-financial business economy. Despite the relatively low average personnel costs in leather manufacturing, the wage adjusted productivity ratio of the leather manufacturing sector (130 %) remained below the level of the non-financial business economy (148 %). This characteristic was common across the majority of Member States for which data are available [7], with the exceptions of France and Italy where the two ratios were similar.

_____

[7] Portugal and Slovenia, 2003; Denmark, Greece, Ireland, Cyprus, Latvia, Luxembourg, Malta, Austria, Romania and Slovakia, not available.

As a measure of profitability, the gross operating rate of the leather manufacturing sector (8.1 %) was the lowest of the three NACE divisions that comprise the textiles, clothing and leather manufacturing sector and a little more than one quarter (26.4 %) less than the rate for the non-financial business economy. The relatively low level of profitability in the activities of leather manufacturing was common to the vast majority of Member States, although the gross operating rate of the sector was higher than the average for the non-financial business economy in France (21.4 % higher) and Finland (8.7 %).

EXTERNAL TRADE

The trade in leather and leather products (CPA Subsection DC) between the EU-27 and non-member countries was EUR 12.3 billion in terms of exports and EUR 20.5 billion in terms of imports (see Table 3.18). The trade deficit increased to EUR 8.2 billion in 2006.

Much of the recent growth in the value of imports was due to a steep rise in the value of footwear imports from China which, together with Vietnam, is now subject to a period of anti-dumping measures.

EU-27 Member States' trade in leather and leather products was focused on the internal market, as two-thirds (67.5 %) of all exports by EU-27 Member States were destined for other EU Member States, the same share as for industrial goods as a whole. Italy was the only Member State that had a trade surplus in leather and leather products with non-member countries as well as with other EU Member States (EUR 1.9 billion and EUR 4.1 billion respectively). Much smaller trade surpluses (generally below EUR 0.5 billion) recorded in Belgium, Bulgaria, Portugal, Romania and Slovakia were all based on surpluses generated by intra-EU trade.

Table 3.18

Leather and leather products (CPA Subsection DC)
External trade, EU-27, 2006

	Extra-EU exports (EUR million)	Extra-EU exports (% share of chapter)	Extra-EU imports (EUR million)	Extra-EU imports (% share of chapter)	Trade balance (EUR million)	Cover ratio (%)
Leather and leather products	12 250	26.8	20 451	21.0	-8 201	59.9
Leather	2 631	5.7	2 591	2.7	39	101.5
Luggage, handbags and the like; saddlery and harness	4 298	9.4	5 854	6.0	-1 557	73.4
Footwear	5 322	11.6	12 005	12.3	-6 684	44.3

Source: Eurostat (Comext)

Table 3.19

Manufacture of textiles (NACE Division 17)
Main indicators, 2004

	EU-27	BE	BG	CZ	DK	DE	EE	IE	EL	ES	FR	IT	CY	LV	LT
No. of enterprises (thousands)	77.3	1.5	0.8	2.7	0.5	3.7	0.2	0.1	:	9.4	5.4	25.6	0.1	0.5	0.4
Turnover (EUR million) (1)	112 000	6 411	488	1 790	1 013	14 341	292	346	:	8 889	13 109	36 586	33	137	359
Production (EUR million) (1)	107 000	6 250	476	1 709	940	13 300	289	321	:	8 703	12 690	35 763	30	136	354
Value added (EUR million) (1)	32 000	1 674	134	537	357	4 519	91	118	:	2 660	3 423	9 478	13	48	113
Gross operating surplus (EUR million) (1)	9 300	498	66	208	99	1 042	32	31	:	775	544	3 377	4	17	33
Purchases of goods & services (EUR million) (1)	80 000	4 752	362	1 290	670	9 707	209	213	:	6 544	9 841	26 975	21	93	256
Personnel costs (EUR million) (1)	22 700	1 176	68	329	258	3 477	59	87	:	1 885	2 879	6 101	9	30	81
Investment in tangible goods (EUR million)	4 433	196	62	188	47	452	18	7	:	359	364	1 223	1	13	26
Employment (thousands)	1 217	36	36	54	7	108	11	3	:	93	94	264	1	9	19
Apparent labour prod. (EUR thousand) (1)	27.0	46.1	3.8	9.9	54.8	41.7	8.2	33.8	:	28.7	36.5	35.8	16.1	5.2	6.0
Average personnel costs (EUR thousand) (1)	20.0	33.7	1.9	6.5	41.1	33.1	5.3	25.7	:	21.7	31.1	27.0	11.6	3.5	4.3
Wage adjusted labour productivity (%) (1)	130.0	136.8	193.3	153.2	133.5	125.9	154.0	131.8	:	132.1	117.4	132.7	138.6	150.5	138.8
Gross operating rate (%) (1)	8.4	7.8	13.6	11.6	9.8	7.3	10.9	8.8	:	8.7	4.1	9.2	12.0	12.5	9.0
Investment / employment (EUR thousand)	3.6	5.4	1.7	3.5	7.2	4.2	1.7	1.9	:	3.9	3.9	4.6	1.6	1.4	1.4

	LU (2)	HU	MT	NL	AT	PL	PT	RO	SI	SK	FI	SE	UK	NO
No. of enterprises (thousands)	0.0	2.3	:	1.5	0.8	5.6	4.9	2.5	0.5	0.2	1.0	2.0	4.9	0.7
Turnover (EUR million)	:	603	:	2 616	2 115	2 708	4 103	890	1 135	282	678	985	10 456	507
Production (EUR million)	:	537	:	2 521	2 033	2 442	4 022	906	657	273	668	940	9 418	452
Value added (EUR million)	:	180	:	711	747	745	1 266	289	187	87	257	342	3 547	174
Gross operating surplus (EUR million)	:	24	:	197	214	352	368	99	31	11	82	64	1 007	42
Purchases of goods & services (EUR million)	:	430	:	1 915	1 426	2 025	2 901	641	936	193	430	657	6 784	341
Personnel costs (EUR million)	:	157	:	515	533	394	898	190	155	76	176	278	2 540	133
Investment in tangible goods (EUR million) (3)	:	38	:	67	65	177	325	139	41	24	32	36	278	13
Employment (thousands)	:	31	:	15	16	90	83	89	13	16	5	8	98	4
Apparent labour prod. (EUR thousand) (4)	:	5.8	:	46.1	45.7	8.3	15.3	3.2	15.0	5.4	47.5	42.5	36.1	43.2
Average personnel costs (EUR thousand) (4)	:	5.2	:	36.2	34.0	4.8	11.1	2.2	11.9	4.7	34.2	37.9	26.8	35.2
Wage adjusted labour productivity (%) (4)	:	110.4	:	127.3	134.3	174.3	138.1	150.2	126.1	114.5	138.7	112.0	134.7	122.6
Gross operating rate (%)	:	3.9	:	7.5	10.1	13.0	9.0	11.1	2.7	3.9	12.1	6.5	9.6	8.2
Investment / employment (EUR thousand) (3)	:	1.2	:	3.9	4.0	2.0	3.9	1.6	3.0	1.5	5.9	4.5	2.8	3.1

(1) EU-27, rounded estimate based on non-confidential data. (2) 2003. (3) Netherlands and Slovenia, 2003. (4) Slovenia, 2003.
Source: Eurostat (SBS)

Table 3.20

Manufacture of wearing apparel; dressing and dyeing of fur (NACE Division 18)
Main indicators, 2004

	EU-27	BE	BG	CZ	DK	DE	EE	IE	EL	ES	FR	IT	CY	LV	LT
No. of enterprises (thousands)	141.8	1.1	4.6	9.5	0.5	3.1	0.4	0.1	:	14.3	12.8	38.8	0.6	0.9	0.9
Turnover (EUR million) (1)	84 500	1 058	750	632	530	10 298	192	287	:	7 260	12 270	31 755	70	126	351
Production (EUR million) (1)	79 000	1 019	731	612	483	9 530	154	228	:	7 129	11 119	30 245	58	124	350
Value added (EUR million) (1)	23 500	260	292	291	137	2 488	72	101	:	2 351	3 117	7 465	25	57	161
Gross operating surplus (EUR million) (1)	7 820	94	81	91	36	757	13	38	:	702	739	2 959	6	18	38
Purchases of goods & services (EUR million) (1)	61 900	784	480	357	401	7 772	120	181	:	5 027	9 149	24 239	47	75	192
Personnel costs (EUR million) (1)	15 600	166	211	203	101	1 731	59	63	:	1 649	2 378	4 506	19	38	123
Investment in tangible goods (EUR million)	2 072	27	63	11	10	116	6	5	:	171	186	787	2	7	12
Employment (thousands)	1 583	8	152	49	3	59	12	2	:	102	80	262	2	14	39
Apparent labour prod. (EUR thousand) (1)	15.0	33.1	1.9	5.9	47.2	42.2	5.8	41.2	:	23.0	39.1	28.5	12.3	3.9	4.1
Average personnel costs (EUR thousand) (1)	11.0	24.3	1.4	6.0	38.8	30.9	4.8	26.2	:	17.8	30.7	21.6	11.4	2.8	3.2
Wage adjusted labour productivity (%) (1)	137.0	136.2	132.4	99.5	121.8	136.7	121.0	157.3	:	128.8	127.4	131.6	108.0	141.4	129.4
Gross operating rate (%) (1)	9.3	8.9	10.8	14.5	6.8	7.4	6.8	13.2	:	9.7	6.0	9.3	8.4	14.3	10.8
Investment / employment (EUR thousand)	1.3	3.4	0.4	0.2	3.3	2.0	0.4	1.9	:	1.7	2.3	3.0	0.8	0.5	0.3

	LU (2)	HU	MT	NL	AT	PL	PT	RO	SI	SK	FI	SE	UK	NO
No. of enterprises (thousands)	0.0	5.4	:	1.3	1.0	19.6	12.0	5.6	1.2	0.3	1.2	1.7	4.5	0.6
Turnover (EUR million)	:	934	:	546	896	2 106	4 042	1 840	258	285	544	320	5 737	150
Production (EUR million)	:	800	:	479	755	1 926	3 868	1 801	232	261	450	296	4 975	138
Value added (EUR million)	:	299	:	142	273	789	1 367	819	116	112	188	93	2 000	56
Gross operating surplus (EUR million)	:	61	:	41	73	266	324	219	-2	7	54	35	1 027	22
Purchases of goods & services (EUR million)	:	641	:	392	650	2 074	2 655	1 109	139	167	362	227	3 712	102
Personnel costs (EUR million)	:	239	:	101	200	523	1 043	601	118	105	134	58	972	34
Investment in tangible goods (EUR million) (3)	:	21	:	7	13	70	150	248	9	6	8	4	104	3
Employment (thousands)	:	55	:	5	9	169	127	320	14	26	5	2	48	1
Apparent labour prod. (EUR thousand) (4)	:	5.5	:	30.2	30.6	4.7	10.8	2.6	8.9	4.3	37.1	49.3	41.6	41.1
Average personnel costs (EUR thousand) (4)	:	4.6	:	35.5	25.0	3.6	8.7	1.9	9.7	4.0	28.3	35.4	21.7	31.9
Wage adjusted labour productivity (%) (4)	:	117.7	:	85.2	122.6	130.1	124.2	135.3	92.4	106.6	130.9	139.1	191.7	128.6
Gross operating rate (%)	:	6.5	:	7.5	8.2	12.6	8.0	11.9	-0.7	2.4	9.9	10.9	17.9	14.5
Investment / employment (EUR thousand) (3)	:	0.4	:	1.5	1.4	0.4	1.2	0.8	0.6	0.2	1.6	1.9	2.2	2.3

(1) EU-27, rounded estimate based on non-confidential data. (2) 2003. (3) Netherlands and Slovenia, 2003. (4) Slovenia, 2003.
Source: Eurostat (SBS)

Table 3.21

Tanning and dressing of leather; manufacture of luggage, handbags, saddlery, harness and footwear (NACE Subsection DC)
Main indicators, 2004

	EU-27 (1)	BE	BG	CZ	DK	DE	EE	IE	EL	ES	FR	IT	CY	LV	LT
No. of enterprises (thousands)	47.0	0.2	0.5	1.0	0.1	1.3	0.1	0.0	:	6.3	2.3	20.5	0.1	0.1	0.1
Turnover (EUR million)	45 000	364	112	209	:	3 569	33	46	:	4 968	4 090	24 037	17	:	40
Production (EUR million)	43 000	358	108	201	:	3 162	30	39	:	4 873	3 584	23 701	12	:	39
Value added (EUR million)	12 000	82	35	77	:	917	13	12	:	1 247	1 361	5 593	5	:	3
Gross operating surplus (EUR million)	3 600	23	7	15	:	268	2	1	:	281	348	2 049	1	:	-5
Purchases of goods & services (EUR million)	33 000	279	81	135	:	2 616	15	30	:	3 723	2 662	18 399	12	:	41
Personnel costs (EUR million)	8 000	59	28	62	:	650	11	11	:	966	1 013	3 544	4	:	8
Investment in tangible goods (EUR million)	1 300	6	8	5	:	44	1	0	:	91	78	715	0	:	3
Employment (thousands)	610	2	20	12	:	23	2	0	:	58	36	179	0	1	2
Apparent labour prod. (EUR thousand)	19.0	42.6	1.8	6.5	:	40.2	6.0	30.2	:	21.4	37.8	31.3	14.1	:	1.4
Average personnel costs (EUR thousand)	14.0	34.1	1.4	5.8	:	29.9	5.0	27.0	:	17.6	28.7	24.0	12.2	:	3.6
Wage adjusted labour productivity (%)	130.0	124.7	122.3	110.9	:	134.3	119.5	111.9	:	121.4	131.9	130.6	115.8	:	39.4
Gross operating rate (%)	8.1	6.4	6.3	7.2	:	7.5	6.6	3.1	:	5.7	8.5	8.5	5.2	:	-12.5
Investment / employment (EUR thousand)	2.1	3.3	0.4	0.4	:	1.9	0.6	1.0	:	1.6	2.2	4.0	0.5	:	1.2

	LU (2)	HU	MT	NL	AT	PL	PT (2)	RO	SI	SK	FI	SE	UK	NO
No. of enterprises (thousands)	0.0	0.9	:	0.3	0.2	5.8	3.4	:	0.3	:	0.3	0.4	0.8	0.1
Turnover (EUR million)	0	257	:	332	:	769	2 299	:	356	:	218	169	1 385	49
Production (EUR million)	0	210	:	278	:	719	2 232	:	328	:	207	166	1 152	45
Value added (EUR million)	0	88	:	90	:	226	666	:	70	:	80	56	462	15
Gross operating surplus (EUR million)	0	10	:	25	:	91	140	:	-4	:	25	14	168	2
Purchases of goods & services (EUR million)	0	160	:	233	:	534	1 624	:	274	:	141	115	904	35
Personnel costs (EUR million)	0	79	:	65	:	136	526	:	75	:	55	42	294	12
Investment in tangible goods (EUR million)	0	21	:	11	:	26	82	:	8	:	6	7	49	0
Employment (thousands) (3)	0	16	:	2	:	40	62	:	8	:	2	1	12	0
Apparent labour prod. (EUR thousand) (3)	:	5.6	:	43.8	:	5.6	10.7	:	11.3	:	36.8	43.8	39.0	38.2
Average personnel costs (EUR thousand) (3)	:	5.1	:	36.8	:	4.0	:	:	11.1	:	26.7	36.2	25.7	35.6
Wage adjusted labour productivity (%) (3)	:	108.9	:	119.2	:	139.3	122.6	:	101.4	:	137.8	120.8	151.9	107.4
Gross operating rate (%)	:	3.7	:	7.6	:	11.8	6.1	:	-1.2	:	11.3	8.0	12.1	4.9
Investment / employment (EUR thousand) (3)	:	1.3	:	5.3	:	0.6	1.3	:	1.5	:	2.8	5.3	4.2	0.9

(1) Rounded estimates based on non-confidential data. (2) 2003. (3) Slovenia, 2003.
Source: Eurostat (SBS)

Wood and paper

In a Communication from the Commission to the Council and the European Parliament in June 2006 concerning an EU Forest Action Plan [1], a five-year (2007-2011) plan was established to support and enhance sustainable forest management and the multifunctional role of forests. Eighteen key actions were detailed under objectives to improve long-term competitiveness, improve and protect the environment, contribute to quality of life and foster co-ordination and communication. The parts of the Action Plan concerning competitiveness and environmental protection are perhaps of most importance for the wood and paper sector, in so far as they concern actions to examine the effects of globalisation on the economic viability and competitiveness of the EU forestry sector, to encourage research

and development, to value and market non-wood forest goods and services, to promote the use of biomass for energy generation, to contribute towards the revised Community biodiversity objectives for 2010 and beyond [2] and to enhance the protection of EU forests. These actions could present business opportunities, such as the development of renewable energy from forest biomass or wood processing residues, which would be supported through instruments like the 7th Framework Programme, a possible Forest-based Technology Platform, LIFE+ and the European Agricultural and Rural Development Fund. However, as the European Confederation of Woodworking Industries noted at its General Assembly in March 2007, this could also create problems of access to affordable raw materials.

[1] COM(2006) 302.

[2] COM(2006) 216.

This chapter covers only the forest-based activities regarding the manufacture of wood and wood products (classified under NACE Division 20) and the manufacture of pulp, paper and paper products (found under NACE Division 21). The former includes all stages of wood processing that follow on from the activity of forestry, while the latter covers downstream activities that use output from the initial processing of wood. Together, these activities are referred to, hereafter, as the wood and paper manufacturing sector. It is important to underline that this sector does not include other forestry activities that are not covered within this publication.

NACE

20: manufacture of wood and of products of wood and cork, except furniture; manufacture of articles of straw and plaiting materials;

20.1: sawmilling and planing of wood; impregnation of wood;

20.2: manufacture of veneer sheets; manufacture of plywood, laminboard, particle board, fibre board and other panels and boards;

20.3: manufacture of builders' carpentry and joinery;

20.4: manufacture of wooden containers;

20.5: manufacture of other products of wood; manufacture of articles of cork, straw and plaiting materials;

21: manufacture of pulp, paper and paper products;

21.1: manufacture of pulp, paper and paperboard;

21.2: manufacture of articles of paper and paperboard.

Table 4.1

Top ten enterprise (groups) in forest and paper activities, EU-27, 2006 (EUR million) (1)

		World ranking (sales)	Sales	Net income	Return on capital employed (%) (2)
Stora Enso	FI	3	14 599	589	7.0
Svenska Cellulosa	SE	5	10 988	589	6.0
UPM	FI	6	10 025	340	3.8
Metsäliitto	FI	8	9 274	-259	0.7
Smurfit Kappa	IE	11	7 035	-272	4.0
Anglo American (Mondi)	UK	12	5 968	370	6.4
Sequana Capital	FR	19	3 981	958	0.9
DS Smith	UK	31	2 426	6	3.2
Cartiere Burgo	IT	33	2 382	22	2.1
Holmen	SE	38	2 014	158	6.4

(1) All figures reported for calendar year 2006, except DS Smith which is the year to 30 April 2006.
(2) Calculated as net income before unusual items, minority interest and interest expense, on an after-tax basis, divided by average total assets less average non-interest-bearing current liabilities.
Source: PricewaterhouseCoopers 2007 Global Forest and Paper Industry Survey, available at: http://www.pwc-global.com/forestry

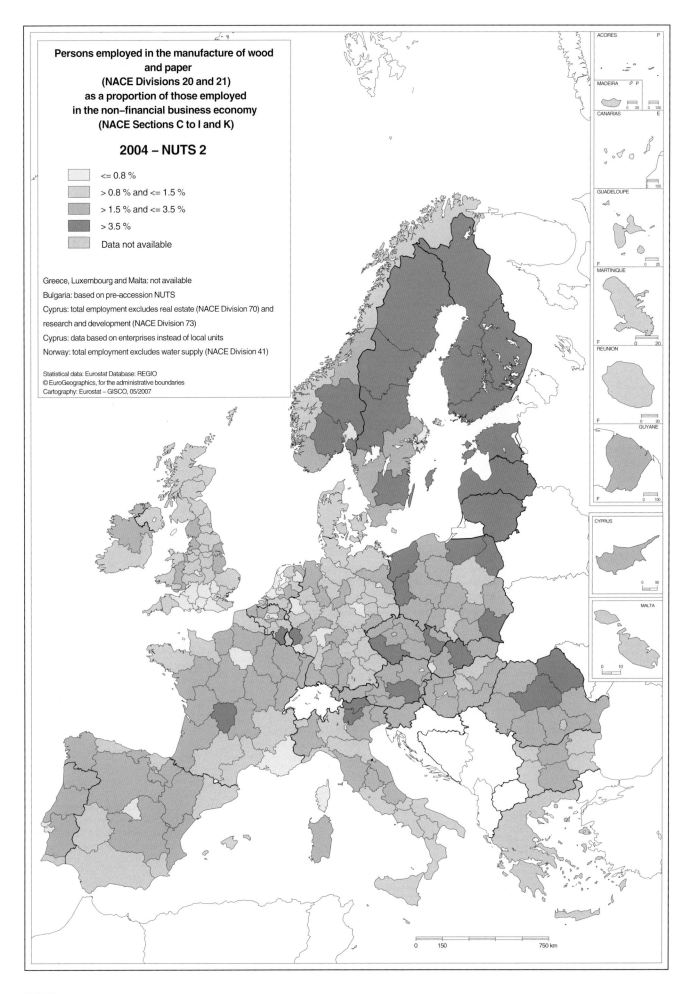

**Persons employed in the manufacture of wood
and paper
(NACE Divisions 20 and 21)
as a proportion of those employed
in the non–financial business economy
(NACE Sections C to I and K)**

2004 – NUTS 2

- <= 0.8 %
- > 0.8 % and <= 1.5 %
- > 1.5 % and <= 3.5 %
- > 3.5 %
- Data not available

Greece, Luxembourg and Malta: not available

Bulgaria: based on pre-accession NUTS

Cyprus: total employment excludes real estate (NACE Division 70) and

research and development (NACE Division 73)

Cyprus: data based on enterprises instead of local units

Norway: total employment excludes water supply (NACE Division 41)

Statistical data: Eurostat Database: REGIO
© EuroGeographics, for the administrative boundaries
Cartography: Eurostat – GISCO, 05/2007

ACORES   P

MADEIRA   P

CANARIAS   E

GUADELOUPE

F

MARTINIQUE

F

REUNION

F

GUYANE

F

CYPRUS

MALTA

0   150   750 km

Multinational enterprises (groups) from the Nordic Member States and North America dominate the global pulp, paper and paper products subsector (see Table 4.1 for the ranking of the largest enterprises (groups) in the EU's forest-based activities). This contrasts with the wood and wood products subsector, which is characterised by relatively small-scale enterprises that are predominantly private-owned and serve local or national markets.

STRUCTURAL PROFILE

Across the EU-27, there were around 217 000 enterprises with wood and paper manufacturing (NACE Divisions 20 and 21) as their main activity in 2004, which generated EUR 77.2 billion of value added, contributing 1.5 % of the value added of the non-financial business economy (NACE Sections C to I and K), and which employed 2.1 million people (1.6 % of the non-financial business economy workforce).

The manufacture of pulp, paper and paper products (NACE Division 21) in the EU-27 was larger than the manufacture of wood and wood products (NACE Division 20) in terms of value added (EUR 42.6 billion compared with EUR 34.6 billion) but it was smaller in terms of employment, representing only 36.6 % of employment in the wood and paper manufacturing sector (see Table 4.2).

The wood and paper manufacturing sector in Germany generated the largest proportion (20.5 %) of value added in the EU-27 among the Member States in 2004, followed by Italy (12.5 %), the United Kingdom (11.8 %) and France (10.5 %). The contribution of the value added generated by the wood and paper manufacturing sector in these four countries to their respective non-financial business economies was generally (Italy apart), however, less than the EU-27 average. In these terms, Finland, Latvia, Estonia and Sweden were the most specialised Member States in wood and paper manufacturing (see Table 4.3), with the relative shares of the value added of the non-financial business economy that were generated by the sector being between four and a half and two and a half times the EU-27 average (1.5 %).

The map on page 88 shows the contribution of the wood and paper products manufacturing sector to employment within the non-financial business economy of each region. The most specialised regions (at the level of detail shown in the map) in the EU-27 were in Finland and Sweden. There was also strong specialisation in the Baltic Member States (each considered as one region at the level of detail in the map), as well as in several regions of Poland, the Czech Republic and Italy.

As shown in Figure 4.1, the production indices for wood and wood products manufacturing on the one hand, and pulp, paper and paper products manufacturing on the other, followed a broadly similar upward trend during the period between 1996 and 2006 (average increases of 2.2 % and 2.0 % per annum respectively), which was also similar to the trend for industry as a whole (NACE Sections C to E). For both of these activities, output growth was strongest in the period through until 2000 (average increases of 3.8 % per annum and 2.8 % per annum respectively). A decline in the output of both activities in 2001 was then followed by a relatively steady upswing (albeit with a temporary fall in the output of pulp, paper and paper products in 2005).

The development of the domestic output price index for the manufacture of wood and wood products during the period between 1996 and 2006 contrasted, however, with the development for pulp, paper and paper products. The output price index of wood and wood products increased relatively steadily (an average 1.1 % per annum), albeit with a small decline in 1999. There was a rollercoaster development in the output price index for the manufacture of pulp, paper and paper products, however, with a decline in 1997 to a low in 1999, before a sharp rebound in 2000 to a relative peak in 2001. There was a subsequent slip in the average price through until 2005 before an upturn in 2006, close to the level in 2000.

Table 4.2

Manufacture of wood and wood products; pulp, paper and paper products (NACE Divisions 20 and 21)
Structural profile, EU-27, 2004 (1)

	No. of enterprises		Turnover		Value added		Employment	
	(thousands)	(% of total)	(EUR million)	(% of total)	(EUR million)	(% of total)	(thousands)	(% of total)
Wood and wood products; pulp, paper and paper products	217.0	100.0	278 000	100.0	77 200	100.0	2 060.0	100.0
Wood and wood products	197.0	90.8	121 000	43.5	34 600	44.8	1 310.0	63.6
Pulp, paper and paper products	19.7	9.1	160 000	57.6	42 600	55.2	753.0	36.6

(1) Rounded estimates based on non-confidential data.
Source: Eurostat (SBS)

Table 4.3

Manufacture of wood and wood products; pulp, paper and paper products (NACE Divisions 20 and 21)
Structural profile: ranking of top five Member States, 2004

Rank	Value added (EUR million) (1)	Employment (thousands) (1)	Share of non-financial business economy			
			No. of enterprises (2)	Turnover (3)	Value added (3)	Employment (3)
1	Germany (15 853)	Germany (315.0)	Czech Republic (3.5 %)	Finland (7.0 %)	Finland (7.0 %)	Latvia (5.9 %)
2	Italy (9 640)	Italy (256.1)	Lithuania (3.1 %)	Latvia (4.9 %)	Latvia (5.4 %)	Estonia (5.4 %)
3	United Kingdom (9 074)	Poland (183.9)	Estonia (3.1 %)	Estonia (3.8 %)	Estonia (4.5 %)	Finland (5.4 %)
4	France (8 091)	France (174.4)	Latvia (2.9 %)	Sweden (3.8 %)	Sweden (3.8 %)	Lithuania (4.0 %)
5	Spain (6 057)	United Kingdom (170.4)	Romania (2.1 %)	Austria (2.7 %)	Austria (2.8 %)	Sweden (3.3 %)

(1) Greece, Luxembourg and Malta, not available.
(2) Ireland, Greece, Cyprus and Malta, not available; Luxembourg, 2003.
(3) Ireland, Greece, Cyprus, Luxembourg and Malta, not available.
Source: Eurostat (SBS)

Figure 4.1

Manufacture of wood and wood products; pulp, paper and paper products (NACE Divisions 20 and 21)
Evolution of main indicators, EU-27 (2000=100)

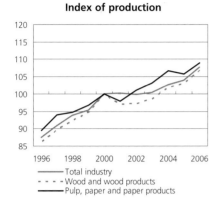
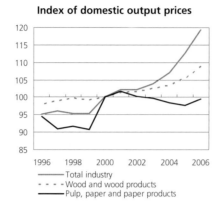
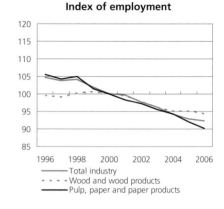

Source: Eurostat (STS)

There were distinct differences in the enterprise size structure between the two subsectors of the wood and paper manufacturing sector in the EU-27; the pulp, paper and paper products subsector is dominated by large enterprises (defined as having 250 or more persons employed) and the wood and wood products subsector by small and medium-sized enterprises (SMEs). SMEs in the pulp, paper and paper products subsector of the EU-27 generated 39.9 % of the total value added of the sector in 2004 (see Figure 4.2), a much lower proportion than that (78.3 %) generated by SMEs in the wood and wood products subsector, the second highest contribution of SMEs to the value added of any industrial NACE division [3] behind recycling (NACE Division 37) and considerably more than the average across the non-financial business economy (57.0 %). In terms of employment, SMEs in the wood and wood products subsector accounted for an even larger share (84.4 %), which was a much higher proportion than for the pulp, paper and paper products subsector (53.1 %) and also well above the non-financial business economy average (67.1 %).

_____

[3] Mining of coal and lignite and the extraction of peat (NACE Division 10), the mining of uranium and thorium ores (NACE Division 12), not available.

Figure 4.2

Manufacture of wood and wood products; pulp, paper and paper products (NACE Divisions 20 and 21)
Share of value added by enterprise size class, EU-27, 2004

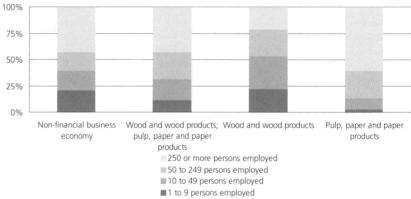

Source: Eurostat (SBS)

EMPLOYMENT CHARACTERISTICS

A significantly higher proportion of the workforce in the wood and paper manufacturing sector (NACE Divisions 20 and 21) of the EU-27 were male than was the case for the non-financial business economy (NACE Sections C to I and K) as a whole in 2006 (79.0 % compared with 65.0 %). This characteristic was common across all of the Member States for which data are available [4]. The proportion of the EU-27 workforce in wood and paper manufacturing working part-time (6.5 %) was less than half of the share (14.4 %) of those working across the non-financial business economy in 2006 (see Figure 4.3), with the clearest exception among the Member States being Hungary where the proportion of part-time workers in the sector (7.3 %) was almost double the proportion of part-time workers in the Hungarian non-financial business economy.

_____

[4] Luxembourg and Malta, not available.

The proportion of employees (paid workers) in persons employed in the wood and paper products manufacturing sector in the EU-27 was 90 % in 2004, which was a slightly higher share than among the non-financial business economy as a whole (86.2 %). Reflecting the importance of small enterprises, working owners, unpaid family workers and other unpaid workers accounted for nearly 15 % of the persons employed in the wood and wood products subsector, but only 3.5 % in pulp, paper and paper products

Figure 4.3

Manufacture of wood and wood products; pulp, paper and paper products (NACE Divisions 20 and 21)
Labour force characteristics, EU-27, 2006

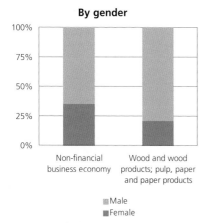

By gender

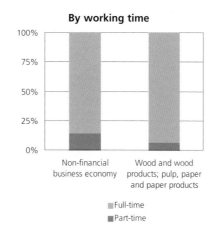

By working time

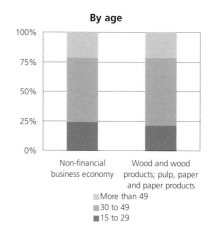

By age

■Male
■Female

■Full-time
■Part-time

■More than 49
■30 to 49
■15 to 29

Source: Eurostat (LFS)

Table 4.4

Manufacture of wood and wood products; pulp, paper and paper products (NACE Divisions 20 and 21)
Productivity and profitability, EU-27, 2004 (1)

	Apparent labour productivity (EUR thousand)	Average personnel costs (EUR thousand)	Wage adjusted labour productivity (%)	Gross operating rate (%)
Wood and wood products; pulp, paper and paper products	37.4	26.1	143.0	10.3
Wood and wood products	26.4	19.8	134.0	10.3
Pulp, paper and paper products	56.6	35.8	158.0	10.4

(1) Rounded estimates based on non-confidential data.
Source: Eurostat (SBS)

COSTS, PRODUCTIVITY AND PROFITABILITY

The proportion of total expenditure (gross operating and tangible investment expenditure) accounted for by personnel costs in the wood and paper manufacturing sector of the EU-27 was a little higher than the average across the non-financial business economy in 2004 (18.3 % compared to 16.4 %), although average personnel costs were a little lower (5.4 % lower at EUR 26 100 per employee). Within the sector, however, the average personnel cost of those working in the pulp, paper and paper products manufacturing subsector (EUR 35 800 per employee) was considerably higher (80.8 %) than the average in the wood and wood products manufacturing subsector (EUR 19 800 per employee) – see Table 4.4.

Despite the slightly lower average personnel costs in the wood and paper manufacturing sector compared to the average across the non-financial business economy, the wage adjusted labour productivity ratio of the wood and paper manufacturing sector of the EU 27 remained a little beneath (3.4 % lower) the average across the non-financial business economy (143 % compared to 148 %). This reflects the fact that the apparent labour productivity of the wood and paper manufacturing sector (EUR 37 400 per person employed) was even more beneath (8.6 %) the average for the non-financial business economy. Within the sector, the apparent labour productivity of the pulp, paper and paper products manufacturing subsector (EUR 56 600 per person employed) was more than double that of the wood and wood products manufacturing subsector (EUR 26 400 per person employed). In all of the Member States for which information is available [5], the apparent labour productivity of the pulp, paper and paper products manufacturing subsector was higher (generally, considerably so) than that for wood and wood products.

The gross operating rate of the wood and paper manufacturing sector of the EU-27 was 10.3 % in 2004, this measure of profitability being similar for both the wood and wood products manufacturing subsector and the pulp, paper and paper products manufacturing subsector.

[5] Greece, Luxembourg and Malta, not available.

EXTERNAL TRADE

The EU-27 imported wood and paper products (CPA Divisions 20 and 21) to the value of EUR 21.4 billion in 2006, mainly from the United States (15.4 %), China (12.4 %), Brazil (11.3 %), Russia (8.9 %) and Switzerland (8.5 %) – see Figure 4.4. However, the EU-27 exported wood and paper products to non-member countries to the value of EUR 29.2 billion in 2006, representing 2.7 % of the value of all industrial exports (CPA Sections C to E). The principal export markets for these products were the United States (14.1 % of EU-27 exports), Switzerland (9.5 %) and Russia (8.4 %). It should be noted, however, that the exports to non-member countries represented only a quarter (26.3 %) of the total trade (intra and extra-EU) of the EU-27 Member States, underlining the importance of the internal market. Exports (intra and extra-EU) of wood and paper products were particularly important in Latvia and Finland, where they represented a little over one fifth (21.7 % and 21.5 % respectively) of the value of industrial exports, as well as in Sweden (12.2 %) and Estonia (11.5 %).

The EU-27 trade surplus in wood and paper products was EUR 7.8 billion in 2006 (see Table 4.5). This overall surplus, however, comprised a large surplus of EUR 8.9 billion for pulp, paper and paper products (CPA Division 21), and a trade deficit of EUR 1.0 billion in the wood and wood products (CPA Division 20). Among the Member States, Finland and Sweden had by far the largest trade surpluses in wood and paper products (EUR 11.1 billion and EUR 10.6 billion respectively), with Germany having the third highest surplus (EUR 5.3 billion). In contrast, the United Kingdom had by far the largest trade deficit in wood and paper products (EUR 8.8 billion in 2006).

Figure 4.4

Wood and wood products; pulp, paper and paper products (CPA Divisions 20 and 21)
Main destination of EU-27 exports and main origin of EU-27 imports, 2006

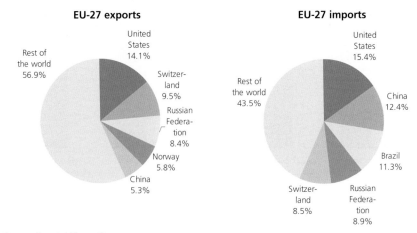

Source: Eurostat (Comext)

Table 4.5

Wood and wood products; pulp, paper and paper products (CPA Divisions 20 and 21)
External trade, EU-27, 2006

	Extra-EU exports		Extra-EU imports			
	(EUR million)	(% share of industrial exports)	(EUR million)	(% share of industrial imports)	Trade balance (EUR million)	Cover ratio (%)
Wood and wood products; pulp, paper and paper products	29 212	2.7	21 367	1.7	7 846	136.7
Wood and wood products	9 376	0.9	10 389	0.8	-1 013	90.2
Pulp, paper and paper products	19 837	1.8	10 978	0.9	8 859	180.7

Source: Eurostat (Comext)

4.1: WOOD AND WOOD PRODUCTS

The wood and wood products sector is classified as NACE Division 20. It is split into five groups that cover the initial processing stages of sawing and planing of wood (NACE Group 20.1), through semi-processed wood products, such as the manufacture of boards and panels (NACE Group 20.2) and builders' carpentry and joinery (NACE Group 20.3), towards finished products such as wooden containers (NACE Group 20.4) and other wood products, including household goods made from wood (NACE Group 20.5). Note that furniture manufacturing (NACE Group 36.1), whether from wood or other materials is not covered here, but in Subchapter 11.1.

The European Commission's Directorate-General for Enterprise [6], recognises that "EU wood-working industries face disadvantages vis-à-vis competing countries in most of the major quantitative competitiveness factors such as wood, labour and distribution costs" but that "qualitative factors, particularly the skills of the EU workforce and product and process innovation, often compensate for these disadvantages". The encouragement of greater training and knowledge transfer through research and development as well as of the use of new technology have been identified as important tools in maintaining a competitive edge.

[6] More information at
http://ec.europa.eu/enterprise/forest_based/.

STRUCTURAL PROFILE

The wood and wood products manufacturing sector (NACE Division 20) of the EU-27 consisted of around 197 000 enterprises, which generated EUR 34.6 billion of value added in 2004, representing a little over two fifths (44.8 %) of the value added generated by the wood and paper sector (NACE Division 20 and 21). In terms of employment, however, it was much more significant, employing 1.3 million people or the equivalent of a little less than two thirds (63.6 %) of all those employed in the activities of wood and paper manufacturing in the EU 27.

Within the wood and wood products manufacturing sector, the largest contribution (45.6 %) of value added came from the manufacture of builder's carpentry and joinery (NACE Group 20.3), which generated EUR 15.8 billion of value added in 2004 (see Table 4.6). This subsector produces a variety of wooden building components (such as doors, window frames, parquet panels and prefabricated wooden buildings). The second largest activity, in terms of value added, was sawmilling, planing and impregnation of wood (NACE Group 20.1), the first stage in the processing of wood, which generated EUR 7.3 billion of value added in 2004 (the equivalent of 21.0 % of the sectoral total). The manufacture of veneer sheets, plywood, laminboard, particle board, fibre board and other panels and boards (NACE Group 20.2) generated a further EUR 5.2 billion of value added in 2004. These are semi-finished products used predominantly as intermediate products in furniture manufacturing or construction.

Among the Member States, Germany had the largest wood and wood products manufacturing sector in terms of value added generated (18.6 % of the EU-27 total), followed by Italy (14.6 %) and the United Kingdom (12.3 %). However, the Baltic Member States were by far the most specialised Member States in this activity in 2004, the value added generated by the wood and wood products manufacturing sector contributing about seven and a half times as much to the value added of the non-financial business economy (NACE Sections C to I and K) than was the average across the EU-27 in Latvia, about six times as much in Estonia and about three times as much in Lithuania. These were also the Member States that were most specialised in terms of the relative numbers of people employed in their wood and wood products manufacturing activities in 2004.

Although there was a relatively steady upward trend in the output of the wood and wood products manufacturing sector in the period between 1996 and 2006, albeit with a temporary decline in 2001, there were some notable contrasts in the output of some of the wood and wood manufacturing subsectors. There was strong and sustained growth (an average increase of 4.1 % per annum) in the production index of the activities of veneer sheets, plywood, laminboard, particle board, fibre board and other panels and boards manufacturing but a sharp decline (an average 3.9 % per annum between 2000 and 2006) in the output of other wood products, articles of cork, straw and plaiting materials (NACE Group 20.5).

Table 4.6

Manufacture of wood and wood products (NACE Division 20)
Structural profile, EU-27, 2004

	No. of enterprises (thousands)	Turnover (EUR million)	Value added (EUR million)	Employment (thousands)
Wood and wood products (1)	197.0	121 000	34 600	1 310.0
Sawmilling and planing of wood, impregnation of wood (1)	35.1	31 000	7 270	321.0
Veneer sheets; plywood panels and boards (1)	2.6	22 000	5 200	130.0
Builders' carpentry and joinery (1)	110.0	46 148	15 786	584.1
Wooden containers	10.4	9 179	2 530	93.8
Other products of wood; cork, straw & plaiting materials (1)	37.0	12 528	3 806	179.6

(1) Rounded estimates based on non-confidential data.
Source: Eurostat (SBS)

Table 4.7

Production of selected products - wood and wood products (CPA Division 20), EU-27, 2006 (1)

	Prodcom code	Production value (EUR million)	Volume of sold production (thousands)	Unit of volume
Builders' joinery and carpentry of wood excluding windows, french-windows and doors, their frames/thresholds, parquet panels, shuttering for concrete constructional work - shingles, shakes	20.30.13.00	8 118	5 790 516	kg
Windows; French-windows and their frames of wood	20.30.11.10	7 464	50 830	units
Doors and their frames and thresholds of wood	20.30.11.50	7 449	115 494	units
Prefabricated buildings of wood	20.30.20.00	6 535	-	-
Particle board and similar board of wood surfaced with melamine resin impregnated paper (excluding waferboard or oriented strand board)	20.20.13.37	4 249	22 958	m³
Coniferous wood; sawn or chipped lengthwise; sliced or peeled; of a thickness > 6 mm; planed (excluding end-jointed or sanded)	20.10.10.34	3 670	18 981	m³
Pine wood: Pinus sylvestris L.	20.10.10.37	3 196	18 403	m³
Parquet panels of wood (excluding those for mosaic floors)	20.30.12.19	2 035	116 775	m²
Coniferous wood in chips or particles	20.10.23.03	1 352	c	kg

(1) Estimated.
Source: Eurostat (PRODCOM)

COSTS, PRODUCTIVITY AND PROFITABILITY

Personnel costs in the wood and wood products sector accounted for 19.4 % of total expenditure (gross operating and tangible investment expenditure) in 2004, a higher proportion than for the activities of wood and paper manufacturing as a whole (18.3 %), despite the fact that average personnel costs (EUR 19 800 per employee) were considerably (24.1 %) lower than the average in wood and paper manufacturing. Within the wood and wood products sector, average personnel costs were particularly low in the sawmilling, planing and impregnation of wood subsector (EUR 15 400 per employee) and the other wood products, articles of cork, straw and plaiting materials manufacturing subsector (EUR 16 700 per employee) – see Table 4.8. In the case of the other wood products, articles of cork, straw and plaiting materials manufacturing subsector, personnel costs nevertheless accounted for a little over one fifth (20.8 %) of gross operating and tangible investment expenditure, suggesting that it is a relatively low-wage and labour intensive subsector.

The apparent labour productivity of the wood and wood products manufacturing sector in the EU-27 was a third (35.5 %) lower than the level of the non-financial business economy as a whole in 2004. Despite the relatively low personnel costs in the sector, the wage adjusted labour productivity ratio of the wood and wood products subsectors therefore generally remained below both the average for the activities of wood and paper manufacturing (NACE Divisions 20 and 21) and of the non-financial business economy in 2004. One exception concerned the sawmilling, planing and impregnation of wood subsector, noted for its particularly low personnel costs, for which the wage adjusted labour productivity level was similar to the level for the non-financial business economy. The other exception was the veneer sheets, plywood, laminboard, particle board, fibre board and other panels and boards manufacturing subsector, noted for its high apparent labour productivity in comparison to the other subsectors, for which the wage adjusted labour productivity level was 170 %, about 15 % higher than the level of the non-financial business economy.

EXTERNAL TRADE

EU-27 exports of wood and wood products (CPA Division 20) reached EUR 9.4 billion in 2006. A little over half (52.9 %) of all such exports were to the United States, Japan, Switzerland and Norway. Nevertheless, with EU-27 imports of EUR 10.4 billion, the EU-27 ran a trade deficit of EUR 1.0 billion in wood and wood products in 2006.

Sawn, planed and impregnated wood (CPA Group 20.1) and other products of wood; articles of cork, straw and plaiting materials (CPA Group 20.5), recorded trade deficits of EUR 1.3 billion and EUR 1.1 billion respectively. The other three CPA product groups within wood and wood products all recorded trade surpluses in the range of about EUR 300 million to EUR 600 million (see Table 4.9).

Among the Member States, Sweden, Finland and Austria had the largest (intra- and extra-EU) trade surpluses (between EUR 2.8 billion and EUR 2.2 billion) for wood and wood products. However, Germany was both the principal exporter (16.6 % of EU trade) of wood and wood products in 2006 and its principal importer (13.8 %).

Table 4.8

Manufacture of wood and wood products (NACE Division 20)
Productivity and profitability, EU-27, 2004

	Apparent labour productivity (EUR thousand)	Average personnel costs (EUR thousand)	Wage adjusted labour productivity (%)	Gross operating rate (%)
Wood and wood products (1)	26.4	19.8	134.0	10.3
Sawmilling and planing of wood, impregnation of wood (1)	22.6	15.4	147.0	8.8
Veneer sheets; plywood panels and boards (1)	40.0	24.0	170.0	9.7
Builders' carpentry and joinery	27.0	22.2	121.8	11.5
Wooden containers	27.0	20.6	131.3	8.8
Other products of wood; cork, straw & plaiting materials	21.2	16.7	127.0	11.1

(1) Rounded estimates based on non-confidential data.
Source: Eurostat (SBS)

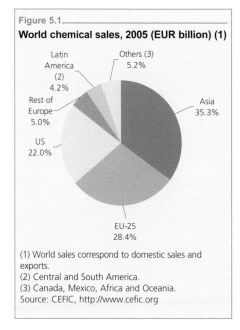

Figure 5.1
World chemical sales, 2005 (EUR billion) (1)

(1) World sales correspond to domestic sales and exports.
(2) Central and South America.
(3) Canada, Mexico, Africa and Oceania.
Source: CEFIC, http://www.cefic.org

STRUCTURAL PROFILE

The chemicals, rubber and plastics manufacturing sector (NACE Subsections DG and DH) of the EU-27 had approximately 100 000 enterprises which generated EUR 250.0 billion of value added in 2004, accounting for 4.9 % of the value added created within the EU-27's non-financial business economy (NACE Sections C to I and K).

The sector employed 3.7 million persons in 2004, representing 3.0 % of the non-financial business economy workforce.

A little over two thirds of the value added of the sector came from the manufacture of chemicals and chemical products (NACE Subsection DG) – see Table 5.2 for a breakdown by NACE group. Indeed, almost one half (49.5 %) of the value added of the sector came from the manufacture of basic industrial chemicals, pesticides and agrochemicals (NACE Groups 24.1 and 24.2) – see Subchapter 5.1 – and from the manufacture of pharmaceuticals (NACE Group 24.4) – see Subchapter 5.2. Within the activities of rubber and plastic products manufacturing (NACE Subsection DH), the principal activity was plastics manufacturing (NACE Group 25.2, Subchapter 5.6) which generated a little under one quarter (24.0 %) of the value added generated by the whole of the chemicals, rubber and plastics manufacturing sector. The workforce in the chemicals, rubber and plastics manufacturing sector was more evenly split between the two subsectors, with 38 % employed in the manufacture of rubber and plastic products.

Germany was by far the leading producer of chemicals, rubbers and plastics among the Member States, accounting for one quarter

(25.2 %) of the value added generated for the EU 27 as a whole in 2004 and employing the largest share (22.9 %) of its workforce. However, in relative terms, the contribution of the value added generated by the chemicals, rubber and plastics manufacturing sector to the value added of the non-financial business economy was higher in Slovenia (9.2 %) and Belgium (8.4 %) than it was in Germany (5.9 %) – see Table 5.3. Nonetheless, it seems likely that Ireland was the most specialised Member State in these activities, based on the limited data available; the chemicals, rubber and plastics sector accounted for 36.6 % of Irish manufacturing (NACE Section D) value added [4] in 2004, considerably more than the shares for Belgium (25.2 %) for example. In the chemicals and chemical products subsector in 2004 Belgium contributed 5.7 % of EU-27 value added and Ireland 7.4 %, in both cases the highest share of the EU-27 total by these

_____
[4] The relatively high proportion of Irish manufacturing value added that is accounted for by the chemicals, plastics and rubber sector may reflect foreign ownership of enterprises, outsourcing of activities, and accounting practices of multinational enterprises. Note that this observation applies throughout this chapter, where Ireland consistently reports very high levels of value added and related indicators (apparent labour productivity, wage adjusted labour productivity, the gross operating surplus, and the gross operating rate).

Table 5.2
Manufacture of chemicals and chemical products; manufacture of rubber and plastic products (NACE Subsections DG and DH)
Structural profile, EU-27, 2004 (1)

	No. of enterprises		Turnover		Value added		Employment	
	(thousands)	(% of total)	(EUR million)	(% of total)	(EUR million)	(% of total)	(thousands)	(% of total)
Chemicals, rubber and plastic products	100.0	100.0	870 000	100.0	250 000	100.0	3 700.0	100.0
Chemicals and chemical products	32.0	32.0	630 000	72.4	170 000	68.0	2 000	54.1
Basic chemicals; pesticides and other agro-chemical products	8.6	8.6	277 000	31.8	64 200	25.7	650.0	17.6
Pharmaceuticals, medicinal chemicals and botanical products	4.4	4.4	180 171	20.7	59 541	23.8	589.8	15.9
Miscellaneous chemical products	19.0	19.0	160 000	18.4	44 000	17.6	650.0	17.6
Man-made fibres	0.4	0.4	11 500	1.3	2 930	1.2	53.0	1.4
Rubber and plastic products	65.3	65.3	243 462	28.0	75 510	30.2	1 748	47.2
Rubber products	7.9	7.9	58 000	6.7	18 000	7.2	370.0	10.0
Plastic products	57.4	57.4	185 000	21.3	60 000	24.0	1 400.0	37.8

(1) Rounded estimates based on non-confidential data.
Source: Eurostat (SBS)

Table 5.3
Manufacture of chemicals and chemical products; manufacture of rubber and plastic products (NACE Subsections DG and DH)
Structural profile: ranking of top five Member States, 2004

			Share of non-financial business economy			
Rank	Value added (EUR million) (1)	Employment (thousands) (1)	No. of enterprises (2)	Turnover (2)	Value added (2)	Employment (2)
1	Germany (62 978)	Germany (846.4)	Slovakia (1.5 %)	Belgium (6.1 %)	Slovenia (9.2 %)	Slovenia (4.6 %)
2	France (36 660)	France (564.6)	Slovenia (1.5 %)	Slovenia (6.1 %)	Belgium (8.4 %)	Germany (4.1 %)
3	United Kingdom (34 668)	United Kingdom (444.4)	Romania (0.9 %)	Germany (5.5 %)	Germany (5.9 %)	Belgium (4.0 %)
4	Italy (24 567)	Italy (408.3)	Lithuania (0.9 %)	France (5.4 %)	Hungary (5.8 %)	France (4.0 %)
5	Spain (15 917)	Spain (260.0)	Bulgaria (0.8 %)	Netherlands (5.4 %)	Luxembourg (5.1 %)	Luxembourg (3.7 %)

(1) Greece and Malta, not available; Luxembourg and Portugal, 2003.
(2) Ireland, Greece, Cyprus and Malta, not available; Luxembourg and Portugal, 2003.
Source: Eurostat (SBS)

Member States in any industrial NACE subsection, while the 5.4 % share of the Netherlands was its second highest share. In the rubber and plastic products manufacturing subsector France generated 15.3 % of the EU-27 total, its second highest share among the industrial NACE subsections.

The regional specialisation of the chemicals, rubber and plastics manufacturing sector in employment terms is shown in the map on page 100. The most specialised region (at the NUTS 2 level of detail shown in the map) were Rheinhessen-Pfalz in Germany followed by Alsace and Auvergne in France, with regions in France and Germany occupying fourteen of the top twenty places [5].

There was a steady and continuous rise in the EU-27 production index of chemicals, rubber and plastics manufacturing during the ten years through until 2006 (see Figure 5.2). The rate of growth (an average 3.3 % per annum) outpaced the industrial (NACE Sections C to E) average (an average 2.1 % per annum) during this period, especially between 2001 and 2003 when industrial output as a whole went through a period of stagnation. Indeed, during this ten year period only in 2004 was the output growth for industry as a whole greater than for chemicals, rubber and plastics manufacturing.

Within the sector, the strongest expansions in output concerned the EU-27 manufacture of pharmaceuticals, which rose by an average 6.1 % per annum during the ten years up to 2006, and the manufacture of basic chemicals, which rose by an average 3.7 % per annum. In contrast, there were notable contractions in the EU-27 production indices of pesticides and other agro-chemical products (NACE Group 24.2) and man-made fibres (NACE Group 24.7) during the same period (both falling 2.4 % per annum on average), although most of the declines came in the period between 2001 and 2005. Output of rubber and plastics (NACE Subsection DG) went down slightly by 0.7 % in 2001 compared with the previous year. The output of these activities then followed a positive and accelerating development through until 2006, with annual growth rates ranging between 0.2 % in 2002 and 4.1 % in 2006.

[5] Note that data is confidential for the regions of Koblenz and Weser-Ems in Germany, although the proportion of their non-financial business economy employment coming from chemical, rubber and plastics activities was among the highest in terms of regional specialisation.

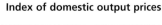

Figure 5.2

Manufacture of chemicals and chemical products; manufacture of rubber and plastic products (NACE Subsections DG and DH)
Evolution of main indicators, EU-27 (2000=100)

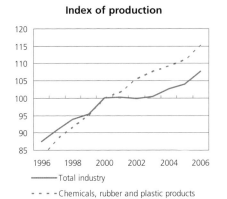
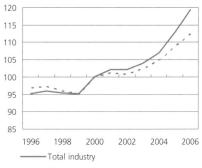

Source: Eurostat (STS)

Figure 5.3

Manufacture of chemicals and chemical products; manufacture of rubber and plastic products (NACE Subsections DG and DH)
Share of value added by enterprise size class, EU-27, 2004

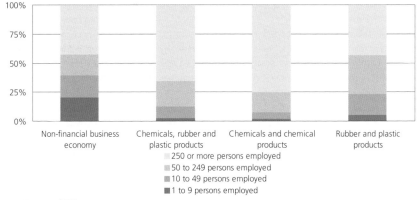

Source: Eurostat (SBS)

The development of the domestic output price index for chemicals, rubber and plastics manufacturing followed a similar pattern to the price index for industry as a whole; after a period of relative stagnation between 1996 and 1999, there was a strong rise in 2000 to levels that were broadly maintained for a couple of years before accelerating higher. The particularly strong price rises for industry as a whole in 2005 and 2006 (an average 5.6 % per annum over these two years), help explain why the average rate of increase in the domestic price index for industry over the ten years as a whole (2.3 % per annum) was above the rate (1.5 % per annum) for chemicals, rubber and plastics manufacturing.

Employment in the manufacture of chemicals and chemical products declined steadily in the EU-27 during the ten year period through until 2006 at a rate (an average 1.5 % per annum) that was similar to the industrial average. In contrast, there was employment growth within the manufacture of rubber and plastic products (an average 0.7 % per annum), although this was restricted to the period before 2000 since when levels have remained relatively steady. Rubber and plastics manufacturing was the only industrial NACE subsection in which there was an overall increase in employment during this period.

Figure 5.4

Manufacture of chemicals and chemical products; manufacture of rubber and plastic products (NACE Subsections DG and DH)
Labour force characteristics, EU-27, 2006

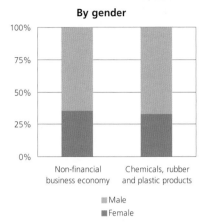

By gender

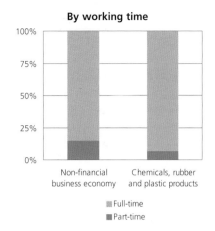

By working time

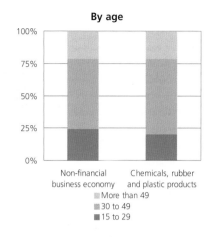

By age

Source: Eurostat (LFS)

The manufacture of chemicals, rubber and plastics in the EU-27 was not only concentrated in the larger Member States, it was also focussed within large enterprises (those employing 250 or more persons), as SMEs (employing less than 250 persons) accounted for only one third (33.6 %) of the value added generated in 2004 (see Figure 5.3). This was a much lower share than the average for SMEs across the non-financial business economy (57.0 %) and the fourth lowest proportion among the chapters of this publication (only higher than communications and media, energy, and transport equipment manufacturing). Within the manufacture of chemicals and chemical products subsector, the dominance of large enterprises was even more apparent, accounting for a little over three quarters (75.9 %) of the value added generated. The importance of large enterprises was particularly marked in Ireland, where they accounted for over four fifths (85.1 %) of all value added in chemicals, rubber and plastics manufacturing, and this share was also over 70 % in Belgium, Germany, Denmark, Hungary and Slovenia. In contrast, a majority of value added in the sector was generated by SMEs in Italy (55.5 %), but more particularly in Portugal (62.9 %, 2003) and Latvia (67.3 %, 2003).

EMPLOYMENT CHARACTERISTICS

As shown in Figure 5.4, the most notable characteristic of the workforce in the chemicals, rubber and plastics manufacturing sector (NACE Subsections DG and DH) that set it apart from the non-financial business economy was the higher proportion of full-time workers (93.4 % compared to 85.6 % in 2006). This characteristic was common to both the chemicals and chemical products subsector (92.9 %) and the rubber and plastics products subsector (94.0 %). The proportion of male

Figure 5.5

Manufacture of chemicals and chemical products; manufacture of rubber and plastic products (NACE Subsections DG and DH)
Labour force characteristics relative to national averages, 2006
(non-financial business economy=100)

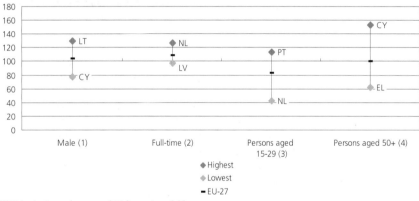

(1) Estonia, Luxembourg and Malta, not available.
(2) Estonia, Ireland and Luxembourg, not available.
(3) Estonia, Cyprus, Latvia, Lithuania, Luxembourg and Malta, not available.
(4) Estonia, Latvia, Lithuania, Luxembourg and Malta, not available.
Source: Eurostat (LFS)

workers (67.5 %) in the chemicals, rubber and plastics workforce was similar to the proportion across the non-financial business economy (65.0 %), although the proportion of male workers in the rubber and plastics products subsector's workforce (72.1 %) was notably higher than in the chemicals and chemical products subsector (64.3 %). Among the Member States, there was quite a mixed picture (see Figure 5.5); the proportion of male workers was low in comparison to other Member States and in comparison to the average of the national non-financial business economy workforce in Cyprus (50.2 %), Denmark (54.0 %), Slovenia (55.8 %) and the Czech Republic (56.2 %), in contrast to the relatively high proportions in Lithuania (76.3 %) and the Netherlands (79.6 %).

The age profile of the workforce in the chemicals, rubber and plastics sector was characterised by a relatively low proportion aged under 30 (20.1 %), 20 % lower than the average of the non-financial business economy (24.2 %) and a correspondingly higher proportion aged between 30 and 49 (58.2 % compared to 54.2 %). Comparing the age structure of the two NACE subsections in this sector, the difference in young workers was pronounced, with the share under 30 years old in the chemicals and chemical products subsector (17.6 %) being much lower than the share (23.5 %) in the rubber and plastic products subsector.

Table 5.4

Manufacture of chemicals and chemical products; manufacture of rubber and plastic products (NACE Subsections DG and DH) Productivity and profitability, EU-27, 2004 (1)

	Apparent labour productivity (EUR thousand)	Average personnel costs (EUR thousand)	Wage adjusted labour productivity (%)	Gross operating rate (%)
Chemicals, rubber and plastic products	66.5	39.0	171.0	12.0
Chemicals and chemical products	90.0	47.0	186.0	12.7
Basic chemicals; pesticides and other agro-chemical products	100.0	48.0	206.0	12.1
Pharmaceuticals, medicinal chemicals and botanical products	100.9	52.7	191.7	15.9
Miscellaneous chemical products	67.0	41.5	160.0	10.4
Man-made fibres	55.0	37.0	149.0	8.4
Rubber and plastic products	43.2	29.8	144.9	10.3
Rubber products	47.6	33.0	145.0	9.9
Plastic products	42.0	29.0	145.0	10.4

(1) Rounded estimates based on non-confidential data.
Source: Eurostat (SBS)

COSTS, PRODUCTIVITY AND PROFITABILITY

The share of gross tangible investment in the total expenditure (personnel costs plus purchases of goods and services plus intangible investment) of the chemicals, rubber and plastics sector of the EU-27 was 4.3 % in 2004. The corresponding share for the chemicals and chemical products subsector was 4.0 % and for the rubber and plastics subsector it was 4.9 % (the same proportion as across the non-financial business economy as a whole). The share of personnel costs for the chemicals, rubber and plastics sector (17.5 %), however, was slightly higher than the average for the non-financial business economy as a whole (16.4 %). However, there was a notable difference between the relative share of personnel costs in the chemical and chemical products subsector (15.7 %) and the share in the rubber and plastic products subsector (21.8 %). Among the Member States, the share of investment in the total expenditure in the chemicals, rubber and plastics sector was relatively high compared to the respective non-financial business economy averages in Hungary (11.8 % compared to 6.7 %) and in Lithuania (12.0 % compared to 7.0 %).

The apparent labour productivity of the chemicals, rubber and plastics manufacturing sector of the EU-27 was EUR 66 500 per person employed in 2004, almost two thirds (62.6 %) higher than the level across the non-financial business economy as a whole, see Table 5.4. The apparent labour productivity of those working in the manufacture of basic chemicals (NACE Groups 24.1 and 24.2) and the manufacture of pharmaceuticals (NACE Group 24.4) in the EU-27 was particularly high (EUR 100 000 per person employed and EUR 100 900 per person employed respectively). In contrast, the apparent labour productivity of plastics products manufacturing (NACE Group 25.2) and rubber products manufacturing (NACE Group 25.1) were much closer to the average level of the non-financial business economy (EUR 40 900). Average personnel costs across the sector (EUR 39 000 per employee) was relatively high (41.3 % above the non-financial business economy average), second highest among the sectoral chapter aggregates of this publication after the manufacture of transport equipment (chapter 10), with the level in the chemical and chemical products subsector (EUR 47 000 per employee) being the highest of all industrial NACE subsections in 2004. However, the value added per person employed created within the EU-27's chemicals, rubber and plastics sector

covered average personnel costs by 171.0 % in 2004, this level of wage adjusted labour productivity being notably higher than the average across the non-financial business economy (148.0 %). Nevertheless, within the sector, the wage adjusted labour productivity of the rubber and plastics subsector (144.9 %) was a little below the non-financial business economy average, and contrasted with the chemical and chemical products subsector where the ratio of 186.0 % was the third highest of all industrial NACE subsections in 2004. The wage adjusted labour productivity of the chemicals, rubber and plastics sector was similar to or higher than the level of the non-financial business economy in all Member States [6] (much higher in the Netherlands, Slovenia, Sweden and the Czech Republic) with the exception of Slovakia, where it was notably lower (12.7 % less).

The gross operating rate of the EU-27's chemicals, rubber and plastics manufacturing sector was 12.0 % in 2004, moderately higher than the non-financial business economy average (11.0 %). However, the rate of rubber and plastic products manufacturing (10.3 %) was below the non-financial business economy average whilst that of chemicals and chemical products (12.7 %) was higher.

[6] Luxembourg and Portugal, 2003; Ireland, Greece, Cyprus and Malta, not available.

The profitability of the pharmaceuticals manufacturing sector in the EU-27, as measured by the gross operating rate, was notably higher than for chemicals, rubber and plastics manufacturing as a whole, with a rate of 15.9 % in pharmaceuticals manufacturing compared to 12.0 %. The highest gross operating rates in this sector were recorded in Ireland (46.8 %, 2003), Sweden (41.7 %), Slovenia, Hungary and Belgium (all three a little over 30 %).

EXTERNAL TRADE

A higher proportion of pharmaceutical products (CPA Group 24.4) were exported by EU-27 Member States to non-member countries than the average for chemicals, rubber and plastic products (CPA Subsections DG and DH) as a whole (39.0 % compared to 32.6 % respectively), although intra-EU exports still dominated trade.

The value of EU-27 exports of pharmaceuticals in 2006 was EUR 69.8 billion, and the main markets for these exports were the United States (35.1 % of extra-EU exports) and Switzerland (13.1 %). Although the value of EU-27 imports of pharmaceutical products increased to a value of EUR 39.9 billion in 2006, the trade surplus widened to EUR 29.8 billion. As well as being the main market for exports of pharmaceutical products, the United States and Switzerland provided the overwhelming majority of pharmaceuticals products (a fairly evenly split total share of 78.8 %) that were imported from outside the EU 27.

Germany and Belgium were the principal exporters of pharmaceutical products, accounting for 20.2 % and 18.1 % respectively of the exports (intra- and extra-EU trade) of EU-27 Member States. However, Ireland had the largest trade surplus in pharmaceutical products (EUR 13.4 billion) among the Member States in 2006, the majority of which was based on a surplus with other Member States. In contrast, the majority of the significant trade surpluses recorded by some other Member States, such as Germany (EUR 7.7 billion), the United Kingdom (EUR 5.6 billion), Sweden (EUR 4.4 billion) and France (EUR 4.1 billion), were based on trade with non-member countries.

5.3: MISCELLANEOUS CHEMICAL PRODUCTS

This subchapter covers three activities that are presented separately. The manufacture of paints, varnishes, enamels, lacquers, solvents, thinners, varnish removers, as well as printing inks (NACE Group 24.3) is the first; hereafter, referred to as paints and printing inks. The manufacture of washing and cleaning products, as well as perfumes, toiletries, cosmetics and related products (NACE Group 24.5) forms the next group; hereafter, referred to as soaps, detergents and toiletries. Finally, NACE Group 24.6 covers other chemical products, a residual grouping that includes the manufacture of photographic materials, explosives, glues and essential oils, as well as intermediate inputs for other manufacturing processes.

There were 19 000 enterprises in the miscellaneous chemical products manufacturing sector (NACE Groups 24.3, 24.5 and 24.6) which employed 650 000 people throughout the EU-27 and generated EUR 44.0 billion of added value, 17.6 % of the added value generated by the whole of the chemicals, rubber and plastics manufacturing sector (NACE Subsections DG and DH). Within the miscellaneous chemical products manufacturing sector, the soaps, detergents and toiletries manufacturing subsector (NACE Group 24.5) was the largest, accounting for a little over

Table 5.14

Miscellaneous chemical products (NACE Groups 24.3, 24.5 and 24.6)
Structural profile, EU-27, 2004 (1)

	No. of enterprises (thousands)	Turnover (EUR million)	Value added (EUR million)	Employment (thousands)
Miscellaneous chemical products	19.0	160 000	44 000	650.0
Paints and printing inks	4.5	39 872	11 340	176.7
Soap, detergents and toiletries	8.2	70 975	17 888	273.7
Soap, detergents, cleaning and polishing preparations	4.4	32 500	8 370	120.0
Perfumes and toilet preparations	3.8	38 500	9 520	150.0
Other chemical products	7.0	51 000	15 000	210.0
Explosives	0.8	2 740	1 030	21.0
Glues and gelatines	0.7	5 780	1 660	23.2
Essential oils	0.6	:	:	:
Photographic chemical material	:	:	:	:
Prepared unrecorded media	0.4	1 320	212	4.8
Other chemical products n.e.c.	4.2	30 800	8 290	120.0

(1) Rounded estimate based on non-confidential data.
Source: Eurostat (SBS)

40 % of value added. The second largest subsector, accounting for about one third of the value added of the sector, concerned other chemical products manufacturing (NACE Group 24.6). The paints and printing inks manufacturing subsector (NACE Group 24.3) was the smallest, generating about one quarter of the value added of the miscellaneous chemical products sector – see Table 5.14.

Table 5.15

Miscellaneous chemical products (NACE Groups 24.3, 24.5 and 24.6)
Structural profile: ranking of top five Member States, 2004

Rank	Share of EU-27 value added (%) (1)	Share of EU-27 employment (%) (2)	Value added specialisation ratio (EU-27=100) (3)	Employment specialisation ratio (EU-27=100) (4)
1	Germany (24.6)	Germany (22.9)	Belgium (156.5)	Belgium (156.7)
2	France (18.9)	France (16.6)	France (134.4)	France (145.1)
3	United Kingdom (16.5)	United Kingdom (13.5)	Poland (119.9)	Germany (138.4)
4	Italy (11.4)	Italy (11.1)	Germany (117.2)	Bulgaria (109.5)
5	Spain (8.2)	Spain (9.1)	Italy (102.4)	Poland (107.5)

(1) Ireland, Greece, Luxembourg, Malta, Slovenia, Slovakia and Finland, not available; Portugal, 2003.
(2) Ireland, Greece, Luxembourg, Malta, Portugal, Slovenia, Slovakia and Finland, not available.
(3) Ireland, Greece, Cyprus, Luxembourg, Malta, Slovenia, Slovakia and Finland, not available; Portugal, 2003.
(4) Ireland, Greece, Cyprus, Luxembourg, Malta, Portugal, Slovenia, Slovakia and Finland, not available.
Source: Eurostat (SBS)

Table 5.16

Production of selected products - paints, varnishes and similar coatings, printing ink and mastics (CPA Group 24.3), EU-27, 2006 (1)

	Prodcom code	Production value (EUR million)	Volume of sold production (thousands)	Unit of volume
Printing inks (excluding black)	24.30.24.70	3 585	1 069 048	kg
Glaziers' putty, grafting putty, resin cements, caulking compounds and other mastics	24.30.22.53	1 385	594 260	kg
Organic composite solvents and thinners used in conjunction with coatings and inks (excluding those based on butyl acetate)	24.30.22.79	1 099	1 043 424	kg
Vitrifiable enamels and glazes; engobes (slips) and similar preparations for ceramics; enamelling or glass	24.30.21.50	884	1 148 225	kg
Prepared pigments; opacifiers; colours and similar preparations for ceramics; enamelling or glass	24.30.21.30	812	226 637	kg
Paints and varnishes, based on polyesters dispersed/dissolved in a non-aqueous medium, weight of the solvent > 50 % of the weight of the solution including enamels and lacquers	24.30.12.25	755	232 277	kg
Prepared water pigments for finishing leather; paints and varnishes (including enamels; lacquers and distempers) (excluding of oil)	24.30.22.15	736	254 909	kg
Black printing inks	24.30.24.50	556	220 206	kg
Paints and varnishes, based on acrylic or vinyl polymers dispersed/dissolved in non-aqueous medium, weight of the solvent > 50 % of the solution weight including enamels and lacquers	24.30.12.30	555	326 830	kg
Pigments, including metallic powders and flakes, dispersed in non-aqueous media, in liquid or paste form, of a kind used in the manufacture of paints; colorants and other colouring matter, n.e.s. put up for retail sale	24.30.22.40	388	86 679	kg

(1) Estimated.
Source: Eurostat (PRODCOM)

MANUFACTURE OF PAINTS AND PRINTING INKS

The activities of paint and printing inks manufacturing generated EUR 11.3 billion of value added in 2004, accounting for 4.5 % of the value added of chemicals, rubber and plastics manufacturing and employed 176 700 people throughout the EU-27, the equivalent of 4.8 % of the chemicals, rubber and plastics workforce.

Germany was the main producer of paints and printing inks in the EU-27, creating a little under one third (30.6 %) of the value added generated across the EU-27. It was also relatively specialised in this activity, although not as specialised as Estonia and Slovenia, where the value added generated by their respective paints and printing inks manufacturing sectors made about twice the contribution to their national non-financial business economies as was the average across the EU-27.

The production index of paints and printing inks followed closely the broader growth in output for chemicals, rubber and plastics in the period between 1996 and 2000 (an average 4.4 % per annum compared to 4.7 % per annum respectively). Although the output of chemicals, rubber and plastics continued to grow at a relatively steady but slower rate through until 2006, there was a distinct stagnation in the production index of paints and printing inks through until 2006, when the output of paints and printing inks surged 6.0 %.

As a proportion of total expenditure (gross operating and tangible investment expenditure), investment in the paints and printing inks manufacturing sector was particularly low (3.0 %) and personnel costs relatively high (19.6 %). With average personnel costs in the sector (EUR 41 600 per employee) being a little higher than the average across all of the activities of chemicals, rubber and plastics manufacturing and the apparent labour productivity (EUR 64 200 per employed) being slightly lower,

the wage adjusted labour productivity of those working in the paints and printing inks manufacturing sector (154.3 %) was about 10 % lower than the average across all the activities covered by this chapter and closer to the average ratio across the non-financial business economy.

Around two thirds (65.6 %) of the exports of paints and printing products (CPA Group 24.3) by the EU-27 Member States was accounted for by intra-EU trade. The value of exports to non-member countries (in other words EU-27 exports) in 2006 was EUR 5.6 billion, and the key non-member country markets for paints and printing inks were Russia (accounting for 17.6 % of EU-27 exports), the United States (7.9 %) and Turkey (6.6 %). Germany accounted for a little less than one third (30.6 %) of all exports (intra- and extra-EU trade) made by EU-27 Member States in 2006, and was, by far, the leading exporter. Imports of paints and printing products from outside the EU-27 were valued at EUR 1.5 billion in 2006, resulting in a trade surplus of EUR 4.1 billion.

Table 5.17

Production of selected products - glycerol; soap and detergents, cleaning and polishing preparations; perfumes and toilet preparations (CPA Group 24.5), EU-27, 2006 (1)

	Prodcom code	Production value (EUR million)	Volume of sold production (thousands)	Unit of volume
Washing preparations and cleaning preparations, with or without soap, p.r.s. including auxiliary washing preparations excluding those for use as soap, surface-active preparations	24.51.32.50	7 952	7 279 269	kg
Toilet waters	24.52.11.70	4 048	181 370	litre
Hair preparations (excluding shampoos, permanent waving and hair straightening preparations, lacquers)	24.52.17.00	2 728	-	-
Non-ionic surface-active agents (excluding soap)	24.51.20.50	1 557	1 053 073	kg
Shampoos	24.52.16.30	1 549	-	-
Perfumed bath salts and other bath preparations	24.52.19.70	1 469	-	-
Anionic surface-active agents (excluding soap)	24.51.20.20	1 160	1 321 831	kg
Lip make-up preparations	24.52.12.50	1 000	-	-
Surface-active preparations; whether or not containing soap; n.p.r.s. (excluding those for use as soap)	24.51.32.60	795	596 298	kg
Cationic surface-active agents (excluding soap)	24.51.20.30	509	482 867	kg

(1) Estimated.
Source: Eurostat (PRODCOM)

MANUFACTURE OF SOAPS, DETERGENTS AND TOILETRIES

Soaps, detergents and toiletries manufacturing generated EUR 17.9 billion of value added in 2004, accounting for 7.2 % of the value added created by the chemicals, rubber and plastics manufacturing activities (NACE Subsections DG and DH). 273 700 people worked in soap, detergents and toiletries manufacturing across the EU-27 in 2004, representing about one in every thirteen workers within the chemicals, rubber and plastics manufacturing workforce.

The activity of perfumes and toiletries manufacturing (NACE Class 24.52) was slightly larger than the activity of soap and detergents manufacturing (NACE Class 24.51), accounting for a small majority of both employment (54.8 %) and value added (53.2 %). This situation, however, is almost entirely due to the relative importance of perfumes and toiletries manufacturing in France; as in nearly every other Member State for which information is available [18], soap and detergents manufacturing was the larger of the two activities. France accounted for 38.7 % of the value added of perfumes and toiletries manufacturing across the EU-27, whereas it only accounted for 12.5 % of the value added created by soap and detergents manufacturing. Poland and France were the only two Member States that were relatively specialised in soaps, detergent and toiletries manufacturing in the EU-27, the contribution of value added to their non-financial business economies being about twice the average across the EU-27.

Average personnel costs in the soaps, detergents and toiletries sector of the EU-27 (EUR 39 000 per employee), as well as apparent labour productivity (EUR 65 400 per person employed) and the wage adjusted labour productivity ratio (167.5 %) were all quite similar to the average for chemicals, rubber and plastics manufacturing as a whole in 2004.

A relatively high proportion (40.3 %) of exports (intra and extra-EU) by EU-27 Member States in perfumes and toilet preparations (CPA Class 24.52) went to non-member countries, particularly compared to the share (25.1 %) for soap and detergents, cleaning and polishing preparations (CPA Class 24.51).

The EU-27 trade surplus in soaps, detergents and toiletries (CPA Group 24.5) widened to EUR 9.6 billion in 2006, a gain of EUR 3.1 billion since 2001. This trade surplus was underpinned by exports valued at EUR 13.3 billion. Almost three quarters (74.9 %) of these exports were accounted for by perfumes and toiletries, for which the United States (17.2 %) and Russia (13.2 %) were the main markets. France was the leading exporter of perfumes and toilet preparations, accounting for 34.7 % of exports (intra- and extra-EU) by EU-27 Member States, whilst Germany had the highest share (24.3 %) of exports for soap and detergents, cleaning and polishing preparations.

MANUFACTURE OF OTHER CHEMICAL PRODUCTS

Other chemical products manufacturing generated EUR 15.0 billion of value added in 2004 in the EU-27, representing 6.0 % of the value added created by the chemicals, rubber and plastics manufacturing as a whole. In the EU-27 210 000 people were employed, representing a similar proportion (5.7 %) of the chemicals, rubber and plastics manufacturing workforce. A majority of the value added generated (55.3 %) and the number of persons employed (57.1 %) came from the manufacture of other chemical products not elsewhere classified (NACE Class 24.66), such as writing inks, lubricating preparations, additives and anti-freezing preparations.

The largest other chemical products manufacturing Member State was Germany, generating almost one quarter (24.8 %) of the EU-27's added value in 2004. However, Belgium was the most specialised Member State, the contribution of value added from this activity to the non-financial business economy in Belgium being almost two and a half times the EU-27 average.

During the period from 1996 to 2006, the overall growth in the output of other chemicals manufacturing was driven by the strong growth in the output of other chemical products not elsewhere classified in the three years after 2003 (a combined rise of 19.1 %).

[18] Portugal, 2003; Latvia, Malta, Slovenia, 2002; Bulgaria, Czech Republic, Ireland, Greece, Luxembourg and Finland, not available.

Table 5.18

Miscellaneous chemical products (CPA Groups 24.3, 24.5 and 24.6)
External trade, EU-27, 2006

	Extra-EU exports		Extra-EU imports			
	(EUR million)	(% share of chapter)	(EUR million)	(% share of chapter)	Trade balance (EUR million)	Cover ratio (%)
Miscellaneous chemical products	39 081	20.1	18 617	14.4	20 464	209.9
Paints and printing inks	5 581	2.9	1 525	1.2	4 056	366.0
Soap, detergents and toiletries	13 292	6.8	3 723	2.9	9 568	357.0
Other chemical products	20 208	10.4	13 368	10.4	6 840	151.2

Source: Eurostat (Comext)

The apparent labour productivity of the other chemical products sector in the EU-27 was EUR 70 000 per person employed in 2004, a slightly higher (5.3 %) figure than that for the chemicals, rubber and plastics manufacturing as a whole. Nevertheless, much higher (17.9 %) average personnel costs of EUR 46 000 per employee, meant that the wage adjusted labour productivity ratio (154.0 %) for the other chemical products sector was below the average for chemicals, rubber and plastics manufacturing (171.0 %).

The EU-27 trade surplus for other chemical products (CPA Group 24.6) in 2006 was valued at EUR 6.8 billion, resulting from exports of EUR 20.2 billion and the much increased imports of EUR 13.4 billion. EU-27 imports came mostly from the United States (34.8 %), Japan (17.5 %), Switzerland (12.1 %) and China (9.9 %). The strong rise in the value of imports from outside the EU-27 mainly concerned prepared unrecorded media (CPA Class 24.65) and other chemicals not elsewhere specified (CPA Class 24.66).

5.4: MAN-MADE FIBRES

This subchapter relates to the manufacture of artificial and synthetic fibres (NACE Group 24.7) in the form of tow, fibres, yarn, or strips. It excludes the manufacture of sewing thread (NACE Class 17.16) and man-made fibres derived from minerals (carbon, ceramic, glass or metal).

Figure 5.9

Manufacture of man-made fibres (NACE Group 24.7)
Evolution of main indicators, EU-27 (2000=100)

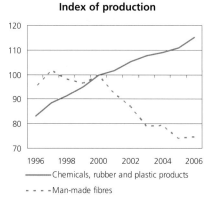

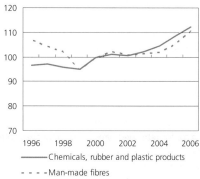

Source: Eurostat (STS)

The man-made fibres covered within this subchapter can be characterised as being made from either natural polymers (such as viscose) or synthetic polymers (such as polyester and nylons), which have different types of production processes.

STRUCTURAL PROFILE

Among the activities of chemicals, rubber and plastics manufacturing (NACE Subsections DG and DH), the man-made fibres manufacturing sector (NACE Group 24.7) was small both in terms of the value added generated and the numbers of people employed; the sector had some 360 enterprises which generated EUR 2.9 billion of added value in 2004 (1.2 % of the value added of chemicals, rubber and plastics manufacturing as a whole) and employed 53 000 people (1.4 % of the workforce). Germany was the principal producer [19] of

man-made fibres, accounting for a little over one third (36.5 %) of the EU-27's value added.

In contrast to the steady rise in the production index of chemicals, rubber and plastics manufacturing throughout the ten years until 2006, there was a marked decline in the output of man-made fibres in the period after 2000 (an

average decline of 5.8 % per annum through until 2005), although the most recent rate of change, for 2006, show a moderate expansion (0.9 %) – see Figure 5.9. There was a relatively strong decline in the output price index for man-made fibres from 1996 through to a low in 1999 and the 1996 index level was not surpassed until 2006.

[19] Bulgaria, the Czech Republic, Denmark, Ireland, Greece, Cyprus, Latvia, Lithuania, Luxembourg, Malta, the Netherlands, Slovenia and Finland, not available.

COSTS, PRODUCTIVITY AND PROFITABILITY

Although average personnel costs in the man-made fibres manufacturing sector of the EU-27 were the lowest (at EUR 37 000 per employee) among the seven NACE groups that comprise the activities of chemicals, chemical products and man-made fibres manufacturing (NACE Subsection DG), they remained a third higher than the average level across the non-financial business economy (NACE Sections C to I and K) in 2004. The apparent labour productivity of the man-made fibres manufacturing sector (EUR 55 000 per person employed) was higher than the average for the non-financial business economy by a similar proportion, which led to almost identical wage adjusted productivity

levels (149 % and 148 % respectively). Among the Member States [20], the highest wage adjusted productivity ratios for the sector in 2004 were for Poland (257.4 %) and the United Kingdom (231.9 %). The gross operating rate of the man-made fibres manufacturing sector (8.4 %) in 2004 was lower than each of the other eight NACE groups that comprise the activities of chemicals, rubber and plastics manufacturing and therefore also well below the average rate for the non-financial business economy (11.0 %).

_____

[20] Bulgaria, the Czech Republic, Denmark, Estonia, Ireland, Greece, Cyprus, Latvia, Lithuania, Luxembourg, Malta, the Netherlands, Slovenia and Finland, not available.

EXTERNAL TRADE

Trade in man-made fibres (CPA Group 24.7) represented only a small part of the trade in chemicals, rubber and plastics (CPA Subsections DG and DH); EU-27 exports of man-made fibres were valued at EUR 1.4 billion in 2006, representing 0.7 % of the chemicals, rubber and plastic goods total. In these products the EU-27 had a small trade deficit (one of only two for the nine NACE groups that comprise chemicals, rubber and plastics) of EUR 537 million in 2006, as imports were valued at EUR 2.0 billion. Italy accounted for the largest proportion of EU-27 Member States' exports (intra- and extra-EU) of man-made fibres in 2006, ahead of Germany, the Netherlands and Belgium.

5.5: RUBBER

> The rubber sector (NACE Group 25.1) has three distinct parts: the manufacture of rubber tyres and tubes; the retreading and rebuilding of rubber tyres; and the manufacture of other rubber products.

Although no natural rubber is grown in the EU, synthetic rubber is produced. According to the International Rubber Study Group [21], the EU produced 2.7 million tonnes of synthetic rubber in 2006 (corresponding to 21.6 % of world production) but consumed 4.0 million tonnes of rubber (both synthetic and natural).

In addition to the REACH legislation, there have been other important policy developments of impact on rubber manufacturing in the EU. In March 2006, a Council decision [22] was taken to adopt the UNECE regulations 108 and 109 on retreaded tyres for motor and commercial vehicles that sets standards of safety and quality control for retreaded tyres as for new tyres. The growing emphasis on retreading or alternative uses of old tyres is important given the mid-July 2006 ban on putting shredded tyres into landfill.

_____

[21] IRSG, http://www.rubberstudy.com/ statistics-geninfo.aspx.
[22] 2006/443/EC.

STRUCTURAL PROFILE

There were 7 900 enterprises in the rubber products manufacturing sector (NACE Group 25.1) which employed 370 000 people across the EU-27 in 2004 and generated EUR 18.0 billion of added value, which corresponded to 7.2 % of the added value generated by activities of chemicals, rubber and plastics manufacturing (NACE Subsections DG and DH). The added value of other rubber products (NACE Class 25.13) accounted for half (49.9 %) of the value added of the rubber products manufacturing sector in 2004, with the added value created by the rubber tyres and tubes manufacturing subsector (NACE Class 25.11) accounting for most of the rest. Indeed, the value added created by these two activities dwarfed the 2.2 % contribution made by the retreading and rebuilding of rubber tyres (NACE Class 25.12).

A little over three quarters (78.4 %) of the EU-27's value added generated by the rubber products manufacturing sector was concentrated in the five largest Member States, with Germany (25.7 % of the EU-27 total) and France (19.9 %) being the largest producers. However, Luxembourg was the Member State where the value added from rubber products manufacturing made the largest proportional contribution (2.8 % in 2003) to the value added of its non-financial business economy (NACE Sections C to I and K), almost eight times the average recorded across the EU-27 (just 0.4 %). Slovakia and the Czech Republic were the next most specialised Member States within this sector (see Table 5.20).

Table 5.19 _____

Manufacture of rubber products (NACE Group 25.1)
Structural profile, EU-27, 2004 (1)

	No. of enterprises (thousands)	Turnover (EUR million)	Value added (EUR million)	Employment (thousands)
Rubber products	7.9	58 000	18 000	370.0
Rubber tyres and tubes	:	30 000	8 600	135.0
Retreading and rebuilding of rubber tyres	1.5	1 420	401	13.2
Other rubber products	5.9	26 200	8 980	222.0

(1) Rounded estimate based on non-confidential data.
Source: Eurostat (SBS)

Table 5.20 _____

Manufacture of rubber products (NACE Group 25.1)
Structural profile: ranking of top five Member States, 2004

Rank	Share of EU-27 value added (%) (1)	Share of EU-27 employment (%) (1)	Value added specialisation ratio (EU-27=100) (2)	Employment specialisation ratio (EU-27=100) (2)
1	Germany (25.7)	Germany (20.8)	Luxembourg (780.5)	Luxembourg (627.6)
2	France (19.9)	France (18.7)	Slovakia (312.6)	Slovakia (254.4)
3	Italy (12.4)	Italy (12.4)	Czech Republic (258.8)	Slovenia (191.8)
4	United Kingdom (10.9)	Spain (8.6)	Slovenia (255.0)	Czech Republic (191.1)
5	Spain (9.6)	United Kingdom (8.4)	Romania (152.3)	France (163.9)

(1) Greece and Malta, not available; Luxembourg and Slovenia, 2003.
(2) Ireland, Greece, Cyprus and Malta, not available; Luxembourg and Slovenia, 2003.
Source: Eurostat (SBS)

The index of production for the rubber products sector followed an upward trend during the period 1996 to 2006, with annual average growth of 2.0 % per annum. However, 1996, 2001 and 2002 were marked by a contraction in the level of production for these activities, with the most significant reduction being recorded in 2001 (-2.7 %).

The domestic output price for rubber products manufacturing declined steadily through until 2000, after which there was a steady and longer rise (an average 1.6 % per annum) which was underlined by the strong rise in 2006 (see Figure 5.10). The development of the domestic output price index, in large part reflected developments in the price of natural rubber and petroleum costs for synthetic rubber.

Figure 5.10 _____

Manufacture of rubber products (NACE Group 25.1)
Evolution of main indicators, EU-27 (2000=100)

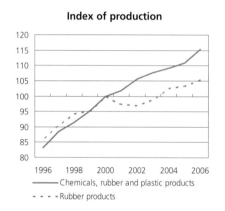

Index of production

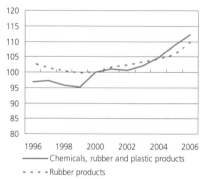

Index of domestic output prices

Source: Eurostat (STS)

Table 5.21 _____

Production of selected products - rubber products (CPA Group 25.1), EU-27, 2006 (1)

	Prodcom code	Production value (EUR million)	Volume of sold production (thousands)	Unit of volume
New pneumatic rubber tyres for motor cars (including for racing cars)	25.11.11.00	10 431	311 457	units
New pneumatic rubber tyres for buses or lorries with a load index > 121	25.11.13.57	2 927	16 173	units
Seals; of vulcanised rubber	25.13.73.23	2 296	228 564	kg
Rubber-to-metal bonded articles for tractors and motor vehicles	25.13.73.45	1 902	248 342	kg
Moulded rubber articles for tractors and motor vehicles	25.13.73.47	1 870	880 192	kg
New pneumatic rubber tyres for buses or lorries with a load index <= 121	25.11.13.55	1 740	38 643	units
Compounded rubber unvulcanised (excluding with carbon black or silica and rubber solutions, dispersions)	25.13.20.19	1 498	766 552	kg
Rubber compounded with carbon black or silica; unvulcanized	25.13.20.13	1 227	619 318	kg
Rubber-to-metal bonded articles for other uses than for tractors and motor vehicles	25.13.73.49	1 133	128 384	kg
Extruded solid rubber rods and profiles	25.13.20.87	987	227 573	kg

(1) Estimated.
Source: Eurostat (PRODCOM)

Table 5.22

Rubber products (CPA Group 25.1)
External trade, EU-27, 2006

	Extra-EU exports		Extra-EU imports		Trade balance	Cover ratio
	(EUR million)	(% share of chapter)	(EUR million)	(% share of chapter)	(EUR million)	(%)
Rubber products	7 400	3.8	7 653	5.9	-252	96.7
New and used rubber tyres and tubes	3 496	1.8	4 411	3.4	-915	79.3
Retreaded pneumatic tyres, of rubber	67	0.0	12	0.0	55	573.0
Other rubber products	3 838	2.0	3 231	2.5	607	118.8

Source: Eurostat (Comext)

COSTS, PRODUCTIVITY AND PROFITABILITY

The value of investment expenditure as a share of total expenditure (gross operating and tangible investment expenditure) within the rubber products manufacturing sector was 4.1 % in 2004, a little below the share for chemicals, rubber and plastics manufacturing as a whole (4.3 %). Personnel costs in the rubber products manufacturing sector accounted for 22.1 % of total expenditure in 2004, a much higher proportion than the average across chemicals, plastics and rubber manufacturing as a whole (17.5 %), despite the fact that average personnel costs of EUR 33 000 per employee were 15.4 % less than the chemicals, plastics and rubber manufacturing average.

Each person employed in the EU-27's rubber products manufacturing sector generated an average of EUR 47 600 of value added in 2004, which more than covered the average personnel costs. The resulting wage adjusted labour productivity ratio of 145.0 % for the sector in 2004 was much less, however, than the ratio of 171.0 % for the chemicals, rubber and plastics manufacturing as a whole, although only marginally less than the average across the non-financial business economy (148.0 %). In Portugal, the Czech Republic and Finland, the wage adjusted labour productivity ratio of the rubber products sector was substantially above (between 40 % and 65 % higher) the ratios of their respective non-financial business economies.

The profitability of the EU-27's rubber products manufacturing sector, as measured by the gross operating rate, was below the average rate across its non-financial business economy in 2004 (9.9 % compared with 11.0 %) and more noticeably below the rate across its chemicals, rubber and plastics manufacturing activities as a whole (12.0 %). The highest gross operating rates for the rubber products manufacturing sector were recorded in Finland (27.3 %) and Portugal (25.4 %) in 2004 [23], at levels that were well over double the average rates across their respective national non-financial business economies.

[23] Luxembourg and Slovenia, 2003; Greece and Malta, not available.

EXTERNAL TRADE

Exports of rubber products (CPA Group 25.1) from the EU-27 were valued at EUR 7.4 billion in 2006, a 3.8 % share of the value of exports from the chemical, rubber and plastics sector as a whole (CPA Subsections DG and DH). With imports of rubber products from non-member countries valued at EUR 7.7 billion, the EU-27 ran a small trade deficit of EUR 252 million in 2006 (see Table 5.22). The make-up of this deficit, however, reflects two distinct trends; the trade deficit for rubber tyres and tubes (CPA Class 25.11) widened to EUR 915 million in 2006, while the trade surplus for other rubber products (CPA Class 25.13) increased to EUR 607 million. It should be noted that there is almost no external trade in retreaded and rebuilt tyres (CPA Class 25.12).

The main exporters of rubber products in 2006 were Germany with 23.0 % of EU-27 Member States exports (intra- and extra-EU) and France with 14.4 %, and these two Member States had the two largest trade surpluses in these goods (EUR 0.9 billion and EUR 1.1 billion respectively). After rapid increases, the trade surpluses for rubber products in the Czech Republic and Poland reached EUR 677 million and EUR 442 million in 2006.

5.6: PLASTICS

This subchapter covers the manufacture of plastic products (NACE Group 25.2), including plastic sheets, pipes and tubes; plastic packaging goods (such as bags, containers and bottles); plastic products for the construction sector (such as doors, frames and baths); and other plastic products (such as insulating and lighting fittings). Note that the manufacture of plastic games, toys, footwear, furniture and linoleum are not considered as part of this sector.

Table 5.23

Manufacture of plastic products (NACE Group 25.2)
Structural profile, EU-27, 2004 (1)

	No. of enterprises (thousands)	Turnover (EUR million)	Value added (EUR million)	Employment (thousands)
Plastic products	57.4	185 000	60 000	1 400.0
Plastic plates, sheets, tubes and profiles	8.3	50 000	14 000	280.0
Plastic packing goods	:	35 500	10 700	250.0
Builders' ware of plastic	11.0	28 700	9 110	240.0
Other plastic products	30.0	72 000	24 000	607.0

(1) Rounded estimate based on non-confidential data.
Source: Eurostat (SBS)

Among the distinct groups of plastics, the five main groups are polyvinylchloride (PVC), polystyrene (PS), polyethylene terephthalate (PET), polyethylene (PE) - including low density, linear low-density and high-density forms – and polypropylene (PP), which according to the European Market Research and Statistics Working Group represented about 74 % of all plastics demand in Europe [24] in 2005. Primary forms of plastics (included as part of Subchapter 5.1), are converted into a very broad range of products. According to the Association of Plastics Manufacturers [25], over one third (37 %) of plastics were used as packaging in 2005 in Europe [26], by far the single largest end-use, ahead of construction (21 %), and automotive applications (8 %).

Policy developments in recent years have tended to concentrate on environmental considerations. The imposition of definitive anti-dumping duties [27] on imports of certain types of PETs originating in India, Indonesia, Malaysia, the Republic of Korea, Thailand and Taiwan by the Council, serve as a reminder of the importance of trade policy developments.

[24] EU-25 plus Norway and Switzerland.
[25] APME, http://www.plasticseurope.org.
[26] EU-25 plus Norway and Switzerland.
[27] Council Regulations 192/2007/EC and 193/2007/EC.

STRUCTURAL PROFILE

The plastics manufacturing sector (NACE Group 25.2) of the EU-27 employed 1.4 million persons in 2004, corresponding to about 38 % of the chemicals, rubber and plastics manufacturing (NACE Subsections DG and DH) workforce. The sector had approximately 57 400 enterprises which generated EUR 60.0 billion of value added in 2004, corresponding to a little less than one quarter (24.0 %) of value added of chemicals, rubber and plastics manufacturing activities in the EU-27.

Other plastics manufacturing (NACE Class 25.24), covering the production of goods such as plastic tableware and kitchenware as well as electrical insulating, was the largest activity within the sector in 2004, generating two fifths of sectoral value added. A little under one quarter (23.3 %) of sectoral value added came from the activity of plastic plates, sheets, tubes and profiles manufacturing (NACE Class 25.21), with the activities of plastic packing goods manufacturing (NACE Class 25.22) and builders' ware of plastic manufacturing (NACE Class 25.23) providing the remainder.

Among the Member States [28], the plastics manufacturing sector in Germany generated the most value added in 2004, accounting for a little more than one quarter (26.7 %) of the EU-27 total. This was a significantly higher proportion that the next highest from the United Kingdom (15.6 %). There was not a particularly strong level of relative specialisation within the plastics manufacturing sector (see Table 5.24), the highest specialisation in value added terms being for Slovenia, where the sector contributed 1.8 % (2003) of non-financial business economy value added compared to an average 1.2 % across the EU-27.

Between 1996 and 2000 the production index of plastics manufacturing in the EU-27 rose in an almost identical way to the index for chemicals, rubber and plastics manufacturing. Thereafter the output of plastics manufacturing at first levelled out, then rose slowly through to 2004, stabilised again in 2005 and returned to strong growth in 2006, at a rate that slightly exceed that for the output of chemicals, rubber and plastics manufacturing as a whole (see Figure 5.11).

[28] Luxembourg and Slovenia, 2003; Greece and Malta, not available.

Table 5.24

Manufacture of plastic products (NACE Group 25.2)
Structural profile: ranking of top five Member States, 2004

Rank	Share of EU-27 value added (%) (1)	Share of EU-27 employment (%) (1)	Value added specialisation ratio (EU-27=100) (2)	Employment specialisation ratio (EU-27=100) (2)
1	Germany (26.7)	Germany (22.1)	Slovenia (155.2)	Slovenia (153.7)
2	United Kingdom (15.6)	United Kingdom (13.3)	Luxembourg (129.7)	Czech Republic (136.4)
3	France (13.2)	France (12.3)	Czech Republic (129.7)	Germany (133.7)
4	Italy (12.1)	Italy (11.7)	Germany (127.4)	Poland (124.7)
5	Spain (6.6)	Poland (7.5)	Hungary (116.0)	Slovakia (119.4)

(1) Greece and Malta, not available; Luxembourg and Slovenia, 2003.
(2) Ireland, Greece, Cyprus and Malta, not available; Luxembourg and Slovenia, 2003.
Source: Eurostat (SBS)

Table 5.25

Production of selected products - plastic products (CPA Group 25.2), EU-27, 2006 (1)

	Prodcom code	Production value (EUR million)	Volume of sold production (thousands)	Unit of volume
Sacks and bags of polymers of ethylene (including cones)	25.22.11.00	6 646	3 133 977	kg
Plastic carboys; bottles; flasks and similar articles for the conveyance or packing of goods; of a capacity <= 2 litres	25.22.14.50	6 181	92 686 681	units
Cellular plates; sheets; film; foil and strip of polyurethanes	25.21.41.50	3 397	2 427 697	kg
Monofilament with any cross-sectional dimension > 1 mm; rods; sticks and profile shapes of polymers of vinyl chloride (including surface worked but not otherwise worked)	25.21.10.70	3 364	1 438 427	kg
Plastic parts for machinery and mechanical appliances excluding internal combustion piston engines, gas turbines	25.24.90.10	3 097	-	-
Plastic stoppers; lids; caps and other closures (excluding for bottles)	25.22.15.27	3 075	763 745	kg
Rigid tubes; pipes and hoses of polymers of vinyl chloride	25.21.21.57	2 813	2 038 466	kg
Cellular plates; sheet; film; foil and strip of polymers of styrene	25.21.41.20	2 581	1 054 453	kg
Plastic baths; shower-baths, sinks and wash-basins	25.23.12.50	1 665	18 520	units

(1) Estimated.
Source: Eurostat (PRODCOM)

Within the plastics manufacturing sector, there were some highly contrasting developments in the production indices of the various activities, most notably after 2000. The production index of builders' ware of plastic declined strongly in 2001 and 2002, from which there had been only a partial recovery by 2006; the output of other plastics products remained little changed in the years after 2000; the output of plastic plates, sheets, tubes and profiles only surpassed 2000 levels in 2004; whilst the steady growth in the output of plastic packing goods continued through until 2006.

COSTS, PRODUCTIVITY AND PROFITABILITY

As a proportion of total expenditure, investment expenditure in the plastics manufacturing sector was 5.1 % in 2004, the highest proportion among the nine NACE groups that comprise the activities of chemicals, rubber and plastics manufacturing. The proportion of total expenditure (gross operating and tangible investment expenditure) taken by personnel costs in the plastics sector was also above the average of chemicals, rubber and plastics manufacturing as a whole (21.6 % compared to 17.5 %), despite the fact that average personnel costs in the sector (EUR 29 000) were an average EUR 10 000 per employee less than across chemicals, rubber and plastics manufacturing in 2004.

Figure 5.11

Manufacture of plastic products (NACE Group 25.2)
Evolution of main indicators, EU-27 (2000=100)

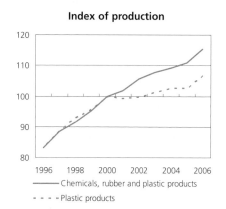

Index of production

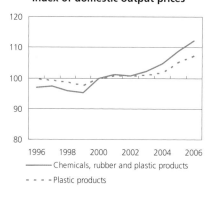

Index of domestic output prices

Source: Eurostat (STS)

Each person employed in the EU-27's plastics manufacturing sector generated an average of EUR 42 000 of value added in 2004, a little more than one third less (36.8 %) than the average across chemicals, rubber and plastics manufacturing as a whole, but very similar to the average across the non-financial business economy. Average personnel costs across the sector were also similar to the level across the non-financial business economy and as a result so was the wage adjusted labour productivity ratio (145.0 %), although it was much less than the 171.0 % across the chemicals, rubber and plastics manufacturing. The wage adjusted labour productivity ratio for the plastics sector was highest [29] in Romania (247.1 %) in 2004,

a little ahead of Poland (224.9 %), Latvia (223.2 %) and Bulgaria (221.9 %). The wage adjusted labour productivity ratio for the plastics sector in Romania was also considerably higher than the average ratio for the national non-financial business economy (52.9 percentage points higher), this being the greatest difference among the Member States.

The gross operating rate of the plastics manufacturing sector in the EU-27 was 10.4 % in 2004, a slightly lower rate than for the non-financial business economy (11.0 %).

[29] Luxembourg and Slovenia, 2003; Greece and Malta, not available.

Table 5.26 _____

Plastic products (CPA Group 25.2)
External trade, EU-27, 2006

	Extra-EU exports		Extra-EU imports		Trade balance	Cover ratio
	(EUR million)	(% share of chapter)	(EUR million)	(% share of chapter)	(EUR million)	(%)
Plastic products	17 279	8.9	13 437	10.4	3 842	128.6
Plastic plates, sheets, tubes and profiles	7 533	3.9	3 859	3.0	3 674	195.2
Packaging products of plastics	2 381	1.2	2 661	2.1	-280	89.5
Builders' ware of plastics	1 551	0.8	819	0.6	732	189.4
Other plastic products	5 814	3.0	6 097	4.7	-283	95.4

Source: Eurostat (Comext)

EXTERNAL TRADE
The value of EU-27 exports of plastics products (CPA Group 25.2) was EUR 17.3 billion in 2006, while imports were valued at EUR 13.4 billion, enabling the EU-27 to register a trade surplus in these goods of EUR 3.8 billion (see Table 5.26). Among the four CPA classes that comprise plastic products, the largest trade surplus (EUR 3.7 billion) in 2006 was for plastic plates, sheets, tubes and profiles (CPA Class 25.21). Indeed, in 2006 the EU-27 recorded small trade deficits for packaging products of plastics (CPA Class 25.22) and other plastic products (CPA Class 25.24).

Germany was the principal exporter of plastic products among the Member States, accounting for 28.3 % of the EU-27 member States' (intra- and extra-EU) exports in 2006. Germany also had the largest trade surplus in plastic products, which widened to EUR 10.0 billion in 2006. The only other Member States with significant trade surpluses in plastic products in 2006 were Italy (EUR 4.5 billion) and Belgium (EUR 1.2 billion).

Table 5.27

Manufacture of chemicals and chemical products (NACE Division 24)
Main indicators, 2004

	EU-27 (1)	BE	BG	CZ	DK	DE	EE	IE	EL	ES	FR	IT	CY	LV	LT
No. of enterprises (thousands)	32.0	0.8	0.6	1.1	0.4	3.3	0.1	0.2	:	4.2	3.9	5.8	0.1	0.1	0.1
Turnover (EUR million)	630 000	34 115	834	4 757	7 717	145 933	308	29 399	:	41 598	116 889	71 834	193	127	463
Production (EUR million)	600 000	33 717	797	4 615	7 856	127 879	257	28 588	:	37 750	105 540	65 984	168	116	475
Value added (EUR million)	170 000	9 650	191	1 191	3 272	42 341	60	12 505	:	10 254	25 134	15 045	67	52	89
Gross operating surplus (EUR million)	80 000	4 948	107	752	1 627	14 632	36	11 287	:	4 570	9 376	5 825	31	29	46
Purchases of goods & services (EUR million)	460 000	25 790	663	3 645	4 910	103 196	249	17 048	:	32 541	92 273	56 714	128	78	378
Personnel costs (EUR million)	90 000	4 702	84	438	1 644	27 710	24	1 217	:	5 684	15 758	9 220	36	23	43
Investment in tangible goods (EUR million)	23 000	721	68	299	673	5 293	13	774	:	1 794	3 622	2 142	15	15	41
Employment (thousands)	2 000	69	25	42	30	460	3	24	:	137	324	199	2	4	5
Apparent labour prod. (EUR thousand)	90.0	140.3	7.7	28.3	110.4	92.1	21.1	517.9	:	75.0	77.7	75.5	35.6	12.3	17.0
Average personnel costs (EUR thousand)	47.0	69.0	3.5	10.7	55.6	60.5	8.5	50.5	:	42.2	48.7	48.2	19.1	5.5	8.3
Wage adjusted labour productivity (%)	186.0	203.3	221.0	263.9	198.7	152.3	247.7	1 025.1	:	177.7	159.4	156.8	186.0	224.9	205.2
Gross operating rate (%)	12.7	14.5	12.8	15.8	21.1	10.0	11.6	38.4	:	11.0	8.0	8.1	15.9	22.8	9.9
Investment / employment (EUR thousand)	12.1	10.5	2.7	7.1	22.7	11.5	4.7	32.1	:	13.1	11.2	10.8	7.8	3.4	7.8

	LU (2)	HU	MT	NL	AT	PL	PT (2)	RO	SI	SK	FI	SE	UK	NO
No. of enterprises (thousands)	0.0	0.7	:	0.9	0.4	2.4	0.8	1.2	0.2	0.2	0.3	0.9	3.7	0.3
Turnover (EUR million)	550	4 433	:	46 904	7 824	10 636	4 091	2 554	2 107	1 000	6 339	13 666	73 933	5 347
Production (EUR million)	369	4 141	:	43 349	7 043	9 777	3 760	1 991	2 043	976	5 987	14 121	65 891	5 160
Value added (EUR million)	98	1 434	:	9 128	2 476	3 084	1 039	431	834	183	1 922	5 978	23 338	1 803
Gross operating surplus (EUR million)	44	871	:	5 262	1 099	2 050	473	208	440	80	1 059	3 438	11 228	946
Purchases of goods & services (EUR million)	463	3 018	:	37 691	5 600	7 941	3 096	2 199	1 356	816	4 661	9 117	50 327	3 762
Personnel costs (EUR million)	54	564	:	3 866	1 377	1 035	566	223	394	104	863	2 540	12 111	858
Investment in tangible goods (EUR million)	21	651	:	1 344	461	634	188	311	236	52	337	586	3 240	322
Employment (thousands)	1	34	:	67	27	102	22	56	13	13	18	44	227	13
Apparent labour prod. (EUR thousand)	67.4	42.5	:	136.8	92.4	30.2	47.8	7.6	64.0	14.0	106.6	135.2	102.9	135.4
Average personnel costs (EUR thousand)	37.3	16.8	:	58.1	51.8	10.5	26.3	4.0	30.4	8.0	48.0	63.2	54.0	64.6
Wage adjusted labour productivity (%)	180.7	253.1	:	235.5	178.5	289.0	181.8	190.8	210.7	176.2	222.2	213.8	190.6	209.6
Gross operating rate (%)	7.9	19.6	:	11.2	14.0	19.3	11.6	8.1	20.9	8.0	16.7	25.2	15.2	17.7
Investment / employment (EUR thousand)	14.6	19.3	:	20.1	17.2	6.2	8.7	5.5	18.1	4.0	18.7	13.3	14.3	24.2

(1) Rounded estimates based on non-confidential data. (2) 2003.
Source: Eurostat (SBS)

Table 5.28

Manufacture of rubber and plastic products (NACE Division 25)
Main indicators, 2004

	EU-27	BE	BG	CZ	DK	DE	EE	IE	EL	ES	FR	IT	CY	LV	LT
No. of enterprises (thousands)	65.3	0.8	1.3	3.1	0.7	6.9	0.2	0.3	:	5.8	5.3	12.6	0.1	0.2	0.4
Turnover (EUR million)	243 462	7 733	385	5 291	3 235	61 552	215	1 382	:	18 193	40 185	36 601	82	136	437
Production (EUR million)	226 397	7 025	368	4 994	3 169	55 938	206	1 308	:	17 111	37 502	34 963	76	131	406
Value added (EUR million)	75 510	2 043	76	1 281	1 344	20 637	52	543	:	5 664	11 526	9 522	35	34	80
Gross operating surplus (EUR million)	25 051	797	41	650	423	5 723	20	224	:	2 061	2 743	3 588	13	19	39
Purchases of goods & services (EUR million)	169 492	5 734	340	4 162	1 856	41 158	168	848	:	12 937	28 176	27 385	51	107	366
Personnel costs (EUR million)	50 459	1 246	35	633	921	14 914	32	319	:	3 603	8 783	5 934	22	15	41
Investment in tangible goods (EUR million)	11 220	213	45	452	240	2 467	13	62	:	985	1 670	1 427	6	18	71
Employment (thousands)	1 748	27	19	75	22	387	4	10	:	123	241	209	1	4	9
Apparent labour prod. (EUR thousand)	43.2	75.0	3.9	17.1	62.0	53.4	12.3	55.6	:	45.9	47.8	45.5	27.2	8.6	9.3
Average personnel costs (EUR thousand)	29.8	47.3	1.9	8.9	42.9	39.0	7.5	33.0	:	29.9	36.5	31.2	17.5	3.9	4.9
Wage adjusted labour productivity (%)	144.9	158.8	205.6	193.3	144.7	136.9	163.3	168.6	:	153.5	131.0	145.9	155.5	219.0	191.1
Gross operating rate (%)	10.3	10.3	10.7	12.3	13.1	9.3	9.4	16.2	:	11.3	6.8	9.8	15.2	14.2	8.8
Investment / employment (EUR thousand)	6.4	7.8	2.3	6.0	11.1	6.4	3.0	6.4	:	8.0	6.9	6.8	5.0	4.6	8.3

	LU (1)	HU	MT	NL	AT	PL	PT	RO	SI	SK	FI	SE	UK	NO
No. of enterprises (thousands)	0.0	2.5	:	1.3	0.6	8.9	1.1	2.2	1.2	0.4	0.7	1.7	7.0	0.4
Turnover (EUR million)	1 464	3 058	:	6 457	4 762	7 346	2 394	1 242	1 279	1 299	2 504	4 227	30 638	975
Production (EUR million)	1 250	2 234	:	5 975	4 250	6 882	2 302	1 160	1 162	1 196	2 507	3 966	29 072	894
Value added (EUR million)	483	656	:	1 951	1 678	1 946	762	289	403	264	1 026	1 456	11 330	312
Gross operating surplus (EUR million)	159	276	:	650	596	1 158	355	172	202	122	433	358	4 022	79
Purchases of goods & services (EUR million)	995	2 412	:	4 546	3 244	5 631	1 697	1 019	920	1 051	1 614	2 874	19 250	673
Personnel costs (EUR million)	306	380	:	1 301	1 083	787	407	117	201	142	592	1 098	7 308	233
Investment in tangible goods (EUR million)	35	199	:	283	235	577	202	212	44	94	158	241	1 161	33
Employment (thousands)	6	42	:	33	28	132	25	45	13	19	16	30	218	5
Apparent labour prod. (EUR thousand)	82.5	15.7	:	58.7	60.3	14.7	30.3	6.5	30.6	14.1	63.4	49.3	52.0	56.9
Average personnel costs (EUR thousand)	52.3	9.3	:	39.8	39.3	6.5	16.3	2.7	16.1	7.6	36.9	42.5	34.4	43.2
Wage adjusted labour productivity (%)	157.7	169.3	:	147.3	153.4	226.5	185.9	244.7	190.2	185.1	171.6	115.9	151.2	131.8
Gross operating rate (%)	10.8	9.0	:	10.1	12.5	15.8	14.8	13.9	15.8	9.4	17.3	8.5	13.1	8.1
Investment / employment (EUR thousand)	6.0	4.8	:	8.5	8.5	4.4	8.1	4.8	3.3	5.0	9.8	8.2	5.3	6.0

(1) 2003.
Source: Eurostat (SBS)

Other non-metallic mineral products

The processes of transforming mineral raw materials such as clay, lime, sand or stone into other non-metallic mineral products (for use, among others, by the construction industry, food and beverages sector, or households in the form of consumer durables) tend to be energy intensive and lead to gas emissions.

Recent policy initiatives of key importance to other non-metallic mineral enterprises have tended to focus on energy strategies, the environment and health and safety. Regarding energy strategies, recent developments (further described in Chapter 13) include ensuring the availability of energy at affordable prices, the need to minimise energy waste and reduce energy use as well as emissions targets. Developments also include the second period for emissions trading (and the implications of possibly incorporating nitrogen and sulphur oxides emissions targets), pollution prevention (existing installations being brought into compliance by 30 October 2007), the start of the classification of chemical substances (REACH) in June 2007 (see Chapter 5), and the December 2006 regulation of the European Commission on the good manufacturing practice for materials and articles that come into contact with food [1].

Other developments include new free trade agreements, such as that agreed in April 2007 with India, Korea and the ASEAN countries [2], offering potential tariff and non-tariff barrier reductions on various ceramic and glass products and further discussions in the Council on the proposal for a regulation on origin marking [3].

STRUCTURAL PROFILE

The other non-metallic mineral products manufacturing (NACE Division 26) sector created EUR 72.9 billion of value added across the EU-27 in 2004 (see Table 6.1), which corresponded to 1.4 % of the value added generated across the EU-27's non-financial business economy (NACE Sections C to I and K). There were 101 500 enterprises which employed 1.6 million people in the other non-metallic mineral products manufacturing sector across the EU-27, which represented a similar proportion (1.3 %) of the non-financial business economy workforce as for value added.

The value added generated by the activities of cement and concrete manufacturing (NACE Groups 26.5 and 26.6, see Subchapter 6.3) in the EU-27 was EUR 31.0 billion in 2004, which was the largest contribution (42.5 %) to the sectoral total. The activities of glass manufacturing (NACE Group 26.1, see Subchapter 6.1) generated a further EUR 16.0 billion of value added (22.0 % of the sectoral total), with ceramic goods and clay products manufacturing (NACE Groups 26.2 to 26.4, see Subchapter 6.2) generating a further EUR 15.0 billion, and stone and miscellaneous non-metallic mineral products (NACE Groups 26.7 and 26.8, see Subchapter 6.4) the remaining EUR 10.6 billion.

This chapter focuses on the manufacture of other non-metallic mineral products (NACE Division 26), which consists of glass manufacturing (NACE Group 26.1); the manufacture of ceramic and clay products (NACE Groups 26.2 to 26.4); the manufacture of cement and concrete (NACE Groups 26.5 and 26.6); and the working of stone and miscellaneous non-metallic mineral products (NACE Groups 26.7 and 26.8). Note that the quarrying of non-metallic mineral products is covered in Chapter 12.

NACE
26: manufacture of other non-metallic mineral products;
26.1: manufacture of glass and glass products;
26.2: manufacture of non-refractory ceramic goods other than for construction purposes; manufacture of refractory ceramic products;
26.3: manufacture of ceramic tiles and flags;
26.4: manufacture of bricks, tiles and construction products, in baked clay;
26.5: manufacture of cement, lime and plaster;
26.6: manufacture of articles of concrete, plaster and cement;
26.7: cutting, shaping and finishing of ornamental and building stone;
26.8: manufacture of other non-metallic mineral products.

[1] 2023/2006/EC.
[2] Philippines, Malaysia, Singapore, Thailand, Indonesia, Brunei, Vietnam, Laos, Myanmar and Cambodia.
[3] 2107/2005/EC.

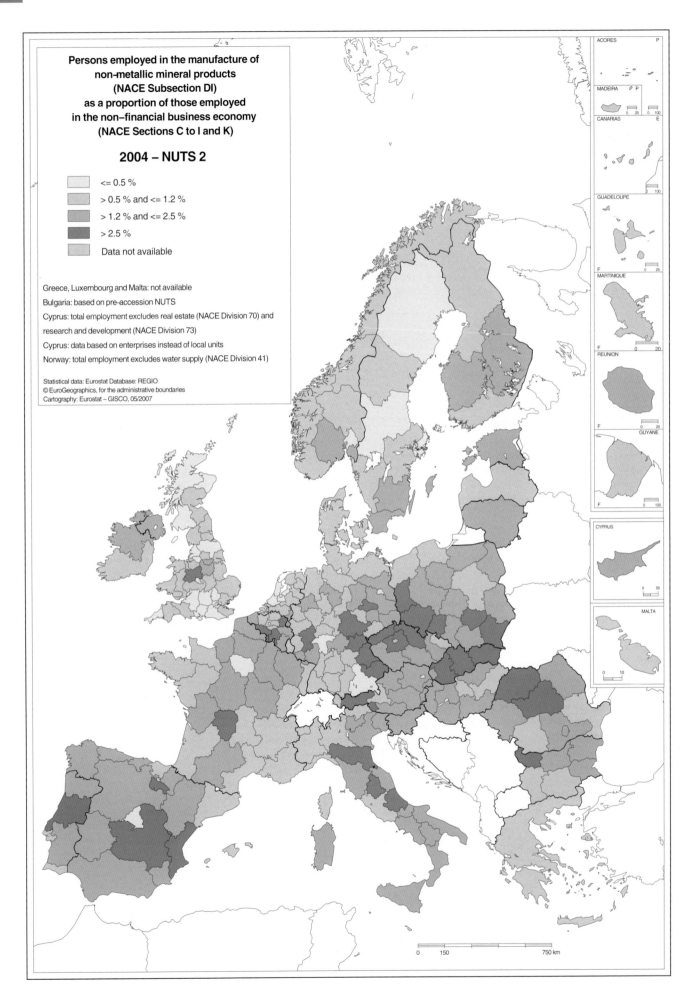

Persons employed in the manufacture of
non-metallic mineral products
(NACE Subsection DI)
as a proportion of those employed
in the non-financial business economy
(NACE Sections C to I and K)

2004 – NUTS 2

- <= 0.5 %
- > 0.5 % and <= 1.2 %
- > 1.2 % and <= 2.5 %
- > 2.5 %
- Data not available

Greece, Luxembourg and Malta: not available

Bulgaria: based on pre-accession NUTS

Cyprus: total employment excludes real estate (NACE Division 70) and
research and development (NACE Division 73)

Cyprus: data based on enterprises instead of local units

Norway: total employment excludes water supply (NACE Division 41)

Statistical data: Eurostat Database: REGIO
© EuroGeographics, for the administrative boundaries
Cartography: Eurostat – GISCO, 05/2007

Table 6.1 _____

Manufacture of other non-metallic mineral products (NACE Subsection DI)
Structural profile, EU-27, 2004 (1)

	No. of enterprises		Turnover		Value added		Employment	
	(thousands)	(% of total)	(EUR million)	(% of total)	(EUR million)	(% of total)	(thousands)	(% of total)
Other non-metallic mineral products	101.5	100.0	211 281	100.0	72 875	100.0	1 600.0	100.0
Glass and glass products	17.8	17.6	44 000	20.8	16 000	22.0	390.7	24.4
Ceramic goods and clay products	20.0	19.7	38 000	18.0	15 000	20.6	400.0	25.0
Cement and concrete	26.0	25.6	94 000	44.5	31 000	42.5	530.0	33.1
Stone and miscellaneous non-metallic mineral products	37.2	36.6	33 000	15.6	10 600	14.5	290.0	18.1

(1) Rounded estimates based on non-confidential data.
Source: Eurostat (SBS)

Table 6.2 _____

Manufacture of other non-metallic mineral products (NACE Subsection DI)
Structural profile: ranking of top five Member States, 2004

Rank	Value added (EUR million) (1)	Employment (thousands) (2)	Share of non-financial business economy			
			No. of enterprises (3)	Turnover (3)	Value added (3)	Employment (4)
1	Germany (13 235)	Italy (249.5)	Lithuania (1.0 %)	Czech Republic (1.9 %)	Czech Republic (3.0 %)	Slovakia (2.5 %)
2	Italy (12 609)	Germany (248.3)	Portugal (0.8 %)	Spain (1.7 %)	Portugal (2.6 %)	Czech Republic (2.3 %)
3	Spain (10 116)	Spain (191.7)	Slovakia (0.8 %)	Slovakia (1.7 %)	Slovakia (2.5 %)	Portugal (2.1 %)
4	France (8 427)	France (143.7)	Poland (0.8 %)	Portugal (1.7 %)	Romania (2.5 %)	Poland (1.8 %)
5	United Kingdom (8 344)	Poland (137.2)	Czech Republic (0.8 %)	Italy (1.6 %)	Bulgaria (2.3 %)	Slovenia (1.8 %)

(1) Greece and Malta, not available; Luxembourg, 2003.
(2) Greece and Malta, not available; Luxembourg and Slovenia, 2003.
(3) Ireland, Greece, Cyprus and Malta, not available; Luxembourg, 2003.
(4) Ireland, Greece, Cyprus and Malta, not available; Luxembourg and Slovenia, 2003.
Source: Eurostat (SBS)

Germany and Italy were the largest producers of other non-metallic mineral products among the Member States, generating EUR 13.2 billion and EUR 12.6 billion of value added respectively in 2004 (see Table 6.2); together they contributed a little over one third (35.5 %) of the value added generated by this sector across the EU-27 in 2004. However, the Czech Republic, Portugal, Slovakia and Romania were the Member States that were the most specialised in the manufacture of other non-metallic mineral products in value added terms; the proportion of the value added generated by each of their respective non-financial business economies which came from this sector being between 2.5 % and 3.0 %.

The map on page 124 shows the contribution of the other non-metallic mineral products manufacturing sector to employment within the non-financial business economy of each region in 2004. Many regions in Germany and Italy, as well as in Poland, Belgium, the Czech Republic, Slovakia and Spain, were specialised in this sector in terms of employment, as well as regional pockets in a number of other Member States among which the Centro region of Portugal showed the highest regional specialisation among all the regions of the EU-27.

Figure 6.1 _____

Manufacture of other non-metallic mineral products (NACE Subsection DI)
Evolution of main indicators, EU-27 (2000=100)

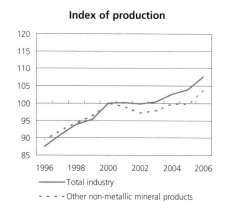
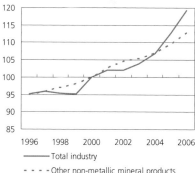

Source: Eurostat (STS)

During the ten years through until 2006, there was a strong similarity between the development of the output of other non-metallic mineral products and that of the output of industry as a whole (see Figure 6.1); in both cases the strong growth came to an end in 2000 before resuming some time later. Where the two production indices differentiated concerned the fact that the output of other non-metallic mineral products declined moderately in 2001 and 2002 whereas industrial output stabilised. It was not until 2006 that the output of other non-metallic mineral products surpassed the level that had been reached in 2000.

There was a continuous rise in the domestic output price index for other non-metallic mineral products manufacturing during the ten years through until 2006 (an average rise of 1.8 % per annum). The steadiness of this increase contrasted with the domestic output price index for industry as a whole, which had some periods of relatively unchanged prices (1996 to 1999 and 2001 to 2002), that were followed by sharper price rises. Furthermore, there was a much stronger rise in the industrial output price index in 2005 and 2006 than for other non-metallic mineral products.

A small majority (52.0 %) of the value added generated within the EU-27's other non-metallic mineral products manufacturing sector came from small and medium-sized enterprises (employing less than 250 people) in 2004. This majority was less strong than that (57.0 %) across the non-financial business economy. The greatest contrast between the SMEs concerned the relative contribution made by micro-enterprises employing less than ten people; they contributed 6.9 % of other non-metallic mineral products manufacturing value added in 2004 but 20.2 % of the value added of the non-financial business economy. Lithuania stood apart from other Member States regarding the importance of SMEs within the other non-metallic mineral products manufacturing sector, as they accounted for 71.8 % of sectoral value added in 2004, a much higher proportion than the average SME contribution across the Lithuanian non-financial business economy (56.7 %).

EMPLOYMENT CHARACTERISTICS

The proportion of men in the workforce of the other non-metallic mineral products manufacturing sector across the EU-27 was considerably higher than across the non-financial business economy workforce (76.4 % in 2006 compared to 65.0 % - see Figure 6.2). This characteristic was common across almost all of the Member States, but particularly evident in Lithuania and Bulgaria. The only exception [4], where the proportion of men was below the non-financial business economy average (albeit moderately so), was the Czech Republic.

Full-time employment was much more common within the other non-metallic mineral products manufacturing workforce in 2006 (94.7 %) than it was across the non-financial business economy as a whole (85.6 %). This was a characteristic common to all of the Member States for which information was available [5], with the exception of Lithuania.

The proportion of workers in the sector under the age of 30 (19.1 %) was notably smaller than the proportion (24.1 %) across the non-financial business economy, the difference largely accounted for by the higher proportion of workers aged between 30 and 49 years old (58.6 % and 54.2 % respectively). These characteristics were common to the vast majority of Member States. In Romania and Slovenia was the proportion of young workers in the sector only a little more than half the average across the national non-financial business economy.

---

[4] Estonia, Latvia and Malta, not available.
[5] Luxembourg, 2003; Estonia, Latvia and Malta, not available.

According to structural business statistics there was relatively little self-employment within the other non-metallic mineral products manufacturing sector; employees (paid workers) accounted for 94.8 % of the number of persons employed in 2004, a notably higher share than that (86.2 %) for the non-financial business economy as a whole.

COSTS, PRODUCTIVITY AND PROFITABILITY

As a proportion of total expenditure within the other non-metallic mineral products manufacturing sector in 2004, investment accounted for a relatively high share (6.3 %) when compared to the average across the non-financial business economy (4.9 %). Similarly, the proportion of total expenditure in the sector accounted for by personnel costs was also relatively high (22.0 %) when compared to the average across the non-financial business economy (16.4 %). This situation occurred despite the fact that average personnel costs in the sector (EUR 28 500 per employee) were only marginally higher than the average across the non-financial business economy as a whole. The labour intensive nature of the sector was particularly apparent for the ceramic and clay products manufacturing subsector (see Subchapter 6.2) and the glass manufacturing subsector (see Subchapter 6.1), where personnel costs accounted for 26.3 % and 24.5 % respectively of their total expenditure, despite slightly lower (ceramic and clay products) or broadly similar (glass) average personnel costs per employee to that of the non-financial business economy as a whole.

Figure 6.2

Manufacture of other non-metallic mineral products (NACE Subsection DI)
Labour force characteristics, EU-27, 2006

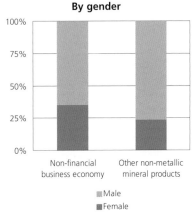

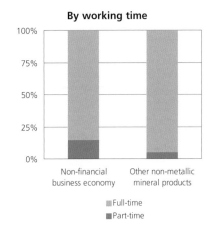

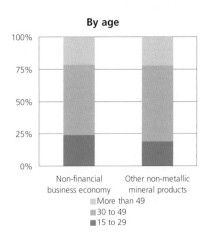

Source: Eurostat (LFS)

Table 6.10

Production of ceramic goods and clay products (CPA Groups 26.2 to 26.4), EU-27, 2006 (1)

	Prodcom code	Production value (EUR million)	Volume of sold production (thousands)	Unit of volume
Glazed stoneware flags and paving; hearth or wall tiles; with a face of > 90 cm²	26.30.10.73	4 004	591 759	m²
Non-refractory clay roofing tiles	26.40.12.50	2 416	3 219 650	units
Glazed ceramic flags and paving, hearth or wall tiles excluding double tiles of the spaltplatten type, stoneware, earthenware or fine pottery flags, paving or tiles with a face of not > 90 cm²	26.30.10.79	2 176	289 093	m²
Glazed earthenware or fine pottery ceramic flags and paving; hearth or wall tiles; with a face of > 90 cm²	26.30.10.75	2 020	364 263	m²
Ceramic sinks... and other sanitary fixtures, of porcelain of china	26.22.10.30	1 864	51 007	units
Porcelain or china tableware and kitchenware (excluding electro-thermic apparatus, coffee or spice mills with metal working parts)	26.21.11.30	1 190	270 084	kg
Refractory cements; mortars; concretes and similar compositions (including refractory plastics, ramming mixes, gunning mixes) (excluding carbonaceous pastes)	26.26.13.00	1 098	2 589 879	kg
Refractory ceramic constructional goods containing >50 % of MgO, CaO or Cr₂O₃ including bricks, blocks and tiles excluding goods of siliceous fossil meals or earths, tubing and piping	26.26.12.10	720	1 119 220	kg
Refractory bricks, blocks..., weight > 50 % Al₂O₃ and/or SiO₂: others	26.26.12.37	573	432 634	kg
Ceramic tableware, other household articles : earthenware or fine pottery	26.21.12.50	500	185 545	kg

(1) Estimated.
Source: Eurostat (PRODCOM)

There were contrasting developments in the production indices of the three NACE groups that comprise ceramic and clay products manufacturing (see Figure 6.4). There was a sharp downward trend in the output of ceramic goods other than for construction purposes in the EU-27 between 1996 and 2006 (an average decline of 1.6 % per annum). From 1999 there was also a steady decline in the output of ceramic tiles and flags, with an average decline of 0.5 % per annum over the ten years to 2006. The development of the production index for clay construction products, however, was similar to the development for other non-metallic mineral products as a whole, albeit with a sharper rate of increase in output between 1996 and 2000, a greater fall in 2001 and 2002, and a more pronounced rebound through until 2006.

Figure 6.4

Manufacture of ceramic goods and clay products (NACE Groups 26.2 to 26.4) Evolution of main indicators, EU-27 (2000=100)

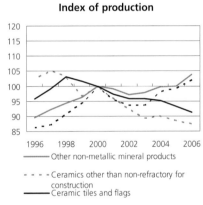
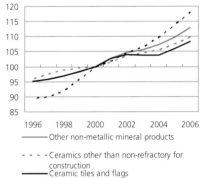

Source: Eurostat (STS)

COSTS, PRODUCTIVITY AND PROFITABILITY

Investment in the ceramic goods and clay products sector accounted for 6.4 % of total expenditure in 2004, a similar proportion to that across other non-metallic mineral products as a whole: this investment share reached 10.7 % in the manufacturing of clay construction products subsector, almost twice the share recorded in the other activities within the sector. Personnel costs within the ceramic goods and clay products sector accounted for a little more than one quarter (26.3 %) of the total expenditure (gross operating and tangible investment expenditure) in 2004, considerably more than the share (16.4 %) across the non-financial business economy as a whole, despite the fact that average personnel costs of EUR 26 000 per employee were a little less than the non-financial business economy average.

The apparent labour productivity of those working in the manufacture of ceramic goods and clay products in the EU-27 was EUR 40 000 per person in 2004 and the wage adjusted labour productivity ratio was 150 %, both measures of productivity being similar to the averages for the non-financial business economy. However, wage adjusted labour productivity ranged from 130.0 % for the manufacture of ceramic goods other than for construction purposes to 197.6 % for the manufacture of clay construction products.

The gross operating rate in ceramic goods and clay products manufacturing was 14.5 % in 2004, although this ratio rose as high as 22.2 % for the manufacture of clay construction products subsector.

EXTERNAL TRADE

The EU-27 had a trade surplus of EUR 3.4 billion in the trade of ceramic and clay products (CPA Groups 26.2 to 26.4) in 2006. Trade surpluses were recorded in 2006 for each of the three CPA groups that comprise ceramic and clay products, with that for ceramic tiles and flags (CPA Group 26.3) being by far the largest at EUR 2.4 billion, although the strongest widening of trade surplus concerned ceramic goods other than for construction (CPA Group 26.2).

6.3: CEMENT AND CONCRETE

This subchapter covers the manufacture of cement, lime and plaster (NACE Group 26.5), as well as the manufacture of articles made from concrete, plaster and cement (NACE Group 26.6).

The production of cement is a two-step process that involves producing a „clinker" from raw materials (mainly limestone and clay) that are heated within a kiln that is set at an intense heat, before being cooled at 100°C – 200°C. In a second step, gypsum and sometimes additions like coal fly ash are added to the clinker and ground to a fine cement powder. Concrete is a solid material that is made of cement, mixed with water, aggregates, sand and usually some admixtures. The products that are manufactured by cement and concrete manufacturers range from construction products that are prefabricated or precast, to mortars and fibre cements (see Table 6.12).

STRUCTURAL PROFILE

There were 26 000 enterprises in the cement and concrete manufacturing sector (NACE Groups 26.5 and 26.6) across the EU-27 which generated EUR 31.0 billion of value added in 2004 (see Table 6.11), representing 42.5 % of the value added generated by the activities of other non-metallic mineral products manufacturing (NACE Division 26). In terms of employment, the sector was smaller; the 530 000 workers in the sector across the EU-27 represented one in every three (33.1 %) workers in other non-metallic mineral products manufacturing activities in 2004.

Table 6.11

Manufacture of cement, lime and plaster; manufacture of articles of concrete, plaster, cement (NACE Groups 26.5 and 26.6)
Structural profile, EU-27, 2004

	No. of enterprises (thousands)	Turnover (EUR million)	Value added (EUR million)	Employment (thousands)
Cement and concrete (1)	26.0	94 000	31 000	530.0
Cement, lime and plaster	1.2	22 616	9 316	86.4
Articles of concrete, plaster, cement (2)	25.0	70 000	22 000	440.1

(1) Rounded estimates based on non-confidential data.
(2) Rounded estimates based on non-confidential data; employment, 2003.
Source: Eurostat (SBS)

Among the Member States for which data are available [(10)], the cement and concrete manufacturing sector in Germany was the largest, contributing 16.3 % of the value added generated by the sector across the whole of the EU-27 in 2004. Other large contributions came from Italy (14.8 %), Spain (14.2 %), the United Kingdom (12.6 %) and France (12.1 %). Romania and Bulgaria were relatively specialised in the manufacture of cement and concrete, the contribution of sectoral value added to the value added generated across their respective non-financial business economies being a little more than double the average across the EU 27. In the absence of structural business statistics for recent years, Greece and Cyprus also appear to be relatively specialised on the basis of their exports (see the section on external trade below).

_____
[(10)] Slovenia, 2003; Denmark, Estonia, Ireland, Greece, Latvia, Luxembourg, Malta, the Netherlands and Austria, not available.

Between 1996 and 2000 there were similar rates of growth in the production indices of cement, lime and plaster and of articles of concrete, plaster and cement. Since 2000, however, the production indices for these two activities have diverged. Despite a contraction in output in 2002, there was further growth in the output of cement, lime and plaster through until 2006 (see Figure 6.5), at a similar average annual rate of increase to that recorded between 1996 and 2000. In contrast, the production index of articles of concrete, plaster and cement did not exceed the output level of 2000 until 2006, after a contraction in output in 2005 had stifled the partial recovery witnessed in 2003 and 2004 from the relative low in 2002.

There were steady increases in the domestic output price indices of both cement, lime and plaster manufacturing (an average 2.4 % per annum, despite a slight decline in 2003) and articles of concrete, plaster and cement (an average 1.9 % per annum), at slightly faster rates than the average (1.8 % per annum) for other non-metallic mineral products manufacturing.

Table 6.12

Production of selected products - cement, lime and plaster; articles of concrete, plaster and cement (CPA Groups 26.5 and 26.6), EU-27, 2006 (1)

	Prodcom code	Production value (EUR million)	Volume of sold production (thousands)	Unit of volume
Ready-mixed concrete	26.63.10.00	26 336	884 225 928	kg
Grey Portland cement (including blended cement)	26.51.12.30	17 320	216 023 151	kg
Prefabricated structural components for building, ..., of cement ...	26.61.12.00	14 673	108 133 935	kg
Tiles; flagstones and similar articles of cement; concrete or artificial stone (excluding building blocks and bricks)	26.61.11.50	8 806	75 566 235	kg
Pipes and other articles of cement, concrete or artificial stone, and accessories	26.60.13.Z1	4 430	19 957 566	kg
Building blocks and bricks of cement; concrete or artificial stone	26.61.11.30	4 391	94 186 373	kg
Articles of cement; concrete or artificial stone for non-constructional purposes (including vases; flower pots; architectural or garden ornaments; statues and ornamental goods)	26.66.12.00	2 815	8 778 571	kg
Boards, sheets, panels, tiles, similar articles of plaster/compositions based on plaster, faced/reinforced with paper/paperboard only, excluding articles agglom. with plaster, ornamented	26.62.10.50	2 785	1 534 504	m²
Prefabricated buildings of cement	26.61.20.00	2 623	-	-
Quicklime	26.52.10.33	2 443	21 665 092	kg

(1) Estimated.
Source: Eurostat (PRODCOM)

Figure 6.5 _____

Manufacture of cement, lime and plaster; manufacture of articles of concrete, plaster, cement (NACE Groups 26.5 and 26.6)
Evolution of main indicators, EU-27 (2000=100)

Index of production

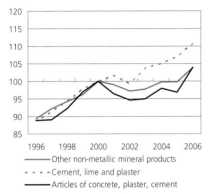

———— Other non-metallic mineral products
- - - - Cement, lime and plaster
———— Articles of concrete, plaster, cement

Index of domestic output prices

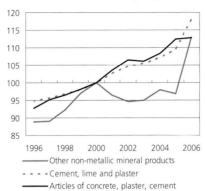

———— Other non-metallic mineral products
- - - - Cement, lime and plaster
———— Articles of concrete, plaster, cement

Source: Eurostat (STS)

The gross operating surplus of the cement and concrete manufacturing sector was the equivalent of 15.0 % of turnover in 2004, a little higher than the average for other non-metallic mineral products manufacturing and also higher, therefore, than the average across the non-financial business economy (11.0 %). Within the sector, the gross operating rate of the cement, lime and plaster manufacturing subsector was 26.2 %, the fifth highest level of profitability (using this measure) among the NACE groups for which 2004 data are available.

EXTERNAL TRADE

In view of the contribution (42.5 %) made by the cement and concrete manufacturing sector to the value added of other non-metallic mineral products as a whole (see the structural profile above), the relatively small share (9.3 %) of EU-27 exports of cement and concrete (CPA Groups 26.5 and 26.6) in the value of total exports of other non-metallic mineral products (CPA Division 26) points to the fact that much of the supply and demand for cement and concrete products is local. EU-27 exports of cement and concrete were valued at EUR 1.6 billion in 2006. There was a relatively small trade surplus of EUR 444 million in 2006, although there was a trade deficit of EUR 337 million for cement, lime and plaster (CPA Group 26.5).

Exports of cement and concrete from Germany (both intra- and extra-EU trade combined) were of greater value than any other Member State, accounting for a little over one fifth (21.9 %) of the trade in these products by the EU-27 Member States combined. However, Greece and Cyprus were the most specialised Member States in exporting cement and concrete, as these products accounted for 1.2 % of their respective industrial exports, much higher than the 0.2 % average for the EU-27 Member States combined.

COSTS, PRODUCTIVITY AND PROFITABILITY

Investment expenditure in the cement, lime and plaster subsector (NACE Group 26.5) represented 9.7 % of total expenditure in 2004, a much higher proportion than the 5.9 % for the articles made from concrete, plaster and cement manufacturing subsector (NACE Group 26.6). Personnel costs as a proportion of total expenditure for both subsectors (see Table 6.13) were lower than the share for the manufacture of other non-metallic mineral products as a whole (22.0 %), despite the fact that average personnel costs in the cement, lime and plaster subsector (EUR 39 500 per employee) and in the manufacture of articles of concrete, plaster and cement manufacturing subsector (EUR 30 000 per employee) were higher than the average (EUR 28 500 per employee) across other non-metallic mineral products manufacturing activities as a whole.

The apparent labour productivity of those working in the EU-27's cement and concrete manufacturing sector was EUR 58 000 per person employed in 2004, which was 26.1 % higher than the average for those within other non-metallic mineral products manufacturing. Within the sector, the apparent labour productivity of those working in the manufacture of cement, lime and plaster subsector (EUR 107 800 per person) was the fourth highest among all industrial NACE groups for which 2004 data are available and more than double the level of apparent labour productivity of those working in the manufacture of articles of concrete, plaster and cement subsector (EUR 49 000 per person). The wage adjusted labour productivity ratio for the cement, lime and plaster manufacturing subsector (272.8 %) was also significantly higher than that for the manufacture of articles of concrete, plaster and cement subsector (170.0 %).

Table 6.13 _____

Manufacture of cement, lime and plaster; manufacture of articles of concrete, plaster, cement (NACE Groups 26.5 and 26.6)
Total expenditure, EU-27, 2004

	Value (EUR million)				Share (% of total expenditure)			
	Total expenditure	Purchases of goods and services	Personnel costs	Investment in tangible goods	Purchases of goods and services	Personnel costs	Investment in tangible goods
Cement and concrete (1)	85 700	64 000	16 000	5 700	74.7	18.7	6.7
Cement, lime and plaster	18 630	13 441	3 385	1 804	72.1	18.2	9.7
Articles of concrete, plaster, cement (1)	68 000	51 000	13 000	4 000	75.0	19.1	5.9

(1) Rounded estimates based on non-confidential data.
Source: Eurostat (SBS)

6.4: STONE AND MISCELLANEOUS NON-METALLIC MINERAL PRODUCTS

This subchapter covers separately the activities of cutting, shaping and finishing stone (NACE Group 26.7), hereafter referred to as the working of stone, and the manufacture of other non-metallic mineral products (NACE Group 26.8), hereafter referred to as the manufacture of miscellaneous non-metallic mineral products; this latter group includes the production of abrasive products, non-metallic mineral yarns, and mineral insulating materials (be they for heat or sound insulation).

WORKING OF STONE

There were 33 600 enterprises engaged within the activities of cutting, shaping and finishing stone (NACE Group 26.7), together they generated EUR 5.7 billion of value added across the EU-27 in 2004 (see Table 6.14), accounting for 7.8 % of the value added generated by the manufacturing activities of other non-metallic mineral products (NACE Division 26). However, the 190 000 people employed in the working of stone in the EU-27 represented a much larger proportion of the other non-metallic mineral products workforce (11.9 %).

Italy accounted for the largest share (29.1 %) of the value added created by the working of stone across the EU-27 in 2004, the next largest contributions coming from Spain (22.3 %), and Germany (13.7 %). Among the Member States for which information was available [11], Portugal was the most specialised Member State in this activity, followed by Italy and Spain, the contributions of working of stone to their respective non-financial business economies (NACE Sections C to I and K) being two and a half to three and a half times the EU-27 average.

---
[11] The Czech Republic, Ireland, Greece, Cyprus, Luxembourg and Malta, not available.

During the ten years through to 2006, the production index for the working of stone reached a high plateau in the years from 1996 to 1998, after which there was fluctuation along a downward trend (see Figure 6.6). There was a steep decline in output in 1999, with further declines between 2002 and 2004 more than offsetting the slight recovery in output in both 2000 and 2001. Although there were further rebounds in 2005 and 2006, the level of output in 2006 remained lower than the level of 2001.

Between 1996 and 2000, the upward evolution of the domestic output price index for the working of stone was similar to that for miscellaneous non-metallic mineral products manufacturing. However, the index for the working of stone subsequently continued to rise between 2001 and 2004, in contrast to the price index for the miscellaneous non-metallic mineral products manufacturing which remained relatively unchanged. The domestic output price index for miscellaneous non-metallic mineral products manufacturing once again started to increase in 2005 and 2006, while prices for the working of stone contracted in 2006.

The EU-27's trade surplus in monumental and building stone products (CPA Group 26.7) narrowed for the fifth consecutive year to a value of EUR 290 million in 2006 (down from EUR 1.1 billion in 2001). This narrowing of the trade surplus was principally due to a rising level of imports rather than a decline in the value of exports to non-member countries. The value of imports reached EUR 1.2 billion in 2006, almost half (48.5 %) of which were from China. Trade surpluses (intra- and extra-EU trade combined) in monumental and building stone products were limited to six Member States, among which those of Italy (EUR 1.5 billion) and Spain (EUR 0.5 billion) were by far the largest.

MANUFACTURE OF MISCELLANEOUS NON-METALLIC MINERAL PRODUCTS

The activities of miscellaneous non-metallic mineral products manufacturing (NACE Group 26.8), with some 3 500 enterprises which generated EUR 4.9 billion of value added across the EU-27 in 2004, accounting for 6.7 % of the value added generated by other non-metallic mineral products manufacturing (NACE Division 26). A little less than one third (31.7 %) of the value added generated by miscellaneous non-metallic mineral products manufacturing across the EU-27 as a whole came from Germany, the next largest contributions coming from Italy (11.2 %) and the United Kingdom (11.0 %). However, the relative contribution of this activity to the value added of the non-financial business economy was greatest in Slovakia (0.5 %), almost five times the average across the EU-27.

In comparison to the production index for other non-metallic mineral products manufacturing as a whole, the output of miscellaneous non-metallic mineral products manufacturing was somewhat more irregular during the period 1996 to 2006 (see Figure 6.6). Output in the miscellaneous non-metallic mineral products manufacturing rose sharply in 2001, since when the development of both production indices has been more similar.

The EU-27's trade surplus in miscellaneous non-metallic mineral products (CPA Group 26.8) widened further to EUR 766 million in 2006, with the increase in the value of exports outweighing the increase in the value of imports from non-member countries. Germany recorded the largest trade surplus (EUR 731 million, intra- and extra-EU trade combined), despite being the largest importer, accounting for a little under one fifth (19.2 %) of the imports of these products by EU-27 Member States.

Table 6.14

Cutting, shaping and finishing of stone; manufacture of other non-metallic mineral products (NACE Groups 26.7 and 26.8)
Structural profile, EU-27, 2004 (1)

	No. of enterprises (thousands)	Turnover (EUR million)	Value added (EUR million)	Employment (thousands)
Stone and miscellaneous non-metallic mineral products	37.2	33 000	10 600	290.0
Cutting, shaping and finishing of ornamental and building stone	33.6	15 300	5 700	190.0
Other non-metallic mineral products	3.5	18 000	4 900	96.0

(1) Rounded estimates based on non-confidential data.
Source: Eurostat (SBS)

Table 6.15

Production of selected products - stone and miscellaneous non-metallic mineral products (CPA Groups 26.7 and 26.8), EU-27, 2006 (1)

	Prodcom code	Production value (EUR million)	Volume of sold production (thousands)	Unit of volume
Bituminous mixtures based on natural and artificial aggregate and bitumen or natural asphalt as a binder	26.82.13.00	3 516	76 109 267	kg
Worked monumental or building stone and articles thereof, of granite excluding tiles, cubes and similar articles, largest surface area is < 7 cm², setts, kerbstones and flagstones	26.70.12.60	3 107	5 773 805	kg
Roofing or water-proofing felts based on bitumen (in rolls)	26.82.12.53	1 855	947 209	m²
Slag wool; rock wool and similar mineral wools and mixtures thereof; in bulk; sheets or rolls	26.82.16.10	1 836	2 157 914	kg
Mixtures and articles of heat/sound-insulating materials n.e.c.	26.82.16.30	1 339	1 936 504	kg
Worked monumental or building stone and articles thereof (excluding of calcareous stone; granite or slate, tiles; cubes and similar articles; of which the largest surface area is < 7 cm²)	26.70.12.80	827	3 709 089	kg
Natural stone setts; kerbstones and flagstones (excluding of slate)	26.70.12.10	744	3 542 603	kg
Articles of stone or other mineral substances, n.e.c.	26.82.16.90	674	5 653 007	kg
Products based on bitumen (excluding in rolls)	26.82.12.90	558	7 908 983	kg
Millstones, grindstones, grinding wheels and the like, without frameworks, of reinforced synthetic/artificial resin, with binder excluding millstones and grindstones for milling, grinding, pulping	26.81.11.30	409	118 706	kg

(1) Estimated.
Source: Eurostat (PRODCOM)

Figure 6.6

Cutting, shaping and finishing of stone; manufacture of other non-metallic mineral products (NACE Groups 26.7 and 26.8)
Evolution of main indicators, EU-27 (2000=100)

Index of production

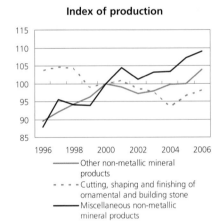

Index of domestic output prices

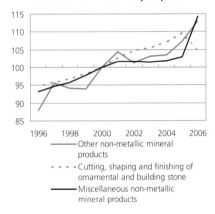

——— Other non-metallic mineral products
- - - - Cutting, shaping and finishing of ornamental and building stone
——— Miscellaneous non-metallic mineral products

Source: Eurostat (STS)

Table 6.16

Manufacture of other non-metallic mineral products (NACE Subsection DI)
Main indicators, 2004

	EU-27	BE	BG	CZ	DK	DE	EE	IE	EL	ES	FR	IT	CY	LV	LT
No. of enterprises (thousands)	101.5	1.5	1.0	6.8	0.7	9.3	0.2	0.3	:	11.7	9.2	26.5	0.3	0.3	0.5
Turnover (EUR million)	211 281	7 513	670	4 460	2 737	38 557	307	2 066	:	29 336	27 063	39 541	430	191	273
Production (EUR million)	200 000	7 344	636	4 231	2 538	35 282	286	1 919	:	28 265	24 948	39 051	426	183	268
Value added (EUR million)	72 875	2 328	193	1 588	1 067	13 235	105	766	:	10 116	8 427	12 609	157	67	93
Gross operating surplus (EUR million)	29 943	875	128	908	308	3 516	60	361	:	4 807	2 761	5 756	86	41	42
Purchases of goods & services (EUR million)	140 025	5 187	501	2 995	1 716	25 291	208	1 291	:	19 952	18 272	27 497	285	134	184
Personnel costs (EUR million)	42 932	1 453	65	683	759	9 719	45	405	:	5 309	5 666	6 853	71	26	52
Investment in tangible goods (EUR million)	12 377	275	109	284	223	1 628	22	177	:	2 067	1 193	2 408	34	47	44
Employment (thousands) (1)	1 600	33	24	81	18	248	5	11	:	192	144	249	3	5	10
Apparent labour prod. (EUR thousand) (1)	46.0	70.1	8.1	19.6	60.9	53.3	21.5	70.7	:	52.8	58.6	50.5	48.8	12.3	9.1
Average personnel costs (EUR thousand) (1)	28.5	46.1	2.8	9.3	44.3	40.2	9.3	37.9	:	28.7	40.2	32.6	22.9	4.8	5.2
Wage adjusted labour productivity (%) (1)	160.0	151.9	286.7	211.1	137.6	132.5	230.8	186.6	:	184.0	146.0	155.3	212.8	254.2	175.5
Gross operating rate (%)	14.2	11.6	19.1	20.4	11.3	9.1	19.6	17.5	:	16.4	10.2	14.6	20.0	21.4	15.3
Investment / employment (EUR thousand) (1)	8.0	8.3	4.6	3.5	12.8	6.6	4.6	16.3	:	10.8	8.3	9.7	10.4	8.7	4.3

	LU (2)	HU	MT	NL	AT	PL	PT	RO	SI	SK	FI	SE	UK	NO
No. of enterprises (thousands)	0.0	2.6	:	1.6	1.5	11.4	4.7	2.4	0.5	0.3	0.9	1.8	5.0	0.8
Turnover (EUR million)	681	1 976	:	6 041	5 830	6 572	4 837	1 571	732	1 077	2 753	3 115	20 013	2 084
Production (EUR million)	651	1 676	:	5 523	5 466	6 183	4 525	1 564	677	1 044	2 647	2 883	19 042	1 975
Value added (EUR million)	230	586	:	2 093	2 468	2 381	1 675	531	252	332	1 002	1 030	8 344	701
Gross operating surplus (EUR million)	90	301	:	767	935	1 506	758	323	100	169	406	268	3 927	220
Purchases of goods & services (EUR million)	448	1 408	:	3 944	3 564	4 328	3 253	1 135	481	758	1 815	2 130	11 549	1 418
Personnel costs (EUR million)	140	285	:	1 326	1 533	876	917	208	152	163	596	762	4 417	480
Investment in tangible goods (EUR million)	154	260	:	241	331	609	416	319	53	181	142	163	966	105
Employment (thousands) (3)	3	31	:	30	36	137	61	71	10	22	16	20	126	10
Apparent labour prod. (EUR thousand) (3)	70.4	18.9	:	68.7	68.8	17.3	27.3	7.4	24.4	14.9	62.6	51.0	66.2	68.6
Average personnel costs (EUR thousand) (3)	43.2	9.6	:	45.9	44.0	7.1	15.4	2.9	14.4	7.3	37.8	44.1	35.8	48.2
Wage adjusted labour productivity (%) (3)	163.0	197.0	:	149.7	156.5	245.5	177.5	253.6	169.6	203.8	165.4	115.5	184.6	142.3
Gross operating rate (%)	13.2	15.3	:	12.7	16.0	22.9	15.7	20.6	13.7	15.7	14.7	8.6	19.6	10.6
Investment / employment (EUR thousand) (3)	47.2	8.4	:	7.9	9.2	4.4	6.8	4.5	3.6	8.1	8.9	8.1	7.7	10.3

(1) EU-27, rounded estimate based on non-confidential data.
(2) 2003.
(3) Slovenia, 2003.
Source: Eurostat (SBS)

Metals and metal products

The EU-27 is largely dependent on imports of ore and concentrates for steel, ferro-alloys and non-ferrous metals production; according to the Directorate-General for Enterprise and Industry, the EU had a dependency rate of 83 % for iron ore (a raw material for steel), 74 % for copper ore, and 76 % for lead ore in 2003 by way of example. This dependency reflects, among other things, the EU's geology, the exhaustion of certain deposits over time and the absence of certain minerals. Domestic supply constraints have been magnified by the strong growth in international demand (largely driven by the industrialisation of countries such as China and India) that has sent prices for most raw materials soaring. As metal is a fundamental material for many manufacturing activities (in transport equipment and chemicals manufacturing, by way of example) and the construction sector, the issue of whether the EU's metals and metal products enterprises will be able to secure supply at affordable prices has clear downstream consequences. These concerns of access to raw materials are being considered by the High-Level Group (HLG) on Competitiveness, Energy and the Environment in 2007. Furthermore, the EU's Competitiveness Council called in May 2007 for further actions in industrial policy to deal with raw materials supply to industry as well as appropriate measures for cost-effective, reliable and environmentally responsible access to and exploitation of natural resources.

NACE Divisions 27 and 28 cover the manufacture of basic metals and fabricated metal products (except machinery and equipment, see Chapter 8).

The manufacture of basic metals (NACE Division 27) includes activities such as the manufacture of iron, steel and ferro-alloys, as well as basic precious and non-ferrous metals; it also includes first processing stages of metal manufacturing (such as the manufacture of tubes, bars, strips, wires, and sheets of metal, as well as casting). The downstream activity of the manufacture of fabricated metal products (NACE Division 28) covers the production of structural metal products; boilers, metal containers and steam generators; forging, pressing, stamping and roll forming of metal; the treatment and coating of metal and general mechanical engineering (such as turning, milling, or welding); the manufacture of cutlery, tools and general hardware; and the manufacture of other fabricated metal products (such as metal drums, metal packaging, wire products, and household articles of metal).

Note that there are no external trade statistics for a number of industrial services covered in this chapter, namely foundry work services (CPA Group 27.5), forging, pressing, stamping and roll forming metal services (CPA Group 28.4) and treatment and coating of metal services and general mechanical engineering services (CPA Group 28.5).

NACE
27:    manufacture of basic metals;
27.1: manufacture of basic iron and steel and of ferro-alloys;
27.2: manufacture of tubes;
27.3: other first processing of iron and steel;
27.4: manufacture of basic precious and non-ferrous metals;
27.5: casting of metals;
28:    manufacture of fabricated metal products, except machinery and equipment;
28.1: manufacture of structural metal products;
28.2: manufacture of tanks, reservoirs and containers of metal; manufacture of central heating radiators and boilers;
28.3: manufacture of steam generators, except central heating hot water boilers;
28.4: forging, pressing, stamping and roll forming of metal; powder metallurgy;
28.5: treatment and coating of metals; general mechanical engineering;
28.6: manufacture of cutlery, tools and general hardware;
28.7: manufacture of other fabricated metal products.

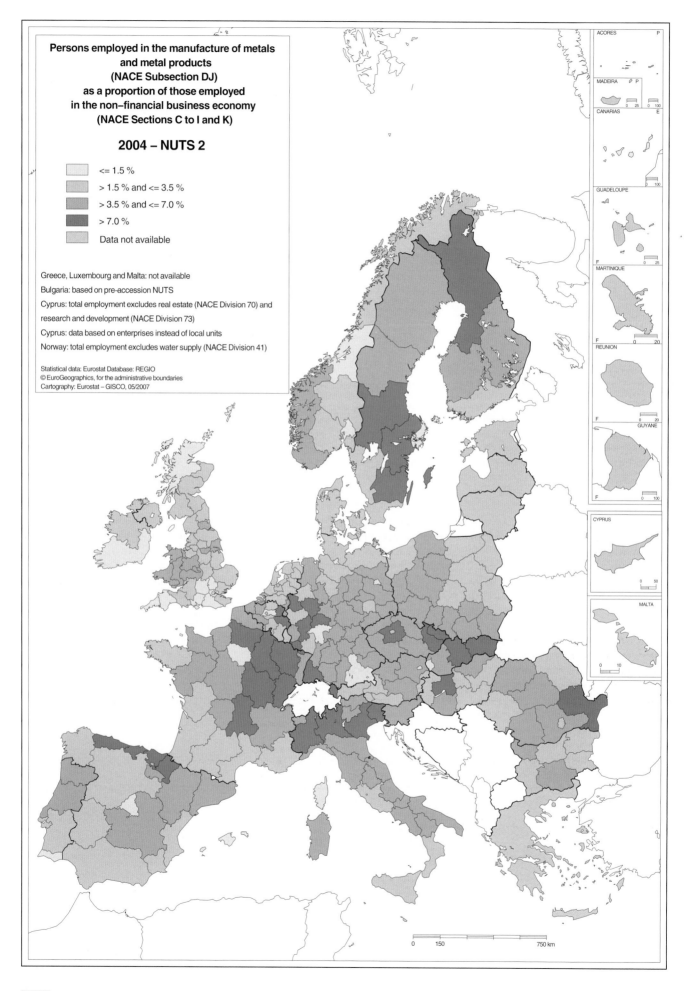

Persons employed in the manufacture of metals
and metal products
(NACE Subsection DJ)
as a proportion of those employed
in the non–financial business economy
(NACE Sections C to I and K)

2004 – NUTS 2

- <= 1.5 %
- > 1.5 % and <= 3.5 %
- > 3.5 % and <= 7.0 %
- > 7.0 %
- Data not available

Greece, Luxembourg and Malta: not available

Bulgaria: based on pre-accession NUTS

Cyprus: total employment excludes real estate (NACE Division 70) and
research and development (NACE Division 73)

Cyprus: data based on enterprises instead of local units

Norway: total employment excludes water supply (NACE Division 41)

Statistical data: Eurostat Database: REGIO
© EuroGeographics, for the administrative boundaries
Cartography: Eurostat – GISCO, 05/2007

Table 7.1 _____

Manufacture of basic metals and fabricated metal products (NACE Subsection DJ)
Structural profile, EU-27, 2004

	No. of enterprises		Turnover		Value added		Employment	
	(thousands)	(% of total)	(EUR million)	(% of total)	(EUR million)	(% of total)	(thousands)	(% of total)
Basic metals and fabricated metal products	398.6	100.0	698 911	100.0	212 567	100.0	4 991.4	100.0
First processing of ferrous metals (1)	6.0	1.5	187 000	26.8	41 000	19.3	630.0	12.6
Basic precious and non-ferrous metals	3.3	0.8	76 646	11.0	14 329	6.7	228.3	4.6
Casting of metals	6.5	1.6	31 294	4.5	10 924	5.1	273.7	5.5
Structural metal products	107.4	27.0	103 944	14.9	33 894	15.9	1 029.6	20.6
Boilers, metal containers and steam generators (1)	14.0	3.5	36 838	5.3	12 463	5.9	306.6	6.1
Other metal processing (1)	154.0	38.6	134 749	19.3	52 920	24.9	1 378.0	27.6
Miscellaneous fabricated metal products (1)	107.2	26.9	130 000	18.6	46 000	21.6	1 150.0	23.0

(1) Rounded estimates based on non-confidential data.
Source: Eurostat (SBS)

Table 7.2 _____

Manufacture of basic metals and fabricated metal products (NACE Subsection DJ)
Structural profile: ranking of top five Member States, 2004

			Share of non-financial business economy			
Rank	Value added (EUR million) (1)	Employment (thousands) (1)	No. of enterprises (2)	Turnover (2)	Value added (2)	Employment (2)
1	Germany (56 424)	Germany (1 041.2)	Slovenia (5.1 %)	Luxembourg (18.0 %)	Slovakia (9.6 %)	Slovenia (7.1 %)
2	Italy (36 172)	Italy (839.2)	Czech Republic (4.1 %)	Slovakia (6.9 %)	Slovenia (7.3 %)	Slovakia (6.8 %)
3	France (26 658)	France (553.6)	Slovakia (3.3 %)	Czech Republic (5.8 %)	Czech Republic (6.9 %)	Czech Republic (6.5 %)
4	United Kingdom (21 922)	Spain (433.7)	Italy (2.7 %)	Slovenia (5.8 %)	Italy (6.4 %)	Italy (5.7 %)
5	Spain (18 288)	United Kingdom (427.3)	Portugal (2.6 %)	Italy (5.5 %)	Romania (5.9 %)	Luxembourg (5.6 %)

(1) Greece and Malta, not available; Luxembourg, 2003.
(2) Ireland, Greece, Cyprus and Malta, not available; Luxembourg, 2003.
Source: Eurostat (SBS)

The metals and metal products manufacturing sector is also energy-intensive, particularly in the early, first processing activities. Another key area of policy and enterprise concern, therefore, is the availability of energy at affordable prices (see Chapter 13). The cost profile for those operating in the sector is further influenced by transport costs, environmental issues on emissions reductions, waste, water, and health and safety issues. The importance of innovation for the sector in order to remain competitive has prompted the establishment of a European Technology Platform on Sustainable Mineral Resources and a European Steel Technology Platform as part of the 7th Framework Programme for research, technological development and demonstration activities.

STRUCTURAL PROFILE
The metal and metal products manufacturing sector (NACE Subsection DJ) of the EU-27 had approximately 398 600 enterprises which created EUR 212.6 billion of value added in 2004, the highest contribution (4.2 %) of any industrial (NACE Sections C to E) NACE subsection to the value added of the non-financial business economy (NACE Sections C to I and K) – see Table 7.1. With 5.0 million persons employed in this sector throughout the EU-27 in 2004, metal and metal products

manufacturing was also the biggest industrial employer and accounted for 4.0 % of the non-financial business economy workforce.

Within the metal and metal products sector the largest subsector (in terms of the activity coverage of Subchapters 7.1 to 7.7) was other metal processing (NACE Groups 28.4 and 28.5, Subchapter 7.6), contributing about one quarter of value added and employment; the manufacture of miscellaneous fabricated metal products (NACE Groups 28.6 and 28.7, Subchapter 7.7) contributed a little more than one fifth of value added and employment; the first processing of ferrous metal (NACE Groups 27.1 to 27.3) generated a little under one fifth of value added but a much smaller proportion (12.6 %) of employment - see Subchapter 7.1; and the manufacture of structural metal products (NACE Group 28.1, Subchapter 7.4) accounted for a little over one fifth of employment but a lower proportion (15.9 %) of value added. The other subsectors presented in Subchapters 7.2, 7.3 and 7.5 each accounted for less than 7 % of sectoral employment and value added.

Germany was by far the leading producer of metals and metal products in 2004, generating EUR 56.4 billion of value added, representing more than a quarter (26.5 %) of the EU-27's

total, and employed 1.0 million persons, which corresponded to slightly more than a fifth (20.9 %) of the sectoral employment throughout the EU-27. Despite this high German contribution, the metals and metal products manufacturing sector was only the fourth largest industrial NACE subsection in value added terms in Germany, while it was the second largest in terms of industrial employment. Italy, France, the United Kingdom and Spain were the next largest producers (see Table 7.2), who together with Germany accounted for exactly three-quarters of the value added generated throughout the EU-27 in 2004.

Almost one-tenth (9.6 %) of the value added generated by the non-financial business economy as a whole in Slovakia came from its metal and metal products manufacturing sector, making it the most specialised Member State in this sector by this measure; the 0.6 % share of EU-27 value added generated by Slovakia in this sector was the highest contribution by Slovakia to the EU-27 total in any industrial NACE subsection in 2004. The metals and metal products manufacturing sector also contributed significant proportions of the value added generated across national non-financial business economies in Slovenia (7.3 %) and the Czech Republic (6.9 %).

Figure 7.1

Manufacture of basic metals and fabricated metal products (NACE Subsection DJ)
Evolution of main indicators, EU-27 (2000=100)

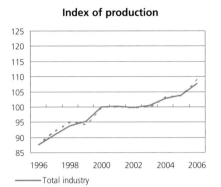

Index of production

Total industry
- - - - Basic metals and fabricated metal products

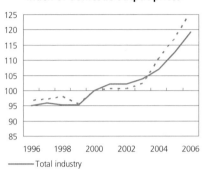

Index of domestic output prices

Total industry
- - - - Basic metals and fabricated metal products

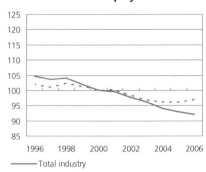

Index of employment

Total industry
- - - - Basic metals and fabricated metal products

Source: Eurostat (STS)

The map on page 138 shows, on a regional basis, the relative size of the metal and metal products manufacturing sector within the non-financial business economy in terms of employment. More than one in every seven workers within the non-financial business economy were employed in the metal and metal products manufacturing sector in Arnsberg (Germany), Východné Slovensko (Slovakia) and Norra Mellansverige (Sweden) in 2004, making them the most specialised regions (at the level of detail shown in the map). There were many regions across the Czech Republic, Germany, Spain, France, Italy, Slovakia and Sweden that were also specialised in this sector.

The development of the production index for metals and metal products manufacturing for the EU-27 during the ten years through until 2006 was very similar to the development of output for industry as a whole (see Figure 7.1), although the index of metals and metal products manufacturing tended to have somewhat larger fluctuations both when expanding and contracting. The average rates of growth in output over the ten years between 1996 and 2006 was 2.2 % per annum for metals and metal products manufacturing compared to 2.1 % per annum for industry as a whole.

Within metal and metal products manufacturing, the average rate of growth (2.6 % per annum) in the output of the manufacture of fabricated metal products (NACE Division 28) during the ten years through until 2006 was much stronger than that (1.5 %) for the manufacture of basic metals (NACE Division 27). Among the dozen NACE groups that comprise metal and metal products manufacturing, the strongest rates of growth in output concerned the two other metal processing activities (see Subchapter 7.6); the annual average rate of growth in the output of forging, pressing, stamping and roll forming of metals (NACE Group 28.4) was 4.4 % per annum and that of the treatment and coating of metal and general mechanical engineering (NACE Group 28.5) was 4.2 % per annum.

The development of the EU-27's domestic output price index for metals and metal products manufacturing during the ten years between 1996 and 2006 reflected three patterns; firstly, there were relatively stable prices between 1996 and 1999, secondly, there was a rise in 2000 to a new plateau that was maintained through 2001 and 2002, and finally there was a strong upsurge in prices through until 2006. The rise in the domestic output price index between 1996 and 2002 was limited to 4.0 % but the index rose by 23.0 % in the last three years of the period under review, partly reflecting price increases for raw materials and energy. The rise in the domestic output price of basic metals was particularly strong after 2002 (a rise of 42.8 %), with the price increase in 2006 being even higher than 2005 in large part due to the surge (up 36.7 %) in the price of basic precious and non-ferrous metals (NACE Group 27.4).

In comparison to industry as a whole, the decline in the index of employment for metals and metal products manufacturing during the period between 1996 and 2006 was rather moderate (an average decline of 0.5 % per year compared with an average fall of 1.3 % per year for industry). Within metals and metal products manufacturing, however, there were net employment gains in the manufacture of fabricated metal products. Indeed, this NACE division was one of only a few industrial divisions for which the index of employment rose during the most recent ten-year period for which data are available, with an average increase of 0.5 % per annum.

Small and medium-sized enterprises (SMEs), which employ less than 250 persons, generated the majority (61.6 %) of value added in the EU-27's metals and metal products manufacturing sector in 2004. Within the sector, however, there was a distinct difference between the dominance of large enterprises (that employ 250 persons or more) in the manufacture of basic metals (accounting for 74.7 % of the value added generated by this activity) and the dominance of SMEs in the manufacture of fabricated metal products (accounting for 77.5 % of value added). This dichotomy placed these two subsectors at odds with the average situation across the non-financial business economy, for which SMEs contributed a relatively small majority (57.0 %) of value added – see Figure 7.2. These structural differences were also apparent in terms of relative shares of employment.

Figure 7.2 _____

Manufacture of basic metals and fabricated metal products (NACE Subsection DJ)
Share of value added by enterprise size class, EU-27, 2004

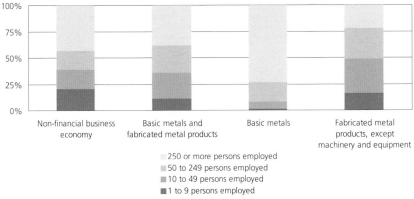

250 or more persons employed
50 to 249 persons employed
10 to 49 persons employed
1 to 9 persons employed

Source: Eurostat (SBS)

EMPLOYMENT CHARACTERISTICS

A little more than eight in every ten workers (84.4 %) within the metals and metal products manufacturing sector of the EU-27 were male, a much higher share than across the non-financial business economy as a whole (65.0 %) – see Figure 7.3 – a characteristic that was noted across all of the Member States for which information was available [1]. Almost all (94.8 %) of the metals and metal products manufacturing workforce of the EU-27 were in full-time employment, a proportion rather more in keeping with the industrial average (92.4%) than the non-financial business economy average (85.6 %), which was a characteristic generally noted among the Member States. The age profile of the metal and metal products manufacturing workforce of the EU-27 was quite similar to the profile among the whole of the non-financial business economy workforce,

albeit with a slightly lower share of workers aged 15 to 29 and slightly higher proportion of workers aged 50 or more. Among the Member States, the share of workers aged under 30 in the metals and metal products sector was closer to half of the share across the non-financial business economy in Bulgaria, Denmark, Latvia, Luxembourg (2003), Romania and the United Kingdom, generally with the share of workers aged over 50 years being disproportionately high.

The proportion of paid employees among the number of persons employed by the metals and metal products sector was 92.5 % in 2004, a higher proportion than across the non-financial business economy as a whole (86.2 %).

COSTS, PRODUCTIVITY AND PROFITABILITY

As a proportion of total expenditure within the metals and metal products manufacturing sector of the EU-27, tangible investment accounted for a share (4.1 %) that was a little less than that (4.9 %) for the non-financial business economy in 2004. In contrast, the share of total expenditure accounted for by personnel costs in the sector (21.1 %) was notably higher than that across the non-financial business economy (16.4 %) in 2004. In part, this reflected the fact that the average personnel costs of EUR 30 400 per employee in the sector across the EU-27 were about one-tenth higher than the average across the non-financial business economy.

_____
[1] Luxembourg and Malta, not available.

Figure 7.3 _____

Manufacture of basic metals and fabricated metal products (NACE Subsection DJ)
Labour force characteristics, EU-27, 2006

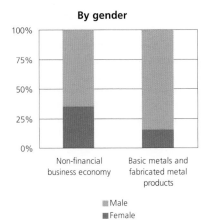 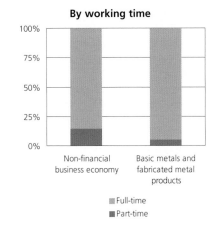 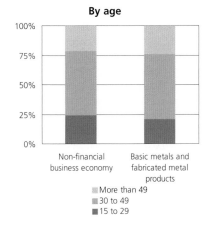

Male / Female | Full-time / Part-time | More than 49 / 30 to 49 / 15 to 29

Source: Eurostat (LFS)

Table 7.3 _____

Manufacture of basic metals and fabricated metal products (NACE Subsection DJ)
Productivity and profitability, EU-27, 2004

	Apparent labour productivity (EUR thousand)	Average personnel costs (EUR thousand)	Wage adjusted labour productivity (%)	Gross operating rate (%)
Basic metals and fabricated metal products	42.6	30.4	140.2	10.3
First processing of ferrous metals (1)	66.0	37.0	180.0	10.3
Basic precious and non-ferrous metals	62.8	40.1	156.4	6.9
Casting of metals	39.9	30.6	130.3	8.7
Structural metal products	32.9	25.2	130.8	10.1
Boilers, metal containers and steam generators	40.7	33.0	123.0	7.0
Other metal processing	38.4	29.7	129.2	12.0
Miscellaneous fabricated metal products (1)	40.0	29.0	138.0	12.4

(1) Rounded estimates based on non-confidential data.
Source: Eurostat (SBS)

Table 7.4 _____

Basic metals and fabricated metal products (CPA Subsection DJ)
External trade, EU-27, 2006

	Extra-EU exports		Extra-EU imports		Trade balance (EUR million)	Cover ratio (%)
	(EUR million)	(% share of industrial exports)	(EUR million)	(% share of industrial imports)		
Basic metals and fabricated metal products	90 147	8.3	104 480	8.3	-14 333	86.3
Basic iron and steel and ferro-alloys; tubes; other iron and steel	36 928	3.4	33 027	2.6	3 901	111.8
Basic precious metals and other non-ferrous metals	23 740	2.2	49 632	4.0	-25 892	47.8
Foundry work services	:	:	:	:	:	:
Structural metal products	5 086	0.5	1 572	0.1	3 515	323.6
Tanks, reservoirs and containers of metal; central heating radiators and boilers; steam generators, except central heating hot water boilers	2 981	0.3	1 060	0.1	1 921	281.3
Other metal processing	:	:	:	:	:	:
Cutlery, tools and general hardware; other fabricated metal products	21 412	2.0	19 190	1.5	2 222	111.6

Source: Eurostat (Comext)

The apparent labour productivity of the EU-27's metals and metal products manufacturing sector was EUR 42 600 per person employed in 2004 (see Table 7.3), a little above (4.2 %) the level of the non-financial business economy but some EUR 6 400 lower than the industrial average. Although the apparent labour productivity of the sector more than covered its average personnel costs, the wage adjusted labour productivity ratio of 140.2 % was lower than the non-financial business economy ratio (148.0 %) and among the lower tier of industrial NACE subsections. The gross operating rate of the EU-27's metals and metal products manufacturing sector was 10.3 %, again a slightly lower rate than the non-financial business economy average (11.0 %), indicating a lower rate of operating profitability.

The highest wage adjusted labour productivity level (180.0 %) was for the first processing of ferrous metals subsector and the lowest (123.0 %) for the boilers, metal containers and steam generators subsector. The highest rates of operating profitability were in the miscellaneous fabricated metals subsector and the other metal processing subsector (both around 12 %), with the lowest rate being in the basic precious and non-ferrous metals subsector (6.9 %).

EXTERNAL TRADE
The EU-27 had a trade deficit of EUR 14.3 billion in metals and fabricated metal products (CPA Subsection DJ) in 2006, following a trade surplus of EUR 2.0 billion in 2005. This turnaround reflected a sharp rise in the value of imports from non-member countries to EUR 104.5 billion, the highest shares of which came from Russia (12.9 %) and China (12.8 %). The value of EU-27 exports of metals and fabricated metal products increased to EUR 90.1 billion in 2006, accounting for 8.3 % of industrial exports (see Table 7.4). In 2006 trade with non-member countries accounted for 26.3 % of all exports (intra- and extra-EU) by the EU-27 Member States and 30.3 % of imports.

Exports (intra- and extra-EU) of metals and fabricated metal products from Germany were valued at EUR 81.1 billion, accounting for a little less than one quarter (23.7 %) of all exports by EU-27 Member States. Among the Member States, Germany also had the largest trade surplus (EUR 12.9 billion) in metal and fabricated metal products, with other sizeable trade surpluses recorded for Belgium (EUR 4.2 billion), the Netherlands, Austria, Finland and Sweden (all between EUR 1.9 billion and EUR 2.4 billion). In contrast, Spain and Italy had the largest trade deficits in these products (EUR 6.7 billion and EUR 5.9 billion respectively).

It is also worth noting that the share of metals and fabricated metal products exports in national industrial exports (intra- and extra-EU) was highest in Bulgaria (28.7 %), where such goods accounted for the highest proportion of industrial exports (at the level of CPA subsections), and Luxembourg (21.3 %), where they accounted for the second highest proportion of industrial exports after electrical and optical equipment (CPA Subsection DL).

7.1: FIRST PROCESSING OF FERROUS METALS

This subchapter includes information on NACE Groups 27.1 to 27.3. The first of these covers the manufacture of basic iron and steel and ferro-alloys (NACE Group 27.1). The manufacture of tubes (be they of iron or steel) is included in NACE Group 27.2, while other first processing activities associated with iron and steel (drawing, rolling, forming, wire drawing) are covered by NACE Group 27.3. The aggregate covering all three of these activities is hereafter referred to as the first processing of ferrous metals.

The consumption of crude steel by China during the current period of rapid industrialisation represented a little less than one-third (30.9 %) of global consumption in 2006 according to the International Iron and Steel Institute [2]. This strong demand at a time of supply bottlenecks has led to sharply higher prices. China was also the largest producer of steel in the world in 2006, accounting for a little over one third (34.0 %) of global production, a little more than double the share (16.5 %) of EU-27 production in 2006.

There has been a recent round of consolidation in the global market, with the merger of Mittal Steel and Arcelor in 2006 creating the largest steel manufacturing enterprise in the world (see Table 7.5). This was followed by the buy-out of the Corus Group by Tata Steel of India.

[2] IISI (International Iron and Steel Institute), more information at: http://www.worldsteel.org.

Table 7.5

Largest global steel producing enterprise (groups) (million tonnes of crude steel output)

	2005	2006
Arcelor Mittal (1)	:	117.2
Nippon Steel	32.0	32.7
JFE	29.9	32.0
POSCO	30.5	30.1
Baosteel	22.7	22.5
U.S. Steel	19.3	21.2
Nucor	18.4	20.3
Tangshan	16.1	19.1
Corus Group	18.2	18.3
Riva Group	17.5	18.2

(1) 2005 tonnages, Mittal Steel (63.0) and Arcelor (46.7).
Source: IISI (International Iron and Steel Institute), http://www.worldsteel.org

STRUCTURAL PROFILE

The first processing of ferrous metals sector (NACE Groups 27.1 to 27.3) had some 6 000 enterprises which generated EUR 41.0 billion of value added across the EU-27 in 2004, accounting for a little less than one fifth (19.3 %) of the value added generated by metals and metal products manufacturing as a whole (NACE Subsection DJ). The sector was much smaller in terms of its workforce, the 630 000 persons employed across the EU-27 accounting for 12.6 % of those employed in metals and metal products manufacturing. Within the first processing of ferrous metals sector, the manufacture of basic iron and steel (NACE Group 27.1) was by far the largest activity among the three NACE groups covered, accounting for about three-quarters (75.2 %) of value added and two-thirds of employment (66.9 %). The next largest activity was the manufacture of tubes (NACE Group 27.2), which generated 14.6 % of sectoral value added and accounted for 20.6 % of the sectoral workforce. The remaining was accounted for by other first processing of iron and steel (NACE Group 27.3).

Table 7.6

Manufacture of basic iron and steel and of ferro-alloys; manufacture of tubes; other first processing of iron and steel (NACE Groups 27.1, 27.2 and 27.3)
Structural profile, EU-27, 2004

	No. of enterprises (thousands)	Turnover (EUR million)	Value added (EUR million)	Employment (thousands)
First processing of ferrous metals (1)	6.0	187 000	41 000	630.0
Basic iron and steel and of ferro-alloys	2.1	141 694	30 866	421.4
Tubes (1)	1.9	25 000	6 000	130.0
Other first processing of iron and steel	1.9	20 372	4 512	74.4

(1) Rounded estimate based on non-confidential data.
Source: Eurostat (SBS)

Table 7.7

Manufacture of basic iron and steel and of ferro-alloys; manufacture of tubes; other first processing of iron and steel (NACE Groups 27.1, 27.2 and 27.3)
Structural profile: ranking of top five Member States, 2004

Rank	Share of EU-27 value added (%) (1)	Share of EU-27 employment (%) (2)	Value added specialisation ratio (EU-27=100) (3)	Employment specialisation ratio (EU-27=100) (4)
1	Germany (24.9)	Germany (20.4)	Romania (410.2)	Sweden (261.2)
2	Italy (14.6)	Italy (12.0)	Bulgaria (276.9)	Romania (246.9)
3	France (10.5)	France (9.0)	Czech Republic (271.0)	Czech Republic (196.6)
4	Spain (8.8)	Romania (7.9)	Finland (230.4)	Belgium (196.1)
5	Belgium (6.0)	Spain (6.2)	Belgium (221.6)	Finland (182.5)

(1) Estonia, Greece, Cyprus, Latvia, Luxembourg, Malta, Netherlands and Slovakia, not available; Portugal and Slovenia, 2003.
(2) Estonia, Greece, Cyprus, Luxembourg, Malta, Netherlands and Slovakia, not available; Portugal and Slovenia, 2003.
(3) Estonia, Ireland, Greece, Cyprus, Latvia, Luxembourg, Malta, Netherlands and Slovakia, not available; Portugal and Slovenia, 2003.
(4) Estonia, Ireland, Greece, Cyprus, Luxembourg, Malta, Netherlands and Slovakia, not available; Portugal and Slovenia, 2003.
Source: Eurostat (SBS)

Almost exactly one-quarter of the value added generated by the first processing of ferrous metals sector across the EU-27 as a whole came from Germany (see Table 7.7), the next largest contributions coming from Italy (14.6 %) and France (10.5 %). These three Member States also had the largest sectoral workforces (a combined 41.4 %). It is interesting to note the contrast between the relative size of the sector in terms of employment and value added in Romania and the Czech Republic; the first processing of ferrous metals sector in Romania accounted for 7.9 % of the EU-27 workforce and in the Czech Republic this share was 5.6 %, whereas these Member States accounted for only 1.7 % and 2.8 % of EU-27 value added. Relative to the value added generated across their respective non-financial business economies, Romania, the Czech Republic and Bulgaria were the most specialised Member States in the activities covered by this sector.

The development of the production index for the manufacture of basic iron and steel in the EU-27 was similar to that for metals and metal products manufacturing as a whole, with average growth of 1.6 % per annum between 1996 and 2006. In contrast, the evolution of the production indices for the other two NACE groups was far more variable. After staggered but strong growth in the output of other first processing of iron and steel activities between 1996 and 2000, there was an almost equally strong decline through until 2005, before a slight rebound in 2006. After the relative low in 1999, there was strong growth (3.5 % per annum) in the production index for the manufacture of tubes through until 2006, albeit with a short-lived cutback in output in 2002.

Figure 7.4 _____

Manufacture of basic iron and steel and of ferro-alloys; manufacture of tubes; other first processing of iron and steel (NACE Groups 27.1, 27.2 and 27.3)
Evolution of main indicators, EU-27 (2000=100)

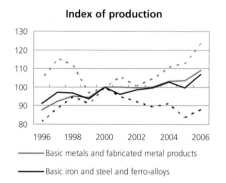

Index of production

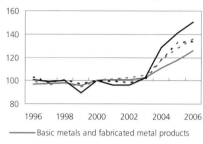

Index of domestic output prices

——— Basic metals and fabricated metal products

——— Basic iron and steel and ferro-alloys

- - - - Tubes

- - - - Other first processing activities associated with iron and steel

Source: Eurostat (STS)

COSTS, PRODUCTIVITY AND PROFITABILITY

The apparent labour productivity of the EU-27's first processing of ferrous metals sector was EUR 66 000 per person employed in 2004, an average EUR 23 400 more than across metals and metal products manufacturing as a whole – see Table 7.8 – the highest level among Subchapters 7.1 to 7.7. Average personnel costs were also relatively high at EUR 37 000 per employee. When comparing these two ratios, personnel costs per employee were more than covered by the value added per person employed, the resulting wage adjusted productivity ratio of 180.0 % being much higher than the average (140.2 %) of metals and metal products manufacturing as a whole. Among the three subsectors, the manufacture of basic iron and steel had the highest wage adjusted labour productivity ratio of 197.3 % in 2004, as well as having the highest gross operating rate (10.8 %).

EXTERNAL TRADE

EU-27 exports of ferrous metals (CPA Groups 27.1 to 27.3) were valued at EUR 36.9 billion in 2006, accounting for 41.0 % of the value of metals and fabricated metal product exports (see Table 7.9). The United States and Turkey were the main export markets for ferrous metals, accounting for a little over one quarter (a combined 26.4 %) of the value of EU-27 exports. During the period between 2001 and 2006, the value of exports of ferrous metals from the EU-27 doubled but the internal market still accounted for the overwhelming majority (74.1 %) of all trade (both intra and extra-EU) by EU-27 Member States in 2006. During the same period, the value of imports from non-member countries tripled to EUR 33.0 billion in 2006, with Russia and China accounting for a little under one-third (a combined 30.3 %) of these imports.

Table 7.8 _____

Manufacture of basic iron and steel and of ferro-alloys; manufacture of tubes; other first processing of iron and steel
(NACE Groups 27.1, 27.2 and 27.3)
Productivity and profitability, EU-27, 2004

	Apparent labour productivity (EUR thousand)	Average personnel costs (EUR thousand)	Wage adjusted labour productivity (%)	Gross operating rate (%)
First processing of ferrous metals (1)	66.0	37.0	180.0	10.3
Basic iron and steel and of ferro-alloys	73.2	37.1	197.3	10.8
Tubes (1)	50.0	35.0	140.0	8.0
Other first processing of iron and steel	60.6	36.5	166.0	9.1

(1) Rounded estimates based on non-confidential data.
Source: Eurostat (SBS)

Table 7.9

Basic iron and steel and ferro-alloys; tubes; other iron and steel (CPA Groups 27.1, 27.2 and 27.3)
External trade, EU-27, 2006

	Extra-EU exports		Extra-EU imports		Trade balance (EUR million)	Cover ratio (%)
	(EUR million)	(% share of chapter)	(EUR million)	(% share of chapter)		
Basic iron and steel and ferro-alloys; tubes; other iron and steel	36 928	41.0	33 027	31.6	3 901	111.8
Basic iron and steel and ferro-alloys	24 106	26.7	26 614	25.5	-2 508	90.6
Tubes	10 869	12.1	3 427	3.3	7 442	317.2
Other first processed iron and steel	1 953	2.2	2 986	2.9	-1 032	65.4

Source: Eurostat (Comext)

The EU-27's trade surplus in ferrous metals narrowed to EUR 3.9 billion in 2006, down from the relative peak of EUR 8.3 billion in 2005. Within ferrous metals, tubes (CPA Group 27.2) generated a trade surplus of EUR 7.4 billion in 2006, a little less than twice as much as the trade surplus in 2004. In contrast, there were trade deficits of EUR 1.0 billion for other first processed iron and steel (CPA Group 27.3) and EUR 2.5 billion for basic iron and steel and ferro-alloys (CPA Group 27.1) in 2006.

Among the EU-27 Member States, a little over one fifth (20.2 %) of ferrous metal exports (intra- and extra-EU) came from Germany in 2006, making it by far the largest exporter. Germany also recorded the largest trade surplus for ferrous metals (EUR 5.4 billion), closely followed by Belgium (EUR 4.7 billion). As a proportion of industrial exports, however, ferrous metals were particularly significant in Luxembourg (15.5 %) and Latvia (10.7 %) compared to other Member States and the EU-27 average (3.4 %).

7.2: BASIC PRECIOUS AND NON-FERROUS METALS

> NACE Group 27.4 covers the manufacture of a wide range of metals other than iron and steel, including precious metals (such as gold, silver and platinum) and common metals (aluminium, lead, zinc, tin, copper, chrome, nickel and manganese), hereafter referred to as basic precious and non-ferrous metals manufacturing.

STRUCTURAL PROFILE

There were some 3 300 enterprises in the EU-27's basic precious and non-ferrous metals manufacturing (NACE Group 27.4) sector, which generated EUR 14.3 billion of value added and employed 228 300 persons across the EU-27 in 2004, making it one of the smaller activities within the manufacturing activities of metals and metal products (NACE Subsection DJ); it accounted for 6.7 % of value added and 4.6 % of the employment within metals and metal products manufacturing. Within the five NACE Classes that make-up the EU-27's basic precious and non-ferrous metals manufacturing sector, aluminium production was the largest activity, with EUR 8.0 billion of value added recorded in 2004.

The value added generated by the basic precious and non-ferrous metals manufacturing sector in Germany was EUR 4.6 billion in 2004, almost one third (32.3 %) of the value added generated by the sector across the EU-27 and a little more than the combined value added of the three next largest Member States, namely Italy, France and the United Kingdom (each with value added of EUR 1.5 billion) - see Table 7.10. The structure of the basic precious and non-ferrous metals manufacturing sector in terms of employment was very similar. As a proportion of the value added generated across their respective non-financial business economies, the precious and non-ferrous metals manufacturing sectors of Slovakia and Bulgaria generated the highest value added in

2004, approaching three times the average contribution (0.3 %) across the EU-27. Romania and Belgium were also relatively specialised in this activity.

There was a similar strong upward development in the production index for basic precious and non-ferrous metals manufacturing between 1996 and 2000 to that of metals and metal products manufacturing as a whole. Whereas the output of metals and metal products manufacturing then stabilised through until 2003 before rising strongly through until 2006, the output of basic precious and non-ferrous metals manufacturing declined steadily through until 2003 after which there was a partial rebound to a level in

Figure 7.5

Manufacture of basic precious and non-ferrous metals (NACE Group 27.4)
Value added, EU-27, 2004 (EUR million) (1)

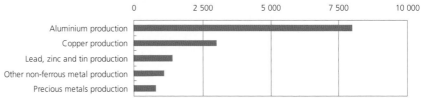

(1) Rounded estimates based on non-confidential data.
Source: Eurostat (SBS)

Table 7.10

Manufacture of basic precious and non-ferrous metals (NACE Group 27.4)
Structural profile: ranking of top five Member States, 2004

Rank	Share of EU-27 value added (%) (1)	Share of EU-27 employment (%) (1)	Value added specialisation ratio (EU-27=100) (2)	Employment specialisation ratio (EU-27=100) (2)
1	Germany (32.3)	Germany (27.5)	Slovakia (285.1)	Belgium (206.9)
2	United Kingdom (10.3)	Italy (10.4)	Bulgaria (276.6)	Slovakia (167.5)
3	Italy (10.1)	France (9.1)	Romania (208.4)	Germany (166.4)
4	France (10.1)	United Kingdom (8.6)	Belgium (192.6)	Sweden (160.6)
5	Spain (6.7)	Spain (6.3)	Hungary (165.5)	Bulgaria (158.5)

(1) Estonia, Greece, Cyprus, Luxembourg and Malta, not available; Lithuania, Portugal and Slovenia, 2003.
(2) Estonia, Ireland, Greece, Cyprus, Lithuania, Luxembourg and Malta, not available; Portugal and Slovenia, 2003.
Source: Eurostat (SBS)

Figure 7.6

Manufacture of basic precious and non-ferrous metals (NACE Group 27.4)
Evolution of main indicators, EU-27 (2000=100)

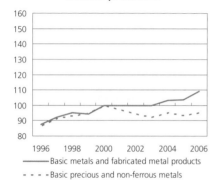

Index of production

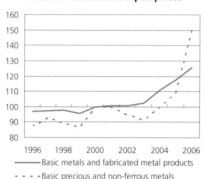

Index of domestic output prices

Source: Eurostat (STS)

EXTERNAL TRADE

The EU-27 had a trade deficit of EUR 25.9 billion in basic precious metals and other non-ferrous metals (CPA Group 27.4) in 2006, which was the fourth largest deficit among all of the CPA groups that comprise industrial (CPA Sections C to E) products and double the deficit that had been recorded in 2005. The considerable widening of the deficit in large part reflected the surge in the value of imports of basic precious metals and other non-ferrous metals to EUR 49.6 billion (see Table 7.11), a large part of which was explained by the sharp rise in prices. The main markets from which the EU-27 imported basic precious metals and non-ferrous metals were Russia (14.8 % of EU-27 imports), Chile (12.4 %) and Norway (10.4 %). The main imports of basic precious metals and other non-ferrous metals to the EU-27 concerned aluminium and aluminium products (CPA Class 27.42), valued at EUR 15.2 billion, copper products (CPA Class 27.44), valued at EUR 14.2 billion, and precious metals (CPA Class 27.41) which were valued at EUR 10.2 billion. Trade of these three types of basic precious metals or other non-ferrous metals generated a deficit between EUR 5.1 billion to EUR 8.4 billion in 2006.

Although the vast majority of the Member States recorded trade deficits (intra- and extra-EU combined) for basic precious metals and other non-ferrous metals, including Germany who was the principal exporter, there were small trade surpluses in Bulgaria (EUR 1.5 billion), Poland (EUR 1.3 billion) and Finland (EUR 1.1 billion), as well as even smaller surpluses below EUR 300 million in Romania, Luxembourg, the Netherlands, Slovakia, Latvia and Ireland.

2006 that remained 4.7 % below the relative peak of 2000 (see Figure 7.6). The domestic output price index for basic precious and non-ferrous metals manufacturing fluctuated within a relatively narrow range during the period between 1996 and 2003, during which growth was limited to an average 0.6 % per annum. After 2003, however, there were very strong price rises of a combined 63.9 % in the three years up to and including 2006, which far outstripped the rate of price increase for metals and metal products manufacturing as a whole.

COSTS, PRODUCTIVITY AND PROFITABILITY

Average personnel costs with the EU-27's basic precious and non-ferrous metals sector were EUR 40 100 per employee in 2004, the highest level among the dozen NACE groups that comprise metals and metal products manufacturing and almost half as much (45.3 %) as the average across the non-financial business economy. Despite these high average personnel costs across the sector, relative to total expenditure, personnel costs accounted for a relatively low share (12.1 %) compared to both the non-financial business economy (16.4 %) and the metals and metal products manufacturing as a whole (21.1 %).

The high personnel costs in the sector were also more than covered by an apparent labour productivity of EUR 62 800 per person employed in the EU-27. As a result, the wage adjusted labour productivity ratio of 156.4 % for the basic precious and non-ferrous metals sector of the EU-27 in 2004 was higher than the non-financial business economy average (148.0 %) and more particularly the ratio for metals and metal products manufacturing (140.2 %).

The wage adjusted labour productivity of the basic precious and non-ferrous metals sector was the same or higher than the non-financial business economy ratio in almost all the Member States (the main exception being Denmark) and was notably higher in Slovakia, where the ratio of 446.0 % for the sector compared to an average 207.0 % across its non-financial business economy.

In contrast, the gross operating rate (6.9 %) of the EU-27's basic precious and non-ferrous metals sector was the lowest among the seven subchapters of this metals and metal products chapter and considerably lower than the rate (11.0 %) for the non-financial business economy.

Table 7.11

Basic precious metals and other non-ferrous metals (CPA Group 27.4)
External trade, EU-27, 2006

	Extra-EU exports		Extra-EU imports			
	(EUR million)	(% share of chapter)	(EUR million)	(% share of chapter)	Trade balance (EUR million)	Cover ratio (%)
Basic precious metals and other non-ferrous metals	23 740	26.3	49 632	47.5	-25 892	47.8
Precious metals	5 152	5.7	10 248	9.8	-5 096	50.3
Aluminium and aluminium products	6 761	7.5	15 173	14.5	-8 411	44.6
Lead, zinc and tin and products thereof	990	1.1	2 386	2.3	-1 396	41.5
Copper production	7 688	8.5	14 237	13.6	-6 549	54.0
Other non-ferrous metal production	3 149	3.5	7 589	7.3	-4 439	41.5

Source: Eurostat (Comext)

7.3: CASTING

NACE Group 27.5 covers the casting of metals (including iron, steel, light metals and other non-ferrous metals). As such, this activity specialises in the manufacture of semi-finished castings for downstream customers. The information presented does not include the manufacture of standardised, finished products (such as tubes, see Subchapter 7.1) or boilers or radiators (see Subchapter 7.5). Note that external trade statistics are not available for foundry work services (CPA Group 27.5).

Foundry work consists of pouring a molten metal alloy into a mould to obtain a part with the same shape as the mould after it solidifies, and uses casting procedures appropriate for the alloy used, the number of parts to be made, and their shape and weight. Main downstream activities for casting enterprises include machinery and equipment and transport equipment manufacturers, as well as the construction and telecommunications sectors.

Table 7.12

Casting of metals (NACE Group 27.5)
Structural profile, EU-27, 2004 (1)

	No. of enterprises (thousands)	Turnover (EUR million)	Value added (EUR million)	Employment (thousands)
Casting of metals	6.5	31 294	10 924	273.7
Casting of iron	1.8	11 600	4 000	110.0
Casting of steel	0.5	3 610	1 410	35.2
Casting of light metals	2.1	11 500	4 080	90.0
Casting of other non-ferrous metals	2.0	4 580	1 430	34.8

(1) Rounded estimate based on non-confidential data.
Source: Eurostat (SBS)

STRUCTURAL PROFILE

The casting of metals (NACE Group 27.5) sector consisted of approximately 6 500 enterprises which generated EUR 10.9 billion of value added across the EU-27 in 2004, making the smallest contribution (5.1 %) to the total value added of the metals and metal products manufacturing sector (NACE Subsection DJ) of all of the activities presented in Subchapters 7.1 to 7.7. The sector employed 273 700 persons across the EU-27 in 2004, corresponding to 5.5 % of the metals and metal products manufacturing workforce, a slightly higher share than that recorded for basic precious and non-ferrous metals (NACE Group 27.4).

The casting of metals sector in Germany generated a little over one third (36.1 %) of the value added generated by the sector across the EU-27, by far the largest contribution and far greater than the next highest shares from Italy (16.2 %) and France (11.9 %) – see Table 7.13. However, the proportional contribution made by the sector to the value added of the non-financial business economy was highest in Slovenia (0.7 % in 2003) – more than three times the average share across the EU-27. In these terms, the Czech Republic and then Germany were the next most specialised Member States in the casting of metals.

Table 7.13

Casting of metals (NACE Group 27.5)
Structural profile: ranking of top five Member States, 2004

Rank	Share of EU-27 value added (%) (1)	Share of EU-27 employment (%) (2)	Value added specialisation ratio (EU-27=100) (3)	Employment specialisation ratio (EU-27=100) (4)
1	Germany (36.1)	Germany (25.6)	Slovenia (319.4)	Slovenia (300.4)
2	Italy (16.2)	Italy (13.2)	Czech Republic (207.7)	Czech Republic (252.6)
3	France (11.9)	France (11.9)	Germany (172.2)	Germany (154.7)
4	Spain (9.6)	Spain (7.9)	Italy (145.6)	Bulgaria (127.7)
5	United Kingdom (8.7)	United Kingdom (7.9)	Austria (135.6)	Poland (122.9)

(1) Greece, Latvia, Luxembourg, Malta, Netherlands and Slovakia, not available; Estonia, Lithuania, Portugal and Slovenia, 2003.
(2) Greece, Luxembourg, Malta, Netherlands and Slovakia, not available; Estonia, Lithuania, Portugal and Slovenia, 2003.
(3) Ireland, Greece, Cyprus, Latvia, Lithuania, Luxembourg, Malta, Netherlands and Slovakia, not available; Estonia, Portugal and Slovenia, 2003.
(4) Ireland, Greece, Cyprus, Lithuania, Luxembourg, Malta, Netherlands and Slovakia, not available; Estonia, Portugal and Slovenia, 2003.
Source: Eurostat (SBS)

The index of production for EU-27 casting of metals followed closely the development in output for the manufacture of metals and metal products as a whole between 1996 and 2006, growing by an average 1.9 % per annum. The development of the domestic output price index was also very similar between the two sets of activities in the period between 1996 and 2003, in that they both remained relatively unchanged, but since then the rise in the price for metals and metals products manufacturing far outpaced that of the casting of metals.

COSTS, PRODUCTIVITY AND PROFITABILITY

Average personnel costs in the EU-27's casting of metals sector were EUR 30 600 per employee in 2004 (see Table 7.14), almost the same as across the manufacture of metals and metal products as a whole. However, as a proportion of total expenditure, personnel costs in the sector accounted for a relatively high share (26.9 %) both in comparison to metals and metal products manufacturing (21.1 %) and more particularly the non-financial business economy (16.4 %). The apparent labour productivity level of EUR 39 900 per person employed in the casting of metals sector was very slightly lower (2.4 %) than the non-financial business economy level but more than covered personnel costs. The wage adjusted labour productivity level of 130.3 % for the EU-27's casting of metals sector, however, was somewhat lower than the level for metals and metal products manufacturing as a whole (140.2 %) and more clearly lower than the level

for the non-financial business economy (148.0 %). The relatively low wage adjusted labour productivity levels for the casting of metals sector in comparison to the non-financial business economy was a characteristic noted in almost all of the Member States [3], with the exception of Spain and Italy where it was slightly higher.

The profitability of the casting of metals sector, as indicated by the gross operating rate, was also lower (at 8.7 %) than for metals and metal products manufacturing as a whole (10.3 %) and the non-financial business economy (11.0 %). The major exception to this characteristic among the Member States concerned Hungary, where the gross operating rate of the sector was 11.4 % and that of its non-financial business economy was 8.8 %.

[3] Estonia, Portugal and Slovenia, 2003; Ireland, Greece, Cyprus, Latvia, Lithuania, Luxembourg, Malta, Netherlands and Slovakia, not available.

Table 7.14

Casting of metals (NACE Group 27.5)
Productivity and profitability, EU-27, 2004 (1)

	Apparent labour productivity (EUR thousand)	Average personnel costs (EUR thousand)	Wage adjusted labour productivity (%)	Gross operating rate (%)
Casting of metals	39.9	30.6	130.3	8.7
Casting of iron	35.0	28.0	120.0	7.2
Casting of steel	40.2	32.0	126.0	8.5
Casting of light metals	45.4	32.7	139.0	10.4
Casting of other non-ferrous metals	41.2	31.9	129.0	8.2

(1) Rounded estimates based on non-confidential data.
Source: Eurostat (SBS)

7.4: STRUCTURAL METAL PRODUCTS

This subchapter includes information on NACE Group 28.1 that covers the manufacture of structural metal products. The vast majority of the products that are produced within this activity are destined for the construction sector (see Chapter 15), for example, as metal supports and structures, prefabricated buildings, metal doors, window frames, or shutters. Demand is therefore closely linked to developments in the construction sector for new housing, renovation and civil engineering projects.

Table 7.15

Manufacture of structural metal products (NACE Group 28.1)
Structural profile, EU-27, 2004

	No. of enterprises (thousands)	Turnover (EUR million)	Value added (EUR million)	Employment (thousands)
Structural metal products	107.4	103 944	33 894	1 029.6
Metal structures and parts of structures (1)	50.0	75 100	23 900	690.0
Builders' carpentry and joinery of metal (1)	57.7	28 900	9 950	340.0

(1) Rounded estimate based on non-confidential data.
Source: Eurostat (SBS)

STRUCTURAL PROFILE

There were 107 400 enterprises with their core activities in the structural metals products (NACE Group 28.1) sector which employed 1.0 million persons across the EU-27 and generated EUR 33.9 billion of value added in 2004, which

corresponded to a little more than one in every five people (20.6 %) within the metals and metal products (NACE Subsection DJ) manufacturing workforce and 15.9 % of its value added. The manufacture of metal structures and parts of structures subsector

(NACE Class 28.11) was much larger than the manufacture of builders' carpentry and joinery of metal subsector (NACE Class 28.12), accounting for two-thirds (67.0 %) of the sectoral workforce and a slightly greater share (70.5 %) of value added.

Table 7.16

Manufacture of structural metal products (NACE Group 28.1)
Structural profile: ranking of top five Member States, 2004

Rank	Share of EU-27 value added (%) (1)	Share of EU-27 employment (%) (1)	Value added specialisation ratio (EU-27=100) (2)	Employment specialisation ratio (EU-27=100) (2)
1	Germany (20.5)	Italy (18.8)	Italy (176.9)	Italy (160.2)
2	Italy (19.7)	Germany (16.3)	Austria (152.5)	Estonia (148.9)
3	Spain (13.5)	Spain (14.9)	Spain (150.3)	Spain (145.4)
4	United Kingdom (11.8)	United Kingdom (7.5)	Slovenia (136.0)	Portugal (139.6)
5	France (7.6)	Poland (6.6)	Estonia (128.1)	Romania (128.9)

(1) Greece and Malta, not available; Luxembourg, 2003.
(2) Ireland, Greece, Cyprus and Malta, not available; Luxembourg, 2003.
Source: Eurostat (SBS)

Table 7.17

Production of selected products - structural metal products (CPA Group 28.1), EU-27, 2006 (1)

	Prodcom code	Production value (EUR million)	Volume of sold production (thousands)	Unit of volume
Aluminium doors, thresholds for doors, windows and their frames	28.12.10.50	11 025	36 612	units
Aluminium structure and parts of structures..., n.e.c.	28.11.23.70	7 055	1 336 637	kg
Iron or steel doors, thresholds for doors, windows and their frames	28.12.10.30	6 458	c	units
Installation in situ of self produced metal structures	28.11.91.00	5 066	-	-
Structures, solely or principally of iron or steel sheet comprising two walls of profiled (ribbed) sheet with an insulating core (excluding prefabricated buildings)	28.11.23.40	3 057	1 648 836	kg
Iron/steel equipment for scaffolding, shuttering, propping/pit-propping including pit head frames and superstructures, extensible coffering beams, tubular scaffolding and similar equipment	28.11.23.10	3 056	2 633 121	kg
Iron or steel towers and lattice masts	28.11.22.00	1 919	c	kg
Iron or steel bridges and bridge-sections	28.11.21.00	1 230	773 377	kg
Prefabricated buildings, of aluminium	28.11.10.50	1 186	-	-
Weirs, sluices, lock-gates, fixed landing stages, fixed docks and other maritime and waterway structures of iron or steel	28.11.23.30	378	131 904	kg

(1) Estimated.
Source: Eurostat (PRODCOM)

The value added generated by the structural metals products sectors in Germany and Italy each accounted for about one-fifth (20.5 % and 19.7 % respectively) of the value added generated by the sector across the EU-27 (see Table 7.16). The contribution (1.2 %) made by the sector to the value added generated across the non-financial business economy was also highest in Italy, making it the most specialised Member State in this activity. Austria and Spain were the next most specialised Member States in structural metals products manufacturing, an activity for which the average contribution to the value added of the non-financial business economy across the EU-27 was 0.7 %.

The development of the production index for structural metals products manufacturing during the ten years through to 2006 was broadly similar to that of metals and metal products manufacturing as a whole, except that the period of relatively unchanged output that started in 2000 extended beyond 2003 to 2005. This helps explain why the average rate of growth (1.9 % per annum) in the output of structural metals products manufacturing was slightly lower than that of metals and metal products manufacturing. Similarly there was little difference in the development of the two domestic output price indices, although that for structural metals products manufacturing was slightly steadier and grew year-on-year throughout the ten years.

Table 7.18

Manufacture of structural metal products (NACE Group 28.1)
Productivity and profitability, EU-27, 2004

	Apparent labour productivity (EUR thousand)	Average personnel costs (EUR thousand)	Wage adjusted labour productivity (%)	Gross operating rate (%)
Structural metal products	32.9	25.2	130.8	10.1
Metal structures and parts of structures (1)	34.7	26.4	132.0	9.3
Builders' carpentry and joinery of metal (1)	29.2	22.5	130.0	12.0

(1) Rounded estimates based on non-confidential data.
Source: Eurostat (SBS)

COSTS, PRODUCTIVITY AND PROFITABILITY

Average personnel costs of EUR 25 200 per employee within the EU-27's structural metal products manufacturing sector were the lowest among the dozen NACE groups that comprise metals and metal products manufacturing and 8.7 % lower than the average across the non-financial business economy. As a proportion of total expenditure, however, personnel costs in the sector accounted for a relatively high share (23.9 %), supporting the notion of this as a relatively low-cost, labour intensive sector. The apparent labour productivity of EUR 32 900 per person employed (see Table 7.18) was also the lowest among the NACE groups within the metals and metal products manufacturing and a fifth lower than the non-financial business economy average. It was enough, nevertheless, to cover personnel costs; as the wage adjusted labour productivity ratio was 130.8 % in 2004. The wage adjusted labour productivity ratio of the sector was lower than that of the national non-financial business economy in each of the Member States [4], except Bulgaria where it was very slightly higher. The gross operating rate for the structural metal products manufacturing sector was 10.1 % in 2004, which was very similar to this profitability measure for the whole of metals and metal products manufacturing and, therefore, a little less than the rate for the non-financial business economy (11.0 %).

___

[4] Luxembourg, 2003; Ireland, Greece, Cyprus and Malta, not available.

EXTERNAL TRADE

The EU-27's exports of structural metal products (CPA Group 28.1) to non-member countries were valued at EUR 5.1 billion in 2006, generating a trade surplus of EUR 3.5 billion. Since 2001, the trade surplus in these products has increased every year. Exports (intra- and extra-EU trade combined) of structural metal products from Germany accounted for a quarter of EU trade and the country recorded the highest trade surplus in these products (EUR 2.3 billion) among the Member States in 2006, more than double the next largest trade surplus that was recorded by Poland.

7.5: BOILERS, METAL CONTAINERS AND STEAM GENERATORS

This subchapter covers NACE Groups 28.2 and 28.3 together, which are referred to as the boilers, metal containers and steam generators manufacturing sector. The first of the groups covered includes the manufacture of metal tanks, reservoirs and containers, as well as central heating radiators and boilers, while the latter covers the manufacture of steam generators (except for central heating), for example, vapour generators, condensers or nuclear reactors.

The manufacture of boilers, containers and steam generators supplies various downstream sectors, most notably the construction (see Chapter 15) and energy (see Chapter 13) sectors.

STRUCTURAL PROFILE

The boilers, metal containers and steam generators manufacturing sector (NACE Groups 28.2 and 28.3) accounted for 14 000 enterprises which generated EUR 12.5 billion of value added in the EU-27, accounting for 5.9 % of the value added generated by metals and metal products manufacturing (NACE Subsection DJ), and employed 306 600 persons. France contributed the largest share (29.5 %) to the value added created by the boilers, metal containers and steam generators manufacturing sector across the EU-27, with Germany contributing the second highest amount (24.6 %) – see Table 7.20. The two NACE groups that compose this subchapter were of similar size both in terms of value added and employment.

Despite declines in the production index for the EU-27's manufacture of steam generators subsector (NACE Group 28.3) in 1997, 1999 and 2003, there was otherwise strong growth in the ten years through to 2006, at an average rate (2.5 % per annum) that was slightly more than the rate for metals and metal products manufacturing (2.2 % per annum). In contrast, there was much slower growth (an average 1.1 % per annum) in the output of boilers, reservoirs, containers and central heating radiators and boilers (NACE Group 28.2) during this period, the rate of growth being restricted by strong declines in 2000 and 2001.

Table 7.19

Manufacture of boilers, metal containers and steam generators (NACE Groups 28.2 and 28.3)
Structural profile, EU-27, 2004 (1)

	No. of enterprises (thousands)	Turnover (EUR million)	Value added (EUR million)	Employment (thousands)
Boilers, metal containers and steam generators	14.0	36 838	12 463	306.6
Tanks, reservoirs and containers of metal; central heating radiators and boilers	6.1	20 322	6 444	160.1
Tanks, reservoirs and containers of metal	3.6	8 560	3 010	86.0
Central heating radiators and boilers	2.6	11 800	3 440	74.3
Steam generators, except central heating hot water boilers	8.2	16 515	6 019	146.5

(1) Rounded estimate based on non-confidential data.
Source: Eurostat (SBS)

Table 7.20

Manufacture of boilers, metal containers and steam generators (NACE Groups 28.2 and 28.3)
Structural profile: ranking of top five Member States, 2004

Rank	Share of EU-27 value added (%) (1)	Share of EU-27 employment (%) (2)	Value added specialisation ratio (EU-27=100) (1)	Employment specialisation ratio (EU-27=100) (2)
1	France (29.5)	France (28.1)	France (209.7)	France (245.9)
2	Germany (24.6)	Germany (17.0)	Czech Republic (158.5)	Finland (196.3)
3	United Kingdom (8.9)	Italy (8.0)	Belgium (149.0)	Czech Republic (185.9)
4	Italy (8.9)	Poland (8.0)	Romania (138.4)	Belgium (152.3)
5	Spain (5.6)	Spain (6.4)	Poland (131.9)	Romania (137.6)

(1) Denmark, Estonia, Ireland, Greece, Cyprus, Lithuania, Luxembourg, Malta and Netherlands, not available; Latvia and Slovenia, 2003.
(2) Denmark, Estonia, Ireland, Greece, Cyprus, Lithuania, Luxembourg and Malta, not available; Slovenia, 2003.
Source: Eurostat (SBS)

Figure 7.7

Manufacture of boilers, metal containers and steam generators (NACE Groups 28.2 and 28.3)
Index of production, EU-27 (2000=100)

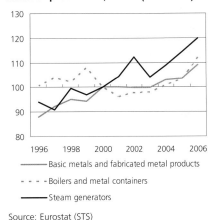

- Basic metals and fabricated metal products
- - - Boilers and metal containers
- Steam generators

Source: Eurostat (STS)

COSTS, PRODUCTIVITY AND PROFITABILITY

The wage adjusted labour productivity of the EU-27's boilers, metal containers and steam generators manufacturing sector was 123.0 % in 2004 (see Table 7.21), the lowest rate of the seven subchapters within this chapter on metals and metal products manufacturing, reflecting average personnel costs (EUR 33 000 per employee) that were a little higher (8.6 %) than the metal and metal products manufacturing average and an apparent labour productivity ratio (EUR 40 700 per person employed) that was a little lower (4.5 %) than the chapter average. The ratio of gross operating surplus to turnover (the gross operating rate) was 7.0 % for the boilers, metal containers and steam generators manufacturing sector, also lower than the metals and metal products manufacturing average (10.3 %).

EXTERNAL TRADE

The EU-27 had a trade surplus of EUR 1.9 billion with non-member countries for boilers, metal containers and steam generators (CPA Groups 28.2 and 28.3) in 2006, two thirds of which came from the surplus for tanks, reservoirs, containers and central heating radiators and boilers (CPA Group 28.2). EU-27 exports of boilers, metal containers and steam generators were valued at EUR 3.0 billion in 2006, about 10 % each to Russia, Turkey and the United States. Among the Member States, Italy and Germany generated the largest trade surpluses (intra- and extra-EU trade) of EUR 1.2 billion and EUR 1.0 billion respectively.

Table 7.21

Manufacture of boilers, metal containers and steam generators (NACE Groups 28.2 and 28.3)
Productivity and profitability, EU-27, 2004 (1)

	Apparent labour productivity (EUR thousand)	Average personnel costs (EUR thousand)	Wage adjusted labour productivity (%)	Gross operating rate (%)
Boilers, metal containers and steam generators	40.7	33.0	123.0	7.0
Tanks, reservoirs and containers of metal; central heating radiators and boilers	40.3	30.3	132.7	8.5
Tanks, reservoirs and containers of metal	35.0	28.6	122.0	7.3
Central heating radiators and boilers	46.3	32.3	143.0	9.4
Steam generators, except central heating hot water boilers	41.1	36.0	114.2	5.2

(1) Rounded estimate based on non-confidential data.
Source: Eurostat (SBS)

7.6: OTHER METAL PROCESSING

Together, NACE Groups 28.4 and 28.5 are referred to as other metal processing. Both activities concern the transformation of metals, with NACE Group 28.4 covering forging, pressing, stamping and roll forming of metal, while NACE Group 28.5 covers the treatment and coating of metal and general mechanical engineering (such as turning, milling, welding or planing).

STRUCTURAL PROFILE

The EU-27's other metal processing sector (NACE Groups 28.4 and 28.5) generated EUR 52.9 billion of value added in 2004, contributing almost a quarter (24.9 %) of the value added generated by metals and metal products (NACE Subsection DJ) manufacturing, thereby being the largest of the activities covered in Subchapters 7.1 to 7.7. There were some 154 000 enterprises in the other metal processing sector which employed 1.4 million persons, representing an even larger share (27.6 %) of the share of metals and metal products manufacturing workforce. About three quarters of the EU-27's value added in the other metal processing sector came from the treatment and coating of metal and general mechanical engineering (NACE Group 28.5) in 2004, while the remaining share was generated by forging, pressing, stamping and roll forming of metal (NACE Group 28.4) – see Table 7.22.

Three quarters (75.4 %) of the value added generated by the EU-27's other metal processing sector came from Germany (23.6 %), Italy (22.4 %), France (16.3 %) and the United Kingdom (13.1 %) - see Table 7.23. Italy was the most specialised Member State in the manufacture of other metal processing, this sector contributing 2.1 % of the value added of the Italian non-financial business economy in 2004, which was slightly more than double the EU-27 average (1.0 %).

The development of the production indices of the two NACE groups that make-up other metal processing were very similar in the ten years through until 2006; the average rate of growth in the output of forging, pressing, stamping and roll forming of metal was 4.4 % per annum for the EU-27, while the corresponding rate for the treatment and coating of metal and general mechanical engineering was 4.2 %, these rates being the highest rates among the twelve NACE groups that comprise metal and metal products manufacturing.

Table 7.22

Forging, pressing, stamping and roll forming of metal; powder metallurgy; treatment and coating of metals; general mechanical engineering (NACE Groups 28.4 and 28.5) Structural profile, EU-27, 2004 (1)

	No. of enterprises (thousands)	Turnover (EUR million)	Value added (EUR million)	Employment (thousands)
Other metal processing	154.0	134 749	52 920	1 378.0
Forging, pressing, stamping and roll forming of metal; powder metallurgy	14.1	45 831	14 286	313.8
Treatment and coating of metals; general mechanical engineering	139.8	88 918	38 634	1 064.2
Treatment and coating of metals	22.0	23 000	10 100	270.0
General mechanical engineering	117.0	66 000	29 000	790.0

(1) Rounded estimates based on non-confidential data.
Source: Eurostat (SBS)

Figure 7.8

Forging, pressing, stamping and roll forming of metal; powder metallurgy; teatment and coating of metals; general mechanical engineering (NACE Groups 28.4 and 28.5) Index of production, EU-27 (2000=100)

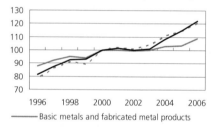

Basic metals and fabricated metal products

- - - - Forging, pressing, stamping and roll forming of metal; powder metallurgy

Teatment and coating of metals; general mechanical engineering

Source: Eurostat (STS)

Table 7.23

Forging, pressing, stamping and roll forming of metal; powder metallurgy; treatment and coating of metals; general mechanical engineering (NACE Groups 28.4 and 28.5) Structural profile: ranking of top five Member States, 2004

Rank	Share of EU-27 value added (%) (1)	Share of EU-27 employment (%) (2)	Value added specialisation ratio (EU-27=100) (3)	Employment specialisation ratio (EU-27=100) (4)
1	Germany (23.6)	Italy (21.8)	Italy (201.0)	Italy (185.9)
2	Italy (22.4)	Germany (20.1)	Slovenia (152.1)	Slovenia (172.5)
3	France (16.3)	France (14.7)	Czech Republic (117.6)	Sweden (128.9)
4	United Kingdom (13.1)	United Kingdom (11.1)	France (115.9)	France (128.4)
5	Spain (7.7)	Spain (7.8)	Germany (112.6)	Czech Republic (126.1)

(1) Estonia, Greece, Luxembourg and Malta, not available.
(2) Estonia, Greece, Luxembourg and Malta, not available; Slovenia, 2003.
(3) Estonia, Ireland, Greece, Cyprus, Luxembourg and Malta, not available.
(4) Estonia, Ireland, Greece, Cyprus, Luxembourg and Malta, not available; Slovenia, 2003.
Source: Eurostat (SBS)

Table 7.24

Forging, pressing, stamping and roll forming of metal; powder metallurgy; treatment and coating of metals; general mechanical engineering (NACE Groups 28.4 and 28.5)
Productivity and profitability, EU-27, 2004

	Apparent labour productivity (EUR thousand)	Average personnel costs (EUR thousand)	Wage adjusted labour productivity (%)	Gross operating rate (%)
Other metal processing	38.4	29.7	129.2	12.0
Forging, pressing, stamping and roll forming of metal; powder metallurgy	45.5	33.7	135.1	8.9
Treatment and coating of metals; general mechanical engineering	36.3	28.4	127.6	13.5

Source: Eurostat (SBS)

COSTS, PRODUCTIVITY AND PROFITABILITY

Personnel costs in the EU-27's other metal processing sector were an average EUR 29 700 per employee (see Table 7.24) in 2004, slightly lower than the average across metal and metal products manufacturing as a whole. As a proportion of total expenditure, however, personnel costs accounted for 29.0 %, the highest share among the activities covered in Subchapters 7.1 to 7.7 and considerably more than the average share across metals and metal products manufacturing as a whole (21.1 %), underlining the labour intensive nature of the sector.

The apparent labour productivity of those employed across the EU-27 in the other metal processing sector was EUR 38 400 per person employed, which covered average personnel costs by 129.2 % in 2004. This wage adjusted labour productivity ratio for the sector was beneath the level for metals and metal products manufacturing (140.2 %) and more particularly the level for the non-financial business economy (148.0 %).

The gross operating rate, one measure of profitability, for other metal processing in the EU-27 was 12.0 % in 2004, a little higher than the rate (11.0 %) for the non-financial business economy.

7.7: MISCELLANEOUS FABRICATED METAL PRODUCTS

Together, NACE Groups 28.6 and 28.7 are referred to as miscellaneous fabricated metal products manufacturing. These two activities concern the manufacture of finished products for use in other industrial and construction activities, as well as final consumer markets. NACE Group 28.6 covers the manufacture of cutlery, tools and general hardware, such as locks and hinges, while NACE Group 28.7 covers the manufacture of other fabricated metal products, such as metal drums, light metal packaging, wire products, fasteners, baths and sinks, and household articles.

STRUCTURAL PROFILE

The miscellaneous fabricated metal products manufacturing (NACE Groups 28.6 and 28.7) sector of the EU-27 consisted of 107 200 enterprises which generated EUR 46.0 billion of value added in 2004, accounting for a little over one fifth (21.6 %) of the value added created across the metals and metal products manufacturing sector (NACE Subsection DJ). 1.2 million persons were employed in this sector, representing a little less than one in every four (23.0 %) of the metals and metal products manufacturing workforce. Miscellaneous fabricated metal products manufacturing was

Table 7.25

Manufacture of cutlery, tools and general hardware; manufacture of other fabricated metal products (NACE Groups 28.6 and 28.7)
Structural profile, EU-27, 2004 (1)

	No. of enterprises (thousands)	Turnover (EUR million)	Value added (EUR million)	Employment (thousands)
Miscellaneous fabricated metal products	107.2	130 000	46 000	1 150.0
Cutlery, tools and general hardware	45.7	41 000	18 000	430.0
Cutlery	2.5	2 340	999	24.0
Tools	14.2	21 000	9 500	218.0
Locks and hinges	29.0	18 000	7 100	183.0
Other fabricated metal products	61.5	86 425	28 681	722.7
Steel drums and similar containers	1.1	2 910	829	23.0
Light metal packaging	1.2	13 700	3 760	68.1
Wire products	3.9	11 200	3 060	70.0
Fasteners, screw machine products, chain and springs	:	14 000	5 500	120.0
Other fabricated metal products n.e.c.	50.0	45 000	15 000	440.0

(1) Rounded estimate based on non-confidential data.
Source: Eurostat (SBS)

the second largest of the activities, therefore, covered by Subchapters 7.1 to 7.7, both in terms of value added and employment, with shares that were just below those of other metal processing (see Subchapter 7.6). Within the sector, the manufacture of other fabricated

metal products (NACE Group 28.7) subsector generated EUR 28.7 billion of value added in 2004, being about 1.5 times as big as the manufacture of cutlery, tools and general hardware (NACE Group 28.6).

Table 7.26

Production of selected products - cutlery, tools and general hardware; other fabricated metal products (CPA Groups 28.6 and 28.7), EU-27, 2006 (1)

	Prodcom code	Production value (EUR million)	Volume of sold production (thousands)	Unit of volume
Cans used for preserving food and drink of iron or steel, < 50 litres, food cans	28.72.11.33	3 174	35 569 738	units
Welded grill, netting and fencing manufactured from wire of a diameter of <= 3 mm, with mesh size of <= 100 cm² including with a backing of paper as used in cementing and plastering	28.73.13.20	2 702	4 910 128	kg
Aluminium articles; inspection traps, gutters and gutter spouts, ladders and steps, thimbles, venetian blinds, cigarette cases, cosmetic/powder boxes and cases excluding of cast aluminium	28.75.27.55	2 411	c	kg
Iron or steel stranded wire, ropes and cables (including stranded wires and wire ropes with or without attached fittings not electrically insulated) (excluding electrically insulated)	28.73.11.30	1 796	1 442 596	kg
Closed-die forged	28.75.27.45	1 703	723 228	kg
Finished products of iron/steel wire; snares, traps, etc., fodder ties, animal nose rings, mattress hooks, butchers' hooks, tile hangers, waste paper baskets excluding lampshade frames	28.75.27.25	1 617	1 511 456	kg
Indexable inserts for tools, unmounted, of sintered metal carbides and cermets	28.62.50.67	911	3 520	kg
Cast aluminium articles such as inspection traps, gutters and gutter spouts, ladders and steps, thimbles, venetian blinds, cigarette cases, cosmetic or powder boxes and cases	28.75.27.53	874	315 562	kg
Cast articles of iron or steel, n.e.c.	28.75.27.19	804	365 996	kg
Rock drilling or earth boring tools with working part of cermets	28.62.50.13	284	38 623	kg

(1) Estimated.
Source: Eurostat (PRODCOM)

Table 7.27

Manufacture of cutlery, tools and general hardware; manufacture of other fabricated metal products (NACE Groups 28.6 and 28.7)
Structural profile: ranking of top five Member States, 2004

Rank	Share of EU-27 value added (%) (1)	Share of EU-27 employment (%) (2)	Value added specialisation ratio (EU-27=100) (3)	Employment specialisation ratio (EU-27=100) (4)
1	Germany (33.0)	Germany (24.6)	Slovenia (311.5)	Slovenia (297.0)
2	Italy (16.0)	Italy (16.1)	Czech Republic (202.5)	Czech Republic (230.0)
3	United Kingdom (10.9)	United Kingdom (8.7)	Germany (157.4)	Germany (148.7)
4	France (10.3)	France (8.4)	Italy (143.9)	Italy (136.6)
5	Spain (7.1)	Poland (7.3)	Austria (138.7)	Slovakia (133.1)

(1) Greece, Lithuania, Luxembourg, Malta and Netherlands, not available; Latvia, 2003.
(2) Greece, Lithuania, Luxembourg and Malta, not available.
(3) Ireland, Greece, Cyprus, Lithuania, Luxembourg, Malta and Netherlands, not available; Latvia, 2003.
(4) Ireland, Greece, Cyprus, Lithuania, Luxembourg and Malta, not available.
Source: Eurostat (SBS)

The miscellaneous fabricated metal products manufacturing sector in Germany created EUR 15.2 billion of value added in 2004, contributing about one third (33.0 %) of the value added generated by the sector across the EU-27 (see Table 7.27). The sector in Italy was the second largest, generating a little less than half of the value created in Germany. As a proportion of the value added of each Member State's non-financial business economy, however, the miscellaneous fabricated metal products manufacturing sector contributed the highest share (2.8 %) in Slovenia, a little more than three times the average share across the EU-27. The Czech Republic was also relatively specialised in this activity in value added terms, the contribution made by the sector being about double the EU-27 average.

The average rate of growth (2.2 % per annum) in the production index for the manufacture of cutlery, tools and general hardware (NACE Group 28.6) between 1996 and 2006 was similar to that for metals and metal products manufacturing as a whole (2.1 % per annum). The development in the respective production indices was also similar through until 2000, after which there were differences in the staggered growth of output; the production index of cutlery, tools and general hardware manufacturing dipped and then stabilised in the period between 2002 and 2005, whereas the period of relative stability in metals and metal products manufacturing was between 2000 and 2003. Although there was also growth (an average 1.0 % per annum) in the output of the manufacture of other fabricated metal products (NACE Group 28.7) during the ten years through to 2006, almost all of this was concentrated at the two ends of this period; between 2000 and 2005 there was relative stability in output and it was only in 2006 that the level of output rose above the level that had been reached in 1998.

Figure 7.9

Manufacture of cutlery, tools and general hardware; manufacture of other fabricated metal products (NACE Groups 28.6 and 28.7)
Index of production, EU-27 (2000=100)

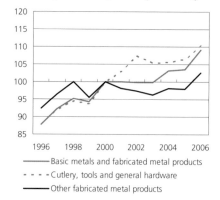

— Basic metals and fabricated metal products
- - - - Cutlery, tools and general hardware
— Other fabricated metal products

Source: Eurostat (STS)

Table 7.28
Cutlery, tools and general hardware; other fabricated metal products (CPA Groups 28.6 and 28.7)
External trade, EU-27, 2006

| | Extra-EU exports | | Extra-EU imports | | Trade balance | Cover ratio |
	(EUR million)	(% share of chapter)	(EUR million)	(% share of chapter)	(EUR million)	(%)
Cutlery, tools and general hardware; other fabricated metal products	21 412	23.8	19 190	18.4	2 222	111.6
Cutlery, tools and general hardware	8 406	9.3	7 204	6.9	1 202	116.7
Other fabricated metal products	13 005	14.4	11 985	11.5	1 020	108.5

Source: Eurostat (Comext)

COSTS, PRODUCTIVITY AND PROFITABILITY

The wage adjusted labour productivity ratio of those working in the miscellaneous fabricated metal products manufacturing sector of the EU-27 was 138.0 % in 2004, similar to the ratio for metals and metal products manufacturing (140 %) but moderately lower than ratio for the non-financial business economy (148.0 %). The similar ratios between the sector and the metals and metal products manufacturing average reflected the fact that both average personnel costs (EUR 29 000 per employee) and apparent labour productivity levels (EUR 40 000 per person employed) were slightly lower than for metals and metal products manufacturing as a whole.

There was a relatively high level of profitability in the EU-27's miscellaneous metal products manufacturing in so far that the gross operating rate was 12.4 % in 2004, the highest rate among the activities grouped in Subchapters 7.1 to 7.7. The relative profitability of the sector was most clearly illustrated in Finland, where there was a gross operating rate for miscellaneous metal products manufacturing of 17.6 % in 2004 compared to a rate of 10.4 % across the Finnish non-financial business economy.

EXTERNAL TRADE

The EU-27 had a trade surplus with non-member countries of EUR 2.2 billion for cutlery, tools and general hardware, and other fabricated metal products (CPA Groups 28.6 and 28.7) in 2006 – see Table 7.28. Although the trade surplus changed little in the period between 2002 and 2006, after widening relatively strongly between 2001 and 2002, there was strong growth in both exports and imports. EU-27 exports of cutlery, tools and general hardware, and other fabricated metal products were valued at EUR 21.4 billion in 2006, with the United States (19.9 % of the value of EU-27 exports) and China (9.0 %) being the main export markets. China was the main origin of EU-27 imports of these products, accounting for a little over one third (37.5 %) of the EUR 19.2 billion of EU-27 imports in 2006.

In contrast to the majority of Member States that recorded trade deficits for cutlery, tools and general hardware, and other fabricated metal products as a whole, Germany and Italy had considerable trade surpluses (intra- and extra-EU combined) of EUR 9.1 billion and EUR 6.9 billion respectively in 2006.

Table 7.29

Manufacture of basic metals (NACE Division 27)
Main indicators, 2004

	EU-27 (1)	BE	BG	CZ	DK	DE	EE	IE	EL	ES	FR	IT	CY	LV	LT
No. of enterprises (thousands)	16.0	0.3	0.2	0.6	0.2	2.7	0.0	0.1	:	1.5	1.1	3.8	0.0	0.0	0.0
Turnover (EUR million)	295 000	14 932	1 803	7 023	1 310	73 607	16	417	:	24 684	31 757	47 078	54	328	18
Production (EUR million)	280 000	15 131	1 861	6 791	1 265	69 802	16	407	:	24 891	30 865	46 380	55	333	16
Value added (EUR million)	66 900	3 395	264	1 481	376	18 762	3	135	:	5 631	7 036	9 204	21	110	6
Gross operating surplus (EUR million)	27 300	1 225	155	839	131	5 889	1	56	:	2 793	2 295	4 333	12	87	1
Purchases of goods & services (EUR million)	235 000	11 870	1 681	5 748	1 002	55 509	13	286	:	20 048	25 201	38 874	35	232	12
Personnel costs (EUR million)	39 700	2 170	108	643	246	12 872	2	79	:	2 837	4 741	4 871	10	23	5
Investment in tangible goods (EUR million)	10 300	294	84	194	49	2 178	2	16	:	1 048	1 006	1 600	16	21	0
Employment (thousands)	1 130	36	22	60	6	262	0	2	:	75	110	135	0	4	1
Apparent labour prod. (EUR thousand)	59.4	95.5	11.8	24.8	65.3	71.7	8.4	64.0	:	75.3	63.9	68.0	48.6	31.0	6.3
Average personnel costs (EUR thousand)	35.9	61.9	4.9	10.9	43.1	49.4	4.8	38.3	:	38.2	43.1	37.6	22.3	6.5	5.3
Wage adjusted labour productivity (%)	165.0	154.3	240.7	227.7	151.6	145.1	175.7	166.9	:	196.9	148.3	181.0	217.8	477.9	118.2
Gross operating rate (%)	9.2	8.2	8.6	11.9	10.0	8.0	8.5	13.3	:	11.3	7.2	9.2	21.2	26.5	5.4
Investment / employment (EUR thousand)	9.1	8.3	3.8	3.3	8.4	8.3	6.5	7.8	:	14.0	9.1	11.8	37.5	5.9	0.4

	LU (2)	HU	MT	NL	AT	PL	PT	RO	SI	SK	FI	SE	UK	NO
No. of enterprises (thousands)	0.0	0.4	:	0.3	0.2	0.8	0.4	0.5	0.1	0.1	0.2	0.5	1.8	0.2
Turnover (EUR million)	8 247	2 460	:	6 667	8 802	7 393	2 055	3 740	1 053	3 129	7 969	11 821	21 626	8 237
Production (EUR million)	2 159	2 399	:	6 606	8 718	7 572	1 969	4 078	1 052	2 926	7 514	11 839	21 140	5 205
Value added (EUR million)	459	532	:	2 099	2 677	1 916	443	865	255	928	1 763	2 851	4 858	1 635
Gross operating surplus (EUR million)	60	276	:	950	1 093	1 339	252	562	106	632	949	1 158	1 604	889
Purchases of goods & services (EUR million)	7 808	1 998	:	4 685	6 390	6 109	1 745	3 177	825	2 334	6 462	9 169	17 053	6 632
Personnel costs (EUR million)	399	256	:	1 150	1 584	577	191	303	149	296	814	1 693	3 254	746
Investment in tangible goods (EUR million)	122	98	:	142	532	181	121	436	61	193	584	350	688	401
Employment (thousands)	7	19	:	21	32	66	11	69	8	28	17	45	78	12
Apparent labour prod. (EUR thousand)	66.2	27.9	:	99.5	82.8	29.0	40.9	12.5	30.4	32.8	102.9	62.8	62.3	133.6
Average personnel costs (EUR thousand)	57.6	13.5	:	54.4	49.1	8.9	17.8	4.4	17.9	10.5	47.5	48.1	42.4	61.1
Wage adjusted labour productivity (%)	115.0	206.3	:	182.8	168.7	327.0	229.1	283.1	170.3	313.2	216.4	130.7	146.9	218.8
Gross operating rate (%)	0.7	11.2	:	14.2	12.4	18.1	12.3	15.0	10.1	20.2	11.9	9.8	7.4	10.8
Investment / employment (EUR thousand)	17.5	5.2	:	6.7	16.5	2.7	11.2	6.3	7.3	6.8	34.1	7.7	8.8	32.7

(1) Rounded estimates based on non-confidential data. (2) 2003.
Source: Eurostat (SBS)

Table 7.30

Manufacture of fabricated metal products, except machinery and equipment (NACE Division 28)
Main indicators, 2004

	EU-27 (1)	BE	BG	CZ	DK	DE	EE	IE	EL	ES	FR	IT	CY	LV	LT
No. of enterprises (thousands)	380.0	6.3	3.1	35.6	4.1	38.5	0.7	0.6	:	42.4	30.5	97.1	1.1	0.5	0.7
Turnover (EUR million)	403 000	10 505	576	6 883	5 471	95 994	468	1 627	:	36 815	55 161	85 977	241	189	340
Production (EUR million)	391 000	10 214	508	6 782	5 225	92 379	426	1 578	:	35 629	53 295	85 300	226	187	335
Value added (EUR million)	146 000	3 364	123	2 147	2 380	37 663	120	632	:	12 657	19 622	26 969	90	60	98
Gross operating surplus (EUR million)	45 000	925	57	993	627	9 914	41	208	:	3 863	3 745	10 496	34	29	30
Purchases of goods & services (EUR million)	262 000	7 241	484	4 935	3 213	58 689	361	1 015	:	25 085	35 350	59 995	158	140	260
Personnel costs (EUR million)	101 000	2 439	66	1 164	1 753	27 748	79	424	:	8 794	15 877	16 473	55	32	68
Investment in tangible goods (EUR million)	16 800	413	50	344	300	3 444	21	45	:	1 597	1 867	4 331	16	15	22
Employment (thousands)	3 860	65	36	173	45	780	11	13	:	359	444	704	4	9	15
Apparent labour prod. (EUR thousand)	37.7	51.7	3.4	12.4	53.1	48.3	10.6	48.1	:	35.3	44.2	38.3	24.3	6.9	6.3
Average personnel costs (EUR thousand)	28.6	41.0	2.0	8.4	41.2	37.1	7.1	32.9	:	26.5	36.3	29.7	18.4	3.8	4.5
Wage adjusted labour productivity (%)	132.0	125.9	169.4	146.7	128.9	130.4	150.0	146.3	:	133.0	121.8	128.9	132.1	181.9	141.8
Gross operating rate (%)	11.2	8.8	9.9	14.4	11.5	10.3	8.8	12.8	:	10.5	6.8	12.2	14.2	15.2	8.8
Investment / employment (EUR thousand)	4.3	6.3	1.4	2.0	6.7	4.4	1.8	3.4	:	4.4	4.2	6.2	4.3	1.7	1.4

	LU (2)	HU	MT	NL	AT	PL	PT	RO	SI	SK	FI	SE	UK	NO
No. of enterprises (thousands)	0.2	10.2	:	7.6	4.0	29.8	14.7	5.3	4.5	1.1	4.6	11.2	27.7	2.4
Turnover (EUR million)	669	3 121	:	15 093	9 625	9 238	4 491	1 498	2 146	1 264	5 048	10 788	38 671	2 614
Production (EUR million)	633	2 612	:	14 631	9 099	8 547	4 403	1 433	2 004	1 193	4 978	10 357	37 366	2 490
Value added (EUR million)	203	833	:	5 094	3 979	2 832	1 481	418	731	339	1 934	4 218	17 064	1 028
Gross operating surplus (EUR million)	50	334	:	1 439	1 395	1 560	493	147	288	129	540	1 146	6 299	235
Purchases of goods & services (EUR million)	447	2 307	:	10 299	5 850	6 723	3 127	1 195	1 483	955	3 268	6 689	21 600	1 613
Personnel costs (EUR million)	152	499	:	3 655	2 585	1 272	989	271	443	210	1 394	3 072	10 765	793
Investment in tangible goods (EUR million)	18	236	:	412	472	390	296	140	110	90	252	483	1 319	87
Employment (thousands)	4	73	:	93	69	235	84	96	32	32	41	84	349	19
Apparent labour prod. (EUR thousand)	47.4	11.5	:	54.9	57.7	12.0	17.7	4.4	22.9	10.4	47.7	50.5	48.8	53.9
Average personnel costs (EUR thousand)	36.4	7.4	:	41.4	39.1	6.4	12.9	2.9	15.3	6.5	35.5	40.3	32.7	43.6
Wage adjusted labour productivity (%)	130.1	154.9	:	132.4	147.7	189.3	137.0	152.3	149.1	160.6	134.5	125.3	149.4	123.6
Gross operating rate (%)	7.5	10.7	:	9.5	14.5	16.9	11.0	9.8	13.4	10.2	10.7	10.6	16.3	9.0
Investment / employment (EUR thousand)	4.3	3.2	:	4.4	6.8	1.7	3.5	1.5	3.4	2.8	6.2	5.8	3.8	4.5

(1) Rounded estimates based on non-confidential data. (2) 2003.
Source: Eurostat (SBS)

8.1: POWER MACHINERY

The manufacture of power machinery (NACE Group 29.1) concerns the manufacture of machinery for the production and use of mechanical power. This includes internal combustion engines, as well as steam, gas, wind and hydraulic turbines, pumps, compressors, taps, valves, bearings and transmission equipment. This NACE group excludes the manufacture of propulsion engines for aircraft, vehicles or cycles. Power machines transform different forms of energy, for example, thermal or electrical energy into motion.

STRUCTURAL PROFILE

The power machinery manufacturing sector (NACE Group 29.1) had some 14 600 enterprises which generated EUR 38.5 billion across the EU-27 in 2004, contributing 22.4 % of the total value added for machinery and equipment manufacturing (NACE Subsection DK). The sector also employed 719 400 persons across the EU-27 in 2004, accounting for about one in every five people within the machinery and equipment workforce.

Among the four NACE classes that comprise the power machinery sector, the manufacture of pumps and compressors (NACE Class 29.12) was the largest in terms of value added, contributing 30.1 % of sectoral value added – see Table 8.5. The next largest activities were the manufacture of bearings, gears, gearing and driving elements (NACE Class 29.14), which contributed 28.3 % of sectoral value added, and then the manufacture of taps and valves (NACE Class 29.13), which contributed a further quarter (24.7 %) of the total. The smallest of the four subsectors was the manufacture of engines and turbines (NACE Class 29.11), which generated 16.7 % of the value added for power machinery manufacturing.

The power machinery manufacturing sector in Germany generated EUR 16.4 billion of value added in 2004, which represented 42.6 % of the value added generated across the EU-27, by far the largest share among the Member States – see Table 8.6. Among the Member States, however, the power machinery manufacturing sector in Slovakia contributed the highest proportion (1.6 %) of the value added of any national non-financial business economy (NACE Sections C to I and K), a little higher than the proportion in Germany, and in both cases a little more than double the average share across the EU-27.

Annual short-term statistics show that the staggered growth in the production index for the manufacture of power machinery (NACE Group 29.1) was very similar to, although slightly more pronounced than that for machinery and equipment manufacturing as a whole (NACE Subsection DK) during the ten years between 1996 and 2006 – see Figure 8.2 in the overview to this chapter. Over the same period, there were also very similar developments in the domestic output price indices for the EU-27's manufacture of power machinery on the one hand and machinery and equipment manufacturing as a whole on the other. Like machinery and equipment manufacturing as a whole, the domestic output price index of power machinery manufacturing increased year-on-year at a relatively even pace (an average 1.5 % per annum over the ten years), although there was some accelerated growth in the output price of power machinery after 2003.

Table 8.5

Manufacture of machinery for the production and use of mechanical power, except aircraft, vehicle and cycle engines (NACE Group 29.1)
Structural profile, EU-27, 2004 (1)

	No. of enterprises (thousands)	Turnover (EUR million)	Value added (EUR million)	Employment (thousands)
Power machinery	14.6	112 000	38 496	719.4
Engines and turbines, except aircraft, vehicle and cycle engines	2.8	22 900	6 430	110.0
Pumps and compressors	5.5	34 100	11 600	214.0
Taps and valves	2.8	26 000	9 500	170.0
Bearings, gears, gearing and driving elements	3.4	29 600	10 900	230.0

(1) Rounded estimates based on non-confidential data.
Source: Eurostat (SBS)

Table 8.6

Manufacture of machinery for the production and use of mechanical power, except aircraft, vehicle and cycle engines (NACE Group 29.1)
Structural profile: ranking of top five Member States, 2004

Rank	Share of EU-27 value added (%) (1)	Share of EU-27 employment (%) (1)	Value added specialisation ratio (EU-27=100) (2)	Employment specialisation ratio (EU-27=100) (2)
1	Germany (42.6)	Germany (33.8)	Slovakia (214.8)	Slovakia (285.2)
2	Italy (15.1)	Italy (13.1)	Germany (203.3)	Denmark (217.1)
3	United Kingdom (10.7)	United Kingdom (9.8)	Denmark (162.3)	Germany (204.3)
4	France (10.1)	France (9.3)	Italy (135.5)	Finland (141.6)
5	Denmark (3.3)	Romania (4.4)	Bulgaria (116.4)	Romania (138.2)

(1) Estonia, Greece, Luxembourg and Malta, not available.
(2) Estonia, Ireland, Greece, Cyprus, Luxembourg and Malta, not available.
Source: Eurostat (SBS)

Table 8.7

Manufacture of machinery for the production and use of mechanical power, except aircraft, vehicle and cycle engines (NACE Group 29.1)
Productivity and profitability, EU-27, 2004 (1)

	Apparent labour productivity (EUR thousand)	Average personnel costs (EUR thousand)	Wage adjusted labour productivity (%)	Gross operating rate (%)
Power machinery	53.5	38.5	138.8	10.0
Engines and turbines, except aircraft, vehicle and cycle engines	59.0	41.0	140.0	9.0
Pumps and compressors	54.5	39.6	137.0	9.7
Taps and valves	56.0	39.0	140.0	11.5
Bearings, gears, gearing and driving elements	48.0	36.0	130.0	9.7

(1) Rounded estimates based on non-confidential data.
Source: Eurostat (SBS)

Table 8.8

Machinery for the production and use of mechanical power, except aircraft, vehicle and cycle engines (CPA Group 29.1)
External trade, EU-27, 2006

	Extra-EU exports (EUR million)	(% share of chapter)	Extra-EU imports (EUR million)	(% share of chapter)	Trade balance (EUR million)	Cover ratio (%)
Power machinery	40 226	23.5	20 602	27.6	19 625	195.3
Engines and turbines except aircraft, vehicle and cycle engines	9 003	5.3	5 775	7.7	3 228	155.9
Pumps and compressors	14 126	8.3	6 403	8.6	7 722	220.6
Taps and valves	9 187	5.4	4 235	5.7	4 952	216.9
Bearings, gears, gearing and driving elements	7 910	4.6	4 188	5.6	3 722	188.9

Source: Eurostat (Comext)

COSTS, PRODUCTIVITY AND PROFITABILITY

The structure of costs across the EU-27's power machinery (NACE Group 29.1) sector was similar to that already described for machinery and equipment manufacturing as a whole, with a relatively low ratio of tangible investment (3.7 %) and much higher ratio of personnel costs (25.7 %) in total expenditure than for the non-financial business economy (4.9 % and 16.4 % respectively) in 2004.

Average personnel costs of EUR 38 500 per employee across the EU-27 power machinery sector were the highest among the NACE groups [6] that comprise machinery and equipment manufacturing, and almost two fifths higher than the average across the non-financial business economy. The apparent

[6] The manufacture of agricultural tractors and other agricultural and forestry machinery (NACE Group 29.3), 2003.

labour productivity of EUR 53 500 per person employed across the sector in the EU-27 in 2004 (see Table 8.7) was also the highest level among the NACE groups within the machinery and equipment manufacturing and 30.8 % higher than the level across the non-financial business economy. Although the wage adjusted labour productivity ratio of the power machinery sector (138.8 %) was also the highest among the NACE groups of this chapter, it remained below the ratio (148.0 %) for the non-financial business economy.

As with the measures of productivity, the gross operating rate of 10.0 % for the EU-27's power machinery sector was also the highest among the NACE groups of this chapter but was a lower rate of profitability than that for the non-financial business economy as a whole (11.0 %).

EXTERNAL TRADE

EU-27 exports of power machinery (CPA Group 29.1) were valued at EUR 40.2 billion in 2006 (see Table 8.8), accounting for a little less than one quarter (23.5 %) of the value of EU-27 exports of machinery and equipment (CPA Subsection DK). With EU-27 imports of power machinery valued at EUR 20.6 billion in 2006, the EU-27 recorded a trade surplus of EUR 19.6 billion in these goods. Each of the four CPA classes comprising power machinery recorded a trade surplus, with that for pumps and compressors (CPA Class 29.12) being largest at EUR 7.7 billion.

As in the majority of machinery and equipment CPA groups, Germany had by far the largest trade surplus in power machinery among the Member States (EUR 16.5 billion), followed by Italy (EUR 7.9 billion) and then France (EUR 1.0 billion). In contrast, the largest trade deficit (EUR 1.8 billion) in power machinery in 2006 was recorded for Spain.

8.2: INDUSTRIAL PROCESSING MACHINERY

The manufacture of industrial processing machinery is made up of the manufacture of general purpose machinery, machine-tools, and special purpose machinery, as covered by NACE Groups 29.2, 29.4 and 29.5.

Other general purpose machinery covers equipment such as lifting and handling equipment, furnaces and furnace burners, and cooling equipment. Such machinery is of general purpose because it is used by a broad range of downstream sectors, such as the distribution and transport sectors and mining and quarrying sectors. In contrast, special purpose machinery is tailored for use within specific sectors of the economy and particularly the various engineering sectors that are covered in other parts of this chapter as well as Chapters 9 and 10 that follow.

STRUCTURAL PROFILE

The EU-27's industrial processing machinery manufacturing sector (NACE Groups 29.2, 29.4 and 29.5) consisted of 122 800 enterprises which generated EUR 110.0 billion of value added in 2004, contributing almost two thirds (64.1 %) of the value added created across machinery and equipment manufacturing (NACE Subsection DK). The 2.3 million employed in the industrial processing machinery manufacturing sector across the EU-27 in 2004 also represented somewhat less than two in every three (62.8 %) of those in the machinery and equipment workforce.

Of the three NACE groups that make up the manufacture of industrial processing machinery, the largest was the manufacture of other general purpose machinery (NACE Group 29.2), which accounted for a little less than half of sectoral value added (46.8 %) in 2004 and a similar proportion (45.9 %) of its workforce. The manufacture of other special purpose

machinery (NACE Group 29.5) was a little smaller, accounting for 38.2 % of sectoral value added and 41.7 % of the industrial processing machinery sector's workforce. The manufacture of machine tools (NACE Group 29.4) was by far the smallest of the three activities covered in this subchapter – see Table 8.9.

The industrial processing sector is made up of 13 NACE classes. Within the EU-27, the largest of these in 2006 was the manufacture of other special purpose machinery not elsewhere classified (NACE Class 29.56), such as printing and book-binding machinery, dryers for wood and centrifugal clothes-dryers, which contributed 18.7 % of the value added generated across the industrial processing machinery manufacturing sector and employed 19.2 % of its workforce. At the NACE class level, three other subsectors contributed one tenth or more of industrial processing value added and employment, all concerning the manufacture of other general purpose

Table 8.9
Manufacture of industrial processing machinery (NACE Groups 29.2, 29.4 and 29.5)
Structural profile, EU-27, 2004 (1)

	No. of enterprises (thousands)	Turnover (EUR million)	Value added (EUR million)	Employment (thousands)
Industrial processing machinery	122.8	324 000	110 000	2 300.0
Other general purpose machinery	63.2	153 425	51 526	1 054.6
Furnaces and furnace burners	3.3	6 000	2 000	41.8
Lifting and handling equipment	16.1	52 100	17 400	350.0
Non-domestic cooling and ventilation equipment	15.0	41 000	13 000	270.0
Other general purpose machinery n.e.c.	28.5	54 400	19 000	390.0
Machine-tools	13.6	40 672	14 568	317.9
Other special purpose machinery	45.9	130 000	42 000	960.0
Machinery for metallurgy	2.5	6 060	2 020	60.0
Machinery for mining, quarrying and construction	6.0	28 600	7 710	190.0
Machinery for food, beverage and tobacco processing	8.4	17 000	5 600	130.0
Machinery for textile, apparel and leather production	5.2	12 000	4 000	95.5
Machinery for paper and paperboard production	1.2	7 640	2 410	45.5
Other special purpose machinery n.e.c.	22.7	58 700	20 600	443.0

(1) Rounded estimates based on non-confidential data, except for machine tools.
Source: Eurostat (SBS)

Table 8.10
Manufacture of industrial processing machinery (NACE Groups 29.2, 29.4 and 29.5)
Structural profile: ranking of top five Member States, 2004

Rank	Share of EU-27 value added (%) (1)	Share of EU-27 employment (%) (2)	Value added specialisation ratio (EU-27=100) (3)	Employment specialisation ratio (EU-27=100) (4)
1	Germany (37.4)	Germany (30.8)	Germany (178.4)	Germany (186.1)
2	Italy (16.6)	Italy (16.3)	Italy (149.5)	Finland (173.5)
3	United Kingdom (9.4)	France (8.2)	Finland (145.6)	Sweden (172.1)
4	France (9.0)	United Kingdom (7.8)	Austria (134.8)	Czech Republic (158.0)
5	Spain (5.2)	Spain (5.9)	Sweden (128.9)	Slovakia (144.5)

(1) Greece, Luxembourg and Malta, not available; Denmark and Slovenia, 2003.
(2) Greece, Luxembourg and Malta, not available; Denmark, 2003.
(3) Ireland, Greece, Cyprus, Luxembourg and Malta, not available; Denmark and Slovenia, 2003.
(4) Ireland, Greece, Cyprus, Luxembourg and Malta, not available; Denmark, 2003.
Source: Eurostat (SBS)

Table 8.11

Production of selected products - industrial processing machinery (CPA Groups 29.2, 29.4 and 29.5), EU-27, 2006 (1)

	Prodcom code	Production value (EUR million)	Volume of sold production (thousands)	Unit of volume
Parts of machines of 8479	29.56.26.70	5 068	-	-
Machinery for packing or wrapping (excluding for filling, closing, sealing, capsuling or labelling bottles, cans, boxes, bags or other containers)	29.24.21.70	4 643	218	units
Parts for earthmoving equipt., ships' derricks, cranes, mobile lifting frames excluding buckets, shovels, grabs, grips, blades (all types of construction equipt.), for boring/sinking machinery	29.52.61.50	4 547	-	-
Parts of machinery of HS 8425, 8427 and 8428 (excluding lift, skip hoists or escalators)	29.22.19.30	4 100	-	-
Self-propelled fork-lift trucks, rough terrain and other trucks, non-electric, with a lifting height <= 1m	29.22.15.33	3 420	83	units
Self-propelled fork-lift trucks powered by an electric motor, with a lifting height <= 1 m	29.22.15.13	2 753	171	units
Wheeled loaders, crawler shovel loaders, front-end loaders	29.52.25.50	2 467	45	units
Self-propelled coal or rock cutters and tunnelling machinery	29.52.12.33	1 421	9	units
Machinery for making pulp of fibrous cellulosic material	29.55.11.13	1 267	c	units
Fully or partly automatic electrical machines for resistance welding of metal	29.43.20.30	806	54	units

(1) Estimated.
Source: Eurostat (PRODCOM)

machinery: the manufacture of other general purpose machinery not elsewhere classified (NACE Class 29.24), such as industrial cleaning and packing machines, centrifuges and gas generators contributed 17.3 % of sectoral value added, the manufacture of lifting and handling equipment (NACE Class 29.22) contributed 15.8 %, and the manufacture of non-domestic cooling and ventilation equipment (NACE Class 29.23) contributed 11.8 % of value added.

The industrial processing machinery manufacturing sector in Germany contributed a little more than one third (37.4 %) of the value added generated by the sector across the EU-27 in 2004, more than double the next highest contribution which was from Italy (16.6 %) – see Table 8.10. Germany had an even greater presence in the manufacture of machine-tools, where it contributed a little over half (52.6 %) of the value added across the EU-27. Germany was also the most specialised Member State in industrial processing machinery manufacturing in 2004, the value added generated by this activity accounting for 3.8 % of the value added generated across its non-financial business economy (NACE Sections C to I and K) in 2004, a much higher share than the average (2.2 %) for the EU-27. In these relative terms, Italy and Finland were also relatively specialised in this sector.

The production indices for the three NACE groups that comprise the manufacture of industrial processing machinery generally followed a similar progression to the index for the manufacture of machinery and equipment as a whole over the period between 1996 and 2001. All three groups then experienced varying declines in output in 2002 and 2003 (and 2004 in the case of the manufacture of machine tools) before a return to strong growth. Over the ten years through until 2006, the growth in output of other general purpose machinery (NACE Group 29.2) was strongest (an average 2.4 %) and most closely followed the broader development for machinery and equipment manufacturing. The lower rates of growth in the output of both other special purpose machinery (NACE Group 29.5) and the manufacture of machine tools (NACE Group 29.4), an average 1.5 % and 1.4 % per annum respectively, in large part reflected the downturns in output after 2001. The domestic output price indices of the three NACE groups developed in a very similar way to that for machinery and equipment manufacturing as a whole throughout the period between 1996 and 2006, with year-on-year rises which averaged between 1.3 % and 1.4 % per annum.

COSTS, PRODUCTIVITY AND PROFITABILITY

The structure of costs within the industrial processing machinery manufacturing sector was very similar to that for machinery and equipment manufacturing as a whole, albeit with a slightly lower proportion of total expenditure accounted for by investment expenditure (2.6 %) and slightly higher proportion accounted for by personnel costs (26.4 %).

Average personnel costs for those working in the sector (EUR 36 900 per employee) across the EU-27 were very similar to the average across machinery and equipment manufacturing as a whole and about one third higher (33.7 %) than the average across the non-financial business economy. Apparent labour productivity of EUR 46 500 per person employed in the sector (see Table 8.12) was also similar to the average across machinery and equipment manufacturing as a whole. As a result, the wage adjusted labour productivity ratio of the industrial processing machinery manufacturing sector (126.0 %) was also similar to the average for the activities covered in this chapter and was notably lower, therefore, than the average ratio (148.0 %) across the non-financial business economy. This characteristic was common to all Member States [7], with the exception of Italy where the wage adjusted labour productivity ratio of the sector was slightly above the ratio for the non-financial business economy.

[7] Denmark and Slovenia, 2003; Ireland, Greece, Cyprus, Luxembourg and Malta, not available.

Table 8.12

Manufacture of industrial processing machinery (NACE Groups 29.2, 29.4 and 29.5)
Productivity and profitability, EU-27, 2004 (1)

	Apparent labour productivity (EUR thousand)	Average personnel costs (EUR thousand)	Wage adjusted labour productivity (%)	Gross operating rate (%)
Industrial processing machinery	46.5	36.9	126.0	8.2
Other general purpose machinery	48.9	37.8	129.1	9.2
Furnaces and furnace burners	48.0	39.0	123.0	8.3
Lifting and handling equipment	49.8	37.9	132.0	9.0
Non-domestic cooling and ventilation equipment	48.0	38.0	129.0	8.4
Other general purpose machinery n.e.c.	48.7	38.1	128.0	10.0
Machine-tools	45.8	37.0	123.8	7.9
Other special purpose machinery	44.1	36.0	123.0	7.2
Machinery for metallurgy	34.0	28.0	120.0	6.9
Machinery for mining, quarrying and construction	40.0	31.0	130.0	7.5
Machinery for food, beverage and tobacco processing	45.0	35.0	127.0	8.4
Machinery for textile, apparel and leather production	42.0	36.0	116.0	6.0
Machinery for paper and paperboard production	52.9	46.9	113.0	4.3
Other special purpose machinery n.e.c.	46.7	38.2	122.0	7.5

(1) Rounded estimates based on non-confidential data.
Source: Eurostat (SBS)

Table 8.13

Industrial processing machinery (CPA Groups 29.2, 29.4 and 29.5)
External trade, EU-27, 2006

	Extra-EU exports		Extra-EU imports		Trade balance (EUR million)	Cover ratio (%)
	(EUR million)	(% share of chapter)	(EUR million)	(% share of chapter)		
Industrial processing machinery	115 097	67.3	42 256	56.6	72 841	272.4
Other general purpose machinery	41 169	24.1	15 787	21.1	25 382	260.8
Furnaces and furnace burners	2 986	1.7	588.0	0.8	2 398.0	508.0
Lifting and handling equipment	11 557	6.8	3 338.0	4.5	8 219.0	346.0
Non-domestic cooling and ventilation equipment	8 827	5.2	6 544.0	8.8	2 283.0	135.0
Other general purpose machinery n.e.c.	17 798	10.4	5 316.0	7.1	12 481.0	335.0
Machine tools	15 628	9.1	9 830	13.2	5 799	159.0
Other special purpose machinery	58 300	34.1	16 639	22.3	41 661	350.4
Machinery for metallurgy	2 547	1.5	323	0.4	2 224	790.0
Machinery for mining, quarrying and construction	17 490	10.2	5 813	7.8	11 677	301.0
Machinery for food, beverage and tobacco processing	5 564	3.3	801	1.1	4 762	694.0
Machinery for textile, apparel and leather production	6 688	3.9	1 204	1.6	5 484	555.0
Machinery for paper and paperboard production	3 282	1.9	739	1.0	2 543	444.0
Other special purpose machinery n.e.c.	22 728	13.3	7 759	10.4	14 969	293.0

Source: Eurostat (Comext)

The gross operating rate, a measure of profitability that compares the gross operating surplus with turnover, for the EU-27's manufacture of industrial processing machinery sector was 8.2 % in 2004. The manufacture of other general purpose machinery (NACE Group 29.2) had the highest gross operating rate (9.2 %) among the three NACE groups covered, although this rate remained below the non-financial business economy average (11.0 %).

EXTERNAL TRADE

EU-27 exports of industrial processing machinery (CPA Groups 29.2, 29.4 and 29.5) were valued at EUR 115.1 billion in 2006 (see Table 8.13), accounting for 10.6 % of the value of industrial (CPA Sections C to E) exports. The EU-27 trade surplus with non-member countries in industrial processing machinery widened to EUR 72.8 billion in 2006, despite the strong rise in the value of imports to EUR 42.3 billion. There were trade surpluses for each of the CPA groups that comprise industrial processing machinery, although the majority (57.2 %) of the surplus came from EU-27 trade in other general purpose machinery (CPA Group 29.2).

Germany had a trade surplus (intra- and extra EU trade) of EUR 52.4 billion in industrial processing machinery in 2006, almost double the surplus recorded by Italy (EUR 27.0 billion) and substantially more than the third highest surplus (EUR 4.4 billion) which was recorded by Sweden.

8.3: AGRICULTURAL AND FORESTRY MACHINERY

NACE Group 29.3 covers the manufacture of agricultural tractors and other agricultural and forestry machinery, but not agricultural hand tools.

Domestic demand for agricultural machinery is closely linked to structural developments and profitability within farming. The number of farms has been declining steeply and steadily for many years (a decline of 14.6 % in the EU-15 [8] between 2000 and 2005 according to statistics from the Structure of Agricultural Holdings), which has had the dual effect of reducing the size of the domestic market and increasing the second-hand market for machinery. There has also been an increasing tendency to use specialist machinery contractors for sowing, harvesting and spraying.

[8] France, not available.

STRUCTURAL PROFILE

The agricultural and forestry machinery manufacturing sector (NACE Group 29.3) was one of the smaller activities within the manufacture of machinery and equipment (NACE Subsection DK); the sector had some 21 400 enterprises and generated EUR 8.0 billion of value added across the EU-27 in 2004, contributing 4.7 % of value added generated by all the manufacturing activities covered by this chapter and the 210 000 people employed accounted for only a slightly higher proportion (5.7 %) of the manufacture of machinery and equipment workforce.

The manufacture of other agricultural and forestry machinery (NACE Class 29.32), generated the bulk (82.5 %) of sectoral value added, the remainder being generated by the manufacture of agricultural tractors (NACE Class 29.31).

A quarter (25.3 %) of sectoral value added was generated in Germany, the largest contribution among Member States, the next largest coming from Italy (18.4 %) and France (15.5 %) – see Table 8.14. In terms of this sector's contribution to the value added of the national non-financial business economies (NACE Sections C to I and K), Finland, Austria and Italy were relatively more specialised in the manufacture of agricultural and forestry machinery than the other Member States [9].

[9] Denmark, Ireland, Greece, Cyprus, Luxembourg, Malta and Netherlands, not available.

Table 8.14

Manufacture of agricultural and forestry machinery (NACE Group 29.3)
Structural profile: ranking of top five Member States, 2004

Rank	Share of EU-27 value added (%) (1)	Share of EU-27 employment (%) (2)	Value added specialisation ratio (EU-27=100) (3)	Employment specialisation ratio (EU-27=100) (4)
1	Germany (25.3)	Germany (18.3)	Finland (272.4)	Finland (229.4)
2	Italy (18.4)	Italy (16.9)	Austria (203.0)	Austria (178.2)
3	France (15.5)	France (13.7)	Italy (165.1)	Slovenia (151.9)
4	United Kingdom (5.2)	Poland (8.6)	Slovenia (132.1)	Czech Republic (146.0)
5	Austria (4.9)	Spain (5.4)	Czech Republic (124.1)	Italy (143.9)

(1) Denmark, Greece, Luxembourg, Malta and Netherlands, not available.
(2) Denmark, Greece, Luxembourg and Malta, not available; Slovenia, 2003.
(3) Denmark, Ireland, Greece, Cyprus, Luxembourg, Malta and Netherlands, not available.
(4) Denmark, Ireland, Greece, Cyprus, Luxembourg and Malta, not available; Slovenia, 2003.
Source: Eurostat (SBS)

Table 8.15

Production of selected products - agricultural and forestry machinery (CPA Group 29.3), EU-27, 2006 (1)

	Prodcom code	Production value (EUR million)	Volume of sold production (thousands)	Unit of volume
New agricultural and forestry tractors, wheeled, of an engine power > 59 kW but <= 75 kW (excluding pedestrian-controlled tractors)	29.31.23.30	1 842	64	units
Combine harvester-threshers	29.32.34.10	1 162	14	units
New agricultural and forestry tractors, wheeled, of an engine power > 75 kW but <= 90 kW (excluding pedestrian-controlled tractors)	29.31.23.50	1 076	20	units
New agricultural and forestry tractors, wheeled, of an engine power > 37 kW but <= 59 kW (excluding pedestrian-controlled tractors)	29.31.22.00	1 059	49	units
Parts of agricultural, horticultural or forestry machinery for soil preparation or cultivation	29.32.70.20	831	-	-
Self-loading or self-unloading trailers for agricultural purposes	29.32.50.40	771	91	units
Self-propelled powered mowers with a seat and with the cutting device rotating in a horizontal plane, for lawns, parks, golf courses or sports grounds (excluding electric mowers)	29.32.20.33	647	918	units
Seeders for agricultural or horticultural use (excluding central driven precision spacing seeders)	29.32.13.35	262	36	units
New agricultural and forestry tractors, wheeled, of an engine power <= 18 kW (excluding pedestrian-controlled tractors)	29.31.21.30	79	40	units

(1) Estimated.
Source: Eurostat (PRODCOM)

The output of the EU-27's manufacture of agricultural and forestry machinery grew during the period between 1996 and 2006, although did so unevenly and in stages. There was strong growth in the production index between 1996 and 1997, which was partly undone by the subsequent year-on-year declines through until 2001. There was then strong growth in the production index in 2002, which was again followed by a small decline, although there was a return to growth in 2004, 2005 and 2006. Over the ten years through until 2006 the average rate of growth in the production index for the manufacture of agricultural and forestry machinery (an average 2.1 % per annum) was very similar to the rate of growth for the manufacture of machinery and equipment as a whole.

COSTS, PRODUCTIVITY AND PROFITABILITY

The apparent labour productivity of those working in the EU-27's manufacture of agricultural and forestry machinery sector was around EUR 38 000 per person employed in 2004, EUR 8 800 per person less than the level across machinery and equipment manufacturing as a whole. Figures for 2003, however, suggest that average personnel costs per employee in the sector were also low, resulting in a wage adjusted labour productivity ratio for the sector (129.9 %) that was slightly above the machinery and equipment average but well below the ratio for the non-financial business economy.

EXTERNAL TRADE

The EU-27 recorded a EUR 4.0 billion trade surplus for agricultural and forestry machinery (CPA Group 29.3) in 2006, resulting from EU-27 exports of EUR 6.3 billion and imports of EUR 2.3 billion (see Table 8.16). Both the CPA classes within agricultural and forestry machinery recorded trade surpluses in 2006, with the surplus for other agricultural and forestry machinery (CPA Class 29.32) accounting for a little less than two thirds (64.7 %) of the total. The largest trade surpluses (intra- and extra-EU trade) for agricultural and forestry machinery among the Member States in 2006 were recorded for Germany (EUR 4.0 billion) and Italy (EUR 2.4 billion).

Table 8.16

Agricultural and forestry machinery (CPA Group 29.3)
External trade, EU-27, 2006

	Extra-EU exports		Extra-EU imports			
	(EUR million)	(% share of chapter)	(EUR million)	(% share of chapter)	Trade balance (EUR million)	Cover ratio (%)
Agricultural and forestry machinery	6 305	3.7	2 270	3.0	4 034	277.7
Agricultural tractors	2 193	1.3	769	1.0	1 424	285.3
Other agricultural and forestry machinery	4 112	2.4	1 502	2.0	2 610	273.8

Source: Eurostat (Comext)

8.4: ARMS AND AMMUNITION

The activity of NACE Group 29.6 covers the manufacture of tanks and other fighting vehicles, artillery material and ballistic missiles, small arms and ammunition. This activity also includes the manufacture of hunting, sporting or protective firearms and ammunition, as well as explosive devices (such as bombs, mines and torpedoes).

In comparison to many of the other sectors of the economy covered by this publication, the availability of data on the arms and ammunition sector is often restricted by issues of confidentiality. Therefore, the likelihood of an under-reporting of arms production and sales must be borne in mind by readers.

STRUCTURAL PROFILE

Among the NACE groups that make up machinery and equipment manufacturing, the manufacture of arms and ammunition sector (NACE Group 29.6) was the smallest in terms of both the value added generated (EUR 4.3 billion) and the size of its workforce (105 800 persons); the sector accounted for only 2.5 % of the value added generated across machinery and equipment manufacturing and 2.9 % of its workforce. There were 1 240 enterprises registered in the EU-27's arms and ammunition sector in 2004.

The manufacture of arms and ammunition sector in the United Kingdom generated more value added than in any other Member State, accounting for a little over a quarter (26.9 %) of the value added generated across the EU-27 in 2004. The next highest contributions came from France (19.5 %) and Germany (19.2 %) – see Table 8.17. Across the EU-27 as a whole, the contribution made by the manufacture of arms and ammunition sector to the value added of the non-financial business economy (NACE Sections C to I and K) was only 0.1 % in 2004. In these terms, Bulgaria was by far the most specialised Member State [10] in this activity, the sector contributing 0.5 % of the value added of its non-financial business economy, followed by Sweden and Romania.

Over the period between 1996 and 2006, the production index for arms and munitions manufacturing (as given in annual short-term statistics) grew by an average 2.9 % per annum, the fastest rate of growth among the NACE groups that comprise machinery and equipment manufacturing. However, there were two distinct periods of output development; the first was characterised by falling output after 1997 through until 2000 and the second by the subsequent, sustained strong growth through until 2006, at an average 6.5 % per annum.

[10] Slovenia, 2003; Denmark, Estonia, Ireland, Greece, Cyprus, Latvia, Luxembourg, Malta and Netherlands, not available.

COSTS, PRODUCTIVITY AND PROFITABILITY

The wage adjusted labour productivity ratio of the EU-27's arms and ammunition manufacturing sector was 119.9 % in 2004, the lowest of any of the NACE groups [11] that make up machinery and equipment manufacturing and much lower than the ratio for the EU-27's non-financial business economy (148.0 %). The wage adjusted labour productivity ratio for the sector in 2004, reflected a relatively low apparent labour productivity level of EUR 40 300 per person employed and relatively high average personnel costs of EUR 33 600 per employee.

EXTERNAL TRADE

Exports of arms and ammunition (CPA Group 29.6) to non-member countries accounted for a small majority (53.3 %) of the EU-27 Member States' trade (intra- and extra-EU), the second highest proportion among the various subchapters of this publication.

The value of exports of arms and ammunition recorded in official external trade statistics was relatively small at EUR 907.5 million in 2006, from which a trade surplus of EUR 619.8 million was recorded.

[11] The manufacture of agricultural tractors and other agricultural and forestry machinery (NACE Group 29.3), 2003.

Table 8.17

Manufacture of arms and ammunition (NACE Group 29.6)
Structural profile: ranking of top five Member States, 2004

Rank	Share of EU-27 value added (%) (1)	Share of EU-27 employment (%) (2)	Value added specialisation ratio (EU-27=100) (3)	Employment specialisation ratio (EU-27=100) (4)
1	United Kingdom (26.9)	United Kingdom (16.0)	Bulgaria (638.2)	Bulgaria (960.1)
2	France (19.5)	Romania (15.7)	Sweden (250.8)	Romania (489.2)
3	Germany (19.2)	Bulgaria (13.6)	Romania (178.0)	Sweden (168.8)
4	Italy (9.6)	France (11.6)	Finland (149.3)	Czech Republic (156.1)
5	Sweden (7.3)	Germany (11.2)	United Kingdom (142.0)	Finland (123.7)

(1) Denmark, Estonia, Greece, Latvia, Luxembourg, Malta and Netherlands, not available; Slovenia, 2003.
(2) Denmark, Estonia, Greece, Luxembourg, Malta and Netherlands, not available; Slovenia, 2003.
(3) Denmark, Estonia, Ireland, Greece, Cyprus, Latvia, Luxembourg, Malta and Netherlands, not available; Slovenia, 2003.
(4) Denmark, Estonia, Ireland, Greece, Cyprus, Luxembourg, Malta and Netherlands, not available; Slovenia, 2003.
Source: Eurostat (SBS)

8.5: DOMESTIC APPLIANCES

The activities of NACE Group 29.7 cover the manufacture of domestic electrical appliances (such as white goods and vacuum cleaners), heating appliances, and non-electric domestic cooking equipment.

Among the activities covered by the machinery and equipment manufacturing sector, the domestic appliances manufacturing sector (NACE Group 29.7) is the only one for which households are the main customers. Product innovations have tended to concentrate on efficiency and environmental considerations, lifestyle changes, the incorporation of new materials, design and ergonomics.

STRUCTURAL PROFILE

The domestic appliances manufacturing sector (NACE Group 29.7) of the EU-27 consisted of 4 300 enterprises which generated EUR 12.4 billion of value added in 2004, accounting for 7.2 % of the value added created by all machinery and equipment manufacturing activities (NACE Subsection DK). The sector employed 286 600 persons throughout all of the Member States, which represented 7.8 % of the machinery and equipment workforce.

The value added generated by the domestic appliances manufacturing sector in Germany was much larger than that in any other Member State, accounting for 29.0 % of the total across the EU-27 in 2004 – see Table 8.18. However, Slovenia was by far the most specialised Member State [12] in the manufacture of domestic appliances, as the sector contributed 2.1 % of the value added of the Slovenian non-financial business economy (NACE Sections C to I and K) in 2004, compared to an average 0.3 % across the EU-27.

_____

[12] Estonia, 2003; Ireland, Greece, Cyprus, Latvia, Luxembourg and Malta, not available.

The production index for the EU-27's domestic appliances manufacturing developed in an almost identical manner to the index for machinery and equipment manufacturing as a whole in the period between 1996 and 2003, after which growth in the output of domestic appliances manufacturing was weaker and more staggered (a slight decline in 2005). Over the ten years through until 2006, the output of domestic appliances manufacturing increased by an average 1.5 % per annum, a slower rate than that for machinery and equipment manufacturing as a whole (an average 2.2 % per annum). For most of this ten-year period, the output price index for domestic appliances remained remarkably flat; average growth was limited to 0.4 % per annum with much of this resulting from an upswing in prices in 2005 and 2006.

Table 8.18 _____

Manufacture of domestic appliances n.e.c. (NACE Group 29.7)
Structural profile: ranking of top five Member States, 2004

Rank	Share of EU-27 value added (%) (1)	Share of EU-27 employment (%) (2)	Value added specialisation ratio (EU-27=100) (3)	Employment specialisation ratio (EU-27=100) (4)
1	Germany (29.0)	Germany (21.8)	Slovenia (868.2)	Slovenia (798.4)
2	Italy (21.4)	Italy (20.7)	Italy (192.7)	Italy (176.2)
3	United Kingdom (12.7)	United Kingdom (9.3)	Hungary (171.3)	Hungary (169.4)
4	Spain (9.4)	Spain (7.6)	Romania (155.3)	Slovakia (167.7)
5	France (8.3)	France (6.8)	Lithuania (152.8)	Sweden (165.2)

(1) Greece, Latvia, Luxembourg and Malta, not available; Estonia, 2003.
(2) Greece, Luxembourg, Malta and Netherlands, not available; Estonia, 2003.
(3) Ireland, Greece, Cyprus, Latvia, Luxembourg and Malta, not available; Estonia, 2003.
(4) Ireland, Greece, Cyprus, Luxembourg, Malta and Netherlands, not available; Estonia, 2003.
Source: Eurostat (SBS)

Table 8.19 _____

Production of selected products - domestic appliances n.e.c. (CPA Group 29.7), EU-27, 2006 (1)

	Prodcom code	Production value (EUR million)	Volume of sold production (thousands)	Unit of volume
Fully-automatic washing machines of a dry linen capacity <= 10 kg (including machines which both wash and dry)	29.71.13.30	4 362	17 818	units
Household dishwashing machines	29.71.12.00	2 487	9 717	units
Combined refrigerators-freezers, with separate external doors	29.71.11.10	1 797	7 326	units
Domestic electric hobs for building-in	29.71.28.33	1 660	20 613	units
Non-electric instantaneous or storage water heaters	29.72.14.00	1 514	5 228	units
Household-type refrigerators (including compression-type, electrical absorption-type) (excluding built-in)	29.71.11.33	1 309	16 923	units
Parts for electro-mechanical domestic appliances with a self-contained electric motor	29.71.30.30	1 258	-	-
Iron or steel solid fuel domestic appliances (including heaters, grates, fires and braziers; excluding cooking appliances and plate warmers)	29.72.12.70	1 146	2 180	units
Drying machines of a dry linen capacity <= 10 kg	29.71.13.70	1 012	5 088	units
Parts of appliances of 8516	29.71.30.70	937	-	-

(1) Estimated.
Source: Eurostat (PRODCOM)

Table 8.20
Domestic appliances n.e.c. (CPA Group 29.7)
External trade, EU-27, 2006

	Extra-EU exports		Extra-EU imports			
	(EUR million)	(% share of chapter)	(EUR million)	(% share of chapter)	Trade balance (EUR million)	Cover ratio (%)
Domestic appliances n.e.c.	8 612	5.0	9 302	12.4	-690	92.6
Electric domestic appliances	7 489	4.4	8 564	11.5	-1 075	87.5
Non-electric domestic appliances	1 122	0.7	738	1.0	384	152.0

Source: Eurostat (Comext)

COSTS, PRODUCTIVITY AND PROFITABILITY

The proportion of total expenditure accounted for by personnel costs in the EU-27's domestic appliances manufacturing sector was 19.1 % in 2004, by far the lowest proportion among the NACE groups within machinery and equipment manufacturing as a whole and much closer to the proportion across the non-financial business economy (16.4 %). This may be explained, in part, by average personnel costs in the sector (EUR 32 000 per employee) that were also relatively low (EUR 4 300 per employee less than across machinery and equipment manufacturing as a whole).

Although the apparent labour productivity level of EUR 44 000 per person employed in the sector in 2004 was also less than the average across all of the EU-27's machinery and equipment manufacturing activities, the wage adjusted labour productivity ratio of 135.0 % for EU-27's domestic appliances manufacturing sector was higher than the chapter average (129.2 %).

EXTERNAL TRADE

EU-27 exports of domestic appliances (CPA Group 29.7) were valued at EUR 8.6 billion in 2006, however, the EU-27 had a small trade deficit in domestic appliances as imports were valued at EUR 9.3 billion. The trade deficit in 2006 reflected a turnaround from the trade surplus of EUR 1.2 billion that was recorded in 2001, brought about by the faster rate of growth in the value of imports than exports. In contrast to the trade deficit of EUR 1.1 billion in electric domestic appliances (CPA Class 29.71) in 2006, there was a small surplus of EUR 384.2 million in non-electric domestic appliances (CPA Class 29.72).

The two largest exporters (intra- and extra-EU combined) of domestic appliances in the EU-27 were Germany and Italy, with exports of these goods valued respectively at EUR 7.6 billion and EUR 7.1 billion. These two Member States also had the largest trade surpluses in these goods, although that for Italy (EUR 5.0 billion) was much larger than that for Germany (EUR 2.4 billion).

Table 8.21

Manufacture of machinery and equipment n.e.c. (NACE Subsection DK)
Main indicators, 2004

	EU-27	BE	BG	CZ	DK	DE	EE	IE	EL	ES	FR	IT	CY	LV	LT
No. of enterprises (thousands)	164.3	1.8	1.9	7.8	2.3	21.0	0.2	0.3	:	13.8	16.4	41.2	0.2	0.3	0.3
Turnover (EUR million)	531 646	9 206	941	7 033	9 552	177 703	182	1 856	:	26 655	59 077	103 544	86	133	246
Production (EUR million)	498 550	8 641	898	6 695	8 895	169 267	166	1 779	:	24 969	52 391	99 107	74	127	243
Value added (EUR million)	171 696	2 746	252	2 054	3 577	63 942	55	681	:	8 506	16 938	28 634	30	48	81
Gross operating surplus (EUR million)	44 553	784	75	707	733	12 344	16	261	:	2 619	3 534	9 980	9	19	24
Purchases of goods & services (EUR million)	366 160	6 461	733	5 189	6 277	115 577	129	1 196	:	18 841	41 841	76 181	56	90	172
Personnel costs (EUR million)	127 143	1 961	176	1 350	2 844	51 597	39	421	:	5 888	13 404	18 654	21	30	57
Investment in tangible goods (EUR million)	14 878	335	65	402	353	4 476	7	55	:	784	1 131	3 014	3	12	11
Employment (thousands)	3 661	42	66	152	63	1 064	5	12	:	194	315	570	1	7	11
Apparent labour prod. (EUR thousand)	46.9	64.8	3.8	13.5	57.0	60.1	10.7	57.9	:	43.9	53.7	50.3	22.0	6.5	7.6
Average personnel costs (EUR thousand)	36.3	48.2	2.8	9.4	46.0	49.1	7.7	36.1	:	31.7	43.1	36.6	16.8	4.0	5.4
Wage adjusted labour productivity (%)	129.2	134.5	138.3	144.3	123.9	122.4	139.5	160.5	:	138.4	124.6	137.5	131.0	160.7	141.3
Gross operating rate (%)	8.4	8.5	8.0	10.0	7.7	6.9	8.8	14.0	:	9.8	6.0	9.6	9.9	14.0	9.9
Investment / employment (EUR thousand)	4.1	7.9	1.0	2.7	5.6	4.2	1.4	4.7	:	4.0	3.6	5.3	2.5	1.6	1.0

	LU (1)	HU	MT	NL	AT	PL	PT	RO	SI	SK	FI	SE	UK	NO
No. of enterprises (thousands)	0.0	6.9	:	4.3	2.2	13.6	3.9	1.5	1.5	0.6	3.5	5.6	12.9	2.6
Turnover (EUR million)	587	3 935	:	17 448	14 234	7 658	3 083	1 796	2 065	1 972	11 075	20 969	49 764	4 483
Production (EUR million)	529	3 170	:	16 624	13 515	7 068	2 952	1 791	1 931	1 922	10 700	18 928	45 367	4 341
Value added (EUR million)	143	939	:	5 365	5 034	2 546	1 115	505	626	515	3 298	6 157	17 573	1 453
Gross operating surplus (EUR million)	37	292	:	1 576	1 468	1 227	371	87	219	195	933	1 276	5 712	315
Purchases of goods & services (EUR million)	442	3 028	:	12 253	9 613	5 670	2 020	1 411	1 495	1 492	8 060	15 229	32 095	3 098
Personnel costs (EUR million)	106	646	:	3 788	3 567	1 319	744	419	408	320	2 366	4 881	11 861	1 138
Investment in tangible goods (EUR million)	16	288	:	347	492	401	190	205	126	131	228	598	1 165	116
Employment (thousands)	2	69	:	85	79	191	43	129	26	44	56	118	304	22
Apparent labour prod. (EUR thousand)	61.8	13.6	:	63.2	63.8	13.4	25.7	3.9	24.4	11.7	59.1	52.2	57.8	64.8
Average personnel costs (EUR thousand)	46.0	9.9	:	46.0	46.0	7.5	17.6	3.4	16.5	7.3	43.0	50.0	40.0	53.5
Wage adjusted labour productivity (%)	134.3	136.4	:	137.6	138.7	178.7	145.9	116.9	147.7	160.7	137.3	104.4	144.3	121.2
Gross operating rate (%)	6.4	7.4	:	9.0	10.3	16.0	12.0	4.8	10.6	9.9	8.4	6.1	11.5	7.0
Investment / employment (EUR thousand)	7.0	4.2	:	4.1	6.2	2.1	4.4	1.6	4.9	3.0	4.1	5.1	3.8	5.2

(1) 2003.
Source: Eurostat (SBS)

Electrical machinery and optical equipment

Electrical machinery and optical equipment enterprises manufacture a diverse range of goods that can be classified as either being consumer goods (for example, telephones, radios, televisions and watches), capital goods (for example, computers and transmission equipment) or intermediate goods (for example, electronic components such as conductors and wiring) that are used by other sectors of the economy. Business investment decisions and consumer demand for electronic goods are greatly influenced by broader developments in the business cycle, and production patterns for electronic machinery and optical equipment goods tend to adapt to these changes more strongly (as shown, by way of example, in Figure 9.1) and perhaps quickly than is the case for many other manufactured goods.

The sector operates within an established legislative framework that covers issues such as product safety, energy labelling, minimum efficiency requirements, eco-design and waste. Changes to sector-specific legislation, such as to the recently re-codified low voltage directive [1], are pending the agreement of the Council and of the European Parliament to proposals made by the European Commission in February 2007 to revisions of the so-called New Approach [2], which aims to iron out product-related legislative weaknesses that prevent consumers and enterprises from fully exploiting the benefits of the Internal Market. Nevertheless, some legislative developments have come into force. In July 2007 the revised

This chapter covers NACE Subsection DL and is referred to as the manufacture of electrical machinery and optical equipment. There are four NACE divisions included, which cover the manufacture of computers and office machinery (NACE Division 30); the manufacture of electrical machinery and equipment (NACE Division 31); the manufacture of radio, television and communication equipment (NACE Division 32); and instrument engineering (NACE Division 33), which includes the manufacture of medical, precision and optical equipment.

NACE

30: manufacture of office machinery and computers;
31: manufacture of electrical machinery and apparatus n.e.c.;
31.1: manufacture of electric motors, generators and transformers;
31.2: manufacture of electricity distribution and control apparatus;
31.3: manufacture of insulated wire and cable;
31.4: manufacture of accumulators, primary cells and primary batteries;
31.5: manufacture of lighting equipment and electric lamps;
31.6: manufacture of electrical equipment n.e.c.;
32: manufacture of radio, television and communication equipment and apparatus;
32.1: manufacture of electronic valves and tubes and other electronic components;
32.2: manufacture of television and radio transmitters and apparatus for line telephony and line telegraphy;
32.3: manufacture of television and radio receivers, sound or video recording or reproducing apparatus and associated goods;
33: manufacture of medical, precision and optical instruments, watches and clocks;
33.1: manufacture of medical and surgical equipment and orthopaedic appliances;
33.2: manufacture of instruments and appliances for measuring, checking, testing, navigating and other purposes, except industrial process control equipment;
33.3: manufacture of industrial process control equipment;
33.4: manufacture of optical instruments, photographic equipment;
33.5: manufacture of watches and clocks.

European Parliament and Council directive [3] relating to electromagnetic compatibility came into force, replacing an existing Council directive on this subject. Furthermore, since July 2006 restrictions (in terms of maximum concentration values) have been in place on the use of hazardous substances (such as lead, cadmium and mercury) in electrical and electronic equipment under the legislation on the restriction of the use of certain hazardous substances in electric and electronic equipment [4].

---

[4] Directive 2002/95/EC.

---

[1] Re-codified to 2006/95/EC in December 2006 from Council Directive 73/23/EEC.
[2] COM(2007) 37.

[3] 89/336/EEC being replaced by 2004/108/EC.

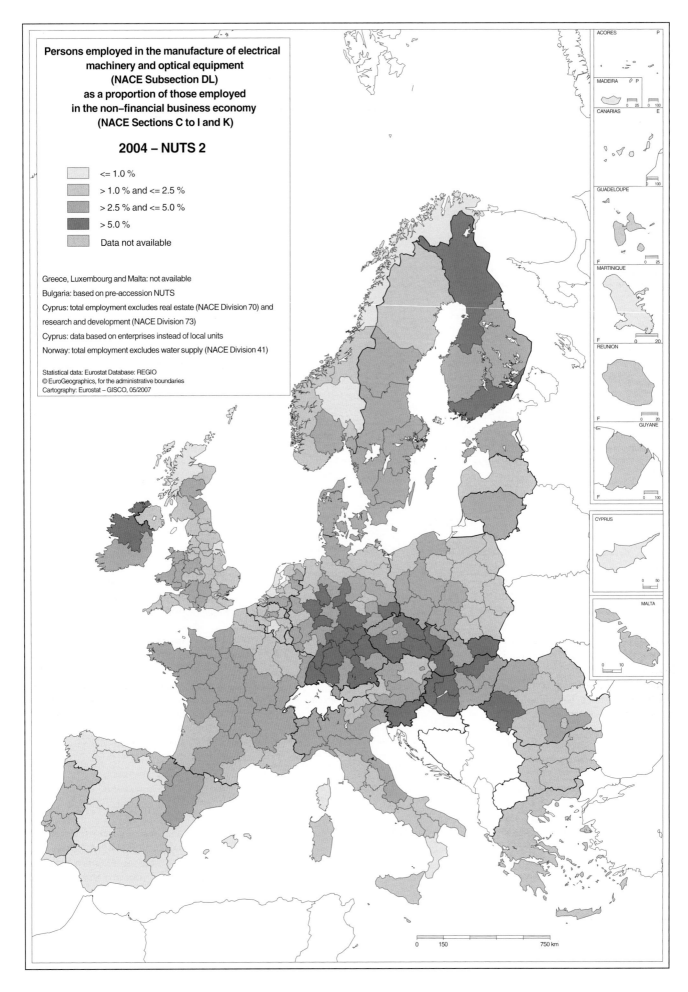

Persons employed in the manufacture of electrical machinery and optical equipment (NACE Subsection DL) as a proportion of those employed in the non–financial business economy (NACE Sections C to I and K)

2004 – NUTS 2

- <= 1.0 %
- > 1.0 % and <= 2.5 %
- > 2.5 % and <= 5.0 %
- > 5.0 %
- Data not available

Greece, Luxembourg and Malta: not available

Bulgaria: based on pre-accession NUTS

Cyprus: total employment excludes real estate (NACE Division 70) and research and development (NACE Division 73)

Cyprus: data based on enterprises instead of local units

Norway: total employment excludes water supply (NACE Division 41)

Statistical data: Eurostat Database: REGIO
© EuroGeographics, for the administrative boundaries
Cartography: Eurostat – GISCO, 05/2007

Table 9.1 ———

Manufacture of electrical and optical equipment (NACE Subsection DL)
Structural profile, EU-27, 2004 (1)

	No. of enterprises		Turnover		Value added		Employment	
	(thousands)	(% of total)	(EUR million)	(% of total)	(EUR million)	(% of total)	(thousands)	(% of total)
Electrical and optical equipment	196.4	100.0	631 408	100.0	189 687	100.0	3 600.0	100.0
Instrument engineering	92.7	47.2	127 680	20.2	51 376	27.1	1 020.0	28.3
Computers and office equipment	9.7	4.9	59 500	9.4	11 500	6.1	161.4	4.5
Electrical machinery and equipment	65.5	33.4	243 000	38.5	76 000	40.1	1 671.4	46.4
Radio, TV & communication equipment	28.5	14.5	201 024	31.8	51 057	26.9	812.4	22.6

(1) Rounded estimates based on non-confidential data.
Source: Eurostat (SBS)

Table 9.2 ———

Manufacture of electrical and optical equipment (NACE Subsection DL)
Structural profile: ranking of top five Member States, 2004

Rank	Value added (EUR million) (1)	Employment (thousands) (2)	Share of non-financial business economy			
			No. of enterprises (3)	Turnover (3)	Value added (3)	Employment (4)
1	Germany (63 173)	Germany (1 012.1)	Czech Republic (2.5 %)	Finland (11.1 %)	Hungary (10.2 %)	Slovakia (6.8 %)
2	France (24 970)	France (432.5)	Slovakia (2.1 %)	Hungary (9.7 %)	Finland (9.8 %)	Hungary (6.0 %)
3	United Kingdom (23 353)	Italy (422.5)	Slovenia (1.9 %)	Czech Republic (5.5 %)	Germany (5.9 %)	Finland (5.4 %)
4	Italy (19 373)	United Kingdom (363.8)	Germany (1.5 %)	Germany (5.2 %)	Slovenia (5.3 %)	Czech Republic (5.2 %)
5	Sweden (7 279)	Czech Republic (186.9)	Hungary (1.3 %)	Slovakia (4.6 %)	Czech Republic (5.1 %)	Slovenia (5.1 %)

(1) Greece and Malta, not available; Luxembourg, 2003.
(2) Greece and Malta, not available; Luxembourg and Slovenia, 2003.
(3) Ireland, Greece, Cyprus and Malta, not available; Luxembourg, 2003.
(4) Ireland, Greece, Cyprus and Malta, not available; Luxembourg and Slovenia, 2003.
Source: Eurostat (SBS)

STRUCTURAL PROFILE

Among the NACE subsections, electrical and optical equipment manufacturing (NACE Subsection DL) in the EU-27 was the third largest industrial activity in 2004 in terms of the value added generated, only behind the manufacture of food, beverages and tobacco (NACE Subsection DA, see Chapter 2) and the manufacture of basic metals and fabricated metal products (NACE Subsection DJ, see Chapter 7). The electrical and optical equipment manufacturing sector generated EUR 189.7 billion value added in 2004, contributing 3.7 % of the value added created across the EU-27's non-financial business economy (NACE Sections C to I and K). The 196 400 enterprises active in the sector employed 3.6 million persons across the EU-27, accounting for 2.9 % of the non-financial business economy workforce.

Among the four NACE divisions that comprise the electrical machinery and optical equipment manufacturing sector, the largest was the electrical machinery and equipment manufacturing (NACE Division 31) subsector, which accounted for two fifths (40.1 %) of sectoral value added in 2004. Instrument engineering (NACE Division 33) and the manufacture of radio, television and

telecommunication equipment and apparatus (NACE Division 32) were similarly sized, both contributing a little over one quarter (27.1 % and 26.9 % respectively) of the value added generated across electrical machinery and optical equipment manufacturing as a whole. By far the smallest subsector of the four was manufacture of office machinery and computers (NACE Division 30), which contributed just 6.1 % of sectoral value added – see Table 9.1.

The electrical and optical equipment manufacturing sector in Germany contributed one third (33.3 %) of the value added generated by the sector across the EU-27, by far the largest contribution and much greater than the next highest (13.2 %) from France. Among the Member States [5] the contribution made by the electrical machinery and optical equipment sector to the value added generated across national non-financial business economies in 2004 was highest, however, in Hungary (10.2 %) and Finland (9.8 %), where it was a little over two-and-a-half times the EU 27 average (3.7 %). In these two Member States, the electrical and optical equipment

manufacturing sector was the largest sector within the industrial economy (at the level of NACE subsections) on the basis of value added data. Germany, Slovenia and the Czech Republic were also relatively specialised in the manufacture of electrical machinery and optical equipment sector (see Table 9.2).

The map on page 176 shows the regional specialisation of the electrical machinery and optical equipment manufacturing sector (NACE Subsection DL) in terms of the proportion of the non-financial business economy workforce employed in this sector. The most specialised regions (at the level of detail shown in the map) were Zapadne Slovensko in Slovakia and Oberpfalz and Mittelfranken in Germany, where at least one in every nine people (11 %) within the non-financial business economy workforce was employed in electrical and optical equipment manufacturing. There were many other regions in Germany that were also specialised in this sector and many regions in the Czech Republic and Hungary, as well as Slovenia (which is considered as a single region at the level of detail in the map).

—————————————————
[5] Luxembourg, 2003; Ireland, Greece, Cyprus and Malta, not available.

Figure 9.1

Manufacture of electrical and optical equipment (NACE Subsection DL)
Evolution of main indicators, EU-27 (2000=100)

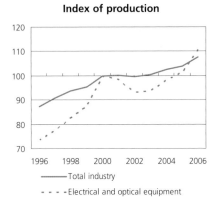
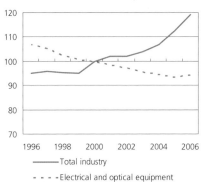

Source: Eurostat (STS)

The development of the production index for EU-27 electrical machinery and optical equipment manufacturing followed, but magnified, the economic cycle for industrial (NACE Sections C to E) output as a whole in the period between 1996 and 2006; the average rate of growth in the production index (4.2 % per annum) for electrical machinery and optical equipment manufacturing in the ten years through to 2006 was double that for industry as a whole (NACE Sections C to E) but there was a more significant downturn in production in the period between 2000 and 2002 than for industry as a whole (see Figure 9.1). The growth in the production index for electrical machinery and optical equipment manufacturing during these ten years was driven by the growth (an average 5.8 % per annum) in the output of radio, television and communication equipment manufacturing (NACE Division 32), which is described in more detail in Subchapter 9.4.

Marking a break from the steady downward trend in the domestic output price index for electrical machinery and optical equipment manufacturing, there was a small price increase in 2006. Nevertheless, the general downward trend in output prices (an average 1.2 % per annum over the ten years from 1996) for electrical machinery and optical equipment contrasted starkly with the relatively steady rise (an average 2.3 % per annum) in the output price index for industry as a whole, and the overall price increases in all the other manufacturing (NACE Section D) NACE subsections. The downward trend in the output price index was particularly apparent (an average decline of 8.3 % per annum) for the manufacture of computers and office machinery (NACE Division 30), which is described in more detail in Subchapter 9.2.

Figure 9.2

Manufacture of electrical and optical equipment (NACE Subsection DL)
Share of value added by enterprise size class, EU-27, 2004

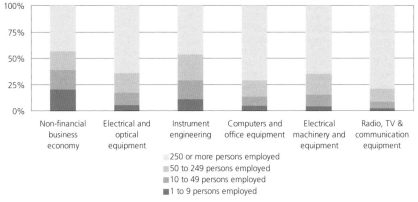

Source: Eurostat (SBS)

There were two distinct developments in the employment index for the manufacture of electrical and optical equipment in the EU-27 during the period between 1996 and 2006; between 1996 and 2001 there was stability and then some growth in employment, which contrasted with the broader decline across industry as a whole, followed by a relatively steady decline in keeping with the developments for industry as a whole, until 2006 when there was a small increase.

Large enterprises (employing more than 250 persons) generated a little under two thirds (64.0 %) of the value added within the EU-27's electrical machinery and optical equipment manufacturing sector in 2004, in stark contrast to their minority contribution (43.0 %) across the non-financial business economy as a whole. This relative importance of large enterprises in the sector was also clear in three of the four electrical machinery and optical equipment manufacturing subsectors, the exception being instrument engineering for which the contribution of large enterprises was more in keeping with that for non-financial business economy –see Figure 9.2. The share of value added coming from large enterprises was particularly high (79.2 %) in the computers and office equipment manufacturing subsector.

Figure 9.3

Manufacture of electrical and optical equipment (NACE Subsection DL)
Labour force characteristics, EU-27, 2006

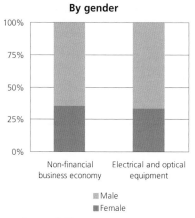
By gender

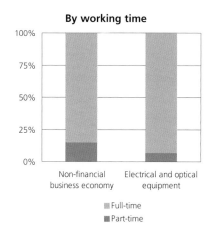
By working time

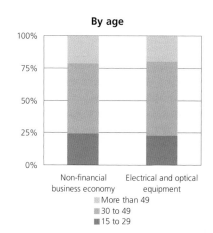
By age

Source: Eurostat (LFS)

EMPLOYMENT CHARACTERISTICS

The general profile of the workforce in the EU-27's electrical machinery and optical equipment manufacturing sector was similar to that of the workforce across the non-financial business economy in terms of both gender and age composition in 2006 (see Figure 9.3). About two thirds (66.8 %) of the EU-27 workforce in the sector were male, slightly above the non-financial business economy average(65.0 %) but below the industrial average (70.1 %) and this was broadly reflected across the four subsectors that comprise the electrical machinery and optical equipment manufacturing sector. Among the Member States, however, there were many notable differences; in Cyprus the proportion of men in the workforce of this sector was particularly high (79.1 %) compared to the non-financial business economy average (64.8 %), whereas in Slovakia men were in the minority (46.3 %) in this sector, in contrast to the situation (63.7 %) across the non-financial business economy.

The proportion of workers engaged in part-time work (6.8 %) in the electrical machinery and optical equipment manufacturing sector was much lower than the proportion (14.4 %) across the non-financial business economy as a whole, although much more in line with the industrial average (7.6 %), and this pattern was replicated across the four subsectors that make up the electrical machinery and optical equipment manufacturing sector.

According to structural business statistics, there was relatively little self-employment within the electrical machinery and optical equipment manufacturing sector; employees accounted for 95.4 % of the number of persons employed in 2004, a much higher share than that (86.2 %) for the non-financial business economy as a whole.

COSTS, PRODUCTIVITY AND PROFITABILITY

As a proportion of total expenditure, investment within the EU-27's electrical machinery and optical equipment manufacturing sector (NACE Subsection DL) in 2004 was relatively low (3.3 %) compared to the average proportion (4.9 %) across the non-financial business economy (NACE Sections C to I and K). Personnel costs within the sector, however, accounted for a relatively high share (21.5 %) of total expenditure compared with the average share (16.4 %) across the non-financial business economy, in large part reflecting the fact that average personnel costs of EUR 37 000 per employee in the sector were about a third higher (34.1 %) than the non-financial business economy average. Ireland, Hungary and Finland stood out from the other Member States, as the proportion of total expenditure in the sector accounted for by personnel costs was relatively low (between 8.4 % and 10.8 %), whereas the proportion accounted for by the purchase of goods and services was relatively high (between 86.0 % and 88.0 %, compared to an EU-27 average of 75.1 %).

Table 9.3

Manufacture of electrical and optical equipment (NACE Subsection DL)
Productivity and profitability, EU-27, 2004 (1)

	Apparent labour productivity (EUR thousand)	Average personnel costs (EUR thousand)	Wage adjusted labour productivity (%)	Gross operating rate (%)
Electrical and optical equipment	52.0	37.0	141.0	9.7
Instrument engineering	50.0	35.0	138.0	13.4
Computers and office equipment	70.0	40.0	179.0	9.0
Electrical machinery and equipment	46.0	35.0	132.0	8.4
Radio, TV & communication equipment	62.9	41.5	151.4	9.2

(1) Rounded estimates based on non-confidential data.
Source: Eurostat (SBS)

Table 9.4

Electrical and optical equipment (CPA Subsection DL)
External trade, EU-27, 2006

	Extra-EU exports		Extra-EU imports			
	(EUR million)	(% share of industrial exports)	(EUR million)	(% share of industrial imports)	Trade balance (EUR million)	Cover ratio (%)
Electrical and optical equipment	197 586	18.3	267 029	21.3	-69 443	74.0
Medical, precision and optical instruments; watches and clocks	54 106	5.0	47 174	3.8	6 932	114.7
Office machinery and computers	28 937	2.7	80 121	6.4	-51 185	36.1
Electrical machinery and equipment	51 061	4.7	40 224	3.2	10 837	126.9
Radio, TV & communication equipment	63 482	5.9	99 510	7.9	-36 028	63.8

Source: Eurostat (Comext)

Although the average apparent labour productivity (EUR 52 000 per person employed) of those working within the EU-27's electrical machinery and optical equipment manufacturing sector was over a quarter (27.1 %) higher than that across the non-financial business economy as a whole in 2004, the wage adjusted labour productivity level of 141.0 % was lower than the non-financial business economy average (148.0 %) due to the sector's relatively high average personnel costs. Among the subsectors, however, the wage adjusted labour productivity level of those working in manufacture of computers and office machinery was particularly high (179.0 %).

The gross operating rate for the EU-27's electrical machinery and optical equipment manufacturing sector was 9.7 %, which was lower than the average rate (11.0 %) for the non-financial business economy. There were a number of Member States, however, for whom the profitability of the sector in 2004 was above the non-financial business average; by way of examples, in Lithuania the gross operating rate of the sector was 13.7 % compared to a non-financial business economy rate of 10.5 %, in Bulgaria it was 11.3 % compared to 8.8 % and in Sweden 12.3 % compared to 9.6 %.

EXTERNAL TRADE

The EU-27 imported electrical and optical equipment (CPA Subsection DL) to the value of EUR 267.0 billion in 2006, which represented a little more than one fifth (21.3 %) of the value of all industrial imports (CPA Sections C to E), mainly from China (30.6 %), the United States (16.9 %) and Japan (10.1 %) – see Table 9.4 and Figure 9.4. The EU-27 exported electrical and optical equipment to non-member countries to the value of EUR 197.6 billion in 2006, representing 18.3 % of all industrial exports, with the single largest export market being the United States (20.4 %). It should be noted, however, that exports to non-member countries represented only one third (33.2 %) of the total trade (intra and extra-EU) of the EU-27 Member States in electrical and optical equipment, underlining the importance of the internal market. Exports (intra and extra-EU) of electrical and optical equipment were particularly important in Malta, where they represented almost two thirds (63.8 %) of the value of national industrial exports, as well as in Luxembourg (44.9 %) and Hungary (38.3 %).

The EU-27 had a trade deficit in electrical and optical equipment of EUR 69.4 billion in 2006. At a more detailed level, however, the EU-27 recorded a trade surplus of EUR 10.8 billion for electrical machinery and apparatus (CPA Division 31) and a surplus of EUR 6.9 billion for medical, precision and optical instruments, watches and clocks (CPA Division 33). These surpluses contrasted starkly with the trade deficit of EUR 36.0 billion for radio, television and communication equipment and apparatus (CPA Division 32) and the deficit of EUR 51.2 billion for computer and office equipment (CPA Division 30).

Among the Member States, Germany recorded the largest trade surplus (EUR 15.9 billion) in electrical and optical equipment in 2006, followed by Ireland (EUR 10.1 billion). In contrast, the largest deficit for these goods was recorded by Spain (EUR 18.5 billion), with other large deficits being posted in France (EUR 10.9 billion) and Italy (EUR 10.3 billion).

Figure 9.4

Electrical and optical equipment (CPA Subsection DL)
Main destination of EU-27 exports and main origin of EU-27 imports, 2006

EU-27 exports

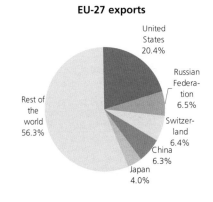

EU-27 imports

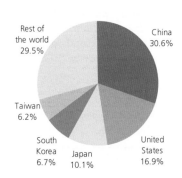

Source: Eurostat (Comext)

9.1: INSTRUMENT ENGINEERING

The manufacture of medical, precision and optical instruments, watches and clocks (NACE Division 33) includes activities related to the manufacture of instruments, industrial process control equipment, watches, clocks and photographic equipment (while photo-chemical products, flashbulbs or television cameras are not included). Together these activities are referred to here as instrument engineering.

STRUCTURAL PROFILE

A little more than one quarter (27.1 %) of the value added generated by all of the electrical machinery and optical equipment manufacturing activities (NACE Subsection DL) in the EU-27 in 2004, came from instrument engineering (NACE Division 33), in value terms some EUR 51.4 billion. There were 1.0 million persons employed in the instrument engineering sector in 2004 spread across 92 700 enterprises, which together accounted for 28.3 % of the electrical machinery and optical equipment manufacturing workforce.

The two largest subsectors in value added terms were the manufacture of instruments and appliances for measuring, checking, testing, navigating and other purposes, except industrial process control equipment (NACE Group 33.2) and the manufacture of medical and surgical equipment and orthopaedic appliances (NACE Group 33.1), which each accounted for around two fifths of the sector's value added – see Table 9.5. The manufacture of optical instruments and photographic equipment (NACE Group 33.4) and the manufacture of industrial process control equipment (NACE Group 33.3) contributed respectively just over and just under 10 % of instrument engineering value added in 2004, leaving the manufacture of watches and clocks (NACE Group 33.5) as by far the smallest instrument engineering subsector. This pattern was closely mirrored in terms of the breakdown of employment within the sector.

The instrument engineering sector in Germany contributed one third (33.6 %) of the value added generated by the sector across the EU-27, slightly more than the combined contribution from the United Kingdom (16.3 %) and France (15.3 %), who had the next largest sectors (see Table 9.6). The value added generated by the instrument engineering sector accounted for 1.6 % of the value added generated across Germany's non-financial business economy, the highest share among the Member States and notably more than the average across the EU-27 (1.0 %). By this measure, Sweden and Slovenia were the Member States that were the next most specialised in instrument engineering.

Table 9.5

Instrument engineering (NACE Division 33)
Structural profile, EU-27, 2004

	No. of enterprises (thousands)	Turnover (EUR million)	Value added (EUR million)	Employment (thousands)
Instrument engineering (1)	92.7	127 680	51 376	1 020.0
Medical and surgical equipment and orthopaedic appliances	59.3	46 821	19 614	434.2
Instr. and appl. for measuring, checking, testing, navigating and other purp. (1)	16.9	52 963	21 062	360.0
Industrial process control equipment	7.4	11 560	4 175	91.9
Optical instruments and photographic equipment (1)	8.0	15 000	6 000	120.0
Watches and clocks (1)	1.2	1 500	540	13.0

(1) Rounded estimates based on non-confidential data.
Source: Eurostat (SBS)

Table 9.6

Instrument engineering (NACE Division 33)
Structural profile: ranking of top five Member States, 2004

Rank	Share of EU-27 value added (%) (1)	Share of EU-27 employment (%) (2)	Value added specialisation ratio (EU-27=100) (3)	Employment specialisation ratio (EU-27=100) (4)
1	Germany (33.6)	Germany (31.8)	Germany (160.6)	Germany (192.1)
2	United Kingdom (16.3)	France (13.1)	Sweden (130.6)	Slovenia (167.9)
3	France (15.3)	Italy (12.2)	Slovenia (124.1)	Sweden (125.4)
4	Italy (10.8)	United Kingdom (11.7)	Denmark (109.9)	Finland (117.8)
5	Ireland (4.4)	Poland (5.0)	France (108.9)	Czech Republic (115.6)

(1) Greece, Malta and Netherlands, not available; Luxembourg, 2003.
(2) Greece and Malta, not available; Luxembourg, 2003.
(3) Ireland, Greece, Cyprus, Malta and Netherlands, not available; Luxembourg, 2003.
(4) Ireland, Greece, Cyprus and Malta, not available; Luxembourg, 2003.
Source: Eurostat (SBS)

Table 9.7

Production of selected products - medical, precision and optical instruments; watches and clocks (CPA Division 33), EU-27, 2006 (1)

	Prodcom code	Production value (EUR million)	Volume of sold production (thousands)	Unit of volume
Radar apparatus	33.20.20.30	4 044	2 013	units
Instruments and apparatus, regulating or controlling, n.e.c.	33.20.70.90	3 387	111 310	units
Apparatus based on the use of X-rays, for medical, surgical, dental or veterinary uses (including radiography and radiotherapy apparatus)	33.10.11.15	3 291	160	units
Instruments and appliances for aeronautical or space navigation (excluding compasses)	33.20.11.55	2 984	193	units
Needles, catheters, cannulae and the like used in medical, surgical, dental or veterinary sciences (excluding tubular metal needles and needles for sutures)	33.10.15.17	2 552	10 025 297	units
Repair and maintenance of instruments and apparatus for measuring, checking, testing, navigating and other purposes (excluding industrial process control equipment)	33.20.92.00	2 301	-	-
Dental fittings (including dentures and part dentures, metal crowns, cast tin bars, stainless steel bars) (excluding individual artificial teeth)	33.10.17.59	2 272	-	-
Instruments and apparatus using optical radiations, n.e.c.	33.20.53.50	817	273	units
Ozone therapy, oxygen therapy, aerosol therapy, respiration apparatus	33.10.16.55	675	222 975	units

(1) Estimated.
Source: Eurostat (PRODCOM)

Figure 9.5

Instrument engineering (NACE Division 33)
Evolution of main indicators, EU-27 (2000=100)

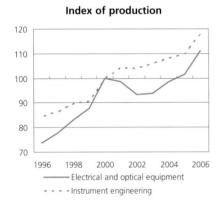
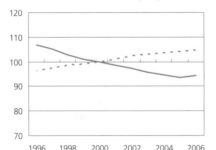
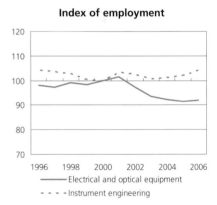

Source: Eurostat (STS)

The production index for instrument engineering in the EU 27 during the period between 1996 and 2006 developed in a way that was similar to the production index for industry as a whole (NACE Sections C to E), avoiding the relatively sharp fall in output in 2001 and 2002 that was recorded for electrical machinery and optical equipment manufacturing as a whole. The average rate of growth (3.4 % per annum) in the output of instrument engineering over the ten years through to 2006 was slower, however, than the rate of growth (an average 4.2 % per annum) in the output for electrical machinery and optical equipment manufacturing.

The domestic output price index for instrument engineering rose steadily year-on-year (an average 0.8 % per annum) throughout the ten-year period to 2006, in contrast to the downward trend in prices already noted for electrical machinery and optical equipment as a whole (see Figure 9.5).

COSTS, PRODUCTIVITY AND PROFITABILITY

The structure of costs for the EU-27's instrument engineering sector was quite different to that of electrical machinery and optical equipment manufacturing as a whole in 2004; personnel costs accounted for a much higher share (29.7 % compared to 21.5 %) of total expenditure, and purchases of goods and services for a much lower share (67.2 % compared to 75.1 %). This cost structure for instrument engineering in the EU-27 was mirrored across its five subsectors.

Although personnel costs in this sector accounted for a high proportion of total expenditure, average personnel costs of EUR 35 000 per employee in the instrument engineering sector across the EU-27 were a

Table 9.8

Instrument engineering (NACE Division 33)
Productivity and profitability, EU-27, 2004

	Apparent labour productivity (EUR thousand)	Average personnel costs (EUR thousand)	Wage adjusted labour productivity (%)	Gross operating rate (%)
Instrument engineering (1)	50.0	35.0	138.0	13.4
Medical and surgical equipment and orthopaedic appliances	45.2	31.4	143.9	16.4
Instr. and appl. for measuring, checking, testing, navigating and other purp. (1)	58.0	43.0	137.0	11.6
Industrial process control equipment	45.4	37.1	122.5	8.5
Optical instruments and photographic equipment (1)	50.0	35.0	140.0	15.0
Watches and clocks (1)	40.0	:	:	8.3

(1) Rounded estimates based on non-confidential data.
Source: Eurostat (SBS)

little beneath the average for electrical machinery and optical equipment manufacturing (EUR 37 000 per employee), which suggests that the sector was relatively labour intensive. The apparent labour productivity (EUR 50 000 per person employed) of those working in the sector was also a little lower than the level across electrical machinery and optical equipment manufacturing, as was the wage adjusted labour productivity level (138.0 % compared to 141.0 %).

The gross operating rate of the instrument engineering sector was 13.4 % in 2004, much higher than the rate (9.7 %) for electrical machinery and optical equipment manufacturing as a whole and also above the average rate for the non-financial business economy (11.0 %). Within the instrument engineering sector, however, the profitability of the five subsectors varied considerably according to this measure (see Table 9.8), from 8.3 % for the manufacture of watches and clocks (NACE Group 33.5) to 16.4 % for the manufacture of medical and surgical equipment and orthopaedic appliances (NACE Group 33.1).

EXTERNAL TRADE

The EU-27 recorded a trade surplus of EUR 6.9 billion in medical, precision and optical instruments, watches and clocks (CPA Division 33) with non-member countries in 2006, resulting from exports valued at EUR 54.1 billion (a little over a quarter of the value of electrical machinery and optical equipment exports) and imports valued at EUR 47.2 billion – see Table 9.9. Exports of medical, precision and optical instruments, watches and clocks as a whole to non-member countries were almost as valuable as trade in these goods between Member States, accounting for 47.9 % of all exports (intra- and extra-EU) by EU-27 Member States.

Among the Member States, Germany recorded the largest trade surplus (EUR 16.6 billion) in these goods (intra- and extra-EU trade), with the next highest being for Ireland (EUR 4.1 billion) and the Netherlands (EUR 2.0 billion). In contrast, the largest trade deficits in these goods were recorded for Slovakia (EUR 2.0 billion) and Spain (EUR 4.1 billion).

Table 9.9

Medical, precision and optical instruments; watches and clocks (CPA Division 33)
External trade, EU-27, 2006

	Extra-EU exports		Extra-EU imports		Trade balance (EUR million)	Cover ratio (%)
	(EUR million)	(% share of chapter)	(EUR million)	(% share of chapter)		
Medical, precision and optical instruments; watches and clocks	54 106	27.4	47 174	17.7	6 932	114.7
Medical and surgical equipment and orthopaedic appliances	22 003	11.1	18 528	6.9	3 475	118.8
Instruments and appliances for measuring, checking, testing, navigating and other purposes	22 619	11.4	17 102	6.4	5 517	132.3
Industrial process control equipment	:	:	:	:	:	:
Optical instruments and photographic equipment	7 768	3.9	6 994	2.6	775	111.1
Watches and clocks	1 717	0.9	4 551	1.7	-2 834	37.7

Source: Eurostat (Comext)

9.2: COMPUTERS AND OFFICE EQUIPMENT

This subchapter covers the manufacture of office machinery, computers and peripherals, such as printers and terminals (NACE Division 30). Note that the manufacture of electronic games is classified under toys and is covered within Subchapter 11.2.

STRUCTURAL PROFILE

The computers and office equipment manufacturing sector (NACE Division 30) was the smallest activity among the four NACE divisions that comprise electrical machinery and optical equipment manufacturing as a whole (NACE Subsection DL), both in terms of the value added generated and in terms of employment; the EUR 11.5 billion of value added generated within the EU-27 in 2004 accounted for 6.1 % of the value added generated by all of the activities covered by this chapter and the 161 400 persons employed across the 9 700 enterprises active in computer and office equipment manufacturing represented less than one person in every twenty (4.5 %) within the electrical machinery and optical equipment manufacturing workforce.

The manufacture of computers and other information processing equipment (NACE Class 30.02) accounted for about four fifths of both the value added (84.4 %) generated in the sector and its workforce (81.4 %), the remaining share being accounted for by the manufacture of office machinery (NACE Class 30.01).

The computers and office equipment manufacturing sector in Germany generated a little over one third (35.3 %) of the value added created by the sector across the EU-27 in 2004, with the sector in the United Kingdom (28.2 %) and Ireland (13.2 %) also contributing significant proportions (see Table 9.11). Among the Member States [6], the contribution made by the sector to the value added of the non-financial business economy was highest (1.1 %) in Hungary, almost five times the average contribution across the EU-27. Nonetheless, based on the limited data available; the computers and office equipment manufacturing sector accounted for 4.2 % of the value added in Irish manufacturing (NACE Section D) in 2004, considerably more than the share for Hungary (2.7 %) and the average share across the EU-27 (0.7 %). This relatively high share for Ireland is at least in part explained by Ireland acting as an entrance point into the EU-27 for some large international manufacturers.

---

[6] Ireland, Greece, Cyprus, Luxembourg and Malta, not available.

Annual short-term statistics show that the index of production for the computer and office equipment manufacturing in the EU-27 rose at a particularly fast pace (an average 11.1 % per annum) between 1996 and its relative peak in 2000 when compared to the otherwise strong rate (an average 7.9 % per annum) for electrical and optical equipment manufacturing – see Figure 9.6. As with many technology related activities, however, the output of computer and office equipment manufacturing then fell; there was a decline in the production index in consecutive years from 2001 to 2004, with a particularly pronounced reduction (down 16.8 %) in 2002. In 2005 and 2006 there were signs of a sustained recovery, with an overall rise of 9.2 % from the relative low in 2004.

Price comparisons over time in this area are particularly difficult because computer specifications are constantly increasing. Nevertheless, in contrast to the large majority of industrial NACE divisions, the domestic output price index for the manufacture of computers and office equipment in the EU-27 fell year-on-year between 1996 and 2006 at an average rate of decline of 8.3 % per annum.

Table 9.10

Manufacture of computers and office equipment (NACE Division 30)
Structural profile, EU-27, 2004 (1)

	No. of enterprises (thousands)	Turnover (EUR million)	Value added (EUR million)	Employment (thousands)
Computers and office equipment	9.7	59 500	11 500	161.4
Office machinery	1.0	5 500	1 800	31.8
Computers and other information processing equipment	8.7	54 000	9 710	130.0

(1) Rounded estimate based on non-confidential data.
Source: Eurostat (SBS)

Table 9.11

Manufacture of computers and office equipment (NACE Division 30)
Structural profile: ranking of top five Member States, 2004

Rank	Share of EU-27 value added (%) (1)	Share of EU-27 employment (%) (2)	Value added specialisation ratio (EU-27=100) (3)	Employment specialisation ratio (EU-27=100) (4)
1	Germany (35.3)	Germany (26.0)	Hungary (489.7)	Hungary (250.6)
2	United Kingdom (28.2)	United Kingdom (18.7)	Germany (168.6)	Slovakia (249.9)
3	Ireland (13.2)	Italy (9.4)	United Kingdom (149.0)	Czech Republic (192.3)
4	Italy (5.8)	Ireland (8.8)	Czech Republic (104.8)	Germany (157.0)
5	France (4.2)	Czech Republic (5.5)	Slovenia (85.3)	United Kingdom (129.9)

(1) Greece, Luxembourg and Malta, not available.
(2) Greece, Luxembourg, Malta and Netherlands, not available.
(3) Ireland, Greece, Cyprus, Luxembourg and Malta, not available.
(4) Ireland, Greece, Cyprus, Luxembourg, Malta and Netherlands, not available.
Source: Eurostat (SBS)

Table 9.12

Production of selected products - office machinery and computers (CPA Division 30), EU-27, 2006 (1)

	Prodcom code	Production value (EUR million)	Volume of sold production (thousands)	Unit of volume
Digital data processing machines: presented in the form of systems	30.02.14.00	c	14 772	units
Parts and accessories for computers and other data processing machines	30.02.19.00	9 601	-	-
Installation of computers and other information processing equipment	30.02.90.00	3 434	-	-
Central storage units	30.02.17.30	3 066	c	units
Input or output units whether or not containing storage units in the same housing (including mouses) (excluding printers and keyboards)	30.02.16.70	1 754	14 317	units
Desktop PCs	30.02.13.00	1 628	2 214	units
Printers	30.02.16.30	745	4 375	units
Parts and accessories for photocopiers incorporating an optical system, contact type photocopiers and thermocopiers	30.01.25.00	554	-	-
Storage units (excluding central storage units, disk storage units and magnetic tape storage units)	30.02.17.90	495	17 557	units
Parts and accessories of the machines of HS 8472	30.01.24.00	228	-	-

(1) Estimated.
Source: Eurostat (PRODCOM)

Figure 9.6

Manufacture of computers and office equipment (NACE Division 30)
Evolution of main indicators, EU-27 (2000=100)

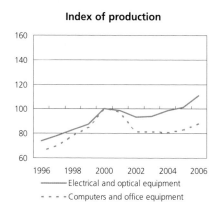

Index of production

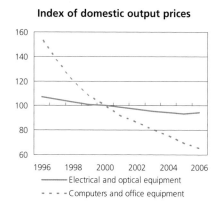

Index of domestic output prices

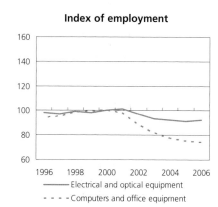

Index of employment

Source: Eurostat (STS)

Table 9.13 ———

Manufacture of computers and office equipment (NACE Division 30)
Productivity and profitability, EU-27, 2004 (1)

	Apparent labour productivity (EUR thousand)	Average personnel costs (EUR thousand)	Wage adjusted labour productivity (%)	Gross operating rate (%)
Computers and office equipment	70.0	40.0	179.0	9.0
Office machinery	56.0	41.0	140.0	9.2
Computers and other information processing equipment	74.9	39.3	191.0	9.0

(1) Rounded estimates based on non-confidential data.
Source: Eurostat (SBS)

Table 9.14 ———

Office machinery and computers (CPA Division 30)
External trade, EU-27, 2006

	Extra-EU exports		Extra-EU imports			
	(EUR million)	(% share of chapter)	(EUR million)	(% share of chapter)	Trade balance (EUR million)	Cover ratio (%)
Office machinery and computers	28 937	14.6	80 121	30.0	-51 185	36.1
Office machinery and parts thereof	2 951	1.5	6 010	2.3	-3 059	49.1
Computers and other information processing equipment	25 986	13.2	74 112	27.8	-48 126	35.1

Source: Eurostat (Comext)

COSTS, PRODUCTIVITY AND PROFITABILITY

As a proportion of total expenditure, gross investment in tangible goods in the EU-27's computers and office equipment manufacturing sector in 2004 was particularly low (1.3 %), both in comparison to the average across electrical machinery and optical equipment manufacturing (3.3 %) and, more particularly, the non-financial business economy (4.9 %). Similarly, personnel costs in the sector in 2004 accounted for the lowest share (11.2 %) of total expenditure among the four NACE divisions that make-up electrical machinery and optical equipment manufacturing (for which the average share was 21.5 %). This was despite the fact that average personnel costs in the sector (an average EUR 40 000 per employee) were a little higher than the average across electrical machinery and optical equipment manufacturing as a whole (EUR 37 000 per employee).

Apparent labour productivity in the sector was EUR 70 000 per person employed across the EU-27, the highest level among the NACE divisions that cover electrical and optical equipment manufacturing and EUR 18 000 per person employed more than the average for electrical machinery and optical equipment manufacturing. The apparent labour productivity level in the sector more than covered average personnel costs, with the wage adjusted labour productivity ratio of 179.0 % being substantially more than the average ratio across electrical and optical equipment manufacturing (141.0 %) as well as the average ratio for the EU-27's non-financial

business economy (148.0 %). The high value of the wage adjusted labour productivity ratio for the whole of the computers and office equipment sector was strongly influenced by the ratio for computers and other information processing equipment (191.0 %), while the ratio for office machinery (140.0 %) was more in line with the electrical and optical equipment manufacturing average (see Table 9.13).

The gross operating rate for the EU-27's computer and office equipment manufacturing sector was 9.0 % in 2004, below both the rate for electrical and optical equipment manufacturing as a whole (9.7 %) and, more clearly, the rate for the non-financial business economy (11.0 %). This pattern was reflected in a majority of Member States, although among the exceptions the most notable concerned Hungary and the United Kingdom for whom the gross operating rates of the sector (14.8 % and 21.0 % respectively) were much higher than those of their non-financial business economies (8.8 % and 14.4 % respectively).

EXTERNAL TRADE

The EU-27 had a trade deficit of EUR 51.2 billion for office machinery and computers (CPA Division 30) in 2006, which represented a substantial widening of the deficit recorded in 2005 (EUR 42.3 billion) and an acceleration of the trend noted since 2001. The trade deficit in 2006 was a result of EU-27 imports valued at EUR 80.1 billion (almost two fifths of which came from China) and exports of EUR 28.9 billion (see Table 9.14). Computers and other information processing equipment (CPA Class 30.02) represented 89.8 % of total exports, while accounting for 92.5 % of total imports in 2006.

Among the Member States, the Netherlands was the largest trader, exporting (intra- and extra-EU trade combined) EUR 39.2 billion worth of office machinery and computers and importing EUR 39.5 billion worth of these products. Only four Member States (Ireland, Hungary, the Czech Republic and Luxembourg) recorded a trade surplus for office machinery and computers in 2006 with that for Ireland (EUR 4.7 billion) being by far the largest. In contrast, the largest trade deficits for office machinery and computers in 2006 were recorded for France (EUR 8.4 billion) and Germany (EUR 7.6 billion).

Table 9.21

Manufacture of radio, television and communication equipment (NACE Division 32)
Structural profile: ranking of top five Member States, 2004

Rank	Share of EU-27 value added (%) (1)	Share of EU-27 employment (%) (1)	Value added specialisation ratio (EU-27=100) (2)	Employment specialisation ratio (EU-27=100) (2)
1	Germany (21.8)	Germany (18.1)	Finland (724.0)	Finland (455.3)
2	France (15.5)	France (15.9)	Hungary (369.8)	Hungary (327.3)
3	Finland (10.3)	Italy (10.8)	Sweden (247.3)	Estonia (235.0)
4	United Kingdom (9.4)	United Kingdom (9.8)	Austria (183.6)	Sweden (180.9)
5	Italy (8.6)	Hungary (6.7)	Lithuania (135.9)	Lithuania (178.6)

(1) Greece, Luxembourg, Malta and Netherlands, not available.
(2) Ireland, Greece, Cyprus, Luxembourg, Malta and Netherlands, not available.
Source: Eurostat (SBS)

Table 9.22

Production of selected products - radio, television and communication equipment and apparatus (CPA Division 32), EU-27, 2006 (1)

	Prodcom code	Production value (EUR million)	Volume of sold production (thousands)	Unit of volume
Radio transmission apparatus with reception apparatus	32.20.11.70	32 230	277 415	units
Flat panel colour TV receivers, lcd/plasma, etc. excluding television projection equipment, apparatus with video recorder/player, video monitors, television receivers with integral tube	32.30.20.60	8 178	13 304	units
Telephonic or telegraphic switching apparatus (excluding relays and switching equipment such as selectors for automatic telephone exchangers)	32.20.20.40	7 477	63 965	units
Digital MOS integrated circuits (ICs): wafers not yet cut into chips	32.10.62.15	7 111	4 205 662	units
Photosensitive semiconductor devices; solar cells, photo-diodes, photo-transistors, etc.	32.10.52.37	3 554	1 137 164	units
Linear (analogue) integrated circuits (ICs)	32.10.62.95	2 720	7 710 022	units
Electronic assemblies, parts, for line telephony or line telegraphy, including for line telephones with cordless receivers, and for videophones (excluding for telephonic or telegraphic carrier-current line systems)	32.20.30.60	2 718	-	-
Radio receivers motor vehicles with sound recording or reproducing apparatus	32.30.12.70	2 567	19 091	units
Telephonic/telegraphic apparatus for carrier-current line systems, n.e.c.	32.20.20.50	2 373	12 415	units
Bare multilayer printed circuit boards	32.10.30.50	2 124	c	units

(1) Estimated.
Source: Eurostat (PRODCOM)

Figure 9.8

Manufacture of radio, television and communication equipment (NACE Division 32)
Evolution of main indicators, EU-27 (2000=100)

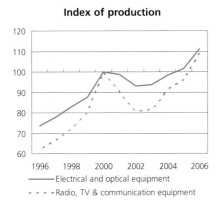

Index of production

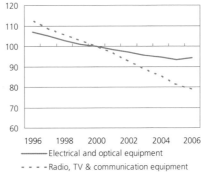

Index of domestic output prices

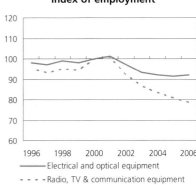

Index of employment

——— Electrical and optical equipment
- - - - Radio, TV & communication equipment

Source: Eurostat (STS)

Table 9.23

Manufacture of radio, television and communication equipment (NACE Division 32)
Productivity and profitability, EU-27, 2004

	Apparent labour productivity (EUR thousand)	Average personnel costs (EUR thousand)	Wage adjusted labour productivity (%)	Gross operating rate (%)
Radio, TV & communication equipment	62.9	41.5	151.4	9.2
Electronic valves and tubes and other electronic components (1)	60.0	36.0	160.0	9.4
Television and radio transmitters and apparatus for line telephony and line telegraphy (2)	:	51.7	:	:
Television and radio receivers, sound or video recording or reproducing apparatus and associated goods (2)	49.7	33.9	146.4	6.3

(1) Rounded estimates based on non-confidential data; gross operating rate, 2003.
(2) Rounded estimates based on non-confidential data.
Source: Eurostat (SBS)

Table 9.24

Radio, television and communication equipment and apparatus (CPA Division 32)
External trade, EU-27, 2006

	Extra-EU exports		Extra-EU imports		Trade balance (EUR million)	Cover ratio (%)
	(EUR million)	(% share of chapter)	(EUR million)	(% share of chapter)		
Radio, TV & communication equipment	63 482	32.1	99 510	37.3	-36 028	63.8
Electronic valves and tubes and other electronic components	23 790	12.0	31 573	11.8	-7 783	75.3
Television and radio transmitters; apparatus for line telephony and telegraphy	27 348	13.8	31 685	11.9	-4 337	86.3
Television and radio receivers; sound or video recording or reproducing apparatus and associated goods	12 343	6.2	36 252	13.6	-23 909	34.0

Source: Eurostat (Comext)

COSTS, PRODUCTIVITY AND PROFITABILITY

The cost structure of the radio, television and communication equipment manufacturing sector was more akin to the structure across the non-financial business economy as a whole than to electrical machinery and optical equipment manufacturing. A much lower proportion of total expenditure went on personnel costs (16.9 %) in the sector than was generally the case across electrical machinery and optical equipment manufacturing (21.5 %), despite the fact that average personnel costs in the sector were EUR 4 500 per employee higher at EUR 41 500 per employee in 2004 – see Table 9.23. However, the wage adjusted productivity ratio of the EU-27's radio, television and communication equipment manufacturing sector remained higher than the ratio across electrical machinery and optical equipment manufacturing as a whole in 2004 (151.4 % compared to 141.0 %), as the apparent labour productivity of the sector (EUR 62 900 per person employed) was EUR 10 900 per person employed higher than for electrical machinery and optical equipment manufacturing.

However, profitability, as measured by the gross operating rate (which is the ratio of gross operating surplus to turnover) was a little lower for the EU-27's radio, television and telecommunication equipment sector (9.2 %) than the average for electrical machinery and optical equipment manufacturing as a whole (9.7 %) and more clearly beneath the average rate for the non-financial business economy (11.0 %).

EXTERNAL TRADE

The EU-27 had a trade deficit for radio, television and communication equipment (CPA Division 32) of EUR 36.0 billion in 2006 – see Table 9.24. Imports of radio, television and communication equipment from non-member countries into the EU-27 were valued at EUR 99.5 billion in 2006, the majority of this coming from Far East countries like China (32.6 %), South Korea (12.6 %) and Japan (10.8 %).

Overall, intra-EU imports accounted for a small majority (54.4 %) of the value of radio, television and communication equipment imports (intra- and extra-EU) by EU-27 Member States, underlining the importance of the internal market for these goods. The United Kingdom and Germany were the main traders in radio, television and communication equipment accounting for a combined share of 41.6 % of the value of EU-27 Member States exports (intra-and extra-EU) and 37.6 % of their imports. However, whereas the United Kingdom recorded the highest trade surplus for these goods (EUR 12.3 billion) among the Member States in 2006, Germany recorded the largest trade deficit (EUR 7.5 billion).

Table 9.25

Manufacture of computers and office equipment (NACE Division 30)
Main indicators, 2004

	EU-27	BE	BG	CZ	DK	DE	EE	IE	EL	ES	FR	IT	CY	LV	LT
No. of enterprises (thousands) (1)	9.7	0.1	0.1	0.4	0.1	1.1	0.0	0.1	:	1.1	0.5	1.9	0.0	0.0	0.0
Turnover (EUR million) (1)	59 500	217	76	2 634	229	16 579	60	15 971	:	781	2 752	4 188	0	14	15
Production (EUR million) (1)	53 300	204	60	2 648	227	13 252	35	15 719	:	732	2 471	3 865	0	10	9
Value added (EUR million) (1)	11 500	53	12	124	90	4 061	5	1 514	:	139	488	666	0	3	4
Gross operating surplus (EUR million) (1)	5 400	21	6	52	34	1 662	1	912	:	1	120	201	0	2	2
Purchases of goods & services (EUR million) (1)	48 000	167	72	2 535	141	12 509	58	14 423	:	660	2 226	3 665	0	12	12
Personnel costs (EUR million) (1)	6 100	33	5	73	56	2 399	3	602	:	138	368	465	0	1	2
Investment in tangible goods (EUR million)	697	5	4	18	3	173	0	125	:	9	36	46	0	0	1
Employment (thousands)	161	1	2	9	1	42	0	14	:	5	9	15	0	0	1
Apparent labour prod. (EUR thousand) (1)	70.0	59.9	6.2	14.0	75.0	96.9	13.0	107.2	:	28.2	56.6	43.8	:	12.0	7.6
Average personnel costs (EUR thousand) (1)	40.0	43.8	3.0	8.6	47.7	58.2	9.3	42.6	:	32.9	42.9	36.4	:	5.1	3.9
Wage adjusted labour productivity (%) (1)	179.0	136.8	207.7	162.2	157.3	166.5	140.4	251.3	:	85.9	131.8	120.3	:	237.7	194.4
Gross operating rate (%) (1)	9.0	9.5	8.3	2.0	14.7	10.0	2.2	5.7	:	0.2	4.3	4.8	:	12.1	12.6
Investment / employment (EUR thousand)	4.3	5.5	2.2	2.0	2.4	4.1	1.2	8.8	:	1.9	4.1	3.0	:	0.7	1.5

	LU (2)	HU	MT	NL	AT	PL	PT	RO	SI	SK	FI	SE	UK	NO
No. of enterprises (thousands)	0.0	0.3	:	0.2	0.1	0.9	0.0	0.5	0.1	0.0	0.1	0.4	1.7	0.0
Turnover (EUR million)	:	2 106	:	1 568	615	406	109	191	128	684	88	703	9 341	49
Production (EUR million)	:	1 966	:	1 439	576	282	90	79	79	676	70	598	8 172	47
Value added (EUR million)	:	399	:	306	42	79	24	12	26	-26	17	221	3 242	15
Gross operating surplus (EUR million)	:	311	:	20	-4	44	6	6	10	-48	4	33	1 961	3
Purchases of goods & services (EUR million)	:	1 734	:	1 305	549	336	86	182	105	727	72	426	6 113	35
Personnel costs (EUR million)	:	88	:	285	46	36	18	6	16	22	13	188	1 281	12
Investment in tangible goods (EUR million)	:	27	:	:	3	8	3	4	3	32	1	14	152	1
Employment (thousands)	:	8	:	:	1	5	1	3	1	3	0	4	30	0
Apparent labour prod. (EUR thousand)	:	47.9	:	:	33.6	15.8	31.1	4.3	31.0	-9.1	44.7	53.0	107.4	80.9
Average personnel costs (EUR thousand)	:	10.6	:	:	38.3	8.9	24.0	2.1	19.8	7.7	36.4	48.3	43.0	68.3
Wage adjusted labour productivity (%)	:	450.3	:	:	87.7	177.7	129.4	199.4	157.0	-118.1	123.0	109.7	250.0	118.3
Gross operating rate (%)	:	14.8	:	1.3	-0.7	10.8	5.3	3.2	7.8	-7.1	4.2	4.7	21.0	6.3
Investment / employment (EUR thousand)	:	3.3	:	:	2.1	1.6	3.5	1.5	3.7	11.2	3.5	3.3	5.0	3.2

(1) EU-27, rounded estimate based on non-confidential data. (2) 2003.
Source: Eurostat (SBS)

Table 9.26

Manufacture of electrical machinery and equipment (NACE Division 31)
Main indicators, 2004

	EU-27	BE	BG	CZ	DK	DE	EE	IE	EL	ES	FR	IT	CY	LV	LT
No. of enterprises (thousands)	65.5	0.7	0.6	13.8	0.9	5.9	0.1	0.2	:	3.1	4.3	17.7	0.1	0.1	0.1
Turnover (EUR million) (1)	243 000	3 510	332	5 303	4 549	95 322	208	3 336	:	16 120	28 873	31 772	29	123	252
Production (EUR million) (1)	227 000	3 401	314	5 078	4 375	86 426	177	3 310	:	15 578	27 534	30 970	25	100	251
Value added (EUR million) (1)	76 000	1 190	76	1 458	1 091	30 713	58	1 687	:	4 478	8 705	8 735	10	32	72
Gross operating surplus (EUR million) (1)	20 300	276	33	627	184	4 717	21	1 363	:	1 717	1 659	3 305	3	15	38
Purchases of goods & services (EUR million) (1)	171 000	2 378	262	4 018	3 368	64 776	164	1 722	:	12 321	20 466	23 839	19	97	183
Personnel costs (EUR million) (1)	55 400	914	43	843	907	25 995	37	325	:	2 761	7 046	5 430	7	17	34
Investment in tangible goods (EUR million)	7 378	52	18	304	130	2 426	21	83	:	442	843	1 215	1	4	5
Employment (thousands)	1 671	20	18	110	21	499	4	9	:	85	161	195	1	3	7
Apparent labour prod. (EUR thousand) (1)	46.0	61.0	4.2	13.2	51.6	61.6	13.4	183.9	:	53.0	54.1	44.9	19.4	9.5	10.3
Average personnel costs (EUR thousand) (1)	35.0	48.3	2.5	8.6	43.7	52.4	8.6	35.6	:	33.2	43.9	32.1	15.1	5.1	4.9
Wage adjusted labour productivity (%) (1)	132.0	126.3	169.8	153.5	118.1	117.5	155.6	516.8	:	159.5	123.0	139.7	128.2	187.7	210.7
Gross operating rate (%) (1)	8.4	7.9	9.8	11.8	4.0	4.9	10.0	40.8	:	10.6	5.7	10.4	9.0	12.0	15.1
Investment / employment (EUR thousand)	4.4	2.6	1.0	2.8	6.2	4.9	4.7	9.0	:	5.2	5.2	6.2	1.3	1.1	0.6

	LU (2)	HU	MT	NL	AT	PL	PT	RO	SI	SK	FI	SE	UK	NO
No. of enterprises (thousands)	0.0	1.7	:	0.9	0.6	4.8	0.9	0.8	0.8	0.4	0.5	1.3	5.2	0.5
Turnover (EUR million)	:	5 110	:	3 737	5 093	5 046	2 272	1 074	1 072	1 435	3 321	4 706	19 813	1 323
Production (EUR million)	:	4 613	:	3 325	4 929	4 673	2 143	1 055	999	1 374	3 259	4 330	18 179	1 198
Value added (EUR million)	:	1 662	:	1 145	1 803	1 450	595	335	354	380	1 073	1 445	6 920	433
Gross operating surplus (EUR million)	:	966	:	345	621	828	141	132	121	136	316	302	2 358	111
Purchases of goods & services (EUR million)	:	3 452	:	2 636	3 652	3 707	1 707	769	748	1 068	2 326	3 282	12 924	914
Personnel costs (EUR million)	:	696	:	800	1 182	622	454	203	233	244	757	1 143	4 562	322
Investment in tangible goods (EUR million) (3)	:	256	:	75	144	200	82	137	67	102	62	72	583	27
Employment (thousands) (3)	:	70	:	17	27	92	27	66	15	41	18	26	134	6
Apparent labour prod. (EUR thousand) (3)	:	23.6	:	66.5	66.3	15.8	22.2	5.1	23.4	9.3	60.7	55.4	51.5	69.9
Average personnel costs (EUR thousand)	:	10.0	:	47.6	43.9	7.2	17.1	3.1	15.5	6.0	43.1	47.8	34.7	52.8
Wage adjusted labour productivity (%) (3)	:	236.4	:	139.6	150.8	220.4	130.0	164.3	151.0	155.8	141.0	115.9	148.5	132.3
Gross operating rate (%)	:	18.9	:	9.2	12.2	16.4	6.2	12.3	11.3	9.5	9.5	6.4	11.9	8.4
Investment / employment (EUR thousand) (3)	:	3.6	:	4.4	5.3	2.2	3.1	2.1	4.6	2.5	3.5	2.8	4.3	4.3

(1) EU-27, rounded estimate based on non-confidential data. (2) 2003. (3) Slovenia, 2003.
Source: Eurostat (SBS)

Table 9.27

Manufacture of radio, television and communication equipment (NACE Division 32)
Main indicators, 2004

	EU-27	BE	BG	CZ	DK	DE	EE	IE	EL	ES	FR	IT	CY	LV	LT
No. of enterprises (thousands)	28.5	0.2	0.2	3.9	0.2	2.5	0.1	0.0	:	1.0	2.6	7.9	0.0	0.0	0.1
Turnover (EUR million)	201 024	5 063	112	3 894	1 117	45 241	202	2 824	:	5 012	31 393	13 709	7	38	325
Production (EUR million)	166 189	5 209	104	3 701	1 066	32 969	202	2 868	:	4 307	27 821	14 190	7	38	337
Value added (EUR million)	51 057	1 799	38	630	383	11 112	60	1 585	:	1 006	7 900	4 402	1	19	95
Gross operating surplus (EUR million)	18 414	596	21	336	81	3 369	20	1 260	:	228	1 070	1 327	0	13	40
Purchases of goods & services (EUR million)	153 140	3 561	73	3 472	746	34 276	128	1 348	:	4 111	23 617	9 740	6	21	251
Personnel costs (EUR million)	32 644	1 203	17	295	301	7 743	40	326	:	779	6 830	3 075	0	6	55
Investment in tangible goods (EUR million)	8 135	80	7	126	41	2 214	28	909	:	144	1 182	970	0	3	46
Employment (thousands)	812	17	6	34	7	147	6	8	:	25	129	88	0	1	9
Apparent labour prod. (EUR thousand)	62.9	102.8	6.4	18.4	54.1	75.6	10.2	203.0	:	40.6	61.2	49.9	23.4	14.5	10.3
Average personnel costs (EUR thousand)	41.5	69.6	3.0	9.7	43.0	53.2	6.8	41.7	:	32.1	53.1	39.4	11.7	4.6	6.0
Wage adjusted labour productivity (%)	151.4	147.7	214.8	190.5	126.0	142.3	149.1	486.7	:	126.4	115.3	126.8	199.5	314.0	172.7
Gross operating rate (%)	9.2	11.8	18.7	8.6	7.3	7.4	9.9	44.6	:	4.5	3.4	9.7	4.7	34.6	12.3
Investment / employment (EUR thousand)	10.0	4.5	1.2	3.7	5.7	15.1	4.8	116.4	:	5.8	9.2	11.0	13.0	2.2	4.9

	LU (1)	HU	MT	NL	AT	PL	PT	RO	SI	SK	FI	SE	UK	NO
No. of enterprises (thousands)	0.0	1.8	:	0.3	0.2	2.6	0.3	0.2	0.3	0.1	0.3	0.8	2.8	0.2
Turnover (EUR million)	:	11 207	:	:	6 240	3 152	3 328	292	524	555	26 619	10 605	16 481	963
Production (EUR million)	:	10 491	:	:	5 509	3 053	3 305	293	443	501	14 864	11 234	14 537	977
Value added (EUR million)	:	1 337	:	:	2 257	539	635	105	163	93	5 274	3 666	4 806	316
Gross operating surplus (EUR million)	:	767	:	:	709	298	322	53	50	28	3 374	1 659	1 592	72
Purchases of goods & services (EUR million)	:	9 976	:	:	4 239	2 745	2 754	202	369	464	22 036	7 604	11 586	666
Personnel costs (EUR million)	:	570	:	:	1 547	241	313	52	113	65	1 900	2 007	3 214	244
Investment in tangible goods (EUR million) (2)	:	552	:	:	292	146	168	34	18	32	261	151	396	35
Employment (thousands)	:	55	:	:	26	31	13	10	6	10	36	30	80	4
Apparent labour prod. (EUR thousand)	:	24.4	:	:	88.4	17.5	50.4	10.8	26.3	9.4	146.9	120.9	60.4	78.3
Average personnel costs (EUR thousand)	:	10.6	:	:	60.9	8.6	25.0	5.4	18.8	6.6	53.0	73.3	41.4	61.0
Wage adjusted labour productivity (%)	:	230.0	:	:	145.1	203.4	202.0	200.7	139.5	142.2	277.1	164.9	146.0	128.3
Gross operating rate (%)	:	6.8	:	:	11.4	9.4	9.7	18.2	9.6	5.0	12.7	15.6	9.7	7.4
Investment / employment (EUR thousand) (2)	:	10.1	:	:	11.4	4.7	13.4	3.5	3.0	3.2	7.3	5.0	5.0	8.7

(1) 2003. (2) Slovenia, 2003.
Source: Eurostat (SBS)

Table 9.28

Instrument engineering (NACE Division 33)
Main indicators, 2004

	EU-27	BE	BG	CZ	DK	DE	EE	IE	EL	ES	FR	IT	CY	LV	LT
No. of enterprises (thousands) (1)	92.7	1.4	0.9	4.2	0.7	15.6	0.1	0.1	:	5.3	12.3	21.5	0.1	0.1	0.2
Turnover (EUR million)	127 680	1 543	101	1 390	2 432	40 352	90	5 509	:	3 428	22 167	15 485	13	34	98
Production (EUR million)	118 793	1 444	91	1 342	2 325	37 662	88	5 066	:	3 319	20 700	14 823	10	32	97
Value added (EUR million)	51 376	468	24	441	1 131	17 288	26	2 266	:	1 296	7 877	5 571	6	12	35
Gross operating surplus (EUR million)	17 064	141	11	179	457	4 479	11	1 486	:	433	1 756	2 288	2	4	15
Purchases of goods & services (EUR million)	76 671	1 071	79	968	1 307	22 950	67	3 324	:	2 221	14 237	10 157	8	21	69
Personnel costs (EUR million)	34 311	327	14	263	675	12 808	15	780	:	863	6 121	3 283	4	7	21
Investment in tangible goods (EUR million)	3 679	50	7	87	107	1 022	3	249	:	112	508	445	0	3	7
Employment (thousands) (1)	1 020	9	7	34	15	324	2	22	:	34	134	124	0	2	4
Apparent labour prod. (EUR thousand) (1)	50.0	53.4	3.6	13.1	77.4	53.3	15.1	104.1	:	38.0	58.9	44.8	20.4	6.6	9.3
Average personnel costs (EUR thousand) (1)	35.0	44.8	2.4	9.1	46.9	40.8	8.8	35.9	:	28.6	47.4	34.6	16.5	4.2	5.7
Wage adjusted labour productivity (%) (1)	138.0	119.2	152.7	143.8	165.1	130.8	171.7	290.3	:	132.9	124.2	129.3	123.5	156.9	162.3
Gross operating rate (%)	13.4	9.1	10.4	12.9	18.8	11.1	12.1	27.0	:	12.6	7.9	14.8	13.2	12.9	14.8
Investment / employment (EUR thousand) (1)	3.6	5.7	1.0	2.6	7.3	3.2	1.9	11.4	:	3.3	3.8	3.6	1.0	1.4	1.9

	LU (2)	HU	MT	NL	AT	PL	PT	RO	SI	SK	FI	SE	UK	NO
No. of enterprises (thousands)	0.1	3.7	:	2.3	1.4	11.1	0.9	0.9	0.5	0.2	0.8	2.2	5.9	0.5
Turnover (EUR million)	165	794	:	:	1 932	1 407	459	225	439	247	1 932	4 867	18 196	1 603
Production (EUR million)	167	630	:	:	1 807	1 302	425	219	403	232	1 969	4 560	16 435	1 538
Value added (EUR million)	81	282	:	:	947	554	155	80	169	73	733	1 947	8 384	584
Gross operating surplus (EUR million)	22	121	:	:	383	273	47	41	53	24	246	564	3 565	98
Purchases of goods & services (EUR million)	90	514	:	:	1 018	821	308	168	286	181	1 261	2 955	9 758	1 050
Personnel costs (EUR million)	60	160	:	:	564	281	108	39	116	49	487	1 383	4 820	486
Investment in tangible goods (EUR million) (3)	8	44	:	76	58	51	29	20	27	9	37	127	582	33
Employment (thousands)	2	20	:	26	16	52	7	13	8	7	12	26	120	8
Apparent labour prod. (EUR thousand)	43.0	13.8	:	:	59.1	10.7	23.3	6.4	21.7	10.8	62.8	73.8	70.0	73.2
Average personnel costs (EUR thousand)	32.0	8.8	:	:	37.5	7.2	16.9	3.2	15.3	7.3	42.7	56.4	41.5	62.1
Wage adjusted labour productivity (%)	134.2	156.2	:	:	157.5	149.8	137.9	201.7	142.1	148.1	147.0	130.8	168.9	117.9
Gross operating rate (%)	13.0	15.3	:	:	19.8	19.4	10.3	18.2	12.2	9.6	12.8	11.6	19.6	6.1
Investment / employment (EUR thousand) (3)	4.1	2.2	:	2.9	3.6	1.0	4.4	1.6	3.6	1.3	3.1	4.8	4.9	4.1

(1) EU-27, rounded estimate based on non-confidential data. (2) 2003. (3) Slovenia, 2003.
Source: Eurostat (SBS)

Transport equipment

The transport equipment manufacturing sector is central to economic development, as it provides the means for transporting both individuals and goods. Demand for transport equipment has risen as the volume of goods transported and the distance travelled by passengers have expanded greatly - see Chapter 20 which provides information on transport flows, as well as information on selected transport equipment stocks. Increased international trade has stimulated demand for goods transport, while deregulation and liberalisation, improved living standards and access to transport equipment/networks have led to rapid expansions in the distances travelled by passengers. These trends have been accompanied by a modal shift towards road transport, reflected in the increased number of goods vehicles and passenger cars on Europe's roads.

The issue of sustainable development is likely to play an important role in future product developments, as transport equipment manufacturers try to meet demands for more environmentally friendly transport solutions, for example, motor vehicles that consume less fuel, consume alternative fuels (see Subchapter 16.2 concerning biofuels for example), produce less emissions, or that are easier to recycle or dispose of at the end of their life.

Most transport equipment manufacturing activities are structured on the basis of complex pyramidal relationships between major manufacturers and several tiers of component suppliers, ranging from fairly large enterprises

that supply whole systems down to very small, specialised manufacturers that may provide a single component for a vehicle. Deliveries from one level of the pyramid to the next are often made on a just-in-time basis and it is common to find clusters of enterprises concentrated in regions around the leading producers.

STRUCTURAL PROFILE

The EU-27's transport equipment manufacturing sector (NACE Subsection DM) consisted of 43 000 enterprises which generated EUR 176.7 billion of value added in 2004, while employing 3.2 million persons. The transport equipment manufacturing sector accounted for 3.5 % of the value added created within the EU-27's non-financial business economy (NACE Sections C to I and K) and 2.6 % of the non-financial business economy workforce. The sector is dominated by the manufacture of motor vehicles, trailers and semi-trailers (NACE Division 34), as this activity represented 75.8 % of sectoral value added and 70.5 % of employment in 2004 - see Subchapter 10.1. Among the EU-27's other transport equipment manufacturing (NACE Division 35) activities, the manufacture of aerospace equipment (NACE Group 35.3; Subchapter 10.2) was by far the largest activity in 2004, with a 14.1 % share of value added for the whole of the transport equipment manufacturing sector, followed by the building and repairing of ships and boats (NACE Group 35.1; Subchapter 10.3) with 5.6 % and the manufacture of railway and tramway locomotives and rolling stock (NACE Group 35.2; see Subchapter 10.4) with a 3.1 % share.

The manufacture of transport equipment is covered by two NACE divisions, the first of which covers the manufacture of motor vehicles (NACE Division 34), while the other covers the manufacture of other types of transport equipment, namely, shipbuilding, railway rolling stock, aerospace equipment, motorcycles and bicycles, and a residual category of other transport equipment (all included under NACE Division 35).

NACE
34:     manufacture of motor vehicles, trailers and semi-trailers;
34.1: manufacture of motor vehicles;
34.2: manufacture of bodies (coachwork) for motor vehicles; manufacture of trailers and semi-trailers;
34.3: manufacture of parts and accessories for motor vehicles and their engines;
35:     manufacture of other transport equipment;
35.1: building and repairing of ships and boats;
35.2: manufacture of railway and tramway locomotives and rolling stock;
35.3: manufacture of aircraft and spacecraft;
35.4: manufacture of motorcycles and bicycles;
35.5: manufacture of other transport equipment n.e.c.

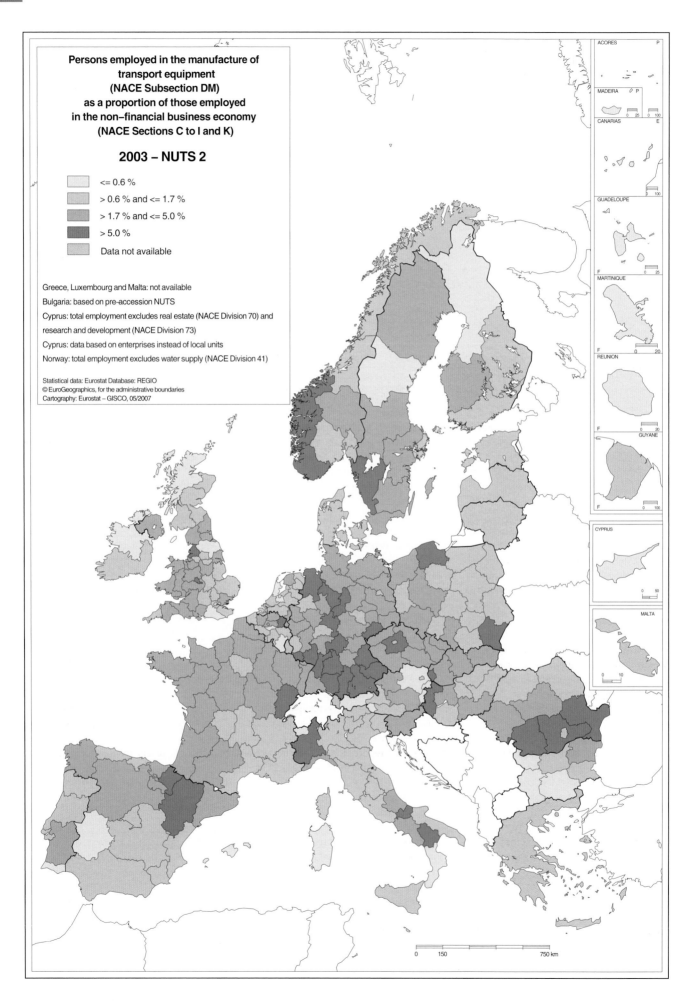

Persons employed in the manufacture of
transport equipment
(NACE Subsection DM)
as a proportion of those employed
in the non–financial business economy
(NACE Sections C to I and K)

2003 – NUTS 2

<= 0.6 %

> 0.6 % and <= 1.7 %

> 1.7 % and <= 5.0 %

> 5.0 %

Data not available

Greece, Luxembourg and Malta: not available

Bulgaria: based on pre-accession NUTS

Cyprus: total employment excludes real estate (NACE Division 70) and
research and development (NACE Division 73)

Cyprus: data based on enterprises instead of local units

Norway: total employment excludes water supply (NACE Division 41)

Statistical data: Eurostat Database: REGIO
© EuroGeographics, for the administrative boundaries
Cartography: Eurostat – GISCO, 05/2007

ACORES   P

MADEIRA   P

CANARIAS   E

GUADELOUPE

F

MARTINIQUE

F

REUNION

F

GUYANE

F

CYPRUS

MALTA

Table 10.1 _____

Manufacture of transport equipment (NACE Subsection DM)
Structural profile, EU-27, 2004 (1)

	No. of enterprises		Turnover		Value added		Employment	
	(thousands)	(% of total)	(EUR million)	(% of total)	(EUR million)	(% of total)	(thousands)	(% of total)
Transport equipment	43.1	100.0	862 231	100.0	176 718	100.0	3 200.0	100.0
Motor vehicles, trailers and semi-trailers	18.3	42.3	704 000	81.6	134 000	75.8	2 256.0	70.5
Aircraft and spacecraft	2.2	5.2	91 000	10.6	25 000	14.1	380.0	11.9
Building and repairing of ships and boats	18.6	43.1	33 000	3.8	9 900	5.6	290.0	9.1
Railway, tramway locomotives, rolling stock	1.1	2.5	20 396	2.4	5 423	3.1	171.5	5.4
Miscellaneous transport equipment	3.0	7.0	12 500	1.4	2 900	1.6	70.0	2.2

(1) Rounded estimates based on non-confidential data.
Source: Eurostat (SBS)

Table 10.2 _____

Manufacture of transport equipment (NACE Subsection DM)
Structural profile: ranking of top five Member States, 2004

Rank	Value added (EUR million) (1)	Employment (thousands) (2)	Share of non-financial business economy			
			No. of enterprises (3)	Turnover (3)	Value added (3)	Employment (4)
1	Germany (70 152)	Germany (1 013.6)	Sweden (0.5 %)	Slovakia (9.3 %)	Germany (6.6 %)	Germany (4.9 %)
2	France (26 623)	France (427.3)	Netherlands (0.5 %)	Germany (8.6 %)	Czech Republic (5.1 %)	Sweden (4.2 %)
3	United Kingdom (24 978)	United Kingdom (356.6)	Finland (0.5 %)	Sweden (6.0 %)	Sweden (5.0 %)	Slovakia (3.4 %)
4	Italy (12 240)	Italy (262.0)	Slovakia (0.4 %)	France (5.6 %)	Hungary (4.8 %)	Czech Republic (3.3 %)
5	Spain (11 686)	Spain (220.8)	Estonia (0.4 %)	Czech Republic (5.3 %)	Slovakia (4.6 %)	Romania (3.2 %)

(1) Greece and Malta, not available; Luxembourg, 2003.
(2) Greece and Malta, not available; Luxembourg and Slovenia, 2003.
(3) Ireland, Greece, Cyprus and Malta, not available; Luxembourg, 2003.
(4) Ireland, Greece, Cyprus and Malta, not available; Luxembourg and Slovenia, 2003.
Source: Eurostat (SBS)

In employment terms the share of aerospace equipment manufacturing was notably lower (11.9 %) while the shares of the building and repairing of ships and boats (9.1 %) and the manufacture of railway and tramway locomotives and rolling stock (5.4 %) were higher. Miscellaneous transport equipment, namely the manufacture of motorcycles and bicycles (NACE Group 35.4) and other transport equipment manufacturing n.e.c. (NACE Group 35.5) had a combined share of just 1.6 % of transport equipment manufacturing value added and 2.2 % of employment - see Subchapter 10.5.

As can clearly be seen from Table 10.2, Germany dominated the EU-27's transport equipment manufacturing sector: Germany's EUR 70.2 billion of value added was just under two fifths of the EU-27 total, and its workforce of just over 1 million persons was just under one third of the EU-27 workforce. It was not just in absolute size that Germany dominated this sector, as it was also the most specialised Member State, in that this sector contributed more to non-financial business economy value added (6.6 %) and non-financial business economy employment (4.9 %) than in any other Member State, and it was in this sector that Germany recorded its highest contribution

to EU-27 value added of any of the industrial NACE subsections. The manufacture of transport equipment was particularly concentrated within the larger Member States, as Germany, France (15.1 % of EU-27 value added) and the United Kingdom (14.1 %) had a cumulative share of EU-27 value added equal to 68.9 % in 2004, compared with their 54.0 % share of non-financial business economy value added. This high level of concentration meant that relatively few of the Member States were specialised in the manufacture of transport equipment, with Germany, the Czech Republic, Sweden, Hungary, Slovakia and France the only Member States [1] to report that their respective transport equipment manufacturing sectors contributed more to national non-financial business economy value added than the EU-27 average in 2004.

The regional specialisation of transport equipment manufacturing in employment terms is shown on the map on page 196. The top three most specialised regions (at the level of detail shown in the map) were all in

_____
[1] Luxembourg, 2003; Greece, Ireland, Cyprus and Malta, not available.

Germany and German regions occupied at least half of the top ten places. Among the other Member States several regions in Romania were relatively specialised in this sector, providing evidence of the importance this activity has reached in parts of Central and Eastern Europe.

Changes in the EU-27 index of production for the manufacture of transport equipment generally took place at a more rapid pace than the industrial average during the ten years to 2006 - see Figure 10.1. On average, output rose by 4.1 % per annum compared with 2.1 % for the industrial economy as a whole. Year on year growth rates recorded for transport equipment manufacturing exceeded those for the industrial economy in each year from 1996 to 2006, except in 2002 when production fell by 0.5 % for the industrial economy as a whole and by 0.6 % for transport equipment manufacturing. Recently, particularly rapid growth was recorded for transport equipment manufacturing in 2004 and in 2006, exceeding 4 % in both years. Several Member States in central and eastern Europe recorded double-digit annual growth in the five years to 2006, ranging from a high of 19.9 % in Lithuania through Poland, Bulgaria, Romania and the Czech Republic, to 11.1 % in Slovakia.

Figure 10.1 _____

Manufacture of transport equipment (NACE Subsection DM)
Evolution of main indicators, EU-27 (2000=100)

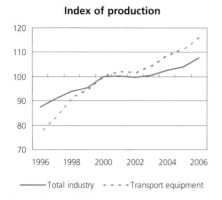

Index of production

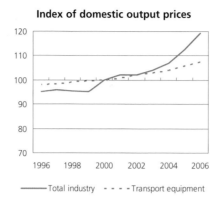

Index of domestic output prices

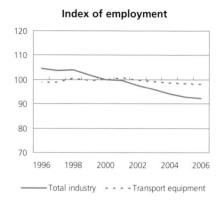

Index of employment

Source: Eurostat (STS)

Figure 10.2 _____

Manufacture of transport equipment (NACE Subsection DM)
Index of production, EU-27 (2000=100)

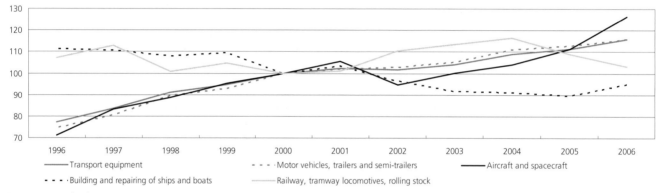

Source: Eurostat (STS)

The growth in output for the EU-27 as a whole was largely driven by the manufacture of motor vehicles, trailers and semi-trailers, where the index of production rose on average by 4.5 % per annum in the ten years to 2006, while for other transport equipment manufacturing growth averaged 3.3 % per annum during the same period. Figure 10.2 provides a more detailed analysis of the development of the production index and this shows a quite varied development for the various parts of other transport equipment manufacturing. The only one of these activities that recorded significant growth over the ten years to 2006 as a whole was aerospace equipment manufacturing, where the EU-27 production index rose by an average of 5.9 % per annum over the period considered. Over the same period the steady decline in output of the building and repairing of ships and boats can be contrasted with the more volatile output of the other transport equipment manufacturing activities shown.

While transport equipment manufacturing employment remained more or less stable in the EU-27 during the ten year period up to 2006, this resulted from a slight increase in the employment index for the manufacture of motor vehicles, trailers and semi-trailers combined with a more rapid decline in the employment index for the smaller activity of other transport equipment manufacturing: employment in the latter increased just once during the ten year period analysed, in 2005. The manufacture of motor vehicles, trailers and semi-trailers recorded an overall annual average growth rate of employment in the EU-27 of 0.5 % in the ten years to 2006 - this activity was one of only four industrial NACE divisions [2] for which the EU-27 recorded an increase in employment levels over this period.

_____
[2] NACE Divisions 11, 12, 13 and 41, not available.

Not only was the manufacture of transport equipment concentrated within the larger Member States, it was also concentrated within relatively large enterprises, as SMEs (employing less than 250 persons) generated just 12.7 % of the EU-27's value added in 2004 (see Figure 10.3), compared with a non-financial business economy average of 57.0 %. This was by far the lowest value added contribution of SMEs recorded for any of the chapters in the present publication. The dominance of large enterprises (with 250 or more persons employed) was particularly prevalent within the manufacture of motor vehicles, trailers and semi-trailers (NACE Division 34) where they accounted for 88.1 % of value added and 82.4 % of employment. The importance of large enterprises was particularly marked in France where they accounted for close to all value added (99.7 %) in transport equipment manufacturing in 2004, and this share was also [3] over 90 % in Germany, Hungary (2003) and the Czech Republic.

_____
[3] Hungary, 2003; Estonia, Greece, Luxembourg, not available.

Energy

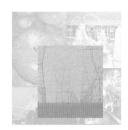

A competitive, reliable and sustainable energy sector is essential for an economy, and this has been put under the spotlight in recent years by a number of issues, notably the volatility in oil prices (see Subchapter 13.1), interruptions to energy supply from non-member countries, blackouts aggravated by inefficient connections between national electricity networks, and the difficulties of market access for suppliers in relation to the gas and electricity markets.

In January 2007 the European Commission adopted a communication proposing an energy policy for Europe [1], with the goal to combat climate change and boost the EU's energy security and competitiveness. One aim is to give energy users greater choice, and another is to spur investment in energy infrastructure. Based on this, in March 2007, the Council endorsed the following targets: reducing greenhouse gas emissions (GHG) by at least 20 % (compared to

[1] COM(2007) 1.

1990 levels) by 2020; improving energy efficiency by 20 % by 2020; raising the share of renewable energy to 20 % by 2020; increasing the level of biofuels in transport fuel to 10 % by 2020.

Figure 13.1 shows the development of the level of GHG emissions from energy industries within the EU-25 since 1990, and the share of all GHG emissions that originate from energy industries. Table 13.1 shows a selection of air emissions for the energy industries including acidifying compounds such as sulphur and nitrogen oxides, as well as the main GHG produced by these industries. It should be noted that trade can affect where emissions are recorded - for example, the substitution of production by imports (for electricity or for products that require a lot of energy in their production) can reduce emissions in a given country (see Figure 13.17 in Subchapter 13.3 for information on trade in electricity), while in fact having little global impact on the level of emissions.

This chapter describes the activities involved in the supply of energy, which include the mining and quarrying of energy producing materials (NACE Subsection CA), the manufacture of coke, refined petroleum products and nuclear fuel (NACE Subsection DF) and the supply of electricity, gas, hot water and steam (NACE Division 40). These are presented in turn in three subchapters.

NACE

10: mining of coal and lignite; extraction of peat;
10.1: mining and agglomeration of hard coal;
10.2: mining and agglomeration of lignite;
10.3: extraction and agglomeration of peat;
11: extraction of crude petroleum and natural gas; service activities incidental to oil and gas extraction, excluding surveying;
11.1: extraction of crude petroleum and natural gas;
11.2: service activities incidental to oil and gas; extraction, excluding surveying;
12: mining of uranium and thorium ores;
23: manufacture of coke, refined petroleum products and nuclear fuel;
23.1: manufacture of coke oven products;
23.2: manufacture of refined petroleum products;
23.3: processing of nuclear fuel;
40: electricity, gas, steam and hot water supply;
40.1: production and distribution of electricity;
40.2: manufacture of gas; distribution of gaseous fuels through mains;
40.3: steam and hot water supply.

Figure 13.1

Greenhouse gas (GHG) emissions by energy industries, EU-25 (1)

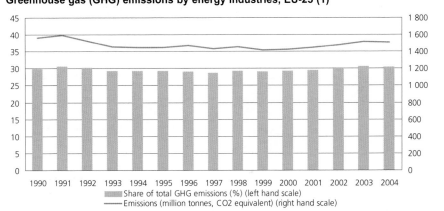

■ Share of total GHG emissions (%) (left hand scale)
— Emissions (million tonnes, CO2 equivalent) (right hand scale)

(1) Energy industries include: public electricity and heat production; petroleum refining; manufacture of solid fuels and other energy industries (IPCC common reporting format sector classification).
Source: Eurostat (Air emissions)

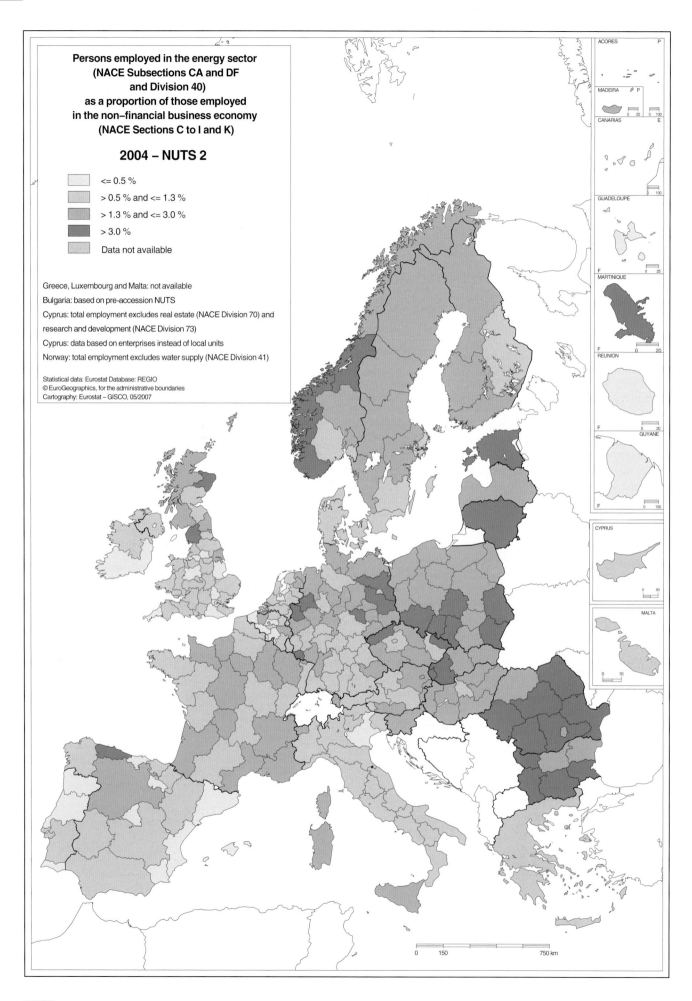

**Persons employed in the energy sector
(NACE Subsections CA and DF
and Division 40)
as a proportion of those employed
in the non–financial business economy
(NACE Sections C to I and K)**

2004 – NUTS 2

- <= 0.5 %
- > 0.5 % and <= 1.3 %
- > 1.3 % and <= 3.0 %
- > 3.0 %
- Data not available

Greece, Luxembourg and Malta: not available

Bulgaria: based on pre-accession NUTS

Cyprus: total employment excludes real estate (NACE Division 70) and
research and development (NACE Division 73)

Cyprus: data based on enterprises instead of local units

Norway: total employment excludes water supply (NACE Division 41)

Statistical data: Eurostat Database: REGIO
© EuroGeographics, for the administrative boundaries
Cartography: Eurostat – GISCO, 05/2007

ACORES   P

MADEIRA   P

CANARIAS   E

GUADELOUPE

F

MARTINIQUE

F

REUNION

F

GUYANE

F

CYPRUS

MALTA

STRUCTURAL PROFILE

In 2004 the energy sector (NACE Subsections CA and DF and Division 41) consisted of 21 500 enterprises, which generated EUR 240.0 billion of gross value added, equivalent to around 4.7 % of the wealth created by the EU-27's non-financial business economy (NACE Sections C to I and K) – see Table 13.2. By comparison, at 1.98 million persons, employment in the EU-27 energy sector accounted for just 1.6 % of non-financial business economy employment, indicating a particularly high apparent labour productivity.

The energy sector is essentially made up of three different activities, concerning extraction, processing, and distribution respectively. The mining and quarrying of energy producing materials (NACE Subsection CA) generated just over one fifth (22.5 %) of EU-27 value added in the energy sector in 2004, the manufacture of coke, refined petroleum products and nuclear fuel (NACE Subsection DF, hereafter referred to as fuel processing) accounted for 15.0 %, and the network supply of electricity, gas, steam and hot water (NACE Division 40) was the largest subsector generating close to two thirds (62.5 %) of the sector's value added.

Table 13.1

Emissions by energy industries, EU-25 (1 000 tonnes) (1)

	1990	2004
Sulphur oxides	14 204	4 285
Nitrogen oxides	3 879	2 199
Ammonium	6	7
Carbon monoxide	619	602
Non-methane volatile organic compounds	81	93
Carbon dioxide	1 545 290	1 494 320
Methane	62	72
Nitrous oxide	50	52

(1) Energy industries include: public electricity and heat production; petroleum refining; manufacture of solid fuels and other energy industries (IPCC common reporting format sector classification).
Source: Eurostat (Air emissions)

In employment terms, the dominance of the network supply part of the energy sector was even clearer, as it accounted for 65.7 % of employment in the EU-27's energy sector in 2004. The mining and quarrying of energy producing materials accounted for 25.3 % of the workforce, also higher than its value added share, and more than double the 9.1 % share of the fuel processing subsector.

The United Kingdom generated over one fifth (20.9 %) of the EU-27's value added in 2004 in the energy sector, just ahead of Germany (19.5 %), while France (11.4 %) was the only other Member State to record a double-digit share of the EU-27 total. In employment terms the contribution of the Member States was very different, with Poland's workforce of 338 000 persons equivalent to 17.1 % of the EU-27 total. The next largest shares for which data are available were 16.4 % in Germany, 10.3 % in France and 8.5 % in the United Kingdom, but it should be noted that Romania had an 11.7 % share of EU-27 employment in the whole energy sector, even excluding the Romanian fuel processing subsector for which data are not available.

Table 13.2

Energy (NACE Subsections CA and DF and Division 40)
Structural profile, EU-27, 2004 (1)

	No. of enterprises		Turnover		Value added		Employment	
	(thousands)	(% of total)	(EUR million)	(% of total)	(EUR million)	(% of total)	(thousands)	(% of total)
Energy	21.5	100.0	1 146 763	100.0	240 000	100.0	1 980.0	100.0
Mining and quarrying of energy producing materials	2.5	11.6	140 000	12.2	54 000	22.5	500.0	25.3
Coke, refined petroleum products and nuclear fuel	1.2	5.4	370 000	32.3	36 000	15.0	180.0	9.1
Electricity, gas, steam and hot water supply	17.8	83.0	636 763	55.5	150 000	62.5	1 300.0	65.7

(1) Rounded estimates based on non-confidential data.
Source: Eurostat (SBS)

Table 13.3

Energy (NACE Subsections CA and DF and Division 40)
Structural profile: ranking of top five Member States, 2004

			Share of non-financial business economy			
Rank	Value added (EUR million) (1)	Employment (thousands) (2)	No. of enterprises (3)	Turnover (1)	Value added (1)	Employment (2)
1	United Kingdom (50 165)	Poland (338.0)	Denmark (1.1 %)	Lithuania (12.2 %)	Poland (14.7 %)	Poland (4.5 %)
2	Germany (46 876)	Germany (324.7)	Finland (0.7 %)	Poland (8.9 %)	Lithuania (12.9 %)	Estonia (3.5 %)
3	France (27 406)	France (204.5)	Latvia (0.7 %)	Hungary (8.3 %)	Hungary (8.0 %)	Lithuania (3.3 %)
4	Italy (22 312)	United Kingdom (169.1)	Estonia (0.6 %)	Germany (8.3 %)	Czech Republic (7.2 %)	Latvia (2.8 %)
5	Spain (17 452)	Italy (126.9)	Lithuania (0.4 %)	Belgium (7.0 %)	Estonia (6.0 %)	Czech Republic (2.4 %)

(1) Bulgaria, Denmark, Ireland, Greece, Cyprus, Latvia, Malta, Austria, Portugal, Romania and Slovakia, not available; Luxembourg, 2003.
(2) Bulgaria, Denmark, Ireland, Greece, Cyprus, Malta, Austria, Portugal, Romania and Slovakia, not available; Luxembourg and Slovenia, 2003.
(3) Ireland, Greece, Cyprus, Malta, Portugal, Romania and Slovakia, not available; Luxembourg, 2003.
Source: Eurostat (SBS)

Figure 13.2

Energy (NACE Subsections CA and DF and Division 40)
Evolution of main indicators, EU-27 (2000=100)

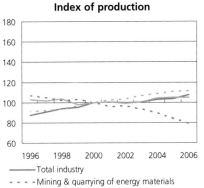

Index of production

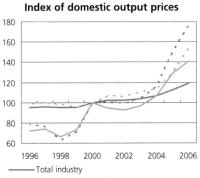

Index of domestic output prices

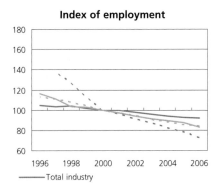

Index of employment

——— Total industry
- - - - Mining & quarrying of energy materials
——— Coke, refined petrol. products & nuclear fuel
- - - - Electricity, gas, steam and hot water supply

——— Total industry
- - - - Mining & quarrying of energy materials
——— Coke, refined petrol. products & nuclear fuel
- - - - Electricity, gas, steam and hot water supply

——— Total industry
- - - - Mining & quarrying of energy materials
——— Coke, refined petrol. products & nuclear fuel
- - - - Electricity, gas, steam and hot water supply

Source: Eurostat (STS)

Several Member States recorded a high value added specialisation in the energy sector, relative to the EU-27 as a whole. In Poland and Lithuania the energy sector accounted for 14.7 % and 12.9 % respectively of non-financial business economy value added in 2004, more than double the share for the EU-27 as a whole. For Slovakia, Romania and Bulgaria data is not available for the fuel processing subsector, but nevertheless the other two energy subsectors together accounted for more than 11 % of non-financial business economy value added in each of these Member States.

The map on page 230 shows the regional specialisation in the energy sector, based on the sector's share of the non-financial business economy employment. This sector was particularly important in several regions of Poland, Romania (which together were home to the three regions most specialised in this sector), and Bulgaria, as well as in Estonia and Lithuania (considered each as one region at the level of detail in the map).

There were contrasting developments in the EU-27 production indices of the three activities involved in the supply of energy. There was steady and successive annual growth for the supply of electricity, gas, hot water and steam over the ten years through until 2006 (at an average rate of 2.0 % per annum). In contrast, there was a downward trend in the production index for the mining and quarrying of energy producing materials (on average by -2.9 % per annum) from a relative peak in 1996, albeit with some temporary upturns in output in 1999 and 2002. The production index for fuel

processing was, by comparison, more stable (rising on average by 0.2 % per annum during the last decade): this index shadowed the overall industrial production index quite closely from 2000 to 2005, but in 2006 the unchanged output in this activity contrasted with the 3.7 % growth recorded for industry as a whole.

Between 1996 and 2006 the employment index fell considerably more strongly for these three energy activities than for industry (NACE Sections C to E) as a whole. The average annual fall in employment was 6.9 % for the mining and quarrying of energy producing materials (1997 to 2006), 3.3 % for fuel processing, and 2.9 % for the supply of electricity, gas, hot water and steam, in all cases a much faster contraction in employment than the industrial average of 1.3 %.

The output price indices of the mining and quarrying of energy producing materials, and of fuel processing, followed quite similar paths during the ten years to 2006. This was characterised by a fall in prices in 1998 followed by large increases in 1999 and 2000. Prices were relatively stable or falling in 2001 and 2002, after which price increases accelerated over the next three years, exceeding 20 % in both of these activities in 2005. In 2006 price increases moderated slightly but were still above the industrial average in both of these activities. In the four years from 2002 to 2006 the annual average output price increase was 15.5 % for the mining and quarrying of energy producing materials, and 11.0 % for fuel processing, more than double the 4.0 % industrial average.

Up to 2000 the output price index for electricity, gas, steam and hot water supply was relatively stable. After 2000 the index developed in a manner similar to the other energy activities, particularly that of mining and quarrying of energy producing materials, with an increase in 2001 followed by a fall in 2002, and then strong growth for the last four years: with an 18.3 % increase in the output price index in 2006 this activity recorded the third highest growth of any industrial NACE division in 2006.

Size class data shows that the EU-27's energy sector is dominated by large enterprises, as SMEs (enterprises with less than 250 persons employed) contributed one fifth (20.4 %) of this sector's value added in 2004, whereas in the non-financial business economy as a whole their contribution was more than half, at 57.0 %. This was the second lowest value added contribution of SMEs among the chapters in the present publication. Large enterprises dominated value added in all three parts of the energy sector, most notably in the fuel processing subsector where they contributed 86.1 % of the total. Unusually, the dominance of large enterprises was even more pronounced in employment rather than value added terms, as 85.0 % of employment in the energy sector was in large enterprises.

Figure 13.3 _____

Energy (NACE Subsections CA and DF and Division 40)
Labour force characteristics, EU-27, 2006

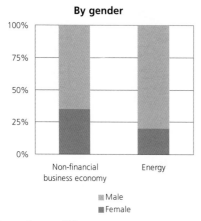

By gender

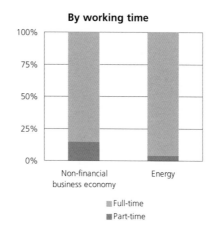

By working time

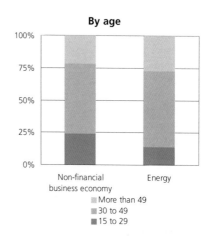

By age

Source: Eurostat (LFS)

EMPLOYMENT CHARACTERISTICS
The energy sector's workforce in the EU-27 can be characterised as male and full-time with a relatively low weight of younger workers - see Figure 13.3. In 2006, according to Labour Force Survey data, 80.0 % of the persons employed in this sector were male, some 15.0 percentage points higher than the non-financial business economy average. The proportion of full-time workers was 96.1 %, 10.5 percentage points higher than the average for the non-financial business economy and the second highest full-time rate among the chapters in the present publication. The proportion of young persons (aged less than 30) in this sector's workforce was only 14.3 %, just under three fifths the average share for the non-financial business economy (24.2 %), and the lowest share among the chapters in the present publication. Instead older workers made up a large part of the workforce, particularly persons aged 50 or over who accounted for more than one quarter (27.2 %) of the workforce.

The characteristics of male, full-time workers with few younger workers were particularly apparent in the energy mining and quarrying subsector, and this is mainly due to the mining of coal and lignite (NACE Division 10). In 2006, 86.2 % of the persons employed in energy mining and quarrying were male, some 6.3 percentage points higher than the energy sector average while the proportion of full-time workers was 97.8 %, 1.6 percentage points higher than the energy sector average. The proportion of the workforce aged under 30 was 10.2 %, the lowest of the energy subsectors and less than half the average for the non-financial business economy. Some 79.2 % of the persons employed in the EU-27's fuel processing activities were male and 96.3 % worked full-time, and in these respects the

employment characteristics of this subsector were typical for the energy sector. Electricity, gas, steam and hot water supply was the least dominated by men and had the lowest proportion of full-time workers, but for both indicators it still reported proportions well above the non-financial business economy average. The proportion of the electricity, gas, steam and hot water supply workforce accounted for by men in the EU-27 was 77.6 % in 2006 and the proportion of full-time employment was 95.4 %.

Structural business statistics for 2004 indicate that the share of paid employees in the total number of persons employed in the EU-27's energy sector was very high. Within the energy mining and quarrying subsector it was 99.7 % and in the electricity, gas, steam and hot water supply subsector it was 99.1 %, while in the fuel processing activities subsector the share for the EU-25 was 99.5 %. As such in all three subsectors the share was close to 100 %, and therefore above the industrial (94.5 %) and non-financial business economy (86.2 %) averages. In all 16 of the Member States for which information on this share is available the share in the energy sector was above the industrial average.

COSTS, PRODUCTIVITY AND PROFITABILITY
Figure 13.4 shows the breakdown of total expenditure (gross tangible investment and operating expenditure) within the EU-27's energy sector. The share of gross tangible investment in total expenditure was 7.1 %, somewhat higher than the 4.9 % non-financial business economy average. This share was particularly high for the mining and quarrying of energy producing materials (12.3 %), the highest of all industrial NACE subsections, and to a lesser extent for electricity, gas, steam and hot water supply (8.6 %). The share of investment was less than half the non-financial business economy average for fuel processing (2.1 %), the lowest of all industrial NACE subsections. Given their processing and distributive natures it is unsurprising that the shares of purchases of goods and services in total expenditure were high in the fuel processing (94.4 %) and electricity, gas, steam and hot water supply (82.3 %) subsectors, and this explains to a large extent their relatively low shares for tangible investment.

Within the EU-27's energy sector there was a range in levels of apparent labour productivity between the subsectors in 2004, but they were all very high. The energy sector's apparent labour productivity was EUR 121 200 per person employed, three times as high as the non-financial business economy average. For mining and quarrying of energy producing materials this ratio was lower, at EUR 109 000 per person employed, while for electricity, gas, steam and hot water supply the ratio was close to the energy sector average, at EUR 120 000 per person employed. For fuel processing apparent labour productivity for the EU-27 was EUR 200 000, by far the highest of all industrial NACE subsections.

Average personnel costs in the EU-25's energy sector were also higher than the non-financial business economy average, reaching EUR 44 200 per employee in 2004. Again fuel processing recorded the highest ratio within the energy sector, at EUR 59 500 per employee, while the lowest average personnel costs were in mining and quarrying of energy producing materials at EUR 33 000 (EUR 25 500 for EU-27). These very high apparent labour productivity ratios and comparatively moderate average personnel costs resulted in particularly high wage adjusted labour productivity ratios, ranging from around 300 % in electricity, gas, steam and hot water supply to 430 % in mining and quarrying of energy producing materials, far above the non-financial business economy average for 2004 of 148 %. The difference was smaller for the gross operating rate (the gross operating surplus relative to turnover) due to the high turnover in the processing and distribution subsectors: the gross operating rate was 14.6 % in the EU-27's energy sector as a whole compared with the non-financial business economy average of 11.0 %. In particular the very low share of personnel costs in total expenditure combined with a high level of turnover in fuel processing resulted in a gross operating rate for this subsector of just 7.0 %, less than half the energy sector's average. The highest gross operating rate among the three energy subsectors was the 29.2 % recorded for mining and quarrying of energy producing materials.

THE ENERGY MIX

Primary energy production in the EU-27 fell on average by 0.5 % per annum between 1995 and 2005 to reach 890 million toe (tonnes of oil equivalent). In contrast gross inland consumption increased over the same period, by an average of 0.9 % per annum to 1.8 billion toe. Consequently the EU-27's dependency on energy imports grew, net imports increasing on average by 2.9 % per annum to 975 million toe in 2005: as such in 2005 net imports were 9.5 % higher than the level of primary production.

Despite the increase in gross inland energy consumption, the energy intensity (measured as gross inland energy consumption divided by GDP) of the EU-25 economy fell on average by 1.3 % per year between 1995 and 2004, meaning that less energy was required to produce the same amount of GDP.

Figure 13.4

Energy (NACE Subsections CA and DF and Division 40)
Structure of total expenditure, EU-27, 2004 (1)

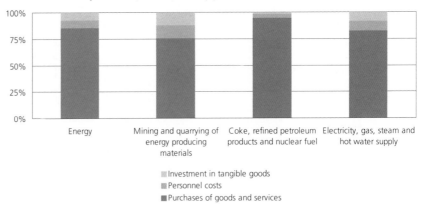

(1) Rounded estimates based on non-confidential data.
Source: Eurostat (SBS)

Box 13.1: definitions

Primary production is the sum of energy extraction, heat produced in reactors as a result of nuclear fission, and the use of renewable energy sources. Primary production, net imports (imports-exports) and stock changes combine to show gross inland consumption. This indicator corresponds to the amount of energy available for final consumption plus the sum of distribution and transformation losses, and consumption by the energy branch itself. Energy available for final consumption is the energy placed at the disposal of consumers including non-energy consumption, for example, the use of some energy products as raw materials by the chemical industry.

Note that unlike the rest of this publication the EU-27's imports and exports of energy products (from Eurostat's energy domain) are generally measured as the sum of the external trade of the Member States. This means that internal trade between EU-27 Member States is counted in the EU-27's total, rather than considering the EU-27 as a whole and only counting extra-EU trade flows.

Figures 13.5 to 13.7 show the change in the ten years between 1995 and 2005 in the energy product mix of the EU-27 in terms of primary production, net imports and gross inland consumption. The share of solid fuels (for example coal and lignite) in primary production fell significantly from nearly three tenths (29.3 %) in 1995 to just over one fifth (21.9 %) in 2005 - see Figure 13.5. The share of crude oil also fell considerably, from 18.0 % to 14.6 % between the same years. These two large falls were compensated by an increase in all of the other sources shown, with renewable energy sources and nuclear energy in particular, but also gas, increasing their shares. In absolute terms, solid fuels and crude oil saw a decrease in primary production over the ten years analysed while gas output was more of less the same in 2005 as in 1995: the output of solid fuels fell on average by 3.4 % per annum and that of crude oil by 2.6 % per annum.

As noted above, the EU-27's net imports of fuels grew significantly between 1995 and 2005: on average (in quantity) net imports of gas grew by 5.9 % per annum, solid fuels by 4.8 % per annum and crude oil and petroleum products by 1.6 % per annum. These different growth rates, in particular the relatively low growth in net imports of crude oil and petroleum products, led to a major change in the product mix in net imports over the period considered (see Figure 13.6), with a 8.6 percentage point drop in the share of crude oil and petroleum products and a 6.5 percentage point increase in the share of gas.

An analysis of the product mix of gross inland consumption in 1995 and in 2005 is shown in Figure 13.7. The product mix in 2005 compared with ten years earlier showed a lower dependence on fossil fuels in relative terms, and a higher use of other sources, in particular gas. The 1997 European Commission White paper on energy for the future targeted the share of renewable sources in gross inland energy consumption at 12 % by 2010, and as noted above, the target of 20 % by 2020 was set in March 2007. Renewable energy sources [2] increased their share from 5.3 % of gross inland consumption in 1995 to 6.8 % in 2005.

Figure 13.8 provides an overview of the change in the destination of final energy use in the ten years between 1995 and 2005. Most notably the share of energy used for transport (including all transport, not just transport by the transport services sector) in the EU-27 increased by 2.8 percentage points, while the share consumed by industry (excluding own-account transport) fell by about the same amount.

Figure 13.9 shows the different changes in the supply of gross inland consumption of the main energy products between 1995 and 2005 for the EU-27. For hard coal and lignite the significant fall in primary production was greater than the increase in net imports, leading to a fall (-12.1 %) in gross inland consumption. A decrease in the primary production of crude oil was more than offset by significantly increased net imports leading to an increase (8.0 %) in gross inland consumption. A large increase in natural gas net imports combined with a stable level of primary production resulted in the significant increase (33.5 %) in gross inland consumption of natural gas. There is no trade in nuclear heat and for renewables net imports are negligible such that primary production and gross inland consumption are effectively the same. Both recorded absolute increases in gross inland consumption between 1995 and 2005, with the increase for renewables (43.8 %) far ahead of that for nuclear heat (15.4 %).

Figures 13.10 to 13.12 show the origin of the EU-27's imports (intra- and extra-EU) of hard coal, crude oil and natural gas in 2005. For all three Russia is the largest or second largest supplier of the EU-27's requirements, providing between 20 % and 30 % of EU-27 net imports.

[2] Hydroelectric, wind, solar, geothermal energy and biomass/waste.

Figure 13.5

Primary production by fuel type, EU-27 (%)

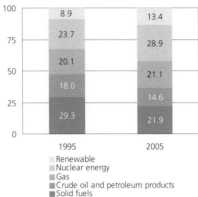

Renewable
Nuclear energy
Gas
Crude oil and petroleum products
Solid fuels

Source: Eurostat (Energy statistics (ES) - quantities)

Figure 13.6

Net imports by fuel type, EU-27 (%)

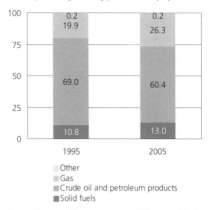

Other
Gas
Crude oil and petroleum products
Solid fuels

Source: Eurostat (Energy statistics (ES) - quantities)

Figure 13.7

Gross inland consumption by fuel type, EU-27 (%)

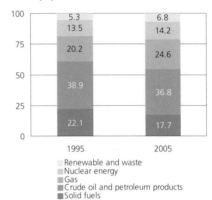

Renewable and waste
Nuclear energy
Gas
Crude oil and petroleum products
Solid fuels

Source: Eurostat (Energy statistics (ES) - quantities)

Figure 13.8

Final energy consumption by end-use, EU-27 (%)

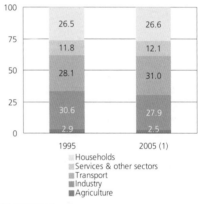

Households
Services & other sectors
Transport
Industry
Agriculture

(1) Provisional.
Source: Eurostat (Energy statistics (ES) - quantities)

Figure 13.9

Main indicators for selected products, EU-27 (million toe)

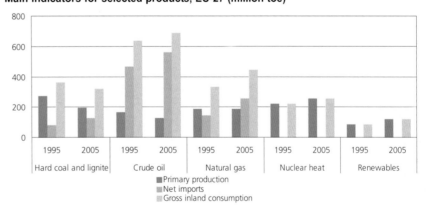

Primary production
Net imports
Gross inland consumption

Source: Eurostat (Energy statistics (ES) - quantities)

Figure 13.10
Hard coal
Sum of EU-27 Member States: origin of imports, 2005 (%)

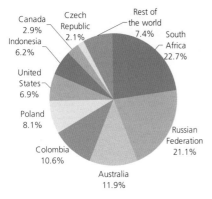

Source: Eurostat (Energy statistics (ES) - quantities)

Figure 13.11
Crude oil
Sum of EU-27 Member States: origin of imports, 2005 (%)

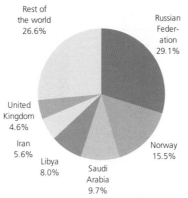

Source: Eurostat (Energy statistics (ES) - quantities)

Figure 13.12
Natural gas
Sum of EU-27 Member States: origin of imports, 2005 (%)

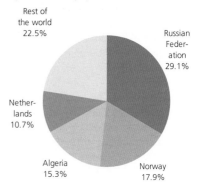

Source: Eurostat (Energy statistics (ES) - quantities)

13.1: MINING AND QUARRYING OF ENERGY PRODUCING MATERIALS

This subchapter looks at the extraction of crude oil and natural gas (NACE Division 11), solid fuels such as coal and lignite (NACE Division 10), as well as mining of uranium and thorium ores (NACE Division 12). The related activities of exploration and surveying are covered in Chapter 22.

The vast majority of hard coal and lignite was consumed as a transformation input in 2005. Most of this was used in conventional thermal power stations, although over one fifth (22.3 %) of the hard coal that was transformed was used as input in coke oven plants. Crude oil is essentially a transformation input, used in refineries (see Subchapter 13.2).

Over several decades the EU's coal mining activity has been in decline due to competition from coal imports and the substitution of other fuels to produce electricity, the latter stimulated recently in part by efforts to reduce emissions. Despite increased prices in recent years stimulating exploration and increasing the economic viability of existing fields, extraction of oil and gas by EU Member States also declined: in the case of crude oil primary production fell sharply from 1999 onwards, and in the case of natural gas more gradually since its most recent peak in 2001.

STRUCTURAL PROFILE

The mining and quarrying of energy producing materials (NACE Subsection CA) was the main activity of 2 500 enterprises which generated EUR 54.0 billion of value added in 2004 in the EU-27 and employed half a million persons, equivalent to 22.5 % of value added in the energy (NACE Subsections CA and DF and Division 40) sector and 25.3 % of the energy sector's workforce. In 2004 the subsector concerning the extraction of crude petroleum and natural gas (NACE Division 11) contributed 83.1 % of the sector's value added but just 30.0 % of employment in the EU-27, while practically all of the remainder was in coal, lignite and peat mining (NACE Division 10): there was negligible activity in the EU-27 in the mining of uranium and thorium ores (NACE Division 12).

Table 13.4

Mining and quarrying of energy producing materials (NACE Subsection CA)
Structural profile: ranking of top five Member States, 2004

Rank	Share of EU-27 value added (%) (1)	Share of EU-27 employment (%) (2)	Value added specialisation ratio (EU-27=100) (3)	Employment specialisation ratio (EU-27=100) (4)
1	United Kingdom (48.0)	Poland (31.3)	Romania (708.3)	Romania (719.6)
2	Netherlands (9.4)	Romania (23.0)	Denmark (380.4)	Poland (522.0)
3	Italy (8.7)	Germany (12.3)	Poland (349.8)	Estonia (337.5)
4	Germany (8.1)	Czech Republic (8.1)	United Kingdom (253.8)	Czech Republic (284.2)
5	Denmark (7.6)	United Kingdom (7.4)	Netherlands (205.9)	Bulgaria (250.0)

(1) Ireland, Greece, Malta and Portugal, not available; Luxembourg, 2003.
(2) Ireland, Greece, Malta and Portugal, not available; Luxembourg and Slovenia, 2003.
(3) Ireland, Greece, Cyprus, Malta and Portugal, not available; Luxembourg, 2003.
(4) Ireland, Greece, Cyprus, Malta and Portugal, not available; Luxembourg and Slovenia, 2003.
Source: Eurostat (SBS)

Figure 13.13 _____

Mining and quarrying of energy producing materials (NACE Subsection CA)
Evolution of main indicators, EU-27 (2000=100)

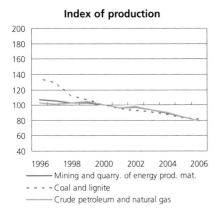

Index of production

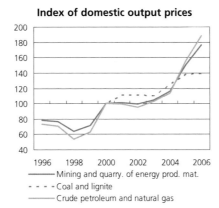

Index of domestic output prices

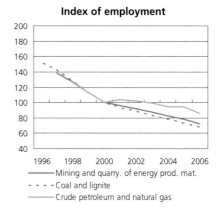

Index of employment

Source: Eurostat (STS)

The United Kingdom generated nearly half (48.0 %) of the EU-27's value added in the mining and quarrying of energy producing materials sector, ahead of the Netherlands (9.4 %), Italy (8.7 %), Germany (8.1 %), Denmark (7.6 %) and Poland (7.2 %). For the United Kingdom, the Netherlands and Denmark this share was their highest share recorded in any industrial NACE subsection as it was also for Romania (3.0 %), while for Poland it was the second highest. In employment terms, Poland and Romania dominated the sector, with 156 300 and 115 200 persons employed respectively in 2004, 31.3 % and 23.0 % of the EU-27 workforce. The third largest workforce was in Germany which represented 12.3 % of the EU-27 total, ahead of the Czech Republic with 8.1 %. Despite its dominance in value added terms, the United Kingdom's share of the EU-27 workforce was just 7.4 %. The large differences between the two variables can be partly explained by the different specialisations within the sector, as the United Kingdom was particularly active in the extraction of crude petroleum and natural gas, whereas the Czech Republic and Poland were almost exclusively active in the mining of coal and lignite, and, as explained below, there was a huge difference in the value added generated per person employed between these subsectors.

Figure 13.13 illustrates clearly the reduction in output and steeper reduction in employment in these activities over several years: output from the mining and quarrying of energy producing materials fell on average 2.9 % per annum in the ten years to 2006, while employment fell an average of 6.9 % per annum in the nine years to 2006. In contrast, the development of output prices was less stable, particularly for crude petroleum and natural gas for which prices increased strongly from 1998 to 2000, fell slightly for two years, and then increased at an average rate of 18.5 % per annum during the four years to 2006. Output prices for coal and lignite followed a similar path, but with less volatile changes.

COSTS, PRODUCTIVITY AND PROFITABILITY

As noted earlier, the share of gross tangible investment in total expenditure was 12.3 % in the EU-27's energy producing materials mining and quarrying sector in 2004, the highest share of all industrial NACE subsections. This share was particularly high for the extraction of crude petroleum and natural gas subsector at 12.5 %.

Average personnel costs in this sector were EUR 25 500 in 2004 and apparent labour productivity was more than four times as high, at EUR 109 000 per person employed. The resulting wage adjusted labour productivity of 430.0 % was the highest of all industrial NACE subsections. For the crude petroleum and natural gas subsector these ratios were all generally much higher, with average personnel costs of EUR 36 000 per employee and apparent labour productivity of EUR 300 000 per person employed resulting in wage adjusted labour productivity of 836.0 %, by far the highest of any non-financial business economy NACE division [3]. It should be noted that the expansion of the EU to include Bulgaria and Romania has had a huge impact on some of these indicators for the crude petroleum and natural gas extraction subsector: for example the average personnel costs and apparent labour productivity of the EU-25 were twice the level of that for the EU-27, reflecting the fact that the Romanian workforce in the extraction of crude petroleum and natural gas subsector is larger than that of all of the EU-25 Member States together, and that the Romanian workforce's apparent labour productivity in this subsector was equivalent to just 2.5 % of EU-25 average, and its average personnel costs equivalent to just 7.1 % of the EU-25 average.

The gross operating rate in the energy producing materials mining and quarrying sector was high (29.2 %), due mainly to a high rate in the extraction of crude petroleum and natural gas subsector (31.2 %), the highest for an industrial NACE division, and third highest for all non-financial business economy divisions [4] in 2004.

_____
[3] NACE Divisions 10, 12, 13 and 14, not available.
[4] NACE Divisions 10, 12 and 62, not available.

FOCUS ON CRUDE OIL PRICES AND RESERVES

One of the most visible characteristics of the energy sector and its products is the volatility in the price of oil, which has risen since 2002 to its high level at the time of writing - see Figure 13.14. High oil prices have an impact on prices of substitutes, notably natural gas, and also feed into the prices of products from other sectors that are heavy users of energy or of energy products as raw materials.

Table 13.5 shows world production and proved reserves of crude oil. The BP Statistical Review of World Energy notes that 'proved reserves are generally taken to be those quantities that geological and engineering information indicates with reasonable certainty can be recovered in the future from known reservoirs under existing economic and operating conditions'.

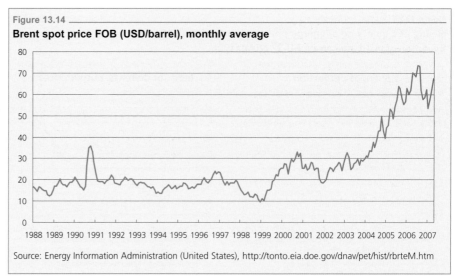

Figure 13.14

Brent spot price FOB (USD/barrel), monthly average

Source: Energy Information Administration (United States), http://tonto.eia.doe.gov/dnav/pet/hist/rbrteM.htm

Table 13.5

Production and proved reserves of oil, 2006 (1)

	Production (million barrels/day)	Proved reserves (billion barrels) (2)	R/P ratio (years) (3)
North America	13.7	59.9	12.0
South and Central America	6.9	103.5	41.2
Africa	10.0	117.2	32.1
EU and Norway (DK, IT, RO, UK, NO)	5.0	14.7	8.1
Central & Eastern Europe, Eurasia	12.6	129.7	28.2
Middle East	25.6	742.7	79.5
Asia Pacific	7.9	40.5	14.0
World	81.7	1 208.2	40.5

(1) Oil includes gas condensate and natural gas liquids as well as crude oil.
(2) As of end 2006.
(3) Ratio of reserves divided by production.
Source: BP Statistical Review of World Energy 2007

13.2: FUEL PROCESSING

This subchapter covers the manufacture of coke oven products (NACE Group 23.1), the manufacture of refined petroleum products (NACE Group 23.2) and the processing of nuclear fuels (NACE Group 23.3). Hereafter these are collectively referred to as fuel processing activities (NACE Subsection DF). Note that these activities essentially involve the processing of products whose extraction was covered in the previous subchapter, such as coal, crude oil, and ores.

Table 13.6

Manufacture of coke, refined petroleum products and nuclear fuel (NACE Subsection DF)
Structural profile, EU-27, 2004

	No. of enterprises (thousands)	Turnover (EUR million)	Value added (EUR million)	Employment (thousands)
Manufacture of coke, refined petroleum products and nuclear fuel (1)	1.2	370 000	36 000	180.0
Coke oven products	0.1	2 857	932	9.4
Refined petroleum products (1)	1.1	360 000	33 000	140.0
Processing of nuclear fuel	0.0	7 531	2 549	31.5

(1) Rounded estimate based on non-confidential data.
Source: Eurostat (SBS)

EU-27 transformation output of petroleum products was 740.2 million tonnes in 2005. Diesel oil accounted for 36.5 % of this output in 2005, motor spirit 21.7 %, residual fuel oil 14.7 %, and jet fuel, naphtha, refinery gas and liquefied petroleum gas (LPG) collectively accounted for a further 19.5 %.

STRUCTURAL PROFILE

In the fuel processing sector (NACE Subsection DF) there were 1 150 enterprises which generated EUR 36.0 billion of value added was generated in 2004 in the EU-27, and employed 180 000 persons, equivalent to 15.0 % of value added in the energy (NACE Subsections CA and DF and Division 40) sector and 9.1 % of the energy sector's workforce. Around nine tenths (91.7 %) of value added was generated in the manufacture of refined petroleum products (NACE Group 23.2) where around three quarters (77.8 %) of the workforce were employed. Close to one fifth (17.5 %) of the workforce was employed in the processing of nuclear fuel (NACE Group 23.3), far greater than this subsector's 7.1 % share of value added. The remaining 2.6 % of value added and 5.2 % of the workforce were accounted for by the manufacture of coke oven products (NACE Group 23.1).

In the fuel processing sector, Germany accounted for 20.2 % of the EU-27's value added in 2004, ahead of Spain (14.2 %), Poland (13.4 %), France (12.8 %) and the United Kingdom (10.5 %). In this sector Spain and Poland recorded their highest contributions to EU-27 value added of any industrial (NACE Sections C to E) NACE subsection, as did Hungary (2.4 %) and Lithuania (1.0 %). In the manufacture of coke, Poland alone contributed 81.4 % of the EU-27 total, although as noted above this is a small part of the fuel processing sector in the EU-27 in general, and even in Poland the coke oven products manufacturing subsector only represented 15.7 % of fuel processing value added in 2004. In value added terms Lithuania and Poland were by far the most specialised EU-27 Member States in the fuel processing sector in 2004 - see Table 13.7.

COSTS, PRODUCTIVITY AND PROFITABILITY

The share of gross tangible investment in the total expenditure was 2.1 % in the EU-27's fuel processing sector in 2004. This very low share was the result of a very high share (94.4 %) of purchases of goods and services (including, in particular, the purchase of the new energy products to be processed). In absolute terms gross tangible investment in this sector was valued at EUR 6.0 billion in 2004, around 0.7 % of the non-financial business economy (NACE Sections C to I and K) total, a similar share to this sector's value added share.

Average personnel costs in the EU-25's fuel processing sector were EUR 59 500 per employee in 2004 well above the energy average and more than double the non-financial business economy average. Nevertheless, within the sector there were large differences, with average personnel costs as low as EUR 17 500 per employee in the manufacture of coke oven products and over EUR 60 000 in the two other subsectors. The low average in coke oven products manufacturing can be attributed to the dominance of this subsector by Poland where average personnel costs were EUR 12 000 per employee, although this was nearly double the

Table 13.7

Manufacture of coke, refined petroleum products and nuclear fuel (NACE Subsection DF)
Structural profile: ranking of top five Member States, 2004

Rank	Share of EU-27 value added (%) (1)	Share of EU-27 employment (%) (2)	Value added specialisation ratio (EU-27=100) (3)	Employment specialisation ratio (EU-27=100) (4)
1	Germany (20.2)	France (18.2)	Lithuania (714.5)	Lithuania (308.6)
2	Spain (14.2)	United Kingdom (14.1)	Poland (652.7)	Finland (194.9)
3	Poland (13.4)	Germany (11.8)	Hungary (344.4)	Hungary (190.4)
4	France (12.8)	Italy (9.8)	Belgium (195.3)	Estonia (180.1)
5	United Kingdom (10.5)	Poland (8.8)	Finland (158.9)	France (159.0)

(1) Bulgaria, Denmark, Ireland, Greece, Latvia, Luxembourg, Malta, Austria, Romania and Slovakia, not available.
(2) Bulgaria, Denmark, Ireland, Greece, Luxembourg, Malta, Austria, Romania and Slovakia, not available.
(3) Bulgaria, Denmark, Ireland, Greece, Cyprus, Latvia, Luxembourg, Malta, Austria, Romania and Slovakia, not available.
(4) Bulgaria, Denmark, Ireland, Greece, Cyprus, Luxembourg, Malta, Austria, Romania and Slovakia, not available.
Source: Eurostat (SBS)

Polish non-financial business economy average. Despite the overall high average personnel costs in the fuel processing sector, the very high levels of apparent labour productivity resulted in a very high wage adjusted labour productivity ratio, 366.9 % in the EU-25 in 2004, the second highest of the industrial NACE subsections. Among the individual Member States, Poland recorded a wage adjusted labour productivity of 1 847.2 %, some five times as high as the EU-25 average. Spain also recorded a remarkably high level for this indicator, 974.6 %.

The gross operating rate (ratio of gross operating surplus to turnover) in the EU-27's fuel processing sector was 7.0 %, the only one of the three main parts of the energy sector where this rate was below the non-financial business economy average (11.0 %). This ratio reached as high as 26.9 % in the coke oven products manufacturing subsector.

Figure 13.15

Manufacture of coke, refined petroleum products and nuclear fuel (NACE Subsection DF) Structure of gross operating and tangible investment expenditure, EU-27, 2004

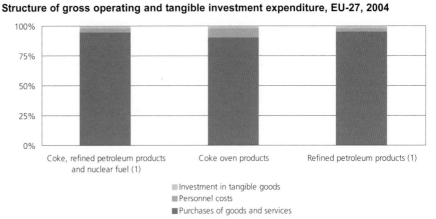

■ Investment in tangible goods
■ Personnel costs
■ Purchases of goods and services

(1) Rounded estimates based on non-confidential data.
Source: Eurostat (SBS)

13.3: NETWORK SUPPLY OF ELECTRICITY, GAS AND HEAT

This subchapter focuses on the production and distribution of electricity, whether generated from fossil, nuclear or renewable fuels (NACE Group 40.1), and the manufacture and distribution of gas via mains (NACE Group 40.2). The manufacture of gas includes the manufacture of gas from the carbonisation of coal, from by-products of agriculture or from waste, but does not include the manufacture of refined petroleum products, or of industrial gases. The distribution of gas concerns only through a mains network, and does not include the bulk sale and transport of gaseous fuels, or its distribution in canisters.

Figure 13.16

Gross electricity generation by type of power plant, EU-27, 2005 (%)

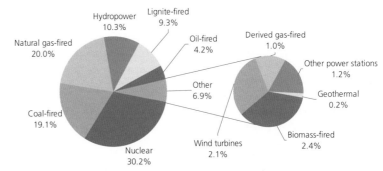

Source: Eurostat (Energy statistics (ES) - quantities)

This subchapter also covers steam and hot water supply (NACE Group 40.3), normally for district heating, also known as city heating. District heating is the distribution of heat through a network to one or several buildings using hot water or steam produced centrally, often from co-generation plants, from waste heat from industry, or from dedicated heating systems. Large scale district heating in Europe is commonly found in central and eastern Europe and in the Nordic countries.

The gas and electricity markets in the EU have been changing through the requirements of the second electricity and gas directives adopted in 2003. The aim is to have gas and electricity markets open for all customers by July 2007, as well as further unbundling the sector's supply

and distribution/transmission enterprises. In January 2007 the European Commission published a communication on the prospects for the internal gas and electricity market [5]. Whilst recognising progress in these markets the European Commission noted the improper implementation of the current legal framework by several Member States. The European Commission outlined its planned actions concerning: ensuring non-discriminatory access to well developed networks; improving regulation of network access at national and EU level; reducing the scope for unfair competition; providing a clear framework for investment; resolving issues relating to households and smaller commercial customers.

The lack of integration between national markets, indicated by the absence of price convergence and the low level of cross-border trade, is generally due to barriers to entry, inadequate use of existing infrastructure and - in the case of electricity - insufficient interconnection between many Member States: in June 2007 Luxembourg and Germany announced their decision to join Belgium, France and the Netherlands to create a single North-West European electricity market.

[5] COM(2006) 841.

Figure 13.17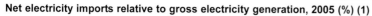

Net electricity imports relative to gross electricity generation, 2005 (%) (1)

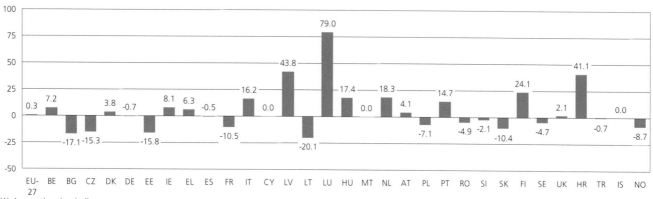

(1) A negative sign indicates net exports.
Source: Eurostat (Energy statistics (ES) - quantities)

Figure 13.18

Contribution of electricity from renewables to total electricity consumption, 2005 and target for 2010 (%) (1)

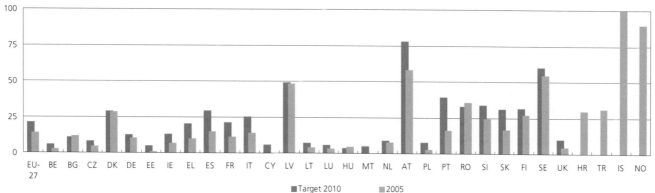

■ Target 2010   ■ 2005

(1) Target 2010 only for EU-27 Member States.
Source: Eurostat (Structural indicators)

FOCUS ON ELECTRICITY

Gross electricity generation (6) in the EU-27 in 2005 was 3 310 TWh. More than half of this was generated in coal, natural gas, lignite-fired, oil fired, derived gas-fired or other thermal power stations (54.8 %) and just over three tenths (30.2 %) in nuclear power stations. The largest part of the remaining generation was in hydroelectric power plants (10.3 %), biomass-fired power stations (2.4 %) and wind turbines (2.1 %) - see Figure 13.16.

Within Europe there are some movements of electricity across borders and in fact some smaller Member States and Candidate countries are particularly dependent on external sources for their electricity supply. For example, in Luxembourg and Latvia, as well as in Croatia, the level of net imports is very high relative to gross electricity generation - see Figure 13.17. Among the Member States the largest net exporters of electricity in 2005 were France, the Czech Republic and Poland, while Norway also recorded significant net exports of electricity.

(6) Gross electricity generation is the electricity measured at the outlet of the main transformers, in other words, including the consumption of electricity in plant auxiliaries and in transformers.

In 2001 a target of 21 % was set for the share of renewable energy sources (wind, solar, geothermal, wave, tidal, hydropower, biomass, landfill gas, sewage treatment plant gas and biogases) in electricity consumption by 2010. Figure 13.18 shows the targets and the contribution to electricity generation from renewables in 2005 in terms of gross national electricity consumption (gross national electricity generation from all fuels plus net electricity imports). For the EU-27 as a whole this share was 14.0 % in 2005, an increase of only 1.0 percentage point since 1995 (13.0 %). Several of the Member States recorded a large increase in the contribution of renewables in the ten years to 2005, with the share more than trebling in Denmark, Estonia, Hungary and the Netherlands. However, seven of the Member States recorded a fall in the contribution of renewables over the period considered, most notably France and Portugal.

Concerns about safety and waste have been issues for nuclear energy for a long time. In November 2006 a directive on the control of shipments of radioactive waste and spent fuel (7) was adopted. The benefits of nuclear fuel have however been boosted as concerns about the security of energy supply have risen along with the increase in EU imports of oil and gas, while at the same time Member States have committed themselves to reduce emissions. According to the World Nuclear Association, as of May 2007, Bulgaria, France, Romania, Slovakia, Finland and Turkey had started construction or planned new nuclear reactors, as had Russia and the Ukraine: outside of Europe most of the countries planning new nuclear reactors were in Asia.

(7) Council Directive 2006/117/Euratom; Official Journal L337 p. 21, of 5 December 2006.

Figure 13.19

Prices (without taxes) for industrial consumers, 1 January 2007

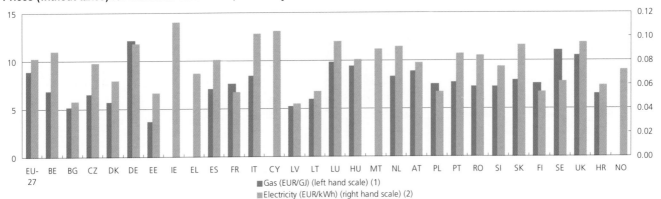

■ Gas (EUR/GJ) (left hand scale) (1)
■ Electricity (EUR/kWh) (right hand scale) (2)

(1) Natural gas prices charged to final industrial consumers defined as follows: annual consumption of 41 860 GJ, and load factor of 200 days (1 600 hours); Ireland, Greece, Cyprus, Malta and Norway, not available.
(2) Electricity prices charged to final industrial consumers defined as follows: annual consumption of 2 000 MWh, maximum demand of 500 kW and annual load of 4 000 hours.
Source: Eurostat (Energy statistics (ES) - prices)

PRICES

Figure 13.19 shows the prices of two types of energy provided to consumers, in this case to industrial consumers. This shows the price per unit (GJ for gas or kWh for electricity) at the beginning of 2007 across the Member States. Bulgaria, Estonia and Latvia recorded the lowest prices for both products. Ireland, Cyprus and Italy had the most expensive electricity prices, and Germany, Sweden and the United Kingdom the highest gas prices.

STRUCTURAL PROFILE

In electricity, gas, steam and hot water supply (NACE Division 40) EU-27 value added in 2004 was EUR 150.0 billion, 62.5 % of the energy (NACE Subsections CA and DF and Division 40) sector total. There were 17 800 enterprises which employed some 1.3 million persons in the electricity, gas, steam and hot water supply sector across the EU-27, 65.7 % of the energy sector's workforce. This activity was more evenly distributed among the Member States than the other energy sectors presented in Subchapters 13.1 and 13.2. Nevertheless, this sector did account for as much as 14.0 % of non-financial business economy (NACE Sections C to I and K) value added in Slovakia and 10.0 % in Bulgaria, and as little as 1.6 % in the Netherlands.

An analysis of the subsectors identifies the production and distribution of electricity (NACE Group 40.1) as the largest in value added terms, as it contributed approximately three quarters (77 %) [8] of the sector's value added in 2004. The data availability for the two remaining subsectors is weaker, but based on an average for 15 Member States [9] the manufacture of gas and distribution of gaseous fuels through mains (NACE Group 40.2) subsector contributed around 17 % of the sectoral value added and the steam and hot water supply subsector (NACE Group 40.3) around 5 %.

[8] EU average, 2004; Latvia, Luxembourg and Slovakia, 2003; excluding Estonia, Ireland, Greece, Cyprus, Malta and the Netherlands.
[9] EU average, 2004; Slovenia, 2003; excluding Belgium, Bulgaria, Estonia, Ireland, Greece, Latvia, Luxembourg, Malta, the Netherlands, Slovakia, Sweden and the United Kingdom.

Table 13.8

Electricity, gas, steam and hot water supply (NACE Division 40)
Structural profile: ranking of top five Member States, 2004 (1)

Rank	Share of EU-27 value added (%)	Share of EU-27 employment (%)	Value added specialisation ratio (EU-27=100)	Employment specialisation ratio (EU-27=100)
1	Germany (23.5)	Germany (18.6)	Slovakia (475.1)	Slovakia (311.2)
2	France (14.3)	Poland (12.8)	Bulgaria (340.4)	Romania (280.8)
3	United Kingdom (13.6)	France (12.4)	Lithuania (239.3)	Lithuania (260.6)
4	Italy (10.1)	Romania (9.0)	Poland (218.2)	Latvia (237.2)
5	Spain (7.7)	United Kingdom (8.2)	Romania (197.5)	Bulgaria (222.7)

(1) Ireland, Greece, Cyprus and Malta, not available; Luxembourg, 2003.
Source: Eurostat (SBS)

Electricity, gas, steam and hot water supply output increased more or less in line with that for total industry, but employment fell faster and output prices grew much faster - see Figure 13.20. The decrease in employment averaged 2.9 % per annum in the ten years to 2006 for electricity, gas, steam and hot water supply, more than twice the industrial average decline of 1.3 %. In contrast output prices for electricity, gas, steam and hot water supply increased at an annual average rate of 4.5 %, close to double the industrial average of 2.3 %. This strong growth in output prices reflects the particularly high increases in 2005 (14.2 %) and 2006 (18.3 %).

COSTS, PRODUCTIVITY AND PROFITABILITY

An analysis of investment and operating expenditure indicates the capital nature of this activity. The share of gross tangible investment in total expenditure was 8.6 % in the electricity, gas, steam and hot water supply sector in 2004, which was approximately 1.7 times as high as the non-financial business economy average. In absolute terms investment in this sector in 2004 reached EUR 50.0 billion, some 5.6 % of the non-financial business economy total, close to double the sector's share of non-financial business economy value added.

Average personnel costs in the EU-27's electricity, gas, steam and hot water supply sector were EUR 40 000 in 2004, more than 40 % higher than the non-financial business economy average (EUR 27 600). The apparent labour productivity was EUR 120 000 per person employed, high in absolute terms, but only average for the energy sector as a whole. The resulting wage adjusted labour productivity ratio was 300.0 % indicating that value added per person employed was three times as high as average personnel costs. In every Member State [10] the wage adjusted labour productivity in this sector was higher than the non-financial business economy average, the largest difference being in Spain where it was approximately 3.7 times as high. Among the three subsectors, the wage adjusted labour productivity was highest in 2004 for the manufacture of gas and distribution of gaseous fuels through mains at 328 % on average in the EU [11]. For the production and distribution

[10] Luxembourg, 2003; Ireland, Greece, Cyprus and Malta, not available.
[11] EU average, 2004; Slovenia, 2003; excluding Belgium, Bulgaria, Estonia, Ireland, Greece, Latvia, Luxembourg, Malta, the Netherlands, Slovakia, Sweden and the United Kingdom.

of electricity it was 278 % on average in the EU [12], while for steam and hot water supply the EU [13] average was 200 %.

The gross operating rate, calculated as the ratio of the gross operating surplus to turnover was 15.7 %, above both the energy sector (14.6 %) and the non-financial business economy (11.0 %) averages.

[12] EU average, 2004; Latvia, Luxembourg and Slovakia, 2003; excluding Estonia, Ireland, Greece, Cyprus, Malta and the Netherlands.
[13] EU average, 2004; Slovenia, 2003; excluding Belgium, Bulgaria, Greece, Luxembourg, Malta, the Netherlands, Sweden and the United Kingdom.

Figure 13.20

Electricity, gas, steam and hot water supply (NACE Division 40)
Evolution of main indicators, EU-27 (2000=100)

Index of production

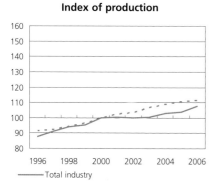

——— Total industry
- - - - Electricity, gas, steam and hot water supply

Index of domestic output prices

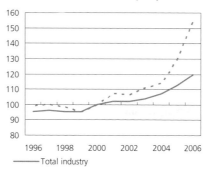

——— Total industry
- - - - Electricity, gas, steam and hot water supply

Index of employment

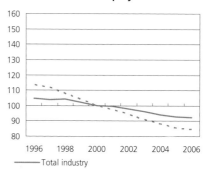

——— Total industry
- - - - Electricity, gas, steam and hot water supply

Source: Eurostat (STS)

Table 13.9

Mining of coal and lignite; extraction of peat (NACE Division 10)
Main indicators, 2004

	EU-27	BE	BG	CZ	DK	DE	EE	IE	EL	ES	FR	IT	CY	LV	LT
No. of enterprises (thousands) (1)	1.5	:	0.0	0.0	0.0	0.1	0.0	:	:	0.1	0.0	0.0	0.0	0.1	:
Turnover (EUR million) (2)	13 698	:	244	1 898	:	4 019	:	:	:	827	369	4	0	44	:
Production (EUR million) (3)	:	:	233	1 636	:	3 675	:	:	:	877	366	32	0	43	:
Value added (EUR million) (4)	9 000	:	122	882	:	2 865	:	:	:	547	-56	3	0	17	:
Gross operating surplus (EUR million) (4)	2 000	:	34	449	:	160	:	:	:	84	-495	-18	0	8	:
Purchases of goods & services (EUR million) (3)	:	:	133	1 008	:	4 016	:	:	:	496	833	9	0	27	:
Personnel costs (EUR million) (4)	7 000	:	87	433	:	2 705	:	:	:	463	439	22	0	9	:
Investment in tangible goods (EUR million) (3)	:	:	25	170	:	469	:	:	:	103	12	1	0	6	:
Employment (thousands) (3)	:	:	17	37	:	55	:	:	:	12	5	1	0	2	:
Apparent labour prod. (EUR thousand) (4)	28.0	:	7.3	24.0	:	51.7	:	:	:	46.8	-10.5	5.5	:	8.4	:
Average personnel costs (EUR thousand) (3)	:	:	5.2	11.8	:	48.9	:	:	:	39.8	82.8	35.4	:	4.7	:
Wage adjusted labour productivity (%) (3)	:	:	139.1	203.0	:	105.8	:	:	:	117.6	-12.7	15.6	:	176.9	:
Gross operating rate (%) (3)	:	:	14.1	23.7	:	4.0	:	:	:	10.2	-134.0	-500.4	:	17.1	:
Investment / employment (EUR thousand) (3)	:	:	1.5	4.6	:	8.5	:	:	:	8.8	2.3	0.9	:	2.9	:

	LU (5)	HU	MT	NL	AT	PL	PT	RO	SI	SK	FI	SE	UK	NO
No. of enterprises (thousands)	0.0	0.0	:	0.0	0.0	0.1	0.0	0.0	0.0	0.0	0.7	0.1	0.1	0.0
Turnover (EUR million)	0	56	:	0	:	5 010	0	337	:	99	343	:	1 283	160
Production (EUR million)	0	42	:	0	:	5 540	0	389	:	87	309	:	1 298	162
Value added (EUR million)	0	15	:	0	:	3 821	0	254	:	53	110	:	442	72
Gross operating surplus (EUR million) (6)	0	6	:	0	:	1 639	0	15	-7	12	66	:	7	34
Purchases of goods & services (EUR million)	0	43	:	0	:	1 761	0	212	:	48	217	:	788	89
Personnel costs (EUR million)	0	9	:	0	:	2 183	0	239	:	41	44	:	434	38
Investment in tangible goods (EUR million)	0	1	:	:	:	374	0	136	:	3	39	:	106	21
Employment (thousands)	0	1	:	0	:	155	0	32	:	6	1	:	9	0
Apparent labour prod. (EUR thousand)	:	21.1	:	4.8	:	24.6	:	8.0	:	9.1	83.9	:	50.5	257.0
Average personnel costs (EUR thousand)	:	13.2	:	6.8	:	14.1	:	7.5	:	7.0	36.2	:	49.9	138.4
Wage adjusted labour productivity (%)	:	160.4	:	70.8	:	174.9	:	106.3	:	130.4	231.9	:	101.2	185.7
Gross operating rate (%)	:	10.4	:	-17.5	:	32.7	:	4.5	:	12.5	19.1	:	0.6	21.2
Investment / employment (EUR thousand)	:	1.7	:	:	:	2.4	:	4.3	:	0.4	30.1	:	12.1	75.6

(1) EU-27, rounded estimate based on non-confidential data. (2) EU-27 and France, 2003. (3) France, 2003. (4) EU-27, rounded estimate based on non-confidential data; France, 2003. (5) 2003. (6) Slovenia, 2003.
Source: Eurostat (SBS)

Table 13.10

Extr. of crude petroleum and natural gas; service activities incidental to oil and gas extr., excluding surveying (NACE Division 11)
Main indicators, 2004

	EU-27 (1)	BE	BG	CZ	DK	DE	EE	IE	EL	ES	FR	IT	CY	LV	LT
No. of enterprises (thousands)	0.9	:	:	0.0	0.0	0.0	0.0	:	:	0.0	0.1	0.0	0.0	0.0	:
Turnover (EUR million)	127 000	:	:	:	:	4 598	:	:	:	365	2 744	47 557	0	0	:
Production (EUR million)	113 000	:	:	:	:	3 705	:	:	:	415	3 931	48 174	0	0	:
Value added (EUR million)	44 900	:	:	:	:	1 487	:	:	:	180	1 575	4 682	0	0	:
Gross operating surplus (EUR million)	39 600	:	:	:	:	959	:	:	:	110	1 395	3 860	0	0	:
Purchases of goods & services (EUR million)	70 000	:	:	:	:	2 690	:	:	:	238	2 243	32 036	0	0	:
Personnel costs (EUR million)	5 360	:	:	:	:	528	:	:	:	71	180	822	0	0	:
Investment in tangible goods (EUR million)	10 800	:	:	:	:	291	:	:	:	9	179	1 025	0	0	:
Employment (thousands)	150	:	:	:	:	6	:	:	:	2	2	11	0	0	:
Apparent labour prod. (EUR thousand)	300.0	:	:	:	:	245.9	:	:	:	94.1	766.5	425.7	:	:	:
Average personnel costs (EUR thousand)	36.0	:	:	:	:	87.6	:	:	:	36.9	87.8	75.2	:	:	:
Wage adjusted labour productivity (%)	836.0	:	:	:	:	280.8	:	:	:	254.8	873.0	566.0	:	:	:
Gross operating rate (%)	31.2	:	:	:	:	20.9	:	:	:	30.1	50.8	8.1	:	:	:
Investment / employment (EUR thousand)	72.0	:	:	:	:	48.2	:	:	:	4.8	86.9	93.2	:	:	:

	LU (2)	HU	MT	NL	AT	PL	PT	RO	SI	SK	FI	SE	UK	NO
No. of enterprises (thousands)	0.0	0.0	:	0.1	0.0	0.0	:	0.1	0.0	0.0	0.0	0.0	0.4	0.2
Turnover (EUR million)	0	65	:	20 447	:	76	:	3 041	:	100	0	:	41 230	49 539
Production (EUR million)	0	59	:	8 837	:	79	:	3 002	:	99	0	:	38 639	50 025
Value added (EUR million)	0	23	:	5 100	:	59	:	1 365	:	69	0	:	25 490	42 018
Gross operating surplus (EUR million)	0	6	:	4 610	:	40	:	923	:	57	0	:	23 015	39 032
Purchases of goods & services (EUR million)	0	43	:	13 716	:	22	:	1 679	:	29	0	:	15 683	5 946
Personnel costs (EUR million)	0	17	:	490	:	19	:	441	:	12	0	:	2 476	2 985
Investment in tangible goods (EUR million)	0	33	:	:	:	3	:	1 010	:	14	0	:	6 244	8 100
Employment (thousands)	0	1	:	6	:	1	:	83	:	1	0	:	28	29
Apparent labour prod. (EUR thousand)	:	25.2	:	811.6	:	51.7	:	16.4	:	63.4	:	:	898.2	1 455.7
Average personnel costs (EUR thousand)	:	18.8	:	78.3	:	17.0	:	5.3	:	10.6	:	:	87.9	103.4
Wage adjusted labour productivity (%)	:	133.9	:	1 036.9	:	303.8	:	309.1	:	597.4	:	:	1 021.9	1 407.4
Gross operating rate (%)	:	9.3	:	22.5	:	52.8	:	30.4	:	57.3	:	:	55.8	78.8
Investment / employment (EUR thousand)	:	35.5	:	:	:	2.4	:	12.1	:	13.3	:	:	220.0	280.6

(1) Rounded estimates based on non-confidential data. (2) 2003.
Source: Eurostat (SBS)

Table 13.11

Manufacture of coke, refined petroleum products and nuclear fuel (NACE Subsection DF)
Main indicators, 2004

	EU-27 (1)	BE	BG	CZ	DK	DE	EE	IE	EL	ES	FR	IT	CY	LV	LT
No. of enterprises (thousands)	1.2	0.0	0.0	0.0	0.0	0.1	0.0	:	:	0.0	0.1	0.4	0.0	0.0	0.0
Turnover (EUR million)	370 000	21 879	:	2 640	:	116 372	46	:	:	27 095	58 018	33 074	66	:	2 201
Production (EUR million)	330 000	20 464	:	1 984	:	94 159	44	:	:	22 222	58 517	31 678	66	:	2 229
Value added (EUR million)	36 000	1 918	:	182	:	7 262	13	:	:	5 116	4 604	2 509	8	:	352
Gross operating surplus (EUR million)	26 000	1 250	:	141	:	5 528	7	:	:	4 591	2 332	1 555	4	:	301
Purchases of goods & services (EUR million)	270 000	20 005	:	2 466	:	76 175	32	:	:	22 352	42 449	25 729	52	:	1 900
Personnel costs (EUR million)	10 000	668	:	41	:	1 734	6	:	:	525	2 272	954	4	:	51
Investment in tangible goods (EUR million)	6 000	150	:	36	:	613	3	:	:	760	943	780	0	:	20
Employment (thousands)	180	5	:	3	:	21	1	:	:	8	33	18	0	0	4
Apparent labour prod. (EUR thousand)	200.0	352.9	:	58.8	:	342.4	12.9	:	:	605.2	140.7	142.8	61.4	:	99.6
Average personnel costs (EUR thousand)	:	123.3	:	13.5	:	81.9	5.6	:	:	62.1	69.4	55.9	31.0	:	14.5
Wage adjusted labour productivity (%)	:	286.1	:	433.9	:	418.1	231.6	:	:	974.6	202.6	255.7	198.1	:	688.3
Gross operating rate (%)	7.0	5.7	:	5.3	:	4.8	16.0	:	:	16.9	4.0	4.7	5.7	:	13.7
Investment / employment (EUR thousand)	32.0	27.5	:	11.6	:	28.9	2.8	:	:	89.9	28.8	44.4	0.0	:	5.6

	LU (2)	HU	MT	NL	AT	PL	PT	RO	SI	SK	FI	SE	UK	NO
No. of enterprises (thousands)	0.0	0.0	:	0.0	0.0	0.1	0.0	:	0.0	:	0.0	0.1	0.2	0.0
Turnover (EUR million)	0	4 940	:	20 457	:	11 572	6 239	:	7	:	5 361	1 093	41 257	374
Production (EUR million)	0	4 507	:	16 977	:	10 471	6 299	:	6	:	4 700	1 098	41 404	391
Value added (EUR million)	0	878	:	1 122	:	4 828	603	:	1	:	816	356	3 786	243
Gross operating surplus (EUR million)	0	649	:	653	:	4 568	456	:	-1	:	628	190	2 124	243
Purchases of goods & services (EUR million)	0	3 263	:	18 399	:	6 927	5 558	:	6	:	4 661	772	23 844	148
Personnel costs (EUR million)	0	229	:	470	:	260	147	:	2	:	188	166	1 662	0
Investment in tangible goods (EUR million) (3)	0	217	:	309	:	361	105	:	0	:	187	142	799	0
Employment (thousands)	0	7	:	7	:	16	2	:	0	:	3	3	25	0
Apparent labour prod. (EUR thousand)	:	124.4	:	167.4	:	305.6	284.4	:	7.2	:	239.6	119.0	149.1	17 383.3
Average personnel costs (EUR thousand)	:	32.5	:	70.0	:	16.5	69.5	:	17.8	:	55.1	58.3	65.7	35.2
Wage adjusted labour productivity (%)	:	382.7	:	239.0	:	1 847.2	409.2	:	40.3	:	434.7	204.3	226.9	49 333.5
Gross operating rate (%)	:	13.1	:	3.2	:	39.5	7.3	:	-13.4	:	11.7	17.4	5.1	64.9
Investment / employment (EUR thousand) (3)	:	30.7	:	46.1	:	22.9	49.3	:	0.3	:	55.0	47.6	31.4	2.8

(1) Rounded estimates based on non-confidential data. (2) 2003. (3) Slovenia, 2003.
Source: Eurostat (SBS)

Table 13.12

Electricity, gas, steam and hot water supply (NACE Division 40)
Main indicators, 2004

	EU-27	BE	BG	CZ	DK	DE	EE	IE	EL	ES	FR	IT	CY	LV	LT
No. of enterprises (thousands)	17.8	0.1	0.2	0.8	2.1	1.4	0.2	:	:	2.3	2.1	1.6	:	0.3	0.2
Turnover (EUR million)	636 763	25 721	3 722	9 584	16 160	186 839	968	:	:	36 724	57 368	86 762	:	727	1 655
Production (EUR million)	587 853	25 728	1 949	9 326	10 422	187 203	551	:	:	28 799	57 733	77 541	:	626	1 410
Value added (EUR million) (1)	150 000	4 862	830	2 703	2 798	35 261	226	:	:	11 608	21 382	15 118	:	307	491
Gross operating surplus (EUR million) (1)	100 000	3 177	561	2 125	2 178	19 944	157	:	:	9 555	10 646	10 331	:	198	311
Purchases of goods & services (EUR million) (1)	480 000	20 866	3 083	6 947	11 543	146 600	725	:	:	26 535	36 096	72 317	:	455	1 170
Personnel costs (EUR million) (1)	53 000	1 685	269	576	619	15 317	69	:	:	2 053	10 737	4 787	:	109	180
Investment in tangible goods (EUR million) (1)	50 000	1 450	530	650	1 725	7 073	195	:	:	6 484	4 425	5 318	:	250	248
Employment (thousands) (1)	1 300	18	41	43	14	242	7	:	:	38	161	98	:	15	22
Apparent labour prod. (EUR thousand) (1)	120.0	273.1	20.2	62.4	204.4	145.7	30.6	:	:	308.1	132.6	154.7	:	21.0	22.8
Average personnel costs (EUR thousand) (1)	40.0	95.1	6.6	13.5	50.7	63.3	9.4	:	:	56.9	66.7	49.9	:	7.5	8.4
Wage adjusted labour productivity (%) (1)	300.0	287.1	307.7	461.3	403.4	230.2	325.4	:	:	541.6	198.9	309.7	:	280.3	272.5
Gross operating rate (%) (1)	15.7	12.3	15.1	22.2	13.5	10.7	16.2	:	:	26.0	18.6	11.9	:	27.2	18.8
Investment / employment (EUR thousand) (1)	38.5	81.5	12.9	15.0	126.0	29.2	26.4	:	:	172.1	27.4	54.4	:	17.1	11.5

	LU (2)	HU	MT	NL	AT	PL	PT	RO	SI	SK	FI	SE	UK	NO
No. of enterprises (thousands)	0.1	0.4	:	0.4	0.9	1.3	0.3	0.2	0.3	0.2	0.6	1.2	0.3	0.5
Turnover (EUR million)	766	11 298	:	27 005	16 380	22 642	9 935	7 215	1 502	5 430	8 555	21 472	69 859	8 312
Production (EUR million)	503	4 385	:	27 337	16 407	14 896	9 659	7 398	1 401	5 473	5 148	13 312	71 037	8 925
Value added (EUR million)	212	1 966	:	3 705	4 705	6 726	2 963	1 254	462	1 844	2 709	6 193	20 446	3 759
Gross operating surplus (EUR million)	150	1 309	:	2 467	2 806	4 791	2 301	674	276	1 513	2 117	4 595	14 943	2 953
Purchases of goods & services (EUR million)	564	9 417	:	23 649	11 630	16 383	7 102	6 286	1 045	3 634	6 145	16 008	48 970	3 697
Personnel costs (EUR million)	62	657	:	1 238	1 899	1 934	661	579	186	331	592	1 597	5 503	806
Investment in tangible goods (EUR million)	141	844	:	:	1 158	1 604	1 241	2 275	170	256	915	2 041	6 022	1 571
Employment (thousands)	1	37	:	23	29	166	12	117	8	29	12	29	107	14
Apparent labour prod. (EUR thousand)	229.2	53.1	:	164.3	162.9	40.5	241.9	10.7	61.0	63.6	217.7	213.1	191.9	271.2
Average personnel costs (EUR thousand)	69.2	17.8	:	54.9	66.7	11.7	55.1	5.0	25.2	11.4	47.7	59.7	51.8	58.1
Wage adjusted labour productivity (%)	331.1	298.5	:	299.5	244.1	345.6	438.7	216.1	241.7	556.5	456.2	356.8	370.5	466.5
Gross operating rate (%)	19.6	11.6	:	9.1	17.1	21.2	23.2	9.3	18.4	27.9	24.7	21.4	21.4	35.5
Investment / employment (EUR thousand)	152.0	22.8	:	:	40.1	9.7	101.3	19.5	22.5	8.8	73.5	70.2	56.5	113.4

(1) EU-27, rounded estimate based on non-confidential data. (2) 2003.
Source: Eurostat (SBS)

Table 15.3 _____
Site preparation (NACE Group 45.1)
Structural profile: ranking of top five Member States, 2004

Rank	Share of EU-27 value added (%) (1)	Share of EU-27 employment (%) (1)	Value added specialisation ratio (EU-27=100) (2)	Employment specialisation ratio (EU-27=100) (2)
1	France (24.2)	France (20.1)	Finland (299.0)	Finland (300.2)
2	Spain (19.3)	Spain (18.8)	Sweden (222.6)	Sweden (249.1)
3	Italy (10.7)	Italy (10.5)	Spain (214.9)	Czech Republic (206.7)
4	Germany (10.7)	Germany (9.0)	France (171.8)	Spain (183.4)
5	United Kingdom (6.9)	Czech Republic (5.9)	Czech Republic (141.2)	France (175.5)

(1) Greece, Cyprus and Malta, not available; Luxembourg, 2003.
(2) Ireland, Greece, Cyprus and Malta, not available; Luxembourg, 2003.
Source: Eurostat (SBS)

15.2: GENERAL CONSTRUCTION

The building of complete constructions (or parts thereof) and civil engineering (NACE Group 45.2), hereafter referred to as general construction, constitute the core activities of the construction sector. These two activities are the first stages of most construction activities, following on from the activities of architects, structural engineers and landscape designers. At the four-digit level of NACE there are five parts to the activity: general construction of buildings and civil engineering (NACE Class 45.21) which includes most building work as well as engineering projects such as bridges, tunnels, and cable and pipe networks; the erection of roof covering and frames (NACE Class 45.22); the construction of motorways, roads, airfields and sports facilities (NACE Class 45.23); the construction of water projects (NACE Class 45.24) including waterways, locks and ports, as well as dredging work; and other special trades construction work (NACE Class 45.25) including for example foundations work, pile-driving and scaffolding.

STRUCTURAL PROFILE
General construction activities (NACE Group 45.2) was the main activity of close to 1.1 million enterprises which generated EUR 251.3 billion of value added in the EU-27 in 2004, and employed 7.2 million persons, in both cases more than half of the construction sector's (NACE Section F) total. A more detailed analysis of the EU-27's general construction sector in 2004 shows that the general construction of buildings and civil engineering work (NACE Class 45.21) was by far the largest part of the general construction activities sector, with 70.4 % of value added and 71.2 % of employment. Other construction work involving special trades (NACE Class 45.25) was the second largest class with 11.5 % of value added and 11.3 % of employment, slightly larger than the main specialised civil engineering activity of road building and the construction of airfields and sports facilities (NACE Class 45.23) which had 10.7 % of value added and 9.8 % of employment. The erection of roof coverings and frames (NACE Class

45.22) accounted for 6.1 % of value added while the smallest activity within general construction activities was the construction of water projects (NACE Class 45.24) which had just 1.3 % of value added.

The largest contributor to EU-27 value added in the general construction sector was the United Kingdom with EUR 51.4 billion of value added, 20.5 % of the EU-27 total, only slightly more than the Spanish general construction sector's share of 19.6 % - see Table 15.5 - Italy, Germany and France all contributed at least 10 % of the EU-27 value added. In employment terms the Spanish general construction sector's workforce was by far the largest, its 1.5 million strong workforce constituted 20.4 % of the EU-27 total. In comparison, the workforce of this sector in the United Kingdom represented just 10.4 % of the EU-27 total, less than in Italy and only slightly more than in Germany.

Table 15.4 _____
General construction (building of complete constructions or parts thereof; civil engineering) (NACE Group 45.2)
Structural profile, EU-27, 2004

	No. of enterprises (thousands)	Turnover (EUR million)	Value added (EUR million)	Employment (thousands)
General construction	1 096.9	832 346	251 338	7 166.7
General construction of buildings and civil engineering works (1)	776.0	621 000	177 000	5 100.0
Erection of roof covering and frames (1)	105.0	39 000	15 400	480.0
Construction of motorways, roads, airfields and sport facilities (1)	39.0	90 000	27 000	700.0
Construction of water projects (1)	12.0	9 100	3 150	:
Other construction work involving special trades (1)	165.0	73 000	29 000	810.0

(1) Rounded estimates based on non-confidential data.
Source: Eurostat (SBS)

Table 15.5

General construction (building of complete constructions or parts thereof; civil engineering) (NACE Group 45.2)
Structural profile: ranking of top five Member States, 2004

Rank	Share of EU-27 value added (%) (1)	Share of EU-27 employment (%) (1)	Value added specialisation ratio (EU-27=100) (2)	Employment specialisation ratio (EU-27=100) (2)
1	United Kingdom (20.5)	Spain (20.4)	Spain (218.0)	Spain (198.8)
2	Spain (19.6)	Italy (12.6)	Portugal (162.2)	Portugal (190.0)
3	Italy (12.5)	United Kingdom (10.4)	Lithuania (134.8)	Luxembourg (151.7)
4	Germany (11.4)	Germany (10.2)	Luxembourg (124.6)	Lithuania (136.3)
5	France (10.5)	France (9.2)	Estonia (119.5)	Slovenia (123.2)

(1) Greece and Malta, not available; Luxembourg, 2003.
(2) Ireland, Greece, Cyprus and Malta, not available; Luxembourg, 2003.
Source: Eurostat (SBS)

In most of the Member States [8] general construction activities generated half or more of the construction sector's value added, although Sweden (44.7 %), France (43.9 %) and Denmark (42.4 %) were all below this level. The highest value added and employment specialisation ratios for general construction were recorded for Spain and Portugal; indeed, Spain was the only Member State to report that the share of non-financial business economy value added that was derived from general construction activities was more than twice the EU-27 average.

At a more detailed level, particular specialisation among various general construction subsectors was notable within the construction of water projects in Romania, the Netherlands, Latvia and Belgium where this subsector contributed more than three times as much to general construction value added than the average for the EU-27 as a whole, while Germany and Austria both recorded a particularly high share of their value added in this sector being derived from the erection of roof coverings and frames.

[8] Luxembourg, 2003; Greece and Malta, not available.

COSTS, PRODUCTIVITY AND PROFITABILITY

Investment by the EU-27's general construction sector represented 3.3 % of total expenditure (gross operating and tangible investment expenditure) in 2004, the same share as the average for the construction sector as a whole. The share of purchases of goods and services represented 76.0 % of total expenditure, the highest of the construction NACE groups.

The EU-27's general construction activity reported apparent labour productivity of EUR 35 100 per person employed in 2004, EUR 2 100 higher than the construction average. Average personnel costs in this activity were EUR 26 500 per employee, only marginally below the construction average. The combination of a higher apparent labour productivity and average personnel costs that were typical for the construction sector as a whole, led to a wage adjusted labour productivity ratio of 132.5 %, some 8.8 percentage points higher than the construction average. Despite this, this sector's gross operating rate in 2004 was 10.6 %, the lowest of the construction NACE groups.

Table 15.6

General construction (building of complete constructions or parts thereof; civil engineering) (NACE Group 45.2)
Productivity and profitability, EU-27, 2004

	Apparent labour productivity (EUR thousand)	Average personnel costs (EUR thousand)	Wage adjusted labour productivity (%)	Gross operating rate (%)
General construction	35.1	26.5	132.5	10.6
General construction of buildings and civil engineering works (1)	35.0	25.6	137.0	10.7
Erection of roof covering and frames (1)	32.3	28.0	114.0	11.3
Construction of motorways, roads, airfields and sport facilities (1)	38.0	29.0	130.0	8.1
Construction of water projects (1)	:	:	:	12.0
Other construction work involving special trades (1)	35.5	29.2	122.0	11.9

(1) Rounded estimates based on non-confidential data.
Source: Eurostat (SBS)

15.3: BUILDING INSTALLATION ACTIVITIES

Installation work is divided into four classes at the NACE four-digit level: installation of electrical wiring and fittings (NACE Class 45.31); insulation (NACE Class 45.32); plumbing (NACE Class 45.33) including all water and gas supply, drainage, heating and ventilation work; and other building installation activities (NACE Class 45.34). Note that the installation of industrial equipment (for example, the installation of industrial furnaces and turbines) is excluded.

Building installation includes activities such as plumbing, installation of heating and air-conditioning systems, aerials, alarm systems and other electrical work, sprinkler systems, elevators and escalators. Also included are insulation work (water, heat, and sound) and the installation of illumination and signalling systems for roads, railways, airports, harbours, etc.

STRUCTURAL PROFILE

Building installation activities (NACE Group 45.3) consisted of 674 000 enterprises which employed 3.1 million persons and generated EUR 96.9 billion of value added in the EU-27 in 2004. As such, building installation activities made up more than one fifth of the construction sector (NACE Section F), contributing 23.8 % of the workforce and 22.4 % of the value added. At the NACE class level the largest activities in value added terms were the installation of electrical wiring and fittings (NACE Class 45.31) and plumbing (NACE Class 45.33) each with more than two fifths of the total, 40.4 % for plumbing and 48.7 % for electrical wiring and fittings. The two remaining classes, namely insulation (NACE Class 45.32) and other building installation activities (NACE Class 45.34) were much smaller, with 5.0 % and 5.8 % of the total respectively.

The United Kingdom, Germany and France had the three largest building installation sectors in the EU-27, each contributing more than 15 % of EU-27 value added within this sector. In employment terms Germany had the largest workforce (15.2 % of the EU-27 total), and the Spanish and Italian workforces were larger than in both France and the United Kingdom. Within the construction sector the building installation sector [9] was most important in value added terms in Sweden where it contributed 31.1 % of construction value added and in Denmark (28.0 %) and Germany (27.7 %). In contrast, this sector contributed just 10.0 % of construction value added in Cyprus.

[9] Luxembourg, 2003; Greece and Malta, not available.

Table 15.7

Building installation (NACE Group 45.3)
Structural profile, EU-27, 2004

	No. of enterprises (thousands)	Turnover (EUR million)	Value added (EUR million)	Employment (thousands)
Building installation	674.3	249 582	96 945	3 125.1
Installation of electrical wiring and fittings (1)	294.0	116 000	47 200	1 480.0
Insulation work activities (1)	27.8	12 700	4 890	156.0
Plumbing (1)	308.0	104 000	39 200	1 310.0
Other building installation (1)	44.0	17 000	5 630	182.0

(1) Rounded estimates based on non-confidential data.
Source: Eurostat (SBS)

Table 15.8

Building installation (NACE Group 45.3)
Structural profile: ranking of top five Member States, 2004

Rank	Share of EU-27 value added (%) (1)	Share of EU-27 employment (%) (1)	Value added specialisation ratio (EU-27=100) (2)	Employment specialisation ratio (EU-27=100) (2)
1	United Kingdom (18.0)	Spain (15.3)	Luxembourg (163.1)	Luxembourg (169.8)
2	Germany (16.2)	Germany (15.2)	Spain (148.0)	Spain (149.2)
3	France (15.3)	Italy (15.0)	Austria (133.5)	Italy (127.9)
4	Spain (13.3)	France (12.4)	Netherlands (118.1)	Austria (122.5)
5	Italy (12.7)	United Kingdom (10.8)	Denmark (116.1)	Sweden (120.1)

(1) Greece and Malta, not available; Luxembourg, 2003.
(2) Ireland, Greece, Cyprus and Malta, not available; Luxembourg, 2003.
Source: Eurostat (SBS)

Table 15.9

Building installation (NACE Group 45.3)
Productivity and profitability, EU-27, 2004

	Apparent labour productivity (EUR thousand)	Average personnel costs (EUR thousand)	Wage adjusted labour productivity (%)	Gross operating rate (%)
Building installation	31.0	27.1	114.6	11.9
Installation of electrical wiring and fittings (1)	32.0	27.8	115.0	11.7
Insulation work activities (1)	31.2	27.4	114.0	10.2
Plumbing (1)	29.9	26.5	113.0	12.0
Other building installation (1)	31.0	24.4	127.0	13.6

(1) Rounded estimates based on non-confidential data.
Source: Eurostat (SBS)

COSTS, PRODUCTIVITY AND PROFITABILITY

In the EU-27's building installation activities tangible investment represented just 2.5 % of total expenditure (gross operating and tangible investment expenditure) in 2004, the lowest share among the construction NACE groups. This share reached its highest in Latvia (7.9 %), Romania (7.0 %) and Bulgaria (6.8 %). The share of personnel costs in total expenditure was 29.5 %, higher than all construction NACE groups except for building completion activities (NACE Group 45.4).

The building installation sector recorded apparent labour productivity of EUR 31 000 per person employed in the EU-27 in 2004. This was higher than in building completion activities, but otherwise was the lowest among the construction NACE groups. Average personnel costs were EUR 27 100 per employee slightly above the construction average. The low apparent labour productivity resulted in a wage adjusted labour productivity ratio for building installation activities of just 114.6 %, well below the construction average of 123.7 %, and again higher only than the building completion sector among construction NACE groups. In Latvia, the building installation sector recorded a wage adjusted labour productivity ratio (203.1 %) that indicated that added value per person employed was just over double the average personnel costs per employee, and Romania and Bulgaria also recorded quite high ratios, but in none of the Member States [10] did this ratio for the building installation sector exceed that for the non-financial business economy as a whole.

At 11.9 %, the EU-27's gross operating rate for the building installation activities was lower than most of the construction NACE groups, but above that for general construction activities (NACE Group 45.2) and slightly above the construction average of 11.6 %.

_____

[10] Luxembourg, 2003; Ireland, Greece, Cyprus and Malta, not available.

15.4: BUILDING COMPLETION ACTIVITIES

Completion work is divided into five classes at the NACE four-digit level: plastering (NACE Class 45.41); joinery installation (NACE Class 45.42); floor and wall covering (NACE Class 45.43); painting and glazing (NACE Class 45.44); and other building completion activities (NACE Class 45.45).

Building completion encompasses activities that contribute to the completion or finishing of a construction, such as glazing, plastering, painting and decorating, floor and wall tiling or covering with other materials like parquet, carpets or wallpaper. As well as work on new structures, the renovation, repair and maintenance markets are also important for enterprises in these activities.

STRUCTURAL PROFILE

Building completion (NACE Group 45.4) was the main activity for around 808 000 enterprises in the EU-27 in 2004. Together these enterprises employed 2.4 million persons, around three quarters of a million fewer than building installation (NACE Group 45.3), thus making it the third largest NACE group within the construction sector (NACE Section F) with an 18.0 % share of the construction workforce. The value added generated by this workforce was EUR 66.3 billion in the EU-27, some 15.3 % of the construction sector total. The largest parts of building completion were painting and glazing (NACE Class 45.44), with 29.7 % of the sector's value added and employment, and joinery installation (NACE Class 45.42) with 28.2 % of the sector's value added and 25.3 % of its employment. Floor and wall covering work (NACE Class 45.43) was the third largest subsector with 16.8 % of value added but nearly one fifth (19.4 %) of employment. Other building completion work (NACE Class 45.45) contributed 13.6 % of the sector's value added and employment, while plastering (NACE Class 45.41) was the smallest building completion activity with 11.7 % of value added and 12.0 % of employment.

Spain and France had the largest workforces in the building completion sector, with 427 200 and 415 600 persons employed, equivalent to 18.0 % and 17.5 % of the EU-27 total. In value added terms, Spain's contribution was only the fourth largest (14.1 % of the EU-27 total), behind France (22.2 %), the United Kingdom (16.4 %) and Germany (15.9 %).

The relative importance of the building completion sector was particularly high in Denmark, France and Spain, with value added specialisation ratios in excess of 150 %, denoting that these activities had a share of national non-financial business economy value added that was at least 50 % higher than the EU-27 average [11]. In contrast, building completion activities contributed less than 5 % of total construction value added in Estonia, Romania, Cyprus and Slovakia. A number of specialisations among the building completion activities can be noted in particular Member States, notably the importance of floor and wall covering work in Latvia and Lithuania where it accounted for 92.1 % and 65.8 % respectively of building completion value added.

_____

[11] Luxembourg, 2003; Ireland, Greece, Cyprus and Malta, not available.

Table 15.10

Building completion (NACE Group 45.4)
Structural profile, EU-27, 2004

	No. of enterprises (thousands)	Turnover (EUR million)	Value added (EUR million)	Employment (thousands)
Building completion	807.9	156 233	66 261	2 371.5
Plastering (1)	94.6	16 800	7 720	285.0
Joinery installation (1)	200.0	50 100	18 700	601.0
Floor and wall covering (1)	162.0	28 400	11 100	459.0
Painting and glazing (1)	213.0	39 900	19 700	704.0
Other building completion (1)	139.0	21 000	8 990	323.0

(1) Rounded estimates based on non-confidential data.
Source: Eurostat (SBS)

Motor trades

The generally high level of competition and the importance of the legislative framework (mainly concerning relations between manufacturers and distributors, environmental issues, as well as taxes) are common characteristics to most of the motor trades activities presented in the following pages. There is a strong link between motor vehicles manufacturers and distributors (see Subchapter 16.1) and also between the main oil suppliers and automotive fuel distributors (see Subchapter 16.2).

The services of motor trades are covered by the European Parliament and the Council Directive on services in the internal market [1], adopted at the end of 2006, with the objective to achieve a genuine internal market in services by breaking down barriers to trade in services across the EU - see Chapter 22 for more information.

STRUCTURAL PROFILE
The motor trades (NACE Division 50) sector had a value added of EUR 150.6 billion in the EU-27 in 2004 and employed 4.1 million persons, equivalent to 3.0 % of the non-financial business economy's (NACE Sections C to I and K) value added and 3.3 % of its employment, underlining the generally low level of apparent labour productivity (value added per person employed) in this sector. However, the wealth generated by the EU-27's motor trades sector represented 15.1 % of distributive trades (NACE Section G) value added and provided a slightly lower share of the workforce (13.3 %). Among all the non-financial business economy sectors

covered by Chapters 2 to 23 of this publication the motor trades sector was one of the smallest in value added terms (ranked 16th), while in turnover terms it was the fifth largest, unsurprisingly, given the distributive nature of many parts of the motor trades sector.

In excess of three quarters of a million enterprises were classified with motor trades as their main activity in the EU-27 in 2004, of which a large majority (approximately 90 %) sold, repaired or maintained motor vehicles and motorcycles as their main activity (NACE Groups 50.1 to 50.4, see Subchapter 16.1), the remainder being enterprises with the retail of automotive fuel as their main activity (NACE Group 50.5, see Subchapter 16.2).

Motor vehicles and motorcycles distribution also accounted for more than nine tenths (91.0 %) of the EU-27's value added for the motor trades sector, while employing a somewhat lower share of the motor trades workforce (88.0 %). As a counterpart, the share of value added generated by the retail sale of automotive fuel was 9.0 %, while the share of total motor trades' workforce was somewhat higher (12.0 %), indicating lower apparent labour productivity in this subsector. Unsurprisingly, given that the retail sale of automotive fuel subsector is a pure retail activity, whereas motor vehicles and motorcycles distribution involves a mixture of distributive trade and repair activities, the retail sale of automotive fuel subsector had an even higher share (13.0 %) of the sector's EUR 1 185 billion of turnover.

Motor trades (NACE Division 50) cover the wholesale, retail sale and repair of motor vehicles and motorcycles, as well as the retailing of automotive fuels and lubricants.

NACE
50: sale, maintenance and repair of motor vehicles and motorcycles; retail sale of automotive fuel;
50.1: sale of motor vehicles;
50.2: maintenance and repair of motor vehicles;
50.3: sale of motor vehicle parts and accessories;
50.4: sale, maintenance and repair of motorcycles and related parts and accessories;
50.5: retail sale of automotive fuel.

---

[1] Directive 2006/123/EC of the European Parliament and of the Council of 12 December 2006 on services in the internal market.

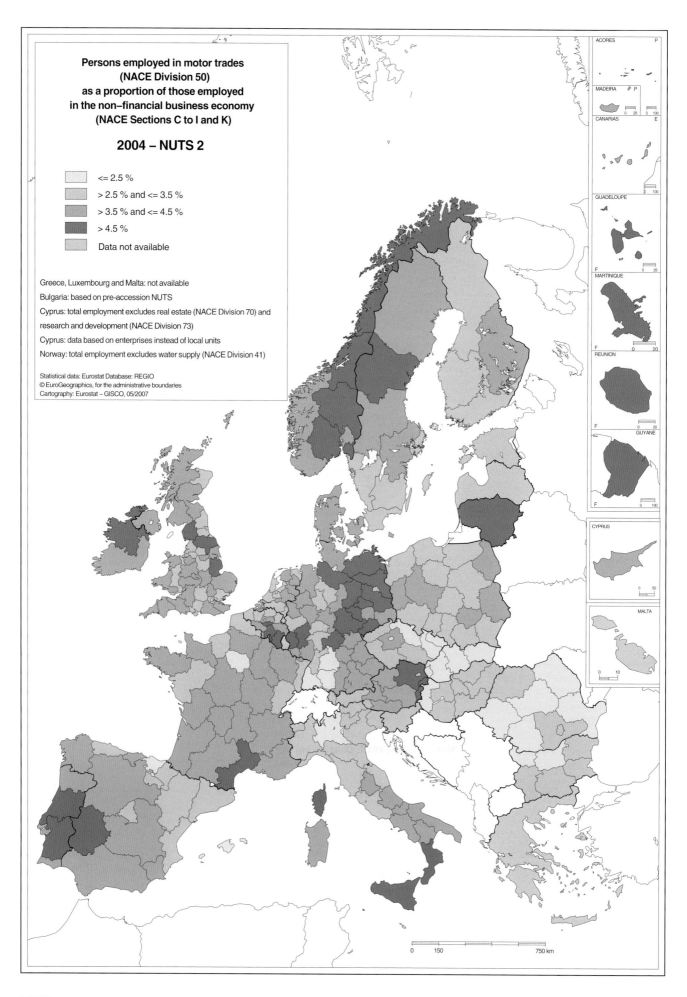

Persons employed in motor trades
(NACE Division 50)
as a proportion of those employed
in the non–financial business economy
(NACE Sections C to I and K)

2004 – NUTS 2

- <= 2.5 %
- > 2.5 % and <= 3.5 %
- > 3.5 % and <= 4.5 %
- > 4.5 %
- Data not available

Greece, Luxembourg and Malta: not available

Bulgaria: based on pre-accession NUTS

Cyprus: total employment excludes real estate (NACE Division 70) and
research and development (NACE Division 73)

Cyprus: data based on enterprises instead of local units

Norway: total employment excludes water supply (NACE Division 41)

Statistical data: Eurostat Database: REGIO
© EuroGeographics, for the administrative boundaries
Cartography: Eurostat – GISCO, 05/2007

ACORES P

MADEIRA P

CANARIAS E

GUADELOUPE

MARTINIQUE

REUNION

GUYANE

CYPRUS

MALTA

0   150   750 km

Table 16.1

Motor trades (NACE Division 50)
Structural profile, EU-27, 2004

	No. of enterprises		Turnover		Value added		Employment	
	(thousands)	(% of total)	(EUR million)	(% of total)	(EUR million)	(% of total)	(thousands)	(% of total)
Motor trades	782.3	100.0	1 185 418	100.0	150 599	100.0	4 066.6	100.0
Motor vehicles and motorcycles distribution (1)	709.0	90.6	1 030 000	86.9	137 000	91.0	3 578.7	88.0
Retail sale of automotive fuel	73.6	9.4	154 284	13.0	13 650	9.1	487.9	12.0

(1) Rounded estimates based on non-confidential data.
Source: Eurostat (SBS)

Table 16.2

Motor trades (NACE Division 50)
Structural profile: ranking of top five Member States, 2004

			Share of non-financial business economy			
Rank	Value added (EUR million) (1)	Employment (thousands) (1)	No. of enterprises (2)	Turnover (2)	Value added (2)	Employment (2)
1	Germany (35 485)	Germany (665.9)	Lithuania (8.1 %)	Belgium (9.7 %)	Slovenia (3.7 %)	Lithuania (5.1 %)
2	United Kingdom (34 444)	United Kingdom (611.3)	Portugal (5.2 %)	Slovenia (9.2 %)	Portugal (3.7 %)	Portugal (4.6 %)
3	France (17 802)	Italy (472.4)	Poland (5.2 %)	Denmark (9.0 %)	United Kingdom (3.6 %)	Denmark (3.8 %)
4	Italy (14 048)	France (462.8)	Finland (4.9 %)	Portugal (8.5 %)	Lithuania (3.5 %)	Luxembourg (3.8 %)
5	Spain (12 755)	Spain (390.2)	Belgium (4.8 %)	Luxembourg (8.5 %)	Latvia (3.4 %)	Austria (3.6 %)

(1) Malta, not available; Luxembourg, 2003.
(2) Ireland, Greece, Cyprus and Malta, not available; Luxembourg, 2003.
Source: Eurostat (SBS)

Among the Member States with available data [2], Germany recorded both the highest levels of value added and employment, while the United Kingdom had the highest level of turnover. However, in terms of relative shares in their non-financial business economy value added [3], Slovenia and Portugal had the largest motor trades' sector (both 3.7 %), closely followed by the United Kingdom (3.6 %), Lithuania (3.5 %) and Latvia (3.4 %). In terms of turnover, Belgium ranked first [4], posting almost one tenth (9.7 %) of its non-financial business economy total generated by the motor trades sector, while this share was slightly lower in Slovenia (9.2 %) and in Denmark (9.0 %). Turning to the impact of motor trades in the workforce, this sector concentrated 5.1 % of non-financial business economy employment in Lithuania, while no other Member State [5] recorded a share above 5.0 %.

Regional specialisation (in some cases the whole country is treated as one region) can be seen from the map on page 272 which is based on the employment share of this sector in the whole non-financial business economy. Motor trades share of non-financial business economy employment was highest (at the level of detail shown in the map) in Brandenburg (both Südwest and Nordost) and in Magdeburg, all in

Germany, while the French islands of Réunion, Guadeloupe and Martinique, as well as Guyane also recorded high shares. It should be noted that specialisation ratios in small regions (and small activities) can be heavily influenced by the location of a few specific producers.

Short-term statistics provide a picture of the evolution of the motor trades sector in the EU-27 over the period 1998 to 2006, in terms of turnover and employment indices. The annual growth rate for the EU-27's motor trades turnover index (in current prices and in working days adjusted data) was between 1.8 % and 6.3 % each year during this period with the slowest growth being recorded in 2000 and the fastest in 2004 – see Figure 16.1.

The index of employment for motor trades in the EU-27 is available for a ten-year period, starting in 1996, see Figure 16.1. After respective year on year growth by 0.7 % and 1.3 % in 1997 and 1998, the index contracted by 2.1 % between 1998 and 1999. Thereafter, the index of employment increased every year. Average employment growth between 1999 and 2006 was 1.3 % per annum, boosted by growth in excess of 2 % in 2004 and 2006. These developments for the index of employment of the motor trades sector contrasted with the EU-27's distributive trades sector as a whole. Indeed, steady and uninterrupted year on year employment growth was recorded from 1997 through to 2006 for the distributive trades sector, never exceeding 2.2 % in any year.

[2] Luxembourg, 2003; Malta, data not available.
[3] Luxembourg, 2003; Cyprus, Greece, Ireland and Malta, not available.
[4] Luxembourg, 2003; Cyprus, Greece, Ireland and Malta, not available.
[5] Luxembourg, 2003; Cyprus, Greece, Ireland and Malta, not available.

Figure 16.1

Motor trades (NACE Division 50)
Evolution of main indicators, EU-27 (2000=100)

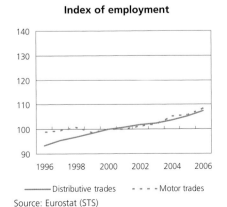

Index of employment

Index of turnover

—— Distributive trades   - - - Motor trades

- - - Motor trades

Source: Eurostat (STS)

Figure 16.2

Motor trades (NACE Division 50)
Share of value added by enterprise size class, EU-27, 2004

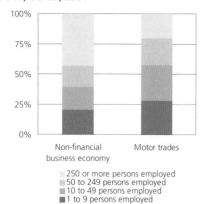

- 250 or more persons employed
- 50 to 249 persons employed
- 10 to 49 persons employed
- 1 to 9 persons employed

Source: Eurostat (SBS)

Figure 16.3

Motor trades (NACE Division 50)
Distribution of value added by size class relative to national averages, 2004 (non-financial business economy=100)

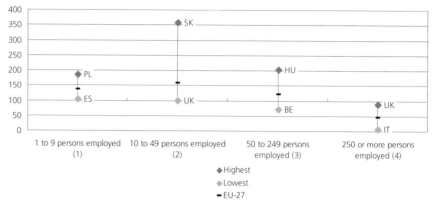

◆ Highest
◆ Lowest
▬ EU-27

(1) Belgium, Denmark, Estonia, Ireland, Greece, Cyprus, Latvia, Lithuania, Luxembourg, Malta, Netherlands, Austria, Portugal, Slovenia, Slovakia and Finland, not available; Bulgaria, Germany and Hungary, 2003.
(2) Belgium, Ireland, Greece, Cyprus, Luxembourg, Malta, Netherlands, Slovenia and Finland, not available; Denmark, Latvia, Hungary, Portugal and Slovakia, 2003.
(3) Estonia, Ireland, Greece, Cyprus, Luxembourg, Malta, Austria, Portugal and Finland, not available; Germany, Latvia and Hungary, 2003.
(4) Belgium, Denmark, Estonia, Ireland, Greece, Cyprus, Latvia, Lithuania, Luxembourg, Malta, Austria, Portugal, Slovenia, Slovakia and Finland, not available; Bulgaria and Germany, 2003.
Source: Eurostat (SBS)

An analysis by enterprise size-classes shows that small and medium-sized enterprises (with less than 250 persons employed, namely SMEs) generated four fifths (79.7 %) of the EU-27's motor trades value added and almost nine tenths (88.5 %) of the employment in 2004. Those shares are significantly higher than for the distributive trades as a whole (respectively 69.9 % and 73.7 %) or compared with the non-financial business economy average (respectively 57.0 % and 67.1 %). All of the Member States with data available had a higher value added share of SMEs within motor trades than the non-financial business economy average. In more details, small enterprises (with between 10 and 49 persons employed) were particularly of note, as these enterprises contributed 29.9 % of sectoral value added in the EU-27, a proportion that was only exceeded in wholesale trade when considering all of the non-financial services NACE divisions. Large enterprises (with 250 or more persons employed) generated 20.4 % of sectoral value

added, which was the second lowest share among the non-financial services NACE divisions, higher only than in real estate activities. However, large enterprises provided just 11.6 % of total employment in motor trades, underlining significantly higher apparent labour productivity than for SMEs.

EMPLOYMENT CHARACTERISTICS
The sector showed atypical employment characteristics compared with both the other distributive trades activities and with the non-financial business economy as a whole, particularly concerning the gender breakdown and the importance of full-time employment. Indeed, according to Labour Force Survey data for motor trades (NACE Division 50) in 2006,

men represented 82.0 % of the EU-27's workforce, therefore 30.5 percentage points above the corresponding share for distributive trades (NACE Section G) average and 17.0 points above the corresponding share for the non-financial business economy average. The high proportion of men that were employed in the motor trades sector was apparent across all the Member States [6], where men accounted for at least 9.5 percentage points more of the workforce in motor trades than for non-financial business economy as a whole.

[6] Luxembourg, 2005.

Figure 16.4

Motor trades (NACE Division 50)
Labour force characteristics, EU-27, 2006

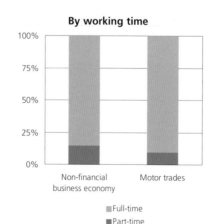
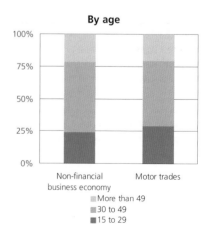

Source: Eurostat (LFS)

Slightly more than nine tenths of the persons employed in the EU-27's motor trade sector in 2006 worked full-time (90.4 %), while this concerned about three quarters (78.3 %) of the distributive trade average and again was well above the non-financial business economy average (85.6 %). Among the Member States [7], only in Bulgaria, Denmark and Romania was the incidence of full-time work lower in motor trades than the non-financial business economy average, and in all three cases the difference was of less than 2 percentage points.

Turning to a breakdown by age of the workforce for the EU-27's motor trades sector in 2006, 29.4 % of those employed were aged between 15 and 29, around half (50.3 %) between 30 and 49, and the remaining one fifth (20.4 %) were persons aged 50 or more. The share of young workers were 20 % higher than the average for the non-financial business economy while these proportions were generally in line with the averages for distributive trades as a whole.

In 2004, the share of the number of paid employees in persons employed for the EU-27's motor trades sector (81.7 %) was very similar to what was registered for the distributive trades as a whole (81.2 %), while these proportions tended to be somewhat below the corresponding share for the non-financial business economy (86.2 %). Among the Member States [8], only in Spain, Latvia, Hungary, Portugal and Slovakia was the share of the number of employees in persons employed higher in motor trades than in the non-financial business economy as a whole, and in all cases it was only slightly higher.

[7] Luxembourg, 2005; Ireland, not available.
[8] Luxembourg, 2003; Ireland, Greece, Cyprus and Malta, not available.

COSTS, PRODUCTIVITY AND PROFITABILITY

Typically for a distributive trades activity, the share of purchases of goods and services relative to total expenditure was high for motor trades (NACE Division 50) in the EU-27 in 2004 (91.0 %), more than 12 percentage points above the non-financial business economy average. This reflects the high purchases and turnover associated with distributive trades (NACE Section G) activities, which generally buy and resell products without transformation. The retail sale of automotive fuel subsector (NACE Group 50.5) recorded a particularly high share for this indicator (94.5 %), while the corresponding share for the motor vehicles and motorcycles distribution subsector (NACE Groups 50.1 to 50.4) was somewhat lower (90.5 %). Among the Member States [9], purchases of goods and services in the Belgian motor trades sector accounted for more than 95 % of total expenditure.

Gross investment in tangible goods in the EU-27's motor trades sector represented 1.8 % of total expenditure in 2004 (4.9 % in the non-financial business economy for comparison), the second lowest share of the activities in the chapters covered in this publication, after wholesale trade. Among national motor trades sectors [10], this share reached 9.1 % in Romania, however four of the five largest EU economies posted a ratio that was lower than the EU-27 average.

[9] Luxembourg, 2003; Malta, not available.
[10] Luxembourg, 2003; Malta, not available.

Apparent labour productivity in the EU-27's motor trades was EUR 37 000 per person employed and average personnel costs were EUR 24 500 per employee, both indicators were below the non-financial business economy average (by at least EUR 2 100). However, wage adjusted labour productivity (the ratio of apparent labour productivity to average personnel costs) was 151.3 % in the EU-27's motor trades sector, slightly above the non-financial business economy average (148.0 %). Nevertheless, this ratio was quite different between the two subsectors, as motor vehicles and motorcycles distribution recorded 148 %, while the corresponding figure for the retail sale of automotive fuel was 186.2 %. Turning to national motor trades sectors, this ratio was above 100 % among all the Member States [11] and reached more than 250 % in Romania and Latvia.

The gross operating rate (the ratio of gross operating surplus to turnover) in the EU-27's motor trades sector was 5.8 % in 2004, ranking as the third lowest rate among all the sectors covered in this publication, after transport equipment and wholesale trade. The gross operating rate in the motor trades sector was low, compared with the non-financial business economy average in all the Member States [12]. The relatively high turnover inherent in the retail sale of automotive fuel subsector resulted in a relatively low gross operating rate for this subsector (4.9 %), compared with a rate of 6.0 % for the motor vehicles and motorcycles distribution subsector.

[11] Luxembourg, 2003; Malta, not available.
[12] Luxembourg, 2003; Ireland, Greece, Cyprus and Malta, not available.

Table 16.3

Motor trades (NACE Division 50)
Total expenditure, EU-27, 2004

	Value (EUR million)				Share (% of total expenditure)			
	Total expenditure	Purchases of goods and services	Personnel costs	Investment in tangible goods		Purchases of goods and services	Personnel costs	Investment in tangible goods
Motor trades	1 129 916	1 028 556	81 317	20 043		91.0	7.2	1.8
Motor vehicles and motorcycles distribution (1)	983 000	890 000	75 000	18 000		90.5	7.6	1.8
Retail sale of automotive fuel (1)	148 709	140 578	6 131	2 000		94.5	4.1	1.3

(1) Rounded estimates based on non-confidential data.
Source: Eurostat (SBS)

Table 16.4

Motor trades (NACE Division 50)
Productivity and profitability, EU-27, 2004

	Apparent labour productivity (EUR thousand)	Average personnel costs (EUR thousand)	Wage adjusted labour productivity (%)	Gross operating rate (%)
Motor trades	37.0	24.5	151.3	5.8
Motor vehicles and motorcycles distribution (1)	38.3	25.8	148.0	6.0
Retail sale of automotive fuel	28.0	15.0	186.2	4.9

(1) Rounded estimates based on non-confidential data.
Source: Eurostat (SBS)

16.1: MOTOR VEHICLES AND MOTORCYCLES DISTRIBUTION

These activities cover the wholesale, retail and commission sale of new and used motor vehicles (NACE Group 50.1), parts and accessories (NACE Group 50.3), as well as motorcycles (part of NACE Group 50.4). Note that motor vehicles include not just passenger cars, but also other passenger vehicles, lorries, trailers and caravans.

This subchapter also covers the maintenance and repair of motor vehicles (NACE Group 50.2) and motorcycles (the remainder of NACE Group 50.4). This includes all types of repairs (mechanical, bodywork and electrical), spraying and painting, regular servicing, as well as the installation of replacement parts and accessories. Equally, the data presented cover tyre repair and fitting, towing, roadside assistance and car cleaning services. The renting of motor vehicles is not covered (see Chapter 23).

The market for vehicles and motorcycles distribution is divided in different segments: passenger cars, motorcycles and caravans are often purchased by households, while large-scale business customers sometimes buy cars directly from manufacturers. However, business customers dominate the market for commercial vehicles and lorries. Taxes strongly influence demand for motor vehicles and motorcycles, including taxes for the registration of a vehicle [13] as well as annual circulation taxes. The demand for new passenger cars is closely linked to the general health of the economy. One way to follow the development of the passenger car market is to look at the annual number of new car registrations, which is shown in Table 16.5.

In terms of environment, the EU strategy for reducing emissions from cars has been based on voluntary commitments by car manufacturers, legislative controls, consumer information (car labelling) and fiscal measures to encourage purchases of more fuel-efficient cars..

According to the European Commission's latest report [14] on car prices based on figures from the second half of 2006, pre-tax prices in the EU-25 (this report does not include results for Bulgaria and Romania) were lowest in Denmark on average followed by Hungary, which was the cheapest market among the ten Member States that joined the EU in 2004. According to

Table 16.5

New registrations of passenger cars in Western Europe by selected manufacturer, 2006 (1)

Group	Main brands	Units	Market share (%)
BMW	BMW	670 379	4.5
	MINI	113 655	0.8
	Others	138	0.0
DAIMLER - CHRYSLER	CHRYSLER	58 156	0.4
	JEEP	38 399	0.3
	MERCEDES	713 711	4.8
	SMART	101 744	0.7
	Others	10 386	0.1
FIAT	ALFA ROMEO	143 448	1.0
	FIAT	854 906	5.8
	LANCIA	115 978	0.8
	IVECO and others	5 783	0.0
FORD	FORD	1 214 751	8.2
	JAGUAR	40 593	0.3
	LAND ROVER	83 140	0.6
	VOLVO	236 454	1.6
	Others	3 844	0.0
GM	CHEVROLET	153 047	1.0
	OPEL	1 257 559	8.5
	SAAB	88 183	0.6
	Others	4 244	0.0
JAPAN	(2)	2 098 242	14.2
KOREA	(3)	553 731	3.8
MG ROVER	ROVER	7 783	0.1
PSA	CITROEN	875 927	5.9
	PEUGEOT	1 067 355	7.2
RENAULT	DACIA	35 071	0.2
	RENAULT	1 230 060	8.3
VOLKSWAGEN	AUDI	627 970	4.3
	SEAT	368 721	2.5
	SKODA	308 198	2.1
	VOLKSWAGEN	1 613 666	10.9
	Others	3 966	0.0
OTHERS		62 586	0.4

(1) EU-15, Iceland, Norway and Switzerland.
(2) Honda, Mazda, Mitsubishi, Nissan, Suzuki, Toyota and others.
(3) Daewoo, Hyundai, Kia and others.
Source: ACEA, http://www.acea.be

the same source, between December 2005 and December 2006, car prices (reflecting actual prices paid by consumers, including VAT and registration taxes) increased by just 0.7 % in the EU-25, well below the overall average for consumer prices. Among the large markets (in terms of volume), car prices increased somewhat more in Spain (1.8 %) than in Germany (1.3 %), France and Italy (both by 1.2 %), but always to a lower extent than for the overall average for consumer prices. Car Prices in the United Kingdom were virtually unchanged (0.2 %).

In terms of legislation on competition, since 30 September 2005, location clauses set in the block exemption from EC competition rules [15] that applied to motor vehicles supply, distribution and servicing arrangements have been abolished and dealers are now free to set-up secondary sales outlets in other areas of the EU, as well as their own countries. Dealers may also sell more than one brand of car at the same site, namely multi- franchising.

[13] Most, but not all, Member States have a registration tax.
[14] See 'Car Price Report' from 1/5/2006, available at: http://ec.europa.eu/comm/competition/sectors/motor_vehicles/prices/report.html.

[15] Commission Regulation 1400/2002 of 31 July 2002.

Table 16.6

Sale, maintenance and repair of motor vehicles (NACE Groups 50.1, 50.2, 50.3 and 50.4)
Structural profile, EU-27, 2004

	No. of enterprises (thousands)	Turnover (EUR million)	Value added (EUR million)	Employment (thousands)
Motor vehicles and motorcycles distribution (1)	709.0	1 030 000	137 000	3 578.7
Sale of motor vehicles	182.0	787 909	81 140	1 587.4
Maintenance & repair of motor vehicles	396.5	102 472	32 632	1 315.0
Sale of motor vehicle parts & accessories (1)	95.0	117 000	20 000	577.8
Sale, maintenance & repair of motorcycles (1)	35.0	23 000	3 100	98.4

(1) Rounded estimates based on non-confidential data.
Source: Eurostat (SBS)

Table 16.7

Sale, maintenance and repair of motor vehicles (NACE Groups 50.1, 50.2, 50.3 and 50.4)
Structural profile: ranking of top five Member States, 2004

Rank	Share of EU-27 value added (%) (1)	Share of EU-27 employment (%) (1)	Value added specialisation ratio (EU-27=100) (2)	Employment specialisation ratio (EU-27=100) (2)
1	Germany (24.1)	Germany (17.1)	Portugal (120.9)	Lithuania (141.7)
2	United Kingdom (22.7)	United Kingdom (15.4)	United Kingdom (119.9)	Portugal (139.6)
3	France (12.4)	France (12.2)	Germany (115.2)	Belgium (110.3)
4	Italy (9.3)	Italy (11.5)	Slovenia (107.1)	Austria (110.1)
5	Spain (8.0)	Spain (9.4)	Belgium (106.1)	Denmark (107.6)

(1) Malta, not available; Luxembourg, 2003.
(2) Ireland, Greece, Cyprus and Malta, not available; Luxembourg, 2003.
Source: Eurostat (SBS)

STRUCTURAL PROFILE

The EU-27's motor vehicles and motorcycles distribution sector (NACE Groups 50.1 to 50.4) had approximately 709 000 enterprises which generated EUR 137.0 billion of value added in 2004 and therefore dominated (91.0 % of the total) motor trades (NACE Division 50). Turnover recorded by the sector was EUR 1 030.0 billion, equivalent to 86.9 % of the motor trades total. There were 3.6 million persons employed by the vehicles and motorcycles distribution sector, some 88.0 % of total motor trades employment.

Alone, the sale of motor vehicles (NACE Group 50.1) generated three fifths (59.2 %) of the motor vehicles and motorcycles distribution value added, while the maintenance and repair of motor vehicles (NACE Group 50.2) contributed more than two fifths of the total (23.8 %). In terms of turnover, the importance of the sale of motor vehicles was even more evident, as the activity totalled about three quarters (76.5 %) of the motor vehicles and motorcycles distribution. The main contributors to the employment in motor vehicles and motorcycles distribution were the sale of motor vehicles (for 44.4 %) and the maintenance and repair of motor vehicles (for 36.7 %). A comparison of these employment and turnover

Figure 16.5

Sale, maintenance and repair of motor vehicles (NACE Groups 50.1, 50.2, 50.3 and 50.4)
Value added, EU-27, 2004 (million EUR)

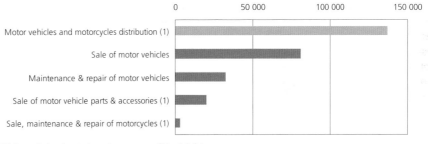

(1) Rounded estimate based on non-confidential data.
Source: Eurostat (SBS)

shares indicates the different characteristics of these activities, particularly between the sale of motor vehicles (which concerns the sale of expensive capital goods) and the maintenance and repair of motor vehicles (which provides labour-intensive services). Among the four NACE groups that make up the motor vehicles and motorcycles distribution sector, the smallest activity was that of sale, maintenance and repair of motorcycles and related parts and accessories (NACE Group 50.4), generating less than 3 % of the sector's total for the main indicators, namely value added, turnover and employment.

Germany and the United Kingdom were the two largest Member States in the motor vehicles and motorcycles distribution sector in terms of value added and employment in 2004. While together they accounted for less than one third of the EU-27's employment (32.5 %), their combined value added share was close to half (46.8 %) the EU-27 total. This high share of value added resulted in both of these large Member States appearing in the top four most specialised Member States [16] in terms of this sector's contribution to non-financial business economy value added; however, Portugal was the most specialised of all.

[16] Luxembourg, 2003; Ireland, Greece, Cyprus and Malta, not available.

Figure 16.6

Motor vehicles and motorcycles distribution
(NACE Groups 50.1, 50.2, 50.3 and 50.4)
Index of turnover, EU-27 (2000=100)

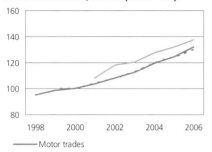

———— Motor trades

- - - - Motor vehicles and motorcycles distribution,
       excl. maintenance & repair of motor vehicles
———— Maintenance & repair of motor vehicles

Source: Eurostat (STS)

Short-term statistics for the index of turnover for motor vehicles and motorcycles distribution (NACE Groups 50.1 to 50.4) as a whole and for some of its parts is shown in Figure 16.6. Motor vehicles and motorcycles distribution, excluding maintenance and repair (NACE Groups 50.1, 50.3 and 50.4) presented in the figure recorded year on year growth from 2001 to 2006. The development of the index for the maintenance and repair (NACE Group 50.2) activity showed the same pattern while the series start a year later, namely continuous year on year growth, with a strikingly faster growth (9.5 %) recorded between 2001 and 2002.

COSTS, PRODUCTIVITY AND PROFITABILITY

Typically for a distributive trades activity, total expenditure dedicated to purchases of goods and services was important (90.5 %) within the EU-27's motor vehicles and motorcycles distribution sector in 2004. Gross investment in tangible goods represented just 1.8 % of this total expenditure. In contrast with the other three NACE groups that make up the motor vehicles and motorcycles distribution sector, maintenance and repair of motor vehicles (NACE Group 50.2) recorded that purchases of goods and services accounted for threequarters of total expenditure, a significantly lower proportion than the sectoral average.

Apparent labour productivity per person employed in the EU-27's motor vehicles and motorcycles distribution sector was EUR 38 300 in 2004 and average personnel costs were EUR 25 800, some EUR 1 300 higher than for motor trades as a whole for both indicators. The wage adjusted labour productivity ratio in the EU-27's motor vehicles and motorcycles distribution sector (148.0 %) was in line with the non-financial business economy average, while the gross operating rate (6.0 %) was in line with the average for distributive trades (NACE Section G) as a whole.

Table 16.8

Sale, maintenance and repair of motor vehicles (NACE Groups 50.1, 50.2, 50.3 and 50.4)
Total expenditure, EU-27, 2004

	Value (EUR million)				Share (% of total expenditure)			
	Total expenditure	Purchases of goods and services	Personnel costs	Investment in tangible goods	Purchases of goods and services	Personnel costs	Investment in tangible goods
Motor vehicles and motorcycles distribution (1)	983 000	890 000	75 000	18 000	90.5	7.6	1.8
Sale of motor vehicles (1)	755 659	701 777	42 382	11 500	92.9	5.6	1.5
Maintenance & repair of motor vehicles	92 411	69 287	19 077	4 047	75.0	20.6	4.4
Sale of motor vehicle parts & accessories (1)	110 205	96 000	12 100	2 105	87.1	11.0	1.9
Sale, maintenance & repair of motorcycles (1)	22 915	21 000	1 600	315	91.6	7.0	1.4

(1) Rounded estimates based on non-confidential data.
Source: Eurostat (SBS)

Table 16.9

Sale, maintenance and repair of motor vehicles (NACE Groups 50.1, 50.2, 50.3 and 50.4)
Productivity and profitability, EU-27, 2004

	Apparent labour productivity (EUR thousand)	Average personnel costs (EUR thousand)	Wage adjusted labour productivity (%)	Gross operating rate (%)
Motor vehicles and motorcycles distribution (1)	38.3	25.8	148.0	6.0
Sale of motor vehicles	51.1	29.6	172.6	4.9
Maintenance & repair of motor vehicles	24.8	20.7	119.8	13.2
Sale of motor vehicle parts & accessories (1)	35.0	25.0	142.0	6.8
Sale, maintenance & repair of motorcycles (1)	32.0	24.2	131.0	6.5

(1) Rounded estimates based on non-confidential data.
Source: Eurostat (SBS)

16.2: RETAIL SALE OF AUTOMOTIVE FUEL

This subsector covers the retail sale of automotive fuel, lubricating and cooling products for motor vehicles and motorcycles (NACE Group 50.5). It does not include the wholesale trade of automotive fuel.

Various business models are found in this sector, the most important being: dealer owned and operated service stations, supplier owned and dealer operated service stations (through exclusive purchasing or agency contracts), and supplier owned and operated service stations (which are owned and operated by the petroleum supplier whose brand they bear).

Table 16.10 provides information on the retail (pump) price of unleaded petrol and automotive diesel. The price of a litre of diesel (including VAT and other taxes) varied considerably between the Member States during the second half of 2006, from a high of EUR 1.44 in the United Kingdom to EUR 0.88 in Estonia. The range of prices for unleaded petrol (95 RON) was rather similar, with the highest price per litre in the Netherlands (EUR 1.54) and the lowest prices again recorded in Estonia (EUR 0.95), closely followed by Latvia (EUR 0.96) and Lithuania (EUR 0.99). Note that the tax and VAT levied on diesel was lower (as a proportion of the final price) than for unleaded petrol in each of the Member States; this helps to explain why diesel prices were lower than unleaded petrol prices in all Member States except for the United Kingdom.

Table 16.10

At the pump prices of petroleum products, second half of 2006

	Premium unleaded gasoline, 95 Ron		Automotive diesel oil	
	EUR/litre	of which, taxes (%)	EUR/litre	of which, taxes (%)
BE	1.41	59.3	1.07	48.0
CZ	1.11	53.3	1.06	49.1
DK	1.39	58.8	1.15	51.9
DE	1.38	61.4	1.15	54.8
EE	0.95	45.5	0.88	43.0
EL	1.17	55.3	1.13	50.0
ES	1.08	45.8	1.01	42.1
FR	1.13	49.8	1.00	44.0
IE	1.32	60.9	1.12	53.7
IT	1.39	57.4	1.21	50.9
CY	1.01	43.1	0.94	39.4
LV	0.96	44.1	0.91	41.1
LT	0.99	44.5	0.92	41.9
LU	1.18	50.6	0.95	42.2
HU	1.11	51.2	1.05	46.9
MT	1.16	42.1	1.02	39.4
NL	1.54	59.3	1.14	49.5
AT	1.16	53.5	1.05	48.7
PL	1.08	50.4	1.00	47.7
PT	1.36	58.4	1.08	48.7
SI	1.04	53.2	0.98	47.6
SK	1.11	51.9	1.09	50.8
FI	1.40	60.0	1.07	48.0
SE	1.37	63.8	1.21	52.8
UK	1.41	66.1	1.44	59.9

Source: Eurostat (Energy)

Other factors influencing the retail sale of automotive fuel include competition in the petroleum retailing market (both among fuel retailers and from other retailers, such as supermarkets), social changes (for example, in terms of the demand for shopping outside of traditional hours), legal requirements relating to environmental protection, and health and safety issues. Some of these have resulted in an expansion of the variety of goods and services retailed alongside automotive fuels, automated payments outside of normal opening hours, and longer opening hours.

One of the main energy policy targets of the EU is to double the share of the Renewable Energy Sources (RES) in gross inland consumption, from 5.4 % in 1997 up to 12.0 % by 2010. By the start of the year 2007 the European Commission made proposals for a new Energy Policy for Europe, including a renewable energy roadmap proposing a binding 10 % target for the share of biofuels in petrol and diesel in each Member State in 2020, to be accompanied by

the introduction of a sustainability scheme for biofuels. At the time of drafting, a public consultation is currently open with the aim for the European Commission to draft proposals to incorporate these targets in legislation [17].

STRUCTURAL PROFILE

Value added generated by the 73 600 enterprises with the retail sale of automotive fuel (NACE Group 50.5) as their main activity in the EU-27 was EUR 13.6 billion in 2004, derived from EUR 154.3 billion of turnover; corresponding to 9.1 % of motor trades (NACE Division 50) value added and 13.0 % of turnover, while with 487 900 persons employed, the sector generated some 12.0 % of the motor trades total.

_____

[17] For more information, see the European Commission Directorate-General for Energy and Transport at: http://ec.europa.eu/energy/energy_policy/index_en.htm

The United Kingdom, Germany, Spain and Italy were systematically in the top four Member States in terms of shares of the EU-27's retail sale of automotive fuel value added, turnover and employment in 2004. However, the contribution of the German sector to the EU-27's turnover was relatively low compared with the other EU large economies. Note that the contribution of France did not exceed 5.6 % for any of these three main variables. In Germany and some other Member States a significant proportion of enterprises that retail automotive fuel do so on a commission basis, and as such their turnover only reflects the commission they receive on sales, and not the value of the fuel itself; whereas in France (and a number of other Member States) a large proportion of fuel is sold through service stations (particularly in out-of-town shopping locations) that belong to retailers classified within retail trade (NACE Division 52) rather than the retailing of automotive fuels. These structural characteristics impact on the analysis that is made of the relative importance of Member States for this sector. This can also be seen in Figure 16.7

Figure 16.7

Retail sale of automotive fuel (NACE Group 50.5) Turnover per enterprise, 2004 (EUR million) (1)

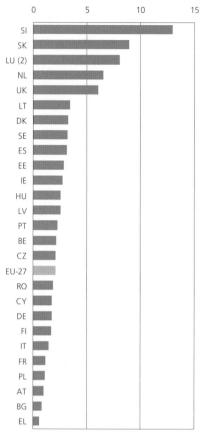

(1) Malta, not available.
(2) 2003.
Source: Eurostat (SBS)

where an analysis of enterprise size is obtained by studying the average turnover per enterprise in 2004. Slovenia, Slovakia and Luxembourg (2003) stood out from the rest of the Member States as having the highest average turnover per enterprise, in excess of EUR 12 million per enterprise for Slovenia and EUR 8 million for the other two Member States, while unsurprisingly Germany and France were among the Member States with the lowest average turnover per enterprise.

Figure 16.8

Retail sale of automotive fuel (NACE Group 50.5) Index of turnover, EU-27 (2000=100)

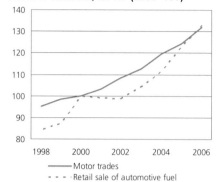

Source: Eurostat (STS)

The evolution of the EU-27 turnover index for the retail sale of automotive fuels was more volatile than that of motor trades as a whole. Indeed, the subsector recorded a strong growth in 2000 compared with the previous year, then contracted slightly in the two following years to 2002, and then accelerated in the three years to 2005, before posting growth of 8.0 % in 2006. Note that the turnover index can only be provided in current prices and therefore reflects price changes. As such, changes in oil prices have to be considered when analysing this data, as the volume of automotive fuel may have fallen while sales in value terms rose (due to significant price increases).

Annual short-term statistics for the index of turnover for retail sale of automotive fuels (NACE Group 50.5) was more volatile than for the motor trades as a whole, growing strongly in 2000, contracting slightly in 2001 and 2002, and then growing increasingly strongly in the three years to 2005 – see Figure 16.8. A slow down in the rhythm of growth was nonetheless registered in 2006 compared with the increase registered the previous year. Note that these indices for turnover need to be interpreted with some care, as they include the effects of price changes as well as changes in volumes (they are therefore likely, at least to some degree, to follow the evolution of oil prices).

COSTS, PRODUCTIVITY AND PROFITABILITY

Purchases of goods and services represented 94.5 % of total expenditure for the EU-27's retail sale of automotive fuel, therefore slightly above the motor trades average. This share was the highest recorded among all the subchapters covered in this publication. As a result, personnel costs for the sector accounted for a relatively low share of the total (4.1 %), as did gross investment in tangible goods (1.3 %).

Given the high incidence of part-time work associated with retailing, it is more relevant to consider wage adjusted labour productivity than apparent labour productivity, the former being less influenced by this characteristic of the workforce than the latter. This ratio was equivalent to 186.2 % in the EU-27's automotive fuel retail sector, above the motor trades ratio of 151.3 %. However, in terms of profitability, the ratio of gross operating surplus to turnover (the gross operating rate) for automotive fuel retailing showed a lower rate (4.9 %) than for the motor trades as a whole (5.8 %) and the non-financial business economy average (11.0 %), reflecting the relatively high turnover inherent in this retail activity. Moreover, among the Member States, the gross operating rate for automotive fuel retailing was above the national non-financial business economy average only in Germany, again reflecting the particular structure of this sector in Germany which results in a relatively low turnover.

Table 16.11

Retail sale of automotive fuel (NACE Group 50.5)
Structural profile: ranking of top five Member States, 2004

Rank	Share of EU-27 value added (%) (1)	Share of EU-27 employment (%) (1)	Value added specialisation ratio (EU-27=100) (2)	Employment specialisation ratio (EU-27=100) (2)
1	United Kingdom (24.6)	Italy (12.5)	Latvia (474.5)	Lithuania (266.4)
2	Germany (17.7)	United Kingdom (12.3)	Bulgaria (462.6)	Bulgaria (265.9)
3	Spain (13.0)	Germany (11.1)	Slovenia (302.0)	Latvia (231.0)
4	Italy (9.5)	Spain (10.9)	Lithuania (294.7)	Luxembourg (225.7)
5	France (5.6)	Poland (9.0)	Luxembourg (293.4)	Denmark (179.4)

(1) Malta, not available; Luxembourg, 2003.
(2) Ireland, Greece, Cyprus and Malta, not available; Luxembourg, 2003.
Source: Eurostat (SBS)

Table 16.12

Sale, maintenance and repair of motor vehicles and motorcycles; retail sale of automotive fuel (NACE Division 50)
Main indicators, 2004

	EU-27	BE	BG	CZ	DK	DE	EE	IE	EL	ES	FR	IT	CY	LV	LT
No. of enterprises (thousands)	782.3	19.0	8.7	31.8	8.5	77.0	1.6	5.8	33.5	76.2	83.8	149.7	3.4	2.6	4.3
Turnover (EUR million)	1 185 418	65 954	2 610	11 402	32 613	171 884	1 799	15 192	17 511	107 760	151 394	154 031	1 631	1 383	2 262
Production (EUR million)	336 744	10 197	524	3 013	18 287	52 652	339	2 053	4 227	23 909	36 214	67 065	390	363	529
Value added (EUR million)	150 599	4 180	222	1 082	2 652	35 485	162	1 229	2 710	12 755	17 802	14 048	233	181	242
Gross operating surplus (EUR million)	69 282	1 792	137	525	857	18 892	71	389	1 774	5 117	3 693	7 452	100	116	108
Purchases of goods & services (EUR million)	1 028 556	62 682	2 473	10 525	17 475	136 248	1 671	14 218	15 763	97 775	134 237	142 932	1 417	1 244	2 044
Personnel costs (EUR million)	81 317	2 388	85	556	1 795	16 654	92	840	936	7 638	14 109	6 596	133	65	134
Investment in tangible goods (EUR million)	20 043	764	143	289	402	2 601	61	304	528	2 447	1 840	2 273	24	77	84
Employment (thousands)	4 067	81	49	95	63	666	12	38	100	390	463	472	9	20	40
Apparent labour prod. (EUR thousand)	37.0	51.6	4.5	11.4	42.3	53.3	13.4	32.4	27.0	32.7	38.5	29.7	27.4	9.0	6.0
Average personnel costs (EUR thousand)	24.5	39.3	2.0	8.9	31.5	28.9	7.8	25.4	17.8	23.4	32.3	25.4	19.5	3.3	3.5
Wage adjusted labour productivity (%)	151.3	131.2	221.8	128.6	134.2	184.2	172.2	127.8	151.7	139.7	118.9	117.1	140.8	271.6	170.0
Gross operating rate (%)	5.8	2.7	5.2	4.6	2.6	11.0	3.9	2.6	10.1	4.7	2.4	4.8	6.1	8.4	4.8
Investment / employment (EUR thousand)	4.9	9.4	2.9	3.0	6.4	3.9	5.1	8.0	5.3	6.3	4.0	4.8	2.8	3.8	2.1

	LU (1)	HU	MT	NL	AT	PL	PT	RO	SI	SK	FI	SE	UK	NO
No. of enterprises (thousands)	0.9	19.6	:	21.5	9.7	75.3	30.4	13.1	3.7	1.0	9.1	20.2	70.3	8.9
Turnover (EUR million)	4 202	13 165	:	64 541	25 636	22 441	24 604	5 486	5 084	3 158	17 637	33 095	228 049	19 605
Production (EUR million)	582	2 455	:	15 521	6 961	9 168	4 626	1 447	1 034	539	3 244	7 267	64 013	5 911
Value added (EUR million)	353	1 002	:	6 236	3 480	2 341	2 354	632	498	222	1 967	3 986	34 444	2 699
Gross operating surplus (EUR million)	120	523	:	2 365	1 043	1 516	708	420	268	112	765	1 191	19 229	788
Purchases of goods & services (EUR million)	3 866	12 127	:	53 373	22 394	20 312	22 806	5 008	4 681	2 991	15 983	29 362	194 138	17 181
Personnel costs (EUR million)	233	479	:	3 871	2 437	824	1 646	213	230	110	1 203	2 796	15 214	1 910
Investment in tangible goods (EUR million)	37	406	:	725	377	479	639	522	112	175	298	786	3 618	541
Employment (thousands)	7	80	:	150	86	250	134	90	16	14	39	86	611	56
Apparent labour prod. (EUR thousand)	47.1	12.5	:	41.4	40.6	9.4	17.5	7.0	31.6	15.4	50.2	46.4	56.3	48.6
Average personnel costs (EUR thousand)	33.6	6.8	:	30.0	31.7	5.1	13.3	2.4	17.3	7.7	33.9	38.1	27.9	36.8
Wage adjusted labour productivity (%)	140.1	184.6	:	138.0	128.4	182.7	132.0	289.3	182.3	200.8	148.3	121.8	201.7	132.0
Gross operating rate (%)	2.9	4.0	:	3.7	4.1	6.8	2.9	7.7	5.3	3.6	4.3	3.6	8.4	4.0
Investment / employment (EUR thousand)	4.9	5.1	:	4.8	4.4	1.9	4.8	5.8	7.1	12.1	7.6	9.2	5.9	9.7

(1) 2003.
Source: Eurostat (SBS)

Wholesale trade

The wholesaling activity consists of selling to retailers or to industrial, commercial, institutional and professional users. Wholesalers can act on a fee or contract basis as agents (which are covered in Subchapter 17.1) or for their own-account, buying and selling goods (as covered by Subchapters 17.2 to 17.6). The own-account wholesale subchapters distinguish the types of product in which the wholesaler is specialised: agricultural products, consumer goods, intermediate goods, machinery and equipment (as covered by Subchapters 17.2 to 17.5), while specialised wholesalers of other products are included in the final subchapter (Subchapter 17.6) along with non-specialised wholesalers.

In the supply chain, wholesalers are located between producers and users, providing know-how and knowledge in markets for which they have expertise. Competition within the wholesale trade activity is often centred on providing more efficient service or more sophisticated value added services. Wholesalers can provide a range of services from basic storage and break of bulk, sorting, grading and logistics to pre- and post-production operations (for instance, labelling, packaging, bottling and installation).

STRUCTURAL PROFILE

Value added generated by the 1.7 million enterprises that made up the EU-27's wholesale trade sector (NACE Division 51) was EUR 462.7 billion in 2004. As such, this was the second largest of all the sectoral chapters covered within this publication in terms of value added, with 9.1 % of the value added generated within the non-financial business economy (NACE Sections C to I and K). Compared with the distributive trades (NACE Section G) total, wholesale trade contributed almost half of the value added (46.4 %). Turnover in the wholesale trade sector was EUR 3 916.1 billion, the largest turnover recorded among all the sectors covered by the publication, accounting for 54.9 % of the distributive trade turnover and for 20.6 % of the non-financial business economy turnover. There were 9.6 million persons employed in the EU-27's wholesale trade sector in 2004, which equated to 7.6 % of the non-financial business economy workforce. Those main indicators showed that this sector's contribution to both distributive trades and non-financial services was much higher in value added and turnover terms than in employment terms, underlining high apparent labour productivity in this sector.

The activities in NACE Division 51 cover all wholesale trade except that concerning motor trade (see the previous chapter). This chapter covers resale (sale without transformation) of new and used products, as well as wholesale activities carried out on a fee or contract basis.

NACE
51: wholesale trade and commission trade, except of motor vehicles and motorcycles;
51.1: wholesale on a fee or contract basis;
51.2: wholesale of agricultural raw materials and live animals;
51.3: wholesale of food, beverages and tobacco;
51.4: wholesale of household goods;
51.5: wholesale of non-agricultural intermediate products, waste and scrap;
51.8: wholesale of machinery, equipment and supplies;
51.9: other wholesale.

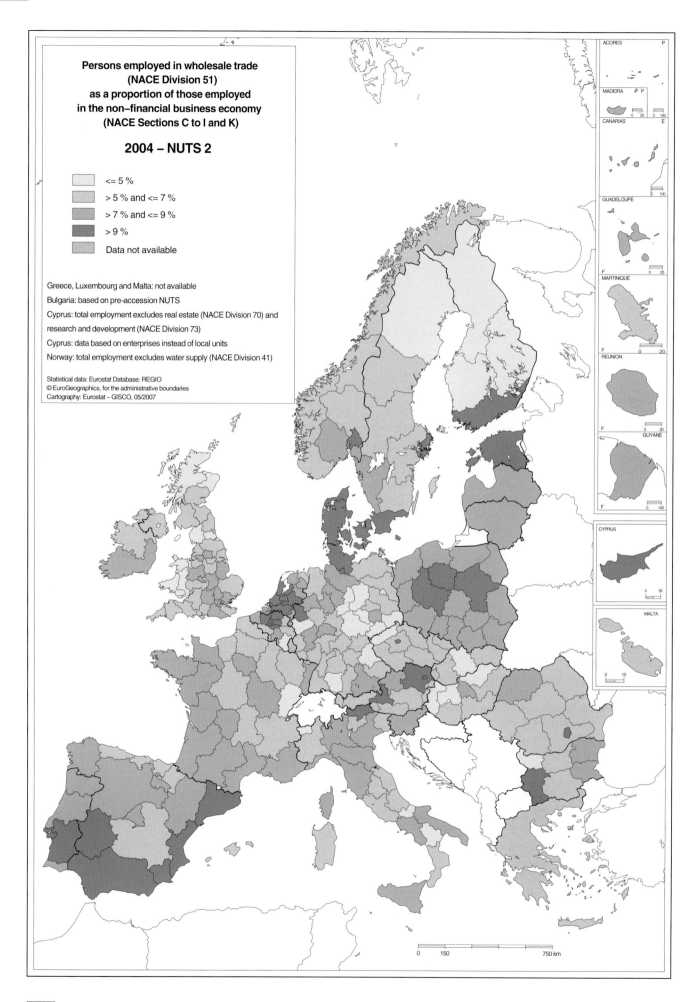

Persons employed in wholesale trade
(NACE Division 51)
as a proportion of those employed
in the non–financial business economy
(NACE Sections C to I and K)

2004 – NUTS 2

<= 5 %

> 5 % and <= 7 %

> 7 % and <= 9 %

> 9 %

Data not available

Greece, Luxembourg and Malta: not available

Bulgaria: based on pre-accession NUTS

Cyprus: total employment excludes real estate (NACE Division 70) and
research and development (NACE Division 73)

Cyprus: data based on enterprises instead of local units

Norway: total employment excludes water supply (NACE Division 41)

Statistical data: Eurostat Database: REGIO
© EuroGeographics, for the administrative boundaries
Cartography: Eurostat – GISCO, 05/2007

Table 17.1

Wholesale trade and commission trade (NACE Division 51)
Structural profile, EU-27, 2004

	No. of enterprises		Turnover		Value added		Employment	
	(thousands)	(% of total)	(EUR million)	(% of total)	(EUR million)	(% of total)	(thousands)	(% of total)
Wholesale trade and commission trade	1 682.2	100.0	3 916 076	100.0	462 707	100.0	9 554.2	100.0
Wholesale on a fee or contract basis	529.4	31.5	203 815	5.2	37 635	8.1	902.3	9.4
Agricultural wholesaling (1)	65.0	3.9	180 000	4.6	14 000	3.0	340.0	3.6
Wholesale of consumer goods	546.5	32.5	1 559 755	39.8	183 393	39.6	4 032.8	42.2
Wholesale of intermediate goods	235.7	14.0	1 182 673	30.2	111 230	24.0	1 988.6	20.8
Wholesale of machinery and equipment (1)	190.0	11.3	600 000	15.3	90 000	19.5	1 600.0	16.7
Other wholesale	118.7	7.1	183 500	4.7	23 507	5.1	669.8	7.0

(1) Rounded estimates based on non-confidential data.
Source: Eurostat (SBS)

Table 17.2

Wholesale trade and commission trade (NACE Division 51)
Structural profile: ranking of top five Member States, 2004

			Share of non-financial business economy			
Rank	Value added (EUR million) (1)	Employment (thousands) (1)	No. of enterprises (2)	Turnover (2)	Value added (2)	Employment (2)
1	United Kingdom (83 996)	Germany (1 208.2)	Slovakia (23.5 %)	Bulgaria (31.9 %)	Latvia (18.5 %)	Netherlands (10.2 %)
2	Germany (78 514)	United Kingdom (1 201.3)	Estonia (22.1 %)	Latvia (31.7 %)	Estonia (13.2 %)	Estonia (10.1 %)
3	France (62 382)	Spain (1 119.6)	Luxembourg (14.6 %)	Netherlands (28.4 %)	Netherlands (13.1 %)	Denmark (9.9 %)
4	Italy (48 573)	Italy (1 076.3)	Romania (13.7 %)	Estonia (26.6 %)	Portugal (11.9 %)	Belgium (9.8 %)
5	Spain (44 125)	France (1 056.2)	Slovenia (12.7 %)	Belgium (25.7 %)	Lithuania (11.9 %)	Portugal (9.3 %)

(1) Malta, not available; Luxembourg, 2003.
(2) Ireland, Greece, Cyprus and Malta, not available; Luxembourg, 2003.
Source: Eurostat (SBS)

Looking in more detail at the activities that make up the wholesale trade sector (in terms of the coverage used for each of the subchapters), the largest wholesale trade subsector in value added and employment terms was the wholesale trade of consumer goods (NACE Groups 51.3 and 51.4), followed by the wholesaling of intermediate goods (NACE Group 51.5) and the wholesaling of machinery and equipment (NACE Group 51.8). However, while the wholesale trade of consumer goods contributed a larger proportion to sectoral employment than to sectoral value added, both of the two other large subsectors made a larger contribution to sectoral value added than employment, indicating their higher apparent labour productivity.

Among the Member States [1] for which data is available for a breakdown of wholesale turnover activities, the share of consumer goods reached 53.5 % in Greece, and also exceeded 50 % in Romania and Portugal. In nine of the Member States, the wholesale of intermediate goods was the largest contributors to national wholesale trade. While the wholesale trade of machinery and equipment generated 15.3 % of the EU-27's wholesale trade, the importance of these activities reached 28.5 % in the Netherlands and this share was above 20 % in Sweden, Denmark, Finland and Luxembourg. Wholesale trade on a fee or contract basis (NACE Group 51.5) was relatively important in Slovenia (24.1 %), France (17.2 %) and Slovakia (15.1 %), compared with the EU-27 average (5.2 %).Other wholesale trade (NACE Group 51.9) accounted for 4.7 % of wholesale trade turnover in the EU-27, although this proportion rose to almost one third in Poland (32.1 %) and was also relatively high in Slovenia (18.9 %), Slovakia (17.9 %) and Finland (16.0 %). Agricultural wholesaling (NACE Group 51.2) was the smallest wholesale trade subsector, accounting for 4.6 % of turnover in the EU-27, while that proportion was 8.0 % in France and 7.9 % in Hungary, with the smallest national share that was recorded in the United Kingdom (1.5 %).

Among the Member States [2], the United Kingdom and Germany had the largest levels of value added, turnover and employment in the wholesale trade sector. However, relative to the whole non-financial business economy, the importance of the wholesale trade sector varied from just 7.3 % of the value added in Germany to 18.5 % in Latvia. For employment, this range was much narrower, the sectoral wholesale trade workforce accounting from 5.8 % of non-financial business economy employment in Germany to 10.2 % in the Netherlands.

[2] Luxembourg, 2003; Malta, not available.

[1] Ireland and Luxembourg, 2003; the Czech Republic, other wholesale trade, not available; Malta, not available.

Figure 17.2 shows the average turnover per enterprise of the EU-27's wholesaling subsectors. In 2004, the highest average for the EU-27 was recorded by the wholesale trade of intermediate goods at EUR 5.0 million per enterprise, while the lowest average was for the wholesale on a fee or contract basis (NACE Group 51.1) at EUR 0.4 million per enterprise. Across the subsectors shown in the figure, the widest range of values for this average was found in the miscellaneous activities of other wholesale, while wholesale on a fee or contract basis registered the narrowest range of values.

Regional employment specialisation (in some cases the whole country is treated as one region) can be seen from the map on page 284 which is based on the non-financial business economy employment share of the wholesale trade sector. Given the essential nature of many parts of wholesale trade, providing services directly to retailers and to industrial consumers, it is unsurprising that most regions tended towards the average. In the regions where the wholesale trade workforce accounted for its highest share of the non-financial business economy workforce (15 % and over in one Dutch and one Spanish region), the relative specialisation was around five times higher than in the least specialised regions (around 3 % in two Finnish and one Italian region).

Annualised short-term statistics for the EU-27's wholesale trade sector showed that the index of turnover grew by 9.8 % in 2006, compared with the previous year, the highest growth rate recorded for the sector since 2000 (when growth reached 10.3 %). During the period 1996-2006, the index of turnover rose on average by 4.4 % per annum. Employment for the EU-27's wholesale trade sector also increased in 2006, up 3.1 % compared with growth of 1.1 % in 2005 and 0.4 % in 2004. Over the period 1996-2006, the index of employment recorded two slight negative year on year rates of change, -0.2 % in 2001 and -0.5 % in 2003, in contrast to the uninterrupted growth of the employment index for the whole of distributive trades - see Figure 17.3.

Turnover indices are available for all of the wholesale trade NACE groups except for wholesale on a fee or contract basis - see Figure 17.4. Focusing only on the developments for the most recent five years, from 2001 to 2006, EU-27 agricultural wholesaling (NACE Group 51.2) maintained a relatively stable level of turnover, the slowest development across the NACE groups shown (average growth of 1.1 % per annum during this period). The two consumer oriented NACE groups, namely the wholesale of food, beverages and tobacco, and of household goods, recorded consecutive years of uninterrupted

growth, resulting in average annual growth rates of 3.4 % and 4.3 % per annum respectively between 2001 and 2006. The turnover index for the wholesaling of intermediate goods developed quickly during the period considered, on average by 9.2 % per annum, the highest average annual growth rate over this period of all available non-financial services [3]. However, note that this activity covers the wholesaling of fuels, and such products have recorded large price increases in recent years and these are also reflected in the turnover index. The wholesaling of machinery, equipment and supplies, and the other wholesale activity showed rather similar average annual growth rates for the period 2001-2006, 3.2 % and 3.4 % respectively. However, the former subsector recorded a fall in its turnover index in the years 2001 through to 2003, followed by strong growth in the three following years up to 2006. In contrast, the latter subsector showed a mixture of periods of stability and stronger growth (7.1 % in both 2004 and 2006).

[3] Note that the services turnover indices are available at a mixture of NACE levels, sometimes, classes, groups, divisions, or special aggregates thereof.

Figure 17.1

Wholesale trade and commission trade (NACE Division 51)
Share of non-financial business economy, EU-27, 2004 (%) (1)

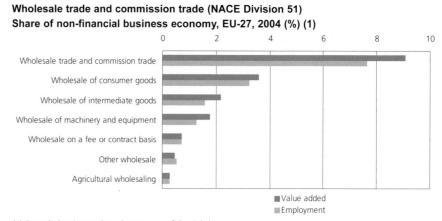

(1) Rounded estimates based on non-confidential data.
Source: Eurostat (SBS)

Figure 17.2

Wholesale trade and commission trade (NACE Division 51)
Turnover per enterprise, 2004 (EUR million)

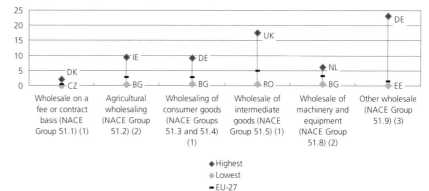

(1) Ireland and Luxembourg, 2003; Malta, not available.
(2) Luxembourg, 2003; Malta, not available.
(3) Luxembourg, 2003; Czech Republic and Malta, not available.
Source: Eurostat (SBS)

Figure 17.3

Wholesale trade and commission trade (NACE Division 51)
Index of employment, EU-27 (2000=100)

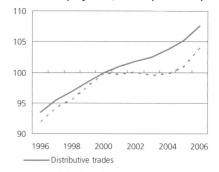

Source: Eurostat (STS)

European business — Facts and figures

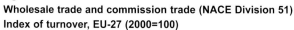

Figure 17.4

Wholesale trade and commission trade (NACE Division 51)
Index of turnover, EU-27 (2000=100)

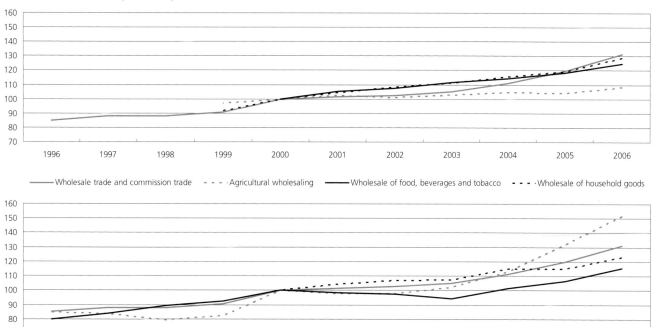

Source: Eurostat (STS)

The size class structure of the wholesale trade sector was quite similar to that of motor trades (NACE Division 50 - see Chapter 16), in that SMEs (enterprises with less than 250 persons employed) contributed just over three quarters (77.2 %) of the EU-27's wholesale trade sector's value added in 2004, the remaining share being generated by large enterprises (with 250 or more persons employed). For comparison, SMEs contribution to value added was smaller in the whole of the distributive trades (69.9 %), as well as in the non-financial business economy (57.0 %). All four of the size classes shown in Figure 17.5 contributed between one fifth and one third of the EU-27's wholesale trade sector's value added in 2004. Small enterprises (with between 10 and 49 persons employed) accounted more (30.3 %) of the sector's value added than any other enterprise size class. This size class structure was in contrast to that of the retail trade and repair sector (NACE Division 52), where the vast majority of sectoral value added was generated by large enterprises or micro enterprises (with less than 10 persons employed). In terms of employment, SMEs provided 83.7 % of the workforce in the wholesale trade sector, a sign of low apparent labour productivity for SMEs relative to large enterprises. However, this low apparent labour productivity resulted essentially from the predominance of micro enterprises

(with less than 10 persons employed) that provided slightly more than one third of the workforce of the wholesale trade sector, while they contributed less than one quarter (23.8 %) of value added.

Figure 17.5

Wholesale trade and commission trade (NACE Division 51)
Share of value added by enterprise size class, EU-27, 2004

Source: Eurostat (SBS)

EMPLOYMENT CHARACTERISTICS
According to Labour Force Survey data for wholesale trade in 2006, men represented two thirds (66.2 %) of the EU-27's workforce, a share that was in line with the gender breakdown for the non-financial business economy as a whole, while this proportion of men employed in the wholesale trade was relatively high compared with the distributive trades average (51.5 %). However in half of the Member States with available data [4] the proportion of men working in the wholesale trade sector was below the average for the national non-financial business economy. Slightly less than nine tenths (89.3 %) of the persons employed in the EU-27's wholesale trade sector in 2006 worked full-time, a proportion that was 11.0 percentage points above the distributive trade average and slightly above the non-financial business economy average (85.6 %) as well. Among the Member States [5], only in Belgium and Bulgaria was the incidence of full-time work slightly lower in wholesale trade than in the non-financial business economy as a whole.

---

[4] Luxembourg, 2005.
[5] Luxembourg, 2005; Ireland, not available.

Figure 17.6

Wholesale trade and commission trade (NACE Division 51)
Labour force characteristics, EU-27, 2006

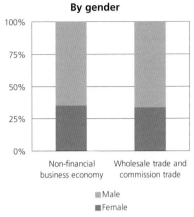

By gender

■ Male
■ Female

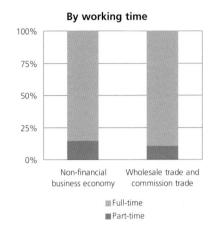

By working time

■ Full-time
■ Part-time

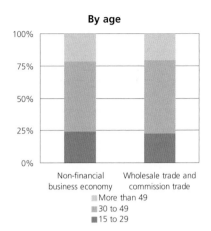

By age

■ More than 49
■ 30 to 49
■ 15 to 29

Source: Eurostat (LFS)

A breakdown by age of the workforce for the EU-27's wholesale trade sector in 2006 shows a quite similar contribution of all the three age classes analysed when compared with the non-financial business economy average. Indeed, 22.6 % of those employed were aged between 15 and 29, more than half (56.7 %) between 30 and 49, and the remaining one fifth (20.8 %) were persons aged 50 or more.

According to structural business statistics for 2004, the share of the number of paid employees in persons employed (85.9 %) for the EU-27's wholesale trade sector was very similar to what was registered for the non-financial business economy as a whole (0.3 percentage points above the share for the wholesale trade). Among the Member States [6], around two thirds recorded a higher share of employees in persons employed in wholesale trade than in the non-financial business economy as a whole, but the difference was slight except in Denmark, Spain and Hungary where the difference was more visible (at least 4.1 percentage points difference). In Italy, the total number of persons employed in the wholesale trade sector was almost equally distributed between paid employees (54.4 %) on one hand and working proprietors and unpaid family workers on the other hand (the counterpart of the share of the number of persons employed). In the Italian wholesale trade sector, this proportion of employees in persons employed was relatively low in contrast to the share for the Italian non-financial business economy as a whole (66.8 %).

COSTS, PRODUCTIVITY AND PROFITABILITY

Purchases of goods and services represented a high share (91.9 %) of total expenditure in the EU-27's wholesale trade sector, the largest share recorded in 2004 among all the non-financial business economy NACE divisions, just above the share for the motor trades sector (see previous chapter), underlining the high volume of purchases for resale characteristic of wholesale trade activities. Consequently the shares of personnel costs (6.8 %) and gross investment in tangible goods (1.3 %) were both particularly low, the lowest of all non-financial services NACE divisions. Among the subsectors that make up the wholesale trade sector, the purchases of goods and services constituted the highest share of total expenditure for agricultural wholesaling, and for wholesaling of intermediate goods, at least 94.0 %, while the lowest share (88.2 %) was recorded by the wholesaling of machinery and equipment.

Apparent labour productivity was EUR 48 400 per person employed in the EU-27's wholesale trade sector in 2004, EUR 7 500 higher than the non-financial business economy average. However, two of the six wholesale trade subsectors recorded apparent labour productivity ratios that were below the non-financial business economy average (EUR 40 900 per person employed), namely agricultural wholesaling and other wholesale trade, as did the part of consumer goods wholesaling concerned with food, beverages and tobacco wholesaling.

Average personnel costs in the wholesale trade sector were EUR 30 700 per employee in the EU-27 in 2004 which, as with apparent labour productivity, were higher than the non-financial business economy average. The wage adjusted labour productivity ratio was 157.6 % in 2004, below the non-financial business economy average.

The ratio of the gross operating surplus to turnover (the gross operating rate) was 5.4 % in the EU-27's wholesale trade sector in 2004, almost half the corresponding rate for the non-financial business economy as a whole (11.0 %), reflecting the high turnover (resale in the same condition as purchased) and relatively low margins typically associated with wholesale trade. Wholesale trade gross operating rates among the Member States [7] were systematically lower than the national non-financial business economy averages.

---

[7] Luxembourg, 2003; Malta, not available.

---

[6] Luxembourg, 2003; Ireland, Greece, Cyprus and Malta, not available.

Table 17.3

Wholesale trade and commission trade (NACE Division 51)
Total expenditure, EU-27, 2004

	Value (EUR million)				Share (% of total expenditure)		
	Total expenditure	Purchases of goods and services	Personnel costs	Investment in tangible goods	Purchases of goods and services	Personnel costs	Investment in tangible goods
Wholesale trade and commission trade	3 726 635	3 426 411	252 229	47 995	91.9	6.8	1.3
Wholesale on a fee or contract basis	179 843	163 482	12 798	3 563	90.9	7.1	2.0
Agricultural wholesaling (1)	180 149	170 000	7 700	2 449	94.4	4.3	1.4
Wholesale of consumer goods	1 498 943	1 375 973	103 916	19 054	91.8	6.9	1.3
Wholesale of intermediate goods	1 110 681	1 043 529	54 658	12 494	94.0	4.9	1.1
Wholesale of machinery and equipment (1)	578 007	510 000	60 000	8 007	88.2	10.4	1.4
Other wholesale	176 374	162 689	11 256	2 429	92.2	6.4	1.4

(1) Rounded estimates based on non-confidential data.
Source: Eurostat (SBS)

Table 17.4

Wholesale trade and commission trade (NACE Division 51)
Productivity and profitability, EU-27, 2004

	Apparent labour productivity (EUR thousand)	Average personnel costs (EUR thousand)	Wage adjusted labour productivity (%)	Gross operating rate (%)
Wholesale trade and commission trade	48.4	30.7	157.6	5.4
Wholesale on a fee or contract basis	41.7	29.4	142.0	12.2
Agricultural wholesaling (1)	40.0	27.0	150.0	3.3
Wholesale of consumer goods	45.5	28.8	157.8	5.1
Wholesale of intermediate goods	55.9	30.4	184.1	4.8
Wholesale of machinery and equipment (1)	56.3	40.0	140.0	5.2
Other wholesale	35.1	19.4	180.5	6.7

(1) Rounded estimates based on non-confidential data.
Source: Eurostat (SBS)

17.1: WHOLESALE ON A FEE OR CONTRACT BASIS

This wholesale sector covers agents trading on behalf and on account of others, those involved in bringing sellers and buyers together and those undertaking commercial transactions on behalf of a principal (NACE Group 51.1). It does not include financial intermediaries such as insurance or real estate agents, nor retail sale by agents.

Wholesalers acting as agents provide a service, acting to bring together the two parties to a transaction, namely the buyer and the seller.

STRUCTURAL PROFILE

The EU-27's wholesale on a fee or contract basis (NACE Group 51.1) consisted of close to 530 000 enterprises which generated EUR 37.6 billion value added in 2004 and EUR 203.8 billion turnover, representing respectively 8.1 % and 5.2 % of total value added and turnover in wholesale trade (NACE Division 51). Both of these shares ranked the wholesale on a fee or contract basis as the third smallest of the wholesale trade NACE groups, ahead of agricultural wholesaling and the residual activities of other wholesale. With 902 300 persons employed in the wholesale on a fee or contract basis sector in the EU-27 in 2004, the sector assembled 9.4 % of the total wholesale trade workforce, a higher proportion than for value added underlining the low apparent labour productivity for this activity. It is likely that a high proportion of persons work part-time in this activity and this could account, in part, for the relatively low level of apparent labour productivity.

Slightly less than one third of the value added generated by the EU-27's wholesale on a fee or contract basis sector in 2004 came from Italy (31.9 %) - see Table 17.6 [8]. Unsurprisingly, with such a large contribution to the EU-27 total, Italian wholesaling was very concentrated in this form of wholesaling, as this sector generated 2.1 % of Italian non-financial business economy value added in 2004. However, this share was even higher in Slovenia, where wholesale on a fee or contract basis accounted for 2.7 % of non-financial business economy value added, a share that was 3.7 times the corresponding share for the EU-27 average.

[8] Luxembourg, 2003; Malta, not available.

Table 17.5 _____

Wholesale on a fee or contract basis (NACE Group 51.1)
Relative weight within wholesale on a fee or contract basis, EU-27, 2003 (%)

	No. of enterprises	Turnover	Value added	Employment
Agents involved in the sale of agricultural raw materials live animals, textile raw materials and semi-finished goods	2.7	:	2.8	3.5
Agents involved in the sale of fuels, ores, metals and industrial chemicals	3.1	:	5.5	4.1
Agents involved in the sale of timber and building materials	5.1	3.2	5.9	5.7
Agents involved in the sale of machinery, industrial equipment ships and aircraft	6.3	7.1	15.3	9.1
Agents involved in the sale of furniture, household goods, hardware and ironmongery	7.7	2.2	5.3	7.2
Agents involved in the sale of textiles, clothing, footwear and leather goods	9.2	3.9	8.9	9.9
Agents involved in the sale of food, beverages and tobacco	10.8	32.3	13.1	12.5
Agents specializing in the sale of particular products or ranges of products n.e.c.	28.6	13.6	23.0	24.0
Agents involved in the sale of a variety of goods	26.5	28.1	20.3	24.0

Source: Eurostat (SBS)

Table 17.6 _____

Wholesale on a fee or contract basis (NACE Group 51.1)
Structural profile: ranking of top five Member States, 2004

Rank	Share of EU-27 value added (%) (1)	Share of EU-27 employment (%) (1)	Value added specialisation ratio (EU-27=100) (2)	Employment specialisation ratio (EU-27=100) (2)
1	Italy (31.9)	Italy (34.4)	Slovenia (369.5)	Slovenia (377.1)
2	United Kingdom (17.7)	France (8.8)	Italy (287.1)	Italy (293.1)
3	France (14.5)	Spain (8.5)	Slovakia (243.8)	Slovakia (243.0)
4	Germany (7.8)	United Kingdom (7.6)	Romania (188.2)	Czech Republic (136.3)
5	Spain (7.2)	Germany (5.6)	Czech Republic (155.5)	Romania (120.4)

(1) Malta, not available; Luxembourg, 2003.
(2) Ireland, Greece, Cyprus and Malta, not available; Luxembourg, 2003.
Source: Eurostat (SBS)

COSTS, PRODUCTIVITY AND PROFITABILITY

There was no great difference between the structure of costs for the EU-27's wholesale trade on a fee or contract basis sector and wholesale trade as a whole in 2004. Nevertheless the slightly lower share of total expenditure accounted for by purchases of good and services (90.9 % compared to a wholesale trade average of 91.9 %), was mainly balanced by a higher share (2.0 % compared to 1.3 %) for investment in tangible goods, which although still small compared to the non-financial business economy average (4.9 %) was the highest for any of the wholesale trade groups. Wage adjusted labour productivity was 142.0 % for the sector, slightly below the non-financial business economy average. However, four of the five EU-27's largest economies recorded higher wage adjusted productivity ratios for their wholesale on a fee or contract basis sector than for their non-financial business economy, namely Germany, France, Italy and the United Kingdom.

Turning to one measure of profitability, the ratio of gross operating surplus to turnover, the gross operating rate in the EU-27's wholesale on a fee or contract basis equalled 12.2 %, well above the rates for the other wholesale trade NACE groups, and also slightly above that for the non-financial business economy as a whole.

17.2: AGRICULTURAL WHOLESALING

NACE Group 51.2 covers the wholesaling of raw materials for agricultural activities (such as seeds and animal feed), as well as live animals. It does not cover the wholesaling of outputs from farming other than hides, skins and leather, and unmanufactured tobacco.

STRUCTURAL PROFILE

Agricultural wholesaling (NACE Group 51.2) with its 65 000 enterprises was the smallest of the wholesale trade NACE groups, whether measured in terms of turnover, value added or employment. Indeed, the turnover generated by agricultural wholesaling was EUR 180.0 billion and value added EUR 14.0 billion in the EU-27 in 2004, which represented 4.6 % of wholesale trade turnover and 3.0 % of wholesale trade value added. The EU-27's sector of agricultural wholesaling employed some 340 000 persons in 2004, some 3.6 % of the total number of persons employed in wholesale trade. Among the activities (NACE Classes) that make up the sector, the wholesale of grain, seeds and animal feeds was the largest, both in terms of value added and employment, followed by the wholesale of flowers and plants. None of the other agricultural wholesaling subsectors accounted with more than EUR 2.0 billion value added or employed more than 80 000 persons in 2004.

Among the Member States [9], France and Germany recorded both the highest value added and number of persons employed in the agricultural wholesale sector - see Table 17.8. France's high shares made it the third most specialised Member States in the agricultural wholesale sector both in terms of the sector's contribution to non-financial business economy value added, while the most specialised was the Netherlands followed by Austria.

According to annualised short-term statistics, after a 3.1 % increase in the turnover index in 2000 (compared to the previous year), a series of modest increases and decreases in turnover were recorded from 2001 to 2005, when the evolution of sales for the agricultural wholesaling sector ranged from -1.0 % in 2002 to 2.5 % in 2001. However, turnover grew by 3.7 % in 2006, the fastest progression over the period observed. Nevertheless, with the exception of 2001, the agricultural wholesaling sector recorded a slower rate of growth in turnover than the wholesale trade average.

COSTS, PRODUCTIVITY AND PROFITABILITY

In 2004, total expenditure in the EU-27's agricultural wholesaling sector was dominated (94.4 %) by purchases of goods and services, with 4.3 % for personnel costs and the remaining 1.4 % for gross investment in tangible goods. The

[9] Luxembourg, 2003; Malta, not available.

apparent labour productivity of the sector was EUR 40 000 per person employed in the EU-27, average personnel costs were EUR 27 000 per employee, while the share of employees in persons employed was 83.0 %, all these figures being below the corresponding wholesale trade averages. The resulting wage adjusted labour productivity ratio in this sector was 150.0 %, some 7.6 percentage points below the average for wholesale trade. The gross operating rate of the EU-27's agricultural wholesaling sector was also relatively low, at 3.3 % in 2004.

Figure 17.7

Wholesale of agricultural raw materials, live animals (NACE Group 51.2)
Index of turnover, EU-27 (2000=100)

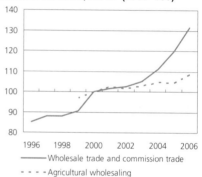

Source: Eurostat (STS)

Table 17.7

Wholesale of agricultural raw materials, live animals (NACE Group 51.2)
Structural profile, EU-27, 2004

	No. of enterprises (thousands)	Turnover (EUR million)	Value added (EUR million)	Employment (thousands)
Agricultural wholesaling (1)	65.0	180 000	14 000	340.0
Wholesale of grain, seeds and animal feeds	28.1	119 149	8 561	192.6
Wholesale of flowers and plants (1)	13.0	19 900	2 720	80.0
Wholesale of live animals (1)	18.5	37 450	1 835	52.0
Wholesale of hides, skins and leather (2)	5.4	7 199	541	16.9
Wholesale of unmanufactured tobacco (1)	:	690	80	:

(1) Rounded estimates based on non-confidential data.
(2) Number of enterprises, turnover and value added, 2003.
Source: Eurostat (SBS)

Table 17.8

Wholesale of agricultural raw materials, live animals (NACE Group 51.2)
Structural profile: ranking of top five Member States, 2004

Rank	Share of EU-27 value added (%) (1)	Share of EU-27 employment (%) (1)	Value added specialisation ratio (EU-27=100) (2)	Employment specialisation ratio (EU-27=100) (2)
1	France (20.9)	France (15.8)	Netherlands (282.2)	Austria (264.2)
2	Germany (20.2)	Germany (15.4)	Austria (174.9)	Netherlands (256.0)
3	Netherlands (12.9)	Spain (10.5)	France (148.4)	France (138.2)
4	Italy (8.1)	Netherlands (9.4)	Bulgaria (148.1)	Denmark (126.9)
5	Spain (7.9)	Italy (7.9)	Hungary (137.2)	Hungary (126.2)

(1) Malta, not available; Ireland and Luxembourg, 2003.
(2) Ireland, Greece, Cyprus and Malta, not available; Luxembourg, 2003.
Source: Eurostat (SBS)

17.3: WHOLESALING OF CONSUMER GOODS

The wholesaling of consumer goods covers NACE Groups 51.3 and 51.4. The first of these groups includes the wholesaling of food, beverages and tobacco, while the latter includes household products, such as textiles, clothing, electrical appliances, games, toys, tableware, furniture and furnishings, as well as cleaning products and personal products. It should be noted that although these two categories are grouped together here as consumer goods, these activities also include the wholesaling of food and beverage products as inputs for further processing.

STRUCTURAL PROFILE

Turnover from the 546 500 enterprises with wholesaling of consumer goods (NACE Groups 51.3 and 51.4) as their main activity was valued at EUR 1 560 billion in the EU-27 in 2004, representing 39.8 % of the wholesale trade total. With EUR 183.4 billion of value added in 2004 this was the largest of the wholesale trade activities presented in Subchapters 17.1 to 17.6, with a 39.6 % share of wholesale value added. However, the contribution to wholesale trade employment was even higher (42.2 %) as there were 4.0 million persons employed in the EU-27's wholesaling of consumer goods sector. The wholesale of household goods (NACE Group 51.4) was the largest of the two NACE groups in this sector, with more than half of the sector's employment and turnover and just over three fifths of the turnover, with the wholesale of food, beverages and tobacco (NACE Group 51.3) recording the smaller share for all three indicators.

Table 17.9

Wholesale of food, beverages, tobacco and household goods (NACE Groups 51.3 and 51.4)
Structural profile, EU-27, 2004

	No. of enterprises (thousands)	Turnover (EUR million)	Value added (EUR million)	Employment (thousands)
Wholesale of consumer goods	546.5	1 559 755	183 393	4 032.8
Food, beverages and tobacco	213.8	728 831	70 518	1 819.1
Fruits and vegetables (1)	42.0	110 000	12 000	370.0
Meat and meat products (1)	22.0	70 000	6 300	170.0
Dairy produce, eggs and edible oils and fats	15.5	67 709	4 924	112.2
Alcoholic and other beverages	39.2	100 909	13 461	277.2
Tobacco products (1)	2.6	53 142	3 253	47.9
Sugar and chocolate and sugar confectionery (1)	11.0	28 957	2 449	67.1
Coffee, tea, cocoa and spices (1)	5.2	10 500	1 750	34.0
Other food including fish, crustaceans and molluscs (1)	43.6	100 000	9 900	260.0
Non-specialized wholesale of food beverages and tobacco	31.9	189 854	16 527	476.6
Household goods	332.7	830 924	112 875	2 213.7
Textiles	28.1	26 714	4 434	124.4
Clothing and footwear	69.8	89 325	14 823	322.6
Electrical household appliances and radio and television goods	38.8	174 362	18 340	328.6
China and glassware, wallpaper and cleaning materials (1)	19.6	27 000	4 800	116.0
Perfume and cosmetics (1)	16.6	36 000	7 100	147.0
Pharmaceutical goods	28.9	261 389	31 348	452.5
Other household goods	130.8	215 173	31 962	722.0

(1) Rounded estimates based on non-confidential data.
Source: Eurostat (SBS)

Table 17.10

Wholesale of food, beverages, tobacco and household goods (NACE Groups 51.3 and 51.4)
Structural profile: ranking of top five Member States, 2004

Rank	Share of EU-27 value added (%) (1)	Share of EU-27 employment (%) (1)	Value added specialisation ratio (EU-27=100) (2)	Employment specialisation ratio (EU-27=100) (2)
1	Germany (18.3)	Spain (14.9)	Latvia (179.1)	Spain (145.1)
2	United Kingdom (17.4)	Germany (13.3)	Portugal (170.5)	Portugal (142.7)
3	France (12.7)	United Kingdom (12.5)	Netherlands (144.5)	Latvia (129.0)
4	Spain (11.1)	Italy (10.4)	Belgium (131.8)	Romania (128.4)
5	Italy (10.0)	France (9.8)	Lithuania (124.4)	Belgium (126.7)

(1) Malta, not available; Luxembourg, 2003.
(2) Ireland, Greece, Cyprus and Malta, not available; Luxembourg, 2003.
Source: Eurostat (SBS)

Germany was to some extent the dominant Member State [10] in the wholesale of consumer goods, with just less than one fifth of both the EU-27 value added and turnover, although Spain had the largest workforce, slightly larger than Germany's. However, Latvia, Portugal, the Netherlands, Belgium, Lithuania and Spain were the most specialised Member States [11] in terms of this sector's contribution to non-financial business economy value added, while Spain and Portugal were the most specialised in employment terms.

Annualised short-term statistics are available for an analysis of the evolution of turnover indices for consumer goods wholesaling, for each of the two NACE groups that compose this sector - see Figure 17.8. The turnover index registered gains for both of these activities in all of the last years. However, turnover growth for both of these activities was higher than for the wholesale trade as a whole in the years 2001 to 2003. In the years 2004 to 2006, this pattern was reversed, namely there was a significantly slower progression of sales for each of the two NACE groups compared with fast growth in the wholesale trade sector.

Figure 17.8

Wholesale of food, beverages, tobacco and household goods
(NACE Groups 51.3 and 51.4)
Index of turnover, EU-27 (2000=100)

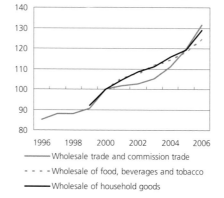

——— Wholesale trade and commission trade

- - - - Wholesale of food, beverages and tobacco

——— Wholesale of household goods

Source: Eurostat (STS)

COSTS, PRODUCTIVITY AND PROFITABILITY

The expenditure structure of the EU-27's wholesaling of consumer goods sector was very similar to wholesale trade as a whole. Apparent labour productivity for consumer goods wholesaling was EUR 45 500 per person employed in the EU-27 in 2004 and average personnel costs were EUR 28 800 per employee, both figures standing below the wholesale trade average. There were significant differences between the two subsectors for these indicators, with the values recorded for the wholesaling of household goods approximately one third higher for both indicators than were recorded for the wholesale of food, beverages and tobacco. In more details, the wholesale of pharmaceutical goods (NACE Class 51.46) stood out from the rest of the wholesale of household goods activities and recorded the highest apparent labour productivity figure (EUR 69 300 per person employed) and personnel costs (EUR 44 000 per employee) among all NACE classes for the sector.

The ratio of wage adjusted labour productivity was almost identical in the wholesaling of consumer goods (157.8 %) and in wholesale trade as a whole (157.6 %). In the large majority of the Member States [12], the ratio for the sector was very similar or higher than national wholesale trade figures. By this measure of productivity, the two subsectors within the wholesaling of consumer goods did not notably diverge, as the ratio for wholesale trade of food, beverages and tobacco (160.2 %) was slightly above that for wholesale trade of household goods (156.1 %).

The gross operating rate was 5.1 % in the EU-27's consumer goods wholesaling sector in 2004, marginally below the wholesale trade average of 5.4 %, while the rate was 2.2 times higher in the non-financial business economy as a whole. Among the Member States with available data, Bulgaria and Romania stood out as they posted gross operating rates for their non-financial business economies that were respectively 3.4 and 4.3 as high as their consumer goods wholesaling sector. According to this measure of profitability the two subsectors performed differently, as the wholesale of food, beverages and tobacco recorded a rate of 4.2 %, while that for the wholesale of household products was approximately 1.4 times as high at 5.9 %, and therefore above the wholesale trade average. Among the NACE classes, the gross operating rate reached 9.7 % for the wholesale of coffee, tea, cocoa and spices (NACE Class 51.37) and was 8.5 % or above for the wholesale of perfume and cosmetics (NACE Class 51.45) and the wholesale of clothing and footwear.

[12] Luxembourg, 2003; Ireland, Greece, Cyprus and Malta, not available.

[10] Luxembourg, 2003; Malta, not available.
[11] Luxembourg, 2003; Ireland, Greece, Cyprus and Malta, not available.

17.4: WHOLESALING OF INTERMEDIATE GOODS

The wholesaling of non-agricultural intermediate products (NACE Group 51.5) (hereafter referred to as wholesaling of intermediate goods) covers the wholesale of all products used as production materials, fuel or other consumables, except for agricultural products (which are treated in Subchapter 17.2). It includes, for example, the wholesaling of fuels, construction materials, hardware and chemical products, as well as the wholesaling of scrap.

STRUCTURAL PROFILE

The EU-27's wholesaling of intermediate goods sector (NACE Group 51.5) consisted of 236 000 enterprises which generated EUR 111.2 billion of value added in 2004, slightly less than one quarter (24.0 %) of the wholesale trade (NACE Division 51) value added. With 2.0 million persons employed, the sector provided about one fifth (20.8 %) of the wholesale trade workforce. Turnover in this sector was valued at EUR 1 182.7 billion. This level of sales was the second highest of the wholesale trade activities, lower only than that of the wholesaling of consumer goods (NACE Groups 51.3 and 51.4), and was equivalent to 30.2 % of the wholesale trade total. Among the seven NACE classes that made up the wholesale of intermediate goods, almost half of the EU-27's turnover, but only one fifth of

the value added was generated by the wholesale of solid, liquid and gaseous fuels and related products (NACE Class 51.51, while the wholesale of wood, construction materials and sanitary equipment (NACE Class 51.53) contributed close to one fifth of the wholesaling of intermediate goods turnover, but more than one quarter of its value added, and two fifths of its workforce.

Among the Member States [13], Germany and the United Kingdom were by far the largest contributors to the EU-27's turnover, value added and employment in intermediate goods wholesaling. However, these two Member States were among the least specialised countries in this activity in terms of their contribution to national non-financial business economy value added and

[13] Luxembourg, 2003; Malta, not available.

Figure 17.9

Wholesale of non-agricultural intermediate products, waste and scrap (NACE Group 51.5) Value added, EU-27, 2004 (million EUR)

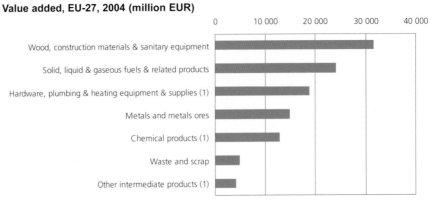

(1) Rounded estimate based on non-confidential data.
Source: Eurostat (SBS)

Table 17.11

Wholesale of non-agricultural intermediate products, waste and scrap (NACE Group 51.5) Structural profile, EU-27, 2004

	No. of enterprises (thousands)	Turnover (EUR million)	Value added (EUR million)	Employment (thousands)
Wholesale of intermediate goods	235.7	1 182 673	111 230	1 988.6
Solid, liquid & gaseous fuels & related products	19.1	531 820	24 175	181.2
Metals and metals ores	16.9	140 781	14 932	208.5
Wood, construction materials & sanitary equipment	102.1	202 369	31 529	797.7
Hardware, plumbing & heating equipment & supplies (1)	36.2	99 108	18 817	404.5
Chemical products (1)	26.0	114 000	13 000	200.0
Other intermediate products (1)	12.6	55 723	4 100	79.5
Waste and scrap	23.0	38 000	4 932	118.0

(1) Rounded estimates based on non-confidential data.
Source: Eurostat (SBS)

Table 17.12

Wholesale of non-agricultural intermediate products, waste and scrap (NACE Group 51.5) Structural profile: ranking of top five Member States, 2004

Rank	Share of EU-27 value added (%) (1)	Share of EU-27 employment (%) (1)	Value added specialisation ratio (EU-27=100) (2)	Employment specialisation ratio (EU-27=100) (2)
1	Germany (19.9)	Germany (15.2)	Latvia (395.7)	Latvia (189.1)
2	United Kingdom (18.8)	United Kingdom (12.6)	Lithuania (207.5)	Lithuania (169.7)
3	France (11.8)	France (11.1)	Estonia (206.1)	Estonia (145.9)
4	Spain (9.8)	Spain (10.9)	Bulgaria (154.0)	Bulgaria (144.4)
5	Italy (9.1)	Italy (9.4)	Belgium (126.0)	Denmark (142.3)

(1) Malta, not available; Luxembourg, 2003.
(2) Ireland, Greece, Cyprus and Malta, not available; Luxembourg, 2003.
Source: Eurostat (SBS)

employment. Indeed, each generated no more than 2.2 % of their non-financial business economy value added in this sector, and no more than 1.5 % of the non-financial business economy workforce was occupied in this sector. In contrast, the Baltic States were the three most specialised Member States [14] in this activity, their intermediate goods wholesaling sectors contributing at least 4.5 % of non-financial business economy value added and at least 2.3 % of employment.

Annualised short-term statistics provide information on the evolution of the turnover index for the wholesale trade of intermediate goods - see Figure 17.10. Looking at the latest 10 year period available for this activity, from 1996 to 2006 the EU-27's index of turnover grew on average by 6.0 % per annum. However, a year on year analysis of the development of the turnover index shows that the wholesale trade of intermediate goods experienced high growth in 1996, almost 10 %, immediately followed by two consecutive years of reductions that reached -5.7 % in 1998. In 1999, the index recovered (3.8 %) and a strong turnover growth occurred in 2000, with an increase of 21.3 % registered for the EU-27. There was a sharp change in fortunes as turnover contracted by 2.1 % in 2001 followed by stagnation in 2002 (-0.1 %). The contraction and relative stagnation experienced in 2001 and 2002 reflected in part the development of output among clients of this sector, namely industrial activities. However, the year 2003 marked the start of an upward development, reinforced in 2004 and 2005 as the EU-27's index of turnover increased by 4.5 %, 10.6 % and 17.0 % respectively. While turnover growth slowed in 2006, it was still substantial at 14.8 %. These growth rates (2003 to 2006 inclusive) were above the corresponding rates for wholesale trade as a whole, which may well reflect in part above average price increases, notably those concerning the wholesaling of fuel which makes up a large part of intermediate goods wholesaling.

[14] Lithuania and Malta, 2002; Greece and Cyprus, not available.

Figure 17.10

Wholesale of non-agricultural intermediate products, waste and scrap (NACE Group 51.5)
Index of turnover, EU-27 (2000=100)

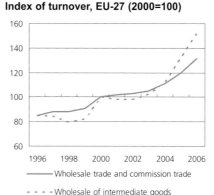

——— Wholesale trade and commission trade

- - - - Wholesale of intermediate goods

Source: Eurostat (STS)

COSTS, PRODUCTIVITY AND PROFITABILITY

The proportion of total expenditure accounted for by purchases of goods and services in the EU-27's intermediate goods wholesaling sector was 94.0 %, the fourth highest proportion across all the non-financial business economy NACE groups in 2004. The wholesale of solid, liquid and gaseous fuels and related products recorded a particularly high share (98.3 %) of this category of expenditure.

Apparent labour productivity was EUR 55 900 per person employed in the EU-27's intermediate goods wholesaling sector, while average personnel costs stood at EUR 30 400 per employee. Those two indicators, resulted in a wage adjusted labour productivity ratio of 184.1 %, well above the wholesale trade ratio (157.6 %) and the non-financial business economy ratio (148.0 %), and the highest of the wholesale trade NACE groups. This ratio was remarkably high in the EU-27's wholesale of solid, liquid and gaseous fuels and related products subsector (402.3 %). Among the Member States [15], the wage adjusted labour productivity ratio was systematically higher for intermediate goods wholesaling than the non-financial business economy average.

The gross operating rate, as measured by the ratio of the gross operating surplus (value added less personnel costs) to turnover, was 4.8 % for the wholesaling of intermediate goods, and although this reached as high as 8.0 % for the wholesale of waste and scrap (NACE Class 51.57) this was still below the non-financial business economy average.

[15] Luxembourg, 2003; Ireland and Greece, not available.

17.5: WHOLESALING OF MACHINERY AND EQUIPMENT

The wholesaling of machinery, equipment and supplies concerns the wholesaling of capital goods and other final durable goods for industrial use, except those covered by motor trade. Wholesaling of installation equipment, as well as electrical and electronic products for industrial use, and the wholesaling of office furniture are all included. In NACE these activities are covered by Group 51.8.

STRUCTURAL PROFILE

Value added in the EU-27's wholesaling of machinery and equipment sector (NACE Group 51.8) was EUR 90.0 billion in 2004, and turnover EUR 600.0 billion. As such, the wholesaling of machinery and equipment represented 19.5 % of wholesale trade (NACE Division 51) value added and 15.3 % of wholesale turnover. The number of persons employed by the 190 000 enterprises with wholesaling of machinery and equipment as their main activity reached 1.6 million persons in the EU-27 in 2004, corresponding to 16.7 % of the wholesale trade workforce. Across the eight NACE classes that make-up the wholesaling of machinery and equipment sector, the miscellaneous category of wholesale of other machinery for use in industry, trade and navigation (NACE Class 51.87) was the largest, accounting for approximately one third

of turnover and two fifths of value added and employment in the EU-27.

Among the Member States [16], the United Kingdom had the largest machinery and equipment wholesaling sector in value added terms, ahead of France, while the latter

[16] Ireland and Luxembourg, 2003; Malta, not available.

contributed the largest proportion to EU-27 turnover and employment. In value added terms, the Netherlands, Belgium, Latvia, as well as the Nordic Member States were all relatively specialised in machinery and equipment wholesaling [17], where these activities contributed at least 2.6 % to the non-financial business economy's value added.

[17] Lithuania and Malta, 2002; Greece and Cyprus, not available.

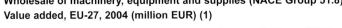

Figure 17.11

Wholesale of machinery, equipment and supplies (NACE Group 51.8)
Value added, EU-27, 2004 (million EUR) (1)

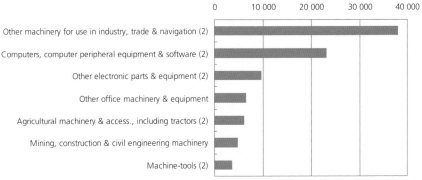

(1) Wholesale of machinery for the textile industry and of sewing and knitting machines, EUR 535 million; the value is too small to be represented in the graph.
(2) Rounded estimate based on non-confidential data.
Source: Eurostat (SBS)

Table 17.13

Wholesale of machinery, equipment and supplies (NACE Group 51.8)
Structural profile, EU-27, 2004 (1)

	No. of enterprises (thousands)	Turnover (EUR million)	Value added (EUR million)	Employment (thousands)
Wholesale of machinery and equipment	190.0	600 000	90 000	1 600.0
Machine-tools	12.2	19 000	3 600	74.0
Mining, construction & civil engineering machinery	8.3	29 096	4 792	78.5
Machinery for the textile industry & of sewing & knitting machines	2.7	2 807	535	12.8
Computers, computer peripheral equipment & software	33.9	198 000	23 200	343.0
Other office machinery & equipment	15.9	39 796	6 512	130.0
Other electronic parts & equipment	14.7	68 100	9 620	153.8
Other machinery for use in industry, trade & navigation	80.0	200 000	38 000	680.0
Agricultural machinery & accessories & implements, including tractors	19.0	43 000	6 200	145.0

(1) Rounded estimates based on non-confidential data.
Source: Eurostat (SBS)

Table 17.14

Wholesale of machinery, equipment and supplies (NACE Group 51.8)
Structural profile: ranking of top five Member States, 2004

Rank	Share of EU-27 value added (%) (1)	Share of EU-27 employment (%) (1)	Value added specialisation ratio (EU-27=100) (2)	Employment specialisation ratio (EU-27=100) (2)
1	United Kingdom (18.9)	France (18.4)	Netherlands (210.1)	Denmark (237.0)
2	France (18.8)	United Kingdom (15.5)	Denmark (193.8)	Netherlands (217.9)
3	Germany (14.2)	Germany (12.2)	Belgium (176.4)	Belgium (194.0)
4	Spain (9.9)	Spain (11.6)	Sweden (160.9)	Sweden (187.3)
5	Netherlands (9.6)	Netherlands (8.0)	Latvia (149.2)	Finland (171.6)

(1) Malta, not available; Ireland and Luxembourg, 2003.
(2) Ireland, Greece, Cyprus and Malta, not available; Luxembourg, 2003.
Source: Eurostat (SBS)

According to annualised short-term statistics, the development over the period 1996-2006 of the turnover index in the EU-27's machinery and equipment wholesaling sector was in contrast with the uninterrupted upward path experienced by the index for wholesale trade as a whole. Indeed, after having decreased by 2.0 % in 1996, the index for machinery and equipment wholesaling grew by at least 3.7 % each year from 1997 to 2000, after which there were three years of contraction with sales falling on average by 1.9 % per annum. In the three following years, from 2004 to 2006, there was renewed turnover growth, as the index increased on average by 6.5 % per annum. The latest year on year growth rate recorded by the index of turnover was 8.1 % in 2006, therefore 1.7 percentage points below the growth rate recorded for wholesale trade as a whole.

Figure 17.12
Wholesale of machinery, equipment and supplies (NACE Group 51.8)
Index of turnover, EU-27 (2000=100)

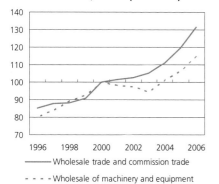

———— Wholesale trade and commission trade

- - - - Wholesale of machinery and equipment

Source: Eurostat (STS)

COSTS, PRODUCTIVITY AND PROFITABILITY

The EU-27's machinery and equipment wholesaling sector had the lowest share of purchases of goods and services in total expenditure (88.2 %) across all the wholesale trade activities presented in Subchapters 17.1 to 17.6, while its share of expenditure dedicated to personnel costs was the highest (10.4 %), the remaining 1.4 % of the total concerning gross investment in tangible goods.

Apparent labour productivity in the EU-27's machinery and equipment wholesaling sector was EUR 56 300 per person employed in 2004, while average personnel costs were EUR 40 000 per employee and 92.9 % of persons employed in the sector were paid employees.

The resulting ratio of wage adjusted labour productivity for EU-27 machinery and equipment wholesaling (140.0 %) was the lowest of the wholesale trade NACE groups, standing below the ratio for the non-financial business economy average (148.0 %) as well. However, in half of the Member States the machinery and equipment wholesaling sector [18] recorded a wage adjusted labour productivity ratio above the national non-financial business economy average.

---

[18] Luxembourg, 2003; Ireland, Greece, Cyprus and Malta, not available.

Among the eight NACE classes that make up the wholesaling of machinery and equipment sector, the wholesale of mining, construction and civil engineering machinery (NACE Class 51.82) had the highest ratio of wage adjusted labour productivity (156.1 %), while the wholesale of computers, computer peripheral equipment and software (NACE Class 51.84) recorded the lowest ratio (133.0 %). Profitability in the EU-27's machinery and equipment wholesaling sector, as measured here by the gross operating rate was 5.2 %, about half the rate for the non-financial business economy average (11.0 %). Among the eight NACE classes, gross operating rates were ranged from 3.4 % for computers, computer peripheral equipment and software to 8.8 % for machinery for the textile industry and of sewing and knitting machines.

17.6: OTHER WHOLESALE TRADE

The other wholesale trade sector covers specialised own-account wholesaling of products not covered in Subchapters 17.2 to 17.5, as well as non-specialised wholesaling, where enterprises resell a variety of products. These activities are covered by NACE Group 51.9.

STRUCTURAL PROFILE

Turnover in the EU-27's other wholesale trade (NACE Group 51.9) sector in 2004 was EUR 183.5 billion, therefore contributing 4.7 % of wholesale trade turnover. According to this measure, this was the second smallest wholesale trade NACE group. There were 669 800 persons employed in total in the 119 000 enterprises that make up the other wholesale trade sector in the EU-27 in 2004, equivalent to 7.0 % of the wholesale trade workforce. The other wholesale trade sector generated EUR 23.5 billion of value added and contributed 5.1 % of the wholesale trade total. The United Kingdom had the largest other wholesale trade sector among the Member States [19], accounting for more than a quarter (27.3 %) of the EU-27's value added, followed by Poland and Germany, both contributing less than one fifth of the sectoral total. In value added terms Poland was indeed the most specialised Member State in that the share of other wholesale trade (4.4 %) in the national non-financial business economy was 9.5 times as high as the corresponding average in the EU-27. Slovakia, Slovenia and Estonia were also relatively specialised, while Spain was the least specialised.

[19] Luxembourg, 2003; the Czech Republic and Malta, not available.

Annualised short-term statistics are available for the other wholesale trade turnover index from 2000 to 2006 and showed an uninterrupted upward trend. The index grew at a faster pace for these activities than for the wholesale trade average in the years 2001, 2002 and 2004. However, a period of relative stagnation of the turnover occurred in 2003 and 2005, while the latest figure available reflected a recovery for this sector, with growth of 7.1 % recorded in 2006 (compared with the previous year).

COSTS, PRODUCTIVITY AND PROFITABILITY

Unsurprisingly for a wholesale trade activity, a breakdown of total expenditure of the EU-27's other wholesale trade sector into the three main components shows that a high percentage (92.2 %) of the total is generated by the purchases of goods and services. Personnel costs constituted 6.4 % of that total and gross investment in tangible goods the remaining 1.4 %. Both apparent labour productivity (EUR 35 100 per person employed) and average personnel costs (EUR 19 400 per employee) were clearly the lowest among the wholesale trade subsectors, well below the non-financial business economy average. The latter more so. As a result, the EU-27's other wholesale trade sector had a wage adjusted labour productivity ratio of 180.5 %, 32.5 percentage points above the non-financial business economy ratio, and the second highest of the wholesale NACE groups. The ratio of the gross operating surplus to turnover was 6.7 % in the EU-27, also the second highest across the wholesale trade NACE groups.

Figure 17.13

Other wholesale (NACE Group 51.9)
Index of turnover, EU-27 (2000=100)

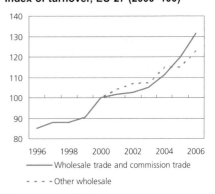

Source: Eurostat (STS)

Table 17.15

Other wholesale (NACE Group 51.9)
Structural profile: ranking of top five Member States, 2004

Rank	Share of EU-27 value added (%) (1)	Share of EU-27 employment (%) (1)	Value added specialisation ratio (EU-27=100) (2)	Employment specialisation ratio (EU-27=100) (2)
1	United Kingdom (27.3)	Poland (34.7)	Poland (950.9)	Poland (578.8)
2	Poland (19.5)	United Kingdom (15.6)	Slovakia (459.4)	Estonia (439.7)
3	Germany (18.3)	Germany (10.8)	Slovenia (349.7)	Slovakia (400.6)
4	Netherlands (5.7)	Romania (4.2)	Estonia (327.0)	Slovenia (242.6)
5	Italy (4.7)	Netherlands (3.8)	Romania (294.6)	Hungary (157.3)

(1) Czech Republic and Malta, not available; Luxembourg, 2003.
(2) Czech Republic, Ireland, Greece, Cyprus and Malta, not available; Luxembourg, 2003.
Source: Eurostat (SBS)

Table 17.16

Wholesale trade and commission trade (NACE Division 51)
Main indicators, 2004

	EU-27	BE	BG	CZ	DK	DE	EE	IE	EL	ES	FR	IT	CY	LV	LT
No. of enterprises (thousands)	1 682.2	43.0	23.1	61.6	16.1	93.5	7.9	7.2	75.6	201.8	183.3	406.8	2.3	6.5	6.6
Turnover (EUR million)	3 916 076	174 864	16 602	48 297	90 999	656 119	6 752	46 134	65 278	344 566	582 277	403 195	3 889	7 601	7 771
Production (EUR million)	1 087 729	49 606	2 376	11 158	31 748	139 850	1 465	10 106	18 590	81 090	157 045	202 515	939	1 698	1 785
Value added (EUR million)	462 707	16 217	744	4 950	11 445	78 514	672	5 683	11 824	44 125	62 382	48 573	623	986	827
Gross operating surplus (EUR million)	210 477	6 823	475	2 861	3 945	34 799	380	2 994	7 300	19 165	18 461	28 861	263	754	463
Purchases of goods & services (EUR million)	3 426 411	156 388	16 285	44 191	70 856	580 234	6 219	40 685	55 171	305 013	517 485	345 712	3 283	6 857	7 133
Personnel costs (EUR million)	252 229	9 394	268	2 089	7 500	43 787	292	2 689	4 524	24 960	43 922	19 712	361	231	365
Investment in tangible goods (EUR million)	47 995	2 106	453	688	1 306	4 242	152	607	2 038	6 948	5 305	6 444	87	241	194
Employment (thousands)	9 554	233	142	237	164	1 208	39	79	312	1 120	1 056	1 076	18	52	71
Apparent labour prod. (EUR thousand)	48.4	69.6	5.2	20.9	69.6	65.0	17.4	71.7	37.9	39.4	59.1	45.1	34.2	18.9	11.7
Average personnel costs (EUR thousand)	30.7	50.3	2.2	11.4	46.9	39.2	8.1	36.6	20.7	25.5	42.1	33.6	20.0	4.6	5.3
Wage adjusted labour productivity (%)	157.6	138.2	238.1	183.0	148.5	165.7	215.4	196.0	182.8	154.7	140.2	134.1	170.4	411.4	220.6
Gross operating rate (%)	5.4	3.9	2.9	5.9	4.3	5.3	5.6	6.5	11.2	5.6	3.2	7.2	6.8	9.9	6.0
Investment / employment (EUR thousand)	5.0	9.0	3.2	2.9	7.9	3.5	3.9	7.7	6.5	6.2	5.0	6.0	4.8	4.6	2.7

	LU (1)	HU	MT	NL	AT	PL	PT	RO	SI	SK	FI	SE	UK	NO
No. of enterprises (thousands)	3.2	33.1	:	57.9	25.6	123.2	59.6	51.7	11.3	8.4	15.1	43.6	111.0	18.5
Turnover (EUR million)	10 827	35 597	:	280 314	94 009	111 303	63 478	27 187	8 902	12 363	50 825	97 397	666 024	65 151
Production (EUR million)	1 699	6 892	:	61 183	27 020	49 531	15 940	5 917	2 623	3 392	12 097	26 566	164 158	18 921
Value added (EUR million)	915	3 051	:	30 570	12 120	11 472	7 663	2 061	1 295	1 458	5 841	14 206	83 996	7 859
Gross operating surplus (EUR million)	395	1 481	:	13 483	4 784	7 719	3 216	1 275	627	872	2 343	4 608	41 991	2 768
Purchases of goods & services (EUR million)	9 931	32 536	:	250 189	79 042	101 711	56 467	25 831	7 709	11 006	46 393	84 318	562 616	55 276
Personnel costs (EUR million)	520	1 570	:	17 087	7 335	3 753	4 447	785	668	586	3 498	9 598	42 005	5 092
Investment in tangible goods (EUR million)	85	763	:	2 168	1 140	1 507	1 678	1 283	194	383	521	1 186	6 245	603
Employment (thousands)	14	169	:	469	193	679	274	311	42	79	82	220	1 201	105
Apparent labour prod. (EUR thousand)	65.9	18.1	:	65.2	62.9	16.9	28.0	6.6	30.7	18.6	71.0	64.4	69.9	75.0
Average personnel costs (EUR thousand)	40.8	9.9	:	39.9	42.1	7.2	17.6	2.6	17.9	7.6	43.9	49.0	37.5	50.8
Wage adjusted labour productivity (%)	161.5	183.6	:	163.5	149.5	233.8	159.2	251.6	171.5	242.7	161.6	131.5	186.6	147.5
Gross operating rate (%)	3.7	4.2	:	4.8	5.1	6.9	5.1	4.7	7.0	7.1	4.6	4.7	6.3	4.2
Investment / employment (EUR thousand)	6.1	4.5	:	4.6	5.9	2.2	6.1	4.1	4.6	4.9	6.3	5.4	5.2	5.7

(1) 2003.
Source: Eurostat (SBS)

Retail trade and repair

In this chapter, a first distinction is made between non-specialised in-store retailers (Subchapter 18.1) and specialised in-store retailers; with the latter further split between food (Subchapter 18.2) and non-food retailers (Subchapter 18.3). In addition, a separate analysis is dedicated to the activity of second-hand goods retailing (Subchapter 18.4), as well as to retailing not in stores (Subchapter 18.5). The last subchapter covers the repair of personal and household goods (Subchapter 18.6).

While the structure of in-store retailing closely follows the NACE classification, the distinction between food and non-food retailing is of analytical interest, and for this reason Subchapter 18.2 contains a special analysis (see Box 18.2) focused on food retailing, contrasting specialised and non-specialised food retailers, while in Subchapter 18.3 there is a similar analysis (see Box 18.3) for non-food items.

Retail trade services are covered by the Directive of the European Parliament and of the Council of 12 December 2006 [1] on services in the internal market, dealing with the right of establishment and the freedom to provide services in a genuine internal market, by removing legal and administrative barriers to the development of service activities between Member States, facilitating the provision and use of cross-border services in the EU.

Retail trade provides an interface between producers and consumers. Typically, one or several distributors intervene before a product which leaves the factory gate reaches the final consumer, the last of which is a retailer. Retailers represent the largest proportion of enterprises within distributive trades (NACE Section G) activities, accounting for slightly over 60 % of all distribution enterprises in the EU-27 in 2004.

Since the development of the Internet, there has been an increasing use of commerce via the web. As such, there has been a gradual shift from traditional methods of purchasing from stores or markets to purchasing remotely. According to Eurostat's information society statistics, some 10 % of the turnover of distributive trades (including motor trades (NACE Division 50) and wholesale trades (NACE Division 51), as well as retail trade and repair) enterprises with ten or more persons employed was derived from e-commerce in 2006. According to the same source 20 % of the EU-27's population ordered or bought goods or services for private use through the Internet in 2006 (during the three months preceding the survey). Note that these figures refer to goods and services supplied to individuals by all sectors of the economy, not just enterprises that are specialised in retail sales.

Division 52 of NACE covers retail trade as well as the repair of personal and household goods (hereafter referred to as retail trade and repair); the retail trade of motor vehicles and motorcycles is covered by NACE Division 50 (see Chapter 16). The activity of retailing covers the resale without transformation of new and used goods to the general public for personal or household use and consumption; note that the renting and hiring of personal and household goods to the public is excluded.

NACE
52:    retail trade, except of motor vehicles and motorcycles; repair of personal and household goods;
52.1: retail sale in non-specialised stores;
52.2: retail sale of food, beverages and tobacco in specialised stores;
52.3: retail sale of pharmaceuticals and medical goods, cosmetic and toilet articles;
52.4: other retail sale of new goods in specialised stores;
52.5: retail sale of second-hand goods in stores;
52.6: retail sale not in stores;
52.7: repair of personal and household goods.

---

[1] Directive 2006/123/EC.

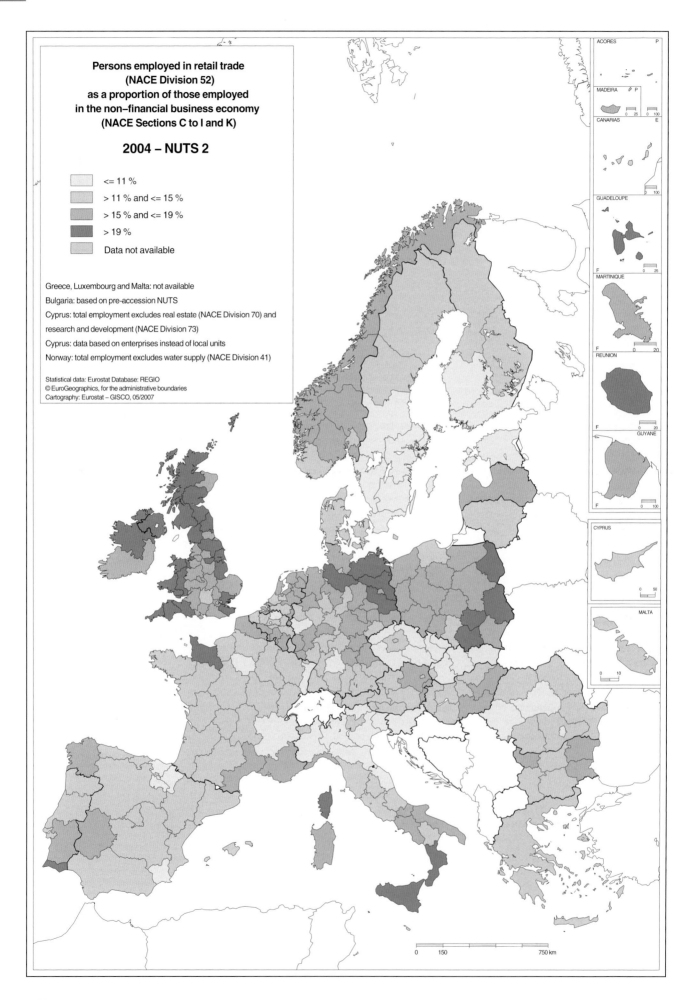

**Persons employed in retail trade
(NACE Division 52)
as a proportion of those employed
in the non–financial business economy
(NACE Sections C to I and K)**

2004 – NUTS 2

<= 11 %

> 11 % and <= 15 %

> 15 % and <= 19 %

> 19 %

Data not available

Greece, Luxembourg and Malta: not available

Bulgaria: based on pre-accession NUTS

Cyprus: total employment excludes real estate (NACE Division 70) and

research and development (NACE Division 73)

Cyprus: data based on enterprises instead of local units

Norway: total employment excludes water supply (NACE Division 41)

Statistical data: Eurostat Database: REGIO
© EuroGeographics, for the administrative boundaries
Cartography: Eurostat – GISCO, 05/2007

In terms of technology, developments in Electronic Data Interchange (EDI) have provided retailers the possibility to ensure that information on orders, schedules and invoices need only to be entered once into their information systems and information can flow rapidly and accurately down the supply chain to all of the parties involved in the delivery of a product to market. A widespread implementation and use of EDI in retail trade might lead to a cut in some operating costs (as the number of intermediaries may be reduced) and an increase in quality.

Figure 18.1

Retail trade (NACE Groups 52.1 to 52.6)
Breakdown of sectoral turnover, 2004 (%)

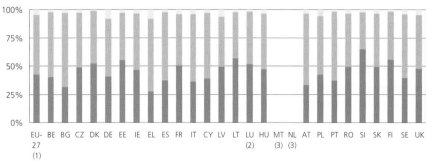

■ Non-specialised in-store retailing   ■ Specialised in-store retailing   Retailing not in stores

(1) 2003, including rounded estimates based on non-confidential data for NACE Group 52.1 and NACE Groups 52.3 and 52.4.
(2) 2002.
(3) Not available.
Source: Eurostat (SBS)

Box 18.1: focus on retail trade turnover

Figure 18.1 shows the breakdown of retail trade turnover (NACE Groups 52.1 to 52.6) between specialised (NACE Groups 52.2 to 52.5) and non-specialised in-store retailing (NACE group 52.1) as well as retailing not in-stores (NACE Group 52.6) for the year 2004 (2003 for EU-27).

Specialised in-store retailing was predominant in EU-27 retailing (2003), generating 53.0 % of retail trade turnover, some 10.7 percentage points more than the share of non-specialised in-store retailing. In 14 of the 25 Member States [2] with data available at least 50 % of their retail trade turnover was generated by specialised in-store retailers, while non-specialised in-store retailers generated 50 % or more of retail trade turnover in nine Member States. The highest share for specialised in-store retailers was 65.2 % in Bulgaria, while many other southern Member States, as well as Austria, also had a majority of their turnover accounted for by specialised in-store retailers. The highest proportion of turnover generated by non-specialised in-store retailers was recorded in Slovenia (65.1 %).

Retailing not in-stores represented 4.6 % of the EU-27's retail trade turnover. In Germany, this proportion reached 8.2 % (where mail order sales were particularly high) while the lowest share was 1.2 % in Denmark.

[2] Luxembourg, 2003; Malta and the Netherlands, not available.

STRUCTURAL PROFILE

In 2004, value added generated by the 3.7 million enterprises that make up the retail trade and repair sector (NACE Division 52) in the EU-27 was EUR 384.4 billion, from a turnover of EUR 2.0 trillion. Some 17.0 million persons were employed in these activities in the EU-27. The retail trade and repair sector accounted for 7.5 % of the non-financial business economy (NACE Sections C to I and K) value added, while it accounted for a larger part in terms of turnover (10.7 %). Moreover, the sector engaged 13.6 % of the non-financial business economy workforce. Compared with the other two distributive trade sectors, namely motor trades (NACE Division 50, see Chapter 16) and wholesale trade (NACE Division 51, see Chapter 17), retail trade and repair was the second largest sector in terms of value added and employment, while it was the largest in terms of employment, underlining the low apparent labour productivity (value added per person employed) associated with these activities.

Based on an analysis at the level of the activities presented in Subchapters 18.1 to 18.6, specialised in-store new goods retailing other than food (NACE Groups 52.3 and 52.4) and non-specialised in-store retailing (NACE Group 52.1) were the largest activities, using the measures of turnover, value added and employment: specialised in-store new goods retailing other than food alone generated about half of the output of the EU-27's retail trade and repair services sector (44.2 % of turnover and 52.0 % of value added) and employed half of the sectoral workforce.

With EUR 82.4 billion value added, the United Kingdom was the largest contributor to the EU-27's retail trade and repair sector in 2004, followed by Germany (EUR 71.1 billion). Moreover, the United Kingdom's retail trade and repair sector employed 3.2 million persons, therefore 600 000 persons above the level recorded in Germany. Italy and France had very similar levels of employment in retail trade and repair, respectively 1.8 million and 1.7 million persons employed. As a share of the non-financial business economy value added total, the retail trade and repair sector was the largest [3] in France (8.8 % of the national total), the United Kingdom and Portugal (both 8.5 %), Latvia and Spain (both 8.0 %), all above the EU-27 average (7.5 %). In terms of turnover, the retail trade and repair sector accounted for a significant part of the national non-financial business economy in two of the Baltic countries (12.8 % in Latvia and 12.2 % in Lithuania), in France (12.3 %) and the United Kingdom (12.1 %). The sector contributed also in relatively high proportions to the national non-financial business economy employment, particularly in the United Kingdom (17.7 %), Latvia (16.7 %), Poland (16.0 %) and the Netherlands (15.3 %). It should be noted that these high contributions of retail trade and repair employment to the non-financial business economy total are affected by the high importance of part-time employment in this sector (see below).

[3] Luxembourg, 2003; Ireland, Greece, Cyprus and Malta, not available.

Table 18.1

Retail trade and repair of personal and household goods (NACE Division 52)
Structural profile, EU-27, 2004

	No. of enterprises		Turnover		Value added		Employment	
	(thousands)	(% of total)	(EUR million)	(% of total)	(EUR million)	(% of total)	(thousands)	(% of total)
Retail trade and repair of personal and household goods	3 735.0	100.0	2 038 052	100.0	384 355	100.0	16 970.0	100.0
Non-specialised in-store retailing (1)	593.8	15.9	872 704	42.8	127 674	33.2	6 031.4	35.5
Specialised in-store food retailing	513.0	13.7	122 843	6.0	26 099	6.8	1 452.6	8.6
Specialised in-store new goods retailing other than food	1 921.2	51.4	900 000	44.2	200 000	52.0	8 164.8	48.1
Second-hand goods retailing in stores	63.2	1.7	7 317	0.4	2 009	0.5	113.3	0.7
Retailing not in stores	512.4	13.7	94 603	4.6	18 930	4.9	939.7	5.5
Repair of personal & household goods	131.4	3.5	11 703	0.6	4 957	1.3	268.1	1.6

(1) Turnover and value added, estimate based on the sum of data for the NACE Classes.
Source: Eurostat (SBS)

Table 18.2

Retail trade and repair of personal and household goods (NACE Division 52)
Structural profile: ranking of top five Member States, 2004

Rank	Value added (EUR million) (1)	Employment (thousands) (1)	Share of non-financial business economy			
			No. of enterprises (2)	Turnover (2)	Value added (2)	Employment (2)
1	United Kingdom (82 371)	United Kingdom (3 176.1)	Bulgaria (39.0 %)	Latvia (12.8 %)	France (8.8 %)	United Kingdom (17.7 %)
2	Germany (71 080)	Germany (2 590.1)	Romania (33.6 %)	France (12.3 %)	United Kingdom (8.5 %)	Latvia (16.7 %)
3	France (62 898)	Italy (1 780.2)	Poland (28.3 %)	Lithuania (12.2 %)	Portugal (8.5 %)	Poland (16.0 %)
4	Italy (40 308)	France (1 736.2)	Portugal (24.9 %)	United Kingdom (12.1 %)	Latvia (8.0 %)	Netherlands (15.3 %)
5	Spain (36 547)	Spain (1 697.7)	Lithuania (24.2 %)	Portugal (11.8 %)	Spain (8.0 %)	Bulgaria (14.2 %)

(1) Malta, not available; Luxembourg, 2003.
(2) Ireland, Greece, Cyprus and Malta, not available; Luxembourg, 2003.
Source: Eurostat (SBS)

The average turnover per enterprise in the EU-27 varied greatly between the various parts of the sector in 2004, from a low of EUR 89 100 in repair of personal and household goods and EUR 115 700 in second-hand goods retailing in stores (NACE Group 52.5) to EUR 1 350 700 for non-specialised in-store retailing (2003). Bulgaria had the smallest average enterprise size (in turnover terms) in all but one of the retail trade activities, while according to the same measure Luxembourg recorded considerably larger enterprises in non-specialised in-store retailing than the average in the EU-27.

The specialisation in each region (in some cases the whole country is treated as one region) can be seen from the map on page 302 which shows the retail trade and repair employment as a share of the non-financial business economy. Even in the regions with the highest share of non-financial business economy employment concentrated in the retail trade and repair sector (around 22 % to 24 % in several regions of the United Kingdom), this share was only around 4 times higher than in the regions with the lowest share (around 5 % to 8 % in several regions in Slovakia), a much lower range than for most of the activities shown in the maps in the other chapters.

Figure 18.2

Retail trade and repair of personal and household goods (NACE Division 52)
Breakdown of sectoral value added and employment, EU-27, 2004 (%) (1)

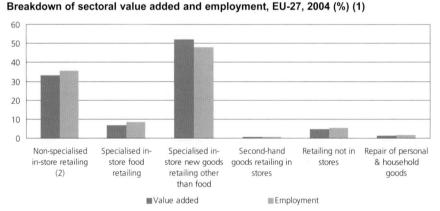

(1) Rounded estimate based on non-confidential data.
(2) Value added, estimate based on the sum of data for the NACE classes.
Source: Eurostat (SBS)

Figure 18.3 _____

Retail trade and repair of personal and household goods (NACE Division 52)
Volume of sales index, EU-27 (2000=100)

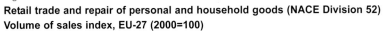

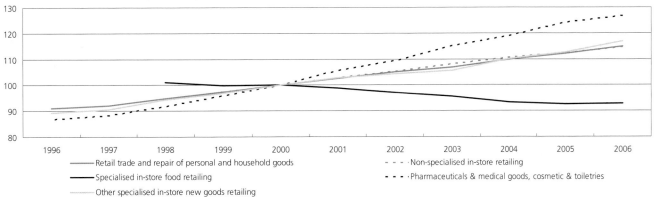

Source: Eurostat (STS)

Annual short-term statistics on the volume of sales, turnover and employment for the retail trade and repair sector are available for the period 1996 to 2006. The index of the volume of retail sales is the retail trade turnover index deflated by appropriate price indices to remove the effect of price changes. The EU-27's volume of sales index for retail trade and repair rose every year between 1996 and 2006, with a modest rate of development in 1996 and 1997, after which the pace of growth was recorded at a faster rhythm, with year on year growth rates ranged between 1.7 % and 3.0 %. In 2006, sales went up by 2.4 % compared to the previous year. At a more detailed level, among the seven NACE groups that make up the retail trade and repair sector, the EU-27's volume of sales index is available for the NACE Groups 52.1 to 52.4. All of these four groups had positive developments for their sales between 2005 and 2006, with growth rates between 2.0 % and 4.0 % for three of the four activities (NACE groups), with the most rapid gains recorded for other retail sale of new goods in specialised stores (NACE Group 52.4). However, the index remained virtually unchanged (0.3 % growth) in specialised in-store food retailing (NACE Group 52.2). Over a longer period, from 2001 to 2006, sales went up on average by 2.2 % per annum for non-specialised in-store retailing, by 2.6 % per annum for other retail sale of new goods in specialised stores, by 3.7 % per annum for the retail sale of pharmaceutical and medical goods, cosmetic and toilet articles, and these rates contrasted with a contraction of sales for specialised in-store food retailing (an average of -1.2 % per annum), which might be explained by consumers opting to shop through other retail formats, for example, non-specialised stores or markets.

The index of employment followed a similar path to that for the volume of sales, with EU-27 growth rates for retail trade and repair between 1.3 % and 2.5 % each year during the period 1997 to 2006, while a slight contraction was recorded in 2006. A peak in the growth of the annualised employment index was reached in the middle of the period considered, as annual growth was 2.5 % in 2001.

A size class analysis for the EU-27's retail trade and repair sector for 2004 shows that small and medium-sized enterprises (SMEs) (with less than 250 persons employed) generated 57.3 % of retail trade and repair value added, the remaining part of sectoral value added being generated by large enterprises (with 250 or more persons employed). This share recorded by SMEs was smaller than the average for distributive trades (12.6 percentage point lower), while it was very similar to the average for non-financial business economy. However, the contribution of micro enterprises (with less than 10 persons employed) to retail trade and repair value added (32.8 %) was well above the distributive trades and the non-financial business economy averages. As a result, the contribution of small enterprises (with 10 to 49 persons employed) and medium-sized enterprises (with 50 to 249 persons employed) to retail trade and repair value added was particularly low; in the case of medium-sized enterprises it was less than half the average for the non-financial business economy. In 10 of the 13 Member States [4] for which data is available, the share of SMEs in retail trade and repair value added was higher than the equivalent share for the non-financial business economy.

_____
[4] Bulgaria and Germany, 2003; Belgium, Denmark, Estonia, Ireland, Greece, Cyprus, Latvia, Lithuania, Luxembourg, Malta, Austria, Portugal, Slovenia and Finland, not available.

Figure 18.4 _____

Retail trade and repair of personal and household goods (NACE Division 52) Evolution of main indicators, EU-27 (2000=100)

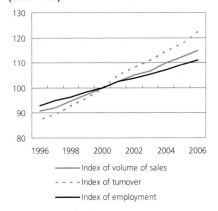

Source: Eurostat (STS)

Figure 18.5 _____

Retail trade and repair of personal and household goods (NACE Division 52) Share of value added by enterprise size class, EU-27, 2004

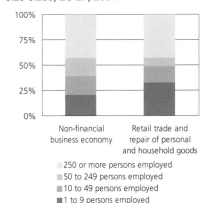

Source: Eurostat (SBS)

Figure 18.6

Retail trade and repair of personal and household goods (NACE Division 52)
Labour force characteristics, EU-27, 2006

By gender

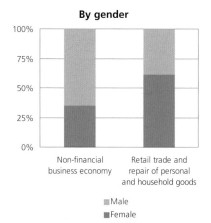

By working time

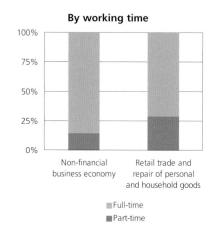

By age

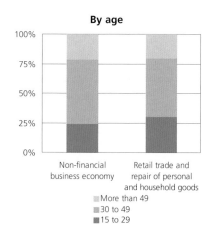

Source: Eurostat (LFS)

EMPLOYMENT CHARACTERISTICS
According to results from the Labour Force Survey, the EU-27's retail trade and repair workforce had a relatively high proportion of women (61.7 %) employed in the sector in 2006, compared with the other two distributive trade sectors (women did not represent more than one third of the workforce for motor trades and wholesale trade). The female workforce in the retail trade and repair sector was also considerably more important than for the non-financial business economy (35.0 %) as a whole. Indeed, the retail trade and repair workforce had the second highest proportion of women in its workforce among all of the NACE divisions that make up the non-financial business economy, just after clothing activities (NACE Division 18, see Subchapter 3.2). The female share of retail trade and repair employment was systematically higher than the average recorded for the non-financial business economy in each of the Member States [5], at least 1.5 times as high in Cyprus, Bulgaria, Slovenia, Romania and Portugal and over two times as high in Poland and Luxembourg.

[5] Luxembourg, 2005.

There was also a high incidence of part-time work (29.0 % of the workforce) in the EU-27's retail trade and repair sector in 2006, when compared with the other two distributive trades sectors where this share stood around 10 %, and also when compared with the non-financial business economy average (14.4 %). The proportion of part-time employment in retail trade and repair activities was the highest among all of the NACE divisions [6] that constitute the non-financial business economy. In relative terms, high part-time employment in this sector was particularly evident in the Nordic Member States, the United Kingdom and Slovakia, where the part-time employment rate was 2.1 times or more the national non-financial business economy average.

There was a relatively high number of young persons employed in the EU-27's retail trade and repair workforce in 2006, as 30.4 % of those employed were aged between 15 and 29, compared with the 24.2 % average for the non-financial business economy. Again this share was higher than the corresponding proportions recorded for the other two distributive trades sectors, while the difference with the motor trades sector share was less evident than for the wholesale trade sector. The retail trade and repair sector reported the second highest share of younger workers among all the NACE divisions of the non-financial business economy [7], just below the share recorded for hotels and restaurants.

[6] NACE Division 12, not available.
[7] NACE Divisions 12, 13 and 13 not available.

With a share of paid employees in persons employed at 78.5 % in 2004 according to structural business statistics, the retail trade and repair sector posted the second highest proportion of self-employed and unpaid family workers of all the non-financial business economy NACE divisions, just after real estate activities (NACE Division 70).

COSTS, PRODUCTIVITY AND PROFITABILITY
Typically for a distributive trade activity, the level of gross investment in tangible goods relative to total expenditure was low in the retail trade and repair sector, at just 2.8 % in the EU-27, in 2004. This was about half the average recorded for the non-financial business economy, although higher than the equivalent ratios for motor trades or wholesale trade. This low share of gross investment reflects the high level of operating expenditure associated with distributive trades activities, boosted by high expenditure on goods purchased for resale in the same condition. An analysis of operating expenditure confirms that purchases of goods and services accounted for 85.1 % of total expenditure in the EU-27's retail trade and repair sector (somewhat below the corresponding ratios for motor trades or wholesale trade). The share of personnel costs within total expenditure in the retail trade and repair sector was 12.1 %, therefore 4.3 percentage points below the non-financial business economy ratio, while well above the equivalent figures for the other two distributive trade sectors. However, note that an analysis of personnel costs only reflects the cost of paid employees, and that the proportion of paid employees in the total number of persons employed within the retail trade and repair sector was relatively low in 2004, both compared with the other two distributive trade sectors and the non-financial business economy average.

Table 18.3

Retail trade and repair of personal and household goods (NACE Division 52)
Total expenditure, EU-27, 2004

	Value (EUR million)				Share (% of total expenditure)			
	Total expenditure	Purchases of goods and services	Personnel costs	Investment in tangible goods	Purchases of goods and services	Personnel costs	Investment in tangible goods
Retail trade and repair of personal and household goods	1 938 548	1 650 471	233 896	54 181	85.1	12.1	2.8
Non-specialised in-store retailing (1)	:	:	90 000	26 464	:	:	:
Specialised in-store food retailing (1)	111 163	96 525	12 078	2 560	86.8	10.9	2.3
Specialised in-store new goods retailing other than food (1)	843 000	700 000	120 000	23 000	83.0	14.2	2.7
Second-hand goods retailing in stores	6 423	5 335	910	179	83.1	14.2	2.8
Retailing not in stores	87 894	76 459	9 722	1 713	87.0	11.1	1.9
Repair of personal & household goods (1)	9 483	6 700	2 471	312	70.7	26.1	3.3

(1) Rounded estimates based on non-confidential data.
Source: Eurostat (SBS)

Table 18.4

Retail trade and repair of personal and household goods (NACE Division 52)
Productivity and profitability, EU-27, 2004

	Apparent labour productivity (EUR thousand)	Average personnel costs (EUR thousand)	Wage adjusted labour productivity (%)	Gross operating rate (%)
Retail trade and repair of personal and household goods	22.6	17.6	129.0	7.4
Non-specialised in-store retailing (1)	21.2	16.0	130.0	4.5
Specialised in-store food retailing	18.0	13.7	131.5	11.4
Specialised in-store new goods retailing other than food (1)	24.0	20.0	132.0	9.1
Second-hand goods retailing in stores	17.7	15.5	114.4	15.0
Retailing not in stores	20.1	21.0	96.1	9.7
Repair of personal & household goods	18.5	17.4	106.2	21.2

(1) Rounded estimates based on non-confidential data.
Source: Eurostat (SBS)

Apparent labour productivity in the retail trade and repair sector was EUR 22 600 in 2004 and average personnel costs were EUR 17 600 per employee in the same year. However, care should be taken when comparing these ratios based on simple head counts across Member States or activities because of the high incidence of part-time employment in the retail trade and repair sector. The resulting wage adjusted labour productivity ratio, which takes into account the share of employees in persons employed, was 129.0 % for the EU-27's retail trade and repair sector in 2004. For comparison, the ratio was above 150 % in the other two distributive trades sectors and was 148.0 % in the non-financial business economy as a whole. In the same year and among the Member States with available data [8], only France and Luxembourg (2003) recorded a wage adjusted labour productivity ratio for their retail trade and repair sector above that for their non-financial business economy. Profitability for the EU-27's retail trade and

repair sector, here measured by the gross operating rate, was 7.4 %, above the other two distributive trades sectors. Nevertheless this was below the average rate for the non-financial business economy (11.0 %), influenced as for all distributive activities by the high levels of turnover.

[8] Luxembourg, 2003; Ireland, Greece, Cyprus and Malta, not available.

Figure 18.7

Retail trade and repair of personal and household goods (NACE Division 52)
Productivity and profitability characteristics relative to national averages, 2004
(non-financial business economy=100) (1)

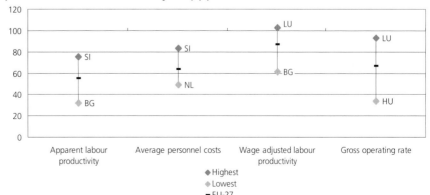

(1) Ireland, Greece, Cyprus and Malta, not available; Luxembourg, 2003.
Source: Eurostat (SBS)

18.1: NON-SPECIALISED IN-STORE RETAILING

This subchapter covers retail sales in non-specialised stores, either with food, beverages and tobacco predominating (NACE Class 52.11) or with non-food products predominating (NACE Class 52.12). The latter NACE class principally includes department stores that stock a general line of merchandise. Together, these activities are referred to as non-specialised in-store retailing within this subchapter.

Non-specialised retailers offer consumers the opportunity to buy a broader range of products at a sole point of purchase (for example, supermarkets, hypermarkets or convenience stores). Large, non-specialised food retailers, in particular, may have greater price flexibility, as they are able to accept lower margins on certain products, as well as exerting greater purchasing power on their suppliers; furthermore, they may have their own integrated wholesale activities. While the number of pan-European brands has increased significantly and consumers can find some of them in a wide range of Member States, it is important to bear in mind that food retailers also work with local suppliers, often reflecting local supply as well as social and cultural characteristics, all of which influence the choice of food and beverages that are available within a particular region.

STRUCTURAL PROFILE

The EU-27's non-specialised in-store retailing sector (NACE Group 52.1) consisted of 594 000 enterprises in 2004 which generated EUR 872.7 billion of turnover and EUR 127.7 billion of value added while employing 6.0 million persons. As such, the EU-27's non-specialised in-store retailing sector accounted for 42.8 % of the turnover and 33.2 % of the value added created by retail trade and repair (NACE Division 52) in 2004. Some 35.5 % of the retail trade and repair workforce was concentrated in this sector.

Turning to the two NACE classes that make up the sector, the wealth generated within non-specialised in-store retailing mainly came from retailers with food, beverages or tobacco predominating (NACE Class 52.11), with EUR 772.7 billion turnover and EUR 105.7 billion value added recorded in 2004. This subsector was dominant in all of the Member States for which data are available [9], frequently generating more than four fifths of sectoral turnover, and only in Slovakia was its share as low as around half, see Figure 18.8.

With EUR 30.4 billion of value added and 1.4 million persons employed in 2004, the United Kingdom was by far the largest contributor to EU-27 value added and employment in this sector. In 2004 the contribution of non-specialised in-store retailing to non-financial business economy value added among the Member States [10] reached 4.1 % in Slovenia, followed by Lithuania (3.9 %), Latvia (3.6 %) and France and the United Kingdom (both 3.2 %). According to the same measure the non-specialised in-store retailing sector was least developed in Bulgaria where it contributed just 1.4 % of non-financial business economy value added.

[9] Luxembourg, 2003; the Czech Republic, Malta and the Netherlands, not available.
[10] Luxembourg, 2003; Ireland, Greece, Cyprus, Malta and the Netherlands, not available.

Figure 18.8

Non-specialised in-store retailing (NACE Group 52.1)
Breakdown of turnover, 2004 (%) (1)

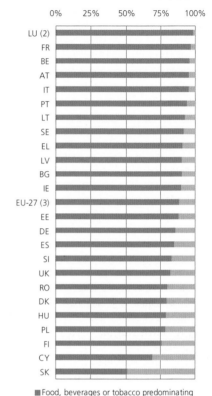

■ Food, beverages or tobacco predominating (NACE Class 52.11)
■ Other (NACE Class 52.12)

(1) Netherlands, incomplete data; Czech Republic and Malta, not available.
(2) 2003.
(3) Rounded estimates based on non-confidential data for NACE Class 52.12.
Source: Eurostat (SBS)

Table 18.5

Retail sale in non-specialized stores (NACE Group 52.1)
Structural profile, EU-27, 2004

	No. of enterprises (thousands)	Turnover (EUR million)	Value added (EUR million)	Employment (thousands)
Non-specialised in-store retailing (1)	593.8	872 704	127 674	6 031.4
Retail sale in non-specialised stores with food beverages or tobacco predominating	479.4	772 704	105 674	5 030.9
Other retail sale in non-specialised stores (2)	114.4	100 000	22 000	1 000.5

(1) Turnover and value added, estimate based on the sum of data for the NACE Classes.
(2) Rounded estimates based on non-confidential data.
Source: Eurostat (SBS)

Table 18.6 _____

Retail sale in non-specialized stores (NACE Group 52.1)
Structural profile: ranking of top five Member States, 2004

Rank	Share of EU-27 value added (%) (1)	Share of EU-27 employment (%) (2)	Value added specialisation ratio (EU-27=100) (3)	Employment specialisation ratio (EU-27=100) (4)
1	United Kingdom (24.3)	United Kingdom (22.9)	Slovenia (163.4)	United Kingdom (158.9)
2	Germany (19.0)	Germany (14.3)	Lithuania (157.6)	Lithuania (156.3)
3	France (18.7)	France (10.6)	Latvia (142.1)	Latvia (151.5)
4	Spain (9.0)	Poland (8.0)	United Kingdom (125.9)	Poland (133.5)
5	Italy (8.7)	Italy (7.3)	France (125.8)	Romania (128.2)

(1) All Member States, 2003, except for Greece, Malta and Netherlands, not available.
(2) Malta, not available; Luxembourg, 2003.
(3) All Member States, 2003, except for Ireland, Greece, Cyprus, Lithuania, Malta, Netherlands and Sweden, not available.
(4) Ireland, Greece, Cyprus and Malta, not available; Luxembourg, 2003.
Source: Eurostat (SBS)

Short-term statistics show that over the period 1998 to 2006 there was consecutive year on year growth in the volume of sales index for EU-27 non-specialised in-store retailing. This growth was recorded at a faster rhythm than for retail trade and repair average in 1999, as well as in the years 2001 to 2003. However, the contrary was observed in the years 2000 and 2004 to 2006.

One indicator of enterprise size is the average turnover generated per enterprise (note the use of the number of enterprises not the number of outlets for which data availability is weak). In 2004, average turnover per enterprise in the EU-27's non-specialised in-store retailing sector was close to EUR 1.5 million. The largest average enterprise size (in turnover terms) was recorded in Luxembourg (2003), at just under EUR 10 million, nearly double the next highest value recorded in France. Relatively high turnover per enterprise was also recorded in some of the north-western Member States, notably in the United Kingdom, Denmark and Germany.

Figure 18.9 _____

Retail sale in non-specialized stores (NACE Group 52.1)
Volume of sales index, EU-27 (2000=100)

Retail trade and repair of personal and household goods
- - - - Retail sale in non-specialised stores with food beverages or tobacco predominating
Other retail sale in non-specialised stores

Source: Eurostat (STS)

COSTS, PRODUCTIVITY AND PROFITABILITY

A breakdown of total expenditure into its three components, namely: purchases of goods and services, personnel costs, and gross tangible investment is available in 2004 for retail sales in non-specialised stores for the EU-25. This breakdown shows that operating expenditures (personnel costs and purchases of goods and services) accounted for 96.8 % of the EU-27's total expenditure, a share that was only slightly below the retail trade and repair share. The 3.2 % share of gross tangible investment was around 15 % higher than the retail trade and repair average.

The apparent labour productivity ratio of the EU-27's non-specialised in-store retailing sector in 2004 was EUR 21 200 per person employed, while average personnel costs were EUR 16 000 per employee, resulting in a wage adjusted ratio of 130 % for the sector. These figures were rather similar to those recorded for retail trade and repair as a whole. In contrast the EU-27's non-specialised in-store retailing sector recorded a 90.5 % share of paid employees in persons employed, significantly higher (12 percentage points above) than the retail trade and repair average.

The wage adjusted labour productivity ratio for non-specialised in-store retailing in 2004 ranged among the Member States [11] from slightly below 100 % in Italy and Bulgaria to just over 180 % in Luxembourg (in 2003). The gross operating rate was 4.5 % in the EU-27's non-specialised in-store retailing sector in 2004, well below the 7.4 % average for retail trade and repair. The gross operating rates in 2004 [12] were lowest in Hungary, Slovakia and Italy (2.0 % or below), while the highest level by far was observed in Greece (11.5 %).

_____
[11] Luxembourg, 2003; Malta and the Netherlands, not available.
[12] Luxembourg, 2003; Malta and the Netherlands, not available.

18.2: SPECIALISED IN-STORE FOOD RETAILING

The activities covered by this subchapter are retail sale in specialised stores of food, beverages or tobacco (NACE Group 52.2).

Food retailing specialists are generally small retail outlets that do not belong to national or international chains, for example, fruit and vegetable shops, bakers, butchers and fishmongers. Contrary to many non-food items, food is a typically inelastic good, which means that when prices rise, consumers generally do not cut back as much on the total quantity purchased, although price changes may influence the choice of brand or retailer chosen by individual customers.

STRUCTURAL PROFILE

The EU-27's specialised in-store food retailing sector (NACE Group 52.2) consisted of 513 000 enterprises in 2004 which generated EUR 122.8 billion of turnover, EUR 26.1 billion of value added while employing 1.5 million people. Therefore, specialised in-store food retailing contributed 6.8 % of retail trade and repair (NACE Division 52) value added and 8.6 % of the workforce, while its contribution to retail trade and repair turnover was 6.0 %.

The specialised in-store food retailing sector was particularly important in Spain which had the highest turnover and employment among the Member States in 2004 [13]. However, Italy generated the largest value added within the EU-27 (19.9 %). Unsurprisingly, Spain was the most specialised of the Member States [14] in this sector as regards its contribution to non-financial business economy in terms of value added and employment, immediately followed by Italy. Indeed, in both Spain and Italy the

[13] Luxembourg, 2003; Malta, not available.
[14] Luxembourg, 2003; Ireland, Greece, Cyprus, Luxembourg and Malta, not available.

proportion of value added generated by these activities in the national non-financial business economy was 1.8 times that for the EU-27 average. In terms of employment specialisation, the proportion of persons employed in these activities in Spain within the national non-financial business economy workforce was again 1.8 times that for the EU-27, while this ratio was 1.3 in Italy.

Box 18.2: food, beverage and tobacco retailing

Note that in-store food, beverages and tobacco retailing is split between Subchapters 18.1 and 18.2, distinguishing specialised (NACE Group 52.2) from non-specialised (NACE Class 52.11) retailers. Among the Member States [15], the Baltic States had the lowest proportion of in-store food, beverages and tobacco retailing turnover from specialised retailers (under 5 % of the total), while the share was also very low in Slovenia (5.6 %). At the other end of the spectrum, specialised retailers generated relatively high shares of turnover in some of the southern Member States – particularly in Greece, Spain and Cyprus - they also accounted for more than one fifth of the turnover generated by the in-store retailing of food, beverages and tobacco in Poland and Austria.

[15] Luxembourg, 2003; the Czech Republic and Malta, not available.

Half of the turnover generated in the EU-27's specialised in-store food retailing sector in 2004 was generated by enterprises with the main activity selling fruit, vegetables, meat, fish and bakery products – see Figure 18.10. The sale of tobacco products generated 18.7 % of total turnover, while beverages and other in-store food products both accounted for slightly more than 15 %. Among the Member States with available data for the same year, the activities of specialised in-store retailing of tobacco

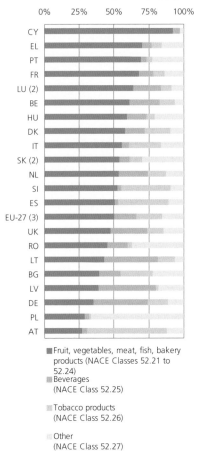

Figure 18.10

Specialised in-store food retailing (NACE Group 52.2)
Breakdown of turnover, 2004 (%) (1)

- Fruit, vegetables, meat, fish, bakery products (NACE Classes 52.21 to 52.24)
- Beverages (NACE Class 52.25)
- Tobacco products (NACE Class 52.26)
- Other (NACE Class 52.27)

(1) Estonia, Ireland, Finland and Sweden, incomplete data; Czech Republic and Malta, not available.
(2) 2003.
(3) Rounded estimates based on non-confidential data for NACE Classes 52.21 to 52.24.
Source: Eurostat (SBS)

products was particularly important in Austria, where the contribution to its specialised in-store food retailing sector turnover was slightly more than 4 times the EU-27 average.

Table 18.7

Retail sale of food, beverages, tobacco in specialized stores (NACE Group 52.2)
Structural profile, EU-27, 2004

	No. of enterprises (thousands)	Turnover (EUR million)	Value added (EUR million)	Employment (thousands)
Specialised in-store food retailing	513.0	122 843	26 099	1 452.6
Retail sale of fruit and vegetables (1)	74.4	12 000	2 370	167.0
Meat and meat products (1)	131.2	31 000	6 800	384.0
Fish, crustaceans and molluscs (1)	36.5	5 960	1 220	77.8
Bread, cakes, flour confectionery & sugar confectionery (1)	67.1	12 300	4 030	257.0
Alcoholic and other beverages (1)	38.0	19 525	2 841	144.2
Tobacco products (1)	66.2	22 865	5 251	151.8
Other specialised in-store food retailing	99.9	18 812	3 551	270.7

(1) Rounded estimates based on non-confidential data.
Source: Eurostat (SBS)

Table 18.8

Retail sale of food, beverages, tobacco in specialized stores (NACE Group 52.2)
Structural profile: ranking of top five Member States, 2004

Rank	Share of EU-27 value added (%) (1)	Share of EU-27 employment (%) (1)	Value added specialisation ratio (EU-27=100) (2)	Employment specialisation ratio (EU-27=100) (2)
1	Italy (19.9)	Spain (18.3)	Spain (182.0)	Spain (178.1)
2	Spain (16.4)	United Kingdom (15.1)	Italy (179.0)	Italy (126.9)
3	United Kingdom (15.8)	Italy (14.9)	Belgium (107.4)	Portugal (126.7)
4	Germany (12.9)	Germany (11.3)	Portugal (104.4)	Poland (121.0)
5	France (12.6)	France (7.3)	Austria (100.2)	Belgium (118.0)

(1) Malta, not available; Luxembourg, 2003.
(2) Ireland, Greece, Cyprus and Malta, not available; Luxembourg, 2003.
Source: Eurostat (SBS)

Figure 18.11

Retail sale of food, beverages, tobacco in specialized stores (NACE Group 52.2)
Index of volume of sales, EU-27 (2000=100)

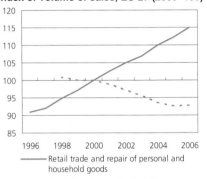

Retail trade and repair of personal and household goods
Specialised in-store food retailing

Source: Eurostat (STS)

Annualised short-term statistics show a general downward trend for the volume of sales index for the EU-27's specialised in-store food retailing sector over the period 1998 to 2006. Indeed, the index contracted nearly every year, with the exception of the years 2000 and 2006. The average decline in the volume of sales index during the period observed was 1.0 % per annum, with the sharpest reduction in 2004 when the index dropped by 2.3 %.

COSTS, PRODUCTIVITY AND PROFITABILITY

The breakdown of total expenditure shows that 86.8 % of the total was allocated to the purchase of goods and services in the EU-27's specialised in-store food retailing, while another 10.9 % was used for personnel costs and the remaining was accounted for by gross investment in tangible goods (2.3 %). The subsector of the retail sale of bread, cakes, flour confectionery and sugar confectionery (NACE Class 52.24) recorded that slightly less than one quarter (74.7 %) of the total expenditure was used for the purchases of goods and services, the lowest proportion recorded within the seven NACE classes that make up the sector. The counterpart of this low figure was a high proportion of expenditure going to personnel costs (21.9 %), the highest across these NACE classes. In contrast purchases of goods and services were predominant in the retail sale of tobacco products, accounting for more than nine tenths (93.1 %) of total expenditure.

The share of employees in persons employed was 60.9 %, substantially below the retail trade and repair average (78.5 %), and lower than the share recorded in both of the other NACE groups concerning specialised in-store retailing of new goods (52.3 and 52.4 - see Subchapter 18.3). EU-27 apparent labour productivity for the specialised in-store food retailing sector was EUR 18 000 per person employed in 2004, while average personnel costs were EUR 13 700 per employee. Both values were below the retail trade and repair (NACE Division 52) average. Nevertheless the resulting wage adjusted labour productivity ratio for this sector was 131.5 % in 2004, slightly above the retail trade and repair average (129.0 %). Among the NACE classes that compose the sector, particularly high wage adjusted labour productivity ratio (230.0 %) was recorded by retail sale of tobacco products. Among the Member States [16], wage adjusted labour productivity in 2004 in specialised in-store food retailing was below national non-financial business economy in all of the Member States except Italy, while in Sweden and Slovenia this ratio was below 100 %, indicating that apparent labour productivity was lower than average personnel costs.

The gross operating rate shows that the ratio of gross operating surplus to turnover for the EU-27's specialised in-store food retailing sector was equivalent to 11.4 % in 2004, higher than the retail trade and repair average (7.4 %), as well as the average of the total non-financial business economy (11.0 %). Again, retail sale of tobacco products recorded the highest ratio (18.6 %) among the NACE classes that make up the sector. However, in 19 of the 23 Member States for which this ratio was available [17] for specialised in-store food retailing, the gross operating rate stood below the national non-financial business economy average. Indeed, only Belgium, France, Italy and Luxembourg (2003) had a higher than average operating rate.

[16] Luxembourg, 2003; Ireland, Greece, Cyprus and Malta, not available.
[17] Luxembourg, 2003; Ireland, Greece, Cyprus and Malta, not available.

Table 18.9 _____

Retail sale of food, beverages, tobacco in specialized stores (NACE Group 52.2)
Productivity and profitability, EU-27, 2004

	Apparent labour productivity (EUR thousand)	Average personnel costs (EUR thousand)	Wage adjusted labour productivity (%)	Gross operating rate (%)
Specialised in-store food retailing (1)	18.0	13.7	131.5	11.4
Retail sale of fruit and vegetables (1)	14.2	12.5	113.0	11.0
Meat and meat products (1)	17.8	15.8	113.0	10.0
Fish, crustaceans and molluscs (1)	15.6	13.4	117.0	11.2
Bread, cakes, flour confectionery & sugar confectionery (1)	15.7	13.3	118.0	12.9
Alcoholic and other beverages	19.7	15.2	129.8	6.0
Tobacco products	34.6	14.9	230.0	18.6
Other specialised in-store food retailing	13.1	9.9	132.1	10.0

(1) Rounded estimates based on non-confidential data.
Source: Eurostat (SBS)

18.3: SPECIALISED IN-STORE NEW GOODS RETAILING OTHER THAN FOOD

The activities covered by this subchapter are retail sale in specialised stores, other than food, beverages and tobacco. Two NACE groups are covered: dispensing chemists, retailers of medical, orthopaedic, cosmetic and toilet articles (NACE Group 52.3); and other specialised in-store retailing of new goods (NACE Group 52.4), for example, shops selling clothes, shoes, furniture, books or electrical items.

This subchapter deals with the retailing of consumer non-durable, semi-durable and durable goods, contrary to the previous subchapter that only covered food items that are by definition non-durables. Among the retailing of non-durable goods are pharmaceuticals, cosmetics and toilet articles, while semi-durable goods include items such as clothing and footwear. Electrical household appliances and radio and television equipment are examples of durable goods.

Compared with food retailing, other new goods retailing is more strongly influenced by the general economic cycle. Most non-food items are bought less frequently or at a certain period of the year, although there are examples (such as newspapers) of non-durable non-food products that are purchased on a frequent basis. For the retail sale of clothes and footwear, promotional sales or changes in seasons determine cycles, while the purchase of some other goods (for example, games and toys) may be concentrated around special events (like Christmas).

Table 18.10 _____

Specialised in-store new goods retailing other than food (NACE Groups 52.3 and 52.4)
Structural profile, EU-27, 2004

	No. of enterprises (thousands)	Turnover (EUR million)	Value added (EUR million)	Employment (thousands)
Specialised in-store new goods retailing other than food (1)	1 921.2	900 000	200 000	8 164.8
Pharmaceuticals & medical goods, cosmetic & toiletries	200.0	183 450	40 111	1 196.4
Dispensing chemists	130.0	140 000	30 000	800.0
Medical and orthopaedic goods	19.7	11 153	3 336	105.0
Cosmetic and toilet articles	52.4	33 000	7 000	310.0
Other specialised in-store new goods retailing (2)	1 721.2	704 287	164 780	6 968.4
Textiles	91.2	12 308	3 049	208.4
Clothing	350.4	156 274	39 011	1 660.5
Footwear and leather goods	84.5	32 818	7 958	394.2
Furniture, lighting equipment and household articles n.e.c.	175.7	99 475	21 640	807.8
Electrical household appliances and radio and television	104.0	83 848	13 587	515.8
Hardware paints and glass	136.1	102 395	20 820	742.3
Books, newspapers and stationery	134.0	41 414	8 717	430.7
Other retail sale in specialized stores	645.2	:	50 000	2 208.7

(1) Rounded estimates based on non-confidential data.
(2) Turnover , 2003; value added, estimate based on the sum of data for the NACE Classes.
Source: Eurostat (SBS)

STRUCTURAL PROFILE

In 2004, the EU-27's sector of specialised in-store new goods retailing other than food (NACE Groups 52.3 and 52.4) consisted of 1.9 million enterprises which generated around EUR 900 billion of turnover, which represented more than two fifths of retail trade and repair (NACE Division 52) turnover. In 2004 around EUR 200 billion of value added was recorded by these activities, 52 % of the retail trade and repair total and 8.2 million persons employed, which equated to 48 % of the retail trade and repair total.

Among the two NACE groups that make up specialised in-store new goods retailing other than food, other specialised in-store retailing of new goods (NACE Group 52.4) was by far the largest activity in terms of turnover, value added and employment, contributing at least four-fifths of the sectoral total for each of these indicators.

Turning to the Member States, specialised in-store new goods retailing other than food were largest in the United Kingdom in terms of value added and employment, followed by Germany. The contribution of both of these Member States was about one fifth of the EU-27 value added total, while they contributed slightly less to total employment – see Table 18.11. In terms of this sector's contribution to non-financial business economy value added, Portugal and France were the most specialised Member States [18], while the Baltic Member States were among the least specialised, along with Slovenia and Slovakia.

[18] Luxembourg, 2003; Ireland, Greece, Cyprus, Malta and the Netherlands, not available.

Box 18.3: in-store retailing of new goods other than food, beverages and tobacco

In-store retailing of new goods other than food, beverages and tobacco has been split across Subchapters 18.1 and 18.3, distinguishing specialised (NACE Groups 52.3 and 52.4) from non-specialised (NACE Class 52.12) retailers. Data for 2004 [19] shows that in Luxembourg (1.4 %, 2003), Austria (2.7 %), Belgium and Italy (3.1 % for both countries) non-specialised retailers generated the lowest proportion of turnover from the in-store retailing of new goods other than food, beverages and tobacco; they were followed by France (3.7 %), Portugal (4.0 %) and Greece (4.6 %). In the other Member States, the proportion of turnover generated by non-specialised retailers was at least 5.0 %, with the highest shares being recorded in Slovenia (27.1 %) and Slovakia (35.9 %).

[19] Luxembourg, 2003, the Czech Republic and the Netherlands, incomplete data; Malta, not available.

Figure 18.12 provides a breakdown of in-store retailing turnover among four main groupings of non-food activities. The specialised in-store retailing of household equipment (NACE Classes 52.44 to 52.46) generated 30.5 % of the sector's turnover in the EU [20] in 2004, slightly more than the share (27.9 %) accounted for by specialised in-store retailing of books, newspapers and other items (NACE Classes 52.47 and 52.48). The specialised in-store retailing of textiles, clothing, footwear and leather goods (NACE Classes 52.41 to 52.43) generated a little more than one fifth (21.8 %) of sectoral turnover, while dispensing chemists, retailers of medical, orthopaedic, cosmetic and toilet articles (NACE Group 52.3) had a share just under one fifth (19.8 %).

[20] EU average; Luxembourg, 2002; excluding the Czech Republic, Malta and the Netherlands.

Figure 18.12

Specialised in-store new goods retailing other than food (NACE Groups 52.3 and 52.4) Breakdown of turnover, 2004 (%) (1)

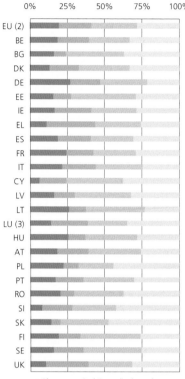

- ■ Pharmaceutical & medical goods, cosmetics & toiletries (NACE Group 52.3)
- ■ Textiles, clothing, footwear and leather goods (NACE Classes 52.41 to 52.43)
- ■ Household equipment (NACE Classes 52.44 to 52.46)
- Books, newspapers and other items (NACE Classes 52.47 and 52.48)

(1) Czech Republic and Netherlands, incomplete data; Malta, not available.
(2) EU average; Luxembourg, 2002; excluding Czech Republic, Malta and Netherlands.
(3) 2003.
Source: Eurostat (SBS)

Table 18.11

Specialised in-store new goods retailing other than food (NACE Groups 52.3 and 52.4)
Structural profile: ranking of top five Member States, 2004

Rank	Share of EU-27 value added (%) (1)	Share of EU-27 employment (%) (2)	Value added specialisation ratio (EU-27=100) (3)	Employment specialisation ratio (EU-27=100) (4)
1	United Kingdom (20.9)	United Kingdom (17.3)	Portugal (127.6)	Austria (125.1)
2	Germany (19.7)	Germany (17.0)	France (117.6)	Netherlands (121.4)
3	France (16.6)	Italy (11.4)	Austria (112.7)	United Kingdom (120.2)
4	Italy (10.9)	Spain (10.8)	United Kingdom (110.4)	Portugal (119.3)
5	Spain (9.6)	France (10.5)	Spain (106.2)	Spain (104.9)

(1) Malta and Netherlands, not available; Luxembourg, 2003.
(2) Malta, not available; Luxembourg, 2003.
(3) Ireland, Greece, Cyprus, Malta and Netherlands, not available; Luxembourg, 2003.
(4) Ireland, Greece, Cyprus and Malta, not available; Luxembourg, 2003.
Source: Eurostat (SBS)

Specialised in-store retailing of household equipment accounted for the highest share of sectoral turnover in Estonia (43.3 %). In contrast, the subsector of specialised in-store retailing of books, newspapers and other items recorded its highest share of sectoral turnover in Slovakia (47.3 %). Specialised in-store retailing of textiles, clothing, footwear and leather goods accounted for its largest proportion of sectoral turnover in Greece (32.7 %), followed by the United Kingdom (28.8 %). The subsector of dispensing chemists, retailers of medical, orthopaedic, cosmetic and toilet articles contributed between 6.2 % of sectoral turnover in Cyprus to over 25 % of the total in Hungary, Lithuania and Germany.

Annualised short-term statistics show the evolution of the volume of sales index in the two NACE groups covered by the EU-27's sector of specialised in-store new goods retailing other than food. In both activities there was uninterrupted growth over the period 1996-2006. Dispensing chemists, retailers of medical, orthopaedic, cosmetic and toilet articles recorded average growth for their volume of sales index of 3.9 % per annum over the period observed, while sales grew at a somewhat slower pace for other specialised in-store retailing of new goods, with average growth of 2.7 % per annum. However, both activities reported faster growth than the retail trade and repair average which was 2.4 % per annum over the same period.

Figure 18.13

Specialised in-store new goods retailing other than food (NACE Groups 52.3 and 52.4)
Index of volume of sales, EU-27 (2000=100)

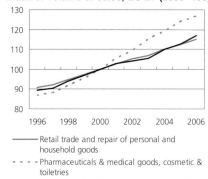

———— Retail trade and repair of personal and household goods
- - - - Pharmaceuticals & medical goods, cosmetic & toiletries
———— Other specialised in-store new goods retailing

Source: Eurostat (STS)

COSTS, PRODUCTIVITY AND PROFITABILITY

A breakdown of total expenditure in 2004 shows that in the EU-27's sector of specialised in-store new goods retailing other than food some 83.0 % of the total was dedicated to purchases of goods and services, the proportion of personnel costs was 14.2 %, and the remaining 2.7 % was for investment in tangible goods – see Table 18.12. These shares were similar to that recorded for the retail trade and repair as a whole, with the most notable difference being the share of personnel costs which was 2.2 percentage points higher.

Paid employees accounted for 77.3 % of all persons employed in this sector in 2004, close to the retail trade and repair average, although this rate was notably higher in the dispensing chemists, retailers of medical, orthopaedic, cosmetic and toilet articles subsector, at 83.0 %. With apparent labour productivity of EUR 24 000 per person employed in 2004, personnel costs of EUR 20 000 per employee, the wage adjusted labour productivity ratio in the EU-27's sector of specialised in-store new goods retailing other than food averaged 132.0 %. Across all the Member States for which data is available [21], the wage adjusted labour productivity ratio for national specialised in-store new goods retailing other than food was systematically lower than the non-financial business economy. Nevertheless this ratio reached 157.1 % for the EU-27's dispensing chemists and retailers of medical, orthopaedic, cosmetic and toilet articles subsector, the highest level of this ratio for any of the retail trade and repair NACE groups, and the only one above the non-financial business economy average (148.0 %).

The sector of specialised in-store new goods retailing other than food recorded a gross operating rate of 9.1 %, which was somewhat higher than for retail trade and repair as a whole (7.4 %), although still lower than the non-financial business economy average of 11.0 %. However, there was some difference between the levels of profitability as measured by this rate in the two subsectors as in the dispensing chemists and retailers of medical, orthopaedic, cosmetic and toilet articles subsector the rate reached 10.3 %.

[21] Luxembourg, 2003; Ireland, Greece, Cyprus, Malta and the Netherlands, not available.

Table 18.12

Specialised in-store new goods retailing other than food (NACE Groups 52.3 and 52.4)
Total expenditure, EU-27, 2004 (1)

	Value (EUR million)				Share (% of total expenditure)		
	Total expenditure	Purchases of goods and services	Personnel costs	Investment in tangible goods	Purchases of goods and services	Personnel costs	Investment in tangible goods
Specialised in-store new goods retailing other than food	843 000	700 000	120 000	23 000	83.0	14.2	2.7
Pharmaceuticals & medical goods, cosmetic & toiletries	166 929	142 872	21 207	2 850	85.6	12.7	1.7
Other specialised in-store new goods retailing	718 108	600 000	98 000	20 108	83.6	13.6	2.8

(1) Rounded estimates based on non-confidential data.
Source: Eurostat (SBS)

18.4: SECOND-HAND GOODS RETAILING IN STORES

The retail sale of second hand products (NACE Group 52.5) includes for example, shops selling antiques, or second-hand books or clothes. Note that the retail sale of second-hand motor vehicles is not covered by this subchapter (see Chapter 16). The retailing of second-hand goods deals by definition with the sale of semi-durable and durable items only.

Turnover was EUR 7.3 billion in the EU-27's sector of second-hand goods retailing in stores (NACE Group 52.5), from which EUR 2.0 billion of added value were generated, the smallest values among the retail trade and repair subchapters. For each of these measures the relative weight of second-hand goods retailing in the retail trade and repair (NACE Division 52) total was 0.5 % or below. Across the 63 000 enterprises with second-hand goods retailing as their main activity there were 113 300 persons employed in the EU-27, therefore equating to 0.7 % of the retail trade and repair workforce.

The United Kingdom alone accounted for 34.9 % of the EU-27's turnover and 47 % of value added in second-hand goods retailing in stores, the largest contributor ahead of France (respectively 27.1 % and 19.7 %). However, the United Kingdom employed only around one fifth of the EU-27's workforce and France 13.0 %. Unsurprisingly, the United Kingdom was the most specialised Member State [22] in terms of the contribution of this sector to non-financial business economy value added.

[22] Luxembourg, 2003; Ireland, Greece, Cyprus and Malta, not available.

The wage adjusted labour productivity ratio was 114.4 % in the EU-27's second-hand goods retailing in stores sector in 2004, compared with a retail trade and repair average of 129.0 % and a non-financial business economy average of 148.0 %. Among the Member States [23], almost all the countries had a lower ratio for their second-hand goods retailing in stores sector than for their non-financial business economy average. The gross operating rate in this sector reached 15.0 % in 2004, double the retail trade and repair average, and this was the highest level of this rate in the EU-27 among the retail trade NACE groups.

[23] Luxembourg, 2003; Ireland, Greece, Cyprus and Malta, not available.

Table 18.13

Retail sale of second-hand goods in stores (NACE Group 52.5)
Structural profile: ranking of top five Member States, 2004

Rank	Share of EU-27 value added (%) (1)	Share of EU-27 employment (%) (1)	Value added specialisation ratio (EU-27=100) (2)	Employment specialisation ratio (EU-27=100) (2)
1	United Kingdom (47.1)	United Kingdom (18.7)	United Kingdom (248.9)	Lithuania (393.4)
2	France (19.7)	Poland (15.5)	Lithuania (236.7)	Latvia (333.5)
3	Germany (10.6)	France (13.0)	Latvia (199.7)	Hungary (261.5)
4	Netherlands (5.6)	Germany (10.3)	Hungary (150.5)	Poland (258.7)
5	Italy (2.5)	Netherlands (6.7)	France (140.0)	Bulgaria (201.0)

(1) Malta, not available; Luxembourg, 2003.
(2) Ireland, Greece, Cyprus and Malta, not available; Luxembourg, 2003.
Source: Eurostat (SBS)

18.5: RETAIL SALES NOT IN STORES

These activities cover retail sales via stalls, markets, and door to door sales, as well as remote sales made via mail order, mobile sales or through vending machines. Enterprises specialising in retail sales via the Internet and via home shopping channels are also included. All of these activities are classified within NACE Group 52.6 and are collectively referred to as the retail trade not in stores sector.

Note that the retailers covered by this subchapter are those which generate the largest part of their output outside of stores. As such, this subchapter does not include retail enterprises that also use remote-selling, but not as their principal activity.

Table 18.14

Retail sale not in stores (NACE Group 52.6)
Structural profile, EU-27, 2004

	No. of enterprises (thousands)	Turnover (EUR million)	Value added (EUR million)	Employment (thousands)
Retailing not in stores	512.4	94 603	18 930	939.7
Retail sale via mail order houses (1)	17.9	50 506	8 781	214.3
Retail sale via stalls and markets (1)	357.0	18 600	4 150	450.0
Other non-store retail sale (1)	137.0	25 000	6 000	280.0

(1) Rounded estimates based on non-confidential data.
Source: Eurostat (LFS)

STRUCTURAL PROFILE

Retail sales not in-stores (NACE Group 52.6) was the main activity of 512 000 enterprises which generated EUR 94.6 billion of turnover in the EU-27 in 2004, which represented 4.6 % of the total turnover for retail trade (NACE Division 52). EU-27 value added was EUR 18.9 billion, or 4.9 % of the retail trade and repair total and there were 939 700 persons employed in this sector in 2004, equivalent to 5.5 % of the retail trade and repair workforce.

Among the Member States [24], Germany contributed more than one quarter of the EU-27's turnover and value added , and the United Kingdom also had a relatively high share for these two indicators, close to one fifth. However, the largest proportion of the retail sales not in-stores workforce was found within Italy (16.3 % of the EU-27 total) and Poland (15.2 %) in 2004.

Across the three NACE classes that make up retail sales not in stores, retail sales via mail order houses (NACE Class 52.61) was the largest activity in terms of turnover and value added in 2004 with around half the sectoral total, while its share of the sector's workforce was just over one fifth. In contrast retail sales via stalls and markets (NACE Class 52.62) had the smallest share of sectoral turnover and value added but its workforce of 450 000 persons employed represented just under half the retail sales not in-stores total. The activity of retail sales via mail order houses was relatively most important in turnover terms in several of the larger Member States (France, Germany and the United Kingdom), the Nordic Member States, and most of all in Austria.

[24] Luxembourg, 2003; Malta, not available.

Figure 18.14

Retailing not in stores (NACE Group 52.6)
Breakdown of turnover, 2004 (%) (1)

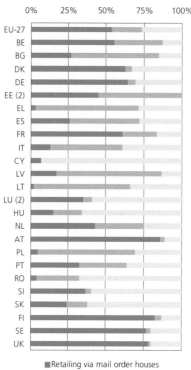

- ■ Retailing via mail order houses (NACE Class 52.61)
- ▨ Retailing via stalls & markets (NACE Class 52.62)
- ▢ Other non-store retailing (NACE Class 52.63)

(1) Czech Republic, Ireland and Malta, not available.
(2) 2003.
Source: Eurostat (SBS)

COSTS, PRODUCTIVITY AND PROFITABILITY

The retail sales not in stores sector recorded a share of paid employees in persons employed that was particularly low, just 49.4 %, the lowest of all retail trade and repair NACE groups. The wage adjusted labour productivity ratio was 96.1 % in the EU-27's retail sales not in stores in 2004, reflecting a level of apparent labour productivity (EUR 20 100 per person employed) that was just insufficient to cover the average personnel costs (EUR 21 000): retail sales not in stores was the only retail trade and repair NACE group where the wage adjusted labour productivity ratio for the EU-27 was below parity (100 %) in 2004.However, the wage adjusted labour productivity was above 100 % in a large majority of Member States for which data is available. The gross operating rate was 9.7 % in the EU-27's retail sales not in store, below the non-financial business economy average of 11.0 %.

Table 18.15

Retail sale not in stores (NACE Group 52.6)
Structural profile: ranking of top five Member States, 2004

Rank	Share of EU-27 value added (%) (1)	Share of EU-27 employment (%) (1)	Value added specialisation ratio (EU-27=100) (2)	Employment specialisation ratio (EU-27=100) (2)
1	Germany (27.1)	Italy (16.3)	Latvia (164.0)	Latvia (314.7)
2	United Kingdom (20.9)	Poland (15.2)	Germany (129.2)	Poland (253.7)
3	France (14.7)	Germany (14.8)	Poland (121.4)	Bulgaria (151.7)
4	Italy (12.2)	United Kingdom (11.2)	United Kingdom (110.5)	Italy (138.9)
5	Spain (6.3)	France (9.8)	Italy (109.3)	Hungary (135.1)

(1) Malta, not available; Luxembourg, 2003.
(2) Ireland, Greece, Cyprus and Malta, not available; Luxembourg, 2003.
Source: Eurostat (SBS)

18.6: REPAIR OF PERSONAL AND HOUSEHOLD GOODS

The repair of personal and household goods is quite different from the other activities covered in this chapter as it does not involve the buying and reselling of goods, but covers the provision of repair services. This activity (NACE Group 52.7) covers specialist repairers only, and excludes enterprises that carry out repair as a secondary activity in combination with other activities.

STRUCTURAL PROFILE

The EU-27's repair of personal and household goods sector (NACE Group 52.7) consisted of 131 000 enterprises in 2004 which employed 268 100 persons and generated EUR 5.0 billion of value added, equivalent to 1.6 % and 1.3 % respectively of retail trade and repair (NACE Division 52).

An analysis at the NACE class level shows that the repair of electrical household goods (NACE Class 52.72) was the largest of the three classes.

The United Kingdom, Germany and France were the largest contributors to the EU-27's total value added in repair of personal and household goods. However, Hungary stood out from the rest of the Member States [25] as being the most specialised in these activities, in terms of its contribution to non-financial business economy value added.

[25] Luxembourg, 2003; Ireland, Greece, Cyprus and Malta, not available.

COSTS, PRODUCTIVITY AND PROFITABILITY

The wage adjusted labour productivity ratio for the EU-27's repair of personal and household goods sector was 106.2 % in 2004. Among the Member States [26] for which data are available, the wage adjusted labour productivity for these activities was below that for the non-financial business economy average in all but one country, with the United Kingdom recording a ratio of 214.2 %. The gross operating rate in this sector was 21.2 % in the EU-27 in 2004, the highest of all of the retail trade and repair NACE groups.

[26] Luxembourg, 2003; Ireland, Greece, Cyprus and Malta, not available.

Table 18.16
Repair of personal and household goods (NACE Group 52.7)
Structural profile, EU-27, 2004

	No. of enterprises (thousands)	Turnover (EUR million)	Value added (EUR million)	Employment (thousands)
Repair of personal & household goods	131.4	11 703	4 957	268.1
Repair of boots, shoes and other articles of leather (1)	22.4	1 100	540	38.0
Repair of electrical household goods	53.7	5 592	2 177	122.2
Repair of watches clocks and jewellery (1)	9.3	500	210	15.0
Repair n.e.c. (1)	46.0	4 469	2 035	93.4

(1) Rounded estimates based on non-confidential data.
Source: Eurostat (SBS)

Table 18.17
Repair of personal and household goods (NACE Group 52.7)
Structural profile: ranking of top five Member States, 2004

Rank	Share of EU-27 value added (%) (1)	Share of EU-27 employment (%) (1)	Value added specialisation ratio (EU-27=100) (2)	Employment specialisation ratio (EU-27=100) (2)
1	United Kingdom (23.2)	United Kingdom (14.1)	Hungary (136.5)	Hungary (228.1)
2	Germany (15.8)	Italy (14.0)	Sweden (123.3)	Latvia (135.5)
3	France (14.3)	Spain (11.0)	United Kingdom (122.7)	Poland (133.1)
4	Italy (11.9)	Germany (10.9)	Denmark (113.4)	Bulgaria (127.2)
5	Spain (9.1)	France (10.1)	Italy (106.8)	Italy (119.2)

(1) Malta, not available; Luxembourg, 2003.
(2) Ireland, Greece, Cyprus and Malta, not available; Luxembourg, 2003.
Source: Eurostat (SBS)

Table 18.18

Retail trade and repair of personal and household goods (NACE Division 52)
Main indicators, 2004

	EU-27	BE	BG	CZ	DK	DE	EE	IE	EL	ES	FR	IT	CY	LV	LT
No. of enterprises (thousands)	3 735.0	72.8	93.7	134.0	24.2	274.2	4.1	17.8	196.3	531.1	427.4	703.6	14.0	13.1	12.9
Turnover (EUR million)	2 038 052	60 536	3 617	21 442	32 182	348 146	2 637	23 052	42 112	183 464	358 325	244 035	3 633	3 062	3 954
Production (EUR million)	724 513	18 671	827	5 419	10 082	125 144	622	7 847	13 014	54 763	115 466	107 107	981	792	960
Value added (EUR million)	384 355	9 504	383	2 926	5 923	71 080	313	5 251	9 161	36 547	62 898	40 308	640	428	515
Gross operating surplus (EUR million)	150 460	4 150	178	1 376	1 715	23 400	106	2 294	6 021	16 246	20 041	20 442	245	191	185
Purchases of goods & services (EUR million)	1 650 471	51 086	3 436	18 710	26 731	266 271	2 383	17 962	36 420	150 375	294 384	208 302	3 055	2 732	3 542
Personnel costs (EUR million)	233 896	5 355	205	1 550	4 208	47 707	207	2 957	3 140	20 301	42 857	19 866	395	237	331
Investment in tangible goods (EUR million)	54 181	1 915	188	599	590	4 165	76	1 146	944	5 891	8 129	6 509	92	134	123
Employment (thousands)	16 970	292	251	377	203	2 590	42	162	479	1 698	1 736	1 780	29	99	113
Apparent labour prod. (EUR thousand)	22.6	32.5	1.5	7.8	29.2	27.4	7.5	32.3	19.1	21.5	36.2	22.6	21.9	4.3	4.6
Average personnel costs (EUR thousand)	17.6	25.2	1.3	6.4	22.7	21.0	5.1	20.5	15.0	17.3	27.2	23.4	17.0	2.5	3.2
Wage adjusted labour productivity (%)	129.0	129.3	117.2	121.9	129.0	130.9	147.5	157.9	127.4	124.3	133.0	97.0	128.9	174.2	143.4
Gross operating rate (%)	7.4	6.9	4.9	6.4	5.3	6.7	4.0	10.0	14.3	8.9	5.6	8.4	6.7	6.2	4.7
Investment / employment (EUR thousand)	3.2	6.6	0.7	1.6	2.9	1.6	1.8	7.1	2.0	3.5	4.7	3.7	3.2	1.4	1.1

	LU (1)	HU	MT	NL	AT	PL	PT	RO	SI	SK	FI	SE	UK	NO
No. of enterprises (thousands)	2.9	108.4	:	78.9	41.6	412.5	145.2	126.3	7.2	4.5	22.1	57.5	200.8	29.8
Turnover (EUR million)	4 353	18 639	:	77 978	43 582	49 733	33 937	10 672	5 380	5 040	27 201	48 720	382 562	32 561
Production (EUR million)	1 307	4 436	:	26 850	15 164	34 113	9 589	2 712	1 584	1 305	8 313	15 440	142 019	10 752
Value added (EUR million)	823	1 992	:	16 376	8 726	6 665	5 491	1 094	866	579	4 717	8 767	82 371	6 120
Gross operating surplus (EUR million)	353	563	:	6 277	2 308	4 019	2 068	494	269	219	1 659	1 909	33 762	1 812
Purchases of goods & services (EUR million)	3 548	16 644	:	61 693	35 281	41 508	29 349	10 110	4 514	4 529	22 770	40 478	294 621	26 742
Personnel costs (EUR million)	471	1 429	:	10 099	6 418	2 646	3 423	600	597	360	3 058	6 858	48 609	4 307
Investment in tangible goods (EUR million)	47	658	:	1 899	928	1 220	1 163	734	279	385	1 048	14 662	747
Employment (thousands)	20	341	:	707	320	1 197	392	440	48	71	131	265	3 176	188
Apparent labour prod. (EUR thousand)	41.4	5.8	:	23.2	27.3	5.6	14.0	2.5	18.0	8.2	35.9	33.1	25.9	32.5
Average personnel costs (EUR thousand)	26.4	5.3	:	16.5	22.9	3.8	10.8	1.5	13.6	5.2	25.1	29.9	16.4	24.4
Wage adjusted labour productivity (%)	156.6	109.3	:	140.3	119.2	145.4	129.8	170.5	132.0	158.1	143.1	110.4	158.3	132.8
Gross operating rate (%)	8.1	3.0	:	8.0	5.3	8.1	6.1	4.6	5.0	4.3	6.1	3.9	8.8	5.6
Investment / employment (EUR thousand)	2.3	1.9	:	2.7	2.9	1.0	3.0	1.7	5.8	5.4	4.6	3.9	4.6	4.0

(1) 2003.
Source: Eurostat (SBS)

Hotels and restaurants

One of the main characteristics of tourism is the high income elasticity of demand, which increases or reduces more easily than for many other products or services. As such, tourism suppliers benefit from rising income with spending on tourism increasing proportionally faster than consumers' income. Moreover, political or economic uncertainties tend to lead to a diversion of tourism demand, leading for example to shifts between outbound tourism and domestic tourism.

On 17 March 2006, the European Commission adopted a communication [1] titled 'a renewed European Union tourism policy: towards a stronger partnership for European tourism', focusing on the competitiveness of tourism suppliers and the creation of jobs through its growth, an approach that was approved by the Council in its conclusions on the 25th of September. In terms of legislation, a Commission working document [2] on package travel, package holidays and package tours sets out the main regulatory problems in the area of package travel. At the time of drafting for this publication, the Commission is collecting stakeholders' views on issues related to the Council Directive 90/314/EEC [3] on package travel, package holidays and package tours which is the main legislative framework, designed to protect consumers who contract

package travel in the EU. The directive regulates the liability of package organisers and retailers, who must accept responsibility for the performance of the services offered. The aim of reviewing this directive is to adapt those three tourism products to recent developments with an impact on tourism products, such as the development of the Internet, the entry of low cost air carriers, the growth within the cruise industry and the increasing trend of consumers putting together their own holiday components from different organisers, instead of opting for packages pre-arranged by an organiser or a retailer.

According to the World Tourism Organisation (WTO), Europe remains the world's most important tourist destination and tourism-generating region. Indeed, according to figures from the same source, more than half (54.8 %) of the worldwide international tourist arrivals in 2005 (estimated at 806 million) were recorded in Europe [4] (441.5 million international arrivals). Most of these were recorded within EU-27 Member States, as France, Spain, Italy, the United Kingdom, Germany and Austria all figured in the top 10 list of international tourist arrivals, altogether accounting for almost 30 % of the worldwide total - Table 19.1.

This chapter covers activities that make up a significant part of the tourism supply (although partly serving also local clients), namely hotels and other provision of short-stay accommodation, restaurants, bars, canteens and catering (NACE Section H or Division 55).

NACE
55: hotels and restaurants;
55.1: hotels;
55.2: camping sites and other provision of short-stay accommodation;
55.3: restaurants;
55.4: bars;
55.5: canteens and catering.

Table 19.1

Top tourism destinations in the EU-27, 2005

Member States [world rank]	International tourist arrivals (millions)	World market share (%)
FR [1]	76.0	9.4
ES [2]	55.6	6.9
IT [5]	36.5	4.5
UK [6]	30.0	3.7
DE [8]	21.5	2.7
AT [10]	20.0	2.5

Source: World Tourism Organization (WTO) ©

[4] Figures for Europe include Northern, Western, Central/Eastern and Southern Europe.

[1] COM(2006) 134.
[2] For more information, see:
http://ec.europa.eu/consumers/cons_int/safe_shop/pack_trav/comm_wd_20072007_en.pdf.
[3] Council Directive 90/314/EEC of 13 June 1990.

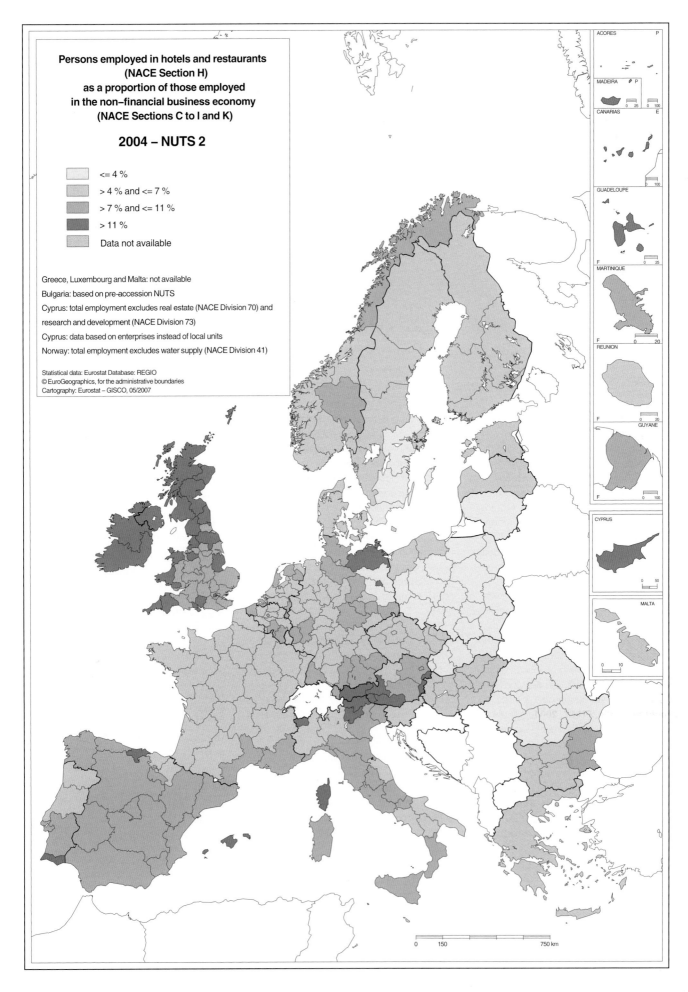

**Persons employed in hotels and restaurants
(NACE Section H)
as a proportion of those employed
in the non–financial business economy
(NACE Sections C to I and K)**

2004 – NUTS 2

- <= 4 %
- > 4 % and <= 7 %
- > 7 % and <= 11 %
- > 11 %
- Data not available

Greece, Luxembourg and Malta: not available

Bulgaria: based on pre-accession NUTS

Cyprus: total employment excludes real estate (NACE Division 70) and

research and development (NACE Division 73)

Cyprus: data based on enterprises instead of local units

Norway: total employment excludes water supply (NACE Division 41)

Statistical data: Eurostat Database: REGIO
© EuroGeographics, for the administrative boundaries
Cartography: Eurostat – GISCO, 05/2007

ACORES   P

MADEIRA   P

CANARIAS   E

GUADELOUPE

MARTINIQUE

REUNION

GUYANE

CYPRUS

MALTA

0   150   750 km

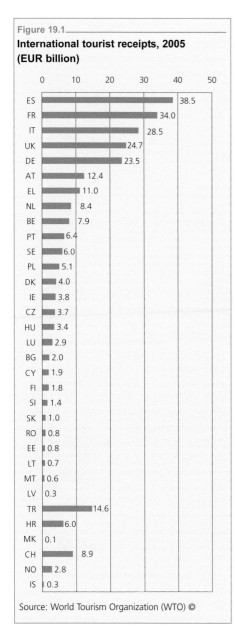

Figure 19.1

International tourist receipts, 2005 (EUR billion)

ES	38.5
FR	34.0
IT	28.5
UK	24.7
DE	23.5
AT	12.4
EL	11.0
NL	8.4
BE	7.9
PT	6.4
SE	6.0
PL	5.1
DK	4.0
IE	3.8
CZ	3.7
HU	3.4
LU	2.9
BG	2.0
CY	1.9
FI	1.8
SI	1.4
SK	1.0
RO	0.8
EE	0.8
LT	0.7
MT	0.6
LV	0.3
TR	14.6
HR	6.0
MK	0.1
CH	8.9
NO	2.8
IS	0.3

Source: World Tourism Organization (WTO) ©

In terms of receipts generated by tourism suppliers among the EU-27 Member States in 2005, the five largest economies occupied the top positions - see Figure 19.1. At the other end of the spectrum, the Baltic countries, Malta and Romania accounted for the lowest levels of receipts in absolute terms. However, relatively to the population of the country, Luxembourg recorded the largest per head receipt in tourism in 2005, followed by Cyprus and Malta. At the other end of the spectrum, Romania, Latvia, Poland and Slovakia stood out from the rest of the Member States as having the lowest per head tourism receipt.

STRUCTURAL PROFILE

The hotels and restaurants sector (NACE Section H) recorded value added of EUR 163.5 billion in the EU-27 in 2004, which represented 3.2 % of the total for the non-financial business economy (NACE Sections C to I and K). However, the contribution of this sector to total employment was about twice its share in total value added, as the 1.6 million enterprises in the hotels and restaurants sector employed 8.7 million people, which is equal to 6.9 % of the EU-27's non-financial business economy workforce. This latter share ranked the sector as the fifth largest employer among all the NACE divisions of the non-financial business economy. Among the two subsectors that make up the hotels and restaurants sector, the activities of restaurants, bars and catering (NACE Groups 55.3 to 55.5) contributed about two thirds (65.4 %) of the EU-27's sectoral value added in 2004, while providing around three quarters (75.4 %) of the sectoral workforce. Accommodation services (NACE Groups 55.1 and 55.2) made up the rest of the sector.

With EUR 40.2 billion of value added in 2004, the United Kingdom was by far the largest Member State in the hotels and restaurants sector, its value added 1.6 times the equivalent figure registered in France, the second largest contributor to the EU-27's sectoral value added. Moreover, across the Member States, the United Kingdom had also the largest workforce in hotels and restaurants, with 1.9 million persons employed in these activities, followed by Germany where some 1.2 million persons were employed - see Table 19.3. In terms of the value added contribution to national non-financial business economy, Spain was the most specialised in hotels and restaurants activities among the countries with data available in 2004 with a 4.9 % contribution. However, data availability for Cyprus is incomplete, but shows that hotels and restaurants contributed 13.8 % of the non-financial business economy value added in Cyprus excluding NACE Divisions 70 and 73, far ahead of the equivalent Spanish figure. Furthermore, data related to specialisation is not at all available for Greece or Malta, while these countries recorded high levels of international tourist receipts according to the WTO when considered on a per head basis. Indeed, per head tourist receipts were about EUR 1 547 per inhabitant in Malta and EUR 996 in Greece in 2005. These two figures were relatively high compared with similar ratios for the five largest EU economies that had the highest levels of tourism receipts in absolute values: Spain (EUR 894 per inhabitant), France (EUR 544), Italy (EUR 487), the United Kingdom (EUR 410) and Germany (EUR 285).

Table 19.2

Hotels and restaurants (NACE Section H)
Structural profile, EU-27, 2004

	No. of enterprises		Turnover		Value added		Employment	
	(thousands)	(% of total)	(EUR million)	(% of total)	(EUR million)	(% of total)	(thousands)	(% of total)
Hotels and restaurants	1 604.7	100.0	386 110	100.0	163 455	100.0	8 651.6	100.0
Hotels; camping sites, other provision of short-stay accommodation	248.4	15.5	116 239	30.1	56 627	34.6	2 127.8	24.6
Restaurants; bars; canteens and catering	1 356.3	84.5	269 872	69.9	106 829	65.4	6 523.8	75.4

Source: Eurostat (SBS)

Figure 19.2 —————————————————————————

Hotels and restaurants (NACE Section H)
Share of non-financial business economy, EU-27, 2004 (%) (1)

(1) Rounded estimate based on non-confidential data.
Source: Eurostat (SBS)

Figure 19.3 ————————

Hotels and restaurants (NACE Section H)
Evolution of main indicators, EU-27
(2000=100)

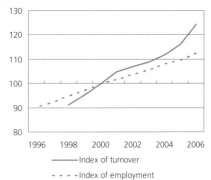

Source: Eurostat (STS)

Among all the Member States with available data [5], the contribution of hotels and restaurants activities to non-financial business economy value added was lower than the equivalent contribution in terms of employment, reflecting the labour intensive nature of these activities although employment figures are boosted by the high degree of part-time employment in this sector (see below).

The map on page 320 shows the contribution of the hotels and restaurants sector to employment within the non-financial business economy (NACE Sections C to I and K) of each region. The importance of this activity in several southern Member States is clear, and the highest proportions of non-financial business economy employment in the hotels and restaurants sector were recorded in the Illes Balears (27.7 %, Spain), the Algarve (23.3 %, Portugal) and the Provincia Autonoma Bolzano-Bozen (21.3 %, Italy). Nevertheless, this sector also provided an important contribution to non-financial business employment in several regions in the United Kingdom and Austria, in both Irish regions, as well as in Cyprus; note, in particular, that data is not available for the Greek regions and for Malta.

Annual short-term statistics are available for the period 1998 to 2006 for the EU-27's turnover index for hotels and restaurants (NACE Section H), while a 10-years series (1996 to 2006) is available for the index of employment - see Figure 19.3. Both of these indices posted uninterrupted upward trends over the periods observed. The index of turnover grew on average by 3.9 % per annum between 1998 and 2006. The years 1999, 2000 and 2001 were characterised by a faster pace of annual growth, compared with more modest increases registered during the following years. However, the rate of growth accelerated steadily from a low 1.8 % in 2003 to 3.8 % by 2005, with the fastest pace of increase being recorded in 2006, when the turnover index went up by 7.2 %. The index of employment showed that there was average growth of 2.2 % per annum between 1996 and 2006. Over the period observed, the fastest annual development for the index of employment was recorded in 1998 (2.8 %) while the slowest increase was registered in 2005 (1.5 %). Among the Member States for which data is available for all of the five years from 2001 to 2006 [6], fast growth of the employment index for hotels and restaurants were recorded for the three Baltic

countries and Bulgaria, where the number of persons employed grew on average by 8.5 % per annum or more over this period of time.

In terms of enterprise size, a large proportion of wealth created in the EU-27's hotels and restaurants sector was concentrated within small and medium-sized enterprises (SMEs, with less than 250 persons employed) as these enterprises generated about three quarters (75.8 %) of the sector's value added in 2004, above the 57.0 % average share in the non-financial business economy. The contribution of SMEs to sectoral employment was even more important than for value added, those enterprises employing 82.3 % of the total workforce, again well above the non-financial business economy average of 67.1 %.

In more detail, micro enterprises (with less than 10 persons employed) contributed the largest part of hotels and restaurants value added and employment. In the EU-27, these enterprises provided 36.5 % of sectoral value added and 45.4 % of the sectoral workforce. These two shares were well above the non-financial business economy averages (29.6 % and 20.2 % respectively).

---

[5] Luxembourg, 2003; Ireland, Greece, Cyprus and Malta, not available.

[6] Belgium, Greece, Italy and the Netherlands, not included in the analysis.

Table 19.3 ———————————————————————

Hotels and restaurants (NACE Section H)
Structural profile: ranking of top five Member States, 2004

| Rank | Value added (EUR million) (1) | Employment (thousands) (1) | Share of non-financial business economy | | | |
			No. of enterprises (2)	Turnover (2)	Value added (2)	Employment (2)
1	United Kingdom (40 152)	United Kingdom (1 923.0)	Austria (16.7 %)	Spain (3.0 %)	Spain (4.9 %)	United Kingdom (10.7 %)
2	France (25 620)	Germany (1 163.9)	Luxembourg (12.2 %)	United Kingdom (2.8 %)	Austria (4.6 %)	Austria (9.6 %)
3	Spain (22 254)	Spain (1 161.2)	Spain (11.4 %)	Portugal (2.8 %)	Portugal (4.2 %)	Spain (9.0 %)
4	Germany (20 852)	Italy (1 035.7)	Portugal (11.2 %)	Austria (2.7 %)	United Kingdom (4.2 %)	Portugal (8.0 %)
5	Italy (18 666)	France (884.4)	Belgium (10.6 %)	France (2.1 %)	Luxembourg (4.0 %)	Luxembourg (7.1 %)

(1) Greece and Malta, not available; Luxembourg, 2003.
(2) Ireland, Greece, Cyprus and Malta, not available; Luxembourg, 2003.
Source: Eurostat (SBS)

Among the Member States, the United Kingdom (46.7 %) and to a lesser extent Poland (32.7 %) and Romania (32.1 %), stood out from the other countries with respect to the relatively high contribution of large enterprises (with 250 and more persons employed) to the hotels and restaurants sector's value added in 2004.

EMPLOYMENT CHARACTERISTICS

There was a majority of women among the hotels and restaurants workforce, as in 2006 they accounted for 55.7 % of those employed in this sector in the EU-27. This proportion was 20.7 percentage points higher than the non-financial business economy (NACE Sections C to I and K) average – see Figure 19.5. Moreover, this pattern was widespread as the proportion of female employment was higher than the non-financial business economy national average in every Member State [7]. Among the EU-27's hotels and restaurants workforce in 2006 some 71.8 % worked on a full-time basis, a share that was clearly below that for the non-financial business economy as a whole (85.6 %). In fact, this was the second lowest full-time rate among all the NACE divisions of the non-financial business economy, higher only than in retail trade (NACE Division 52). This low proportion of full-time employment reflects the need for employment flexibility in this sector, including adaptability to atypical working hours. In all of the Member States the proportion of the persons working full-time in this sector was close to or below the national average for the non-financial business economy.

The hotels and restaurants workforce tended to be younger than in other activities of the non-financial business economy, a characteristic linked to the relatively low-skilled and low paid

[7] Latvia, Lithuania and Luxembourg, 2003; Estonia, not available.

Figure 19.4

Hotels and restaurants (NACE Section H)
Share of value added by enterprise size class, EU-27, 2004

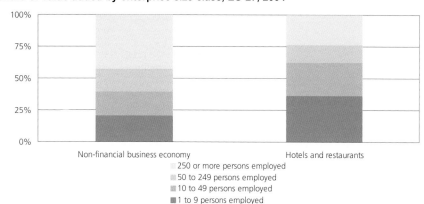

Source: Eurostat (SBS)

nature of many of the jobs and the flexibility and irregularity of working hours and the seasonal nature of work in this sector, that often peaks during periods when higher education establishments are closed. Indeed, in 2006 those aged 15 to 29 accounted for over one third (35.8 %) of the sector's workforce in the EU-27, while the equivalent share for the non-financial business economy as a whole was 11.6 percentage points lower. Indeed, this was the highest share of younger workers in the workforce of all of the NACE divisions of the non-financial business economy. Among the Member States, the share of younger workers in the hotels and restaurant workforce was systematically higher than in the non-financial business economy as a whole except in Cyprus.

In 2004, according to structural business statistics data, the share of employees (paid workers) in persons employed was 80.6 % in the EU-27's hotels and restaurants sector, which was somewhat lower than for the non-financial

business economy as a whole (86.2 %) reflecting a higher incidence of working proprietors and unpaid family workers in this sector.

COSTS, PRODUCTIVITY AND PROFITABILITY

A breakdown of total expenditure shows that purchases of goods and services accounted for slightly more than three fifths (61.9 %) of the total in the EU-27's hotels and restaurants sector in 2006 – see Table 19.4. This share was significantly lower than the non-financial business economy average (78.7 %) and ranked among the lowest shares recorded across all the NACE divisions within the non-financial business economy. Instead, personnel costs accounted for three tenths (30.2 %) of the total expenditure, the fourth largest share dedicated to this category of expenditure among the non-financial business economy NACE divisions, almost twice the average share (16.4 %) for the non-financial business economy. The remaining category of expenditure for the breakdown considered in this

Figure 19.5

Hotels and restaurants (NACE Section H)
Labour force characteristics, 2006

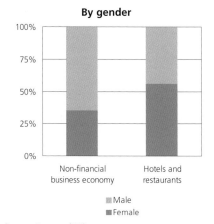
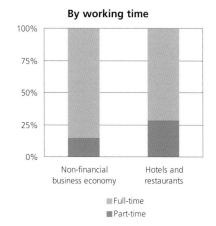
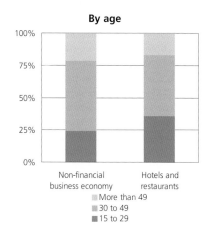

Source: Eurostat (LFS)

Table 19.4

Hotels and restaurants (NACE Section H)
Total expenditure, EU-27, 2004

	Value (EUR million)				Share (% of total expenditure)		
	Total expenditure	Purchases of goods and services	Personnel costs	Investment in tangible goods	Purchases of goods and services	Personnel costs	Investment in tangible goods
Hotels and restaurants	343 232	212 430	103 764	27 038	61.9	30.2	7.9
Hotels; camping sites, other provision of short-stay accommodation	104 861	56 713	34 805	13 344	54.1	33.2	12.7
Restaurants; bars; canteens and catering	238 373	155 720	68 959	13 694	65.3	28.9	5.7

Source: Eurostat (SBS)

Table 19.5

Hotels and restaurants (NACE Section H)
Productivity and profitability, EU-27, 2004

	Apparent labour productivity (EUR thousand)	Average personnel costs (EUR thousand)	Wage adjusted labour productivity (%)	Gross operating rate (%)
Hotels and restaurants	18.9	14.9	127.0	15.5
Hotels; camping sites, other provision of short-stay accommodation	26.6	18.4	144.9	18.8
Restaurants; bars; canteens and catering	16.4	13.6	120.6	14.0

Source: Eurostat (SBS)

analysis was that of gross investment in tangible goods, which represented 7.9 % of the total in the EU-27's hotels and restaurants sector, a share that was more than 60 % higher than the average share for the non-financial business economy. In the accommodation services subsector the share of purchases of goods and services was particularly low, as it represented only slightly more than half of the total expenditure; in this subsector the share of tangible investment was 12.7 %, a share that was higher than that recorded in most of the non-financial business economy NACE divisions and groups.

Apparent labour productivity in the EU-27's hotels and restaurants sector was EUR 18 900 per person employed in 2004, this low level reflecting to some extent the high use of part-time and seasonal employment. Equally, these characteristics and the relatively low or unskilled workforce have an impact on average personnel costs per employee which were EUR 14 900 in the hotels and restaurants sector. Both of these indicators were significantly lower than for the non-financial business economy average (EUR 40 900 and EUR 27 600 respectively) and in fact the average personnel costs were the third lowest among the non-financial business economy NACE divisions and the apparent labour productivity was the second lowest.

The wage adjusted labour productivity ratio is less affected by the incidence of part-time and seasonal employment. For the EU-27's hotels and restaurants sector this was 127.0 %, still

below the equivalent ratio for the non-financial business economy (148.0 %) but by a much smaller margin than for the two previous indicators. In all the Member States [8] for which a comparison of this ratio between the hotels and restaurants sector and the non-financial business economy can be made, the ratio recorded by the hotels and restaurants sector was systematically lower – see Figure 19.6. Among the two subsectors that make up the hotels and restaurants sector, the EU-27's accommodations services recorded a wage adjusted labour productivity ratio (144.9 %) that was close to the non-financial business economy average while the activities of restaurants, bars and catering recorded a ratio of just 120.6 %. Despite the relatively low

[8] Luxembourg, 2003; Ireland, Greece, Cyprus and Malta, not available.

productivity figures, in terms of profitability the EU-27's hotels and restaurants sector recorded a gross operating surplus (value added less personnel costs) equivalent to 15.5 % of turnover in 2004, some way above the non-financial business economy average (11.0 %). However, this was not the case in all the Member States for which data are available, as in Lithuania, Hungary, and Sweden and to a lesser extent in Finland, the gross operating rate for the hotels and restaurants sector were below the non-financial business economy average. Again, the highest level for this indicator was registered for the accommodation services subsector, at 18.8 % in the EU-27, while the rate for the activities of restaurants, bars and catering was lower at 14.0 % but nevertheless above the non-financial business economy average.

Figure 19.6

Hotels and restaurants (NACE Section H)
Productivity and profitability characteristics relative to national averages, 2004
(non-financial business economy=100) (1)

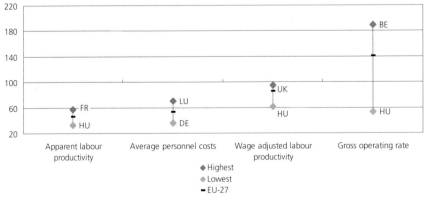

(1) Ireland, Greece, Cyprus and Malta, not available; Luxembourg, 2003.
Source: Eurostat (SBS)

19.1: ACCOMMODATION SERVICES

Accommodation services are covered by two NACE groups: Group 55.1 includes the provision of short-stay lodging in hotels, motels and inns, excluding the rental of long-stay accommodation and timeshare operations; Group 55.2 covers camping sites and other short-stay accommodation, including self-catering holiday chalets or cottages.

One of the major developments both on the supply and demand side for accommodation services is the emergence in the last decade of new channels of purchase and sales coming from new information and communication technologies, for example on-line booking. This is reflected in the most recent results from the annual survey on e-commerce, with an increasing share of total turnover for accommodation services generated via the Internet. Indeed, in 2004 the EU-25 accommodation services (NACE Groups 55.1 and 55.2) generated just 3 % of their turnover via the Internet, while the

equivalent share for the business economy [9] was 9 %. In 2005, the share passed to 8 % for accommodation services, closer to the average for the business economy recorded at 10 % and in 2006 the difference narrowed further, 11 % for accommodation services and 12 % for the business economy. Note however that this survey is limited to enterprises with 10 persons employed and more and, as was shown earlier, micro enterprises (with less than 10 persons employed) are much more important in the hotels and restaurant sector than in other activities.

There are four main types of accommodation: hotels, camping sites, holiday dwellings and other collective establishments. The Member States that had the largest number of hotels and similar establishments in 2005 were Germany, Italy and the United Kingdom with

[9] Defined as NACE Sections D to K and Division 92 for the purpose of this analysis.

over 32 000 establishments each, which combined accounted for close to half the total number in the EU-27 – see Table 19.6. In terms of the number of arrivals (combining resident and non-resident arrivals), France and Germany were the largest markets. A number of southern Member States recorded the longest average stays (nights per arrival) for non-residents, notably in Cyprus, Malta, Bulgaria and Greece where this exceeded 5 nights. Figure 19.7 shows the seasonality of demand for hotels and similar accommodation in the EU-27 through the months of the year 2005: the number of nights spent in August 2005 was 2.5 times that recorded in December the same year. Table 19.7 provides an overview of the supply of other types of collective accommodation, where there were approximately 13.7 million bed-places in the EU-27 in 2005, 1.2 times as many as in hotels and similar establishments.

Table 19.6

Main indicators for hotels and similar establishments, 2005

	Infrastructure (1)			Arrivals (thousands) (2)			Nights spent (thousands) (3)		Nights spent per arrival (2)	
	Establishments	Bedrooms	Bed places	Residents	Non-residents	Non-residents share (%)	Residents	Non-residents	Residents	Non-residents
EU-27	195 338	5 616 459	11 671 209	:	:	:	791 375	657 220	:	:
BE	1 899	54 226	120 668	2 364	5 409	69.6	4 313	10 297	1.8	1.9
BG	1 230	90 593	200 940	1 721	1 909	52.6	3 957	11 471	2.3	6.0
CZ	4 279	99 966	232 295	3 595	5 781	61.7	8 854	17 035	2.5	2.9
DK	480	35 659	69 932	1 903	1 350	41.5	5 328	4 787	2.8	3.5
DE	36 593	890 153	1 621 118	73 777	18 761	20.3	161 895	38 872	2.2	2.1
EE	317	12 312	25 228	428	1 358	76.0	751	2 791	1.8	2.1
IE	4 296	63 087	148 077	:	:	:	8 174	17 024	:	:
EL	9 111	364 179	693 252	5 933	7 143	54.6	13 942	40 075	2.4	5.6
ES	18 304	814 891	1 614 237	47 539	34 492	42.0	114 825	151 763	2.4	4.4
FR	19 811	629 597	1 739 518	72 930	32 304	30.7	123 105	68 821	1.7	2.1
IT	33 527	1 020 478	2 028 452	41 295	30 870	42.8	138 222	102 098	3.3	3.3
CY	785	45 209	91 264	449	1 750	79.6	1 040	13 899	2.3	7.9
LV	337	9 219	19 229	354	680	65.8	796	1 507	2.2	2.2
LT	331	10 134	19 940	347	623	64.2	728	1 334	2.1	2.1
LU	284	7 474	14 349	29	673	95.9	77	1 284	2.7	1.9
HU	1 921	64 769	154 060	2 778	3 140	53.1	6 622	9 127	2.4	2.9
MT	173	18 533	39 518	135	1 004	88.1	314	6 977	2.3	6.9
NL	3 099	94 509	192 067	8 301	8 081	49.3	14 375	15 143	1.7	1.9
AT	14 051	282 002	572 514	7 399	14 947	66.9	20 277	57 114	2.7	3.8
PL	2 200	84 865	169 609	6 805	3 723	35.4	12 464	7 869	1.8	2.1
PT	2 012	116 123	263 814	5 274	5 355	50.4	11 648	23 873	2.2	4.5
RO	4 125	110 937	226 383	:	:	:	:	:	:	:
SI	358	16 402	31 145	484	1 247	72.0	1 746	3 401	3.6	2.7
SK	885	28 231	57 071	1 244	1 203	49.1	3 183	3 650	2.6	3.0
FI	938	54 354	117 605	5 948	1 828	23.5	10 388	3 887	1.7	2.1
SE	1 857	100 155	197 470	11 096	2 736	19.8	17 518	5 382	1.6	2.0
UK	32 926	518 028	1 062 342	52 611	17 009	24.4	117 926	58 909	2.2	3.5
HR	1 015	80 743	203 464	1 002	3 744	78.9	2 862	18 415	2.9	4.9
IS	308	8 025	16 849	245	714	74.5	387	1 341	1.6	1.9
LI	46	646	1 263	1	55	97.6	3	115	2.0	2.1
NO	1 119	69 477	151 252	8 122	2 841	25.9	12 859	4 896	1.6	1.7
CH	5 643	139 941	259 004	:	:	:	:	:	:	:

(1) Ireland, Greece, Spain, Luxembourg, Hungary, Malta, the Netherlands, Austria, Romania, Slovenia, Iceland, Liechtenstein and Norway, 2006; Switzerland, 2002.
(2) The Czech Republic, Spain, France, Luxembourg, Malta, Austria, Slovenia, Iceland, Liechtenstein and Norway, 2006.
(3) EU-25 instead of EU-27; the Czech Republic, Spain, France, Luxembourg, Malta, Austria and Slovenia, 2006; Italy, provisional.
Source: Eurostat (Tourism)

Figure 19.7

Number of nights spent in hotels and similar establishments, EU-27, 2005 (millions)

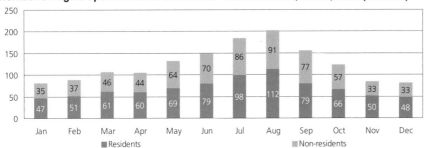

■ Residents   ■ Non-residents

Source: Eurostat (Tourism)

Table 19.7

Main indicators for collective accommodation establishments other than hotels, 2005 (1)

	Number of establishments (units)				Number of bed places: total
	Total	**Tourist campsites**	**Holiday dwellings**	**Other collective accomodations**	
EU-27	208 009	:	:	:	13 721 113
BE	1 550	554	75	921	294 501
BG	325	18	:	:	20 204
CZ	3 329	499	331	2 499	203 698
DK	608	430	77	101	320 832
DE	18 756	2 461	10 844	5 451	1 695 735
EE	467	80	143	244	12 860
IE	4 805	105	4 505	195	60 401
EL	333	333	:	:	93 639
ES	17 895	1 216	4 524	12 155	1 460 288
FR	9 244	8 138	922	184	3 039 178
IT	96 409	2 411	68 385	25 613	2 322 081
CY	134	4	130	0	4 128
LV	81	22	46	13	4 816
LT	193	7	173	13	11 314
LU	252	100	114	38	51 937
HU	940	235	365	340	146 331
MT	6	:	:	:	684
NL	4 055	2 462	806	787	994 826
AT	6 406	542	3 329	2 535	362 157
PL	4 523	136	315	4 072	400 287
PT	288	227	:	:	182 656
RO	585	68	:	:	60 775
SI	349	43	79	227	35 038
SK	1 131	73	66	992	103 124
FI	459	284	128	47	92 608
SE	2 089	1 065	309	715	537 381
UK	33 877	3 874	28 578	1 425	1 162 789
HR	515	224	126	165	295 678
IS	287	140	32	115	:
LI	111	2	100	9	:
NO	1 163	792	297	74	341 874

(1) Ireland, Greece, Spain, Luxembourg, Hungary, Malta, the Netherlands, Austria, Romania, Slovenia, Iceland, Liechtenstein and Norway, 2006; Hungary, provisional.
Source: Eurostat (Tourism)

STRUCTURAL PROFILE

There were 248 400 enterprises in the accommodation services (NACE Groups 55.1 and 55.2) sector which generated EUR 116.2 billion of turnover in the EU-27 in 2004 and EUR 56.6 billion of value added, with a workforce of just over 2 million persons. The contribution of this sector to the hotels and restaurants (NACE Section H) total was about three tenths (30.1 %) for turnover, over one third (34.6 %) for value added, and a smaller share of the workforce, around one quarter (24.6 %). Among the Member States, the United Kingdom created the highest value added for accommodation services in 2004 (EUR 10.7 billion, 18.9 % of the EU-27 total), and had the largest workforce (17.2 % of the EU-27 total). In terms of the contribution of accommodation services to the non-financial business economy (NACE Sections C to I and K) value added in 2004 Austria stood out as being most specialised, as its accommodation services contribution (2.5 %) was more than twice (2.2 times) the EU-27's average (1.1 %) – see Table 19.8. Austria's specialisation on accommodation services was also evident from the contribution of this sector's workforce to its non-financial business economy workforce (4.1 %), some 2.4 times as high as the equivalent EU-27 average (1.7 %). The next most specialised Member State [10] was Spain, both in terms of value added and employment, while Italy also appeared in the top five of the most specialised Member States for both measures.

[10] Luxembourg, 2003; Ireland, Greece, Cyprus and Malta, not available.

Table 19.8

Hotels; camping sites, other provision of short-stay accommodation (NACE Groups 55.1 and 55.2)
Structural profile: ranking of top five Member States, 2004

Rank	Share of EU-27 value added (%) (1)	Share of EU-27 employment (%) (1)	Value added specialisation ratio (EU-27=100) (2)	Employment specialisation ratio (EU-27=100) (2)
1	United Kingdom (18.9)	United Kingdom (17.2)	Austria (224.3)	Austria (242.1)
2	France (15.1)	Germany (16.9)	Spain (160.1)	Spain (119.9)
3	Germany (14.5)	Italy (12.4)	Portugal (131.5)	United Kingdom (119.5)
4	Spain (14.4)	Spain (12.3)	Bulgaria (125.7)	Italy (105.5)
5	Italy (12.9)	France (11.3)	Italy (116.1)	Germany (102.0)

(1) Greece and Malta, not available; Luxembourg, 2003.
(2) Ireland, Greece, Cyprus and Malta, not available; Luxembourg, 2003.
Source: Eurostat (SBS)

Behind these averages for the transport services sector lies a distinction, essentially between air and rail transport on one hand which are dominated by large enterprises, and the remaining transport services which are characterised by an employment contribution from SMEs closer to, but generally still above, the average for the non-financial business economy. Due to the dominance of rail transport by a few enterprises in most Member States an analysis of the size structure of the sector is difficult for reasons of statistical confidentiality. Nevertheless, the information that is available for a few Member States illustrates that this activity is dominated by large enterprises to a greater extent than in nearly any other activity: in Germany large enterprises contributed 90.6 % of value added in rail transport in 2004, while the equivalent share in the United Kingdom was 96.5 % and in Italy it reached 99.2 %. Equally, for air transport services large enterprises accounted for a large share of the sector's value added in 2004, exceeding 50 % in all of the Member States with data available except for Slovakia. The importance of large enterprises in the EU-27's air transport sector was such that they accounted for 90.0 % of employment in 2004; this was the highest employment share of large enterprises among all of the non-financial business economy NACE divisions (5) in 2004.

TRANSPORT OF GOODS AND PASSENGERS
Over several decades, road and sea transport of goods increased strongly in the EU, while the volume of goods transported by inland waterways was relatively stable and rail freight transport declined. For the EU-25 around ten years of data is now available for most modes of transport, and this provides an insight into the changes in more recent periods for both goods and passengers - see Figures 20.4 to 20.7. Since 1995 the use of road and sea freight transport increased steadily and strongly, and in 2005 they together accounted for 83 % of freight transport (in terms of tonne-kilometres). Rail, pipeline and inland water freight transport increased in terms of tonne-kilometres transported but their share of total freight transport decreased.

(5) NACE Divisions 10, 12 to 14, 16, 19, 23 and 61, not available.

Figure 20.3

Transport services (NACE Divisions 60, 61, 62 and 63)
Share of value added by enterprise size class, EU-27, 2004 (1)

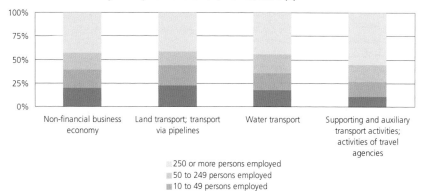

(1) Air transport, not available.
Source: Eurostat (STS)

Figure 20.4

Modal split of goods transport, EU-25
(% of billion tonne-kilometres) (1)

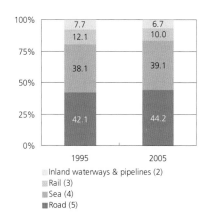

(1) Excluding air.
(2) Germany, crude oil only.
(3) Excluding Northern Ireland.
(4) Domestic and intra-EU-25 transport only; data under revision.
(5) Haulage by vehicles registered in the EU-25.
Source: Eurostat, ECMT, UIC, national statistics, estimates, in European Union Energy and Transport in Figures pocketbook 2006, European Commission, Directorate-General for Energy and Transport

Figure 20.5

Index of the evolution of goods transport
(billion tonne-kilometres), EU-25
(1995=100)

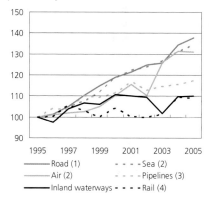

(1) Haulage by vehicles registered in the EU-25.
(2) Domestic and intra-EU-25 transport only; data under revision.
(3) Germany, crude oil only.
(4) Excluding Northern Ireland.
Source: Eurostat, ECMT, UIC, national statistics, estimates, in European Union Energy and Transport in Figures pocketbook 2006, European Commission, Directorate-General for Energy and Transport

Sea passenger transport displayed a fall in the number of passenger-kilometres transported between 1995 and 1999, since when this volume remained stable. Rail passenger transport recorded growth through until 2000 followed by a period of relative stability. Other collective land passenger transport such as bus, metro, tram and coaches recorded more stable increases in their respective volumes of passenger transport. In the EU-25 the fastest increase in passenger transport over the period considered was recorded for air transport, as its share of total passenger transport (in terms of passenger-kilometres) rose from 6.3 % in 1995 to 8.0 % by 2004. The relatively stable modal share of passenger cars reflects a growth rate in the use of passenger cars that was slightly higher than the rates recorded by most forms of passenger transport other than air transport.

EMPLOYMENT CHARACTERISTICS

On the basis of Labour Force Survey data, transport services clearly stand out from most other service activities in terms of their gender profile (see Figure 20.8). Only 20.8 % of those persons employed in this sector in 2006 in the EU-27 were women, which was around three fifths the average for the non-financial business economy, where women accounted for 35.0 % of those employed. In land transport and transport via pipelines (NACE Division 60) the share of women in the workforce was just 13.7 %, among the lowest shares across the non-financial business economy NACE divisions, higher only than in construction and a number of industrial (NACE Sections C to E) divisions. Among the four transport services NACE divisions, the share of women in the workforce was highest in air transport, at 41.4 %, above the non-financial business economy average.

Figure 20.6

Estimated modal split of passenger transport, EU-25
(% of billion passenger-kilometres)

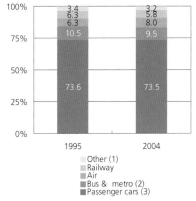

(1) Powered two wheelers and sea.
(2) Includes also coach and tram; only inter-urban bus and coach traffic for Poland and Slovakia; excluding Northern Ireland for bus and coach.
(3) Excluding Northern Ireland.
Source: Eurostat, ECMT, IUPT, UIC, national statistics, estimates, in European Union Energy and Transport in Figures pocketbook 2006, European Commission, Directorate-General for Energy and Transport

Part-time work was also less common in transport services than in other activities, since 90.7 % of those employed in transport services in the EU-27 in 2006 worked on a full-time basis, compared with a non-financial business economy average of 85.6 %. The high incidence of full-time employment was observed in all transport services NACE divisions, but particularly so in water transport (94.0 %) and land transport and transport via pipelines (92.5 %), while the lowest rate of full-time employment was recorded for air transport (82.6 %), some 3.0 percentage points below the non-financial business economy average.

Figure 20.7

Index of the estimated evolution of passenger transport (billion passenger-kilometres), EU-25 (1995=100)

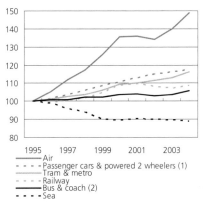

(1) Passenger cars, excluding Northern Ireland.
(2) Only inter-urban traffic for Poland and Slovakia; excluding Northern Ireland.
Source: Eurostat; ECMT, IUPT, UIC, national statistics, estimates, in European Union Energy and Transport in Figures pocketbook 2006, European Commission, Directorate-General for Energy and Transport

The age profile of the transport services workforce was also markedly different from the non-financial business economy average. The proportion of the transport services workforce aged 15 to 29 was 17.6 % in 2006, some 6.6 percentage points below the average for the non-financial business economy. The share of the transport services workforce aged 30 to 49 was 57.3 %, 3.1 percentage points higher than the non-financial business economy average, while persons aged 50 or more accounted for one quarter (25.1 %) of the workforce, compared with just over one fifth (21.6 %) for the non-financial business economy as a whole. All of the transport services NACE divisions recorded a relatively low proportion of younger

Figure 20.8

Transport services (NACE Divisions 60, 61, 62 and 63)
Labour force characteristics, EU-27, 2006

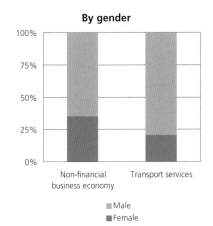

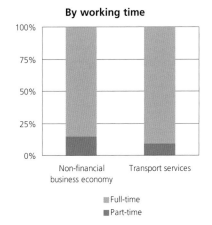

Source: Eurostat (LFS)

Table 20.4

Transport services (NACE Divisions 60, 61, 62 and 63)
Total expenditure, EU-27, 2004

	Value (EUR million)				Share (% of total expenditure)		
	Total expenditure	Purchases of goods and services	Personnel costs	Investment in tangible goods	Purchases of goods and services	Personnel costs	Investment in tangible goods
Transport services (1)	1 040 000	700 000	230 000	110 000	67.3	22.1	10.6
Transport via railways (1)	83 000	40 000	28 000	15 000	48.2	33.7	18.1
Other land transport (1)	323 000	200 000	92 000	31 000	61.9	28.5	9.6
Water transport (1)	72 200	56 000	7 200	9 000	77.6	10.0	12.5
Air transport (1)	105 000	73 000	25 000	7 000	69.5	23.8	6.7
Transport via pipelines (1) (2)	3 944	2 600	386	959	65.9	9.8	24.3
Auxiliary transport activities	325 074	213 874	64 849	46 351	65.8	19.9	14.3
Activities of travel agencies (1)	132 300	120 000	11 000	1 300	90.7	8.3	1.0

(1) Rounded estimates based on non-confidential data.
(2) EU-25.
Source: Eurostat (SBS)

workers, but this was most notable in land transport and transport via pipelines where the proportion was as low as 14.2 %, one of the lowest among the non-financial business economy NACE divisions, higher only than in water supply (NACE Division 41) and some mining and quarrying (NACE Section C) divisions. Air transport was the only transport services NACE division where the proportion of older workers (18.5 %) was below the non-financial business economy average, while the highest proportion of older workers was recorded for water transport services (28.3 %).

Structural business statistics indicate that the proportion of paid employees in the total number of persons employed (which also includes working proprietors and unpaid family workers) was around 88.0 % in the EU-27 transport services sector in 2004, which was marginally higher than the non-financial business economy average (86.2 %). All of the EU-27's transport services subsectors recorded a higher proportion of paid employees than the non-financial business economy average except for road and other land transport (80.0 %), as the share of employees in persons employed was close to or exceeded 90 % in 2004 in the remaining transport services subsectors presented in Subchapters 20.1 to 20.7.

COSTS, PRODUCTIVITY AND PROFITABILITY

Transport services reported high investment expenditure compared with operating expenditure (see Figure 20.9), underlying the capital intensive nature of some parts of the sector: gross tangible investment in EU-27 transport services was equivalent to 10.6 % of total expenditure, over double the non-financial business economy average (4.9 %). One subsector stood out from the others based on this ratio, and that was the EU-27's travel agencies subsector where gross tangible investment was equivalent to just 1.0 % of total expenditure. In the other transport subsectors [6] this ratio was in all cases above

[6] Transport via pipelines, not available.

the non-financial business economy average, and it was particularly high for rail transport at 18.1 %. Personnel costs accounted for over one fifth (22.1 %) of total expenditure in transport services, notably more than the 16.4 % non-financial business economy average. Again this share was high in rail transport where it reached 33.7 % and low among travel agencies where it was just 8.3 %. The distributive nature of travel agencies was evident from the high share of purchases of goods and services in total expenditure which was 90.7 %, compared with a transport services average of 67.3 %.

Figure 20.9

Transport services (NACE Divisions 60, 61, 62 and 63)
Total expenditure, EU-27, 2004 (1)

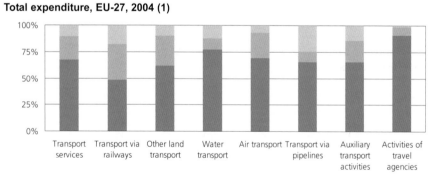

(1) Rounded estimates based on non-confidential data; transport via pipelines, EU-25.
Source: Eurostat (SBS)

Table 20.5

Transport services (NACE Divisions 60, 61, 62 and 63)
Productivity and profitability, EU-27, 2004 (1)

	Apparent labour productivity (EUR thousand) (2)	Average personnel costs (EUR thousand) (2)	Wage adjusted labour productivity (%) (3)	Gross operating rate (%) (4)
Transport services	42.0	30.0	140.0	13.3
Transport via railways	38.0	30.7	124.0	11.0
Other land transport	30.0	26.0	120.0	13.0
Water transport	110.0	:	270.0	19.5
Air transport	70.0	60.0	120.0	4.4
Transport via pipelines	374.8	42.1	890.0	52.0
Auxiliary transport activities	60.4	34.1	177.2	17.3
Activities of travel agencies	43.0	25.9	166.0	7.0

(1) Rounded estimates based on non-confidential data, except for auxiliary transport activities.
(2) Transport via railways and transport via pipelines, EU-25.
(3) Air transport and transport via pipelines, EU-25.
(4) Air transport, EU-25.
Source: Eurostat (SBS)

The high levels of full-time employment may to some extent explain why average personnel costs faced by transport services enterprises were generally high: in transport services they averaged EUR 30 000 per employee in 2004 in the EU-27 compared with EUR 27 600 for the non-financial business economy as a whole. Among the transport services subsectors average personnel costs were notably higher for air transport services where, at EUR 60 000 per employee, they were double the transport services average (see Table 20.5).

As might be expected for a capital intensive sector, the apparent labour productivity in the transport services sector (EUR 42 000 per person employed) was slightly higher than the non-financial business economy average (EUR 40 900 per person employed). However, the relatively high level of average personnel costs impacted on the wage adjusted labour productivity ratio, which represents the extent to which value added per person employed covers average personnel costs per employee. In the EU-27's transport services sector, this ratio was 140.0 % in 2004, below the non-financial business economy average of 148.0 %. A further analysis shows that there were considerable differences in the value of this ratio between the transport services subsectors, with a particularly high ratio for transport via pipelines (890.0 %, EU-25) and to a lesser extent for water transport (270.0 %).

In contrast, the gross operating rate (gross operating surplus relative to turnover) was higher for transport services (13.3 %) in 2004 than the non-financial business economy average (11.0 %). Once more water transport recorded a high value (19.5 %), but this was well below the exceptionally high gross operating rate (52.0 %) recorded for transport via pipelines, comfortably the highest rate among all non-financial business economy NACE groups.

20.1: RAIL TRANSPORT

This subchapter includes information on the transport of passengers and goods by railways (NACE Group 60.1). The activities relating to the operation of the rail infrastructure are classified as auxiliary transport activities and are covered by Subchapter 20.6. Equally, this subchapter does not cover urban and suburban rail transport of passengers, which is included in the following subchapter on road and other land transport.

Considerable legislative efforts have been made to open up and revitalise the rail transport sector, motivated in part by the wish to take advantage of lower emissions from rail transport, and to reduce road congestion. The European Commission proposed three packages of legislation for rail transport. The first was adopted by the European Parliament and Council in 2001 and focused on a drive to open up the international rail freight network. The second package was adopted by the European Parliament and Council in 2004 and concerned opening-up the national rail freight transport market, as well as legislation aimed at improving interoperability (between networks) and safety. It also included the establishment of a railway agency to support the work on issues relating to safety and interoperability. Proposals for a third package were adopted by the European Commission in 2004 and concern, among other issues, opening up international passenger services to competition within the European Union, as such completing the integration of rail transport. It is hoped that improvements in rail passenger services will allow rail transport to compete more effectively with road transport as well as some segments of air transport. In June 2007 the European Parliament and Council reached agreement under the conciliation procedure on the proposals and, at the time of writing, these are expected to be adopted shortly.

In December 2006 the European Commission adopted a series of measures [7] to support the revitalisation of the railway sector by removing obstacles to the circulation of trains throughout the European rail network.

---
[7] COM(2006) 783, 784 and 785.

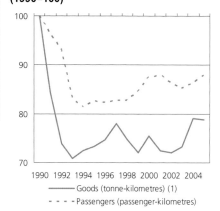

Figure 20.10

Evolution of rail transport, EU-27 (1990=100)

— Goods (tonne-kilometres) (1)
- - - Passengers (passenger-kilometres)

(1) Excluding Northern Ireland.
Source: Eurostat, ECMT, UIC, national statistics, estimates, in European Union Energy and Transport in Figures pocketbook 2006, European Commission, Directorate-General for Energy and Transport

STRUCTURAL PROFILE
Value added in the EU-27's rail transport (NACE Group 60.1) sector reached EUR 34.0 billion in 2004, equivalent to 9.4 % of the transport services (NACE Divisions 60 to 63) total. In the EU-25, there were 640 enterprises in this sector with a total of 900 900 persons employed, equivalent to 11.0 % of the EU-25's transport services workforce. Although data availability among the Member States is weak in this sector, it is clear that the rail transport sector is particularly important in Austria, Hungary and Poland, as this sector accounted for 2.1 %, 1.5 % and 1.4 % respectively of national non-financial business economy value added, between two and three times the 0.7 % share for the EU-27 as a whole.

TRANSPORT OF GOODS AND PASSENGERS
During several decades rail transport volumes declined in the EU, both for goods and passenger transport, but this decline reversed during the 1990s. Figure 20.10 shows the development of both types of rail transport between 1990 and 2005 and the reversal in fortunes can be clearly seen: passenger transport volumes reached a low in 1994, since when average growth was 0.7 % per annum; goods transport volumes stabilised in 1993 since when average growth was 0.9 % per annum.

COSTS, PRODUCTIVITY AND PROFITABILITY
Average personnel costs in the EU-25 rail transport sector reached EUR 30 700 per employee in 2004, around EUR 1 000 below the EU-25's transport services average. The wage adjusted labour productivity ratio in the EU-27 was 124.0 % in the rail transport sector, which was some way below the 140.0 % average for all transport services. The gross operating rate, calculated as the ratio of gross operating surplus (value added less personnel costs) to turnover, for the EU-27's rail transport sector stood at 11.0 % in 2004, the same as the non-financial business economy average and therefore below the transport services average of 13.3 %.

20.2: ROAD AND OTHER LAND TRANSPORT

Road and other land transport activities (NACE Group 60.2) cover road freight transport, urban and suburban passenger transport by bus, coach, tram, trolleybus, underground or elevated railway, inter-city land passenger transport (other than railways), as well as taxi operations and charters. This definition includes a diverse number of enterprises, ranging from independent lorry or taxi drivers to large national or metropolitan public transport enterprises.

Road freight transporters have over a long period expanded beyond simple transport services, to provide other supporting activities, notably logistics and warehousing, competing with specialists in these activities as well as wholesalers who have also extended the range of their operations into transport and supporting activities - see Chapter 17. Road transport has been one of the main areas of growth in the transport services sector as it benefited from increased demand for mobility and flexibility from private individuals and enterprises alike. In May 2007 the European Commission adopted three proposals [8] aimed at modernising the rules governing road transport operators and access to the road transport market. The proposals aim to reduce distortions of competition and improve transport operators' compliance with the provisions of social legislation and road safety rules.

A proposal [9] for a regulation on public passenger transport services by rail and by road was adopted by the European Commission in July 2005: at the time of writing a common position had been reached on this.

[8] COM(2007) 263 to 265.
[9] COM(2005) 319.

Early in 2007 the European Commission announced plans to publish a Green paper on urban transport in the autumn of 2007, to look among others at the questions of congestion and pollution linked to this type of transport. This will address all transport modes, including walking, cycling, motor cycles and motor vehicles, and will cover both urban freight (and logistics) and passenger transport.

The European Commission's communication [10] on alternative fuels for road transport in 2001 identified biofuels as one possible transport fuel, and later targets were set for biofuel use. To further stimulate the use of biofuels the European Commission presented a biomass action plan in December 2005 and in February 2006 it adopted a communication on an EU strategy for biofuels.

STRUCTURAL PROFILE

Some 900 000 enterprises were registered in the road and other land transport (NACE Group 60.2) sector which generated value added of EUR 135 billion in 2004 in the EU-27. As such, road and other land transport accounted for close to two fifths (37.5 %) of all value added generated by transport services (NACE Divisions 60 to 63) in

[10] COM(2001) 547.

2004. Table 20.6 shows that within road and other land transport services, by far the largest activity in value added terms was the road freight transport (NACE Class 60.24) subsector which accounted for around two thirds of the value added created by the EU-27's road and other land transport sector in 2004, the remainder being generated by other passenger land transport activities (NACE Classes 60.21 to 60.23). The relative importance of the road freight transport subsector on the one hand and other passenger land transport on the other differed considerably between the Member States [11]: the share of road freight (in value added terms) rose above 80 % of the sector total in Estonia (2003), the Czech Republic and Slovenia, while the other passenger land transport subsector generated around half of sectoral value added in Slovakia, and Cyprus - it should be noted that Cyprus has no rail network as an alternative form of inland passenger transport, and many residents and tourists therefore use other forms of public transport (notably buses, coaches, minibuses and taxis).

[11] Estonia, Luxembourg and Portugal, 2003; Bulgaria, Denmark, Ireland, Greece and Malta, not available.

Table 20.6

Other land transport (NACE Group 60.2)
Structural profile, EU-27, 2004 (1)

	No. of enterprises (thousands)	Turnover (EUR million)	Value added (EUR million)	Employment (thousands) (2)
Other land transport	900.0	320 000	135 000	4 299.3
Other scheduled passenger land transport; taxi operation; other land passenger transport	:	80 000	50 000	1 700.0
Freight transport by road	600.0	240 000	90 000	2 600.0

(1) Rounded estimates based on non-confidential data.
(2) EU-25.
Source: Eurostat (SBS)

Table 20.7

Other land transport (NACE Group 60.2)
Structural profile: ranking of top five Member States, 2004

Rank	Share of EU-27 value added (%) (1)	Share of EU-25 employment (%) (2)	Value added specialisation ratio (EU-27=100) (3)	Employment specialisation ratio (EU-25=100) (4)
1	France (15.6)	Germany (13.3)	Lithuania (189.6)	Lithuania (163.7)
2	Germany (14.9)	France (13.0)	Finland (146.6)	Finland (142.9)
3	United Kingdom (14.2)	Spain (12.3)	Austria (141.0)	Latvia (136.9)
4	Italy (12.5)	United Kingdom (11.9)	Spain (136.7)	Sweden (133.3)
5	Spain (12.3)	Italy (11.1)	Czech Republic (134.9)	Hungary (133.2)

(1) Bulgaria, Denmark, Estonia, Ireland, Greece, Luxembourg, Malta and Portugal, not available.
(2) Denmark, Estonia, Ireland, Greece, Luxembourg, Malta, Netherlands and Portugal, not available.
(3) Bulgaria, Denmark, Estonia, Ireland, Greece, Cyprus, Luxembourg, Malta and Portugal, not available.
(4) Denmark, Estonia, Ireland, Greece, Cyprus, Luxembourg, Malta, Netherlands and Portugal, not available.
Source: Eurostat (SBS)

Employment in the road and other land transport sector in the EU-25 was about 4.3 million in 2004. As such, the road and other land transport sector supplied just over half (52.5 %) the workforce in transport services in the EU-25.

Unsurprisingly, the larger Member States contributed the greatest shares of EU-27 value added in this sector (see Table 20.7). France, the United Kingdom and Germany all accounted for around 15 % of EU-27 value added in 2004. However, an analysis based on relative specialisation highlights the importance of the road and other land transport sector in several other Member States [12]. For example, this activity contributed 5.0 % of non-financial business economy value added in Lithuania, and over 3.5 % in Finland, Luxembourg (2003), Austria, Spain, the Czech Republic, the Netherlands and Hungary. In contrast, the road and other land transport sector was notably smaller in relative terms in Slovakia and Germany where it accounted for less than 2.0 % of the value added created within the non-financial business economy.

TRANSPORT OF GOODS AND PASSENGERS

When analysing statistics on land transport traffic volumes it is important to bear in mind that this includes own account transport as well as transport services marketed to clients (for hire and reward). Figure 20.11 highlights the growth in the stock of road transport vehicles (buses, coaches and road freight vehicles) between 1995 and 2004 for the EU-27. Road freight vehicles in particular experienced very strong growth whereas for buses and coaches the growth was more subdued, with the stock of such vehicles falling in 2004.

The volume of traffic within the EU-25 is shown in Figure 20.12 for the main collective land passenger transport modes and for road freight. As can be seen the volume of passenger transport by trams and metros increased significantly faster since 1995 than for buses and coaches, but both of these were outstripped by the growth in road freight. Table 20.8 shows the development of road freight transport in the Member States over a shorter period, between 2000 and 2005. Only Belgium, Denmark and Finland witnessed a fall in road freight transport volumes, while the strongest growth was recorded in the two Member States that joined the EU in 2007, with the volume of road haulage more than trebling in Romania and more than doubling in Bulgaria during the five years considered.

[12] Estonia, Luxembourg and Portugal, 2003; Bulgaria, Denmark, Ireland, Greece, Cyprus and Malta, not available.

Figure 20.11

Evolution of the end of year stock of road vehicles, EU-27 (1995=100) (1)

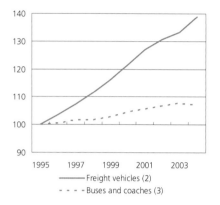

(1) Belgium, stock as of 1 August.
(2) The data is not fully comparable between countries.
(3) Includes all public or private vehicles able to carry 9 or more passengers.
Source: Eurostat, national statistics, study for Energy and Transport DG, in European Union Energy and Transport in Figures pocketbook 2006, European Commission, Directorate-General for Energy and Transport

COSTS, PRODUCTIVITY AND PROFITABILITY

The road and other land transport sector is characterised by a relatively low apparent labour productivity: in 2004, this was EUR 30 000 per person employed in the EU-27, well below the transport services average of EUR 42 000 and also the non-financial business economy average of EUR 40 900. Average personnel costs were also low at EUR 26 000 per employee, resulting in a wage adjusted labour productivity ratio of 120.0 %, among the lowest of the transport services activities. Despite these low average personnel costs per employee, expenditure on personnel accounted for 28.5 % of total expenditure in the EU-27's road and other land transport sector, which was approximately 1.3 times the share recorded for transport services as a whole.

Some four fifths (80.0 %) of persons employed in this sector in the EU-27 were paid employees, the lowest share of all of the transport services presented in Subchapters 20.1 to 20.7. This may in part explain why, despite low levels of productivity, the gross operating rate for the EU-27's road and other land transport sector (13.0 %) in 2004 was only slightly below the transport services average (13.3 %) and above the non-financial business economy average (11.0 %) - see Table 20.9.

Figure 20.12

Evolution of the volume (passenger/tonne-kilometres) of other land transport, EU-25 (1995=100)

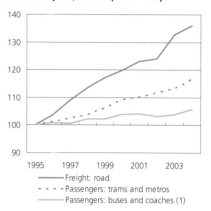

(1) Poland and Slovakia, only inter-urban traffic; excluding Northern Ireland.
Source: Eurostat, ECMT, IUPT, national statistics, estimates in European Union Energy and Transport in Figures pocketbook 2006, European Commission, Directorate-General for Energy and Transport

Table 20.8

Road freight transport traffic; national and international haulage by vehicles registered in the country (billion tonne-kilometres)

	2000	2001	2002	2003	2004
EU-27	1 507.5	1 545.0	1 594.4	1 612.8	1 731.9
BE	51.0	53.2	52.9	50.5	47.9
BG	6.4	8.0	8.8	9.5	12.0
CZ	37.3	39.1	43.7	46.5	46.0
DK	24.0	22.2	22.5	23.0	23.1
DE	280.7	289.0	285.2	290.7	303.8
EE (1)	3.9	4.7	4.4	4.0	5.1
IE	12.3	12.3	14.3	15.7	17.1
EL	17.5	18.5	19.3	20.2	21.1
ES	148.7	161.0	184.5	192.6	220.8
FR	204.0	206.9	204.4	203.6	212.2
IT (2)	184.7	186.5	192.7	174.1	197.0
CY	1.3	1.3	1.3	1.4	1.1
LV	4.8	5.4	6.2	6.8	7.4
LT	7.8	8.3	10.7	11.5	12.3
LU	7.6	8.7	9.2	9.6	9.6
HU	19.1	18.5	17.9	18.2	20.6
MT	0.5	0.5	0.5	0.5	0.5
NL	79.6	78.5	77.4	79.8	89.7
AT	35.1	37.5	38.5	39.6	39.2
PL (2)	75.0	77.2	80.3	86.0	102.8
PT (2)	38.9	40.5	40.2	39.8	40.8
RO	14.3	18.5	25.4	30.8	37.2
SI (3)	5.3	7.0	6.6	7.0	9.0
SK	14.3	13.8	14.9	16.7	18.5
FI	32.0	30.5	32.0	30.9	32.3
SE	35.6	34.2	36.7	36.6	36.9
UK	165.6	163.3	164.0	167.1	167.8

(1) Break in series 2002/2003.
(2) Break in series 2003/2004.
(3) Break in series 2000/2001.
Source: Eurostat, ECMT, national statistics, estimates, in European Union Energy and Transport in Figures pocketbook 2006, European Commission, Directorate-General for Energy and Transport

Table 20.9

Other land transport (NACE Group 60.2)
Productivity and profitability, EU-27, 2004 (1)

	Apparent labour productivity (EUR thousand)	Average personnel costs (EUR thousand)	Wage adjusted labour productivity (%)	Gross operating rate (%)
Other land transport	30.0	26.0	120.0	13.0
Other scheduled passenger land transport; taxi operation; other land passenger transport (2)	:	25.0	110.0	13.1
Freight transport by road	33.0	26.0	130.0	13.0

(1) Rounded estimates based on non-confidential data.
(2) Gross operating rate, EU-25.
Source: Eurostat (SBS)

20.3: WATER TRANSPORT

This subchapter covers all water transport activities, both sea and coastal transport (NACE Group 61.1) and inland water transport (NACE Group 61.2). For information on water transport networks and ports see Subchapter 20.6.

Maritime freight shipping is made up of line (generally scheduled services) and tramp shipping, with a distinction between tankers (liquid and gas) and bulk carriers, and between containerised and general cargo. As well as freight, maritime transport activities also cover passenger transport, for example, scheduled ferry services and cruises. The EU relies heavily on maritime transport for its external trade. Inland navigation traditionally holds a strong market share in the transport of bulk cargo (such as iron ores, construction materials and metal products). In addition to these traditional markets, inland navigation is expanding into new markets such as the hinterland transport of maritime containers, waste and recycling, dangerous goods, and the transport of vehicles.

In December 2006 the European Parliament and Council adopted a directive [13] on technical criteria for inland waterway vessels, which aims to improve safety and promote inland waterway transport.

In May 2007 the European Commission published a Green paper [14] on better ship dismantling in response to concerns about environmental protection and safety measures.

[13] Directive 2006/87/EC of 12 December 2006, Official Journal L389 p. 1 of 30.12.2006.
[14] COM(2007) 269.

Table 20.10

Water transport (NACE Division 61)
Structural profile, EU-27, 2004 (1)

	No. of enterprises (thousands)	Turnover (EUR million)	Value added (EUR million)	Employment (thousands)
Water transport	16.0	80 000	22 000	200.0
Sea and coastal water transport	7.5	72 000	20 000	150.0
Inland water transport	8.6	5 000	1 800	40.0

(1) Rounded estimates based on non-confidential data.
Source: Eurostat (SBS)

STRUCTURAL PROFILE

In 2004 there some 16 000 enterprises in water transport services (NACE Division 61) in the EU-27, while their value added equated to EUR 22.0 billion, which represented 6.1 % of the wealth created in all transport services (NACE Divisions 60 to 63). Employment in the water transport services sector was 200 000 persons, which represented just 2.3 % of the transport services' total, less than two fifths the contribution of this sector in terms of value added. Sea and coastal transport (NACE Group 61.1) dominated the water transport services sector, with EUR 20.0 billion value added and 150 000 persons employed in 2004, the remainder accounted for by inland water transport (NACE Group 61.2) - see Table 20.10.

Naturally, the importance of water transport services may depend largely on geographical, climatic, or historical reasons. For example, as much as one third of transport services' value added was accounted for by the water transport services sector in Denmark (35.5 %), and in Cyprus the share was 25.4 %. In contrast, all of the Member States with no coastline reported only limited activity within the water transport services sector. Consequently, within the EU-27 Denmark had the second largest water transport sector (18.1 % of the EU-27 total) behind Germany (26.6 %), and the Netherlands had the fifth largest share (9.1 %), not far behind the United

Kingdom and Italy - see Table 20.11. In the four Member States with the largest water transport services sectors the sea and coastal transport subsector dominated, generating over nine tenths of sectoral value added (a share reaching 99.5 % in Denmark). In the Netherlands, inland water transport was much more significant, accounting for more than one third (35.1 %) of Dutch water transport value added; this was reflected in the fact that the Netherlands had the largest inland water transport subsector in the EU-27, with nearly two fifths of the EU-27's total value added in this subsector.

Within the EU-27 water transport recorded the strongest growth in the turnover indices between 2000 and 2006 among the transport services NACE divisions, an average increase of 6.8 % per annum over this period. In contrast, the employment index recorded an average fall of 2.9 % per annum over the period shown (1998 to 2006) in Figure 20.13, with considerable contractions in 1999 and 2000 (around -10 % each year) followed by a period of relative stability. In 2006 the employment index in water transport contracted by 1.3 %, and as such this was the only transport services NACE division to record a fall in the EU-27 in this year, and only one of two non-financial services NACE divisions [15] that recorded a reduction in employment in 2006.

[15] Short-term business statistics in services cover NACE Sections G, H and I and Divisions 72 and 74.

Table 20.11

Water transport (NACE Division 61)
Structural profile: ranking of top five Member States, 2004

Rank	Share of EU-27 value added (%) (1)	Share of EU-27 employment (%) (2)	Value added specialisation ratio (EU-27=100) (3)	Employment specialisation ratio (EU-27=100) (4)
1	Germany (26.6)	Germany (13.3)	Denmark (902.1)	Denmark (490.8)
2	Denmark (18.1)	Italy (12.3)	Netherlands (199.4)	Finland (418.7)
3	United Kingdom (13.2)	United Kingdom (8.9)	Finland (187.4)	Sweden (412.6)
4	Italy (11.9)	Sweden (8.5)	Bulgaria (179.6)	Bulgaria (216.5)
5	Netherlands (9.1)	France (8.3)	Lithuania (152.6)	Estonia (197.1)

(1) Czech Republic, Ireland, Greece, Luxembourg, Malta and Romania, not available.
(2) Czech Republic, Ireland, Greece, Luxembourg, Malta, Netherlands and Romania, not available.
(3) Czech Republic, Ireland, Greece, Cyprus, Luxembourg, Malta and Romania, not available.
(4) Czech Republic, Ireland, Greece, Cyprus, Luxembourg, Malta, Netherlands and Romania, not available.
Source: Eurostat (SBS)

Figure 20.13

Water transport (NACE Division 61)
Evolution of main indicators, EU-27 (2000=100)

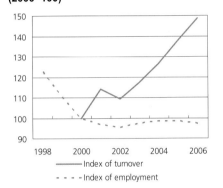

Source: Eurostat (STS)

Table 20.12

Merchant fleet, EU-27, 2005 (1)

	Number of ships (units)	Tonnage (million DWT)
Total fleet controlled	9 741	317
National flag	3 283	104
Foreign flag	6 458	213

(1) Ships of 1 000 GRT and over, as of 1 January 2005; including international registers like the Danish International Ship Register; including vessels registered at territorial dependencies.
Source: ISL merchant fleet databases, based on the Lloyd's Maritime Information System, in European Union Energy and Transport in Figures pocketbook 2006, European Commission, Directorate-General for Energy and Transport

Table 20.13

Seaborne transport of goods and passengers, 2005

	Goods (million tonnes)		Passengers (thousands)	
	Inward	Outward	Inward	Outward
EU-27 (1)	2 342.3	1 375.5	193 924	192 684
BE	116.6	89.9	461	461
BG	14.3	10.5	8	4
CZ	-	-	-	-
DK	53.5	46.1	23 963	23 961
DE	172.3	112.6	14 677	14 813
EE	4.6	42.0	3 454	3 432
IE	37.7	14.5	1 666	1 609
EL	88.2	63.1	42 915	43 153
ES	290.5	109.5	11 880	10 530
FR	243.7	97.7	12 849	12 955
IT	348.2	160.7	39 476	39 277
CY	6.0	1.3	97	97
LV	4.7	55.0	68	75
LT	4.7	21.4	82	85
LU	-	-	-	-
HU	-	-	-	-
MT	3.3	0.2	89	89
NL	351.0	110.0	1 058	1 057
AT	-	-	-	-
PL	16.4	38.4	816	831
PT	47.5	17.8	332	330
RO	25.2	22.7	:	:
SI	9.0	3.6	18	18
SK	-	-	-	-
FI	54.7	44.8	8 582	8 530
SE	95.8	82.3	16 380	16 237
UK	354.4	231.3	15 062	15 145

(1) Passengers, EU-25.
Source: Eurostat (Maritime transport)

TRANSPORT OF GOODS AND PASSENGERS Table 20.13 shows the size of sea transport. The total movement of goods, both inward and outward reached 3 700 million tonnes in the EU-27 in 2005. The United Kingdom accounted for the largest share of sea transport of goods (both inward and outward), with 15.8 % of the EU-27 total, followed by Italy (13.7 %) and the Netherlands (12.4 %). Only in the Baltic States and Poland did the outward volume of sea freight transport exceed the inward volume, with Malta having by far the highest ratio of inward to outward sea freight transport.

The total number of sea passengers in the EU-25 was 386.6 million in 2005 (inward plus outward), of which Greece (22.3 %) and Italy (20.4 %) provided by far the largest shares. The Nordic trio of Denmark (12.4 %), Sweden (8.4 %) and Finland (4.4 %) also contributed relatively high shares.

COSTS, PRODUCTIVITY AND
PROFITABILITY

Like several other transport services, water transport services reported relatively high investment expenditure as a share of total expenditure, 12.5 % for the EU-27 in 2004, above the transport services average of 10.6 %. This share was as high as 16.5 % in inland water transport. In contrast, the share of personnel costs in total expenditure was just 10.0 % in water transport, less than half the transport services average (22.1 %). This share was 9.5 % in the sea and coastal transport subsector, compared with 19.3 % for the smaller inland water transport subsector.

Water transport services were characterised by high apparent labour productivity. Value added per person employed was EUR 110 000 in the EU-27's water transport sector in 2004, with the sea and coastal transport subsector recording a value of EUR 133 300 per person employed, approximately three times as high as the value of EUR 45 000 per person employed that was recorded for inland water transport. The wage adjusted labour productivity ratio for the sector as a whole was 270.0 % in the EU-27, with the sea and coastal transport subsector recording a ratio of 290.0 % and the inland water transport subsector a ratio of 160.0 %, both well above the transport services average. The gross operating rate was also high in this activity in the EU-27, as the gross operating surplus, despite high personnel costs, was equivalent to 19.5 % of turnover in 2004.

20.4: AIR TRANSPORT

The air transport sector comprises enterprises engaged in the transport of passengers and freight by air on scheduled (NACE Group 62.1) as well as unscheduled services (NACE Group 62.2). Space transport activities (NACE Group 62.3), which essentially include the launching of satellites and space vehicles are also covered by the air transport sector. For information on airports see Subchapter 20.6.

The expansion of air traffic has faced criticism, notably because of the growing levels of emissions and noise from this means of transport, although emissions have grown more slowly than air traffic volumes due to technological improvements. Following on from its September 2005 communication [16] on reducing the climate change impact of

aviation, in December 2006 the European Commission adopted proposals [17] to include aviation in the existing emissions trading scheme for carbon dioxide.

Growth in EU air traffic has occurred during a period of market liberalisation and structural change, with an increased number of operators, particularly low cost carriers. The development of low cost carriers has expanded the market for air travel, by offering the possibility of relatively cheap flights for the leisure market. The three largest low cost carriers in Europe in 2005 in terms of passenger-kilometres were easyJet (26.2 billion passenger-kilometres), Ryanair (25.2 billion passenger-kilometres) and Air-Berlin (19.4

billion passenger-kilometres) [18]. The growth in the activity of low cost airlines can be seen for example through a time series for Air-Berlin [19] passenger numbers, which shows double-digit annual growth each and every year during the last ten years, with growth of 40 % or more in some years, most notably in 2006.

In April 2007 the European Union and the United States of America signed the first EU-US aviation agreement [20] which will be applied from March 2008 and is a first step in opening up the EU and US air services markets so that airlines can provide air services in the combined market without restrictions.

---

[16] COM(2005) 459.

[17] COM(2006) 818.

[18] Association of European Airlines, International Air Transport Association, air companies, in European Union Energy and Transport in Figures pocketbook 2006, European Commission, Directorate-General for Energy and Transport.
[19] http://www.airberlin.com.
[20] Air transport agreement, Official Journal L134 p. 4, of 25.5.2007.

Table 20.14

Air transport (NACE Division 62)
Structural profile: ranking of top five Member States, 2004

Rank	Share of EU-25 value added (%) (1)	Share of EU-27 employment (%) (2)	Value added specialisation ratio (EU-25=100) (3)	Employment specialisation ratio (EU-27=100) (4)
1	United Kingdom (35.3)	United Kingdom (21.4)	Luxembourg (528.6)	Denmark (219.9)
2	France (16.7)	France (18.1)	Netherlands (180.7)	Finland (190.1)
3	Netherlands (9.4)	Germany (13.3)	United Kingdom (161.1)	Sweden (172.6)
4	Spain (8.7)	Spain (9.0)	Portugal (147.4)	France (158.0)
5	Italy (5.0)	Italy (6.2)	Finland (126.6)	United Kingdom (148.9)

(1) Ireland, Greece and Malta, not available; Czech Republic and Luxembourg, 2003.
(2) Czech Republic, Ireland, Greece, Luxembourg, Malta, Netherlands and Romania, not available.
(3) Ireland, Greece, Cyprus and Malta, not available; Czech Republic and Luxembourg, 2003.
(4) Czech Republic, Ireland, Greece, Cyprus, Luxembourg, Malta, Netherlands and Romania, not available.
Source: Eurostat (SBS)

STRUCTURAL PROFILE

In 2004 there were 3 200 enterprises in the air transport sector (NACE Division 62) in the EU-27 which employed 400 300 persons; this was the equivalent of 4.9 % of the transport services' (NACE Divisions 60 to 63) workforce. In the EU-25, the air transport sector contributed an 8.2 % share of transport services' value added in 2004, some EUR 30.0 billion. More than one third (35.3 %) of the EU-25's value added was generated in the United Kingdom alone, while France's contribution was 16.7 % with the Netherlands (9.4 %) and Spain (8.7 %) the next largest contributors in value added terms. Germany recorded a negative value added in 2004, and this Member State's relative size can be better expressed by its 13.2 % share of the EU-25 workforce: the low (and in some years negative) German value added may partly reflect the situation where some of the revenue for German air transport operators is recorded in non-German subsidiaries.

Luxembourg (2003) was the most specialised Member State [21] in this sector as air transport represented 3.6 % of non-financial business economy value added. In value added terms the Netherlands and the United Kingdom were also relatively specialised in this sector as were the Nordic Member States of Denmark, Finland and Sweden in employment terms - see Table 20.14. Although precise shares of the air transport sector in non-financial business economy value added and employment can not be calculated for Ireland and Cyprus it is likely that these two Member States were also relatively specialised in air transport.

At 4.3 % per annum air transport recorded the slowest average growth among the transport services NACE divisions between 2000 and 2006. This was composed of a period of falling turnover in 2001 followed by three years of relatively moderate growth, reflecting a general economic slowdown as well as a number of exceptional circumstances such as terrorist attacks and the SARS outbreak. The two most recent years show that the air transport sector experienced growth of 11.8 % in 2005 and 12.1 % in 2006, the highest growth rates among transport services NACE divisions in both years. The employment index grew strongly in 1999 and 2000, followed by a more gentle decline most years since then, with the 0.5 % increase of 2006 the only significant recent employment gain in this sector.

[21] Czech Republic and Luxembourg, 2003; Ireland, Greece, Cyprus, Malta and Romania, not available.

Figure 20.14
Air transport (NACE Division 62) Evolution of main indicators, EU-27 (2000=100)

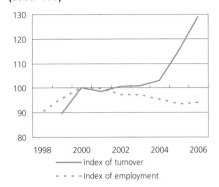

Source: Eurostat (STS)

TRANSPORT OF GOODS AND PASSENGERS

Turning to traffic figures, Table 20.15 shows the number of passengers, with the United Kingdom accounting for one quarter (24.8 %) of passengers flying outside of the EU-25, and Germany just over one fifth (20.5 %), while for intra-EU air travel the United Kingdom again topped the ranking (39.0 % of EU-25 passengers) followed by Spain (30.0 %). Tables 20.16 and 20.17 show the scheduled [22] volume of passenger traffic on a selection of airlines represented by the Association of European Airlines (AEA) and by the European Regions Airline Association (ERA).

[22] Passenger traffic on scheduled services that are performed according to a published timetable, or services that are so regular or frequent as to constitute a recognisably systematic service, which is open to direct booking by members of the public; and extra flights, section flights occasioned by overflow traffic from scheduled flights.

Table 20.15
Air passenger numbers, 2005 (thousands)

	Total	National	Intra-EU-25	Extra-EU-25
EU-25 (1)	704 159	160 784	298 334	245 042
BE	17 814	1	12 885	4 928
BG	:	:	:	:
CZ	11 266	195	8 042	3 029
DK	22 173	1 672	14 254	6 247
DE	145 977	21 901	73 904	50 172
EE	1 393	21	1 192	180
IE	24 254	641	21 023	2 590
EL	30 799	5 763	21 398	3 638
ES	143 680	39 005	89 483	15 191
FR	107 955	26 661	42 995	38 300
IT	87 906	24 664	46 152	17 091
CY	6 782	0	5 643	1 139
LV	1 872	0	1 589	282
LT	1 434	3	1 194	237
LU	1 538	:	1 313	225
HU	8 049	2	5 951	2 096
MT	2 757	8	2 444	305
NL	46 433	82	26 173	20 178
AT	19 685	575	12 265	6 844
PL	7 080	861	4 597	1 622
PT	20 272	2 966	13 954	3 352
RO (2)	3 494	274	:	:
SI	1 217	0	786	431
SK	1 519	63	1 101	355
FI	12 348	2 819	7 476	2 053
SE	20 997	6 191	11 138	3 669
UK	204 013	26 688	116 438	60 887

(1) For intra-EU transport, passengers are counted only once, not at departure and arrival.
(2) Total international transport (extra- and intra-EU combined) was 3.22 million passengers.
Source: Eurostat (Air transport)

Table 20.16
Scheduled passenger traffic - selected airlines, 2006

		(million passengers boarded)	Annual growth, rel. to 2005 (%)
Lufthansa	DE	51.2	4.6
Air France	FR	49.3	4.7
British Airways	UK	36.1	1.6
Iberia	ES	27.2	0.6
SAS	DK/SE/NO	25.1	0.3
Alitalia	IT	24.1	0.2
KLM	NL	22.4	4.4
Turkish airlines	TR	20.6	20.8
Swiss International airlines	CH	10.6	10.3

Source: AEA, http://www.aea.be

Table 20.17
Scheduled passenger traffic - selected regional airlines, 2006

	(million passengers)	Annual growth, rel. to 2005 (%)
Lufthansa Regional	11.2	-0.4
Lufthansa CityLine	6.2	4.2
Air Nostrum	5.3	12.4
Tyrolean Airways	4.1	7.8
Aegean Airlines	4.0	10.1
Brit Air (+ Air France)	4.0	14.0
Régional	3.9	3.7

Source: ERA, http://www.eraa.org

Table 20.18

Air transport (NACE Division 62)
Total expenditure, EU-27, 2004 (1)

	Value (EUR million)				Share (% of total expenditure)		
	Total expenditure	Purchases of goods and services	Personnel costs	Investment in tangible goods	Purchases of goods and services	Personnel costs	Investment in tangible goods
Air transport	105 000	73 000	25 000	7 000	69.5	23.8	6.7

(1) Rounded estimates based on non-confidential data.
Source: Eurostat (SBS)

COSTS, PRODUCTIVITY AND PROFITABILITY

Gross tangible investment by the EU-27's air transport sector in 2004 was equivalent to just 6.7 % of total expenditure (see Table 20.18), well below the transport services average (10.6 %) but above the non-financial business economy average (4.9 %). Investment figures can be volatile, particularly in activities that make occasional, very large purchases such as the air transport sector: a snapshot of investment in just one year needs therefore to be interpreted with care. In 2004 the shares of personnel costs (23.8 %) and of purchases of goods and services (69.5 %) in total expenditure recorded by the EU-27's air transport sector were both slightly higher than the average shares recorded for all transport services.

Practically all (99.1 %) of the persons employed in the EU-27's air transport sector were paid employees in 2004, and among the Member States [23] with data available, only in Sweden (85.4 %) was this share below 95 % in 2004. Average personnel costs were significantly higher in the air transport sector than in the other transport services' NACE divisions. In the EU-27, enterprises in the air transport sector faced average personnel costs of EUR 60 000 per employee in 2004, double the average of EUR 30 000 per employee recorded for transport services as a whole. These high figures for average personnel costs were only partly compensated for by higher apparent

labour productivity, which reached EUR 70 000 per person employed in 2004. This was reflected in a wage adjusted labour productivity ratio that was 120.0 % for the EU-25, below the EU-25's transport services average of 140.1 %. High average personnel costs also resulted in a relatively low gross operating surplus (value added minus personnel costs), and when compared with turnover this gave a gross operating rate of 4.4 % for the EU-25 for the air transport sector, the lowest of the transport activities presented in Subchapters 20.1 to 20.7, and only around one third the average rate for EU-25 transport services as a whole.

_____
[23] Czech Republic and Luxembourg, 2003; Ireland, Greece, Malta, the Netherlands and Romania, not available.

20.5: PIPELINES

Transport via pipelines (NACE Group 60.3) includes the transport of gases, liquids, slurry and other commodities via pipelines and the operation of pump stations; it does not include the distribution (as opposed to the transport) of natural or manufactured gas via mains, or of water or steam.

STRUCTURAL PROFILE

The EU-27's transport via pipelines (NACE Group 60.3) sector had approximately 120 enterprises which together generated EUR 3.5 billion of value added in 2004 and as such its share in transport services (NACE Divisions 60 to 63) value added was 1.0 %. Although data is only available for a few Member States it is clear that in value added terms this sector is dominated by Italy which accounted for 45.7 % of the EU-27's value added in 2004, while Poland also recorded a relatively large share (11.2 %). Employment in this sector in the EU-25 was around 9 200 persons in 2004, just 0.1 % of the transport services total.

COSTS, PRODUCTIVITY AND PROFITABILITY

In 2004 transport via pipelines recorded apparent labour productivity of EUR 374 800 per person employed in the EU-25, an extremely high level reflecting the capital intensive nature of this activity. Average personnel costs in the EU-25's transport via pipelines sector were EUR 42 100 per employee, and the combination of these two indicators resulted in an exceptionally high wage adjusted labour productivity ratio of 890.0 %, many times greater than the EU-25 transport services average of 140.1 %. Likewise, the EU-27's gross operating rate was very high in this sector, with this profitability ratio showing that the gross operating surplus was equivalent to 52.0 % of turnover in 2004.

An analysis of expenditure for the EU-25 underlines the capital intensive nature of this sector, as tangible investment accounted for 24.3 % of total expenditure (gross operating and tangible investment expenditure) in 2004, more than double the average share for transport services as a whole (10.6 %).

20.6: AUXILIARY TRANSPORT ACTIVITIES

This subchapter includes information on auxiliary and supporting transport activities as covered by NACE Groups 63.1, 63.2 and 63.4, hereafter referred to as auxiliary transport activities. Note that travel agencies are covered in Subchapter 20.7.

The services covered by this subchapter are very diverse: they include a number of support services for all modes of transport, such as baggage and cargo handling, storage/warehousing, and freight forwarding/brokerage. Note that these services may be provided by enterprises with their principal activity in auxiliary transport activities or by enterprises classified to other activities, often transporters or wholesalers (in which case they will not be included in the statistics described below). Auxiliary and supporting transport activities include the operation of terminals (rail and bus stations, ports and airports) and infrastructure (notably for inland waterways, railways, roads, tunnels and bridges), as well as the provision of navigational services (notably for air and water transport), towing, berthing and parking services (including car parks).

In December 2006 the European Commission adopted a communication [24] on airport capacity, efficiency and safety in Europe to address a number of issues related with congestion and the environmental impact linked to the growth in air transport. At the same time the European Commission adopted a proposal [25] for a European Parliament and Council directive on airport charges, which addresses a number of issues concerning for example non-discrimination and consultation with users when establishing charges, exchange of information between airports and users, and criteria for the differentiation of charges.

Based on the results of inspections carried out concerning the application of a 2002 regulation on civil aviation security, the European Commission adopted in September 2005 proposals [26] to refine this legislation, allowing quicker technical updates, to simplify and clarify existing rules, and to extend it to cover freight and in-flight security: at the time of writing this proposal is still being discussed.

---

[24] COM(2006) 819.
[25] COM(2006) 820.
[26] COM(2005) 429.

STRUCTURAL PROFILE

Auxiliary transport activities (NACE Groups 63.1, 63.2 and 63.4) constitute a significant part of the transport services sector, with 103 000 enterprises which collectively generated EUR 120.3 billion of value added in the EU-27 in 2004, which equated to 33.4 % of the wealth created in the transport services sector (NACE Divisions 60 to 63). Auxiliary transport activities were less important in their contribution to transport services' employment, as their 2.0 million strong workforce in the EU-27 represented around 23.1 % of the transport services total in 2004.

The four largest Member States collectively accounted for 70.2 % of the EU-27's value added in this sector in 2004, compared with a 63.4 % share for the same Member States in all transport services. This was almost entirely due to the domination of the sector by Germany which generated more than one quarter (25.7 %) of EU-27 value added in auxiliary transport activities, compared with its transport services average of 18.5 %. In relative terms, Malta (2002), Estonia and Latvia were the most specialised in this sector, as auxiliary transport activities contributed more than 5 % of the non-financial business economy's value added in these Member States [27]. At the other end of the range, auxiliary transport activities contributed only around 1 % to non-financial business economy value added in Slovakia, Luxembourg (2003), Poland and the Czech Republic.

---

[27] Luxembourg, 2003; Ireland, Greece, Cyprus and Malta, not available.

Table 20.19 _____

Cargo handling and storage; other supporting transport activities; activities of other transport agencies (NACE Groups 63.1, 63.2 and 63.4)
Structural profile: ranking of top five Member States, 2004

Rank	Share of EU-27 value added (%) (1)	Share of EU-27 employment (%) (1)	Value added specialisation ratio (EU-27=100) (2)	Employment specialisation ratio (EU-27=100) (2)
1	Germany (25.7)	Germany (22.1)	Estonia (246.1)	Latvia (183.5)
2	United Kingdom (19.2)	Italy (14.8)	Latvia (221.1)	Estonia (150.3)
3	France (13.9)	United Kingdom (14.3)	Bulgaria (142.5)	Germany (133.7)
4	Italy (11.4)	France (13.0)	Lithuania (124.2)	Italy (126.1)
5	Spain (8.0)	Spain (8.0)	Germany (122.8)	Bulgaria (123.9)

(1) Greece and Malta, not available; Luxembourg, 2003.
(2) Ireland, Greece, Cyprus and Malta, not available; Luxembourg, 2003.
Source: Eurostat (SBS)

Table 20.20

Density of land transport networks, 2003 (m/km²) (1)

	Motorways	Railway lines
EU-27	14	49
BE	57	116
BG	3	40
CZ	7	124
DK	24	54
DE	34	101
EE	2	23
IE	3	28
EL	:	18
ES	21	29
FR	19	54
IT	22	55
CY	29	-
LV	-	36
LT	7	28
LU	57	107
HU	6	89
MT	-	-
NL	75	83
AT	20	68
PL	1	65
PT	22	31
RO	0	49
SI	24	61
SK	7	76
FI	2	19
SE	4	24
UK	15	71

(1) Based on land area, except for EU-27, Germany and Portugal, for which total area is used.
Source: Eurostat (Transport)

Table 20.21

Inland waterways network, 2004 (1)

	Length in use (km)
BE	1 516
CZ	664
DE	7 565
EE	320
FR	5 372
IT	1 477
LT	290
HU	1 439
NL	6 595
AT	351
PL	3 638
SK	172
FI	8 018
UK	1 065

(1) Czech Republic, 2003; Italy, 2002.
Source: Eurostat (Inland waterways transport)

Table 20.22

Top 10 sea ports ranked by freight traffic, EU-27 (million tonnes)

		2000	2001	2002	2003	2004	2005
Rotterdam	NL	302.5	296.6	302.7	307.4	330.9	345.8
Antwerp	BE	116.0	114.8	113.9	126.1	135.5	145.8
Hamburg	DE	77.0	82.9	86.7	93.6	99.5	108.3
Marseille	FR	91.3	89.5	89.2	92.4	90.8	93.3
Le Havre	FR	63.9	65.4	63.8	67.4	71.9	70.8
Grimsby & Immingham	UK	52.5	54.8	55.7	55.9	57.6	60.7
Tees & Hartlepool	UK	51.5	50.8	50.4	53.8	53.8	55.8
Algeciras	ES	:	41.1	42.2	48.3	52.6	55.2
London	UK	47.9	50.7	51.2	51.0	53.3	53.8
Dunkerque	FR	44.3	41.9	44.3	45.8	46.4	48.5

Source: Eurostat (Maritime transport)

FOCUS ON TRANSPORT NETWORKS

While the transport services described in Subchapters 20.1 to 20.5 use transport infrastructure, infrastructure management enterprises are considered as supporting transport activities (within NACE Group 63.2). Tables 20.20 and 20.21 provide information on three of the transport networks, namely rail, road and inland waterways.

Rail transport services relied on an EU-27 network encompassing 213 500 km of lines in 2003. In density terms, in other words the length of railway line in relation to area, this was the equivalent of 49 m of track per square kilometre. The Czech Republic, Belgium, Luxembourg and Germany had the most dense rail networks, all in excess of 100 m per square kilometre. Cyprus and Malta had no rail network, and the least dense networks were unsurprisingly found in Finland, Estonia and Sweden (the three Member States with the lowest population densities), as well as in Greece.

Road transport services could count on approximately 58 500 km of motorways in the EU-27 in 2003. While Germany (12 000 km), France (10 400 km), Spain (10 300 km) and Italy (6 500 km) had by far the most extensive motorway networks, accounting together for two thirds (67.0 %) of the EU-27 total in 2003, the Benelux countries had the highest densities of motorways in 2003. Note that there was no motorway network in Latvia or Malta. A low density of motorway networks was also recorded in the three least densely populated Member States, as well as in Romania, Poland, Ireland and Bulgaria.

Inland waterways used for transport constituted a network in excess of 38 000 km in the EU-27 in 2004: note that when such waterways constitute a border between two countries they are counted by both countries. Among the Member States, Finland (8 000 km), Germany (7 600 km) and the Netherlands (6 600 km) had the longest inland waterways on their territory.

FOCUS ON PORTS AND AIRPORTS

Eight of the ten largest EU-27 sea ports were in the North Sea (see Table 20.22). Rotterdam (the Netherlands) was the largest of all, with 345.8 million tonnes of freight loaded and unloaded in 2005, almost two and a half times the volume of the next largest port, Antwerp (Belgium) with 145.8 million tonnes.

The largest airport in the EU-27 in 2005 in passenger terms was London Heathrow (the United Kingdom) with 67.7 million passengers - see Table 20.23. As regards freight traffic, the largest EU-27 airport was Frankfurt (Germany) with 2.0 million tonnes of loaded and unloaded freight and mail in 2005 - see Table 20.24.

Table 20.23

Top 10 airports by number of passengers, EU-27, 2005 (million passengers)

		2005
London Heathrow	UK	67.7
Paris Ch. de Gaulle	FR	53.4
Frankfurt Rhein-Main	DE	51.8
Amsterdam Schiphol	NL	44.1
Madrid Barajas	ES	41.6
London Gatwick	UK	32.7
München F.J. Strauss	DE	28.5
Roma Fiumicino	IT	28.0
Barcelona Transoceanico	ES	27.0
Paris Orly	FR	24.9

Source: Eurostat (Air transport)

Table 20.24

Top 10 airports by goods loaded and unloaded, EU-27, 2005 (thousand tonnes) (1)

		2005
Frankfurt Rhein-Main	DE	1 950.6
Amsterdam Schiphol	NL	1 495.9
London Heathrow	UK	1 389.3
Paris Ch. de Gaulle	FR	1 217.9
Bruxelles National	BE	702.7
Köln/Bonn	DE	646.8
Luxembourg Findel	LU	624.8
Milano Malpensa	IT	384.0
Madrid Barajas	ES	365.3
Liège	BE	329.7

(1) Total freight and mail loaded and unloaded; Swedish airports, not available.
Source: Eurostat (Air transport)

COSTS, PRODUCTIVITY AND PROFITABILITY

The auxiliary transport activities sector reported high tangible investment expenditure compared with operating expenditure: gross tangible investment in the EU-27's auxiliary transport activities sector was equivalent to 14.3 % of total expenditure, 3.7 percentage points above the transport services average and nearly three times as high as the non-financial business economy average. This tangible investment share rose to between 35 % and 36 % in Hungary, Portugal and Slovakia.

In 2004 paid employees accounted for 95.5 % of all persons employed in this sector in the EU-27, while this share was above 90 % in all Member States [28] except Poland (84.3 %) and the Czech Republic (87.7 %). Average personnel costs in the auxiliary transport activities sector were EUR 34 100 per employee in the EU-27 in 2004, somewhat higher than the EUR 30 000 average for transport services. Nevertheless, above average apparent labour productivity (EUR 60 400 per person employed) more than compensated for the high average personnel costs, and this was reflected in the ratio of wage adjusted labour productivity, which was 177.2 % in the EU-27, some 37.2 percentage points above the average for transport services. Equally the gross operating rate for auxiliary transport activities was high, as the gross operating surplus represented 17.3 % of turnover in the EU-27 in 2004, some 4.0 percentage points above the transport services average.

[28] Luxembourg, 2003; Greece and Malta, not available.

20.7: TRAVEL AGENCIES

Travel agencies are enterprises that are engaged in arranging transport, accommodation and catering on behalf of travellers (NACE Group 63.3).

Travel agents act as retailers selling travel services or packaged trips to the customer. Traditionally, tour operators acted as wholesalers to travel agents, while more recently they have moved towards selling directly to customers. Tourist guides and tourist information services play a supporting role, offering information and services usually at the tourism destination. Unlike most of the other services presented in this chapter, the services of travel agents are not covered by sector specific legislation, only by the directive of the European Parliament and the Council on services in the internal market - see Chapter 22 for more information.

In the first half of 2007, there were two major mergers involving top ten European travel operators/agents: Thomas Cook and MyTravel merged, as did TUI and First Choice.

STRUCTURAL PROFILE

There were approximately 70 000 travel agencies (NACE Group 63.3) in the EU-27 in 2004 which generated EUR 21.0 billion of value added and employed half a million persons, accounting for 5.8 % of the transport services (NACE Divisions 60 to 63) total for both measures. The United Kingdom and Germany were by far the largest contributors to the wealth and employment generated by travel agencies in the EU-27 as together they accounted for 57.9 % of the value added and 39.2 % of the workforce - see Table 20.25. In value added terms these two Member States were also relatively specialised in the travel agencies sector, each generating 0.6 % of their non-financial business economy value added in this sector, more than any other Member State [29].

_____

[29] Luxembourg, 2003; Malta, Ireland, Greece, Cyprus and Malta, not available.

COSTS, PRODUCTIVITY AND PROFITABILITY

The travel agencies sector may be contrasted with the other transport services covered in this chapter in that its tangible investment expenditure was particularly low as a share of total expenditure (gross operating and tangible investment expenditure), just 1.0 % in the EU-27 in 2004. This low share results from the combination of a relatively low level of tangible investment and a high level of purchases of goods and services as many enterprises in this activity are distributors and as such their purchases include a large proportion of services purchased for resale. Nearly nine tenths (88.0 %) of the persons employed in the EU-27's travel agencies sector were paid employees in 2004, the same as the transport services average. This share of paid employees was particularly low in the Czech Republic, Bulgaria, Italy and Poland where it was below 80 %. Apparent labour productivity in the travel agencies sector in the EU-27 was EUR 43 000 per person employed, while average personnel costs were EUR 25 900, the former just above the transport services average and the later below it. The combination of these two indicators results in a wage adjusted labour productivity ratio of 166.0 %, some 26.0 percentage points above the transport services average. Despite relatively low average personnel costs, the gross operating surplus (value added minus personnel costs) of the travel agencies sector was equivalent to just 7.0 % of turnover, only a little more than half the average rate for transport services, reflecting the high turnover in this sector (mirroring the distributive trades sector). Nevertheless, several Member States reported a high gross operating rate, for example 25.8 % in Cyprus, 24.4 % in Germany, and 16.5 % in Slovakia.

Table 20.25

Activities of travel agencies and tour operators; tourist assistance activities n.e.c. (NACE Group 63.3)
Structural profile: ranking of top five Member States, 2004

Rank	Share of EU-27 value added (%) (1)	Share of EU-27 employment (%) (1)	Value added specialisation ratio (EU-27=100) (2)	Employment specialisation ratio (EU-27=100) (2)
1	United Kingdom (29.0)	United Kingdom (27.0)	United Kingdom (153.4)	United Kingdom (187.2)
2	Germany (28.9)	Germany (12.3)	Germany (137.9)	Austria (129.4)
3	France (8.3)	Spain (10.2)	Estonia (88.5)	Netherlands (123.0)
4	Italy (7.4)	Italy (8.7)	Slovakia (81.9)	Sweden (116.8)
5	Spain (7.3)	France (8.2)	Spain (81.6)	Estonia (110.5)

(1) Ireland, Greece and Malta, not available; Luxembourg, 2003.
(2) Ireland, Greece, Cyprus and Malta, not available; Luxembourg, 2003.
Source: Eurostat (SBS)

Table 20.26

Land transport; transport via pipelines (NACE Division 60)
Main indicators, 2004

	EU-27	BE	BG	CZ	DK	DE	EE	IE	EL	ES	FR	IT	CY	LV	LT
No. of enterprises (thousands)	928.4	10.0	18.9	35.8	10.9	58.3	1.9	4.3	:	197.4	80.2	124.9	2.8	2.1	4.4
Turnover (EUR million)	390 529	13 575	1 861	8 233	7 469	52 927	851	2 880	:	38 600	63 707	54 786	144	800	1 380
Production (EUR million)	378 870	13 894	1 759	6 662	7 568	50 125	826	2 292	:	31 578	64 440	57 532	144	804	1 337
Value added (EUR million)	173 991	6 910	450	2 873	3 894	24 930	233	1 127	:	18 986	30 070	22 098	77	254	515
Gross operating surplus (EUR million)	53 073	1 572	226	1 149	1 169	8 194	100	227	:	9 067	4 765	8 222	3	71	260
Purchases of goods & services (EUR million)	237 320	8 353	1 493	5 749	4 532	32 270	596	1 737	:	22 198	34 103	35 067	66	533	875
Personnel costs (EUR million)	120 919	5 338	223	1 724	2 725	16 737	133	900	:	9 919	25 305	13 876	73	183	255
Investment in tangible goods (EUR million) (1)	47 000	1 462	201	844	1 065	5 842	79	540	:	4 690	6 294	6 290	15	225	162
Employment (thousands)	5 545	136	113	229	79	657	22	31	:	566	737	548	5	45	59
Apparent labour prod. (EUR thousand)	31.4	50.7	4.0	12.5	49.4	38.0	10.4	36.4	:	33.5	40.8	40.3	16.4	5.6	8.7
Average personnel costs (EUR thousand)	26.1	42.3	3.1	8.9	39.0	28.2	6.0	33.8	:	26.0	36.7	35.6	28.8	4.1	4.5
Wage adjusted labour productivity (%)	120.4	119.7	127.5	141.1	126.6	134.7	171.5	107.6	:	128.9	111.3	113.2	56.7	136.6	192.1
Gross operating rate (%)	13.6	11.6	12.2	14.0	15.6	15.5	11.7	7.9	:	23.5	7.5	15.0	2.4	8.9	18.8
Investment / employment (EUR thousand) (1)	8.5	10.7	1.8	3.7	13.5	8.9	3.5	17.4	:	8.3	8.5	11.5	3.2	5.0	2.7

	LU (2)	HU	MT	NL	AT	PL	PT	RO	SI	SK	FI	SE	UK	NO
No. of enterprises (thousands)	0.6	30.4	:	13.7	11.5	124.6	22.7	19.1	7.5	0.7	19.9	24.3	45.6	16.8
Turnover (EUR million)	1 267	5 418	:	19 952	11 914	13 164	5 331	3 779	1 683	1 354	6 588	14 305	54 191	7 370
Production (EUR million)	971	4 266	:	19 782	10 475	12 530	5 335	3 659	1 599	1 325	6 688	14 429	55 128	7 368
Value added (EUR million)	643	1 958	:	9 129	7 280	4 537	2 170	1 308	531	544	3 319	5 487	22 300	4 320
Gross operating surplus (EUR million)	133	547	:	2 440	2 243	2 378	519	658	142	75	1 244	1 511	5 237	2 486
Purchases of goods & services (EUR million)	792	3 500	:	12 083	7 096	8 883	3 374	2 756	1 131	973	3 372	9 153	34 302	3 457
Personnel costs (EUR million)	510	1 411	:	6 689	5 037	2 159	1 650	650	389	469	2 075	3 977	17 063	1 835
Investment in tangible goods (EUR million) (3)	44	739	:	1 417	4 327	1 203	1 437	1 339	67	333	890	1 644	5 197	1 348
Employment (thousands)	13	177	:	197	150	475	100	223	31	66	71	133	569	65
Apparent labour prod. (EUR thousand)	50.2	11.0	:	46.3	48.7	9.6	21.6	5.9	17.1	8.3	46.6	41.3	39.2	66.5
Average personnel costs (EUR thousand)	41.1	9.2	:	36.5	36.2	6.3	17.3	3.0	15.6	7.2	37.2	36.1	32.4	35.3
Wage adjusted labour productivity (%)	122.3	120.2	:	126.8	134.5	151.7	124.8	197.6	109.4	115.8	125.2	114.1	121.0	188.3
Gross operating rate (%)	10.5	10.1	:	12.2	18.8	18.1	9.7	17.4	8.4	5.5	18.9	10.6	9.7	33.7
Investment / employment (EUR thousand) (3)	3.4	4.2	:	7.2	28.9	2.5	14.3	6.0	2.2	5.1	12.5	12.4	9.1	20.8

(1) EU-27, rounded estimate based on non-confidential data. (2) 2003. (3) Slovenia, 2003.
Source: Eurostat (SBS)

Table 20.27

Water transport (NACE Division 61)
Main indicators, 2004

	EU-27 (1)	BE	BG	CZ (2)	DK	DE	EE	IE	EL	ES	FR	IT	CY	LV	LT
No. of enterprises (thousands)	16.0	0.4	0.0	0.1	0.4	2.4	0.0	:	:	0.2	2.0	1.5	0.1	0.0	0.0
Turnover (EUR million)	80 000	2 909	218	25	13 960	17 640	320	:	:	1 499	7 250	8 369	260	33	113
Production (EUR million)	73 000	2 906	212	26	14 000	14 680	268	:	:	1 335	7 224	8 765	256	34	114
Value added (EUR million)	22 000	244	64	6	3 976	5 856	-8	:	:	504	1 407	2 627	152	12	46
Gross operating surplus (EUR million)	15 000	175	40	1	3 263	4 754	-23	:	:	269	653	1 565	74	4	21
Purchases of goods & services (EUR million)	56 000	2 660	150	19	10 250	12 187	335	:	:	1 071	5 924	6 165	104	22	68
Personnel costs (EUR million)	7 200	70	24	5	713	1 102	15	:	:	235	755	1 062	78	8	25
Investment in tangible goods (EUR million)	9 000	216	28	1	2 215	716	16	:	:	161	910	1 688	5	19	19
Employment (thousands)	200	1	6	1	13	27	1	:	:	7	17	25	4	1	2
Apparent labour prod. (EUR thousand)	110.0	181.9	10.5	7.7	305.0	219.5	-6.4	:	:	69.1	84.6	107.1	43.3	18.5	25.4
Average personnel costs (EUR thousand)	:	72.8	3.9	7.2	56.3	44.1	12.5	:	:	32.6	48.1	46.7	22.2	13.1	13.6
Wage adjusted labour productivity (%)	270.0	249.9	268.3	106.8	542.2	497.9	-51.2	:	:	212.1	175.8	229.3	194.7	140.5	186.4
Gross operating rate (%)	19.5	6.0	18.6	4.5	23.4	26.9	-7.1	:	:	17.9	9.0	18.7	28.4	10.8	18.9
Investment / employment (EUR thousand)	45.0	160.6	4.6	1.1	170.0	26.8	13.4	:	:	22.1	54.7	68.8	1.4	29.4	10.2

	LU (3)	HU	MT	NL	AT	PL	PT	RO	SI	SK	FI	SE	UK	NO
No. of enterprises (thousands)	0.0	0.1	:	4.1	0.1	0.5	0.1	:	0.0	0.0	0.3	1.0	1.3	1.6
Turnover (EUR million)	29	61	:	6 777	87	485	400	:	37	30	2 172	3 784	9 131	12 841
Production (EUR million)	29	46	:	6 721	63	480	407	:	35	24	2 000	3 680	8 942	12 683
Value added (EUR million)	10	12	:	2 013	31	104	89	:	8	12	588	924	2 900	3 569
Gross operating surplus (EUR million)	8	1	:	1 450	19	72	48	:	4	7	233	316	1 742	2 293
Purchases of goods & services (EUR million)	18	48	:	4 779	60	325	330	:	29	13	1 640	2 875	6 250	9 576
Personnel costs (EUR million)	2	11	:	563	11	32	41	:	4	6	356	608	1 159	1 276
Investment in tangible goods (EUR million) (4)	0	13	:	813	37	9	105	:	23	1	370	590	872	2 978
Employment (thousands)	0	1	:	:	0	3	2	:	0	1	8	17	18	23
Apparent labour prod. (EUR thousand)	139.3	9.3	:	:	87.2	33.1	51.8	:	39.6	15.6	72.4	54.3	162.9	158.1
Average personnel costs (EUR thousand)	44.6	8.5	:	:	37.9	12.5	24.5	:	24.0	7.3	44.2	43.5	68.6	57.0
Wage adjusted labour productivity (%)	312.4	109.4	:	:	229.9	264.5	211.7	:	164.8	213.1	163.9	124.8	237.6	277.3
Gross operating rate (%)	27.0	2.2	:	21.4	22.0	14.9	12.0	:	10.1	21.5	10.7	8.3	19.1	17.9
Investment / employment (EUR thousand) (5)	0.5	9.5	:	:	106.4	2.8	60.9	:	122.7	1.8	45.5	34.6	49.0	131.9

(1) Rounded estimates based on non-confidential data. (2) 2003, except for number of enterprises. (3) 2003. (4) Netherlands and Slovenia, 2003. (5) Slovenia, 2003.
Source: Eurostat (SBS)

Table 20.28

Air transport (NACE Division 62)
Main indicators, 2004

	EU-27 (1)	BE	BG	CZ (2)	DK	DE	EE	IE	EL	ES	FR	IT	CY	LV	LT
No. of enterprises (thousands)	3.2	0.1	0.0	0.0	0.1	0.4	0.0	:	:	0.1	0.5	0.3	0.0	0.0	0.0
Turnover (EUR million)	100 000	2 173	244	658	2 560	10 780	98	:	:	7 754	15 389	8 884	392	95	94
Production (EUR million)	99 000	2 173	243	745	2 547	10 107	100	:	:	7 686	15 351	8 990	382	106	95
Value added (EUR million)	:	430	18	212	648	-1 030	12	:	:	2 615	5 001	1 486	92	31	16
Gross operating surplus (EUR million)	:	134	9	111	-13	-4 609	1	:	:	630	664	33	-32	23	3
Purchases of goods & services (EUR million)	73 000	1 760	227	586	1 877	12 751	86	:	:	5 364	10 072	7 271	290	73	80
Personnel costs (EUR million)	25 000	296	9	101	660	3 579	11	:	:	1 986	4 337	1 453	124	9	13
Investment in tangible goods (EUR million)	7 000	109	29	31	105	1 396	1	:	:	514	1 672	336	3	9	4
Employment (thousands)	400	5	2	5	12	53	1	:	:	36	72	25	3	1	1
Apparent labour prod. (EUR thousand)	70.0	87.3	8.4	39.7	55.4	-19.4	19.7	:	:	72.5	69.3	60.4	36.4	42.6	15.9
Average personnel costs (EUR thousand)	60.0	62.1	4.3	19.3	56.6	67.9	17.8	:	:	55.0	60.1	59.8	49.1	11.9	13.4
Wage adjusted labour productivity (%)	:	140.6	194.6	206.2	97.9	-28.6	110.2	:	:	131.7	115.3	101.1	74.0	358.4	119.1
Gross operating rate (%)	:	6.2	3.6	16.9	-0.5	-42.8	1.2	:	:	8.1	4.3	0.4	-8.2	24.0	2.7
Investment / employment (EUR thousand)	17.5	22.1	13.6	5.8	9.0	26.3	2.2	:	:	14.2	23.2	13.7	1.3	12.7	4.2

	LU (3)	HU	MT	NL	AT	PL	PT	RO	SI	SK	FI	SE	UK	NO
No. of enterprises (thousands)	0.0	0.1	:	0.2	0.1	0.1	0.0	:	0.0	0.0	0.1	0.2	0.9	0.1
Turnover (EUR million)	1 206	647	:	7 650	2 698	897	1 945	:	143	107	1 999	2 852	26 578	2 570
Production (EUR million)	1 122	573	:	7 574	1 943	898	1 995	:	143	100	2 012	2 846	26 618	2 538
Value added (EUR million)	404	73	:	2 809	504	180	541	:	42	-11	455	916	10 584	897
Gross operating surplus (EUR million)	184	-36	:	752	-9	63	114	:	13	-21	62	159	5 738	158
Purchases of goods & services (EUR million)	791	570	:	4 837	2 377	727	1 479	:	95	113	1 557	2 070	15 573	1 716
Personnel costs (EUR million)	220	109	:	2 057	514	117	427	:	29	10	392	757	4 846	740
Investment in tangible goods (EUR million) (4)	10	15	:	:	230	43	66	:	5	6	101	162	961	133
Employment (thousands)	3	4	:	:	8	5	9	:	1	1	7	14	86	10
Apparent labour prod. (EUR thousand)	124.4	17.8	:	:	59.8	36.8	61.1	:	68.5	-16.5	61.6	64.3	123.4	86.7
Average personnel costs (EUR thousand)	68.0	26.9	:	:	61.3	24.4	48.3	:	47.6	15.5	53.2	62.2	56.9	71.5
Wage adjusted labour productivity (%)	183.1	66.1	:	:	97.4	150.9	126.5	:	143.8	-106.4	115.8	103.4	217.0	121.3
Gross operating rate (%)	15.2	-5.6	:	9.8	-0.3	7.0	5.8	:	9.1	-19.9	3.1	5.6	21.6	6.1
Investment / employment (EUR thousand) (4)	3.2	3.8	:	:	27.3	8.8	7.5	:	8.1	9.4	13.7	11.4	11.2	12.8

(1) Rounded estimates based on non-confidential data. (2) 2003, except for number of enterprises. (3) 2003. (4) Slovenia, 2003.
Source: Eurostat (SBS)

Table 20.29

Supporting and auxiliary transport activities; activities of travel agencies (NACE Division 63)
Main indicators, 2004

	EU-27 (1)	BE	BG	CZ	DK	DE	EE	IE	EL	ES	FR	IT	CY	LV	LT
No. of enterprises (thousands)	170.0	3.5	2.8	10.0	1.9	22.3	1.0	:	:	21.0	12.1	27.1	1.0	1.6	1.1
Turnover (EUR million)	460 000	18 556	912	5 118	9 810	85 265	1 471	:	:	40 954	61 521	47 372	382	1 205	769
Production (EUR million)	400 000	18 321	884	3 868	5 317	56 471	1 330	:	:	19 066	61 225	50 061	382	521	748
Value added (EUR million)	140 000	3 898	302	760	2 688	37 009	313	:	:	11 180	18 457	15 234	275	292	219
Gross operating surplus (EUR million)	65 000	1 500	129	408	1 303	20 469	199	:	:	4 955	7 397	5 433	114	191	122
Purchases of goods & services (EUR million)	330 000	14 757	640	4 356	7 297	54 851	1 153	:	:	30 146	44 513	34 467	105	920	554
Personnel costs (EUR million)	75 000	2 399	173	352	1 385	16 540	114	:	:	6 225	11 060	9 801	161	101	97
Investment in tangible goods (EUR million)	50 000	818	173	233	417	8 400	250	:	:	4 521	8 204	6 231	20	138	100
Employment (thousands)	2 500	50	40	42	31	502	11	:	:	211	299	338	8	19	14
Apparent labour prod. (EUR thousand)	57.0	78.5	7.5	18.2	86.5	73.8	28.8	:	:	53.1	61.7	45.0	36.6	15.4	15.7
Average personnel costs (EUR thousand)	32.6	51.1	4.8	10.8	45.3	34.2	10.6	:	:	31.4	37.1	33.0	23.2	5.6	7.1
Wage adjusted labour productivity (%)	174.0	153.5	156.5	167.8	191.1	215.6	270.8	:	:	169.0	166.5	136.7	157.9	275.5	221.6
Gross operating rate (%)	14.0	8.1	14.1	8.0	13.3	24.0	13.6	:	:	12.1	12.0	11.5	29.8	15.8	15.9
Investment / employment (EUR thousand)	19.3	16.5	4.3	5.6	13.4	16.7	22.9	:	:	21.5	27.4	18.4	2.7	7.3	7.2

	LU (2)	HU	MT	NL	AT	PL	PT	RO	SI	SK	FI	SE	UK	NO
No. of enterprises (thousands)	0.2	5.2	:	5.5	2.6	13.6	2.9	3.4	0.9	0.7	2.2	5.5	16.4	3.2
Turnover (EUR million)	670	3 332	:	19 837	14 648	5 840	6 600	1 402	1 088	748	5 633	18 219	104 460	9 446
Production (EUR million)	204	1 227	:	19 661	4 433	4 536	6 729	1 392	973	715	5 016	14 906	106 607	9 232
Value added (EUR million)	130	643	:	6 068	2 644	1 261	2 078	426	280	165	1 500	3 098	29 153	2 348
Gross operating surplus (EUR million)	25	347	:	2 576	1 029	641	988	209	114	91	502	798	13 890	1 057
Purchases of goods & services (EUR million)	541	2 635	:	14 912	12 191	4 132	4 654	959	813	581	4 213	11 912	77 627	7 277
Personnel costs (EUR million)	105	297	:	3 492	1 615	620	1 090	217	166	74	998	2 300	15 263	1 292
Investment in tangible goods (EUR million)	89	1 230	:	1 722	567	237	1 884	197	94	278	288	592	10 491	350
Employment (thousands)	3	29	:	92	41	84	40	42	9	9	27	58	419	28
Apparent labour prod. (EUR thousand)	49.6	21.9	:	66.1	64.8	15.0	52.6	10.2	31.7	18.9	56.0	53.3	69.5	84.8
Average personnel costs (EUR thousand)	41.3	10.9	:	40.0	41.1	9.4	28.2	5.2	19.4	8.6	37.9	43.3	37.5	47.9
Wage adjusted labour productivity (%)	120.2	200.4	:	165.4	157.5	160.6	186.6	194.0	163.3	219.7	147.6	123.0	185.6	177.0
Gross operating rate (%)	3.7	10.4	:	13.0	7.0	11.0	15.0	14.9	10.4	12.1	8.9	4.4	13.3	11.2
Investment / employment (EUR thousand)	34.0	41.8	:	18.8	13.9	2.8	47.7	4.7	10.6	31.8	10.7	10.2	25.0	12.6

(1) Rounded estimates based on non-confidential data. (2) 2003.
Source: Eurostat (SBS)

Communications and media

This chapter gathers together several activities linked to communication and media activities, however, within this group a distinction has to be made between traditional activities (for example, postal services) for which growth is rather stable and other newer activities (such as mobile telephony and electronic publishing), for which growth developments are more marked.

The uptake of digital (radio and television) transmission as well as delivery over the Internet is intertwined with the development of digital content, allowing content to be more easily shared across devices, facilitating more tailored products, and a greater possibility of on-demand services. Nevertheless, digital technologies also make content easier to share not just between devices but between consumers, which may play an important role in terms of its impact on intellectual property rights, an issue which has been widely debated with respect to downloading and sharing of music files. The management of digital rights is an issue faced by many of the activities covered in this chapter, and in April 2006 the European Commission adopted a revised proposal [1] for a directive of the European Parliament and of the Council to combat intellectual property offences.

_____

[1] COM(2006) 168.

STRUCTURAL PROFILE

Communications and media (NACE Divisions 22 and 64) consisted of 270 000 enterprises which together generated EUR 340.0 billion of value added in the EU-27 in 2004 and employed 4.9 million persons. Value added per person employed (apparent labour productivity) was high in these activities as they accounted for 6.7 % of value added in the non-financial business economy (NACE Sections C to I and K), but just 3.9 % of employment.

With EUR 187.2 billion value added, telecommunications (NACE Group 64.2) was the largest subsector in 2004, accounting for over half (55.1 %) of the communications and media total, while the second largest subsector was publishing, printing, and the reproduction of recorded media (NACE Division 22), with more than one quarter (27.4 %) of value added; while the smallest subsector was post and courier activities (NACE Group 64.1) which generated less than one fifth (17.5 %) of sectoral value added. However, telecommunications accounted for the smallest share of the sectoral workforce, with less than one quarter (24.3 %) of the persons employed, while post and courier activities had the largest workforce of the three subsectors covered, with 38.1 % of the communications and media total, somewhat above the share recorded for publishing, printing, and the reproduction of recorded media (36.7 %).

This chapter focuses on activities whose principal characteristic is to provide services related to the exchange of information. It includes postal, courier and telecommunication services (NACE Division 64) and the activities of publishing, printing, and the reproduction of recorded media (NACE Division 22). Note that compared to the previous edition of this publication, the subchapter on audio-visual activities (NACE Groups 92.1 and 92.2) has been removed from this publication. As in the previous issue, statistics on information and communication technologies (ICT) are split between this chapter and Subchapter 22.1 on computer services.

NACE

22: publishing, printing and reproduction of recorded media;
22.1: publishing;
22.2: printing and service activities related to printing;
22.3: reproduction of recorded media;
64: post and telecommunications;
64.1: post and courier activities;
64.2: telecommunications.

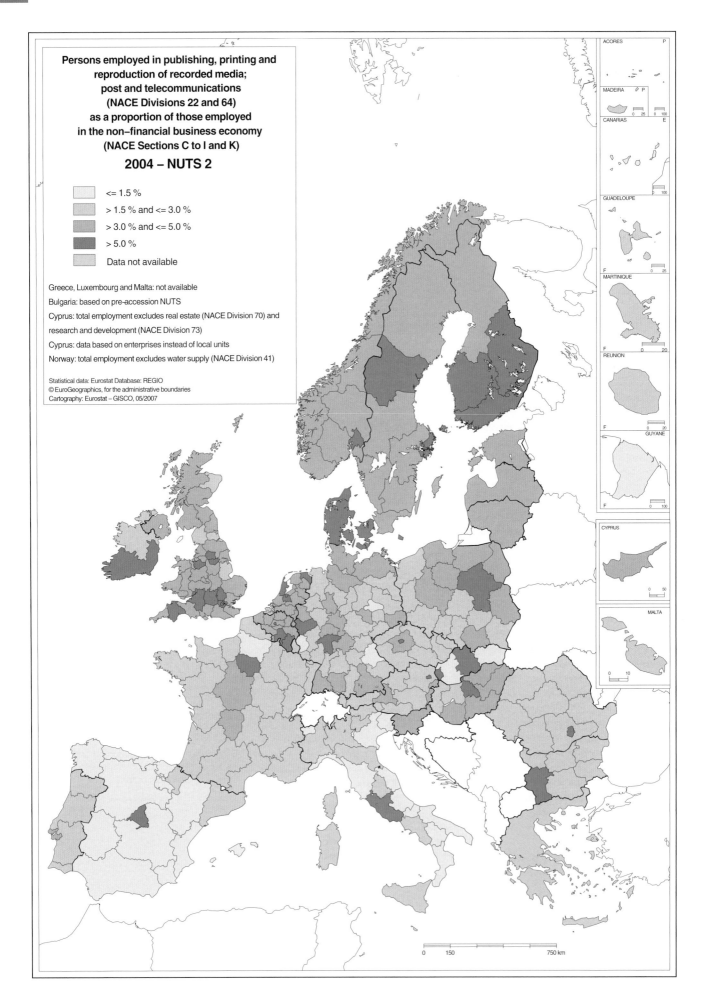

**Persons employed in publishing, printing and
reproduction of recorded media;
post and telecommunications
(NACE Divisions 22 and 64)
as a proportion of those employed
in the non–financial business economy
(NACE Sections C to I and K)**

2004 – NUTS 2

- <= 1.5 %
- > 1.5 % and <= 3.0 %
- > 3.0 % and <= 5.0 %
- > 5.0 %
- Data not available

Greece, Luxembourg and Malta: not available

Bulgaria: based on pre-accession NUTS

Cyprus: total employment excludes real estate (NACE Division 70) and
research and development (NACE Division 73)

Cyprus: data based on enterprises instead of local units

Norway: total employment excludes water supply (NACE Division 41)

Statistical data: Eurostat Database: REGIO
© EuroGeographics, for the administrative boundaries
Cartography: Eurostat – GISCO, 05/2007

ACORES   P

MADEIRA   P

CANARIAS   E

GUADELOUPE

MARTINIQUE   F

REUNION   F

GUYANE   F

CYPRUS

MALTA

Table 21.1

Publishing, printing, reproduction of recorded media; post and telecommunications (NACE Divisions 22 and 64)
Structural profile, EU-27, 2004 (1)

	No. of enterprises		Turnover		Value added		Employment	
	(thousands)	(% of total)	(EUR million)	(% of total)	(EUR million)	(% of total)	(thousands)	(% of total)
Communications, publishing and printing	269.6	100.0	743 000	100.0	340 000	100.0	4 900.0	100.0
Post and courier activities	40.0	14.8	98 199	13.2	59 574	17.5	1 868.6	38.1
Telecommunications	24.0	8.9	398 612	53.6	187 228	55.1	1 189.8	24.3
Publishing, printing, reproduction of recorded media	206.5	76.6	246 000	33.1	93 000	27.4	1 800.0	36.7

(1) Rounded estimates based on non-confidential data.
Source: Eurostat (SBS)

Among the Member States with available data, Germany and the United Kingdom were the largest Member States in this sector in 2004, each of these countries accounting for around one fifth of the EU-27's value added within the communications and media sector. Looking at the contribution of this sector within the non-financial business economy, the most specialised Member States [2] in value added terms, were Bulgaria, Latvia, Romania and Hungary, in which communications and media activities contributed to at least 8.0 % of non-financial business economy value added. Nevertheless, the sector was quite important in all Member States, as even in the least specialised countries it accounted for more than 5 % of non-financial business economy value added.

The regional specialisation of these activities is shown in the map on page 354 which is based on the non-financial business economy employment share of this sector. Countries with many regions specialised in these activities include United Kingdom, Germany, the Netherlands, Belgium, the Nordic countries and Slovakia. These activities were often particularly centred in or around the capital, with the capital region in 17 of the 24 Member States with data available being among the most specialised regions (5 % or more of the workforce in this activity). Some regions were

[2] Ireland, Greece, Cyprus, Luxembourg and Malta, not available.

particularly specialised in communications and media and this is notably the case in Köln (Germany), Lazio (Italy), Île de France (France) and Bruxelles-Capitale/Brussels Hoofdstedelijk (Belgium), where this sector accounted for over one fifth of total employment in the non-financial business economy.

Annualised short-term statistics are available for the EU-27 starting in 1998 (employment) and 2000 (turnover) for the services activity of post and telecommunications (NACE Division 64), while a longer series is available for the industrial activity of publishing, printing, and the reproduction of recorded media (NACE

Division 22), starting from 1996 - see Figure 21.2. Looking first at turnover, postal and courier activities (NACE Group 64.1) and telecommunications (NACE Group 64.2) both developed strongly in the last five years, between 2001 and 2006, averaging growth of 3.8 % per annum for postal and courier activities and 4.5 % per annum for telecommunications in the EU-27. In contrast, the turnover index for publishing, printing, and the reproduction of recorded media grew on average by 1.6 % per year over the same period in the EU-27, resulting from a period of stability between 2000 and 2003, with year on year growth rates below 1 %, followed by

Figure 21.1

Publishing, printing, reproduction of recorded media; post and telecommunications (NACE Divisions 22 and 64)
Share of non-financial business economy, EU-27, 2004 (%) (1)

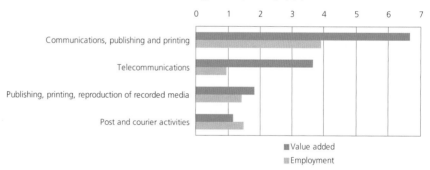

(1) Rounded estimates based on non-confidential data.
Source: Eurostat (SBS)

Table 21.2

Publishing, printing, reproduction of recorded media; post and telecommunications (NACE Divisions 22 and 64)
Structural profile: ranking of top five Member States, 2004

Rank	Value added (EUR million) (1)	Employment (thousands) (1)	Share of non-financial business economy			
			No. of enterprises (2)	Turnover (3)	Value added (3)	Employment (3)
1	Germany (69 797)	Germany (978.8)	United Kingdom (2.8 %)	United Kingdom (4.7 %)	Bulgaria (12.2 %)	Finland (6.0 %)
2	United Kingdom (68 175)	United Kingdom (856.4)	Slovenia (2.4 %)	Finland (4.2 %)	Latvia (9.0 %)	Denmark (5.5 %)
3	France (47 910)	France (645.2)	Lithuania (2.2 %)	Germany (3.8 %)	Romania (8.3 %)	Belgium (4.9 %)
4	Italy (38 549)	Italy (428.3)	Belgium (2.2 %)	Latvia (3.8 %)	Hungary (8.0 %)	Sweden (4.8 %)
5	Spain (25 212)	Spain (318.4)	Netherlands (2.1 %)	Portugal (3.8 %)	Portugal (7.4 %)	United Kingdom (4.8 %)

(1) Greece, Luxembourg and Malta, not available.
(2) Ireland, Greece, Cyprus and Malta, not available; Luxembourg, 2003.
(3) Ireland, Greece, Cyprus, Luxembourg and Malta, not available.
Source: Eurostat (SBS)

more rapid annual growth of at least 1.8 % in the three years that followed. In employment terms, two similar phases of development could be observed for communications (postal and courier activities, and telecommunications) and publishing, printing, and the reproduction of recorded media, both activities showing a period of growth until 2001, followed by a reduction in employment levels. Between 2001 and 2006, annual contractions of the employment index for publishing, printing, and the reproduction of recorded media were ranged between -0.7 % (2004) and -3.2 % (2003), while they were slightly more pronounced for post and telecommunications (between -1.1 % in 2006 and -4.0 % in 2004).

Large enterprises (with 250 and more persons employed) were predominant in the EU-27 as they contributed for more than three quarters (78.0 %) of total value added generated in the communications and media sector in 2004. Hence, the contribution of large enterprises was notably higher (35 percentage points difference) than for the non-financial business economy as a whole - see Figure 21.3. Post and telecommunications (NACE Division 64) was dominated by large enterprises, as these accounted for 92.3 % of value added in the EU-27. This was the second highest proportion of value added accounted for by large enterprises across all non-financial business economy NACE divisions [3] in 2004, just after mining of metal ores (NACE Division 13). In contrast, the value added share of large enterprises in publishing, printing and the reproduction of recorded media (NACE Division 22) was 40.2 %, marginally below the non-financial business economy average. Moreover, given that the share of value added generated by micro enterprises (with less than 10 persons employed) in publishing, printing and the reproduction of recorded media (13.3 %) was below the non-financial business economy average (20.2 %), small enterprises (with between 10 and 49 persons employed), and particularly medium-sized enterprises (with between 50 and 249 persons employed) made a relatively high contribution within this subsector.

_____
[3] NACE Divisions 12 and 62, not available.

Figure 21.2 _____

Publishing, printing, reproduction of recorded media; post and telecommunications (NACE Divisions 22 and 64)
Evolution of main indicators, EU-27 (2000=100)

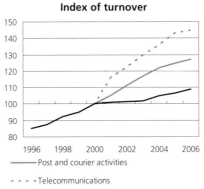
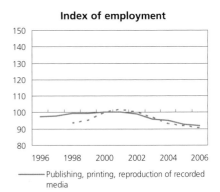

Source: Eurostat (STS)

Figure 21.3 _____

Publishing, printing, reproduction of recorded media; post and telecommunications (NACE Divisions 22 and 64)
Share of value added by enterprise size class, EU-27, 2004

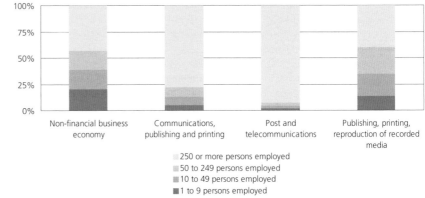

Source: Eurostat (SBS)

EMPLOYMENT CHARACTERISTICS
Labour force statistics show that the characteristics of the workforce in the EU-27's communications and media sector (NACE Divisions 22 and 64) did not diverge greatly from those for the non-financial business economy as a whole. Indeed, about three fifths (59.9 %) of the sectoral workforce were men, a proportion slightly lower than that for the non-financial business economy as a whole (65.0 %) – see Figure 21.4.

The proportion of part-time employment in the sector (17.7 %) in 2006 was also rather similar to that for the non-financial business economy average (14.4 %). However, the activity of publishing, printing, and the reproduction of recorded media (NACE Division 22) engaged more than one fifth (20.7 %) of its workforce on a part-time basis, the fifth largest proportion recorded among the NACE divisions of the non-financial business economy. However, among the Member States with available data [4], about one third of the countries had a lower proportion of part-time employment in their publishing, printing, and reproduction of recorded media activities than in their national non-financial business economy as a whole.

_____
[4] Estonia, Lithuania, Luxembourg and Malta, 2005; Ireland, not available.

Figure 21.4 _____

Publishing, printing, reproduction of recorded media; post and telecommunications (NACE Divisions 22 and 64)
Labour force characteristics, EU-27, 2006

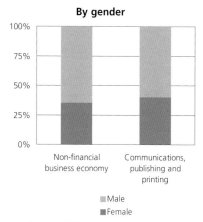
By gender

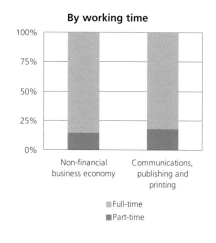
By working time

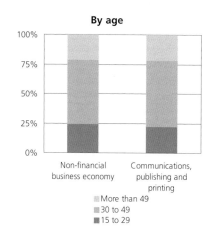
By age

Source: Eurostat (LFS)

Table 21.3 _____

Publishing, printing, reproduction of recorded media; post and telecommunications (NACE Divisions 22 and 64)
Total expenditure, EU-27, 2004

	Value (EUR million)				Share (% of total expenditure)		
	Total expenditure	Purchases of goods and services	Personnel costs	Investment in tangible goods	Purchases of goods and services	Personnel costs	Investment in tangible goods
Communications, publishing and printing (1)	627 600	410 000	165 000	52 600	65.3	26.3	8.4
Post and courier activities	91 387	39 133	48 931	3 323	42.8	53.5	3.6
Telecommunications	320 882	222 352	57 432	41 099	69.3	17.9	12.8
Publishing, printing, reproduction of recorded media (1)	219 210	153 000	58 000	8 210	69.8	26.5	3.7

(1) Rounded estimates based on non-confidential data.
Source: Eurostat (SBS)

A breakdown by age of the workforce for the EU-27's communications and media sector shows that slightly more than one fifth (21.9 %) of those employed in 2006 were aged between 15 and 29, some 56.0 % between 30 and 49, while the remainder were persons aged 50 or more; these proportions were rather similar to respective non-financial business economy averages. Only in Ireland and to a lesser extent in France and Austria did persons employed aged between 15 and 29 account for a significantly lower proportion of the sectoral workforce than the national non-financial business economy average, a low share that was generally accompanied by a larger share for persons aged between 30 and 49. The reverse situation was observed in Portugal, where the youngest age-class of persons employed in the communications and media sector accounted for a remarkably higher proportion in the workforce than the Portuguese non-financial business economy average (10.2 percentage points above).

According to structural business statistics paid employees accounted for 95.4 % of the persons employed in the EU-27's communications and media sector in 2004, a working status that was dominant when compared with the equivalent share for the non-financial business economy average (86.2 %).

COSTS, PRODUCTIVITY AND PROFITABILITY

In 2004 the communications and media sector recorded a share of gross tangible investment in total expenditure (personnel costs plus purchases of goods and services plus intangible investment) of 8.4 % in the EU-27, with a 3.6 % share for post and courier activities, a 3.7 % share for publishing, printing and reproduction of media, and a 12.8 % share for telecommunications; for comparison, the average ratio for the non-financial business economy was 4.9 %. The share of personnel costs was also considerably higher for

communications and media (26.3 %) than for the non-financial business economy as a whole (16.4 %). This was the case in all the three subsectors that make up the communications and media sector, where the share of total expenditure dedicated to personnel costs was lowest at 17.9 % in telecommunications and reached as high as 53.5 % for post and courier activities. As a result of higher shares dedicated to gross investment in tangible goods and personnel costs in the communications and media sector, the share of purchases of goods and services was notably lower for the sector (65.3 %), compared with the non-financial business economy average (78.7 %). The EU-27 pattern was valid among all the Member States with data available (5).

_____
(5) Ireland, Greece, Cyprus, Luxembourg and Malta, not available.

Table 21.4

Publishing, printing, reproduction of recorded media; post and telecommunications (NACE Divisions 22 and 64)
Productivity and profitability, EU-27, 2004

	Apparent labour productivity (EUR thousand)	Average personnel costs (EUR thousand)	Wage adjusted labour productivity (%)	Gross operating rate (%)
Communications, publishing and printing (1)	69.4	35.3	197.0	23.6
Post and courier activities	31.9	26.9	118.4	10.8
Telecommunications	157.4	49.0	321.0	32.6
Publishing, printing, reproduction of recorded media (1)	51.0	34.7	146.0	14.1

(1) Rounded estimates based on non-confidential data.
Source: Eurostat (SBS)

Apparent labour productivity in the EU-27's communications and media sector was EUR 69 400 per person employed in 2004 (see Table 21.4), which was around 70 % higher than the non-financial business economy average. Average personnel costs were EUR 35 300 per employee, which was 28 % higher than the non-financial business economy average. As a result, the wage adjusted labour productivity ratio within the EU-27's communications and media sector was 197.0 % in 2004, some 49.0 percentage points above the average for the non-financial business economy. This high ratio for the sector resulted mainly from a high value registered by the telecommunications subsector (321.0 %),

as for the other two subsectors the ratio was below the non-financial business economy average. Among the Member States several recorded an above average wage adjusted labour productivity ratio in the communications and media sector, notably in some of the Southern Member States. In Bulgaria, Italy, Spain and Portugal this ratio was more than two thirds higher in communications and media than the national non-financial business economy average.

In a similar manner, the gross operating rate for the EU-27's communications and media sector stood at 23.6 % in 2004, which was more than twice the non-financial business economy

average (11.0 %). Note that the gross operating rate was particularly high in telecommunications (32.6 %), and in fact in post and courier activities the gross operating rate was below the non-financial business economy average in 2004. Bulgaria, Romania and Portugal recorded the highest gross operating rate in the communications and media sector relative to the non-financial business economy average. However, all the other Member States for which data is available [6] recorded a gross operating rate in communications and media above their non-financial business economy average.

[6] Ireland, Greece, Cyprus, Luxembourg and Malta, not available.

21.1: POSTAL AND COURIER SERVICES

This subchapter covers NACE Group 64.1, which includes both national post activities (NACE Class 64.11) and other courier activities (NACE Class 64.12). National post activities include the pick-up, transport and delivery (domestic or international) of mail and parcels, and other services such as P.O. boxes or poste restante. Courier activities other than national post activities include mainly express courier services, where enterprises have widened their initial focus on business documents towards the transfer of packages and freight, blurring the distinction between courier and transport enterprises.

In most Member States, Universal service providers (USPs) [7] still operate as a monopoly and have exclusive rights, balanced by the fact that they have a universal service obligation. Private operators dominate the express services market, providing letter and parcel services, specifically to the business-to-business, direct mail and business-to-private segments of the market. However, since the middle of the 1990's there have been gradual developments towards market liberalisation for the postal and courier services, with parcels and express services markets now fully open to competing operators. In October 2006, the European Commission presented plans to abolish

remaining restrictions on mail deliveries under 50 grams (known as the 'reserved area' for national operators) and open up Europe's postal sector to full competition, while liberalisation has already begun or been finalised in few Member States, including the United Kingdom, Sweden, the Netherlands and Germany. At the time of drafting for this publication, the Parliament rejected the Commission's proposal of 2009 as the deadline for removing the remaining 'reserved area' and opted for market opening by 31 December 2010, with an exemption for the new Member States and Member States with a 'difficult topography' who can liberalise their markets by 31 December 2012.

[7] The term USP takes account of the possibility that operators are no longer public organisations.

Table 21.5
Postal services in the EU-25

	2001	2002	2003	2004	2005
Total number of permanent post offices (units)	103 535	102 708	101 602	99 690	98 971
of which, staffed by people from outside the administration (%)	34.4	35.1	35.3	35.6	36.0
Number of letter-post items, domestic service (millions)	112 283	113 223	114 209	118 343	116 936
Number of letter-post items, international service-dispatch (millions)	3 284	2 984	2 916	2 713	2 687
Ordinary parcels, domestic services (millions)	1 098	1 080	1 052	1 077	1 018
Ordinary parcels, international service-dispatch (millions)	14	14	14	14	14

Source: UPU, http://www.upu.int, Postal statistics database

Table 21.6
Selected indicators for Universal Service Providers (USPs), European postal market, 2005

	Letter-post services (thousands) (1)	of which (%): Ordinary letters and postcards	of which (%): Reserved area (2)	Price for standard letter (EUR)	On-time delivery (D+1) (%)
BE	:	:	:	0.50	91.4
BG (3)	80 798	64.0	83.6	0.23	88.0
CZ	887 363	62.9	60.3	0.25	96.0
DK (3)	1 454 053	81.5	68.9	0.60	95.2
DE	15 760 000	54.7	80.5	0.55	>80.0
EE	76 004	76.4	:	0.28	95.3
IE	655 000	90.1	87.9	0.48	73.0
EL	633 793	76.0	81.0	0.50	70.8
ES	5 150 875	73.2	59.3	0.30	88.4
FR	18 199 000	62.6	81.6	0.53	79.1
IT	6 080 648	55.0	:	0.60	88.3
CY	52 805	98.3	:	0.34	64.0
LV	74 285	93.9	91.0	0.23	62.0
LT	52 706	:	75.3	0.29	72.8
LU	133 300	69.3	60.0	0.50	97.8
HU	789 611	73.1	86.9	0.36	99.5
MT	c	c	c	0.16	92.0
NL (4)	5 300 000	56.0	:	0.39	96.6
AT	:	:	:	0.55	95.9
PL	3 158 775	47.1	48.1	0.50	93.3
PT	1 301 058	c	82.5	0.45	95.6
RO	282 391	62.5	50.6	0.14	:
SI	392 800	75.0	72.3	0.20	88.1
SK	374 433	38.7	55.4	0.37	94.3
FI	2 166 000	40.8	:	0.70	94.8
SE	2 754 287	96.4	:	0.60	95.2
UK	c	c	:	0.44	94.1
HR	278 414	70.7	67.1	0.31	98.0
IS	62 462	94.6	85.6	0.64	87.5
NO	1 510 774	c	66.9	0.75	99.0

(1) Letter-post services: the indicator covers items of correspondence (ordinary letters and postcards, direct mail, registered mail, insured mail) and other letter-post items (books, catalogues, newspapers and periodicals); reserved area: mail deliveries under 50 grams for national operators; the price for standard letter: payable for the handling of a standard (first class) letter weighting less than 20 g (universal service) for domestic service, prices of letters vary significantly between EU Member States according to various criteria; On-time delivery: the indicator refers to the share of priority letters delivered on-time according to national performance indicators, the standard measured is D+1, except for Spain, Croatia and Norway, where it is D+3 and for Hungary, where it is D+15, the figure for Germany is to be read as >80.0 % and shows that the requirements according to the German Postal Universal Service Ordinance are fulfilled (D+1 > 80.0 %).
(2) Reserved area: refers to the standard letter-post service, where USPs enjoy exclusive rights to provide services. The reserved area is delineated at country level within weight/price limits given by the EC postal directives (97/67/EC and 2002/39/EC). Country definitions for the reserved area vary, so direct comparisons between countries should be made with prudence. In this publication it is expressed in terms of the percentage of the total letter post services.
(3) 2004.
(4) Share of ordinary letters and postcards in letter-post services, 2004.
Source: Eurostat, Inquiry on Postal Services 2006

FOCUS ON POSTAL INFRASTRUCTURE AND TRANSPORT OF POSTAL ITEMS
According to data collected by the UPU (8) from its postal administration members, there were about 99 000 permanent post offices in the EU-25 in 2005 - see Table 21.5, therefore 4.4 % less when compared with the number in 2001. The number of letter-items for both domestic and international dispatch reached 119.6 billion letters in the EU-25 in 2005, an increase of 3.5 % when compared with 2001. Ordinary parcels for both domestic and international dispatch amounted to 1.0 billion items in 2005, of which 98.6 % were handled within the domestic market. The number of parcels dispatched fell consecutively in 2002 and 2003, but increased in 2004 by 2.4 %, before falling again in 2005 by 5.3 %. According to Eurostat's Inquiry on Postal Services, among the Member States for which data is available, mail deliveries over 50 grams (the 'reserved area') represented around half or more of the letter-post services for national operators in 2005 – see Table 21.6.

(8) UPU (Universal Post Union), more information at: http://www.upu.int.

STRUCTURAL PROFILE

Post and courier activities (NACE Group 64.1) consisted of 40 000 enterprises which generated EUR 59.6 billion of value added in the EU-27 in 2004, which equated to 17.5 % of the communications and media sector (NACE Divisions 22 and 64) total. Nevertheless, with 1.9 million persons employed, these activities represented 38.1 % of the communications and media sectoral workforce, more than twice the value added contribution. National post activities (NACE Class 64.11) was the largest of the two subsectors within the post and courier activities sector, accounting for slightly less than two thirds both of sectoral value added and employment, the remainder being accounted for by courier activities other than national post activities (NACE Class 64.12) – see Table 21.7.

The five largest EU economies were also the five largest contributors to the post and couriers sector in 2004, whether measured in value added or employment terms - see Table 21.8. However, looking at the relative contribution of post and courier activities to the national non-financial business economy value added, these activities were most important in Luxembourg (2003) and France. Indeed, in these two countries post and courier activities generated at least 1.6 % of non-financial business economy value added, a share that was well above the 1.2 % average for the EU-27.

Annual short-term statistics for post and courier activities in the EU-27 provide a picture of the development of the turnover index over the period 2000 to 2006 - see Figure 21.5. There was continuous growth for this index, although at a somewhat slower rhythm than for telecommunications (NACE Group 64.2). Indeed, turnover rose on average by 4.1 % per annum in post and courier activities during the period observed, compared with an average growth rate of 6.4 % per annum for telecommunications. Year on year growth rates for the index of turnover in post and courier activities were in excess of 5 % in the years 2001 to 2003, after which growth slowed to 4.4 % in 2004, 2.2 % in 2005 and 1.9 % in 2006.

Table 21.7

Post and courier activities (NACE Group 64.1)
Structural profile, EU-27, 2004 (1)

	No. of enterprises (thousands)	Turnover (EUR million)	Value added (EUR million)	Employment (thousands)
Post and courier activities	40.0	98 199	59 574	1 868.6
National post activities	:	56 000	39 000	1 200.0
Courier activities other than national post activities	37.0	42 000	20 300	630.0

(1) Rounded estimates based on non-confidential data.
Source: Eurostat (SBS)

Figure 21.5

Post and courier activities (NACE Group 64.1)
Index of turnover, EU-27 (2000=100)

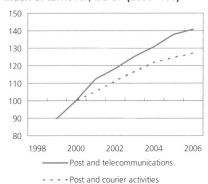

Source: Eurostat (STS)

Table 21.8

Post and courier activities (NACE Group 64.1)
Structural profile: ranking of top five Member States, 2004

Rank	Share of EU-27 value added (%) (1)	Share of EU-27 employment (%) (2)	Value added specialisation ratio (EU-27=100) (3)	Employment specialisation ratio (EU-27=100) (4)
1	Germany (21.6)	Germany (21.5)	Luxembourg (190.4)	Belgium (140.9)
2	France (19.8)	United Kingdom (16.1)	France (140.9)	France (134.7)
3	United Kingdom (18.8)	France (15.4)	Belgium (115.2)	Slovakia (134.5)
4	Italy (11.4)	Italy (8.5)	Germany (102.9)	Finland (133.3)
5	Spain (4.2)	Spain (5.6)	Italy (102.3)	Germany (129.6)

(1) Denmark, Ireland, Greece, Malta, Netherlands, Poland and Slovenia, not available; Luxembourg and Portugal, 2003.
(2) Denmark, Ireland, Greece, Malta, Netherlands, Poland and Slovenia, not available; Czech Republic, Luxembourg and Portugal, 2003.
(3) Denmark, Ireland, Greece, Cyprus, Malta, Netherlands, Poland and Slovenia, not available; Luxembourg and Portugal, 2003.
(4) Denmark, Ireland, Greece, Cyprus, Malta, Netherlands, Poland and Slovenia, not available; Czech Republic, Luxembourg and Portugal, 2003.
Source: Eurostat (SBS)

Table 21.9

Post and courier activities (NACE Group 64.1)
Total expenditure, EU-27, 2004

	Value (EUR million)				Share (% of total expenditure)			
	Total expenditure	Purchases of goods and services	Personnel costs	Investment in tangible goods	Purchases of goods and services	Personnel costs	Investment in tangible goods
Post and courier activities	91 387	39 133	48 931	3 323	42.8	53.5	3.6
National post activities (1)	52 500	16 400	34 000	2 100	31.2	64.8	4.0
Courier activities other than national post activities (1)	38 520	22 600	14 700	1 220	58.7	38.2	3.2

(1) Rounded estimate based on non-confidential data.
Source: Eurostat (SBS)

Table 21.10

Post and courier activities (NACE Group 64.1)
Productivity and profitability, EU-27, 2004

	Apparent labour productivity (EUR thousand)	Average personnel costs (EUR thousand)	Wage adjusted labour productivity (%)	Gross operating rate (%)
Post and courier activities	31.9	26.9	118.4	10.8
National post activities (1)	32.5	28.3	114.0	8.9
Courier activities other than national post activities (1)	32.0	25.0	129.0	13.4

(1) Rounded estimate based on non-confidential data.
Source: Eurostat (SBS)

COSTS, PRODUCTIVITY AND PROFITABILITY

In the EU-27's post and courier activities, more than half (53.5 %) of total expenditure was accounted for by personnel costs – see Table 21.9; this was the fourth largest share of personnel costs recorded among all NACE groups in the non-financial business economy, mainly influenced by the high share recorded in national post activities (NACE Class 64.11) where personnel costs took up more than two thirds (64.8 %) of total expenditure. However, in other courier activities (NACE Class 64.12), purchases of goods and services accounted for the largest proportion (58.7 %) of total expenditure, while personnel costs still represented more than two thirds (38.2 %).

With EUR 31 900 of value added generated per person employed in 2004, the EU-27's post and courier services recorded a relatively low level of apparent productivity compared with most other activities, as the non-financial business economy average was EUR 9 000 above this value. Average personnel costs were EUR 26 900 per employee in the EU-27, only slightly below the non-financial business economy (EUR 700 below) in 2004. As a consequence, the wage adjusted labour productivity ratio for post and courier services was 118.4 % in the EU-27, significantly below the non-financial business economy average of 148.0 %, and a long way below the communication and media average of 197.0 %. The ratio of operating surplus (value added less personnel costs) to turnover is the gross operating rate, and this was 10.8 % for the EU-27's post and courier activities in 2004, only slightly below the non-financial business economy average (11.0 %), although considerably below the average for communications and media (23.6 %). This rate reached 13.4 % for other courier activities while it was 8.9 % for national post activities.

21.2: TELECOMMUNICATION SERVICES

Telecommunications services (NACE Group 64.2) embrace the distribution of sound, images, data and other information via cables, broadcasting, relay or satellite. These services include both the management and maintenance of networks and the provision of services using these networks, including the provision of radio and television services, but not the production of radio and television programmes.

Growing access to broadband Internet among consumers and the increased use of mobile devices for receiving electronic content are important aspects in the development of on-demand services, as is effective management of the radio spectrum. Two recent European Commission decisions concern the distribution of information by radio waves, one on the harmonisation of the radio spectrum for use by short-range devices [9] and another one on the harmonisation of the radio spectrum for radio frequency identification (RFID) devices operating in the ultra high frequency (UHF) band [10].

[9] 2006/771/EC of 09.11.2006.
[10] 2006/804/EC of 23.11.2006.

The regulatory framework for electronic communications in the EU started in 2001 with the adoption by the Council of a new regulatory package. This package was reviewed by the European Commission in 2006 for the first time and a public consultation on the review of the EU regulatory framework ended on 31 January 2006. Negotiation in and between the European Parliament and the Council then started in the first quarter of 2007 and it is expected that the revised framework will be effective around 2010.

This subchapter covers for a large part the activities of the so-called information society, a society whose wealth is based on its ability to process, store, retrieve and communicate information in whatever form - oral, written or visual. However, note that enterprises acting in computer and related activities, such as hardware, software or data processing, are covered in Subchapter 22.1.

FOCUS ON MOBILE AND FIXED LINE TELEPHONY

Information on the market shares of operators in fixed and mobile telecommunications in the Member States [11] is presented in Table 21.11. Unsurprisingly, incumbents (those enterprises that were active before the liberalisation of the market, generally formerly state-owned telecom operators) still dominate, and across the EU as a whole they occupy more than half of the market in 2005, whether for local, long-distance or international calls (in terms of minutes of connection or turnover). An average for the EU-25 shows that incumbent operators accounted for 72 % of local calls (note that local calls also include dial-up Internet connections) some 66 % of long-distance calls, and 56 % of international calls. However, in some countries the dominance of the incumbent operator is less marked, for example in Finland the incumbent accounted for less than half of the market for both long-distance calls (45 %) and international calls (41 %), while in Germany, Italy, the Netherlands and Austria international calls tended to be less dominated by incumbent operators (with market shares ranged from 39 % to just 50 %). In some Member States, the same operators for the fixed network offer local and long distance national and international telecommunications, while in other markets some operators specialise in particular services. Most recent data for leading operators in mobile telecommunications are for 2006 – again, see Table 21.11. Based on the number of subscriptions, leading operators in mobile telecommunications generally accounted for significantly lower market shares compared with the incumbent fixed telecommunication operators, and in a large majority of the Member States they provided less than half of the subscriptions in 2006. Slovenia and Cyprus stood out from the rest of the countries as their leading operators in mobile telecommunications accounted for 71 % and 90 % respectively of the mobile phone subscriptions.

Table 21.12 provides information on the cost of three types of fixed line calls for August 2006. The difference in the cost between Member States is considerable. Cyprus recorded the lowest costs for national calls (EUR 0.22 for a 10 minute call on a weekday, including VAT) and the second lowest cost for local calls (EUR 0.22) and for calls to the United States (EUR 0.66). On the basis of a comparison between the highest and lowest prices, local calls were 3.2 times as high in Slovakia as they were in France, national calls were 5.9 times as high in Slovakia as they were in Cyprus, and international calls to the United States were 12.9 times as high in Latvia as they were in Germany.

[11] Bulgaria and Romania, not available.

Table 21.11

Market shares of operators in telecommunication (NACE Group 64.2) (%) (1)

	Incumbent operator in fixed telecommunications, 2005			Leading operator in mobile telecom-munications, 2006
	Local calls (incl. To the Internet) (2)	Long-distance calls (3)	International calls (4)	
EU-25	72	66	56	39
BE	68	68	58	45
BG	:	:	:	:
CZ	76	63	65	41
DK	:	:	:	32
DE	56	57	39	37
EE	:	:	:	46
IE	83	63	62	47
GR	78	73	74	41
ES	78	75	62	46
FR	80	68	67	46
IT	71	73	47	41
CY	100	100	86	90
LV	97	98	72	35
LT	97	88	76	36
LU	:	:	:	51
HU	92	90	87	45
MT	99	99	98	52
NL	75	75	45	48
AT	53	59	50	39
PL	85	70	71	34
PT	:	78	80	46
RO	:	:	:	:
SI	100	100	83	71
SK	99	100	88	56
FI	95	45	41	45
SE	:	:	40	43
UK	60	52	53	26

(1) The incumbent is defined as the enterprise active on the market just before liberalisation; local call: calls within local networks; long distance: calls from one local network to another; estimate of leading operators' market share, minutes of connection or retail revenues, for the fixed market; shares of the Mobile market, based on the number of mobile subscriptions.
(2) Austria and Finland, 2004; Cyprus, 2003; Estonia, Luxembourg and Sweden, confidential data.
(3) Finland, 2004; Cyprus, 2003; Estonia, Luxembourg and Sweden, confidential data.
(4) Finland and Sweden, 2004; Estonia and Luxembourg, confidential data.
Source: Eurostat (Information society statistics)

Concerning mobile phone charges, the regulation of the European Parliament and of the Council of 27 June 2007 on roaming on public mobile telephone networks within the Community [12] aims to reduce the cost of using mobile phones abroad (roaming charges), with the goal of capping charges by the middle of 2007. Providers of international roaming services will then have two months to implement provisions related to wholesale roaming tariffs and three months to implement provisions related to the transparency obligations at retail level. The regulation sets an EU-wide maximum average price per minute for wholesale charge, not exceeding EUR 0.30. This charge will decrease to EUR 0.28 and

EUR 0.26 after one and two years respectively. The regulation also introduces a Eurotariff [13] at retail level (excluding VAT) not exceeding EUR 0.49 per minute for any call made and EUR 0.24 per minute for any call received for the first year of the regulation. Then, in the second and third years, the price ceiling for calls made will be reduced to EUR 0.46 and EUR 0.43, and for calls received to EUR 0.22 and EUR 0.19, respectively.

[13] For more details, see:
http://www.consilium.europa.eu/ueDocs/cms_Data/docs/pressData/en/misc/94533.pdf.

[12] Regulation (EC) no 717/2007, amending Directive 2002/21/EC, of 27 June 2007.

Table 21.12

Cost including VAT of a 10 minute call at 11 a.m. on a weekday, August 2006 (EUR)

	Local calls	National calls	International calls to USA
EU-25	0.36	0.74	1.79
BE	0.57	0.57	1.98
BG	:	:	:
CZ	0.56	0.56	2.02
DK	0.37	0.37	2.38
DE	0.39	0.49	0.46
EE	0.23	0.23	2.13
EL	0.49	0.82	1.91
ES	0.31	0.74	3.49
FR	0.19	0.85	1.53
IE	0.36	0.89	2.32
IT	0.22	1.15	2.12
CY	0.22	0.22	0.66
LV	0.36	1.03	5.94
LT	0.39	0.79	4.07
LU	0.31	:	1.37
HU	0.40	1.04	2.88
MT	0.25	:	1.64
NL	0.33	0.49	0.85
AT	0.49	0.59	1.90
PL	0.50	1.00	1.23
PT	0.37	0.65	3.11
RO	:	:	:
SI	0.26	0.26	1.40
SK	0.60	1.29	1.23
FI	0.24	0.94	4.90
SE	0.29	0.29	1.18
UK	0.44	0.44	2.23

Source: Eurostat (Information society statistics, Structural indicators - original source Teligen Ltd.)

FOCUS ON THE ICT AND THE DIGITAL ECONOMY

As part of the initiatives to support the development of the information society, the European Commission launched the i2010 strategy, the digitally-led strategy for growth and jobs and the EU's policy strategy to boost the digital economy by combining research, regulatory tools and public-private partnerships, a strategy adopted by the European Commission in June 2005. Progress towards the objectives of that strategy among the Member States are followed in annual reports issued by the European Commission and provides a benchmark on the effectiveness of the European Commission's policy to build sustainable economic growth in information and communication technology (ICT). Hence, the 2007 report [14] shows that EU enterprises are investing both in new and more mature ICT solutions and households broadband connections increased in the year to October 2006. However, further effort is still needed for the EU to reach its 3 % target of GDP for research spending. At a national level, the report shows that Italy leads in 3G mobile phone and fibre development while the most households with digital TV are found in the United Kingdom. Six countries, namely Denmark, the Netherlands, Finland, Sweden, the United Kingdom and Belgium, all have higher broadband penetration rates than the United States and Japan, while ICT deployment in Danish schools is the highest in the EU, and the British and Swedish workforce are the most skilled in ICT, according to this report. Finland has the EU's highest use of public access points and invests the most in ICT research (64.3 % of its R&D enterprise expenditure), while Sweden and Finland also dedicated respectively 3.9 % and 3.5 % of their GDP on research, both shares being above the EU's 3 % target set by the i2010 initiative.

[14] For more details, see: http://ec.europa.eu/ information_society/eeurope/i2010/annual_report/ index_en.htm.

STRUCTURAL PROFILE

The EU-27's telecommunication services sector (NACE Group 64.2) was made up of 24 000 enterprises which generated EUR 398.6 billion turnover and 187.2 billion of value added in the EU-27 in 2004, accounting for more than half of both indicators in the communications and media sector (NACE Divisions 22 and 64), making it the third largest non-financial business economy (NACE Sections C to I and K) activity at the NACE group level (based on available data) in terms of value added and the seventh in terms of turnover. Some 1.2 million persons were employed in telecommunication services, equivalent to just below one quarter (24.3 %) of the communications and media workforce, a share that was considerably lower than that for value added, indicating high apparent labour productivity (value added per person employed).

The five largest EU economies also had the largest telecommunications sectors in 2004, both in terms of value added and turnover. The United Kingdom and Germany ranked first, contributing at least 17.6 % of the EU-27's total for both of these indicators. For these two largest contributors, as well as for Italy and Spain, their share of the EU-27's value added in the telecommunication services sector was higher than their equivalent share in the total workforce, which was not the case in France, where both shares were similar – see Table 21.13. However, among the Member States [15], the contribution of telecommunication services to the non-financial business economy value added was highest in Bulgaria (10.5 %), in Romania and Latvia (6.7 % for both countries), and to a lesser extent in Luxembourg (5.5 %, 2003) and in Hungary (5.4 %).

[15] Luxembourg and Portugal, 2003; Denmark, Ireland, Greece, Cyprus, Malta, Netherlands, Poland and Slovenia, not available.

Table 21.13

Telecommunications (NACE Group 64.2)
Structural profile: ranking of top five Member States, 2004

Rank	Share of EU-27 value added (%) (1)	Share of EU-27 employment (%) (2)	Value added specialisation ratio (EU-27=100) (3)	Employment specialisation ratio (EU-27=100) (4)
1	Germany (20.5)	Germany (17.6)	Bulgaria (286.5)	Bulgaria (210.2)
2	United Kingdom (17.9)	United Kingdom (17.6)	Romania (183.1)	Finland (166.9)
3	France (13.3)	France (13.3)	Latvia (182.0)	Belgium (144.1)
4	Italy (12.2)	Italy (8.5)	Luxembourg (151.5)	Slovakia (125.7)
5	Spain (8.6)	Spain (5.5)	Hungary (147.2)	Romania (124.8)

(1) Denmark, Ireland, Greece, Malta, Netherlands, Poland and Slovenia, not available; Luxembourg and Portugal, 2003.
(2) Denmark, Ireland, Greece, Malta, Netherlands, Poland and Slovenia, not available; Czech Republic, Luxembourg and Portugal, 2003.
(3) Denmark, Ireland, Greece, Cyprus, Malta, Netherlands, Poland and Slovenia, not available; Luxembourg and Portugal, 2003.
(4) Denmark, Ireland, Greece, Cyprus, Malta, Netherlands, Poland and Slovenia, not available; Czech Republic, Luxembourg and Portugal, 2003.
Source: Eurostat (SBS)

Annual short-term statistics are available for the index of turnover for telecommunication services for the years 2000 to 2006 - see Figure 21.6. The EU-27's turnover growth was uninterrupted during this period; with annual average growth over the five most recent years (between 2001 and 2006) at 4.5 %, some way above the 3.8 % average for post and courier activities (NACE Group 64.1). Growth was particularly strong in 2001 (16.1 %) since when it ranged between 4.7 % and 6.0 % each year through to 2005, with the pace of growth slowing substantially in 2006 (1.1 %).

COSTS, PRODUCTIVITY AND PROFITABILITY

A breakdown of total expenditure for the EU-27's telecommunications services sector in 2004 shows that more than two thirds of the total was dedicated to the purchase of goods and services (69.3 %), while the next largest item of expenditure was accounted for by personnel costs (17.9 %), the remaining being used for investment in tangible goods (12.8 %). This was a very different cost structure to postal and courier services (see previous subchapter) where personnel costs were more than half of total expenditure and gross investment in tangible goods below 4 %.

Apparent labour productivity, wage adjusted labour productivity and the gross operating rate were particularly high in the EU-27's telecommunications subsector in 2004, both relative to other activities within the communications and media sector, but also relative to the non-financial business economy as a whole. Value added per person employed in the EU-27 was EUR 157 400, the wage adjusted labour productivity ratio was 321.0 % (indicating that apparent labour productivity was over three times as high as average personnel costs), the fourth largest level of the non-financial business economy NACE groups for which data are available. The gross operating rate was 32.6 % in telecommunications services, the third highest level for this indicator among the non-financial business economy NACE groups in 2004. However, the telecommunications services sector had relatively high average personnel costs, at EUR 49 000 per employee, compared with EUR 27 600 per employee in the non-financial business economy. Among all the Member States with available data, all of these four indicators had higher values for telecommunication services compared with national non-financial business economy averages.

Figure 21.6

Telecommunications (NACE Group 64.2)
Index of turnover, EU-27 (2000=100)

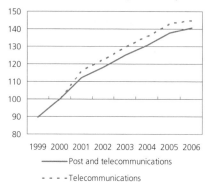

—— Post and telecommunications

- - - - Telecommunications

Source: Eurostat (STS)

Figure 21.7

Telecommunications (NACE Group 64.2)
Productivity and profitability characteristics relative to national averages, 2004
(non-financial business economy=100)

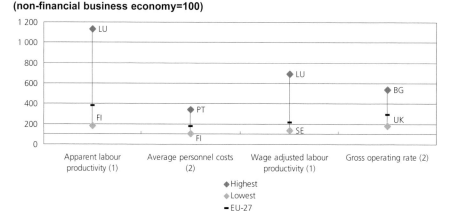

◆ Highest
◆ Lowest
▬ EU-27

(1) Denmark, Ireland, Greece, Cyprus, Malta, Netherlands, Poland and Slovenia, not available; Czech Republic, Luxembourg and Portugal, 2003.
(2) Denmark, Ireland, Greece, Cyprus, Malta, Netherlands, Poland and Slovenia, not available; Luxembourg and Portugal, 2003.
Source: Eurostat (SBS)

21.3: PUBLISHING, PRINTING AND REPRODUCTION OF RECORDED MEDIA

Publishing can be defined as the act of producing and issuing informative material. Printing involves placing the material on paper or other supports. These activities are covered by NACE Group 22.1 (for publishing) and NACE Group 22.2 (for printing and service activities related to printing). Note that publishing activities include not only the publishing of printed matter, but also the publishing of music.

As well as printing and publishing, this subchapter also includes the reproduction of recorded media (NACE Group 22.3), including reproduction services for sound and video recording (NACE Classes 22.31 and 22.32) and reproduction services for software (NACE Class 22.33).

In terms of coverage, the publishing, printing and reproduction of recorded media sector diverges from the previous two subchapters in that it is classified as a manufacturing sector, according to the NACE classification (NACE Division 22 is part of Section D, which covers manufacturing).

Information technologies (IT) have revolutionised publishing and printing activities in the past couple of decades. These activities comprise all the stages necessary to transform a piece of creative writing, music or information into a product available for distribution to the public and in this area IT has created a number of electronic alternatives to traditional printing and enabled smaller and more flexible print-runs. The Internet was initially seen by many as a direct competitor to printed matter, but enterprises that traditionally published printed and other off-line media (such as CDs and DVDs) have often diversified into online media too, creating new products for new markets. For instance, newspapers, magazines, books or reference material are increasingly consulted online or through some other type of electronic medium. In terms of market size, printed matter continues to dominate. For example, according to PRODCOM (statistics by product), the production value of electronic books, brochures, leaflets and the like (excluding dictionaries, atlases and similar products; PRODCOM 22112170 and 22112180) was EUR 518 million in the EU-27 in 2006, with the production value for printed books, brochures, leaflets and the like (PRODCOM 22112200) around EUR 24.7 billion, suggesting that electronic versions accounted for a 2.1 % share of the total market for these products. However, there is increased competition between printed and online media for readers and hence for advertising revenue.

Digital rights management is a major issue for this sector, particularly for sound and video recordings, whether online or offline. Indeed, Digital Rights Management Systems (DRMs) are technologies that describe and identify digital content protected by intellectual property rights, and enforce usage rules set by right-holders or prescribed by law for digital content.

STRUCTURAL PROFILE
Value added generated by the 206 500 enterprises that make up the EU-27's publishing, printing and reproduction of recorded media sector (NACE Division 22) equated to EUR 93 billion value added in 2004, some 27.4 % of the communications and media (NACE Divisions 22 and 64) total. There were 1.8 million persons employed in these activities in the EU-27, which represented a notably higher share of the workforce (36.7 %). Among the three NACE groups that make up the publishing, printing and reproduction of recorded media sector, publishing (NACE Group 22.1) accounted for more than half of the sectoral total value added, while printing and service activities related to printing (NACE Group 22.2, hereafter referred to as printing) gathered more than half of the sectoral workforce – see Table 21.14. In contrast, reproduction of recorded media (NACE Group 22.3) accounted for less than 6 % of the sectoral value added and just 2.0 % of sectoral employment.

Table 21.14

Publishing, printing and reproduction of recorded media (NACE Division 22)
Structural profile, EU-27, 2004 (1)

	No. of enterprises (thousands)	Turnover (EUR million)	Value added (EUR million)	Employment (thousands)
Publishing, printing and reproduction of recorded media	206.5	246 000	93 000	1 800.0
Publishing	73.5	127 108	46 868	810.2
Publishing of books	27.9	32 000	11 000	180.0
Publishing of newspapers	7.8	45 000	19 000	310.0
Publishing of journals and periodicals	16.9	40 200	14 400	249.0
Publishing of sound recordings	9.3	4 360	1 170	19.0
Other publishing	11.6	4 950	1 910	47.7
Printing and service activities related to printing	127.0	101 000	41 000	1 000.0
Printing of newspapers	2.7	5 000	2 100	42.0
Printing n.e.c.	79.0	80 000	31 000	730.0
Bookbinding	7.4	4 160	2 110	66.1
Pre-press activities	16.5	6 000	2 930	74.1
Ancillary activities related to printing	21.2	6 160	2 460	68.4
Reproduction of recorded media	5.8	18 000	5 399	37.8
Reproduction of sound recording	3.7	3 010	1 110	19.0
Reproduction of video recording	1.2	:	433	8.2
Reproduction of computer media	0.9	13 600	3 850	10.3

(1) Rounded estimate based on non-confidential data, except for publishing.
Source: Eurostat (SBS)

Within the publishing subsector the largest contribution to value added in the EU-27 in 2004 was from the publishing of newspapers (NACE Class 22.12) with EUR 19.0 billion of value added, followed by the publishing of journals and periodicals (NACE Class 22.13) with EUR 14.4 billion and the publishing of books (NACE Class 22.11) with EUR 11.0 billion. The printing and service activities related to printing subsector was dominated by printing not elsewhere classified (NACE Class 22.22, hereafter referred to as miscellaneous printing) with EUR 31.0 billion of added value, while none of the remaining four NACE classes covered generated in excess of EUR 3 billion of value added. Finally, within the reproduction of recorded media, the highest level of value added was registered for the reproduction of computer media (NACE Class 22.33) at EUR 3.85 billion in 2004. Within the publishing and printing subsectors those NACE classes that recorded the highest levels of value added also employed the most persons; the largest workforce (at the level of NACE classes) was that of miscellaneous printing, where there were 730 000 persons employed in 2004. The reproduction of sound recording (NACE Class 22.31) was the largest employer within the reproduction of recorded media subsector with 19 000 persons, compared with 10 300 for those employed within the reproduction of computer media (which had the highest level of value added).

Figure 21.8

Publishing, printing and reproduction of recorded media (NACE Division 22)
Relative weight within communications, publishing and printing, EU-27, 2004 (%) (1)

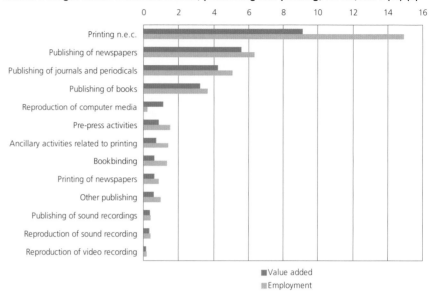

(1) Rounded estimate based on non-confidential data.
Source: Eurostat (SBS)

Slightly more than one quarter of the EU-27's value added in the publishing, printing and reproduction of recorded media sector in 2004 was concentrated in the United Kingdom (25.1 % of the EU-27 total) while one fifth came from Germany (20.0 %) – see Table 21.15. However, Germany was the largest employer in the sector, accounting for slightly more than one fifth (20.5 %) of the EU-27's sectoral workforce, followed by the United Kingdom with slightly less than one fifth (19.3 %). Unsurprisingly, the United Kingdom ranked as the most specialised Member State in publishing, printing and reproduction of recorded media in value added terms, as these activities generated 2.4 % of its non-financial business economy value added. Among the Member States with available data [16], Finland (2.3 %) was the next most specialised, followed by the Netherlands (2.0 %), Slovenia (1.9 %) and Latvia (1.8 %).

[16] Ireland, Greece, Cyprus, Luxembourg and Malta, not available.

There was no clear pattern as to the importance of one or other of the subsectors (as defined as NACE groups) among the Member States. In 2004, publishing accounted for more than half of sectoral value added in 12 of the 24 Member States for which data is available [17], reaching a high of 64.2 % of the value added for publishing, printing and reproduction of recorded media in both Finland and Latvia. Printing generated more than half of sectoral value added in the 11 remaining Member States and was dominant in Cyprus, Romania and Belgium, where it generated more than 60 % of the sector's value added. Only in Ireland was the reproduction of recorded media the most important subsector, where its contribution to Irish sectoral value added was 81.9 %.

[17] Slovenia, incomplete data; Greece, Luxembourg and Malta, not available.

Table 21.15

Publishing, printing and reproduction of recorded media (NACE Division 22)
Structural profile: ranking of top five Member States, 2004

Rank	Share of EU-27 value added (%) (1)	Share of EU-27 employment (%) (1)	Value added specialisation ratio (EU-27=100) (2)	Employment specialisation ratio (EU-27=100) (2)
1	United Kingdom (25.1)	Germany (20.5)	United Kingdom (132.7)	Finland (166.0)
2	Germany (20.0)	United Kingdom (19.3)	Finland (128.6)	Denmark (156.6)
3	France (12.0)	France (11.1)	Netherlands (110.3)	Sweden (135.4)
4	Italy (9.7)	Italy (9.3)	Slovenia (101.6)	United Kingdom (133.8)
5	Spain (7.0)	Spain (8.3)	Latvia (97.4)	Latvia (133.7)

(1) Greece, Luxembourg and Malta, not available.
(2) Ireland, Greece, Cyprus, Luxembourg and Malta, not available.
Source: Eurostat (SBS)

Table 21.16

Production of selected printer matter and recorded media products (CPA Divison 22), EU-27, 2006 (1)

	Prodcom code	Production value (EUR million)	Volume of sold production (thousands)	Unit of volume
Printing of books, brochures, children's picture or colouring books and music printed or in manuscript	22.22.31.00	7 611	-	
Commercial catalogues	22.22.12.30	5 181	-	
Printing of newspapers; journals and periodicals; appearing at least four times a week	22.21.10.00	3 957	-	
Compact discs, with sound recordings	22.14.11.50	2 222	833 210	units
New stamps; stamp-impressed paper; cheque forms; banknotes, etc	22.22.11.00	1 912	-	
Binding and finishing of brochures, magazines, catalogues, samples and advertising literature including folding, assembling, stitching, gluing, cutting cover laying	22.23.10.30	1 737	-	
Printing components	22.24.20.00	1 675	-	
Reproduction of sound on compact discs	22.31.10.70	1 625	-	
Continuous multi-part business forms, including interleaved carbon sets, carbonless paper and books	22.22.20.75	718	315 263	kg

(1) Estimated.
Source: Eurostat (PRODCOM)

Annual short-term statistics show that the EU-27's production index for publishing, printing and reproduction of recorded media developed positively from 1996 to 2000, during this period it grew at an average rate of 3.5 % per annum - see Figure 21.9. This upward trend was reflected in each of the three NACE groups, with the strongest year on year growth over this period recorded within the reproduction of recorded media. In 2001 all three NACE groups recorded a fall in production, and whereas the reproduction of recorded media returned to growth the next year, it was not until 2004 that publishing and printing recorded growth. This period of output growth was short-lived for the publishing activity, as the production index contracted by 2.5 % in 2005 and 0.8 % in 2006, while for printing the period of expansion was only slightly longer, the 2.6 % growth in 2004 and 0.4 % growth in 2005 followed by a contraction of 0.9 % in 2006. In contrast the reproduction of recorded media posted growth of 9.3 % in 2006, its fifth successive year on year increase, an average increase of 12.2 % per annum during the five years to 2006.

COSTS, PRODUCTIVITY AND PROFITABILITY
The breakdown of total expenditure between purchases of goods and services, personnel costs and gross investment in tangible goods was rather similar for the publishing (NACE Group 22.1) and printing (NACE Group 22.2) subsectors, while the reproduction of recorded media subsector diverged from these two subsectors – see Table 21.17. Indeed, purchases of goods and services accounted for 89.0 % of total expenditure for the reproduction of recorded media, a share that was 17.7 percentage points above the highest share of the two other subsectors. As a counter part,

Figure 21.9

Publishing, printing and reproduction of recorded media (NACE Division 22) Index of production, EU-27 (2000=100)

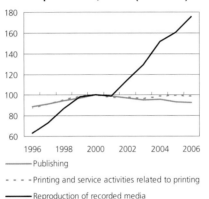

— Publishing

- - - - Printing and service activities related to printing

—— Reproduction of recorded media

Source: Eurostat (STS)

personnel costs accounted for 8.7 % of total expenditure in reproduction of recorded media activities, well below that for the other two subsectors.

Apparent labour productivity for the EU-27's publishing subsector was EUR 57 800 per person employed and EUR 41 200 for printing, while the ratio reached EUR 143 000 for the reproduction of recorded media in 2004. Among the three subsectors, personnel costs ranged between EUR 30 700 (printing) and EUR 39 200 (publishing) per employee. These figures lead to wage adjusted labour productivity ratios below 150 % for the publishing and printing subsectors, while the reproduction of recorded media had a wage adjusted labour productivity of 394 %, meaning that the value added per person employed in this subsector covered average personnel costs nearly four times over. This was

the third highest wage adjusted labour productivity ratio recorded among the NACE groups of the non-financial business economy. For comparison, the average wage adjusted labour productivity was 148.0 % for the non-financial business economy, and within communications and media it was 197.0 %.

In a similar manner, the gross operating rate for the reproduction of recorded media subsector (23.5 %) was also high in 2004, close to the average for communications and media (23.6 %), while for the other two subsectors it was just above 13 %, nevertheless above the non-financial business economy average of 11.0 %.

EXTERNAL TRADE
The EU-27 ran a significant trade surplus with non-member countries for printed matter and printing services (CPA Groups 22.1 and 22.2) which was valued at EUR 2.7 billion in 2006, resulting from EUR 6.4 billion exports and EUR 3.7 billion imports from non-member countries. This level of trade surplus was relatively stable in the five years through to 2006. Among the two categories of products that make up printed matter and printing services (at the level of CPA groups), about three quarters (74.7 %) of exports were accounted for by books, newspapers and other printed matter and recorded media (CPA Group 22.1), while the remaining share was accounted for by printing services and services related to printing (CPA Group 22.2) – see Table 21.18.

Table 21.17

Publishing, printing and reproduction of recorded media (NACE Division 22)
Total expenditure, EU-27, 2004 (1)

	Value (EUR million)				Share (% of total expenditure)		
	Total expenditure	Purchases of goods and services	Personnel costs	Investment in tangible goods	Purchases of goods and services	Personnel costs	Investment in tangible goods
Publishing, printing & reproduction of recorded media	219 210	153 000	58 000	8 210	69.8	26.5	3.7
Publishing	113 197	80 707	29 980	2 510	71.3	26.5	2.2
Publishing of books	28 527	22 000	6 100	427	77.1	21.4	1.5
Publishing of newspapers	41 000	26 700	13 000	1 300	65.1	31.7	3.2
Publishing of journals and periodicals	35 368	25 800	9 030	538	72.9	25.5	1.5
Publishing of sound recordings	4 235	3 500	630	105	82.6	14.9	2.5
Other publishing	4 340	3 080	1 120	140	71.0	25.8	3.2
Printing and service activities related to printing	92 400	60 000	27 000	5 400	64.9	29.2	5.8
Printing of newspapers	4 467	2 700	1 400	367	60.4	31.3	8.2
Printing n.e.c.	74 210	50 000	20 000	4 210	67.4	27.0	5.7
Bookbinding	3 835	2 050	1 570	215	53.5	40.9	5.6
Pre-press activities	5 313	3 020	2 020	273	56.8	38.0	5.1
Ancillary activities related to printing	5 490	3 720	1 460	310	67.8	26.6	5.6
Reproduction of recorded media	13 932	12 400	1 212	320	89.0	8.7	2.3
Reproduction of sound recording	2 593	1 900	529	164	73.3	20.4	6.3
Reproduction of video recording	1 035	700	265	70	67.6	25.6	6.8
Reproduction of computer media	10 271	9 770	417	84	95.1	4.1	0.8

(1) Rounded estimate based on non-confidential data.
Source: Eurostat (SBS)

Among the Member States, Germany was the largest exporter of printed matter and printing services, with exports valued at EUR 5.0 billion (intra and extra-EU trade combined) in 2006, followed by the United Kingdom (EUR 3.7 billion). However, the United Kingdom was the largest importer, with imports of printed matter and printing services valued at EUR 2.9 billion in 2006, followed by France (EUR 2.3 million) and Germany (EUR 2.2 billion). Hence, Germany recorded the largest trade surplus for printed matter and printing services in 2006 (EUR 2.9 billion), followed by the United Kingdom (EUR 0.8 billion). At the other end of the spectrum, Austria (EUR 381.4 million) and France (EUR 378.4 million) registered the largest trade deficits for these products.

Figure 21.10

Publishing, printing and reproduction of recorded media (NACE Division 22)
Productivity and profitability characteristics relative to national averages, 2004
(non-financial business economy=100) (1)

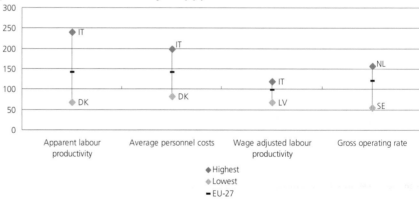

◆ Highest
◆ Lowest
■ EU-27

(1) Ireland, Greece, Cyprus, Luxembourg and Malta, not available; Slovenia, 2003.
Source: Eurostat (SBS)

Table 21.18

Printed matter and printing services (CPA Groups 22.1 and 22.2)
External trade, EU-27, 2006

	Extra-EU exports		Extra-EU imports		Trade balance (EUR million)	Cover ratio (%)
	(EUR million)	(% share of chapter)	(EUR million)	(% share of chapter)		
Printed matter and printing services	6 388	100.0	3 704	100.0	2 684	172.4
Books, newspapers and other printed matter and recorded media	4 770	74.7	2 699	72.9	2 071	176.8
Printing services and services related to printing	1 618	25.3	1 005	27.1	612	160.9

Source: Eurostat (Comext)

Table 21.19

Publishing, printing, reproduction of recorded media (NACE Division 22)
Main indicators, 2004

	EU-27 (1)	BE	BG	CZ	DK	DE	EE	IE	EL	ES	FR	IT	CY	LV	LT
No. of enterprises (thousands)	206.5	5.1	1.5	9.9	2.5	16.3	0.5	0.5	:	23.2	32.3	26.8	0.4	0.8	0.9
Turnover (EUR million)	246 000	6 475	305	2 017	4 244	48 332	233	14 257	:	17 209	34 290	27 409	145	248	275
Production (EUR million)	241 000	6 321	290	1 952	4 164	47 704	219	13 502	:	16 944	33 075	27 471	146	241	266
Value added (EUR million)	93 000	2 166	84	675	1 795	18 562	84	4 281	:	6 543	11 132	8 993	68	95	95
Gross operating surplus (EUR million)	35 000	780	43	341	503	5 049	26	3 575	:	2 530	2 122	4 093	22	42	41
Purchases of goods & services (EUR million)	153 000	4 300	228	1 397	2 535	29 304	150	9 953	:	11 072	23 316	18 551	81	153	179
Personnel costs (EUR million)	58 000	1 386	41	337	1 292	13 513	58	707	:	4 013	9 010	4 900	46	53	54
Investment in tangible goods (EUR million)	8 210	277	37	93	260	1 493	14	107	:	614	827	817	14	21	18
Employment (thousands)	1 800	34	15	42	37	368	6	16	:	149	199	168	2	11	11
Apparent labour prod. (EUR thousand)	51.0	62.8	5.4	16.1	48.0	50.4	13.9	261.7	:	44.0	55.9	53.7	28.6	8.3	8.8
Average personnel costs (EUR thousand)	34.7	46.6	2.9	10.2	35.5	37.9	9.8	43.7	:	29.9	46.3	38.1	20.1	4.7	5.2
Wage adjusted labour productivity (%)	146.0	134.9	185.7	157.8	135.0	132.8	141.8	598.8	:	147.4	120.7	141.0	142.5	174.9	171.2
Gross operating rate (%)	14.1	12.1	14.1	16.9	11.8	10.4	11.1	25.1	:	14.7	6.2	14.9	15.2	16.8	15.0
Investment / employment (EUR thousand)	4.5	8.0	2.4	2.2	6.9	4.1	2.3	6.5	:	4.1	4.2	4.9	6.1	1.8	1.7

	LU (2)	HU	MT	NL	AT	PL	PT	RO	SI	SK	FI	SE	UK	NO	
No. of enterprises (thousands)	0.2	8.0	:	6.7	2.0	17.6	4.5	4.0	1.6	0.6	2.7	9.3	28.3	3.3	
Turnover (EUR million)	:	2 028	:	12 349	4 534	4 267	2 714	790	712	526	4 076	7 188	49 620	4 300	
Production (EUR million)	:	1 580	:	12 234	4 408	4 131	2 708	742	663	494	4 074	7 126	48 859	4 326	
Value added (EUR million)	:	502	:	4 706	1 824	1 516	1 058	241	250	150	1 706	2 390	23 357	1 907	
Gross operating surplus (EUR million)	:	208	:	1 595	693	884	354	142	80	69	569	413	10 308	549	
Purchases of goods & services (EUR million)	:	1 462	:	7 636	2 742	2 740	1 714	571	462	376	2 493	4 893	25 714	2 507	
Personnel costs (EUR million)	:	294	:	3 111	1 131	632	705	99	171	81	1 137	1 977	13 049	1 358	
Investment in tangible goods (EUR million)	:	118	:	336	148	192	215	98	40	31	176	289	1 827	124	
Employment (thousands)	:	36	:	81	26	99	37	34	10	11	29	50	347	29	
Apparent labour prod. (EUR thousand)	:	13.8	:	58.4	69.9	15.3	28.7	7.1	26.1	13.8	58.8	47.5	67.4	64.7	
Average personnel costs (EUR thousand)	:	8.9	:	44.0	45.8	8.4	19.8	3.0	19.4	7.5	39.9	44.1	40.2	47.6	
Wage adjusted labour productivity (%)	:	155.2	:	132.8	152.8	182.4	144.5	237.4	134.9	183.7	147.3	107.6	167.5	136.0	
Gross operating rate (%)	:	10.2	:	12.9	15.3	20.7	13.0	17.9	11.2	13.0	14.0	5.7	20.8	12.8	
Investment / employment (EUR thousand)	:	3.2	:	4.2	5.7	1.9	5.8	2.9	4.2	2.8	6.1	5.7	5.3	4.2	

(1) Rounded estimates based on non-confidential data, except for number of enterprises. (2) 2003.
Source: Eurostat (SBS)

Table 21.20

Post and telecommunications (NACE Division 64)
Main indicators, 2004

	EU-27	BE	BG	CZ	DK	DE	EE	IE	EL	ES	FR	IT	CY	LV	LT
No. of enterprises (thousands)	63.1	3.5	1.1	0.9	1.2	8.1	0.1	1.5	:	6.9	4.9	3.4	0.1	0.2	0.3
Turnover (EUR million)	496 811	14 938	1 565	4 575	7 998	95 531	592	9 079	:	37 705	70 470	60 695	478	665	778
Production (EUR million)	462 606	15 091	1 497	4 450	7 598	85 722	589	7 032	:	29 799	71 159	60 951	477	624	705
Value added (EUR million)	246 803	7 657	925	2 463	3 816	51 235	277	4 899	:	18 670	36 778	29 556	380	385	347
Gross operating surplus (EUR million)	140 440	4 078	710	1 683	1 644	29 196	206	3 781	:	13 328	16 551	19 440	256	301	246
Purchases of goods & services (EUR million)	261 485	7 817	716	2 170	4 718	51 433	317	4 191	:	19 017	33 626	31 395	93	284	437
Personnel costs (EUR million)	106 362	3 579	215	780	2 173	22 039	71	1 118	:	5 342	20 228	10 116	123	84	101
Investment in tangible goods (EUR million)	44 422	765	325	438	1 089	6 886	46	605	:	3 492	4 979	5 057	150	85	86
Employment (thousands)	3 058	83	53	72	54	611	8	30	:	170	446	261	4	13	15
Apparent labour prod. (EUR thousand)	80.7	92.4	17.4	34.4	71.2	83.9	35.7	165.4	:	109.9	82.5	113.4	101.9	28.8	22.8
Average personnel costs (EUR thousand)	35.6	45.1	4.2	11.9	41.1	36.9	9.2	39.7	:	32.4	45.5	39.4	33.7	6.3	6.7
Wage adjusted labour productivity (%)	226.7	205.0	414.1	289.8	173.2	227.2	388.4	417.0	:	339.6	181.5	287.8	302.6	457.3	341.1
Gross operating rate (%)	28.3	27.3	45.3	36.8	20.6	30.6	34.8	41.6	:	35.3	23.5	32.0	53.6	45.3	31.6
Investment / employment (EUR thousand)	14.5	9.2	6.1	6.1	20.3	11.3	5.9	20.4	:	20.6	11.2	19.4	40.2	6.4	5.7

	LU (1)	HU	MT	NL	AT	PL	PT	RO	SI	SK	FI	SE	UK	NO	
No. of enterprises (thousands)	0.1	2.3	:	3.6	0.5	3.3	0.4	2.4	0.6	0.1	0.6	0.9	14.8	1.4	
Turnover (EUR million)	2 144	5 179	:	23 135	9 187	10 265	8 121	2 911	1 221	1 569	8 031	12 415	98 917	8 638	
Production (EUR million)	1 961	3 749	:	22 734	6 225	9 645	7 749	2 754	1 118	1 432	7 831	12 474	91 838	8 560	
Value added (EUR million)	882	2 381	:	11 353	4 269	5 962	3 743	1 560	586	787	2 905	5 135	44 819	3 573	
Gross operating surplus (EUR million)	659	1 470	:	7 199	2 195	4 200	2 606	1 053	325	529	1 476	1 907	22 141	1 857	
Purchases of goods & services (EUR million)	1 224	2 797	:	11 873	5 252	4 631	4 560	1 356	621	777	5 338	7 608	54 547	5 059	
Personnel costs (EUR million)	223	911	:	4 154	2 074	1 762	1 137	508	260	258	1 429	3 229	22 678	1 716	
Investment in tangible goods (EUR million)	124	669	:	1 710	889	1 118	821	724	223	308	518	1 675	10 923	652	
Employment (thousands)	4	64	:	120	51	167	34	83	11	29	43	74	510	37	
Apparent labour prod. (EUR thousand)	214.3	37.0	:	94.4	84.4	35.8	110.0	18.7	51.0	27.4	66.8	69.0	87.9	97.0	
Average personnel costs (EUR thousand)	54.5	14.5	:	35.1	41.3	11.1	33.5	6.2	23.6	9.0	33.0	47.7	45.5	47.5	
Wage adjusted labour productivity (%)	392.9	255.7	:	269.2	204.3	321.6	328.1	302.8	216.1	304.8	202.8	144.5	193.4	204.5	
Gross operating rate (%)	30.8	28.4	:	31.1	23.9	40.9	32.1	36.2	26.6	33.7	18.4	15.4	22.4	21.5	
Investment / employment (EUR thousand)	30.2	10.4	:	14.2	17.6	6.7	24.1	8.7	19.4	10.7	11.9	22.5	21.4	17.7	

(1) 2003.
Source: Eurostat (SBS)

Business services

The freedom to provide services and the freedom of establishment are central principles to the internal market for services and are set out in the EC Treaty. They guarantee to EU enterprises the freedom to establish themselves in other Member States, and the freedom to provide services on the territory of another EU Member State. Box 22.1 presents developments regarding the directive of services, whose goal is to create a real internal market in services.

Business services are mainly supplied to other enterprises, while the public sector and households can also make use of these services, especially legal, architectural and engineering, and technical testing activities. Many of these services could be provided in-house by enterprises themselves or purchased (outsourced) from service providers, which enables the client enterprise to focus on its core activities. Given the considerable political interest and the flexibility and dynamics of the business services sector, in 2000 Eurostat launched a development project to collect data on these key areas of the economy, in particular as regards type of service supplied and type and residence of clients. From this source it can be seen that in 2004 some 86 % of turnover generated by business services enterprises in the EU [1] came from services supplied to enterprises, 10 % from services to the public sector and 4 % from services to households. The manufacturing sector's increased degree of outsourcing has made it into an important client of the business services sector. Indeed, enterprises active in the manufacturing sector (NACE Section D) represented 19 % of the total turnover of the business services sector. The ratio of payments for business services to total operating expenditure (here defined as personnel costs plus purchases of goods and services) for manufacturing enterprises reached 10 % in Denmark and ranged between 2 % and 6 % in most available countries, while outsourcing by manufacturing enterprises was not very widespread in 2004 in Latvia and Romania.

---

[1] Average based on data for Denmark, Germany, Greece, Spain, Latvia, Lithuania, Malta, Portugal, Romania, Slovenia, Slovakia, Finland, Sweden, the United Kingdom and Norway.

In this chapter, the term 'business services' is used to refer to the aggregate of two NACE divisions: computer services (NACE Division 72, as covered by Subchapter 22.1) and other business activities (NACE Division 74, the components of which are covered in Subchapters 22.2 to 22.6). As for the previous edition of this publication, renting and leasing, research and development activities, and real estate services (NACE Divisions 70, 71 and 73) are covered in Chapter 23, such that Chapters 22 and 23 cover the whole of NACE Section K.

NACE
72:   Computer and related activities;
72.1: hardware consultancy;
72.2: software consultancy and supply;
72.3: data processing;
72.4: database activities;
72.5: maintenance and repair of office, accounting and computing machinery;
72.6: other computer related activities;
74:   other business activities;
74.1: legal, accounting, book-keeping and auditing activities; tax consultancy; market research and public opinion polling; business and management consultancy; holdings;
74.2: architectural and engineering activities and related technical consultancy;
74.3: technical testing and analysis;
74.4: advertising;
74.5: labour recruitment and provision of personnel;
74.6: investigation and security activities;
74.7: industrial cleaning;
74.8: miscellaneous business activities n.e.c.

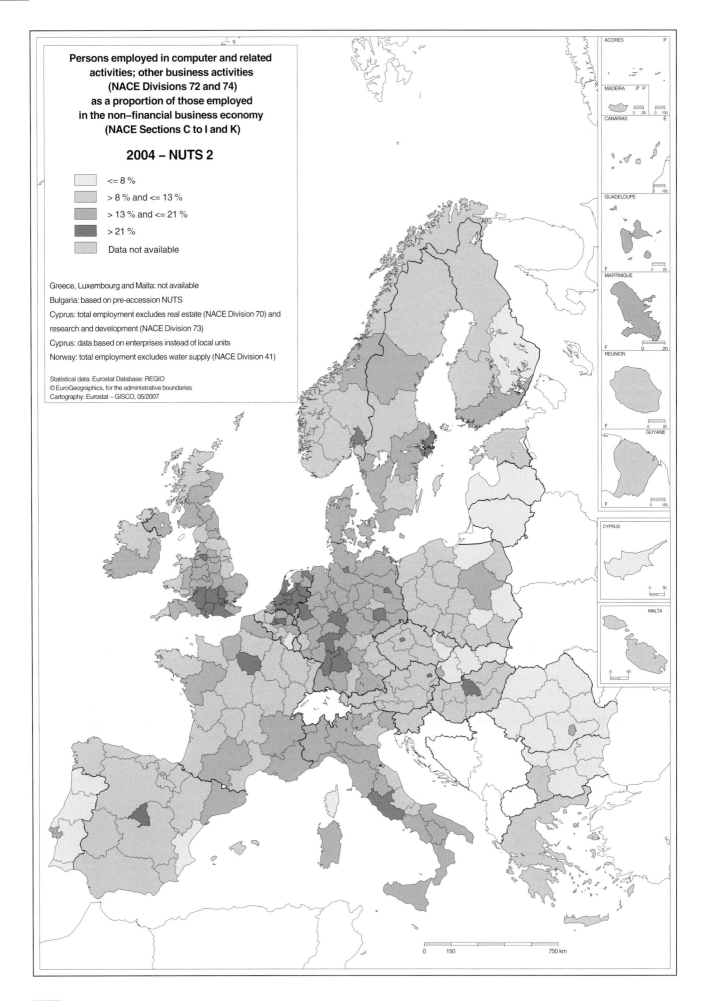

Persons employed in computer and related
activities; other business activities
(NACE Divisions 72 and 74)
as a proportion of those employed
in the non–financial business economy
(NACE Sections C to I and K)

2004 – NUTS 2

- <= 8 %
- > 8 % and <= 13 %
- > 13 % and <= 21 %
- > 21 %
- Data not available

Greece, Luxembourg and Malta: not available
Bulgaria: based on pre-accession NUTS
Cyprus: total employment excludes real estate (NACE Division 70) and
research and development (NACE Division 73)
Cyprus: data based on enterprises instead of local units
Norway: total employment excludes water supply (NACE Division 41)

Statistical data: Eurostat Database: REGIO
© EuroGeographics, for the administrative boundaries
Cartography: Eurostat – GISCO, 05/2007

Box 22.1: internal market in services

The main objective of the directive [2] of the European Parliament and of the Council of 12 December 2006 on services in the internal market is to make progress towards a genuine internal market in services. The directive will have to be implemented by Member States within three years of its publication, therefore by 28 December 2009 at the latest.

In terms of activity coverage, the directive applies to a wide variety of services, whether provided to enterprises or to households. Without being exhaustive, the following can be mentioned as examples of services covered by the directive: industrial services such as the installation and maintenance of equipment; construction; distributive trades; hotels and restaurants; services of travel agencies; business services, such as computer services, most regulated professional activities, advertising, labour recruitment; real estate and renting services; as well as leisure and entertainment services (such as services provided by sports centres and amusement parks), information services (such as news agency activities and publishing), services in the area of training and education; and household support services (such as private nannies or gardening services).

However, the scope of the directive excludes: non-economic services of general interest (services which are not performed for an economic agent), financial services, electronic communication services and networks, services in the field of transport, services of temporary work agencies, healthcare, audiovisual and broadcasting services, gambling activities, activities which are connected with the exercise of official authority (such as notaries), social services relating to social housing, childcare and support of families and persons permanently or temporarily in need, and private security services.

[2] Directive 2006/123/EC of the European Parliament and of the Council of 12 December 2006 on Services in the Internal Market, Official Journal L376 of 27.12.2006, p. 36.

Table 22.1

Business services (NACE Divisions 72 and 74)
Structural profile, EU-27, 2004

	No. of enterprises		Turnover		Value added		Employment	
	(thousands)	(% of total)	(EUR million)	(% of total)	(EUR million)	(% of total)	(thousands)	(% of total)
Business services	3 900.6	100.0	1 450 148	100.0	739 621	100.0	19 433.3	100.0
Computer services	500.6	12.8	313 023	21.6	154 257	20.9	2 570.1	13.2
Other business activities	3 400.1	87.2	1 137 124	78.4	585 364	79.1	16 863.1	86.8
Legal, accounting & management services	1 409.0	36.1	404 343	27.9	221 644	30.0	4 390.6	22.6
Architectural & engineering activities; technical testing & analysis	833.0	21.4	220 633	15.2	108 250	14.6	2 442.1	12.6
Advertising	193.6	5.0	131 569	9.1	33 852	4.6	844.5	4.3
Labour recruitment & provision of personnel	65.4	1.7	97 196	6.7	74 526	10.1	2 911.8	15.0
Other business services	899.0	23.0	283 384	19.5	147 092	19.9	6 274.2	32.3

Source: Eurostat (SBS)

STRUCTURAL PROFILE

The EU-27's business services (NACE Divisions 72 and 74) sector comprised 3.9 million enterprises, about 7 % more than in the previous year, compared with an increase in the number of enterprises for the whole of the non-financial business economy of around 2 %. These enterprises together generated EUR 739.6 billion of value added and employed 19.4 million persons in 2004. As such, the business services sector accounted for 15.5 % of the persons employed in the non-financial business economy (NACE Sections C to I and K), while accounting for a slightly lower proportion of value added (14.5 %).

Among the two NACE divisions that make up the business services sector, computer services (NACE Division 72, see Subchapter 22.1) accounted for about one fifth (20.9 %) of sectoral value added in 2004, while the remainder was generated by the other business activities (NACE Division 74, as presented in Subchapters 22.2 to 22.6). Of these activities, the largest was legal, accounting and

management services (NACE Group 74.1) which alone provided 30.0 % of all business services value added – see Subchapter 22.2, followed by the miscellaneous activities of other business services (NACE Groups 74.6 to 74.8), presented in Subchapter 22.6, that together contributed 19.9 % of business services value added. Architectural and engineering activities and technical testing (NACE Groups 74.2 and 74.3 – see Subchapter 22.3) contributed 14.6 % of business services value added. The two remaining subsectors are advertising (NACE Group 74.4 – see Subchapter 22.4) and labour recruitment and provision of personnel (NACE Group 74.5 - see Subchapter 22.5) which had shares of 4.6 % and 10.1 % of value added respectively. However, in employment terms, the importance of other business services (NACE Groups 74.6 to 74.8) and labour recruitment and provision of personnel (NACE Group 74.5) was much greater – see Table 22.1.

The United Kingdom was by far the largest contributor to the EU-27's business services sector in 2004: with EUR 203.5 billion of value added and 3.8 million persons employed, it generated 27.5 % of the EU-27's sectoral value added and employed 19.5 % of its workforce; indeed, for each of the business services covered in Subchapters 22.1 to 22.6, the United Kingdom contributed the greatest share of EU-27 value added.

Germany had the second largest business services sector, generating the equivalent of about two thirds of the British value added, while the level of employment (3.4 million) was closer to that recorded in the United Kingdom. France, Italy and Spain were the only other Member States that recorded more than EUR 50 billion of value added in 2004 in this sector. Unsurprisingly, in terms of the contribution to national non-financial business economy value added, the United Kingdom was the most specialised Member State, with business services contributing 21.1 % of non-financial business economy value added, compared with the EU-27's average of 14.5 % – see Table 22.3. Luxembourg, where business services contributed 16.8 % (2003) of the non-financial business economy value added, was also relatively highly specialised in these activities, closely followed by the Netherlands (16.3 %) and France (16.1 %). Note that none of the remaining Member States for which data are available recorded a contribution of business services to the non-financial business economy value added above the EU-27 average.

Table 22.2

Business services (NACE Divisions 72 and 74)
Share of non-financial business economy, EU-27, 2004 (%) (1)

	No. of enterprises	Turnover	Value added	Employment
Business services	20.6	7.6	14.5	15.5
Computer services	2.6	1.6	3.0	2.1
Other business activities	18.0	6.0	11.5	13.5
Legal, accounting & management services	7.5	2.1	4.3	3.5
Architectural & engineering activities; technical testing & analysis	4.4	1.2	2.1	2.0
Advertising	1.0	0.7	0.7	0.7
Labour recruitment & provision of personnel	0.3	0.5	1.5	2.3
Other business services	4.8	1.5	2.9	5.0

(1) Rounded estimate based on non-confidential data.
Source: Eurostat (SBS)

Table 22.3

Business services (NACE Divisions 72 and 74)
Structural profile: ranking of top five Member States, 2004

Rank	Value added (EUR million) (1)	Employment (thousands) (1)	Share of non-financial business economy			
			No. of enterprises (2)	Turnover (2)	Value added (2)	Employment (2)
1	United Kingdom (203 519)	United Kingdom (3 783.3)	Sweden (31.4 %)	United Kingdom (11.0 %)	United Kingdom (21.1 %)	Netherlands (23.9 %)
2	Germany (137 526)	Germany (3 428.2)	United Kingdom (30.4 %)	France (8.7 %)	Luxembourg (16.8 %)	Luxembourg (23.1 %)
3	France (115 933)	France (2 457.4)	Hungary (28.5 %)	Netherlands (8.4 %)	Netherlands (16.3 %)	United Kingdom (21.0 %)
4	Italy (74 657)	Italy (2 223.3)	Netherlands (25.6 %)	Sweden (8.2 %)	France (16.1 %)	France (17.2 %)
5	Spain (50 646)	Spain (1 921.5)	Luxembourg (25.6 %)	Slovenia (7.4 %)	Sweden (14.4 %)	Belgium (17.1 %)

(1) Greece and Malta, not available; Luxembourg, 2003.
(2) Ireland, Greece, Cyprus and Malta, not available; Luxembourg, 2003.
Source: Eurostat (SBS)

The regional specialisation in business services is shown in the map on page 372 which is based on the non-financial business economy employment share of this sector. The region with the highest specialisation in business services in 2004 was Inner London where two fifths (40.5 %) of non-financial business economy employment was within this sector. As well as parts of the United Kingdom, several other countries had many regions specialised in these services, notably in the Netherlands and Germany. In a number of countries one region was particularly specialised in these services, typically around the capital city: for example in Praha (Czech Republic), Madrid (Spain), Île de France (France), Lazio (Italy), Budapest (Hungary), Wien (Austria), Lisboa (Portugal) and Stockholm (Sweden).

Figures 22.1 and 22.2 show the development of business services and some of its parts based on annual short-term statistics. The index of employment is available for the business services sector and the two NACE divisions that make up the sector. Developments show that the business services sector offered new employment opportunities, as the EU-27's index of employment for these activities grew, on average, by 2.9 % per annum between 2001 and 2006. Employment growth was particularly strong for other business activities where the index of the number of persons employed rose by an average of 3.2 % per annum over the same period, with the highest gain in employment being recorded in 2006 (5.0 %). Employment grew on average by 1.6 % per annum between 2001 and 2006 for computer services: with a high increase in the workforce recorded in 2001 (10.4 %), while more modest growth occurred in the following years (including a slight contraction of 0.8 % in 2003).

Figure 22.1

Business services (NACE Divisions 72 and 74)
Index of employment, EU-27 (2000=100)

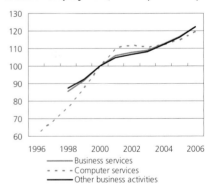

Source: Eurostat (STS)

Figure 22.2

Business services (NACE Divisions 72 and 74)
Index of turnover, EU-27 (2000=100)

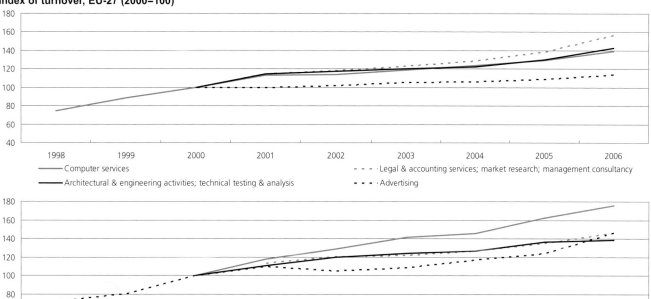

Source: Eurostat (STS)

A more detailed breakdown is available for an analysis of the turnover index for business services – see Figure 22.2. Although time-series are often short they generally show widespread turnover growth throughout the business services sector. Even advertising (NACE Group 74.4), where the turnover index fell slightly in 2001, and labour recruitment and provision of personnel (NACE Group 74.5), where the index contracted by 4.4 % in 2002, recorded consecutive year on year growth in the following years up to 2006. Over the period 2001 to 2006, investigation and security activities (NACE Group 74.6) recorded the fastest developments for the turnover index, with average growth of 8.4 % per annum. The next highest expansion occurred for legal and accounting services; market research and management consultancy, with average growth for the turnover index of 6.5 % per annum. For the remaining activities, the annual average growth rate for the index of turnover between 2001 and 2006 ranged between 2.6 % per annum for advertising (NACE Group 74.4) and 5.9 % per annum for labour recruitment and the provision of personnel (NACE Group 74.5).

In 2004, a size class breakdown of EU-27's business services value added showed that large enterprises (with more than 250 persons employed) generated about one third (33.6 %) of the total, a somewhat lower share than the non-financial business economy average (43.0 %) – see Figure 22.3. The contribution of medium-sized enterprises (with between 50 and 249 persons employed) and small enterprises (with between 10 to 49 persons employed) to sectoral value added was in both cases rather similar to that for the non-financial

business economy as a whole. However, micro enterprises (with less than 10 persons employed) brought some 28.4 % of value added to the sector, 8.2 percentage points above the non-financial business economy average: nevertheless, micro enterprises in computer services generated just 19.4 % of this subsector's value added, whereas in other business activities, the share of micro enterprises was 30.8 %.

Figure 22.3

Business services (NACE Divisions 72 and 74)
Share of value added by enterprise size class, EU-27, 2004

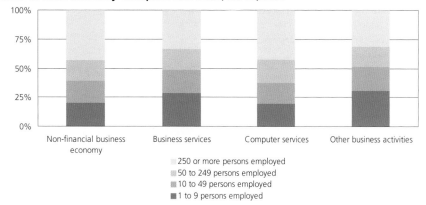

Source: Eurostat (SBS)

Figure 22.4

Business services (NACE Divisions 72 and 74)
Labour force characteristics, EU-27, 2006

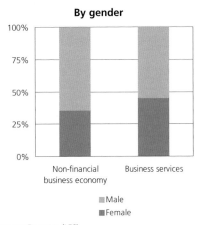

By gender

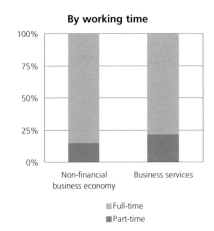

By working time

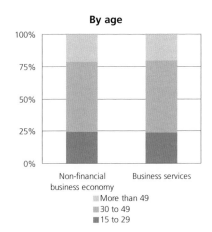

By age

Source: Eurostat (LFS)

EMPLOYMENT CHARACTERISTICS

According to Labour Force Survey data (see Figures 22.4 and 22.5), male employment represented 55.4 % of the total number of persons employed in the EU-27's business services sector in 2006; a share that was 9.6 percentage points lower than that for the non-financial business economy (NACE Sections C to I and K) as a whole. However, among the two NACE divisions that compose the business services sector, male employment was considerably higher (77.6 %) for computer services (NACE Division 72), but much lower (50.9 %) for the other business activities (NACE Division 74).

More than three quarters (78.7 %) of those employed in the EU-27's business services sector worked on a full-time basis, a working status that was less represented in this sector than in the non-financial business economy as a whole (85.6 %). There were significant differences between the two NACE divisions that make up the business services sector, as computer services recorded a full-time employment rate of 90.4 %, compared with a 76.4 % rate for other business activities. The full-time employment rate for computer services was similar to the rates recorded for several industrial NACE divisions.

The age structure of the EU-27's business services workforce was quite similar to that of the non-financial business economy as a whole in 2006, although the proportions of young persons (aged less than 30) and older persons (aged 50 or more) were both somewhat lower in business services, balanced by a slightly higher proportion of those aged between 30 and 49. In the computer services' workforce this age class was significantly more represented, 62.4 % compared with 54.2 % on average in the non-financial business economy, while the proportion of older persons (11.9 %) was almost half that for the whole of the non-financial business economy (21.6 %).

According to structural business statistics, the share of paid employees in the number of persons employed in the EU-27's business services sector in 2004 was 84.0 %, slightly lower than for non-financial business economy as a whole (86.2 %), and there was no great difference in this share between two NACE divisions that make up the sector.

Figure 22.5

Business services (NACE Divisions 72 and 74)
Labour force characteristics relative to national averages, 2006 (non-financial business economy=100)

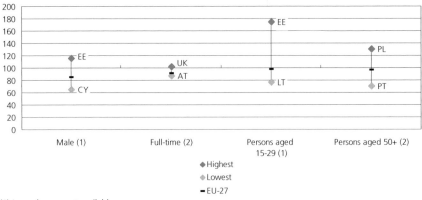

(1) Luxembourg, not available.
(2) Ireland and Luxembourg, not available.
Source: Eurostat (LFS)

Table 22.4

Business services (NACE Divisions 72 and 74)
Total expenditure, EU-27, 2004

	Value (EUR million)				Share (% of total expenditure)		
	Total expenditure	Purchases of goods and services	Personnel costs	Investment in tangible goods	Purchases of goods and services	Personnel costs	Investment in tangible goods
Business services	1 247 915	705 189	490 049	52 678	56.5	39.3	4.2
Computer services	276 603	157 819	107 553	11 231	57.1	38.9	4.1
Other business activities	971 312	547 370	382 495	41 447	56.4	39.4	4.3
Legal, accounting & management services	336 609	184 472	131 713	20 424	54.8	39.1	6.1
Architectural & engineering activities; technical testing & analysis	191 527	116 720	67 733	7 074	60.9	35.4	3.7
Advertising (1)	115 726	93 962	19 544	2 220	81.2	16.9	1.9
Labour recruitment & provision of personnel	80 635	17 769	62 098	769	22.0	77.0	1.0
Other business services (1)	246 854	134 447	101 408	11 000	54.5	41.1	4.5

(1) Rounded estimates based on non-confidential data.
Source: Eurostat (SBS)

Table 22.5

Business services (NACE Divisions 72 and 74)
Productivity and profitability, EU-27, 2004

	Apparent labour productivity (EUR thousand)	Average personnel costs (EUR thousand)	Wage adjusted labour productivity (%)	Gross operating rate (%)
Business services	38.1	30.0	126.8	17.2
Computer services	60.0	48.6	123.5	14.9
Other business activities	34.7	27.1	128.1	17.8
Legal, accounting & management services	50.5	40.2	125.6	22.2
Architectural & engineering activities; technical testing & analysis	44.3	38.3	115.8	18.4
Advertising	40.1	28.4	141.1	10.9
Labour recruitment & provision of personnel	25.6	21.7	117.7	12.8
Other business services	23.4	18.3	127.8	16.1

Source: Eurostat (SBS)

COSTS, PRODUCTIVITY AND PROFITABILITY

A breakdown of total expenditure for the EU-27's business services sector shows that more than half (56.5 %) was dedicated to the purchases of goods and services in 2004, compared with more than three quarters (78.7 %) for the non-financial business economy as a whole (NACE Sections C to I and K). Personnel costs represented almost two fifths (39.3 %) of total expenditure for this sector, more than twice the equivalent share for the non-financial business economy. The two NACE divisions that make up the business services sector displayed a similar breakdown to that of the sector as a whole.

In 2004, apparent labour productivity and average personnel costs for the EU-27's business services sector (respectively EUR 38 100 per person employed and EUR 30 000 per employee) were almost the same as the non-financial business economy averages. Among the two NACE divisions that make up the sector, apparent labour productivity reached EUR 60 000 per person employed for computer services, where average personnel costs were EUR 48 600 per employee, while both indicators for other business activities were slightly below the sectoral and the non-financial business economy averages.

The combination of such levels of apparent labour productivity and average personnel costs led to a wage adjusted labour productivity ratio of 126.8 % for the business services sector in 2004 for the EU-27, therefore 21.2 percentage points below the non-financial business economy average. The ratio of gross operating surplus to turnover (the gross operating rate) was 17.2 % in 2004, significantly higher than the non-financial business economy average of 11.0 %.

EXPORTS OF BUSINESS SERVICES

In 2005, as part of a development project, a number of Member States [3] carried out a survey (reference year 2004) with the aim of gathering more detailed information on exports of business services. An analysis based on the location of clients gives information on the proportion of turnover for business services coming from clients residing in the same country as the supplier, or from exports (clients in another Member State or a non-Community country) – see Figure 22.6. The results show that the market for business services was mainly local, as customers residing in the same country as their service provider contributed at least four fifths of business services' turnover in 2004. Such results can be explained, in part, by the requirement of geographical proximity for some services, as well as cultural (language and consumption characteristics, for instance), economic (such as taxes) and legal factors. Labour recruitment (NACE Group 74.5), advertising (NACE Group 74.4) and accounting and auditing (NACE Class 74.12) were among the business services most locally sold (more than 90 % of total turnover), while 20.1 % of turnover for market research and polling (NACE Class 74.13) activities came from exports; this figure was broken down as 11.5 % from intra-EU customers and 8.6 % from extra-EU customers. Other activities that derived a relatively high share of their turnover from exports of business services included architectural and engineering activities (17 %),

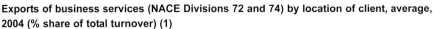

Figure 22.6

Exports of business services (NACE Divisions 72 and 74) by location of client, average, 2004 (% share of total turnover) (1)

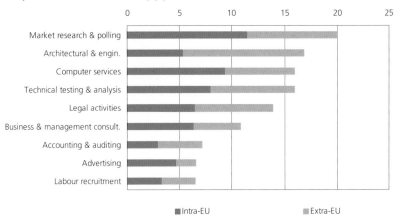

(1) Weighted average based on data for Denmark, Germany, Greece, Spain, Latvia, Lithuania, Romania, Slovenia, Slovakia, Finland, Sweden, the United Kingdom and Norway.
Source: Eurostat (SBS)

technical testing and analysis (16 %) and computer services (16 %). Among the Member States, the share of exports reached 30.7 % in Denmark, while four other relatively small Member States also showed high shares of business services turnover coming from exports: namely, Latvia, Slovakia, Malta and Lithuania, all with an export contribution to turnover that ranged from 15.6 % to 23.0 %. The United Kingdom was the only other participant to report that exports of business services were in excess of 15 % of sectoral turnover.

The qualitative part of the survey aimed to investigate reasons for business services enterprises' exports. The most frequently reported reason for exporting business services was that the products were cutting edge or in a specialised niche, as this was reported by 47 % of the enterprises exporting business services, while 22 % reported that they did so because they belonged to a multi-national group, and 18 % because their domestic market was too small; note that for this part of the survey, multiple answers were allowed.

[3] Denmark, Germany, Greece, Spain, Latvia, Lithuania, Romania, Slovenia, Slovakia, Finland, Sweden, the United Kingdom and Norway.

22.1: COMPUTER SERVICES

Computer services (NACE Division 72) covers software and computing services, which include consultancy activities for hardware or software, data processing activities, database activities and the maintenance and repair of office and information technology machinery. Note that although this subchapter includes the repair of computers it does not cover their actual manufacture (NACE Class 30.02), nor their wholesaling, retailing, or renting (NACE Classes 51.84, 52.48 and 71.33).

Table 22.6

World's top software and IT services enterprise (groups), 2006 (1)

	Software and IT services revenue (EUR million)	Corporate revenue (EUR million)	Number of employees (units)
IBM	50 263	72 582	366 345
Microsoft	29 106	31 688	61 000
EDS	15 735	15 735	117 000
Hewlett-Packard	13 842	69 047	150 000
Accenture	13 615	13 615	123 000
Computer Sciences	11 197	11 197	79 000
Oracle	9 397	9 397	49 872
SAP	7 960	8 028	32 205
Hitachi	7 186	64 428	35 600
Capgemini (2)	7 077	7 077	59 324

(1) Revenue converted at USD 1.2556 = EUR 1.
(2) Number of employees, 2005.
Source: Software Magazine's Annual Software 500, King Content Co., Newton, Mass., 2006

This sector is at the forefront of the information society along with telecommunications – see Subchapter 21.2. Enterprises delivering software and computer services support clients in a broad range of areas, in almost all economic activities. It is quite common for enterprises to out-source their requirements for hardware and software to specialist providers. The ability of such services to be traded across borders has been assisted by improved telecommunications, notably growing access to broadband Internet. The world's top software and IT services enterprise (groups) in 2005 are shown in Table 22.6.

Issues faced by this sector include notably the development of open source technology, anti-trust rulings concerning the bundling of applications and operating systems, the protection of intellectual property rights and patentability of software, and the security of software – particularly in relation to the use of the Internet.

Free and open-source software has become an alternative source of software to traditional software providers that dominate the market overall. The European Commission has encouraged interoperability of software, and the enforcement of this has been one of the main points behind its long-running dispute with Microsoft stemming from the 2004 anti-trust ruling concerning the Windows® operating system: daily fines of EUR 1.5 million were imposed by the European Commission in July 2006, backdated to December 2005. Microsoft and the European Commission are discussing compliance with the anti-trust ruling in the context of the Vista version of Windows.

The protection of intellectual property rights is a double issue for this sector, as software suppliers provide solutions to manage digital rights for other content providers, as well as being concerned about protecting their own rights – see Chapter 21 for information on intellectual property rights in general.

One of the broader issues facing the information society is the security of communication networks and IT, and computer services have a leading role to play in this area. In May 2006 the European Commission adopted a communication [4] on a strategy for a secure information society – dialogue, partnership and empowerment. The proposed strategy emphasises the virtue of technological diversity, as well as the importance of openness and interoperability. In tackling security challenges, a three-pronged approach has been developed embracing specific network and information security measures, the regulatory framework for electronic communications (which includes privacy and data protection issues), and the fight against cyber-crime.

[4] COM(2006) 251.

Table 22.7

Computer services (NACE Division 72)
Structural profile: ranking of top five Member States, 2004

Rank	Share of EU-27 value added (%) (1)	Share of EU-27 employment (%) (1)	Value added specialisation ratio (EU-27=100) (2)	Employment specialisation ratio (EU-27=100) (2)
1	United Kingdom (30.5)	United Kingdom (22.3)	United Kingdom (161.0)	Sweden (184.7)
2	Germany (18.4)	Germany (14.4)	Sweden (154.1)	United Kingdom (155.0)
3	France (14.7)	Italy (13.9)	France (104.1)	Finland (147.8)
4	Italy (9.9)	France (13.4)	Denmark (103.5)	Netherlands (132.7)
5	Spain (5.2)	Spain (7.2)	Netherlands (95.5)	Denmark (126.5)

(1) Greece and Malta, not available; Luxembourg, 2003.
(2) Ireland, Greece, Cyprus and Malta, not available; Luxembourg, 2003.
Source: Eurostat (SBS)

STRUCTURAL PROFILE

The EU-27's computer services (NACE Division 72) sector generated EUR 154.3 billion of value added and employed 2.6 million persons in 2004, therefore contributing 20.9 % of business services (NACE Divisions 72 and 74) value added and 13.2 % of its workforce. There were slightly more than half a million enterprises reported within the computer services sector in the EU-27 in 2004.

The United Kingdom had by far the largest computer services sector within the EU-27, providing about three tenths of EU-27's value added and somewhat more than one fifth of the employment total – see Table 22.7. The next largest national sector was found in Germany, with a significantly lower proportion of both the EU-27's value added and employment than in the United Kingdom. Unsurprisingly, the United Kingdom was the most specialised Member State [5] within computer services in so far as the contribution of this activity to national non-financial business economy value added is concerned, it was 4.9 %, compared with an EU-27 average of 3.0 %. The second highest contribution among the Member States was recorded in Sweden (4.7 %). In terms of employment specialisation, this ranking was reversed with Sweden being the most specialised, followed by the United Kingdom.

Annualised short-term statistics show that computer services (NACE Division 72) were a very dynamic activity within the EU-27 up until 2001, as witnessed by the 14.8 % annual average growth rate for the turnover index during the period 1998 to 2001 and the 12.4 % annual average growth rate for the employment index between 1996 and 2001. In 2002 however, EU-27 turnover and employment indices developed much more sedately (0.6 % and 1.2 % growth respectively). In the following year, employment even contracted by 0.8 %, before recovering gradually and accelerating to 4.5 % growth by 2006. From 2003 to 2006, year on year growth rates for the index of turnover were posted between 4.1 % (2004) and 7.2 % (2006) – see Figure 22.7.

[5] Luxembourg, 2003; Ireland, Greece, Cyprus and Malta, not available.

Figure 22.7
Computer services (NACE Division 72) Evolution of main indicators, EU-27 (2000=100)

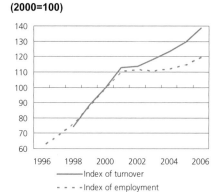

Source: Eurostat (STS)

Figure 22.8
Computer services (NACE Division 72) Breakdown of turnover in computing services by product, average, 2004 (%) (1)

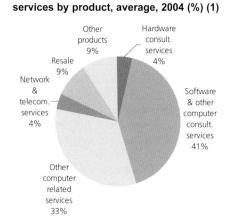

(1) Weighted average based on data for Denmark, Germany, Greece, Spain, Lithuania, Malta, Portugal, Romania, Slovenia, Slovakia, Finland, Sweden and the United Kingdom.
Source: Eurostat (SBS)

A PRODUCT ANALYSIS

An analysis of the breakdown of turnover in computer services is available for a subset of Member States [6], based on the data from a development project compiled on a voluntary basis. The results show that software and other computer consultancy services generated the largest share (41 %) of the sector's turnover – see Figure 22.8 – followed by other computer related activities (33 %) that includes: computer facilities management and data processing services; database services; systems maintenance services; and computer hardware servicing, repair and maintenance of computing machinery and equipment.

COSTS, PRODUCTIVITY AND PROFITABILITY

In 2004 purchases of goods and services accounted for almost three fifths (57.1 %) of total expenditure in the EU-27's computer services sector, while personnel costs accounted for 38.9 %.

Apparent labour productivity in the EU-27's computer services sector was EUR 60 000 per person employed in 2004 and average personnel costs were EUR 48 600 per employee, the highest levels for both of these indicators among the business services subsectors presented in Subchapters 22.1 to 22.6. The wage adjusted labour productivity ratio, derived from these two indicators, was 123.5 % for computer and related activities sector, while the gross operating rate (calculated as the gross operating surplus divided by turnover) was 14.9 %, both of these measures were slightly below the business services average (126.8 % and 17.2 % respectively).

[6] Denmark, Germany, Greece, Spain, Lithuania, Malta, Portugal, Romania, Slovenia, Slovakia, Finland, Sweden and the United Kingdom.

22.2: LEGAL, ACCOUNTING AND MANAGEMENT SERVICES

This subchapter extends across a variety of professional activities that include legal services, accounting, book-keeping, auditing, tax consultancy, market research, public opinion polling, business and management consultancy services, as well as management activities relating to holding companies; these are all classified within NACE Group 74.1.

Enterprises in this sector are generally small, and a common legal form is that of partnerships. Another characteristic of these activities is that households are more likely to use these services than most of the other activities within the business services sector, for instance when they need an accountant, a lawyer, a notary or a tax adviser. Note that activities connected with the exercise of official authority (including part of the work of notaries) are excluded from the scope of the Directive on services in the internal market.

Legal services cover the activities of advocates, barristers, solicitors, notaries, registered lawyers and legal consultants. According to figures from CCBE [7], there were about 1.1 million lawyer members of the Bar in the EU in 2006.

---
[7] CCBE (the Council of Bars and Law Societies of Europe), more information at: http://www.ccbe.org; approximate figures for the EU-27; excluding Malta.

STRUCTURAL PROFILE

The 1.4 million enterprises active in the EU-27's legal, accounting and management services sector (NACE Group 74.1) generated EUR 221.6 billion of value added in 2004, accounting for 30.0 % of the business services total (NACE Divisions 72 and 74). With some 4.4 million persons employed in this sector, it contributed more than one fifth (22.6 %) of the business services workforce. Legal, accounting and management services had therefore the largest value added among the business services activities covered in Subchapters 22.1 to 22.6 and was the second largest employer across these activities in 2004.

The United Kingdom generated more than one quarter (26.8 %) of the EU-27's value added in this sector in 2004, the largest contribution among the Member States, followed by Germany that contributed another fifth (20.2 %). Those two Member States were also the largest employers in the sector – see Table 22.8. However, this activity was also particularly important in the Benelux countries and in Italy, which together with the United Kingdom were the five most specialised Member States in this activity in terms of this sector's contribution to non-financial business economy value added as a whole. Indeed, the legal, accounting and management services sector accounted for 7.2 % (2003) of non-financial business economy value added in Luxembourg, 6.2 % of the total in the United Kingdom, 5.5 % in the Netherlands, and 4.5 % in both Italy and Belgium, compared with an average 4.3 % for the EU-27.

A PRODUCT ANALYSIS

Tables 22.9 to 22.12 provide, for a limited set of countries, a product analysis for four of the five NACE classes covered by the legal, accounting and management services sector. In all of the countries shown in Table 22.9 concerning the legal activities subsector, legal advisory and representation services accounted for the highest proportion of turnover, except in Latvia, Lithuania, Malta and Romania. Among legal advisory and representation services the most popular was services in relation to business/commercial law. For enterprises in accounting, book-keeping, auditing and tax consultancy activities (Table 22.10), there was roughly a three-way split in terms of the most important products contributing to turnover among auditing services, tax consultancy services (including tax returns) and accounting and book-keeping services (excluding tax returns). In the market research and public opinion polling subsector, market research services were clearly the most important products, of which quantitative ad-hoc surveys generally accounted for the largest share of turnover among the Member States with available data – see Table 22.11 – followed by quantitative continuous/regular surveys. The turnover derived by those enterprises operating within business and management consultancy activities was spread across a wide range of products, as shown in Table 22.12.

Table 22.8

Legal, accounting, book-keeping and auditing activities; tax consultancy; market research and public opinion polling; business and management consultancy; holdings (NACE Group 74.1)
Structural profile: ranking of top five Member States, 2004

Rank	Share of EU-27 value added (%) (1)	Share of EU-27 employment (%) (1)	Value added specialisation ratio (EU-27=100) (2)	Employment specialisation ratio (EU-27=100) (2)
1	United Kingdom (26.8)	United Kingdom (20.9)	Luxembourg (163.5)	Netherlands (167.7)
2	Germany (20.2)	Germany (17.8)	United Kingdom (141.9)	United Kingdom (145.3)
3	France (13.9)	Italy (12.3)	Netherlands (126.1)	Luxembourg (137.5)
4	Italy (11.6)	France (10.9)	Italy (104.2)	Belgium (123.3)
5	Spain (6.0)	Spain (8.8)	Belgium (102.8)	Germany (107.4)

(1) Greece and Malta, not available; Luxembourg, 2003.
(2) Ireland, Greece, Cyprus and Malta, not available; Luxembourg, 2003.
Source: Eurostat (SBS)

Table 22.9

Legal activities (NACE Class 74.11)
Breakdown of turnover by product, 2004 (%) (1)

	Average	DK	DE	EL	ES	LV	LT	MT	PL	RO	SI	SK	FI	SE	UK
Legal advisory and representation services	66	87	61	59	42	26	7	33	52	5	74	87	35	73	76
In criminal law	3	4	6	5	5	c	0	2	3	0	8	1	3	7	1
In business/commercial law	39	57	18	29	15	23	4	11	25	5	38	83	23	53	56
In labour law	7	2	12	12	6	c	3	1	4	0	8	2	2	1	5
In civil law	17	23	25	14	16	1	1	19	20	0	20	3	7	12	13
Other legal advisory and information services	7	2	9	10	11	9	80	13	19	14	13	11	0	3	4
Patent and copyright consultancy services	5	1	11	0	3	20	11	2	4	0	6	1	57	16	2
Notarial services	11	0	16	9	39	43	0	15	16	0	4	1	0	0	1
Other products	11	10	3	22	5	3	3	37	9	80	3	0	7	8	16

(1) c: confidential.
Source: Eurostat (SBS)

Table 22.10

Accounting, book-keeping and auditing activities; tax consultancy (NACE Class 74.12)
Breakdown of turnover by product, 2004 (%) (1)

	Average	DK	DE	EL	ES	LV	LT	MT	PT	RO	SI	SK	FI	SE	UK
Accounting, book-keeping & auditing; tax consultancy	79	87	93	93	92	92	85	c	64	90	83	71	92	87	60
Auditing services	23	38	18	20	12	c	39	20	2	34	17	23	18	44	32
Tax consultancy services, including tax returns	20	12	22	43	23	14	17	20	5	15	9	33	9	8	20
Accounting and book-keeping services, except tax returns	22	33	36	9	21	28	24	8	50	40	44	4	45	26	4
Payroll services	6	1	9	9	14	c	1	30	0	0	6	8	9	1	1
Other accounting, book-keeping & auditing services	8	3	8	12	23	4	4	c	6	0	7	3	10	7	2
Business and management consultancy services	14	12	5	5	4	5	10	18	16	9	7	14	4	8	27
Other products	7	2	2	2	4	4	5	c	20	1	10	14	4	5	13

(1) c: confidential.
Source: Eurostat (SBS)

Table 22.11

Market research and public opinion polling activities (NACE Class 74.13)
Breakdown of turnover by product, 2004 (%) (1)

	Average	DK	DE	EL	ES	LV	LT	MT	PL	PT	RO	SI	SK	FI	SE	UK
Market research services	87	79	94	84	89	83	79	38	68	47	78	43	36	89	89	90
Qualitative surveys	11	15	19	27	9	7	5	27	14	10	16	5	5	3	12	7
Quantitative ad-hoc surveys	29	29	36	25	19	6	13	c	20	38	9	12	17	17	32	30
Quantitative continuous/regular surveys	21	22	24	11	17	12	6	c	14	0	28	12	9	65	20	22
Market research other than surveys	11	13	10	15	22	51	52	0	3	0	2	11	0	2	3	10
Other market research services	15	0	5	6	23	7	1	0	17	0	23	4	6	1	22	20
Public opinion polling services	4	3	4	11	7	6	13	c	10	17	1	4	1	2	2	2
Other products	9	18	2	5	4	11	8	c	22	35	20	52	63	10	9	8

(1) c: confidential.
Source: Eurostat (SBS)

COSTS, PRODUCTIVITY AND PROFITABILITY

The pattern of expenditure in the EU-27's legal, accounting and management services sector was very similar to that displayed for the whole of the business services sector, namely a little more than half (54.8 %) of total expenditure was dedicated to purchases of goods and services, less than two fifths (39.1 %) to personnel costs, and the remaining share to investment in tangible goods.

The EU-27's legal, accounting and management services sector registered apparent labour productivity of EUR 50 500 per person employed in 2004, the second highest level of productivity recorded among all the activities that make up the business services activities covered in Subchapters 22.1 to 22.6. Average personnel costs were EUR 40 200 per employee in the EU-27, and the combination of these two indicators led to a wage adjusted labour productivity ratio of 125.6 % in the EU-27, a fairly typical ratio for business services. Among the Member States [8] only the Belgian and Portuguese legal, accounting

and management services sectors had a wage adjusted labour productivity ratio below 100 % in 2004, meaning that in these two Member States apparent labour productivity was lower than average personnel costs.

The gross operating rate of the EU-27's legal, accounting and management services sector was 22.2 % in 2004, the highest rate among the business services sectors, and 5.0 percentage points above the business services average (17.2 %). In several Member States, the gross operating rate stood above 25 % for this sector, reaching a high of 43.6 % in Italy.

[8] Luxembourg, 2003; Greece and Malta, not available.

Table 22.12

Business and management consultancy activities (NACE Class 74.14)
Breakdown of turnover by product, 2004 (%) (1)

	Average	DK	DE	EL	ES	LV	LT	MT	PT	RO	SI	SK	FI	SE	UK
Business and management consultancy services	59	78	93	91	92	88	84	78	56	41	53	80	53	66	35
Business organisation consultancy services	11	5	19	12	14	7	55	19	13	9	11	14	7	17	5
Strategic consult. services, including mergers & acquisitions	6	12	12	7	13	c	4	1	4	1	2	1	14	5	2
Financial management consulting services	4	5	7	8	11	4	4	3	2	4	4	0	2	2	2
Human resources management consulting services	7	9	13	4	4	4	1	1	2	0	3	1	14	3	4
Marketing management consulting services	3	4	7	14	4	c	3	15	:	5	8	6	3	2	1
Production management consulting services	3	6	8	2	2	1	0	1	:	1	4	3	1	1	0
Public relations services	4	5	7	7	5	18	5	0	:	1	1	0	1	2	2
Project management services other than for construction	3	5	6	4	0	15	3	1	:	1	3	23	1	2	1
Other business and management consultancy services	19	27	12	34	38	12	9	36	35	19	17	31	12	32	17
Accounting, book-keeping & auditing; tax consultancy	11	3	0	5	3	3	4	:	18	45	6	6	1	2	18
Other products	31	19	7	3	5	9	12	c	27	13	41	15	46	32	47

(1) c: confidential.
Source: Eurostat (SBS)

22.3: ARCHITECTURAL AND ENGINEERING ACTIVITIES; TECHNICAL TESTING AND ANALYSIS

Architectural and engineering activities covered by NACE Group 74.2 include architectural consulting activities (such as building design and drafting, supervision of construction, town and city planning, and landscape architecture) and various engineering and technical activities related to construction, as well as geological and prospecting activities, weather forecasting activities and geodetic surveying. Technical testing and analysis activities (NACE Group 74.3) include environmental measuring, testing of food hygiene, buildings and equipment, as well as the periodic testing of vehicles for roadworthiness.

Table 22.13 shows the ten largest architectural enterprises (groups) in the EU, based on information compiled by the Swedish Federation of Consulting Engineers and Architects (STD). As can be seen, the United Kingdom dominated the market in 2006, as the four largest groups and several other top ten groups were British. However, even the largest groups were relatively small, with only the three largest having 600 or more employees.

Table 22.13

Top ten architectural groups, EU-25, 2006

		Number of employees (units)	Turnover (EUR million)
AEDAS Architects Group	UK	1 329	99.2
Foster & Partners Ltd	UK	625	65.1
RMJM	UK	600	:
Broadway Malyan Ltd	UK	500	:
White Architects AB	SE	322	29.2
PRP Architects Ltd	UK	320	30.1
SWECO FFNS	SE	310	36.7
Nightingale Associates	UK	310	28.0
Chapman Taylor LLP	UK	300	38.0
gmp-Architekten von Gerkan, Marg und Partner	DE	300	38.0
INBO Architects/consultants	NL	272	26.0
Barton Willmore Group	UK	270	30.1

Source: Swedish Federation of Consulting Engineers and Architects (STD), Sector Review, November 2006

Table 22.14 ———

Architectural and engineering activities and related technical consultancy; technical testing and analysis (NACE Groups 74.2 and 74.3)
Structural profile: ranking of top five Member States, 2004

Rank	Share of EU-27 value added (%) (1)	Share of EU-27 employment (%) (1)	Value added specialisation ratio (EU-27=100) (2)	Employment specialisation ratio (EU-27=100) (2)
1	United Kingdom (23.7)	Germany (17.1)	United Kingdom (125.2)	Sweden (136.5)
2	Germany (19.3)	United Kingdom (15.8)	Sweden (119.6)	Finland (129.5)
3	France (14.3)	Italy (14.1)	Netherlands (114.1)	Netherlands (120.2)
4	Italy (10.5)	France (10.9)	Slovenia (113.9)	Italy (119.8)
5	Spain (8.4)	Spain (10.1)	Denmark (113.2)	Luxembourg (119.6)

(1) Greece and Malta, not available; Luxembourg, 2003.
(2) Ireland, Greece, Cyprus and Malta, not available; Luxembourg, 2003.
Source: Eurostat (SBS)

STRUCTURAL PROFILE

Some EUR 108.3 billion of added value was generated in 2004 by the EU-27's architectural, engineering and technical activities sector (NACE Groups 74.2 and 74.3), corresponding to 14.6 % of the total value added for business services (NACE Divisions 72 and 74). There were 2.4 million persons employed across the 833 000 enterprises that were reported in this sector, equivalent to 12.6 % of the EU-27's business services' workforce. Among the six business services sectors covered in Subchapters 22.1 to 22.6, the architectural, engineering and technical activities sector was the fourth largest in terms of value added and the fifth largest in terms of employment.

Unsurprisingly, the United Kingdom contributed the greatest share (23.7 %) of EU-27 value added in architectural, engineering and technical activities, the second largest contribution being recorded by Germany (19.3 %). However, Germany had a larger workforce in this sector than the United Kingdom – see Table 22.14. In value added terms, the United Kingdom and Sweden were the most specialised Member States in these activities in 2004, as this sector contributed 2.7 % and 2.5 % respectively to national non-financial business economy value added.

A PRODUCT ANALYSIS

Tables 22.15 and 22.16 provide, for a limited set of countries, a product analysis of the two NACE groups covered by this subchapter. In almost all of the countries shown in Table 22.15 concerning architectural and engineering activities and related technical consultancy, engineering design services generated the highest share of turnover. However, in Malta, construction services generated almost half of all sales made by those enterprises within architectural and engineering activities and related technical consultancy. Table 22.16 shows a similar breakdown for the technical testing and analysis subsector where most countries reported that the largest proportion of their turnover from technical testing and analysis services came from the miscellaneous category of other technical testing inspection and analysis services. However, technical automobile inspection services contributed the largest proportion of technical testing and analysis services turnover in Finland (67 %), Lithuania (27 %) and Slovenia (16 %). Only in Slovakia did composition and purity testing and analysis services generate the largest proportion of technical testing and analysis services turnover (35 %).

Table 22.15 ———

Architectural and engineering activities and related technical consultancy (NACE Group 74.2)
Breakdown of turnover by product, 2004 (%) (1)

	Average	DK	DE	EL	ES	LV	LT	MT	PT	RO	SI	SK	FI	SE	UK
Architectural services	14	12	21	26	26	23	18	14	24	25	6	7	18	7	5
Advisory and pre-design architectural services	2	4	2	4	4	4	1	1	9	5	2	2	2	2	1
Architect. design services for buildings & other structures	10	8	18	20	18	18	15	11	12	16	3	1	15	4	2
Other architectural services	2	1	2	2	4	0	2	2	2	4	0	4	1	1	2
Engineering design services incl. for turnkey projects	c	45	58	43	30	c	30	8	33	32	27	50	63	44	c
Urban planning services	2	4	1	2	2	1	2	0	3	1	2	1	2	0	3
Project management services	8	10	7	3	16	9	30	7	9	5	10	1	1	4	7
Other architectural and engineering services	c	16	8	18	21	c	14	10	0	21	12	5	4	27	c
Construction	7	0	0	6	1	4	3	47	5	4	13	24	2	13	13
Technical testing and analysis services	1	0	1	0	1	c	2	c	0	0	1	1	0	0	2
Other products	c	13	4	1	3	c	1	c	27	12	29	11	11	4	c

(1) c: confidential.
Source: Eurostat (SBS)

Table 22.16

Technical testing and analysis (NACE Group 74.3)
Breakdown of turnover by product, 2004 (%) (1)

	Average	DK	DE	EL	ES	LV	LT	MT	PL	RO	SI	SK	FI	SE	UK
Technical testing and analysis services	77	90	93	94	92	c	90	c	71	75	58	87	89	97	42
Composition and purity testing and analysis services	15	14	20	23	12	16	26	c	12	5	9	35	3	13	12
Testing & analysis services of physical properties	8	4	11	24	11	c	13	0	4	2	6	7	2	6	4
Testing & analysis, integr. mechan. & electr. systems services	6	19	8	3	5	28	11	c	6	4	16	1	5	14	c
Technical automobile inspection services	13	0	16	2	17	18	27	c	10	5	16	12	67	27	c
Other technical testing inspection and analysis services	32	52	37	42	47	25	13	87	40	58	10	32	12	37	13
Engineering design services incl. for turnkey projects	1	4	1	3	1	c	0	7	1	0	c	0	0	3	c
Other architectural and engineering services	2	2	1	0	4	c	3	:	6	0	5	2	1	0	c
Other products	c	4	5	3	3	c	7	c	22	25	c	11	11	1	c

(1) c: confidential.
Source: Eurostat (SBS)

COSTS, PRODUCTIVITY AND PROFITABILITY

The share of purchases of goods and services in total expenditure was 60.9 %, while 35.4 % of the total was accounted for by personnel costs and the remaining 3.7 % by investment in tangible goods.

In 2004, apparent labour productivity was relatively high in the EU-27's architectural, engineering and technical activities sector (EUR 44 300 of value added per person employed) compared with a business services average (EUR 38 100). However, average personnel costs were also relatively high in this sector at EUR 38 300 per employee compared with a EUR 30 000 average for business services. As a result, the wage adjusted labour productivity ratio for the EU-27s architectural, engineering and technical activities sector was 115.8 %, which was the lowest among the business services sectors presented in Subchapters 22.1 to 22.6. Only in Romania was the wage adjusted labour productivity ratio for architectural, engineering and technical activities sector above the national average for the non-financial business economy – see Figure 22.9.

Contrasting with the relatively low wage adjusted labour productivity ratios, the gross operating rate of the EU-27's architectural, engineering and technical activities sector was high, reaching 18.4 % in 2004, which was the second highest rate among the business services sectors presented in Subchapters 22.1 to 22.6. This indicator was notably high in Italy (37.8 %), particularly when compared with the national non-financial business economy average (11.4 %). At the other end of the spectrum, in Slovakia, France and Denmark, sectoral profitability (as measured by the gross operating rate) was lower than for the national non-financial business economy as a whole.

Figure 22.9

Architectural and engineering activities and related technical consultancy; technical testing and analysis (NACE Groups 74.2 and 74.3)
Productivity and profitability characteristics relative to national averages, 2004 (non-financial business economy=100) (1)

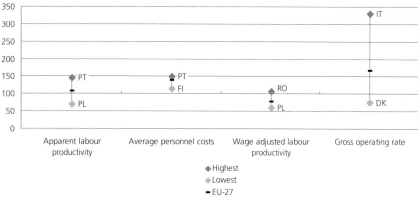

(1) Ireland, Greece, Cyprus and Malta, not available; Luxembourg, 2003.
Source: Eurostat (SBS)

22.4: ADVERTISING AND DIRECT MARKETING

Advertising and direct marketing enterprises engage in services aimed at promoting ideas, goods and services, be it to the general public, specific target groups or other enterprises. These activities are covered by NACE Group 74.4 which includes the creation and placing of outdoor advertising, the sale of advertisement time and space, and the distribution or delivery of advertising material, as well as direct marketing, sponsorship and sales promotion services. Note that advertising enterprises buying and reselling sales time or space tend to have relatively high level of turnover (and therefore a relatively low gross operating rate), while purchases of goods and services tend to be high relative to personnel costs, reflecting the distributive nature of this part of their activity.

Advertising and direct marketing are among the activities for which expenditures tend to rapidly decrease when the economic climate is not favourable. Nonetheless, when an upturn is foreseen, expenditure on these services tends to increase faster than the economy in general. This sector was affected by the slowdown observed in the EU (and global) economy in 2001 and 2002, and in particular by the collapse in 2001 of the dot.com boom, however short-term statistics indicate that there has been growth since.

Recent changes in terms of legislation affecting the advertising activities occurred in May 2007, when both the European Parliament and Council agreed on the main aims of the European Commission's original proposal for the new directive on audiovisual media services without frontiers. It will offer a comprehensive legal framework that covers all audiovisual media services, including TV advertising; the directive should enter into force by the end of 2007.

STRUCTURAL PROFILE

The 193 600 enterprises that took part in advertising activities (NACE Group 74.4) generated EUR 33.9 billion of value added in the EU-27 in 2004, contributing 4.6 % of the business services (NACE Divisions 72 and 74) wealth creation. The advertising sector employed 844 500 persons, 4.3 % of the business services workforce.

With EUR 7.5 billion, the United Kingdom was the largest contributor to the EU-27's value added in advertising activities in 2004, equivalent to 22.1 % of the total – see Table 22.17. France (19.0 %) and Germany (18.1 %) were the next largest contributors. However, the contribution of this sector to non-financial business economy value added in the United Kingdom (0.8 %) was not much above the EU-27 average of 0.7 %. Using this measure, the Czech Republic, France and Sweden (each 0.9 %) were more specialised [9].

A number of Member States provided turnover data for 2004 in the advertising sector broken down by media – see Figure 22.10. This sector's turnover was dominated by advertising in newspapers, magazines and journals and advertising on television which both represented more than one quarter (28 %) of total turnover, while outdoor and transport-based media accounted for almost one fifth (19 %) of total advertising turnover. At the other end of the spectrum, the Internet accounted for 3 % of total sales from advertising activities in 2004, the smallest share of all the media covered, with a share just below that of radio (4 %). Another type of analysis, providing a breakdown of the advertising sector's turnover by product, shows

[9] Luxembourg, 2003; Ireland, Greece, Cyprus and Malta, not available.

that sales were dominated by the sale or leasing of advertising space/time which represented almost half of all turnover – it should be noted that this product is similar to a retail or wholesale product, in that a large proportion of the turnover represents the reselling (normally with a margin) of space/time purchased from a media organisation, rather than income for the provision of a service produced directly by advertising enterprises themselves.

The series for annual short-term statistics for the EU-27's advertising activities starts in 2000 and shows a downturn in the developments of turnover in 2001 (-0.1 % compared with the previous year) that may be associated with a general slowdown in economic activity. In the following years to 2006, the turnover index for advertising activities grew by at least 1.8 % each year except in 2004 when the index remained virtually unchanged (0.7 %); nevertheless, growth rates for advertising activities were systematically lower or similar to those for business services between 2001 and 2006.

Figure 22.10

Advertising activities (NACE Group 74.4) Breakdown of turnover by type of media, 2004 (1)

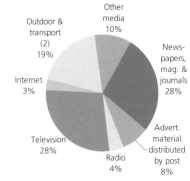

(1) Average based on data for Germany, Spain, Latvia, Lithuania, Romania, Slovenia, Slovakia, Finland, Sweden and United Kingdom.
(2) Airplanes, buses, taxis, posters etc.
Source: Eurostat (SBS)

Table 22.17

Advertising (NACE Group 74.4)
Structural profile: ranking of top five Member States, 2004

Rank	Share of EU-27 value added (%) (1)	Share of EU-27 employment (%) (1)	Value added specialisation ratio (EU-27=100) (2)	Employment specialisation ratio (EU-27=100) (2)
1	United Kingdom (22.1)	Germany (25.1)	Czech Republic (140.7)	Denmark (188.0)
2	France (19.0)	France (12.6)	Sweden (136.1)	Netherlands (160.1)
3	Germany (18.1)	Spain (11.9)	France (134.9)	Germany (151.4)
4	Spain (9.2)	United Kingdom (11.3)	United Kingdom (116.6)	Sweden (150.5)
5	Italy (7.5)	Italy (6.0)	Netherlands (112.5)	Austria (121.6)

(1) Greece and Malta, not available; Luxembourg, 2003.
(2) Ireland, Greece, Cyprus and Malta, not available; Luxembourg, 2003.
Source: Eurostat (SBS)

COSTS, PRODUCTIVITY AND
PROFITABILITY

A large proportion of total expenditure within advertising activities was accounted for by purchases of goods and services (81.2 %), the highest share among the business services covered in Subchapters 22.1 to 22.6, while personnel costs accounted for less than one fifth of the total (16.9 %) and investment in tangible goods for less than 2 %.

In 2004, apparent labour productivity in the EU-27's advertising activities was EUR 40 100 per person employed and average personnel costs were EUR 28 400 per employee. As a result, the wage adjusted labour productivity ratio for EU-27 advertising activities in 2004 was 141.1 %, the highest ratio among the business services presented in this chapter; nevertheless, still below the non-financial business economy average (148.0 %). Among the Member States with available data, only in Germany, Hungary, Italy, Portugal, the United Kingdom, Lithuania and France was the wage adjusted labour productivity ratio for advertising activities above the national non-financial business economy average.

The gross operating rate of advertising activities was relatively low, at just 10.9 % for the EU-27 in 2004; the lowest rate among business services sectors. In Romania and Luxembourg (2003), personnel costs exceeded value added, leading to a negative gross operating surplus and therefore a negative gross operating rate.

22.5: LABOUR RECRUITMENT AND TEMPORARY WORK SERVICES

Activities covered in this subchapter include personnel search, selection referral, head-hunting and job placement services, be they supplied to an individual looking for work or to an enterprise trying to hire (NACE Group 74.5). The data presented also cover labour-contracting activities (for example, temporary work agencies); however, they do not comprise farm labouring or the performing arts.

Labour recruitment and temporary work services have grown mainly as a consequence of the outsourcing trend, using the flexibility and expertise provided by enterprises in this sector (for example, knowledge of the employment market and selection procedures) instead of trying to employ personnel directly. Activities of temporary work agencies are excluded from the scope of the Directive on services in the internal market, but not other parts of this sector, notably labour recruitment/placement services.

On 27 June 2007, the European Commission proposed in a Communication the establishment of eight common principles of flexicurity [10], a policy approach that gains growing importance as an instrument that combines labour market flexibility with employment security and the need to respect workers rights and working conditions. This policy is a response to the challenges posed by globalisation, with the aim of making EU labour markets more flexible while providing employment security at the same time. In this framework, enterprises acting in labour recruitment and temporary work services are directly concerned.

[10] For more information, see: http://ec.europa.eu/employment_social/news/2007/jun/flexicurity_en.pdf.

STRUCTURAL PROFILE

The EU-27's labour recruitment and provision of personnel sector (NACE Group 74.5) generated EUR 74.5 billion of value added in the EU-27 in 2004 and therefore contributed 10.1 % of the wealth that was created in the business services sector. With 2.9 million persons employed across 65 400 enterprises, the sector of labour recruitment and provision of personnel represented a much larger share of the EU-27's business services workforce (15 %) than its corresponding share of value added, reflecting the nature of much of this sector – namely, to employ people to undertake work for clients in other sectors.

Among the Member States, more than one third of the EU-27's value added came from the United Kingdom (34.8 %), the largest market for labour recruitment and provision of personnel, as well as the largest employer – see Table 22.18. France and Germany were respectively the second and third largest

Table 22.18

Labour recruitment and provision of personnel (NACE Group 74.5)
Structural profile: ranking of top five Member States, 2004

Rank	Share of EU-27 value added (%) (1)	Share of EU-27 employment (%) (1)	Value added specialisation ratio (EU-27=100) (2)	Employment specialisation ratio (EU-27=100) (2)
1	United Kingdom (34.8)	United Kingdom (25.2)	France (186.0)	Luxembourg (379.4)
2	France (26.2)	France (20.9)	United Kingdom (183.9)	Netherlands (292.4)
3	Germany (10.9)	Germany (12.4)	Belgium (159.8)	Belgium (192.6)
4	Netherlands (6.6)	Netherlands (10.8)	Netherlands (144.2)	France (182.5)
5	Italy (4.9)	Spain (8.0)	Luxembourg (104.4)	United Kingdom (175.1)

(1) Greece and Malta, not available; Luxembourg, 2003.
(2) Ireland, Greece, Cyprus and Malta, not available; Luxembourg, 2003.
Source: Eurostat (SBS)

Table 22.19

Labour recruitment services (NACE Group 74.5)
Breakdown of turnover of by product, 2004 (%) (1)

	Average	DK	DE	EL	ES	LV	LT	PL	RO	SI	SK	FI	SE	UK
Placement services of personnel	10	12	3	38	7	76	60	30	46	7	22	3	6	12
Executive search services	2	6	2	12	3	8	17	19	28	0	15	0	3	2
Office support personnel and other workers	8	6	1	26	5	67	42	11	17	7	7	3	3	11
Supply services of personnel	85	86	94	51	92	18	30	48	31	91	76	91	93	82
Commercial/trade	9	1	4	8	8	6	2	4	3	8	8	7	2	11
Industrial/manufacturing	24	21	37	1	36	7	19	7	6	40	49	17	18	19
Horeca	2	3	1	c	7	0	0	1	1	7	0	20	1	2
Medical	4	29	3	0	1	0	0	2	0	1	0	0	3	5
Education	1	0	0	2	0	0	0	2	0	1	2	0	0	2
Transport/warehousing/logistics	12	4	19	c	7	c	0	20	7	4	2	1	13	10
Computer and telecommunication	7	0	2	3	3	c	0	2	1	6	2	5	16	9
Other office support personnel	12	23	5	19	20	0	9	2	6	14	4	11	26	13
Others	14	4	22	18	10	c	0	8	7	11	9	32	14	12
Other additional products	5	2	3	11	1	6	10	22	24	2	3	6	1	6

(1) c: confidential.
Source: Eurostat (SBS)

contributors, both in terms of value added or employment, while none of the remaining Member States contributed more than 10 % to EU-27 value added. Given the share of EU-27 value added provided by France and the United Kingdom, it is not surprising that these two Member States [11] were the most specialised in labour recruitment and provision of personnel in terms of this sector's contribution to non-financial business economy (NACE Sections C to I and K) value added. They were joined by Belgium, the Netherlands and Luxembourg, which were the only other Member States to report some degree of specialisation in these activities.

According to annual short-term business statistics, the index of turnover for the EU-27's labour recruitment and provision of personnel sector grew at a rapid pace from 1996 to 2001, on average by 18.6 % per annum, before contracting by 4.4 % in 2002. The turnover index subsequently recovered and an upward trend was observed through to 2006, with sales growth of 18.1 % in the latest year for which data are available.

[11] Luxembourg, 2003; Ireland, Greece, Cyprus and Malta, not available.

Table 22.20

Number of hours supplied by labour recruitment services, breakdown by type of personnel, 2004 (% of total)

	DK	DE	GR	ES	LV	LT	PL	RO	SI	SK	FI	SE	UK
Commercial, trade	0.7	4.1	15.4	9.4	33.8	3.3	1.1	41.8	6.6	10.1	8.4	2.5	8.5
Industrial, manufacturing	28.3	44.2	:	39.1	37.8	75.9	91.2	12.8	17.0	51.9	21.4	14.0	22.6
Horeca	4.4	1.2	0.0	7.6	0.0	0.0	0.2	7.4	22.2	2.6	22.7	1.5	6.0
Medical	23.8	2.1	1.3	0.6	0.0	0.0	0.6	0.0	2.2	0.0	:	2.3	4.7
Education	0.0	0.0	5.1	0.1	0.0	0.0	0.0	2.7	0.3	0.5	:	0.2	2.8
Transport, warehousing, logistics	6.3	18.1	:	6.1	:	0.0	3.7	10.4	12.5	2.6	0.7	7.9	7.4
Computer and telecommunication	1.0	1.9	2.9	2.7	:	0.0	0.3	7.3	11.6	6.7	2.3	11.3	11.1
Other office support personnel	27.6	4.3	43.8	20.9	1.9	1.4	0.5	12.8	14.0	5.6	11.7	10.5	36.3
Others	7.9	24.2	31.0	13.3	:	19.4	2.4	4.7	13.5	20.0	32.6	49.7	0.6

Source: Eurostat (SBS)

A PRODUCT ANALYSIS

Table 22.19 presents a breakdown of turnover by product for the labour recruitment and temporary work services sector for a limited set of Member States. In 2004, supply services of personnel generated the largest share of turnover in most of the Member States for which data are available, as compared with placement services. Only in Latvia and Lithuania, did the placement services of personnel (executive search services and office support personnel and other workers) generate more than half of the total sales. However, placement services of personnel were also the most important labour recruitment and temporary work services in terms of turnover in Romania, where they accounted for 46 % of total sales.

NUMBER OF HOURS WORKED SUPPLIED BY LABOUR RECRUITMENT SERVICES

Table 22.20 provides an analysis of the number of hours worked by type of personnel. The country coverage is limited to those countries with complete or nearly complete data sets for 2004. Hours worked supplied to the industrial activities represented the largest proportion of the total number of hours supplied in a majority of Member States for which data are available, with shares that reached 75.9 % in Lithuania and 91.2 % in Poland. In Denmark, while the largest proportion of hours worked supplied by labour recruitment services was also for the industrial sector (28.3 %), other office support personnel was also important (27.6 % of the total hours supplied), as well as medical personnel (23.8 %).

COSTS, PRODUCTIVITY AND PROFITABILITY

About three quarters (77.0 %) of total expenditure in the EU-27's labour recruitment and provision of personnel sector was dedicated to personnel costs, a little above one fifth to purchases of goods and services (22.0 %), and the remaining 1 % in the form of investment in tangible goods.

Apparent labour productivity, average personnel costs and the wage adjusted labour productivity were all lower in the EU-27's labour recruitment and provision of personnel sector than respective averages for business services (NACE Divisions 72 and 74) in 2004. Indeed, apparent labour productivity was EUR 25 600 per person employed for labour recruitment and provision of personnel (EUR 38 100 for the business services), average personnel costs were EUR 21 700 per employee (EUR 30 000 for business services) and the wage adjusted

labour productivity ratio was 117.7 % (126.8 % for business services). However, note that the first two ratios are to some extent influenced by the high incidence of part-time and temporary work in the labour recruitment and provision of personnel sector, as both of these measures are based on simple head counts of persons employed or employees, while the wage adjusted labour productivity ratio is less affected by these characteristics of the workforce.

22.6: OTHER BUSINESS SERVICES

The business services covered here include security services, such as the transport of valuables and security guard/watchman activities (NACE Group 74.6), industrial cleaning, including interior and exterior cleaning of buildings of all types as well as cleaning of public means of transport (NACE Group 74.7), and miscellaneous business activities (NACE Group 74.8) which includes professional business services such as photographic, secretarial and translation activities, and operational business services such as packaging services.

Security services are excluded from the scope of the latest Directive on services in the internal market, but not other parts of this sector such as industrial cleaning and miscellaneous business activities.

Table 22.21

Other business services (NACE Groups 74.6, 74.7 and 74.8)
Structural profile, EU-27, 2004

	No. of enterprises (thousands)	Turnover (EUR million)	Value added (EUR million)	Employment (thousands)
Other business services	899.0	283 384	147 092	6 274.2
Investigation & security activities	53.2	32 697	22 753	1 153.0
Industrial cleaning	161.5	61 292	43 216	2 883.6
Miscellaneous business activities n.e.c.	684.3	189 395	81 122	2 237.6

Source: Eurostat (SBS)

STRUCTURAL PROFILE

The other business services sector (NACE Groups 74.6 to 74.8) created EUR 147.1 billion of value added in the EU-27's in 2004, which represented 19.9 % of the business services total; this wealth was generated by almost 900 000 enterprises. This sector's contribution to business services employment was 6.3 million persons or a 32.3 % share. Among the three subsectors covered (at the NACE group level) by the other business services sector, miscellaneous business activities (NACE Group 74.8) was the largest in value added terms (EUR 81.1 billion), accounting for a 55.2 % share of the sectoral total. However, industrial cleaning (NACE Group 74.7) had the largest workforce of the three subsectors covered, employing 2.9 million persons – see Table 22.21.

More than one quarter of the EU-27's value added in the other business services sector came from the United Kingdom (25.8 %), which was also most specialised in terms of this sector's share of non-financial business economy value added – see Table 22.22.

Annual short-term business statistics shows positive developments for the index of turnover from 2000 to 2006 for each of the three subsectors (in terms of NACE groups) that make up the other business services sector. The most rapid pace of sales growth was recorded for investigation and security activities, where turnover rose by an average of 9.9 % per annum, followed by industrial cleaning (8.0 % per annum) and miscellaneous business activities (6.7 % per annum). For comparison, the index of turnover for business services as a whole grew on average by 7.6 % per annum.

Table 22.22

Other business services (NACE Groups 74.6, 74.7 and 74.8)
Structural profile: ranking of top five Member States, 2004

Rank	Share of EU-27 value added (%) (1)	Share of EU-27 employment (%) (1)	Value added specialisation ratio (EU-27=100) (2)	Employment specialisation ratio (EU-27=100) (2)
1	United Kingdom (25.8)	Germany (20.5)	United Kingdom (136.4)	Germany (123.9)
2	Germany (19.8)	United Kingdom (17.2)	Luxembourg (111.2)	Spain (119.6)
3	France (14.3)	Spain (12.3)	Spain (103.1)	United Kingdom (119.3)
4	Italy (11.1)	Italy (11.7)	France (101.7)	Hungary (107.8)
5	Spain (9.3)	France (10.4)	Italy (99.5)	Luxembourg (105.0)

(1) Greece and Malta, not available; Luxembourg, 2003.
(2) Ireland, Greece, Cyprus and Malta, not available; Luxembourg, 2003.
Source: Eurostat (SBS)

COSTS, PRODUCTIVITY AND PROFITABILITY

A breakdown of expenditure within the EU-27's other business services sector was very similar to that for the business services as a whole. The largest item of expenditure was purchases of goods and services, which accounted for more than half (54.5 %) of total expenditure in this sector. The share of purchases of goods and services in total expenditure varied considerably between the three subsectors, from a high of 66.1 % for miscellaneous business activities n.e.c., to 31.7 % and 31.6 % for investigation and security activities and for industrial cleaning.

Apparent labour productivity and average personnel costs were relatively low for the EU-27's other business services sector (NACE Groups 74.6 to 74.8). In 2004, apparent labour productivity was EUR 23 400 per person employed and average personnel costs were EUR 18 300 per employee, in both cases these values were lower than for any of the other business services sectors presented in Subchapters 22.1 to 22.5; note these ratios are given for headcounts and that the relatively low figure may reflect, to some degree, a high propensity to employ on a part-time basis within these activities. Among the three subsectors, the lowest values were recorded for industrial cleaning, while the highest values

were recorded for miscellaneous business activities (although both ratios nevertheless remained below business services' averages). The combination of these two indicators resulted in a wage adjusted labour productivity ratio of 127.8 % for the EU-27's other business services sector in 2004, very similar to that for the whole of business services (126.8 %). The other business services sector recorded a gross operating rate of 16.1 %, slightly below the business services average (17.2 %). Among the three subsectors, these two indicators were lowest for investigation and security activities (NACE Group 74.6), and (once again) highest for miscellaneous business activities.

Table 22.23

Computer services (NACE Division 72)

Main indicators, 2004

	EU-27	BE	BG	CZ	DK	DE	EE	IE	EL	ES	FR	IT	CY	LV	LT
No. of enterprises (thousands)	500.6	10.9	2.6	23.4	7.0	45.2	0.8	4.3	:	26.4	49.1	86.8	0.2	0.9	0.9
Turnover (EUR million)	313 023	7 570	204	2 601	6 615	56 841	173	6 742	:	17 266	46 766	35 704	111	151	209
Production (EUR million)	277 688	7 423	183	2 129	5 651	46 882	146	3 749	:	13 760	43 184	34 505	102	131	161
Value added (EUR million)	154 257	3 283	77	1 029	3 197	28 375	71	2 713	:	7 982	22 605	15 246	68	71	68
Gross operating surplus (EUR million)	46 704	867	33	403	787	9 021	21	1 524	:	1 883	2 861	5 550	20	24	30
Purchases of goods & services (EUR million)	157 819	4 290	132	1 596	3 522	29 711	102	4 031	:	9 451	24 486	20 469	43	81	141
Personnel costs (EUR million)	107 553	2 416	44	627	2 410	19 354	51	1 189	:	6 100	19 744	9 696	48	47	38
Investment in tangible goods (EUR million)	11 231	388	14	174	261	2 518	8	91	:	536	1 133	1 296	3	11	11
Employment (thousands)	2 570	49	12	51	43	370	4	29	:	185	345	358	2	6	6
Apparent labour prod. (EUR thousand)	60.0	66.6	6.3	20.3	74.0	76.6	16.5	93.8	:	43.1	65.4	42.6	39.2	12.8	12.0
Average personnel costs (EUR thousand)	48.6	62.8	4.6	17.5	60.6	57.7	12.8	45.8	:	37.1	57.7	38.6	28.2	9.1	7.2
Wage adjusted labour productivity (%)	123.5	106.1	136.0	116.1	122.3	132.7	129.3	205.0	:	116.1	113.4	110.2	139.2	141.0	166.7
Gross operating rate (%)	14.9	11.4	15.9	15.5	11.9	15.9	11.9	22.6	:	10.9	6.1	15.5	18.0	15.7	14.5
Investment / employment (EUR thousand)	4.4	7.9	1.2	3.4	6.0	6.8	1.9	3.2	:	2.9	3.3	3.6	1.9	2.0	2.0

	LU (1)	HU	MT	NL	AT	PL	PT	RO	SI	SK	FI	SE	UK	NO
No. of enterprises (thousands)	1.0	22.2	:	18.5	12.9	27.5	3.2	9.3	2.1	1.2	4.4	28.9	103.2	9.4
Turnover (EUR million)	762	2 639	:	13 669	5 895	3 692	2 161	849	647	529	4 474	14 928	80 366	5 460
Production (EUR million)	581	1 401	:	13 339	4 531	2 842	1 844	626	471	464	4 323	13 095	75 206	5 026
Value added (EUR million)	283	707	:	6 761	2 628	1 322	763	312	240	233	1 742	6 898	47 006	2 770
Gross operating surplus (EUR million)	19	258	:	1 521	736	712	180	149	71	91	-130	1 390	18 593	648
Purchases of goods & services (EUR million)	496	1 881	:	4 626	3 383	2 245	1 457	550	400	292	2 809	8 282	32 867	2 725
Personnel costs (EUR million)	264	449	:	5 240	1 892	610	583	163	169	142	1 872	5 509	28 413	2 122
Investment in tangible goods (EUR million)	6	108	:	330	196	102	87	71	13	25	106	404	2 960	199
Employment (thousands)	5	51	:	126	47	78	21	35	8	11	37	98	573	35
Apparent labour prod. (EUR thousand)	60.1	13.9	:	53.8	56.0	16.9	36.0	9.0	31.6	21.7	47.2	70.4	82.0	79.0
Average personnel costs (EUR thousand)	60.7	12.0	:	46.7	52.8	13.2	28.7	4.9	26.2	13.6	52.0	63.2	55.9	66.0
Wage adjusted labour productivity (%)	99.0	116.2	:	115.1	106.1	128.9	125.2	182.2	120.7	159.4	90.8	111.4	146.7	119.7
Gross operating rate (%)	2.4	9.8	:	11.1	12.5	19.3	8.3	17.6	11.0	17.1	-2.9	9.3	23.1	11.9
Investment / employment (EUR thousand)	1.4	2.1	:	2.6	4.2	1.3	4.1	2.0	1.8	2.3	2.9	4.1	5.2	5.7

(1) 2003.
Source: Eurostat (SBS)

Table 22.24

Other business activities (NACE Division 74)

Main indicators, 2004

	EU-27	BE	BG	CZ	DK	DE	EE	IE	EL	ES	FR	IT	CY	LV	LT
No. of enterprises (thousands)	3 400.1	79.6	18.5	191.0	33.2	323.7	5.0	17.8	:	364.0	386.7	693.2	2.6	7.1	5.0
Turnover (EUR million)	1 137 124	41 359	1 174	10 821	18 546	183 683	765	14 011	:	78 977	204 750	120 750	651	657	807
Production (EUR million)	1 069 220	41 046	1 113	10 597	17 502	163 790	734	9 917	:	61 004	197 845	129 022	645	618	796
Value added (EUR million)	585 364	15 541	325	4 392	9 728	109 151	359	6 838	:	42 664	93 328	59 412	431	259	347
Gross operating surplus (EUR million)	202 869	4 553	133	2 251	2 727	40 236	125	3 223	:	14 956	12 008	33 309	190	121	145
Purchases of goods & services (EUR million)	547 370	25 608	913	6 663	9 282	81 865	418	7 162	:	38 005	116 851	65 791	209	413	480
Personnel costs (EUR million)	382 495	10 988	192	2 141	7 001	68 914	234	3 615	:	27 708	81 321	26 103	241	138	202
Investment in tangible goods (EUR million)	41 447	1 993	125	448	675	6 577	53	669	:	2 923	8 305	4 517	27	58	75
Employment (thousands)	16 863	358	110	359	223	3 058	33	127	:	1 736	2 112	1 865	12	36	41
Apparent labour prod. (EUR thousand)	34.7	43.4	3.0	12.2	43.6	35.7	10.8	53.7	:	24.6	44.2	31.9	36.8	7.2	8.5
Average personnel costs (EUR thousand)	27.1	39.4	2.1	9.8	34.4	25.5	7.3	32.6	:	19.6	39.2	23.8	25.9	4.4	5.3
Wage adjusted labour productivity (%)	128.1	110.1	139.9	124.5	126.7	140.2	147.2	164.5	:	125.6	112.8	134.0	141.9	164.9	160.4
Gross operating rate (%)	17.8	11.0	11.3	20.8	14.7	21.9	16.3	23.0	:	18.9	5.9	27.6	29.1	18.4	18.0
Investment / employment (EUR thousand)	2.5	5.6	1.1	1.2	3.0	2.2	1.6	5.3	:	1.7	3.9	2.4	2.3	1.6	1.8

	LU (1)	HU	MT	NL	AT	PL	PT	RO	SI	SK	FI	SE	UK	NO
No. of enterprises (thousands)	4.6	138.4	:	105.9	49.1	217.6	40.3	42.0	15.1	5.6	29.9	129.3	362.2	42.5
Turnover (EUR million)	2 742	10 511	:	69 316	21 920	14 035	12 145	3 191	3 430	1 661	10 405	28 580	265 069	15 476
Production (EUR million)	2 388	5 660	:	68 544	17 124	13 014	11 745	2 834	2 465	1 541	9 681	28 675	259 972	15 402
Value added (EUR million)	1 623	2 709	:	31 380	11 030	5 539	4 750	1 036	996	641	5 429	14 451	156 513	8 176
Gross operating surplus (EUR million)	412	992	:	7 178	3 435	3 165	756	511	330	241	1 406	2 961	64 831	2 300
Purchases of goods & services (EUR million)	1 093	7 528	:	19 018	11 761	8 769	7 590	2 193	2 379	1 014	5 173	14 704	106 794	7 515
Personnel costs (EUR million)	1 211	1 716	:	24 202	7 595	2 375	3 994	525	666	401	4 023	11 490	91 682	5 876
Investment in tangible goods (EUR million)	46	407	:	1 704	846	512	1 386	399	90	187	327	991	7 373	518
Employment (thousands)	41	315	:	977	269	663	290	226	48	58	128	317	3 210	154
Apparent labour prod. (EUR thousand)	39.3	8.6	:	32.1	40.9	8.4	16.4	4.6	20.7	11.0	42.5	45.6	48.8	52.9
Average personnel costs (EUR thousand)	31.2	7.9	:	27.2	33.6	5.6	14.6	2.4	16.8	7.1	34.2	42.6	31.6	42.8
Wage adjusted labour productivity (%)	125.8	109.0	:	118.1	122.0	148.9	112.4	192.2	123.0	155.3	124.0	107.1	154.3	123.8
Gross operating rate (%)	15.0	9.4	:	10.4	15.7	22.5	6.2	16.0	9.6	14.5	13.5	10.4	24.5	14.9
Investment / employment (EUR thousand)	1.1	1.3	:	1.7	3.1	0.8	4.8	1.8	1.9	3.2	2.6	3.1	2.3	3.4

(1) 2003.
Source: Eurostat (SBS)

Real estate, renting and R&D

Like the business services enterprises covered in the previous chapter, R&D enterprises enable their clients to focus on their own activities and reduce the need to occupy their own personnel with ancillary or supporting tasks. In a similar fashion, renting and leasing services could be used to increase financial flexibility, including the need to commit own capital. While research and development enterprises provide essentially business services, a large part of real estate, renting and leasing services are provided to households. The services included in the present chapter are covered by the directive on services in the internal market - see Chapter 22 for more information.

STRUCTURAL PROFILE

Value added generated by the 1.1 million enterprises active in the EU-27's real estate, renting and R&D sector (NACE Divisions 70, 71 and 73) was EUR 304 billion in 2004 and there were 3.5 million persons employed in these activities (see Table 23.1). As such, the real estate, renting and R&D sector accounted for 6.0 % of value added in the non-financial business economy (NACE Sections C to I and K), but less than half this much in terms of employment, just 2.8 %. Real estate (NACE Division 70) accounted for close to three quarters (72.4 %) of the sector's value added and a slightly smaller share of employment (71.4 %). Renting and leasing (NACE Division 71) generated more than one fifth (21.5 %) of the sector's value added and also had a smaller

share in employment terms (17.1 %). Consequently, research and development (R&D) activities' (NACE Division 73) share of sectoral employment was considerably greater than its share of value added, contributing 11.1 % of those employed and just over half this level (6.1 %) in terms of sectoral value added.

Germany, with EUR 77.2 billion of value added, accounted for the largest share (25.4 %) of the EU-27's real estate, renting and R&D sector in 2004 (see Table 23.2). The United Kingdom generated EUR 59.8 billion of value added and was the second largest contributor with a 19.7 % share. The only other Member States with more than one tenth of EU-27 value added were France (14.8 %) and Spain (10.5 %). In terms of its contribution to value added in the non-financial business economy, the real estate, renting and R&D sector represented 11.2 % of the total in Denmark, 8.7 % in Sweden and 8.2 % in Estonia [(1)]. At the other end of the spectrum, these activities accounted for 1.3 % of non-financial business economy value added in Bulgaria and 1.6 % in Slovenia. In most Member States real estate, renting and R&D accounted for a smaller proportion of non-financial business economy employment than of value added, the only exception being Latvia.

[(1)] Ireland, Greece, Cyprus, Luxembourg and Malta, not available.

In this chapter, the term 'real estate, renting and R&D' is used to refer to the aggregate of three activities: real estate services (NACE Division 70), renting and leasing (NACE Division 71) and research and development (NACE Division 73), each of which are covered in turn in a subchapter. As well as these three divisions, NACE Section K also covers computer services (NACE Division 72) and other business activities (NACE Division 74) which together form Chapter 22 Business services.

NACE
70:    real estate activities;
70.1: real estate activities with own property;
70.2: letting of own property;
70.3: real estate activities on a fee or contract basis;
71:    renting of machinery and equipment without operator and of personal and household goods;
71.1: renting of automobiles;
71.2: renting of other transport equipment;
71.3: renting of other machinery and equipment;
71.4: renting of personal and household goods n.e.c.;
73:    research and development;
73.1: research and experimental development on natural sciences and engineering;
73.2: research and experimental development on social sciences and humanities.

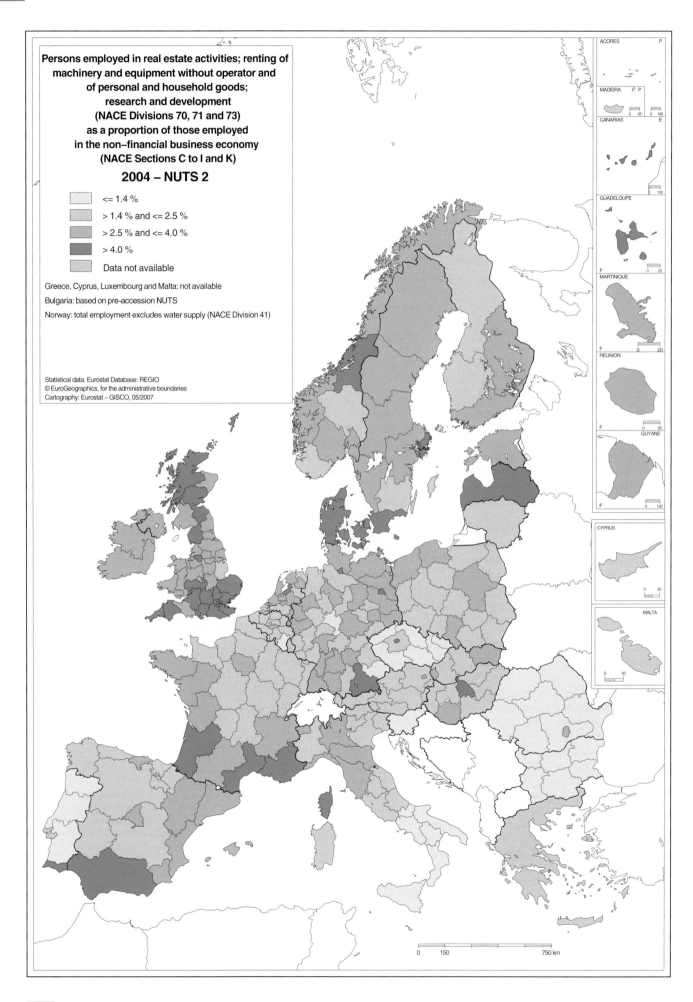

Persons employed in real estate activities; renting of
machinery and equipment without operator and
of personal and household goods;
research and development
(NACE Divisions 70, 71 and 73)
as a proportion of those employed
in the non–financial business economy
(NACE Sections C to I and K)

2004 – NUTS 2

<= 1.4 %

> 1.4 % and <= 2.5 %

> 2.5 % and <= 4.0 %

> 4.0 %

Data not available

Greece, Cyprus, Luxembourg and Malta: not available

Bulgaria: based on pre-accession NUTS

Norway: total employment excludes water supply (NACE Division 41)

Statistical data: Eurostat Database: REGIO
© EuroGeographics, for the administrative boundaries
Cartography: Eurostat – GISCO, 05/2007

Table 23.1 _____

Real estate, renting and research and development (NACE Divisions 70, 71 and 73)
Structural profile, EU-27, 2004 (1)

	No. of enterprises		Turnover		Value added		Employment	
	(thousands)	(% of total)	(EUR million)	(% of total)	(EUR million)	(% of total)	(thousands)	(% of total)
Real estate, renting and research and development	1 072.0	100.0	620 000	100.0	304 000	100.0	3 500.0	100.0
Real estate activities	897.8	83.7	460 000	74.2	220 000	72.4	2 500.0	71.4
Renting and leasing	137.0	12.8	126 310	20.4	65 498	21.5	598.4	17.1
Research and development	37.2	3.5	37 000	6.0	18 400	6.1	390.0	11.1

(1) Rounded estimates based on non-confidential data.
Source: Eurostat (SBS)

Table 23.2 _____

Real estate, renting and research and development (NACE Divisions 70, 71 and 73)
Structural profile: ranking of top five Member States, 2004

			Share of non-financial business economy			
Rank	Value added (EUR million) (1)	Employment (thousands) (1)	No. of enterprises (2)	Turnover (3)	Value added (3)	Employment (3)
1	Germany (77 177)	United Kingdom (740.1)	Latvia (17.7 %)	Spain (5.3 %)	Denmark (11.2 %)	Latvia (6.0 %)
2	United Kingdom (59 763)	Germany (551.2)	Denmark (12.4 %)	Sweden (5.0 %)	Sweden (8.7 %)	United Kingdom (4.1 %)
3	France (44 977)	France (447.3)	Luxembourg (11.7 %)	France (3.9 %)	Estonia (8.2 %)	Denmark (4.0 %)
4	Spain (31 888)	Spain (412.4)	Germany (11.5 %)	Denmark (3.6 %)	Germany (7.2 %)	Sweden (3.6 %)
5	Italy (16 619)	Italy (321.8)	Estonia (9.4 %)	Netherlands (3.5 %)	Netherlands (7.1 %)	Estonia (3.4 %)

(1) Greece, Cyprus, Luxembourg and Malta, not available.
(2) Ireland, Greece, Cyprus and Malta, not available; Luxembourg, 2003.
(3) Ireland, Greece, Cyprus, Luxembourg and Malta, not available.
Source: Eurostat (SBS)

The regional specialisation of the real estate, renting and R&D sector is shown in the map on page 394 which is based on the non-financial business economy employment share of this sector. The most specialised regions (at the level of detail shown in the map) were inner London and Latvia (the latter considered as one region at the level of detail in the map). Many other regions in the United Kingdom were specialised in this sector, particularly in southern England and central Scotland.

A breakdown of EU-27 value added in the real estate, renting and R&D sector shows that small and medium-sized enterprises (SMEs, with less than 250 persons employed) generated 83.1 % of the total added value in 2004 (see Figure 23.1), a much higher proportion than the non-financial business economy average (57.0 %). Micro enterprises (with less than 10 persons employed) alone contributed 47.7 % of the added value in this sector, more than double the non-financial business economy average of 20.2 %. Nevertheless, the size class structures of the three subsectors covered in Subchapters 23.1 to 23.3 were quite different from each other. The dominance of micro enterprises was particularly pronounced for real estate services where they generated more than half of the value added (54.7 %), whereas the micro enterprises' share was notably lower (but still well above the non-financial business economy average) for renting and leasing activities

Figure 23.1 _____

Real estate, renting and research and development (NACE Divisions 70, 71 and 73)
Share of value added by enterprise size class, EU-27, 2004

Source: Eurostat (SBS)

(35.1 %); these were respectively the highest and third highest value added contributions of micro enterprises among the non-financial business economy NACE divisions (2) in 2004. In the EU-27's research and development subsector the micro enterprise contribution to value added was very low (9.8 %), as large enterprises dominated the sector generating 52.5 % of value added and employing 46.0 %

of the workforce in 2004. Medium-sized enterprises (with 50 to 249 persons employed) were also relatively important in this subsector, their 26.5 % contribution to value added being among the highest shares recorded across the non-financial business economy NACE divisions in 2004, lower only than some of the industrial (NACE Sections C to E) NACE divisions.

_____
(2) NACE Divisions 10 to 14, 16, 23 and 62, not available.

Figure 23.2 _____

Real estate, renting and research and development (NACE Divisions 70, 71 and 73)
Labour force characteristics, EU-27, 2006

By gender	By working time	By age
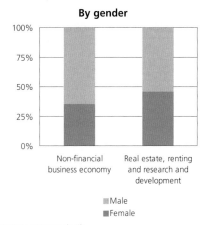	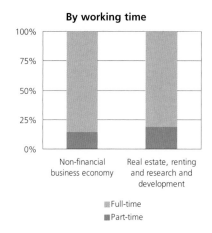	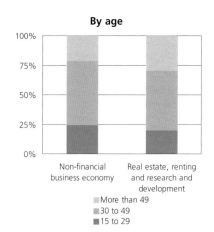
▪Male ▪Female	▪Full-time ▪Part-time	▪More than 49 ▪30 to 49 ▪15 to 29

Source: Eurostat (LFS)

EMPLOYMENT CHARACTERISTICS

The characteristics of the real estate, renting and R&D sector's workforce in the EU-27 was those of a fairly typical services sector, in that the shares of male workers and full-time workers were below the non-financial business economy average. Nevertheless, a more complex picture is revealed when analysing the individual NACE divisions that make up the sector. In 2006, according to the Labour Force Survey (see Figure 23.2), 54.4 % of the persons employed in the sector as a whole were male, some 10.6 percentage points lower than the non-financial business economy average (65.0 %). However, the proportion of male workers within the renting and leasing subsector was higher at 69.7 %, while it was as low as 50.6 % in the real estate subsector. The workforce in the research and development subsector was characterised by a high proportion of full-time employment (87.2 %), the only one of the three subsectors where this proportion was higher than the non-financial business economy average (85.6 %).

In terms of age profile, there was a much higher proportion of the real estate, renting and R&D workforce that were aged 50 or over (29.8 %) than the average for the non-financial business economy (21.6 %). This difference reflects, to a large degree, the fact that over one third (34.2 %) of workers in real estate services were aged 50 or more in 2006, while in the renting and leasing subsector the proportion (18.3 %) was in fact below the non-financial business economy average.

According to structural business statistics the share of paid employees in the total number of persons employed was just 74.3 % in the EU-27's real estate, renting and R&D sector in 2004, some 11.9 percentage points below the non-financial business economy average. A great diversity in this share was recorded across the three activities that make up this sector, ranging from 69.2 % for real estate, through 83.6 % for renting and leasing, to a high of 92.6 % for the research and development activities.

COSTS, PRODUCTIVITY AND PROFITABILITY

The three subsectors within the real estate, renting and R&D sector were all relatively capital intensive services, but to quite different degrees (see Figure 23.3). In 2004 gross tangible investment in the renting and leasing subsector was equivalent to 45.4 % of total expenditure in the EU-27, while in the real estate services subsector the share was 28.8 %: these were the two highest shares of tangible investment among all of the non-financial business economy NACE divisions [3] in 2004. Even in the research and development subsector, where at 7.9 % this ratio was noticeably lower than for the other subsectors covered in this chapter, it was still well above the non-financial business economy average of 4.9 %.

_____

[3] NACE Divisions 10, 12 and 13, not available.

Table 23.3 _____

Real estate, renting and research and development (NACE Divisions 70, 71 and 73)
Productivity and profitability, EU-27, 2004

	Apparent labour productivity (EUR thousand)	Average personnel costs (EUR thousand)	Wage adjusted labour productivity (%)	Gross operating rate (%)
Real estate, renting and research and development (1)	87.0	31.0	280.0	35.8
Real estate activities (1)	88.0	28.1	315.0	37.0
Renting and leasing	109.5	28.9	378.4	40.4
Research and development (1)	46.9	47.1	99.0	3.4

(1) Rounded estimate based on non-confidential data.
Source: Eurostat (SBS)

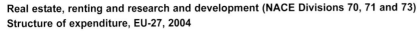

Figure 23.3

Real estate, renting and research and development (NACE Divisions 70, 71 and 73)
Structure of expenditure, EU-27, 2004

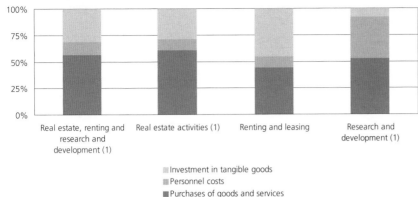

(1) Rounded estimates based on non-confidential data.
Source: Eurostat (SBS)

In 2004, apparent labour productivity for the EU-27 real estate, renting and R&D sector was around EUR 87 000 per person employed, more than double the non-financial business economy average of EUR 40 900. This productivity measure was notably lower in the research and development subsector where it was EUR 46 900.

Average personnel costs were also high, but not to the same extent: around EUR 31 000 per employee in real estate, renting and R&D compared with EUR 27 600 for non-financial business economy. In contrast to productivity, average personnel costs for the research and development subsector were significantly higher, at EUR 47 100 per employee.

For the sector as a whole, the combination of particularly high apparent labour productivity and slightly higher than average personnel costs led to a wage adjusted labour productivity ratio of 280.0 % in 2004 for the EU-27, well above the non-financial business economy average (148.0 %). This ratio was highest for the renting and leasing subsector (378.4 %) and a little lower in the real estate subsector (315.0 %), and as such these two subsectors recorded the second and fourth highest wage adjusted labour productivity ratios among the non-financial business economy NACE divisions [4]. For the research and development subsector, high average personnel costs outstripped the apparent labour productivity resulting in a wage adjusted labour productivity ratio of 99.0 %, the only non-financial business economy NACE division in which this ratio was below 100 %.

[4] NACE Divisions 10, 12 to 14, 23 and 62, not available.

The gross operating rate shows the percentage relationship between the gross operating surplus (value added minus personnel costs) and turnover. The gross operating rate of the EU-27's real estate, renting and R&D sector was 35.8 % in 2004, more than three times as high as the non-financial business economy average of 11.0 %. This rate was particularly high for the renting and leasing (40.4 %) and real estate (37.0 %) subsectors, while it was just 3.4 % in the research and development subsector: these were respectively the two highest, and the lowest levels for this rate among the non-financial business economy NACE divisions [5] in 2004. Care has to be taken with the ratios based on value added for the renting and leasing subsector, as in this subsector the activity of enterprises is to own a good that is then rented or leased out to customers, and financial costs and depreciation charges may constitute the main element of total costs; a similar situation is true for some parts of the real estate sector (letting of own property). These financial costs and depreciation charges are not considered when calculating gross value added and the gross operating surplus. In addition, changes in price levels on the property market have a large impact on the turnover and value added in real estate agencies (which operate on commission).

[5] NACE Divisions 10, 12 and 62, not available.

23.1: REAL ESTATE SERVICES

Within NACE, real estate services are covered by Division 70, which is classified alongside a range of business services within NACE Section K. However, some parts of the activity have a close relationship with the construction sector (Chapter 15) and others with architectural activities (Subchapter 22.3).

The activities of real estate services are very diverse: real estate agents sell on a commission basis; traders buy and sell property; surveyors, valuers, facilities and estate managers provide professional services; and finally owners let property. Most of these activities are related to the secondary market concerned with existing property, although some, such as property developers are active in the primary market and are therefore more closely related to construction. The wide range of real estate service activities have very different cost structures and revenue streams and care has to be taken when comparing them, particularly when trying to measure the size of each subsector or their labour productivity. In particular, when enterprises are the owner of a good that they rent or lease, their financial costs and depreciation charges may constitute the main element of their total costs, but these are not considered when calculating gross value added, the gross operating surplus or indicators of productivity or profitability that are based on these.

One indicator of the level of activity in the residential property market is lending for house purchases. Data from the European Central Bank (ECB) shown in Figure 23.4 indicate how the stock of such lending, was increasing at a progressively stronger rate throughout the period 2003 to 2005, and peaked at 12.1 % in March and April 2006; since when the rate of growth slowed mirroring the increase in interest rates that started in December 2005.

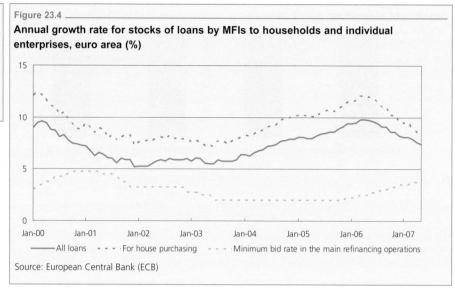

Figure 23.4

Annual growth rate for stocks of loans by MFIs to households and individual enterprises, euro area (%)

Source: European Central Bank (ECB)

STRUCTURAL PROFILE

There were almost 900 000 enterprises active in the EU-27's real estate services sector in 2004. Together they generated EUR 220 billion of value added and employed 2.5 million persons. As such, their contributions to real estate, renting and R&D was 72.4 % in terms of value added and 71.4 % of employment, making real estate services by far the largest of the three activities presented in Subchapters 23.1 to 23.3.

The largest real estate services' sector in the EU-27 was found in Germany (25.3 % of the EU-27 total), followed by the United Kingdom (17.0 %), France (14.5 %) and Spain (12.0 %) - see Table 23.4. As a proportion of value added in the non-financial business economy, the real estate services sector in 2004 was largest [6] in Denmark, Sweden and Estonia (all in excess of 7 %), while it was smallest in Bulgaria, Slovenia and Romania (all just over 1 %).

[6] Ireland, Greece, Cyprus, Luxembourg and Malta, not available.

COSTS, PRODUCTIVITY AND PROFITABILITY

In 2004 gross tangible investment in the real estate services sector was equivalent to 28.8 % of total expenditure in the EU-27, the second highest share of tangible investment among all of the non-financial business economy NACE divisions [7] in 2004, underlying the capital intensive nature of some parts of the sector; the share of tangible investment exceeded 50 % in Denmark, Romania and Austria. The share of personnel costs in operating and tangible investment expenditure was just 10.2 % in real estate services, only three fifths of the average share for the non-financial business economy (16.4 %).

[7] NACE Divisions 10, 12 and 13, not available.

Table 23.4

Real estate activities (NACE Division 70)
Structural profile: ranking of top five Member States, 2004

Rank	Share of EU-27 value added (%) (1)	Share of EU-27 employment (%) (1)	Value added specialisation ratio (EU-27=100) (2)	Employment specialisation ratio (EU-27=100) (2)
1	Germany (25.3)	United Kingdom (18.5)	Denmark (233.4)	Latvia (256.7)
2	United Kingdom (17.0)	Germany (15.3)	Sweden (174.0)	Denmark (161.0)
3	France (14.5)	France (13.0)	Estonia (167.8)	Estonia (149.9)
4	Spain (12.0)	Spain (12.6)	Spain (133.4)	Sweden (132.8)
5	Italy (5.8)	Italy (10.4)	Germany (120.8)	United Kingdom (128.6)

(1) Greece, Cyprus, Luxembourg and Malta, not available.
(2) Ireland, Greece, Cyprus, Luxembourg and Malta, not available.
Source: Eurostat (SBS)

As noted in the overview, 69.2 % of those persons employed in the EU-27's real estate sector were paid employees, the lowest share among the activities covered in Subchapters 23.1 to 23.3, and some 17.0 percentage points below the non-financial business economy average. Average personnel costs in real estate services were EUR 28 100 per employee in the EU-27 in 2004. In the majority of the Member States [8], average personnel costs were close to the national non-financial business economy average, with only the Netherlands recording average personnel costs that were notably higher. Apparent labour productivity was EUR 88 000 per person employed for real estate services in the EU-27 in 2004. The

combination of high apparent labour productivity yet typical average personnel costs resulted in a very high EU-27 wage adjusted labour productivity ratio of 315.0 %, which was more than twice as high as the non-financial business economy average (148.0 %). Only Latvia recorded a wage adjusted labour productivity ratio lower in real estate services (218.0 %) than in its non-financial business economy average (230.1 %), while Denmark recorded the highest ratio (651.4 %) in this sector among the Member States, which was four times higher than the average for the Danish non-financial business economy (163.1 %). Alongside the high wage adjusted labour productivity ratio, real estate services

recorded a high gross operating rate: the gross operating surplus of EUR 170.0 billion was equivalent to 37.0 % of turnover in the EU-27 in 2004; which was 3.4 times as high as the average for the non-financial business economy (11.0 %). Indeed, the gross operating rate for real estate services was the second highest recorded for any NACE division [9] in the non-financial business economy [10], just 3.4 percentage points below the level for renting and leasing activities (see the next subchapter).

---

[9] NACE Divisions 10, 12 and 62, not available.
[10] NACE Divisions 50 to 52, 2002.

---

[8] Ireland, Greece, Cyprus, Luxembourg and Malta, not available.

23.2: RENTING AND LEASING

This subchapter covers the activities of renting of machinery and equipment without operators and the renting of personal and household goods (NACE Division 71). The most important items that are rented or leased include transport equipment (motor vehicles, ships, aircraft, etc.) and agricultural, construction or office equipment. It should be noted that a distinction is generally made between operational leasing (or long-term rental), which is included in this subchapter, and financial leasing which is considered as a special form of credit granting and is hence covered as part of the financial services sector (see Chapter 24). The renting and leasing of real estate is covered in Subchapter 23.1.

Table 23.5

Renting and leasing (NACE Division 71)
Structural profile, EU-27, 2004

	No. of enterprises (thousands)	Turnover (EUR million)	Value added (EUR million)	Employment (thousands)
Renting and leasing	137.0	126 310	65 498	598.4
Renting of automobiles; renting of other transport equipment	34.1	66 948	34 318	171.1
Renting of other machinery and equipment	60.7	45 071	24 507	257.5
Renting of personal and household goods n.e.c.	42.3	14 291	6 674	169.8

Source: Eurostat (SBS)

In general, durable goods can be purchased, leased or rented. In the case of leasing, the two parties involved in the transaction are the lessor and the lessee (the person or enterprise that uses the good in leasing). In exchange for the transfer of user rights, the lessor receives payments. Leasing, contrary to renting, often foresees the possibility of the acquisition of the good at the end of the leasing term; renting is also usually for shorter periods than leasing.

STRUCTURAL PROFILE
Value added in EU-27 renting and leasing activities (NACE Division 71) was EUR 65.5 billion in 2004, of which 25.9 % was generated in Germany, 25.2 % in the United Kingdom and 16.5 % in France, a combined share of 67.6 % compared with a 54.0 % share for the same three Member States in non-financial business economy (NACE Sections C to I and K) value added. In 2004, EU-27 value added in renting and leasing activities accounted for 21.5 % of the wealth generated by real estate, renting and R&D (NACE Divisions 70, 71 and 73). The renting and leasing workforce of 598 400 persons employed represented 17.1 % of the real estate, renting and R&D workforce; the workforce was spread across 137 000 enterprises whose main activity was classified within renting and leasing.

The renting of transport equipment (NACE Groups 71.1 and 71.2) generated EUR 34.3 billion of value added in the EU-27 in 2004, while the renting of other machinery and equipment (NACE Group 71.3) generated EUR 24.5 billion, with the renting of personal and household goods (NACE Group 71.4) clearly the smallest subsector with value added of EUR 6.7 billion (Table 23.5). The renting of transport equipment, and the renting of personal and household goods each employed around 170 000 persons, while the workforce in the renting of other machinery and equipment subsector was larger, at around a quarter of a million strong.

Table 23.6

Renting and leasing (NACE Division 71)
Structural profile: ranking of top five Member States, 2004

Rank	Share of EU-27 value added (%) (1)	Share of EU-27 employment (%) (1)	Value added specialisation ratio (EU-27=100) (2)	Employment specialisation ratio (EU-27=100) (2)
1	Germany (25.9)	United Kingdom (29.5)	Austria (148.3)	United Kingdom (204.7)
2	United Kingdom (25.2)	France (14.5)	Luxembourg (136.0)	Spain (128.8)
3	France (16.5)	Germany (13.4)	United Kingdom (133.4)	France (126.7)
4	Spain (7.2)	Spain (13.2)	Germany (123.7)	Netherlands (118.1)
5	Netherlands (5.5)	Italy (6.1)	Netherlands (118.8)	Denmark (105.9)

(1) Greece and Malta, not available; Luxembourg, 2003.
(2) Ireland, Greece, Cyprus and Malta, not available; Luxembourg, 2003.
Source: Eurostat (SBS)

Austria was particularly specialised in the renting and leasing sector (11), which accounted for 1.9 % of value added in the Austrian non-financial business economy in 2004. The three largest Member States in this sector (Germany, the United Kingdom and France), as well as the Benelux Member States were also relatively specialised, each generating at least 1.5 % of their national non-financial business economy value added in the renting and leasing sector. In these terms, Slovenia was the least specialised Member State in this sector, as value added from renting and leasing activities contributed less than 0.1 % of Slovenian non-financial business economy value added.

An analysis of the three subsectors shows that the renting of transport equipment accounted for 70 % or more of the renting and leasing sector's total value added in Cyprus, Portugal and the Netherlands. In Sweden, Bulgaria and Latvia the renting of other machinery and equipment subsector generated 60 % or more of sectoral value added, while only in the small Slovenian renting and leasing sector was the renting of personal and household goods the largest subsector, with a 43.1 % share of Slovenian renting and leasing value added.

(11) Luxembourg, 2003; Ireland, Greece, Cyprus and Malta, not available.

COSTS, PRODUCTIVITY AND PROFITABILITY

The share of gross tangible investment in total expenditure for the renting and leasing sector was 45.4 % in the EU-27 in 2004, by some way the highest value for this indicator across the non-financial business economy NACE divisions (12). This share was over 60 % in Austria, the Netherlands and Portugal. Among the three subsectors that make up the renting and leasing sector, the share of gross tangible investment in total expenditure varied considerably, ranging from 17.6 % for the renting of personal and household goods n.e.c. to 55.2 % for the renting of automobiles; renting of other transport equipment.

Reflecting this high level of use of capital, apparent labour productivity for EU-27 renting and leasing activities soared to EUR 109 500 per person employed in 2004 (Table 23.7). This ratio was particularly high for the renting of transport equipment subsector at EUR 200 600 per person employed, and lowest for the renting of personal and household goods subsector at EUR 39 300, which was just below the non-financial business economy average.

(12) NACE Divisions 10, 12 and 13, not available.

Personnel costs averaged EUR 28 900 per employee in the renting and leasing sector in 2004, with the renting of personal and household goods subsector significantly below this with an average of EUR 20 900 per employee. The resulting wage adjusted labour productivity ratio was 378.4 % for the EU-27's renting and leasing sector in 2004, the second highest of any NACE division (13) in the non-financial business economy. This ratio was above the non-financial business economy average in all three subsectors, but by far the highest for the renting of transport equipment subsector at 640.5 %. These high values can, in part, be explained by the specific nature of this activity, where the main costs of enterprises are likely to be financial ones covering borrowing as well as depreciation charges, neither of which impact on gross value added or the gross operating surplus. The gross operating rate in the EU-27's renting and leasing sector in 2004 was 40.4 %, 3.7 times as high as the non-financial business economy average, and the highest rate among the non-financial business economy NACE divisions (14). As with the wage adjusted labour productivity ratio all three subsectors recorded a gross operating rate above the non-financial business economy average, and again the highest level was recorded for the renting of transport equipment subsector at 44.4 %.

(13) NACE Divisions 10, 12 to 14, 23 and 62, not available.
(14) NACE Divisions 10, 12 and 62, not available.

Table 23.7

Renting and leasing (NACE Division 71)
Productivity and profitability, EU-27, 2004

	Apparent labour productivity (EUR thousand)	Average personnel costs (EUR thousand)	Wage adjusted labour productivity (%)	Gross operating rate (%)
Renting and leasing	109.5	28.9	378.4	40.4
Renting of automobiles; renting of other transport equipment	200.6	31.3	640.5	44.4
Renting of other machinery and equipment	95.2	32.3	294.2	38.7
Renting of personal and household goods n.e.c.	39.3	20.9	188.2	26.8

Source: Eurostat (SBS)

23.3: RESEARCH AND DEVELOPMENT

Research and development (R&D) activities are classified within NACE according to the field of investigation of the research. A distinction is made between research and experimental development within natural sciences and engineering (NACE Group 73.1) and research and experimental development within social sciences and humanities (NACE Group 73.2). Note that market research activities are not covered and that these are included as part of Subchapter 22.2. Furthermore, it should be noted that the statistics presented for the research and development sector in this subchapter concern exclusively those enterprises whose main activity consists of carrying out R&D activities, and thus excludes R&D departments of universities, public administrations and enterprises whose main activity is otherwise classified.

Increased levels of research and development expenditure are seen as one of the means to achieve the goals set out by the European Council in Lisbon in 2000: in 2002 a target that investment in R&D should reach 3 % of GDP by 2010 was set; the Lisbon objectives were re-launched in 2005 to focus on growth and employment in Europe.

In December 2006 the seventh framework programme of the European Community for research and technological development for the period 2007 to 2013 (FP7) was established, to be applied from January 2007. FP7 will be implemented through specific programmes corresponding to the main themes of European research policy, with funding amounting to around EUR 51 billion.

In January 2000 the European Commission proposed the creation of a European Research Area (ERA), to create an 'internal market' in research, improve coordination of research activities and policies, and develop a European research policy. In April 2007 the European Commission adopted a Green paper titled 'The European Research Area: New Perspectives' [15]. This opens discussions on a number of issues, notably the mobility of researchers, developing research infrastructure and institutions; as well as improvements in the circulation and sharing of knowledge, research programmes, and global research cooperation. It aims to tackle underinvestment, and fragmentation. It is expected that this Green paper will be followed up by specific proposals in 2008.

STRUCTURAL PROFILE

Value added in the EU-27's research and development activities (NACE Division 73) was EUR 18.4 billion in 2004, making this the smallest of the three NACE divisions that compose real estate, renting and R&D (NACE Divisions 70, 71 and 73), with a 6.1 % share of real estate, renting and R&D value added. There were 390 000 persons employed in the EU-27's research and development activities in 2004, just over one tenth (11.1 %) of the real estate, renting and R&D workforce, a significantly higher share than that recorded for value added; the workforce was spread across 37 200 enterprises.

The United Kingdom and Germany had the largest research and development sectors in the EU-27 in 2004, generating 31.6 % and 24.5 % respectively of the EU-27's value added in 2004 (see Table 23.8). Only in a few Member States [16] did this sector's contribution to non-financial business economy value added approach or exceed 0.5 % in 2004, notably in the Netherlands (0.7 %), the United Kingdom (0.6 %) and Slovakia (0.5 %).

[15] COM(2007) 161.
[16] Ireland, Greece, Cyprus, Luxembourg and Malta not available.

COSTS, PRODUCTIVITY AND PROFITABILITY

One characteristic of its cost structure sets the research and development sector apart from many other activities in the non-financial business economy, and that is the very high share of personnel costs in total expenditure, likely to be in part a result of the relatively highly qualified labour force. In 2004 the share of personnel costs was 39.7 % in the EU-27, approximately 2.4 times as high as the non-financial business economy average, and the highest of all of the non-financial business economy NACE divisions [17], just ahead of both computer services and other business activities (NACE Divisions 72 and 74). This high share also reflects the high proportion of paid employees among all persons employed, a proportion which was 92.6 % in the EU-27's research and development sector in 2004, 6.4 percentage points above the non-financial business economy average.

Apparent labour productivity in the EU-27's research and development sector was EUR 46 900 per person employed in 2004, slightly lower than average personnel costs (EUR 47 100 per employee). The higher average personnel costs resulted in a wage adjusted labour productivity ratio below 100 %, which at 99.0 % was the lowest ratio among the non-financial business economy NACE divisions [18] in 2004. This ratio was particularly low in Latvia (64.2 %) and Sweden (69.1 %).

[17] NACE Divisions 10, 12 and 13, not available.
[18] NACE Divisions 10, 12 to 14, 23 and 62, not available.

Table 23.8

Research and development (NACE Division 73)
Structural profile: ranking of top five Member States, 2004

Rank	Share of EU-27 value added (%) (1)	Share of EU-27 employment (%) (1)	Value added specialisation ratio (EU-27=100) (2)	Employment specialisation ratio (EU-27=100) (2)
1	United Kingdom (31.6)	United Kingdom (25.9)	Netherlands (185.2)	Netherlands (244.9)
2	Germany (24.5)	Germany (22.5)	United Kingdom (166.9)	Slovakia (218.5)
3	France (12.4)	Netherlands (9.0)	Slovakia (136.1)	Romania (194.2)
4	Netherlands (8.5)	France (9.0)	Romania (118.5)	United Kingdom (180.0)
5	Italy (5.5)	Italy (6.7)	Germany (117.1)	Latvia (153.0)

(1) Greece, Cyprus, Luxembourg and Malta, not available.
(2) Ireland, Greece, Cyprus, Luxembourg and Malta, not available.
Source: Eurostat (SBS)

Table 23.9

Real estate activities (NACE Division 70)
Main indicators, 2004

	EU-27 (1)	BE	BG	CZ	DK	DE	EE	IE	EL	ES	FR	IT	CY	LV	LT
No. of enterprises (thousands)	897.8	11.1	3.7	32.7	21.1	175.6	2.9	5.4	:	121.0	97.4	164.4	:	9.4	2.0
Turnover (EUR million)	460 000	7 573	216	2 997	10 375	91 711	672	4 822	:	80 051	85 812	33 647	:	557	450
Production (EUR million)	432 000	6 837	231	3 137	13 301	83 941	603	4 034	:	54 855	82 253	40 608	:	549	511
Value added (EUR million)	220 000	3 100	89	1 141	10 287	55 691	367	3 151	:	26 407	31 895	12 864	:	227	210
Gross operating surplus (EUR million)	170 000	2 477	60	822	9 083	47 239	308	2 799	:	20 839	21 966	11 420	:	148	146
Purchases of goods & services (EUR million)	290 000	4 615	164	2 008	5 833	39 307	498	3 051	:	81 775	51 416	26 450	:	347	314
Personnel costs (EUR million)	48 300	623	29	318	1 204	8 452	60	352	:	5 567	9 928	1 444	:	79	64
Investment in tangible goods (EUR million)	137 000	1 804	187	1 458	13 229	18 903	420	1 526	:	15 178	26 615	8 003	:	341	294
Employment (thousands)	2 500	28	14	50	53	383	12	18	:	315	326	259	:	30	17
Apparent labour prod. (EUR thousand)	88.0	110.4	6.3	23.0	192.4	145.4	31.9	174.8	:	83.9	98.0	49.6	:	7.5	12.7
Average personnel costs (EUR thousand)	28.1	35.8	2.7	9.1	29.5	35.9	5.8	37.7	:	24.8	39.0	31.2	:	3.4	4.0
Wage adjusted labour productivity (%)	315.0	308.3	236.6	252.6	651.4	404.7	554.5	464.3	:	337.7	251.1	159.1	:	218.0	319.6
Gross operating rate (%)	37.0	32.7	27.9	27.4	87.5	51.5	45.8	58.0	:	26.0	25.6	33.9	:	26.6	32.4
Investment / employment (EUR thousand)	55.0	64.2	13.3	29.3	247.4	49.3	36.5	84.7	:	48.2	81.8	30.9	:	11.2	17.8

	LU (2)	HU	MT	NL	AT	PL	PT	RO	SI	SK	FI	SE	UK	NO
No. of enterprises (thousands)	2.3	23.2	:	12.6	10.2	27.2	15.5	8.5	1.3	1.8	10.8	38.4	92.5	34.4
Turnover (EUR million)	:	4 868	:	23 812	9 715	7 869	4 375	601	406	582	5 725	22 501	60 931	11 672
Production (EUR million)	:	2 583	:	23 155	8 322	7 847	3 957	729	365	524	5 766	23 115	63 870	11 622
Value added (EUR million)	:	1 237	:	11 432	4 871	3 035	1 169	262	156	217	2 923	11 110	37 416	5 788
Gross operating surplus (EUR million)	:	873	:	8 634	3 851	2 074	751	191	104	127	2 226	8 728	26 174	4 850
Purchases of goods & services (EUR million)	:	3 670	:	12 798	5 398	4 116	3 741	352	283	361	2 965	12 153	25 055	5 744
Personnel costs (EUR million)	:	364	:	2 798	1 020	961	418	71	52	90	698	2 382	11 243	938
Investment in tangible goods (EUR million)	:	1 241	:	5 239	7 239	1 271	630	552	7	137	2 042	10 697	19 375	4 819
Employment (thousands)	:	64	:	75	38	154	37	31	4	14	22	68	463	24
Apparent labour prod. (EUR thousand)	:	19.3	:	153.3	127.3	19.7	31.8	8.4	43.2	15.7	133.6	162.2	80.9	238.9
Average personnel costs (EUR thousand)	:	7.1	:	41.7	32.5	7.5	15.1	2.4	17.1	6.7	35.1	43.4	30.9	46.7
Wage adjusted labour productivity (%)	:	274.1	:	367.8	392.0	262.9	210.4	356.1	252.3	233.2	380.2	373.3	261.8	511.9
Gross operating rate (%)	:	17.9	:	36.3	39.6	26.4	17.2	31.8	25.7	21.8	38.9	38.8	43.0	41.6
Investment / employment (EUR thousand)	:	19.4	:	70.3	189.2	8.2	17.2	17.8	2.1	9.9	93.3	156.2	41.9	198.9

(1) Rounded estimate based on non-confidential data, except for number of enterprises. (2) 2003.
Source: Eurostat (SBS)

Table 23.10

Renting and leasing (NACE Division 71)
Main indicators, 2004

	EU-27	BE	BG	CZ	DK	DE	EE	IE	EL	ES	FR	IT	CY	LV	LT
No. of enterprises (thousands)	137.0	2.9	0.6	4.3	2.4	14.5	0.4	1.9	:	22.0	26.9	14.7	0.4	0.8	0.4
Turnover (EUR million)	126 310	4 570	68	494	2 071	26 421	101	1 694	:	9 695	22 533	7 886	70	52	57
Production (EUR million)	117 295	4 459	64	431	1 582	24 366	95	898	:	8 390	21 833	7 824	67	46	54
Value added (EUR million)	65 498	2 104	20	213	866	16 973	45	615	:	4 745	10 799	2 735	42	26	19
Gross operating surplus (EUR million)	51 020	1 790	17	165	632	15 005	35	414	:	3 327	7 929	2 120	27	19	12
Purchases of goods & services (EUR million)	59 602	2 415	51	297	1 261	9 918	58	1 101	:	4 953	13 227	4 879	27	28	40
Personnel costs (EUR million)	14 478	314	3	49	234	1 968	11	201	:	1 419	2 871	615	14	7	6
Investment in tangible goods (EUR million)	61 488	2 877	21	253	1 050	12 774	31	329	:	5 807	11 903	3 652	12	43	17
Employment (thousands)	598	10	2	7	8	80	1	10	:	79	87	36	1	2	2
Apparent labour prod. (EUR thousand)	109.5	207.0	9.3	32.0	102.9	211.6	33.3	60.8	:	59.9	124.7	74.9	40.9	11.2	11.0
Average personnel costs (EUR thousand)	28.9	42.6	1.7	11.3	32.0	29.8	8.9	24.2	:	23.2	35.0	31.9	17.4	4.0	4.2
Wage adjusted labour productivity (%)	378.4	486.2	543.1	282.4	322.1	711.1	372.4	251.2	:	258.7	356.4	235.1	235.0	277.3	264.7
Gross operating rate (%)	40.4	39.2	24.9	33.4	30.5	56.8	34.7	24.4	:	34.3	35.2	26.9	39.0	35.9	21.4
Investment / employment (EUR thousand)	102.8	283.1	9.9	38.0	124.7	159.2	22.8	32.5	:	73.3	137.4	100.1	12.3	18.9	10.3

	LU (1)	HU	MT	NL	AT	PL	PT	RO	SI	SK	FI	SE	UK	NO
No. of enterprises (thousands)	0.3	3.4	:	4.7	2.0	4.1	2.5	1.1	0.3	0.3	1.1	5.5	16.1	2.6
Turnover (EUR million)	416	590	:	7 520	4 518	773	1 345	165	31	166	831	2 539	30 844	1 434
Production (EUR million)	333	439	:	7 196	3 299	781	1 272	162	25	153	826	2 397	29 723	1 373
Value added (EUR million)	195	319	:	3 570	2 338	393	737	98	10	66	363	1 226	16 536	556
Gross operating surplus (EUR million)	142	272	:	2 870	2 058	329	573	87	6	47	245	847	11 678	339
Purchases of goods & services (EUR million)	216	268	:	1 367	2 263	429	642	68	21	99	491	1 363	13 910	883
Personnel costs (EUR million)	52	47	:	700	280	65	163	11	4	20	118	379	4 857	217
Investment in tangible goods (EUR million)	102	304	:	3 415	4 676	185	1 214	26	0	43	328	792	11 317	509
Employment (thousands)	1	8	:	26	9	12	11	4	1	2	4	12	176	6
Apparent labour prod. (EUR thousand)	230.0	41.4	:	137.0	265.1	34.0	68.4	27.0	20.2	28.4	96.6	103.8	93.8	91.4
Average personnel costs (EUR thousand)	70.0	8.3	:	31.9	38.2	9.3	16.6	3.1	13.5	9.0	33.5	38.4	29.9	41.0
Wage adjusted labour productivity (%)	328.5	497.4	:	430.1	694.8	364.4	412.4	865.6	149.1	313.9	288.1	270.4	313.2	222.8
Gross operating rate (%)	34.3	46.1	:	38.2	45.6	42.5	42.6	52.6	20.1	28.1	29.4	33.3	37.9	23.6
Investment / employment (EUR thousand)	119.9	39.5	:	131.1	530.3	16.0	112.7	7.1	0.0	18.4	87.5	67.1	64.2	83.6

(1) 2003.
Source: Eurostat (SBS)

Table 23.11

Research and development (NACE Division 73)
Main indicators, 2004

	EU-27 (1)	BE	BG	CZ	DK	DE	EE	IE	EL	ES	FR	IT	CY	LV	LT
No. of enterprises (thousands)	37.2	0.2	0.1	0.5	0.3	4.2	0.0	0.3	:	1.5	2.9	10.8	:	0.1	0.1
Turnover (EUR million)	37 000	918	5	168	615	6 412	7	266	:	1 036	6 189	1 837	:	17	12
Production (EUR million)	39 000	935	6	168	719	6 520	7	237	:	977	5 709	2 124	:	16	11
Value added (EUR million)	18 400	486	2	69	250	4 513	3	151	:	736	2 283	1 021	:	7	5
Gross operating surplus (EUR million)	1 300	112	1	1	-67	686	1	71	:	113	261	358	:	-4	2
Purchases of goods & services (EUR million)	22 500	484	3	104	476	3 953	4	114	:	706	4 704	1 041	:	8	7
Personnel costs (EUR million)	17 000	373	1	68	317	3 827	3	80	:	623	2 022	663	:	12	3
Investment in tangible goods (EUR million)	3 370	44	0	18	64	871	0	25	:	184	521	157	:	4	0
Employment (thousands)	390	5	0	6	5	88	0	2	:	18	35	26	:	3	0
Apparent labour prod. (EUR thousand)	46.9	98.1	5.4	11.3	48.8	51.4	14.1	73.1	:	40.1	65.0	39.3	:	2.6	9.5
Average personnel costs (EUR thousand)	47.1	78.2	3.8	12.1	61.9	46.3	11.7	44.6	:	36.5	57.6	47.0	:	4.1	6.4
Wage adjusted labour productivity (%)	99.0	125.4	142.5	93.2	78.8	111.0	121.0	163.7	:	109.9	112.7	83.6	:	64.2	149.9
Gross operating rate (%)	3.4	12.2	15.9	0.4	-10.9	10.7	10.8	26.7	:	10.9	4.2	19.5	:	-24.7	14.6
Investment / employment (EUR thousand)	8.6	8.9	0.8	2.9	12.4	9.9	1.3	12.0	:	10.0	14.8	6.0	:	1.3	0.6

	LU (2)	HU	MT	NL	AT	PL	PT	RO	SI	SK	FI	SE	UK	NO
No. of enterprises (thousands)	0.0	2.7	:	2.0	0.5	0.7	0.1	0.4	0.4	0.1	0.3	2.8	2.9	0.4
Turnover (EUR million)	:	214	:	2 795	489	149	11	173	112	159	405	1 317	13 156	647
Production (EUR million)	:	166	:	2 666	408	143	9	202	102	154	376	1 376	16 090	635
Value added (EUR million)	:	75	:	1 564	281	66	7	92	48	65	185	517	5 811	437
Gross operating surplus (EUR million)	:	24	:	178	46	32	1	15	8	12	-7	-118	-459	-5
Purchases of goods & services (EUR million)	:	136	:	1 352	409	68	10	113	64	93	240	956	7 262	346
Personnel costs (EUR million)	:	51	:	1 386	236	34	6	78	40	53	192	634	6 270	442
Investment in tangible goods (EUR million)	:	15	:	118	95	6	1	32	3	27	16	83	936	26
Employment (thousands)	:	6	:	35	5	3	0	24	2	6	4	11	101	7
Apparent labour prod. (EUR thousand)	:	13.0	:	44.4	55.6	19.6	28.0	3.8	27.3	10.6	47.7	45.5	57.5	58.6
Average personnel costs (EUR thousand)	:	12.6	:	40.2	50.0	13.5	26.4	3.5	24.1	8.7	50.8	65.8	63.0	59.7
Wage adjusted labour productivity (%)	:	102.6	:	110.3	111.1	144.6	105.8	109.2	113.1	121.8	94.0	69.1	91.3	98.2
Gross operating rate (%)	:	11.3	:	6.4	9.3	21.5	12.3	8.4	7.5	7.4	-1.7	-8.9	-3.5	-0.8
Investment / employment (EUR thousand)	:	2.7	:	3.3	18.7	1.8	4.5	1.3	1.8	4.3	4.2	7.3	9.3	3.4

(1) Rounded estimate based on non-confidential data, except for number of enterprises. (2) 2003.
Source: Eurostat (SBS)

Financial services

Financial services provide instruments to businesses and households in the form of products that are essentially savings or loans, or products to transfer and pool risk. Changes in financing techniques have increased the possibilities open to business to fund investment, while consumers have a wider array of choices for credit, savings and payment methods.

There has been considerable EU legislative activity in the sphere of financial services centred upon the creation of an internal market for financial services. This work has been conducted through the financial services action plan (FSAP), which was published by the European Commission in 1999 and the legislative phase completed in 2006.

The absence of cross-border consolidation within the financial services sector has drawn attention and in September 2006 the European Commission adopted a proposal for a directive of the European Parliament and Council [1] that would tighten the procedures that Member States' supervisory authorities have to follow when assessing proposed mergers and acquisitions in banking, insurance and securities activities; the Council adopted the proposal in June 2007. The proposed directive aims to clarify the criteria against which supervisors should assess possible mergers and acquisitions in order to improve clarity and transparency in supervisory assessment and help to ensure a consistent handling of mergers and acquisitions requests across the EU.

---

[1] COM(2006) 507.

In May 2007 the European Commission published a Green paper on retail finance [2] outlining future policy on retail financial services (products provided to individual consumers), essentially to address issues relating to market integration and competition, focusing on good regulation, consumer protection and education. This builds on the 2005 White paper on financial services 2005-2010, and the sector inquiries into retail banking and business insurance (see Subchapters 24.1 and 24.2).

STRUCTURAL PROFILE

Note that within the other sectoral chapters of this publication, the benchmark used for comparison is the non-financial business economy, which by definition excludes the activities that are covered in this chapter. To show the relative importance of financial services within the business economy as a whole, sources other than structural business statistics are used, namely national accounts and the labour force survey.

According to national accounts, the contribution of financial services (NACE Section J) to employment within the business economy (NACE Sections C to K) was around 4.5 % in the EU [3] in 2004, and the level of employment was in excess of 5.8 million persons. According to results from the Labour Force Survey for 2006 just over three fifths (62.7 %) of the persons employed in financial services were employed in financial intermediation activities

---

[2] COM(2007) 226.
[3] EU-27 average, 2004; excluding Bulgaria, Malta and Romania.

Financial services encompass financial intermediation as offered by credit institutions, financial leasing and other credit granting enterprises, and financial intermediaries such as securities and derivatives dealers (all included within NACE Division 65), insurance and pension funding services (NACE Division 66), as well as activities providing financial auxiliary services, such as the administration of financial markets, security brokering, fund management and the various activities of brokers and agents for financial products (NACE Division 67).

NACE
65: Financial intermediation, except insurance and pension funding;
65.1: monetary intermediation;
65.2: other financial intermediation;
66: insurance and pension funding, except compulsory social security;
67: activities auxiliary to financial intermediation;
67.1: activities auxiliary to financial intermediation, except insurance and pension funding
67.2: activities auxiliary to insurance and pension funding.

other than insurance and pension funding (NACE Division 65), almost one fifth (19.1 %) in insurance and pension funding activities (NACE Division 66), while the remainder (18.2 %) were employed in activities auxiliary to financial intermediation (NACE Division 67).

Table 24.1

Financial intermediation (NACE Section J)
Structural profile, EU-27, 2005

	Value added (EUR million)	Share of business economy value added (%)	Number of persons employed (thousands) (1)	Share of business economy employment (%) (1)
Financial intermediation	550 947	7.5	5 815	4.5

(1) 2004; EU-27, excluding Bulgaria, Malta and Romania.
Source: Eurostat (Economy and finance)

Figure 24.1

Financial intermediation (NACE Section J)
Share of value added and employment in the business economy
(NACE Sections C to K), EU-27 (%)

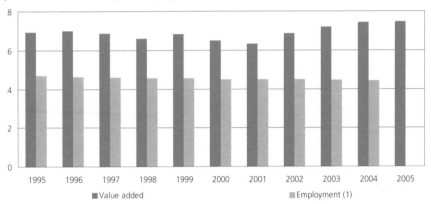

(1) EU average based on available data, excluding Bulgaria, Malta, Portugal and Romania; 2005, not available.
Source: Eurostat (Economy and finance)

Figure 24.2

Financial intermediation (NACE Section J)
Share of value added and employment in the business economy
(NACE Sections C to K), 2005 (%)

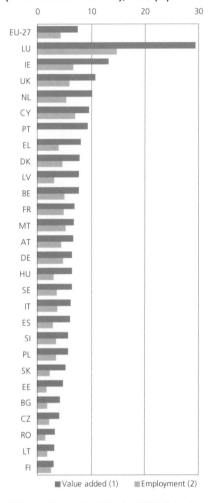

(1) Greece, Portugal and Sweden, 2004; Bulgaria, 2000.
(2) EU average based on available data for 2005; Greece and Sweden, 2004; Romania, 2002; Bulgaria and Malta, 2000; Portugal, not available.
Source: Eurostat (Economy and finance)

Financial services generated EUR 550.9 billion of value added in 2005 according to national accounts: Figure 24.1 shows how this sector's contribution to business economy value added developed from 1995, falling from a high of 7.0 % in 1996 to a low of 6.3 % in 2001, before increasing its share in four consecutive years to 7.5 % by 2005.

In value added terms, the largest Member State in the financial services sector was the United Kingdom, which generated one quarter (24.9 %) of the EU-27's value added in 2005, ahead of Germany (18.2 %). The contribution of this sector to value added within the business economy in 2005 was particularly high in Luxembourg (29.4 %), and this sector also contributed more than 10 % of business economy value added in Ireland, the United Kingdom and the Netherlands. Its contribution was lowest in Finland, Lithuania and Romania where the financial services sector accounted for just over 3 % of value added (see Figure 24.2). The contribution of financial services to the business economy was greater in value added terms than in employment terms in every Member State.

Figure 24.3
Financial intermediation (NACE Section J)
Labour force characteristics, EU-27, 2006

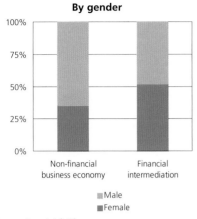

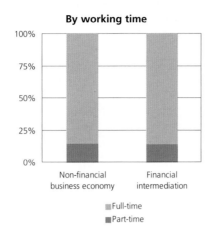

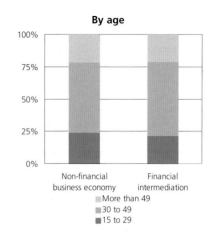

Source: Eurostat (LFS)

EMPLOYMENT CHARACTERISTICS

Only in terms of the gender breakdown did the characteristics of the labour force in this sector differ significantly from those displayed by the non-financial business economy (NACE Sections C to I and K) - see Figure 24.3. The proportion of the financial services sector's workforce that was female was 51.9 %, well above the 35.0 % share recorded for the non-financial business economy. In all Member States [4] the female proportion of the financial services workforce was above the non-financial business economy average. In three fifths of the Member States more than half of the financial services workforce was female; the share of women in the financial services workforce rose to its highest level in Poland (72.0 %).

Unlike other sectors where female employment was high (such as retail trade or hotels and restaurants), the rate of full-time employment in the EU-27's financial services sector was also relatively high in 2006, as 85.9 % of those employed worked on a full-time basis, almost the same as the 85.6 % average for the non-financial business economy. Among the three subsectors covered in this chapter the highest full-time employment rate was recorded for financial intermediation activities other than insurance and pension funding (87.0 %), whereas the proportion of persons working full-time was just below 85 % in the other two subsectors.

The age structure of the EU-27's workforce in financial services displayed a relatively low proportion of younger workers (less than 30 years of age) compensated by a slightly larger share of workers aged between 30 and 49. In 2006 some 21.7 % of the workforce was aged less than 30, which was 2.5 percentage points lower than the non-financial business economy average, while 57.1 % were aged between 30 and 49, 2.9 percentage points above the non-financial business economy average. In all three financial services' subsectors the proportion of workers aged less than 30 was below the non-financial business economy average, but it was particularly low in insurance and pension funding activities at 18.7 %.

[4] Luxembourg, 2005; Estonia, 2004.

24.1: FINANCIAL INTERMEDIATION

The activities covered by this subchapter include financial intermediation activities classified within NACE Division 65, whether they are monetary (NACE Group 65.1) or not (NACE Group 65.2); in particular it includes credit institutions and financial leasing.

Table 24.2

Proportion of individuals (aged 16 to 74) who in the three months prior to the survey used the Internet for financial services (Internet banking, share purchasing) (%)

	Share of all individuals			Share of individuals who used the Internet in the 3 months prior to the survey		
	2004	2005	2006	2004	2005	2006
EU-27	:	:	21	:	:	40
EU-25	18	19	22	36	38	41
BE	:	23	28	:	41	46
BG	1	:	1	4	:	6
CZ	5	5	10	15	16	22
DK	45	49	57	59	63	69
DE	26	:	32	43	:	46
EE	35	45	48	69	75	79
IE	10	13	21	31	34	40
EL	1	1	2	7	6	9
ES	12	14	15	30	31	32
FR	:	:	18	:	:	39
IT	:	8	9	:	23	25
CY	4	6	6	13	18	18
LV	12	16	22	35	37	44
LT	7	10	15	23	30	35
LU	35	37	41	53	54	58
HU	3	6	8	10	16	18
MT	:	:	:	:	:	:
NL	:	50	59	:	63	73
AT	18	22	27	35	40	44
PL	4	6	9	14	17	23
PT	8	8	10	26	26	27
RO	0	:	1	3	:	3
SI	9	12	16	23	25	32
SK	10	10	13	22	20	25
FI	50	56	63	72	77	81
SE	40	51	57	49	62	66
UK	22	27	28	36	41	42
MK	1	:	0	5	:	1
TR	2	2	:	16	13	:
IS	54	61	67	65	71	76
NO	55	62	67	73	77	82

Source: Eurostat (Information society statistics)

Figure 24.4

Breakdown of number of credit institutions by balance sheet total, EU average, 2005 (%) (1)

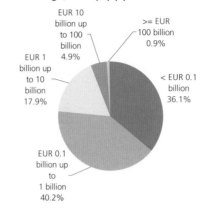

(1) EU average based on available data for 2005; Ireland, Italy, Portugal, 2004; Ireland and Latvia, NACE Class 65.12 only; Luxembourg NACE Class 65.22 only; excluding Spain, Cyprus, Malta and Slovakia.
Source: Eurostat (SBS)

The capital requirements directive for credit institutions and investment firms [5] has been applied since the start of 2007. This introduced a new supervisory framework in the EU reflecting the Basel II rules (a global regulatory framework designed to encourage best practice in risk management and minimum capital requirements in the banking sector) on capital measurement and capital standards.

In December 2005 the European Commission adopted a proposal [6] for a directive of the European Parliament and Council for a new legal framework for payments, to create the Single Payments Area, with the objectives to make electronic payments quicker and easier, to guarantee fair and open access to payments markets, and to increase and standardise consumer protection. The proposal was adopted by the European Parliament in April 2007.

In October 2005 the European Commission adopted a second revised proposal [7] for a directive of the European Parliament and Council on consumer credit, taking into account many of the comments from the European Parliament on the original and first revised proposals. The revised proposal covers consumer credit (not mortgages) of up to EUR 50 000 and aims to introduce a harmonised method for calculating the cost of credit and to establish a set of rights for all borrowers. Agreement on this proposal was reached by the Council in May 2007.

---

[5] Directive 2006/49/EC.
[6] COM(2005) 603.
[7] COM(2005) 483.

Figure 24.5

Breakdown of number of credit institutions by legal status, EU (%) (1)

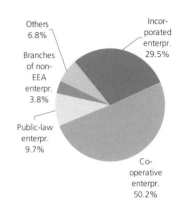

(1) EU average based on available data for 2005; Ireland, Italy, Portugal, 2004; Ireland and Latvia, NACE Class 65.12 only; Luxembourg NACE Class 65.22 only; excluding Spain, Cyprus, Hungary, Malta and Slovakia.
Source: Eurostat (SBS)

In June 2006 the European Commission announced the creation of an expert group to further examine obstacles to a single European mortgage funding market, and this group delivered its final report in December 2006, concluding that mortgage funding markets are already relatively competitive and efficient, although national or EU measures could further improve their operation. A second group created in 2006, the Mortgage Credit Industry and Consumer Dialogue, was established to explore the extent to which consumer and mortgage funding professionals could agree on certain consumer protection provisions, namely information, advice, early repayment, and a standard for the calculation of annual percentage rates (APRs). Building on the work of both groups and the 2005 Green paper, at the time of writing the European Commission is expected to publish a White paper on mortgage credit later in 2007.

Retail banking was also chosen as part of a sector inquiry launched in June 2005 by the European Commission into competition in financial services. The final report was published in January 2007 and noted fragmentation and barriers concerning current accounts and related services and also payment cards.

One particular characteristic of the development of the Internet has been the use of e-banking. Table 24.2 shows results from Eurostat's information society statistics indicating the use of the Internet for financial services, notably e-banking and share purchasing. In 2006 more than one fifth (21 %) of all persons (aged 16 to 74) in the EU-27 used the Internet for financial services, a share that was twice as high (40 %) when limited to Internet users. In all Member States with data available (see Table 24.2 for availability), the proportion of persons using the Internet for financial services grew during the years studied.

EMPLOYMENT IN FINANCIAL INTERMEDIATION
According to Labour Force Survey data, the number of persons employed in the EU-27's sector for financial intermediation excluding insurance and pension funding (NACE Division 65) was 3.9 million in 2006. This equated to 62.7 % of those employed in the financial services (NACE Section J) sector as a whole. Germany and the United Kingdom dominated this sector in employment terms, each with just under one fifth of the EU-27's workforce. In employment terms, the most specialised Member State [8] in this sector was by far Luxembourg where 14.8 % (2005) of those employed within the business economy were working in financial intermediation excluding insurance and pension funding. The next highest share was 6.0 % in Cyprus, while the lowest shares were 1.1 % in Lithuania, 1.2 % in Romania and 1.3 % in Estonia (2004).

CREDIT INSTITUTIONS
Credit institutions are defined in the first indent of Article 1 of Council directive 77/780/EEC: 'credit institution means an undertaking whose business is to receive deposits or other repayable funds from the public and to grant credits for its own account'. In terms of the NACE Rev. 1.1 classification, credit institutions mainly correspond to NACE Class 65.12 (other monetary intermediation). However, due to the different implementation of the EU directives into national law, in some Member States credit institutions might also comprise a number of enterprises whose main activity should be classified under NACE Class 65.22 (other credit granting).

[8] Luxembourg, 2005; Estonia, 2004.

Table 24.3 ————————————————————

Credit institutions network access, 2005 (units)

	Number of local units	Number of ATMs	Ratio of ATMs to local units
BE (1)	3 284	7 256	2.2
BG	1 706	4 631	2.7
CZ	1 164	2 504	2.2
DK	2 106	3 001	1.4
DE	46 158	53 361	1.2
EE	244	841	3.4
IE (2) (3)	909	2 648	2.9
EL	3 543	6 230	1.8
ES	:	:	:
FR	26 685	27 986	1.0
IT (2)	30 951	36 774	1.2
CY (3) (4)	951	470	0.5
LV (3)	371	877	2.4
LT	830	1 056	1.3
LU (5)	500	379	0.8
HU	3 162	3 531	1.1
MT	:	:	:
NL	4 100	7 889	1.9
AT	5 112	3 065	0.6
PL	9 249	8 150	0.9
PT (1) (2)	5 522	12 627	2.3
RO	3 691	4 415	1.2
SI	755	1 490	2.0
SK	:	:	:
FI	1 807	4 713	2.6
SE	2 022	2 851	1.4
UK	13 694	32 029	2.3

(1) Provisional for ATMs.
(2) 2004.
(3) NACE Class 65.12 only.
(4) Provisional.
(5) NACE Class 65.22 only; 2004 for ATMs.
Source: Eurostat (SBS)

An analysis of the number of credit institutions according to the size of their balance sheets in 2005 in the Member States with data available indicates that on average less than 1 % had a balance sheet total that was EUR 100 billion or more, while more than three quarters of credit institutions reported a balance sheet total of less than EUR 1 billion - see Figure 24.4.

An analysis of the legal status of credit institutions in 2005 shows that the most common legal form was a co-operative enterprise (50.2 % of all credit institutions), followed by incorporated enterprises (29.5 %) - see Figure 24.5 for country coverage.

Access to the retail banking network has changed, with a move away from services provided in branches to services provided through automatic teller machines (ATMs), phone and Internet banking. Table 24.3 indicates that there were well in excess of 230 000 ATMs in the EU-27 by 2005, and that in only four of the 24 Member States with data available were there less ATMs than local units. Estonia, Ireland (2004) and Bulgaria reported the highest ratios of ATMs to local units, while the lowest ratios were in Cyprus and Austria.

Looking at the output of credit institutions, the United Kingdom and Germany recorded the highest value added in 2005, with EUR 90.7 billion and EUR 86.4 billion respectively - see Table 24.4.

Table 24.5 shows clearly the importance of the United Kingdom in the credit institutions sector: for example, capital and reserves in British credit institutions were valued at EUR 511.0 billion in 2005, whereas capital and reserves in the next largest Member States, namely Italy (2004), Germany and France ranged between EUR 200 billion and EUR 300 billion. The combined net income (income less payments) of interest and commissions was particularly low relative to equity (capital and reserves) in Sweden, Luxembourg, the Netherlands, Finland and the United Kingdom (below 18 %), whereas it was highest in Greece, Romania, Hungary, Bulgaria and the Czech Republic (45 % or more). In all Member States net income from interest (essentially income from lending) was higher than net income from commissions (fee based business) except in Luxembourg where these values were the same; Greece and Cyprus reported the highest ratios of net interest to net commissions. For the Member States shown in Table 24.5 the total value of loans to customers was around one fifth higher than the value of amounts owed to customers. By far the highest ratios of loans to amounts owed were recorded in Denmark and Sweden, while the situation was reversed in Luxembourg, the Czech Republic and Cyprus, where amounts owed were around 50 % or more higher than loans.

Table 24.4 _____

Credit institutions

Structural profile: ranking of top five Member States, 2005 (1)

Rank	Value added (EUR million)	Employment (units) (2)
1	United Kingdom (90 667)	Germany (691 724)
2	Germany (86 379)	United Kingdom (482 888)
3	France (57 711)	France (387 109)
4	Italy (47 138)	Italy (337 286)
5	Netherlands (20 601)	Poland (153 274)

(1) Belgium and Cyprus, provisional; Ireland, Italy, Portugal, 2004; Ireland, Cyprus and Latvia, NACE Class 65.12 only; Luxembourg, NACE Class 65.22 only; Spain, Malta and Slovakia, not available.
(2) Estonia, Luxembourg and Sweden, also not available.
Source: Eurostat (SBS)

Table 24.5 _____

Credit institutions

Selected net income and balance sheet items, 2005 (EUR million)

	Net income		Balance sheet items		
	Net interest and similar income	Net commissions	Loans and advances to customers	Amounts owed to customers	Total of capital and reserves
BE	8 085	2 510	334 851	448 182	32 599
BG	696	222	9 397	11 680	1 973
CZ	2 154	1 070	39 884	61 295	7 187
DK	6 732	2 362	410 576	158 807	39 374
DE	66 689	24 989	3 246 069	2 715 620	234 589
EE	192	101	8 025	6 092	1 120
IE (1) (2)	7 516	3 029	240 007	174 605	43 987
EL	6 653	1 346	147 764	185 557	15 993
ES	:	:	:	:	:
FR	31 329	19 034	1 487 491	1 177 918	224 536
IT (1)	32 925	18 013	1 208 200	774 692	249 691
CY (2) (3)	937	278	26 669	39 958	3 824
LV (2)	356	167	9 995	8 906	1 352
LT	231	116	7 584	7 367	941
LU (4)	3 203	3 204	144 883	239 911	43 129
HU	2 856	919	47 204	41 587	7 853
MT	:	:	:	:	:
NL	16 374	5 129	945 775	614 921	126 504
AT	6 999	3 505	326 878	209 880	49 640
PL	4 614	1 875	76 002	98 868	16 183
PT (1)	4 883	1 819	194 798	145 577	29 460
RO	1 307	651	16 711	21 981	4 000
SI	593	284	16 002	16 112	2 663
SK	:	:	:	:	:
FI	2 856	879	121 158	84 561	21 363
SE	5 825	2 595	355 975	148 281	61 891
UK	55 056	33 321	7 202 488	7 677 160	510 962

(1) 2004.
(2) NACE Class 65.12 only.
(3) Provisional.
(4) NACE Class 65.22 only.
Source: Eurostat (SBS)

PENSION FUNDS

Official statistics on autonomous pension funds are scarce. The information presented in Table 24.10 indicates that Hungary, the Netherlands and the United Kingdom were among the Member States where this activity was most important, and Ireland (no recent data available) also appears to be particularly specialised in this activity.

Table 24.10 _____

Main indicators for autonomous pension funds, 2004 (EUR million) (1)

	Number of active members (thousands)	Pension contributions receivable from members	Pension contributions receivable from employers	Investment income	Total expenditure on pensions	Investments
BE	:	:	:	:	:	:
BG	:	:	:	:	:	:
CZ	2 714	444	96	120	244	2 477
DK	19	12	99	369	216	5 117
DE	:	:	:	:	:	:
EE	353	17	:	4	0	64
IE	724	:	:	:	:	:
EL	:	:	:	:	:	:
ES	8 468	5 246	1 607	2 300	6 100	40 369
FR	:	:	:	:	:	:
IT	2 127	1 255	1 395	:	2 213	22 249
CY	:	:	:	:	:	:
LV	39	1	8	2	1	40
LT	553	40	0	1	0	40
LU	:	:	:	:	:	:
HU	1 249	132	51 740	63 619	29 101	352 788
MT	:	:	:	:	:	:
NL	14 952	4 404	17 925	42 337	14 494	362 758
AT	447	72	466	594	312	6 858
PL	53	2	27	:	1	63
PT	379	176	1 198	1 094	736	11 016
RO	:	:	:	:	:	:
SI	161	0	0	15	0	218
SK	604	56	48	13	29	265
FI	137	3	94	277	263	3 419
SE	:	:	:	694	:	9 349
UK	:	7 927	37 381	:	53 127	1 095 123
IS	228	191	346	1 352	351	10 113
CH	4 060	9 362	12 561	12 985	29 481	311 741

(1) Czech Republic, Estonia, Ireland, Italy, Poland, Portugal, Slovakia and Sweden, 2003.
Source: Eurostat (SBS)

24.3: FINANCIAL AUXILIARIES

Activities auxiliary to financial intermediation have a supporting function in capital markets, performing a complementary role to banking and insurance activities. The activities covered in this subchapter are classified under NACE Division 67, covering the provision of services involved in or closely related to financial intermediation, but not themselves involving financial intermediation. Activities included are the administration of financial markets, securities and mortgage broking, and fund management (NACE Group 67.1), and activities of insurance brokers and agents (NACE Group 67.2).

EMPLOYMENT IN FINANCIAL AUXILIARIES

According to the results of the Labour Force Survey, employment in the EU-27's financial auxiliaries sector (NACE Division 67) covered 1.1 million persons in 2006. This sector was dominated by the United Kingdom and Germany, with workforces of 400 700 and 259 000 persons respectively, accounting for more than one third and more than one fifth of the EU-27's

workforce: Italy (12.3 %) was the only other Member State [12] with a double-digit share of the EU-27's financial auxiliaries employment. Although in the EU-27 as a whole this sector contributed 18.2 % of financial services (NACE Section J) employment, in most Member States this sector's contribution was less than 15 % and the relatively high EU-27 average was influenced by the dominance of the United Kingdom, Germany and Italy where this sector contributed 33.0 %, 20.1 % and 20.6 % of financial services employment respectively.

FUND MANAGEMENT

An investment fund is a financial investment vehicle that spreads risks by use of a portfolio, with investments spread across shares, bonds or property. Funds can be distinguished between open-ended funds and closed-ended ones, the latter having a fixed number of shares/units that are quoted on an exchange,

---

[12] Luxembourg, 2005; Denmark, 2004; Bulgaria, Estonia, Latvia, Lithuania, Malta and Portugal, not available.

and the former having an unlimited number of shares/units. A major step in the development of open-ended funds within Europe came with the introduction of Council directive 85/611/EEC of 20 December 1985 on the co-ordination of laws, regulations and administrative provisions relating to undertakings for collective investment in transferable securities (UCITS). Other funds are permitted within the EU, according to national regulations.

In November 2006 the European Commission adopted a White paper on investment funds [13], identifying measures designed to simplify the operating environment for investment funds, to create new opportunities for cross-border operators, and also identifying the need to give investors better tools to make informed decisions and to ensure that they receive objective and impartial assistance from fund distributors.

---

[13] COM(2006) 686.

Table 24.11

Total net assets of UCITS and non-UCITS, end 2006 (EUR billion)

	Total net assets	of which, UCITS
BE	127.9	120.5
CZ	5.5	5.5
DK	123.5	73.1
DE	1 013.4	271.6
IE	729.6	582.7
EL	24.8	23.9
ES	287.8	279.4
FR	1 491.8	1 343.4
IT	388.4	343.8
LU	1 844.9	1 661.6
HU	10.1	7.4
NL	101.9	82.5
AT	168.9	114.9
PL	25.8	22.2
PT	38.9	25.8
SK	3.1	3.0
FI	60.9	51.5
SE	140.8	137.8
UK	744.6	602.1
Total	**7 332.4**	**5 752.5**

Source: European Fund and Asset Management Association, Fact Book 2007

Figure 24.6

Net assets of the European investment funds industry, Europe (EUR billion) (1)

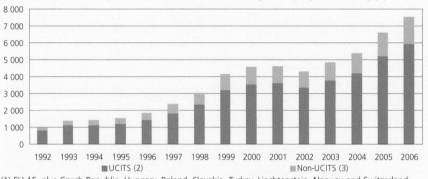

(1) EU-15, plus Czech Republic, Hungary, Poland, Slovakia, Turkey, Liechtenstein, Norway and Switzerland.
(2) Undertaking for collective investment in transferable securities: a collective investment fund that complies with Directive (85/611/EEC) of 20 October 1985.
(3) Non-UCITS regroups funds that are regulated in accordance with specific national requirements.
Source: European Fund and Asset Management Association, Fact Book 2007

Figure 24.7

Total net assets of UCITS, Europe (%) (1)

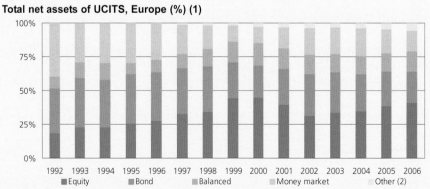

(1) EU-15 excluding Ireland, plus Czech Republic, Hungary, Poland, Slovakia, Turkey, Liechtenstein, Norway and Switzerland.
(2) Including funds of funds.
Source: European Fund and Asset Management Association, Fact Book 2007

Figure 24.6 shows the growth in net assets over more than a decade (from 1992 to 2006) for UCITS and non-UCITS funds among 23 European countries, according to EFAMA [14]. Together the two categories of assets recorded year on year growth during the whole of this period, except in 2002. Growth averaged 15.5 % per annum, which could be broken down as 16.6 % per annum for non-UCITS net assets and 15.2 % per annum for UCITS net assets. By 2006 the net assets managed in investment funds in the 23 European countries for which information are available were valued at EUR 7 552 billion, of which 78.7 % were UCITS.

Table 24.11 shows the same breakdown for 2006 for most of the Member States. The largest values of UCITS funds managed in the EU were in Luxembourg and France, with more than EUR 1 000 billion of UCITS net assets each; the relatively high value of UCITS assets managed in Ireland (EUR 583 billion) is also worth noting.

As well as the classification between open and closed-ended funds, a further distinction can be made between funds specialising in investments in equities, bonds and money markets, or balanced funds with a mix of these three types of investments. Figure 24.7 shows the change in the composition of UCITS assets, notably an increase in the importance of equity funds throughout the 1990s and their subsequent decline in 2001 and 2002 as stock market indices fell, followed by a more modest increase in their share in the four most recent years for which information is available.

EXCHANGES

In recent years European exchanges have undergone a period of consolidation, most notably with the creation of Euronext (exchanges in Amsterdam, Brussels, Lisbon, London and Paris) and OMX (which has exchanges in Copenhagen, Helsinki, Riga, Stockholm, Tallinn, Vilnius and Iceland), and this continued with the London stock exchange buying Borsa Italiana during the summer of 2007. However, this period of consolidation has extended to include trans-Atlantic consolidation, with the completion in April 2007 of the New York Stock Exchange's merger with Euronext and Nasdaq's offer in May 2007 for OMX.

---

[14] EFAMA (the European Fund and Asset Management Association), more information at: http://www.efama.org; data refer to the EU-15, the Czech Republic, Hungary, Poland, Slovakia, Turkey, Liechtenstein, Norway and Switzerland.

Table 24.12

Capitalisation (year end) and domestic equity trading, 2006 (EUR million)

Exchange		Market capital- isation	Electronic order book transactions	Negotiated deals	Total value of equity trading
Prague Stock Exchange	CZ	34 693	28 361	1 655	30 015
Deutsche Börse	DE	1 241 963	1 592 747	572 100	2 164 848
Irish Stock Exchange	IE	123 824	9 238	55 355	64 593
Athens Exchange	EL	157 941	68 034	17 020	85 054
Spanish Exchanges (BME)	ES	1 003 299	1 150 565	385 069	1 535 634
Borsa Italiana	IT	778 501	1 145 650	112 378	1 258 028
Cyprus Stock Exchange	CY	12 254	2 893	450	3 343
Luxembourg Stock Exchange	LU	60 290	187	:	187
Budapest Stock Exchange	HU	31 687	22 525	2 101	24 626
Malta Stock Exchange	MT	3 416	205	:	205
Euronext		2 812 261	2 375 475	672 112	3 047 587
Wiener Börse	AT	146 197	64 893	:	64 893
Warsaw Stock Exchange	PL	112 826	40 401	2 834	43 235
Bucharest Stock Exchange	RO	18 858	1 164	105	1 269
Ljubljana Stock Exchange	SI	11 513	801	650	1 452
Bratislava Stock Exchange	SK	4 214	33	37	70
OMX Nordic exchange (Copenhagen, Tallinn, Riga, Vilnius, Helsinki, Stockholm)		851 460	775 659	261 303	1 036 962
London Stock Exchange	UK	2 876 986	2 215 963	3 774 529	5 990 492
Total of available data		10 282 182	9 494 795	5 857 696	15 352 491

Source: Federation of European Securities Exchange

Table 24.13

Bond turnover, 2006 (EUR million)

Exchange		Electronic order book transactions	Negotiated deals	Total
Prague Stock Exchange	CZ	3	21 186	21 189
Deutsche Börse	DE	10	227 920	227 930
Irish Stock Exchange	IE	-	18 728	18 728
Athens Exchange	EL	5	0	5
Spanish Exchanges (BME)	ES	179 968	3 759 054	3 939 022
Borsa Italiana	IT	123 436	:	123 436
Cyprus Stock Exchange	CY	5	0	5
Luxembourg Stock Exchange	LU	1 292	-	1 292
Budapest Stock Exchange	HU	1 309	7	1 315
Malta Stock Exchange	MT	170	:	170
Euronext		12 336	280 407	292 743
Wiener Börse	AT	494	-	494
Warsaw Stock Exchange	PL	705	6	712
Bucharest Stock Exchange	RO	42	0	42
Ljubljana Stock Exchange	SI	79	1 136	1 216
Bratislava Stock Exchange	SK	151	26 611	26 762
OMX Nordic exchange (Copenhagen, Tallinn, Riga, Vilnius, Helsinki, Stockholm)		5 985	2 276 233	2 282 218
London Stock Exchange	UK	:	2 614 843	2 614 843
Total of available data		325 989	9 226 132	9 552 121

Source: Federation of European Securities Exchange

According to FESE [15] the main stock exchanges in the EU in 2006 in terms of capitalisation and trading were London, Euronext, the Deutsche Börse, the Spanish exchanges (BME, which include Barcelona, Bilbao, Madrid and Valencia), OMX and Borsa Italiana - see Table 24.12 for more details.

In turnover terms, the Spanish exchanges, London and OMX had the largest bond markets in the EU: together these exchanges accounted for more than 92 % of bond-trading among the exchanges listed in Table 24.13.

---

[15] FESE (the Federation of European Securities Exchanges), more information at: http://www.fese.be.

Table 24.14

Credit institutions (NACE Class 65.12 and Group 65.2)
Main indicators, 2005

	EU-27	BE (1)	BG	CZ	DK	DE	EE	IE (2,3)	EL	ES	FR	IT (2)	CY (1,3)	LV (3)	LT
No. of enterprises (units)	:	107	34	56	170	2 014	20	80	61	:	874	778	389	25	77
Production (EUR million)	:	13 841	1 038	4 159	11 514	129 070	375	14 272	9 158	:	92 439	79 333	1 382	696	426
Value added (EUR million)	:	8 695	652	2 972	8 637	86 379	256	10 624	7 223	:	57 711	47 138	1 116	459	271
Gross operating surplus (EUR million)	:	4 013	454	2 087	5 336	46 261	163	7 298	4 381	:	28 136	24 681	602	305	163
Purchases of goods & services (EUR million)	:	5 147	386	1 187	2 878	42 691	120	3 648	1 935	:	34 728	32 195	267	237	156
Personnel costs (EUR million)	:	4 682	199	885	3 301	40 118	93	3 325	2 842	:	29 575	22 457	514	154	107
Investment in tangible goods (EUR million)	:	360	120	88	362	3 115	8	:	:	:	2 311	:	34	50	18
Employment (thousands)	:	69	23	37	48	692	:	36	61	:	387	337	11	11	8
Apparent labour prod. (EUR thousand)	:	126	28	80	182	125	:	299	118	:	149	140	103	43	35
Average personnel costs (EUR thousand)	:	68	9	25	69	58	:	:	:	:	76	:	48	15	14
Wage adjusted labour productivity (%)	:	185	324	327	262	215	:	:	:	:	195	:	217	297	252
Investment / employment (EUR thousand)	:	5	5	2	8	5	:	:	:	:	6	:	3	5	2

	LU (4)	HU	MT	NL	AT	PL	PT (2)	RO	SI	SK	FI	SE	UK	NO
No. of enterprises (units)	155	215	:	91	812	652	198	173	25	:	363	191	394	210
Production (EUR million)	9 256	4 736	:	31 496	14 283	8 721	8 388	2 473	1 127	:	4 946	11 709	148 102	10 558
Value added (EUR million)	6 170	3 228	:	20 601	9 185	6 104	5 919	1 653	811	:	3 379	7 564	90 667	6 046
Gross operating surplus (EUR million)	4 227	2 166	:	11 903	4 361	3 656	3 659	932	472	:	2 259	4 288	48 491	4 020
Purchases of goods & services (EUR million)	3 086	1 509	:	10 895	5 098	2 616	2 469	820	317	:	1 567	4 145	57 435	4 512
Personnel costs (EUR million)	1 943	1 062	:	8 698	4 824	2 448	2 260	721	339	:	1 120	3 276	42 176	2 026
Investment in tangible goods (EUR million)	0	214	:	3 257	1 194	381	179	590	74	:	28	279	5 996	0
Employment (thousands)	:	38	:	126	75	153	53	50	12	:	25	:	483	24
Apparent labour prod. (EUR thousand)	:	84	:	163	122	40	112	33	70	:	138	:	188	257
Average personnel costs (EUR thousand)	:	28	:	69	64	16	43	14	30	:	46	:	87	86
Wage adjusted labour productivity (%)	:	300	:	237	190	249	260	228	236	:	299	:	215	298
Investment / employment (EUR thousand)	:	6	:	26	16	2	3	12	6	:	1	:	12	0

(1) Includes provisional data.
(2) 2004.
(3) NACE Class 65.12 only.
(4) NACE Class 65.22 only.
Source: Eurostat (SBS)

Table 24.15

Life insurance (NACE Class 66.01)
Main indicators, 2005

	EU-27	BE	BG	CZ	DK (1)	DE	EE (2)	IE	EL	ES	FR (1)	IT	CY (3)	LV (2)	LT
No. of enterprises (units)	:	:	11	4	69	:	5	:	16	:	83	71	3	5	8
Gross premiums written (EUR million)	:	:	76	221	9 692	:	52	:	1 030	:	35 252	60 510	113	14	82
Value added (EUR million)	:	:	59	:	:	:	6	:	:	:	:	:	:	5	:
Gross operating surplus (EUR million)	:	:	55	:	:	:	3	:	:	:	:	:	:	3	:
Purchases of goods & services (EUR million)	:	:	14	:	:	:	6	:	:	:	:	10 264	:	5	:
Personnel costs (EUR million)	:	:	4	10	183	:	2	:	32	:	596	293	1	2	5
Employment (thousands)	:	:	1	0	2	:	0	:	2	:	:	5	0	0	1
Apparent labour prod. (EUR thousand)	:	:	66.0	:	:	:	25.0	:	:	:	:	:	:	16.5	:
Gross operating rate (%)	:	:	73.0	:	:	:	6.6	:	:	:	:	:	:	22.2	:

	LU	HU	MT	NL	AT	PL	PT (2)	RO	SI (2)	SK (2)	FI	SE	UK	NO
No. of enterprises (units)	53	8	:	75	5	32	14	9	0	5	15	45	:	10
Gross premiums written (EUR million)	9 770	508	:	24 824	900	3 809	4 342	249	0	89	3 095	14 153	:	7 519
Value added (EUR million)	:	38	:	4 734	:	:	387	:	:	142	1	:	:	:
Gross operating surplus (EUR million)	:	19	:	1 638	:	:	346	:	:	139	-68	:	:	:
Purchases of goods & services (EUR million)	:	97	:	5 494	:	:	119	:	:	14	0	:	:	:
Personnel costs (EUR million)	120	19	:	3 096	:	100	41	14	0	3	69	377	:	235
Employment (thousands)	2	1	:	5	:	7	1	1	0	0	1	4	:	:
Apparent labour prod. (EUR thousand)	:	64	:	986	:	:	440	:	:	444	1	:	:	:
Gross operating rate (%)	:	3.8	:	6.6	:	:	8.0	:	:	155.8	-2.2	:	:	:

(1) 2003.
(2) 2004.
(3) Provisional.
Source: Eurostat (SBS)

Table 24.16

Autonomous pension funding (NACE Class 66.02) (1)
Main indicators, 2004

	EU-27	BE	BG	CZ	DK	DE	EE	IE	EL	ES	FR	IT	CY	LV	LT
No. of enterprises (units)	:	:	:	12	44	:	15	:	:	1 007	:	483	:	5	34
Turnover (EUR million)	:	:	:	771	111	:	51	:	:	12 487	:	3 904	:	9	40
Production (EUR million)	:	:	:	250	584	:	5	:	:	721	:	:	:	10	41
Value added (EUR million)	:	:	:	225	581	:	4	:	:	-9	:	:	:	10	40
Gross operating surplus (EUR million)	:	:	:	216	579	:	:	:	:	-9	:	:	:	10	:
Purchases of goods & services (EUR million)	:	:	:	24	3	:	1	:	:	730	:	:	:	0	1
Personnel costs (EUR million)	:	:	:	9	2	:	:	:	:	0	:	:	:	0	:
Investment in tangible goods (EUR million)	:	:	:	2	:	:	0	:	:	137	:	:	:	0	0
Employment (units)	:	:	:	487	38	:	0	:	:	0	:	:	:	32	0
Apparent labour prod. (EUR thousand)	:	:	:	462.0	15 289	:	:	:	:	:	:	:	:	312.5	:
Gross operating rate (%)	:	:	:	28.0	521.6	:	:	:	:	-0.1	:	:	:	111.1	:
Investment / employment (EUR thousand)	:	:	:	4.1	:	:	:	:	:	:	:	:	:	0.0	:

	LU	HU	MT	NL	AT	PL	PT	RO	SI	SK	FI	SE	UK	NO
No. of enterprises (units)	:	74	:	842	20	5	229	:	4	4	93	51	:	:
Turnover (EUR million)	:	372	:	24 016	773	28	1 441	:	72	103	99	647	48 840	:
Production (EUR million)	:	16	:	69 315	127	:	1 785	:	13	14	117	:	:	:
Value added (EUR million)	:	5	:	68 760	68	:	1 663	:	10	8	113	:	:	:
Gross operating surplus (EUR million)	:	0	:	68 500	50	:	1 663	:	8	7	111	:	:	:
Purchases of goods & services (EUR million)	:	11	:	555	60	:	122	:	2	5	4	12	:	:
Personnel costs (EUR million)	:	5	:	260	18	:	0	:	2	1	2	9	:	:
Investment in tangible goods (EUR million)	:	:	:	:	1	:	0	:	0	12	0	:	2 372	:
Employment (units)	:	241	:	6 000	324	:	0	:	60	549	130	142	:	:
Apparent labour prod. (EUR thousand)	:	21	:	11 460	210	:	:	:	167	15	869	:	:	:
Gross operating rate (%)	:	0.0	:	285.2	6.5	:	115.4	:	11.1	6.8	112.1	:	:	:
Investment / employment (EUR thousand)	:	:	:	:	3.1	:	:	:	0.0	21.9	0.0	:	:	:

(1) Czech Republic, Estonia, Italy, Poland, Portugal, Slovakia and Sweden, 2003.
Source: Eurostat (SBS)

Table 24.17

Non-life insurance (NACE Class 66.03)
Main indicators, 2005

	EU-27	BE	BG	CZ	DK (1)	DE	EE (2)	IE	EL	ES	FR (1)	IT	CY (3)	LV (2)	LT
No. of enterprises (units)	:	:	20	23	121	:	8	:	14	:	286	82	23	12	17
Gross premiums written (EUR million)	:	:	471	132	5 668	:	153	:	205	:	54 041	11 529	251	182	222
Value added (EUR million)	:	:	107	:	:	:	35	:	:	:	:	:	:	108	:
Gross operating surplus (EUR million)	:	:	85	:	:	:	19	:	:	:	:	:	:	83	:
Purchases of goods & services (EUR million)	:	:	176	:	:	:	45	:	:	:	:	5 238	:	75	:
Personnel costs (EUR million)	:	:	22	15	786	:	16	:	21	:	4 460	847	27	25	31
Employment (thousands)	:	:	3	1	9	:	1	:	1	:	:	10	1	6	5
Apparent labour prod. (EUR thousand)	:	:	30.6	:	:	:	29.1	:	:	:	:	:	:	17.3	:
Gross operating rate (%)	:	:	18.1	:	:	:	12.6	:	:	:	:	:	:	45.3	:

	LU	HU	MT	NL	AT	PL	PT (2)	RO	SI	SK (2)	FI	SE	UK	NO
No. of enterprises (units)	27	8	:	227	18	36	22	32	:	4	111	122	:	80
Gross premiums written (EUR million)	1 263	51	:	23 710	2 437	3 892	2 063	971	:	16	3 163	10 281	:	4 332
Value added (EUR million)	:	1	:	7 531	:	:	564	:	:	11	2	:	:	:
Gross operating surplus (EUR million)	:	-8	:	6 019	:	:	375	:	:	9	-354	:	:	:
Purchases of goods & services (EUR million)	:	37	:	2 592	:	:	289	:	:	11	0	:	:	:
Personnel costs (EUR million)	96	9	:	1 512	:	219	189	99	:	1	356	388	:	392
Employment (thousands)	1	0	:	41	:	23	5	12	:	0	8	6	:	:
Apparent labour prod. (EUR thousand)	:	3	:	185	:	:	116	:	:	119	0	:	:	:
Gross operating rate (%)	:	:.8	:	25.4	:	:	18.2	:	:	59.2	-11.2	:	:	:

(1) 2003.
(2) 2004.
(3) Provisional.
Source: Eurostat (SBS)

Background information

GEOGRAPHICAL COVERAGE

This publication covers the European Union, including the 27 Member States (EU-27): Belgium (BE), Bulgaria (BG), the Czech Republic (CZ), Denmark (DK), Germany (DE), Estonia (EE), Ireland (IE), Greece (EL), Spain (ES), France (FR), Italy (IT), Cyprus (CY), Latvia (LV), Lithuania (LT), Luxembourg (LU), Hungary (HU), Malta (MT), the Netherlands (NL), Austria (AT), Poland (PL), Portugal (PT), Romania (RO), Slovenia (SI), Slovakia (SK), Finland (FI), Sweden (SE) and the United Kingdom (UK). Where data availability permits, information is also included in the statistical annexes at the end of each sectoral chapter for Norway.

The order of the EU Member States used in this publication follows their order of protocol; in other words, the alphabetical order of the countries' names in their respective languages; in some graphs the data has been ranked according to the values of a particular indicator.

EU-27 totals cover the EU composed of 27 Member States since 1 January 2007, while EU-25 totals cover the EU composed of 25 Member States as between 1 May 2004 and the end of 2006. Wherever possible, EU-27 totals have been included and the vast majority of series have been back-calculated so that no break in series occurs. As such, unless otherwise stated, all EU-27 data refer to a sum or an average for all 27 Member States for all reference periods, as if all 27 countries had been members of the EU-27 in earlier periods. This is particularly important for external trade data where information on trade by partner has been adapted in order to treat the EU-27 as a single trading block for all reference periods.

All data for Germany is provided on the basis of re-unified Germany unless otherwise stated.

EXCHANGE RATES

All data are reported in ECU/EUR terms, with national currencies converted using average exchange rates prevailing for the year in question. As of 1 January 1999, 11 of the Member States entered into an economic and monetary union (EMU). These countries formed what has become known as the euro area. Technically data available prior to that date should continue to be denominated in ECU terms, while data available afterwards should be denominated in euro. However, as the conversion rate was ECU 1 = EUR 1, for practical purposes the terms may be used interchangeably and this publication denotes all such monetary series in euro. On 1 January 2001, Greece became a member of the euro area. On 1 January 2006, Slovenia also became a member of the euro area.

While the conversion to a common currency of data originally expressed in national currencies facilitates comparison, large fluctuations in currency markets are partially responsible for movements identified when looking at the evolution of a series in euro terms (especially at the level of an individual country). For the exchange rates used, please refer to Table 1.

NON–AVAILABILITY

The colon (:) is used in tables to represent data that is not available, either because it is not available in the source used or because it is confidential. In figures (graphs), missing information is footnoted as being not available.

The dash (-) is used to represent information that is non-applicable (for example, exchange rates against the euro for those countries that changed their currency denomination to the euro).

In the event that data for a particular reference year is not available, attempts have been made to fill the missing values by making recourse to the previous reference period – for example, for structural business statistics reference period 2003 has been used in the event that no data are available for 2004.

Table 1 _____

Average exchange rates against the euro (1 EUR = ... national currency) (1)

	1996	1997	1998	1999	2000	2001	2002	2003	2004	2005	2006
Belgian Franc (BEF)	39.2986	40.5332	40.6207	40.3399	40.3399	40.3399	-	-	-	-	-
New Bulgarian Lev (BGN)	0.22255	1.89099	1.96913	1.95580	1.95220	1.94820	1.94920	1.94900	1.95330	1.95580	1.95580
Czech Koruna (CZK)	34.4572	35.9304	36.0487	36.8840	35.5990	34.0680	30.8040	31.8460	31.8910	29.7820	28.3420
Danish Krone (DKK)	7.35934	7.48361	7.49930	7.43550	7.45380	7.45210	7.43050	7.43070	7.43990	7.45180	7.45910
German Mark (DEM)	1.90954	1.96438	1.96913	1.95583	1.95583	1.95583	-	-	-	-	-
Estonian Kroon (EEK)	15.2730	15.7130	15.7481	15.6466	15.6466	15.6466	15.6466	15.6466	15.6466	15.6466	15.6466
Irish Pound (IEP)	0.793448	0.747516	0.786245	0.787564	0.787564	0.787564	-	-	-	-	-
Greek Drachma (GRD)	305.546	309.355	330.731	325.763	336.630	340.750	-	-	-	-	-
Spanish Peseta (ESP)	160.748	165.887	167.184	166.386	166.386	166.386	-	-	-	-	-
French Franc (FRF)	6.49300	6.61260	6.60141	6.55957	6.55957	6.55957	-	-	-	-	-
Italian Lira (ITL)	1 958.96	1 929.30	1 943.64	1 936.27	1 936.27	1 936.27	-	-	-	-	-
Cypriot Pound (CYP)	0.591904	0.582433	0.579340	0.578840	0.573920	0.575890	0.575300	0.584090	0.581850	0.576830	0.575780
Latvian Lats (LVL)	0.699605	0.659401	0.660240	0.625600	0.559200	0.560100	0.581000	0.640700	0.665200	0.696200	0.696200
Lithuanian Litas (LTL)	5.07899	4.53615	4.48437	4.26410	3.69520	3.58230	3.45940	3.45270	3.45290	3.45280	3.45280
Luxembourg Franc (LUF)	39.2986	40.5332	40.6207	40.3399	40.3399	40.3399	-	-	-	-	-
Hungarian Forint (HUF)	193.758	211.654	240.573	252.770	260.040	256.590	242.960	253.620	251.660	248.050	264.260
Maltese Lira (MTL)	0.457684	0.437495	0.434983	0.425800	0.404100	0.403000	0.408900	0.426100	0.428000	0.429900	0.429300
Dutch Guilder (NLG)	2.13973	2.21081	2.21966	2.20371	2.20371	2.20371	-	-	-	-	-
Austrian Schilling (ATS)	13.4345	13.8240	13.8545	13.7603	13.7603	13.7603	-	-	-	-	-
New Polish Zloty (PLN)	3.42232	3.71545	3.91647	4.22740	4.00820	3.67210	3.85740	4.39960	4.52680	4.02300	3.89590
Portuguese Escudo (PTE)	195.761	198.589	201.695	200.482	200.482	200.482	-	-	-	-	-
New Romanian Leu (RON)	0.39222	0.81085	0.99849	1.63450	1.99220	2.60040	3.12700	3.75510	4.05100	3.62090	3.52580
Slovenian Tolar (SIT)	171.778	180.986	185.948	194.473	206.613	217.980	225.977	233.849	239.087	239.568	-
Slovak Koruna (SKK)	38.9229	38.1129	39.5407	44.1230	42.6020	43.3000	42.6940	41.4890	40.0220	38.5990	37.2340
Finnish Markka (FIM)	5.82817	5.88064	5.98251	5.94573	5.94573	5.94573	-	-	-	-	-
Swedish Krona (SEK)	8.51472	8.65117	8.91593	8.80750	8.44520	9.25510	9.16110	9.12420	9.12430	9.28220	9.25440
Pound Sterling (GBP)	0.813798	0.692304	0.676434	0.658740	0.609480	0.621870	0.628830	0.691990	0.678660	0.683800	0.681730
Croatian Kuna (HRK)	:	:	:	7.58046	7.64316	7.48200	7.41300	7.56880	7.49670	7.40080	7.32470
FYR of Macedonia Denar (MKD)	51.8900	61.2000	60.4800	60.6200	60.7900	60.9600	61.0700	61.2900	61.3100	61.1702	61.1900
New Turkish Lira (TRY)	0.13504	0.22663	0.36575	0.54464	0.62427	1.26950	1.73800	1.77164	1.83620	1.59240	1.86400
Icelandic Krona (ISK)	84.6558	80.4391	79.6976	77.1800	72.5800	87.4200	86.1800	86.6500	87.1400	78.2300	87.7600
Norwegian Krone (NOK)	8.19659	8.01861	8.46587	8.31040	8.11290	8.04840	7.50860	8.00330	8.36970	8.00920	8.04720
Swiss Franc (CHF)	1.56790	1.64400	1.62203	1.60030	1.55790	1.51050	1.46700	1.52120	1.54380	1.54830	1.57290
Japanese Yen (JPY)	138.084	137.076	146.415	121.320	99.470	108.680	118.060	130.970	134.440	136.850	146.020
United States Dollar (USD)	1.26975	1.13404	1.12109	1.06580	0.92360	0.89560	0.94560	1.13120	1.24390	1.24410	1.25560

(1) MKD and TRY: year-end and not annual average.
Source: Eurostat (Economy and finance)

NOTES ON DATA SOURCES

Two types of data sources can be distinguished: those originating from official sources (collected normally by the national statistical institutes in each Member State) and those provided by professional trade associations (representative organisations of various activities) and other non-official bodies. Tables and figures presenting data from non-official sources are easily recognised as they appear in a shaded box. The European business publication has benefited from the co-operation of a wide variety of professional trade association bodies representing industrial and service activities within the EU. However, it should be noted that non-official data may be based on different standards to those used in the European Statistical System, notably in that

they may not: follow the NACE classification, use standard statistical units, cover the same geographical area, cover the activities of other enterprises in an activity that are not members of the organisation (for example, small and medium-sized enterprises may be under-represented). As a result of these differences, users are recommended not to combine directly data from official and non-official sources.

The main official data sources used in this edition of the publication are structural business statistics, short-term statistics and PRODCOM, as well as the labour force survey and external trade statistics. In addition to these sources which are used for many chapters, use has also been made of specialist sources for particular areas, notably transport, energy,

research and development, environment, tourism and information society statistics, as well as national accounts.

Classifications

The statistical information contained within European business is structured according to the NACE Rev. 1.1 classification of economic activities. During the 1990s a thorough revision of international statistical classifications took place, with the result that new classifications were developed as an integrated system of statistical classifications, whereby (a) various product classifications were harmonised and (b) the central product classifications were related to the classifications of economic activities by the economic origin criterion.

To view the complete listing for NACE, access: http://ec.europa.eu/eurostat/ramon/ nomenclatures/index.cfm?TargetUrl= ACT_OTH_DFLT_LAYOUT&StrNom= NACE_1_1&StrLanguageCode=EN.

The maps included in this edition of European business are based on regional structural business statistics. They show in each region of the EU and Norway the concentration of employment within a particular activity. Regions are classified according to the NUTS (Nomenclature of Territorial Units for Statistics). NUTS has been used since 1988 in Community legislation, although it was not until 2003 that a Regulation of the European Parliament and of the Council on the NUTS was adopted. From 1 May 2004, the regions of those Member States that joined the EU in 2004 were also added to the NUTS and the legislation was modified in October 2005. To view the complete listing for NUTS, access:

http://ec.europa.eu/eurostat/ramon/nuts/ splash_regions.html.

While the majority of the data in European business are based on the NACE classification, there are a number of exceptions. External trade data are based on the statistical classification of products by activity in the European Economic Community (CPA). The version of this classification used in this publication dates from 2002. To view the complete listing of CPA, access:

http://ec.europa.eu/eurostat/ramon/ nomenclatures/index.cfm?TargetUrl= ACT_OTH_DFLT_LAYOUT&StrNom= CPA&StrLanguageCode=EN.

The data on industrial products is classified according to the PRODCOM list, which is revised on an annual basis. To view the complete listing for PRODCOM 2006, access:

http://ec.europa.eu/eurostat/ramon/ nomenclatures/index.cfm?TargetUrl= ACT_OTH_DFLT_LAYOUT&StrNom= PRD_2006&StrLanguageCode=EN.

Short-term business statistics for construction are often classified according to the classification of types of construction (CC). To view the complete listing, access:

http://ec.europa.eu/eurostat/ramon/ nomenclatures/index.cfm?TargetUrl= ACT_OTH_DFLT_LAYOUT&StrNom= CC_1998&StrLanguageCode=EN.

Structural business statistics (SBS)

The majority of the analysis contained within European business is derived from structural business statistics (SBS). These data have been collected within the legal framework provided by Council Regulation No 58/97 of 20 December 1996 concerning structural business statistics (hereafter referred to as the SBS Regulation). This instrument aims to provide a common framework for the collection, transmission and evaluation of structural business statistics and should result in the national statistical authorities transmitting to Eurostat data which is comparable between the Member States on the structure, activity, competitiveness and performance of businesses. The SBS Regulation lays down the necessary norms, standards and definitions without detailing the actual collection methods to be used. As such the national statistical authority in each Member State may conduct the data collection exercise in the manner most appropriate to its own situation. SBS data are therefore mainly compiled through statistical surveys and the use of administrative sources. The national statistical authorities may use one or several sources according to the strategy they have adopted, taking into account the costs, the quality and the response burden on enterprises.

The SBS Regulation has been modified three times, twice by other Council regulations (one of which with the European Parliament) and once by a Commission regulation.

1. Council Regulation (EC, Euratom) No 410/98 of 16 February 1998 amending regulation (EC, Euratom) No 58/97 concerning structural business statistics;

2. Regulation (EC) No 2056/2002 of the European Parliament and of the Council of 5 November 2002 amending Council Regulation (EC, Euratom) No 58/97 concerning structural business statistics;

3. Commission Regulation (EC) No 1614/2002 of 6 September 2002 adjusting Council Regulation (EC, Euratom) No 58/97 to economic and technical developments and amending Commission Regulations (EC) No 2700/98, (EC) No 2701/98 and (EC) No 2702/98.

The SBS Regulation can be broken down into its core part and seven annexes. The first annex concerns structural statistics in all business sectors. The remaining annexes are sectoral, covering industry, distributive trades, construction, insurance, credit institutions and pension funds.

At the time of writing a European Commission proposal [1] for a recast of the SBS Regulation is under discussion in the European Parliament and the Council.

_____
[1] COM(2006) 66 final, of 20.02.2006.

Table 2
Deviations from standard SBS survey characteristics - all enterprises

Country	Industry (NACE Sections C - E)	Construction (NACE Section F)	Distributive trades (NACE Section G)	Services (NACE Sections H - K)
Bulgaria	From 2002: reporting units that outsource production on a fee or contract basis are treated as production units and classified on the basis of their turnover			
Spain	Activity in Division 41 is difficult to separate from that in Division 90	No major deviations	No major deviations	No major deviations
Ireland	Enterprises with 3 persons employed or more	Enterprises with 20 persons employed or more	No major deviations	
Cyprus	Class 14.11 includes Class 14.12; Class 14.22 includes Group 14.3; Class 15.13 includes Group 15.2; Class 15.71 includes Class 15.72; Class 15.91 includes Classes 15.93 and 15.96; Class 17.21 includes Class 17.54 and Group 17.6; Class 17.71 includes Class 17.72; Group 19.1 includes Group 19.2; Class 20.51 includes Class 20.52; Class 22.22 includes Classes 22.11 and 22.15; Class 24.11 includes Class 24.13 and Group 24.2; Class 24.41 includes 24.42; Class 24.62 includes Class 24.66; Class 26.11 includes Classes 26.13 and 26.15; Class 27.22 includes Classes 27.42 and 27.44; Class 28.21 includes Group 28.3; Class 28.61 includes Class 28.62; Class 28.74 includes Class 28.75; Class 29.53 includes Class 29.54; Group 31.4 includes Class 31.62; Group 32.2 includes Group 32.3; Group 33.1 includes Groups 33.2 and 33.3; Class 36.21 includes Class 36.22; Group 36.3 includes Group 36.5 and Class 36.61; Class 55.21 includes Class 55.22			
Latvia	It is recommended not to use 4-digit data as a random sampling scheme is used with stratification at the 3-digit level			
Netherlands	Number of enterprises: data for this variable are rounded to multiples of 5; a 0 therefore means 2 or less enterprises			
	2003: statistics for Section K do not include wages and salaries for Class 74.15			
Poland	No correction for non-response for enterprises with more than 10 persons employed			
Romania	Group 13.2 (and therefore Division 13 and Subsection CB) includes Division 12			
Slovenia	Data for tangible investment cover only enterprises with 20 persons employed or more			

Source: Eurostat (SBS)

Table 3 _____

Deviations from standard SBS survey characteristics - size class breakdowns

Country	Industry (NACE Sections C - E)	Construction (NACE Section F)	Distributive trades (NACE Section G)	Services (NACE Sections H - K)
Bulgaria	From 2002: reporting units that outsource production on a fee or contract basis are treated as production units and classified on the basis of their turnover			
Ireland	Enterprises with 3 persons employed or more	Enterprises with 20 persons employed or more	No major deviations	
Cyprus	Size class thresholds are calculated as full-time equivalents; data for size class 500-999 includes data for size class 1 000+; data for size class 100-249 includes data for size class 250-499			
Netherlands	Number of enterprises: data for this variable are rounded to multiples of 5; a 0 therefore means 2 or less enterprises			
	Size classes are derived from business register; ratio between the number of persons employed and the number of enterprises may not fit with the corresponding employment size class			
	2003: statistics for Section K do not include wages and salaries for Class 74.15			
Poland	No correction for non-response for enterprises with more than 10 persons employed			
Romania	Group 13.2 (and therefore Division 13 and Subsection CB) includes Division 12			
Slovenia	Data for tangible investment cover only enterprises with 20 persons employed or more			

Source: Eurostat (SBS)

There are three main SBS data sets that have been used in this publication. The first is a set of annual enterprise statistics which covers enterprises of all sizes; these data were generally used for reference year 2004. Not all Member States transmitted data relating to this population, with some providing data for units with employment above a certain size threshold. Table 2 presents the main deviations from the standard population as laid down in the SBS Regulation (all enterprises, regardless of their size).

The second collection of SBS data covers information broken down by employment size class. Again, not all Member States transmitted data to Eurostat that fully conforms to the statistical units or population requested. In particular, some Member States provided data for units with different employment thresholds. Table 3 summarises the main deviations from the standard statistical units and coverage for enterprise data by size class.

The third collection of SBS data relates to regional information; this information was used to construct the maps that appear in the overview of each chapter.

Statistical unit

The type of statistical unit is generally the enterprise. An enterprise carries out one or more activities at one or more locations. Enterprises are classified by NACE according to their main (or principal) activity. The enterprise should not be confused with the local unit, which is an enterprise or part thereof situated in one geographically identified place. Note that the main exception to the use of the enterprise as the type of statistical unit is with respect to the information published in the maps derived from SBS regional data, which are generally based on local units.

Main definitions

Standard definitions of variables within structural business statistics are laid down in Commission Regulation (EC) No 2700/98 of 17 December 1998 concerning the definitions of characteristics for structural business statistics. As such, the data presented are largely comparable across activities and countries. There are nevertheless some known divergences from these standard definitions; Table 4 presents the main discrepancies. The following standard definitions are taken from Commission Regulation (EC) No 2700/98.

Turnover: comprises the totals invoiced by the observation unit during the reference period, and this corresponds to market sales of goods or services supplied to third parties. Turnover includes all duties and taxes on the goods or services invoiced by the unit with the exception of the VAT invoiced by the unit vis-à-vis its customer and other similar deductible taxes directly linked to turnover. It also includes all other charges (transport, packaging, etc.) passed on to the customer, even if these charges are listed separately in the invoice. Reductions in prices, rebates and discounts as well as the value of returned packing must be deducted. Income classified as other operating income, financial income and extraordinary income in company accounts is excluded from turnover. Operating subsidies received from public authorities or the institutions of the European Union are also excluded.

Production value: measures the amount actually produced by the unit, based on sales, including changes in stocks and the resale of goods and services. The production value is defined as turnover, plus or minus the changes in stocks of finished products, work in progress and goods and services purchased for resale, minus the purchases of goods and services for

Table 4 _____

Deviations from standard SBS variable definitions

Country	Year	Variable	Discrepancy
Czech Republic	All years	Personnel costs	Data are inconsistent with its components (wages and salaries, and social security contributions)
France	From 2004	Payments for agency workers	Definition has been revised, data are expected to be higher
Ireland	All years	Apparent labour productivity, wage adjusted labour productivity, gross operating surplus, gross operating rate, value added	For Groups 22.3, 24.1 and 24.4, and Division 30 - high values may reflect foreign ownership of enterprises, outsourcing of activities, and accounting practices of multinational enterprises
Hungary	All years	Employment variables (persons employed and employees)	Data are derived from annual labour survey; at detailed level they may not be comparable with other SBS data
Netherlands	All years	Number of employees	This is determined by the number of jobs provided; corrections for the number of secondary jobs and the number of unpaid persons employed (working proprietors, unpaid family members) may result in a number of employees actually exceeding the number of persons employed
Poland	All years	Number of persons employed	The number of persons employed is not calculated as an annual average but as the number of persons employed on the last day of the reference year; this may yield results that are incoherent with the number of employees
Slovenia	All years	Tangible investment	In extractive activities (Divisions 11 and 13) excludes expenditure for rehabilitation of abandoned mining and quarrying sites

Source: Eurostat (SBS)

resale, plus capitalised production, plus other operating income (excluding subsidies). Income and expenditure classified as financial or extraordinary in company accounts is excluded from production value. Included in purchases of goods and services for resale are the purchases of services purchased in order to be rendered to third parties in the same condition.

Value added at factor cost: can be calculated from turnover, plus capitalised production, plus other operating income, plus or minus the changes in stocks, minus the purchases of goods and services, minus other taxes on products which are linked to turnover but not deductible, minus the duties and taxes linked to production. Alternatively it can be calculated from gross operating surplus by adding personnel costs. Income and expenditure classified as financial or extraordinary in company accounts is excluded from value added. Value added at factor costs is calculated gross, as value adjustments (such as depreciation) are not subtracted.

Gross operating surplus: is the surplus generated by operating activities after the labour factor input has been recompensed. It can be calculated from value added at factor cost less personnel costs. It is the balance available to the unit which allows it to recompense the providers of own funds and debt, to pay taxes and eventually to finance all or a part of its investment. Income and expenditure classified as financial or extraordinary in company accounts is excluded from the gross operating surplus.

Personnel costs: are defined as the total remuneration, in cash or in kind, payable by an employer to an employee (regular and temporary employees as well as home-workers) in return for work done by the latter during the reference period. All remuneration paid during the reference period is included, regardless of whether it is paid on the basis of working time, output or piecework, and whether it is paid regularly or not. Included are all gratuities, workplace and performance bonuses, ex gratia payments, 13th month pay (and similar fixed bonuses), payments made to employees in consideration of dismissal, lodging, transport, cost of living and family allowances, commissions, attendance fees, overtime, night work, etc., as well as taxes, social security contributions and other amounts owed by the employees and retained at source by the employers. Also included are the social security costs for the employer. These include employer's social security contributions to schemes for retirement pensions, sickness, maternity, disability, unemployment, occupational accidents and diseases, family

allowances as well as other schemes. These costs are included regardless of whether they are statutory, collectively agreed, contractual or voluntary in nature. Payments for agency workers are not included in personnel costs.

Purchases of goods and services: include the value of all goods and services purchased during the reference period for resale or consumption in the production process, excluding capital goods the consumption of which is registered as consumption of fixed capital. The goods and services concerned may be either resold with or without further transformation, completely used up in the production process or, finally, be stocked. Included in these purchases are the materials that enter directly into the goods produced (raw materials, intermediary products, components), plus non-capitalised small tools and equipment. Also included is the value of ancillary materials (lubricants, water, packaging, maintenance and repair materials, office materials) as well as energy products. Included in this variable are the purchases of materials made for the production of capital goods by the unit. Services paid for during the reference period are also included regardless of whether they are industrial or non-industrial. In this figure are payments for all work carried out by third parties on behalf of the unit including current repairs and maintenance, installation work and technical studies. Amounts paid for the installation of capital goods and the value of capitalised goods are excluded. Also included are payments made for non-industrial services such as legal and accountancy fees, patents and licence fees (where they are not capitalised), insurance premiums, costs of meetings of shareholders and governing bodies, contributions to business and professional associations, postal, telephone, electronic communication, telegraph and fax charges, transport services for goods and personnel, advertising costs, commissions (where they are not included in wages and salaries), rents, bank charges (excluding interest payments) and all other business services provided by third parties. Included are services which are transformed and capitalised by the unit as capitalised production. Expenditure classified as financial expenditure or extraordinary expenditure in company accounts is excluded from total purchases of goods and services. Purchases of goods and services are valued at the purchase price excluding deductible VAT and other deductible taxes linked directly to turnover. All other taxes and duties on the products are therefore not deducted from the valuation of the purchases of goods and services.

Gross investment in tangible goods: includes all new and existing tangible capital goods, whether bought from third parties or produced for own use (in other words capitalised production of tangible capital goods), having a useful life of more than one year including non-produced tangible goods such as land. The threshold for the useful life of a good that can be capitalised may be increased according to company accounting practices where these practices require a greater expected useful life than the one year threshold indicated above. All investments are valued prior to (in other words gross of) value adjustments, and before the deduction of income from disposals. Purchased goods are valued at purchase price, in other words transport and installation charges, fees, taxes and other costs of ownership transfer are included. Own produced tangible goods are valued at production cost. Goods acquired through restructuring (such as mergers, take-overs, break-ups, split-off) are excluded. Purchases of small tools which are not capitalised are included under current expenditure. Also included are all additions, alterations, improvements and renovations which prolong the service life or increase the productive capacity of capital goods. Current maintenance costs are excluded as is the value and current expenditure on capital goods used under rental and lease contracts. Investment in intangible and financial assets is excluded. Concerning the recording of investments where the invoicing, delivery, payment and first use of the good may take place in different reference periods, the following method is proposed as an objective:

1. investments are recorded when the ownership is transferred to the unit that intends to use them;
2. capitalised production is recorded when produced;
3. concerning the recording of investments made in identifiable stages, each part-investment should be recorded in the reference period in which they are made.

In practice this may not be possible and company accounting conventions may mean that the following approximations to this method need to be used:

1. investments are recorded in the reference period in which they are delivered;
2. investments are recorded in the reference period in which they enter into the production process;
3. investments are recorded in the reference period in which they are invoiced;
4. investments are recorded in the reference period in which they are paid for.

Number of persons employed: is defined as the total number of persons who work in the observation unit (inclusive of working proprietors, partners working regularly in the unit and unpaid family workers), as well as persons who work outside the unit who belong to it and are paid by it (for example, sales representatives, delivery personnel, repair and maintenance teams). It includes persons absent for a short period (for example, sick leave, paid leave or special leave), and also those on strike, but not those absent for an indefinite period. It also includes part-time workers who are regarded as such under the laws of the country concerned and who are on the payroll, as well as seasonal workers, apprentices and home workers on the payroll. The number of persons employed excludes manpower supplied to the unit by other enterprises, persons carrying out repair and maintenance work in the unit on behalf of other enterprises, as well as those on compulsory military service. Unpaid family workers refer to persons who live with the proprietor of the unit and work regularly for the unit, but do not have a contract of service and do not receive a fixed sum for the work they perform. This is limited to those persons who are not included on the payroll of another unit as their principal occupation.

Number of employees: is defined as those persons who work for an employer and who have a contract of employment and receive compensation in the form of wages, salaries, fees, gratuities, piecework pay or remuneration in kind. The relationship of employer to employee exists when there is an agreement, which may be formal or informal, between an enterprise and a person, normally entered into voluntarily by both parties, whereby the person works for the enterprise in return for remuneration in cash or in kind. A worker is considered to be a wage or salary earner of a particular unit if he or she receives a wage or salary from the unit regardless of where the work is done (in or outside the production unit). A worker from a temporary employment agency is considered to be an employee of the temporary employment agency and not of the unit (customer) in which they work. In particular the following are considered as employees: paid working proprietors; students who have a formal commitment whereby they contribute to the unit's process of production in return for remuneration and/or education services; employees engaged under a contract specifically designed to encourage the recruitment of unemployed persons; home workers if there is an explicit agreement that the home worker is remunerated on the basis of the work done and they are included on the payroll. The number of employees includes part-time workers, seasonal workers, persons on strike or on short-term leave, but excludes those persons on long-term leave. The number of employees does not include voluntary workers. The number of employees is calculated in the same manner as the number of persons employed, namely as the number of jobs and is measured as an annual average.

Apparent labour productivity: is defined as value added divided by the number of persons employed; the result is usually expressed in terms of EUR thousand per person employed.

Average personnel costs: are defined as personnel costs divided by the number of employees; the result is usually expressed in terms of EUR thousand per employee.

Total expenditure: is defined as the sum of gross operating expenditure (purchases of goods and services and personnel costs) and gross investment in tangible goods.

Gross operating rate: is defined as gross operating surplus divided by turnover; the result is expressed as a percentage.

Investment in tangible goods as a share of total investment expenditure: is defined as gross tangible investment divided by total expenditure; the result is expressed as a percentage.

Investment per person employed: is defined as gross investment in tangible goods divided by the number of persons employed; the result is expressed in EUR thousand per person employed.

Personnel costs as a share of total expenditure: is defined as purchases of goods and services divided by total expenditure; the result is expressed as a percentage.

Purchases of goods and services as a share of total investment expenditure: is defined as purchases of goods and services divided by total expenditure; the result is expressed as a percentage.

Wage adjusted labour productivity ratio: is defined as the ratio of value added divided by personnel costs (the latter having been divided by the share of employees in the number of persons employed); the result is expressed as a percentage. The ratio can also be calculated by dividing apparent labour productivity by average personnel costs and expressing the result as a percentage.

EU estimates

EU-27 aggregates including estimates for missing country data

EU-27 aggregates include estimates for missing Member States where necessary; the individual country estimates are not themselves published.

Rounded EU-27 aggregates

EU-27 aggregates are sometimes missing in the SBS databases for annual enterprise statistics and for enterprise statistics broken down by size class due to confidentiality. With the aim of providing a more complete set of data, an exercise was conducted in the spring of 2007 to create a set of harmonised EU-27 estimates for reference year 2004 for both of these data sets. Because the share of the confidential cells is often very low, proxies for the missing EU-27 aggregates were calculated by summing up the non-confidential information and then rounding the results (note that no attempt was made to estimate the confidential values). Rounding creates intervals, within which the 'true' value lies. In the case where very little information is missing, simple rounding would be sufficient. However, if more information is missing due to confidentiality, more 'noise' has to be created to avoid the disclosure of the confidential values, and subsequently greater intervals are needed to ensure that the result is a valid proxy for the missing EU-27 aggregate, although with reduced precision. A rounding of all figures was made to three, two and one significant figures to allow for differences in precision of the proxy EU-27 figure (sum of non-confidential data compared with the EU-27 figure). These calculations were made for a selection of variables and derived ratios for the annual enterprise series and for a selection of variables for the data broken down by size class, with the rounding applied after the calculation of the share of each size class in the total in order to increase precision. This method was carried out down to the most detailed activity level, as well as for special sectoral aggregates created specifically for use in this publication.

Within European business, these rounded EU-27 estimates based on non-confidential data are identified in the tables or graphs by the following footnote 'rounded estimates based on non-confidential data'. Note that the inclusion of rounded EU-27 estimates means that there may be discrepancies between values published at different levels of the NACE hierarchy, as well as between derived indicators and basic variables. Contrary to the previous edition of the publication, the commentary, tables and graphs in this edition of the publication are based on rounded estimates without any adjustment being made for discrepancies. Hence, it is possible that the share of several NACE groups within a NACE division do not sum exactly to 100 %, or that, in extreme cases, values for a derived indicator for a set of NACE groups are all lower (or all higher) than the value reported for the NACE division to which they belong. Note that a combination of available rounded and non-rounded estimates (for example to fill gaps in data availability) could generate estimates which are not a good proxy of the true value.

EU averages

In the absence of sufficient information to compile or estimate EU-27 aggregates, averages or sums have been calculated on the basis of information available for an incomplete set of the Member States. In those cases where neither an EU-27 total nor a rounded EU-27 aggregate are available, a partial EU total, or a ratio derived from a partial EU total has been created. In the event that this method has been used then a footnote has been systematically added to both the commentary and the tables and graphs to show the coverage of the partial total/average that has been used.

Regions of the EU

For regional business statistics there are also difficulties related to a large number of confidential cells. A somewhat different approach was adopted in order to construct the maps that are presented in the overview of each sectoral chapter. For each region and activity, the share of non-financial business economy employment was ranked, for both confidential and non-confidential values. These values were then assigned to an interval which was used for the construction of the maps; the size of the interval being considered large enough to protect the confidential nature of some values. Four intervals were used for each map, with the lowest and highest intervals being based on approximately 30 of the 260 regions for which data are available at the NUTS 2 level and the remaining two intermediate categories based on roughly 100 regions each. This approach has both the advantage of highlighting the most interesting results at the top and the bottom of the rankings and at the same time maximising the protection of confidential cells. Nevertheless, there were a small number of cases where the interval could not be disclosed.

SHORT-TERM BUSINESS STATISTICS

Tracking the business cycle is indispensable for many economic actors. Short-term business statistics provide politicians, government agencies, the financial community, business managers, consumers and trade unionists with information that is crucial when making decisions on whether activities and output prices grow, stagnate or decline. The legal basis of the European system of quantitative short-term business statistics is Council Regulation (EC) No 1165/98, which was adopted on 19 May 1998, and amended by Regulation (EC) No 1158/2005 of the European Parliament and of the Council of 6 July 2005.

Several variables from the short-term business statistics database are presented in this publication. To measure output the following indices are used: the industrial production index, the index of production for construction, the volume of sales for retail trade, the services' turnover index; these indices are often available at a fine level of detail, often for NACE groups or even classes. An employment index is also available for most activities within industry, construction and services, generally at the NACE division level.

Eurostat estimate EU-27 aggregates for short-term statistics once country indices covering more than 60 % of the EU-27 weights are available. Eurostat have also back-calculated the EU-27 indices so they are available for lengthy time-series; data in this edition of European business are generally presented from 1996 to 2006 (subject to availability). As this publication is based on annual statistics the presentation of short-term statistics is largely based on either working-day adjusted or gross indices. Users who wish to exploit monthly or quarterly data may be interested to know that seasonally adjusted and trend-cycle presentations are also available in Eurostat's database.

Main definitions

The following standard definitions are taken from Commission Regulation (EC) No 1503/2006 of 28 September 2006 implementing and amending Council Regulation (EC) No 1165/98 concerning short-term statistics as regards definitions of variables, list of variables and frequency of data compilation.

Index of production for industrial activities: is defined to show the evolution of value added at factor cost, at constant prices. Value added at factor cost can be calculated from turnover (excluding VAT), plus capitalised production, plus other operating income, plus or minus the changes in stocks, minus the purchases of goods and services, minus other taxes on products and taxes linked to production. This index of production should take account of: variations in type and quality of the commodities and of the input materials; changes in stocks of finished goods and work in progress; changes in technical input–output relations (processing techniques); and services such as the assembling of production units, mounting, installations, repairs, planning, engineering, creation of software.

Index of production for construction: the objectives and characteristics of production indices for industrial activities also apply to the indices for building construction and civil engineering. The division of production between building construction and civil engineering is based on the classification of types of construction (CC). These indices aim to show the evolution of value added for each of the two main sections in construction, namely buildings and civil engineering works. The indices are calculated by assigning the basic information (for example, deflated output, hours worked, authorisations/permits) to products in the CC and then aggregating the product indices in accordance with the CC.

Volume of sales index for retail trade: represents the value of turnover in constant prices and as such is a volume index. It is generally calculated as turnover at current prices, deflated by the deflator of sales.

Turnover index for services: the objective of this index is to show the evolution of the market for goods and services. Turnover comprises the totals invoiced by the observation unit during the reference period. This corresponds to market sales of goods or services supplied to third parties. Turnover also includes all other charges (transport, packaging, etc.) passed on to the customer, even if these charges are listed separately in the invoice. Turnover excludes VAT and other similar deductible taxes directly linked to turnover as well as all duties and taxes on the goods or services invoiced by the unit.

Domestic output price index: measures the average price development of all goods and related services resulting from that activity and sold on the domestic market. All price-determining characteristics of the products should be taken into account when compiling these indices, including the quantity of units sold, transport provided, rebates, service conditions, guarantee conditions and destination. The specification must be such that in subsequent reference periods, the observation unit is able to identify the product and to provide the appropriate price per unit. The appropriate price is the basic price that excludes VAT and similar deductible taxes directly linked to turnover as well as all duties and taxes on the goods and services invoiced by the unit, whereas subsidies on products received by the producer, if there are any, should be added.

Construction costs index: an output price index for construction can be used as an approximation for the construction cost variable. These indices measure only the developments for residential buildings, thus excluding residences for communities, non-residential buildings. Land prices and architects' and other fees should also be excluded. The indices reflect the prices paid by the client to the construction enterprise. They therefore do not only reflect the variations in the cost factors of construction, but also the changes in productivity and profit margins.

Index of employment: is based on the total number of persons working in an observation unit (inclusive of working proprietors, partners working regularly in the unit and unpaid family workers), which also includes persons who work outside the unit who belong to it and are paid by it (for example, sales representatives, delivery personnel, repair and maintenance teams). It includes persons absent for a short period (for example, sick leave, paid leave or special leave), and also those on strike, but not those absent for an indefinite period. It also includes part-time workers who are regarded as such under the laws of the country concerned and who are on the payroll, as well as seasonal workers, apprentices and home workers on the payroll. The number of persons employed excludes manpower supplied to the unit by other enterprises, persons carrying out repair and maintenance work in the unit on behalf of other enterprises, as well as those on compulsory military service.

PRODCOM

The data on industrial products from PRODCOM (PRODucts of the European COMmunity) are provided for EU-27 totals. The legal basis of the PRODCOM data is Council Regulation (EEC) No 3924/91 on the establishment of a Community survey of industrial production (the PRODCOM regulation). This regulation requires that production be reported to Eurostat according to the product headings of the PRODCOM list. Each PRODCOM code is identified by an eight-digit code. The first six digits are the CPA code (classification of products by activity). The last two digits provide a further breakdown of the products. Normally each PRODCOM heading also corresponds to one or more Combined Nomenclature (CN) headings, thus enabling the external trade corresponding to one PRODCOM heading to be calculated.

The production concept used is production sold during the survey period, although total production is also required for some headings (total production includes production that is retained by the enterprise for further processing, as well as production that is sold). PRODCOM statistics aim to cover enterprises classified to NACE Sections C, D and E which manufacture products contained in the PRODCOM list. Among the rules on representativeness, the regulation stipulates that the reported production should account for all enterprises employing at least 20 persons. In addition, at least 90 % of production in each (four-digit) NACE class must be recorded.

For this edition of European business the PRODCOM data are given in both value and volume terms; note that volume measures can vary between products depending upon the characteristics of the product in question (for example the volume unit can be a weight, surface area, cubic measure of volume, etc.). The data presented in statistical tables results from a selection process based on available EU-27 totals. For each CPA group all of the available EU-27 totals were extracted from the PRODCOM database and these products were then ranked according to their value of production sold, with the ten most important products being maintained. Note that any ancillary categories (others, not elsewhere specified, etc.) were not included in this ranking procedure. Once the rankings had been made (based on non-confidential, publicly-available information), the tables were cross-checked by Eurostat staff. In cases where a confidential EU-27 total should have been included, tables were adjusted to include additional rows with the PRODCOM description and PRODCOM code – although the confidential values are not published.

EXTERNAL TRADE

EU-27 external trade statistics are available in the Comext database, and can be compiled according to various classifications. For the purpose of this publication the classification of products by activity (CPA) has been used; the 2002 version of this classification is currently in use.

The focus of the external trade data presented in European business is for reference year 2006. No estimates are made for external trade statistics, although it is possible that subsequent revisions may occur. The data are processed by summing together the detailed combined nomenclature (CN) product statistics (using a conversion table from CN to CPA - note that this table can change between reference years).

The data for the EU-27 are reported in terms of trade flows with the rest of the world, in other words EU-27 trade with non-member countries (extra-EU trade). However, for the individual Member States total trade flows are used, in other words, intra- and extra-EU trade combined. All trade figures are given in current price euro terms.

Main definitions

Cover ratio: is defined as the ratio of exports/imports; this indicator is expressed as a percentage.

Trade balance: is defined as the value of exports – the value of imports.

LABOUR FORCE SURVEY

The legal basis for the collection of data is Council Regulation (EC) No 577/98 of 9 March 1998 on the organisation of a sample survey in the Community, which was subsequently amended by Regulation (EC) No 1991/2002 of the European Parliament and of the Council of 8 October 2002. This amending regulation introduced a deadline for the period of transition given to the Member States to introduce a continuous quarterly labour force survey.

The main statistical objective of the Labour Force Survey is to divide the population of working age (generally 15 years and above) into three mutually exclusive and exhaustive groups: persons in employment, unemployed persons, and inactive persons, and to provide descriptive and explanatory data on each of these categories. Respondents are assigned to one of these groups on the basis of the most objective information possible, obtained through a survey questionnaire, which relates principally to their actual activity within the reference period. It is important to note that the information is not collected from enterprises (as with most of the business statistics presented in this publication), but instead through a survey addressed to households.

The national statistical institutes are responsible for selecting the sample, preparing the questionnaires, conducting the interviews and forwarding the results to Eurostat in accordance with a common coding scheme. Eurostat devises the programme for analysing the results and is responsible for processing and disseminating the information. The results are subject to the usual types of errors associated with sampling techniques. Eurostat implements basic guidelines intended to avoid the publication of figures which are statistically unreliable (see Table 5); and figures below these thresholds are not published. A second threshold is applied to data that may only be published with a warning concerning its reliability; for the purpose of this edition of European business these data have also been omitted from the publication.

Table 5

Reliability limits for publishing Labour Force Survey (LFS) data, 2006 (number of observations)

	A	B
EU	20 000	:
Belgium	2 500	4 500
Bulgaria	5 600	12 700
Czech Republic	750	4 500
Denmark	3 500	7 000
Germany	20 000	:
Estonia	6 800	15 200
Ireland	2 500	4 500
Greece	2 500	4 500
Spain	2 500	5 000
France	7 000	21 000
Italy	3 500	7 500
Cyprus	500	1 500
Latvia	4 500	7 500
Lithuania	7 400	29 300
Luxembourg	500	1 500
Hungary	2 600	4 800
Malta	1 500	3 000
Netherlands	4 500	10 000
Austria	4 000	8 000
Poland	5 000	20 000
Portugal	7 500	:
Romania	6 500	11 500
Slovenia	1 000	10 500
Slovakia	2 500	4 500
Finland	2 000	4 000
Sweden	3 000	5 000
United Kingdom	10 000	:

A: threshold for publishing data.
B: threshold for reliable data.
Source: Eurostat (LFS)

Note that the LFS data used in this publication refers to information from the spring reference period, in other words, the second quarter, and not to annual averages based on four quarterly observations. There are a few exceptions that should be noted: all data from 2003 onwards for Luxembourg are based on annual averages. Up to and including 2004, the data for France and Austria refer to the first and not the second quarter of the reference year. The data for France for the second quarter of 2006 are provisional.

For more information, the methodological basis and the contents of this survey are described at the following address:
http://forum.europa.eu.int/irc/dsis/employment/info/data/eu_lfs/index.htm.

Main definitions

Employed persons: are persons aged 15 years and over (16 and over in Spain and the United Kingdom; 15 to 74 years old in Denmark, Estonia, Hungary, Latvia, Finland and Sweden) who during the reference week performed work, even for just one hour a week, for pay, profit or family gain or were not at work but had a job or business from which they were temporarily absent because of, for example, illness, holidays, industrial dispute and education and training.

Gender breakdown: information shown on those in employment is broken down according to the proportion of the workforce that is male or female.

Full-time/part-time: this variable refers to the main job. The distinction between full-time and part-time work is based on a spontaneous response by the respondent (except in the Netherlands, Iceland and Norway where part-time work is determined to be the case if the usual hours are fewer than 35 hours and full-time if the usual hours are 35 hours or more, and in Sweden where this criterion is applied to the self-employed). It is impossible to establish a more precise distinction between full-time and part-time employment, since working hours differ from one Member State to the next and from one activity to the next.

Age: the age of the respondent is calculated from the year of birth. For persons born in the same year, those whose birthdays fall between 1 January and the end of the reference week are, for the purposes of survey results analysis, regarded as being one year older than those whose birthdays fall after the end of the reference week. The presentation of data is made according to a breakdown of the proportion of those in employment according to three age groups, defined as follows: those aged less than 30 years; those aged 30 to 49 years old; and those aged 50 or more.

ABBREVIATIONS
COUNTRIES

EU-27	European Union of 27 Member States
EU-25	European Union of 25 Member States
EU-15	European Union of 15 Member States
BE	Belgium
BG	Bulgaria
CZ	the Czech Republic
DK	Denmark
DE	Germany
EE	Estonia
IE	Ireland
EL	Greece
ES	Spain
FR	France
IT	Italy
CY	Cyprus
LV	Latvia
LT	Lithuania
LU	Luxembourg
HU	Hungary
MT	Malta
NL	the Netherlands
AT	Austria
PL	Poland
PT	Portugal
RO	Romania
SI	Slovenia
SK	Slovakia
FI	Finland
SE	Sweden
UK	the United Kingdom
HR	Croatia
MK	the former Yugoslav Republic of Macedonia
TR	Turkey
IS	Iceland
NO	Norway
CH	Switzerland
JP	Japan
US	United States (of America)

INTERNATIONAL ORGANISATIONS AND TRADE ASSOCIATIONS

ACEA	Association of European Automobile Manufacturers
AEA	Association of European Airlines
APME	Association of Plastics Manufacturers
CCBE	Council of bars and law societies of Europe
CEFIC	European Chemical Industry Council
CIAA	Confederation of food and drink industries
ECMT	European conference of ministers of transport
EFAMA	European fund and asset management association
ERA	European Regions Airline Associations
EU	European Union
FESE	Federation of European Securities Exchanges
FIEC	European Construction Industry Federation
IISI	International Iron and Steel Institute
ISL	Institute of shipping economics and logistics
IUPT	International union of public transport
NAFTA	North American Free Trade Agreement
UIC	International union of railways
UPU	Universal Post Union
VDA	German motor vehicle manufacturers association
WTO	World Tourism Organization

WEIGHTS AND MEASURES

DWT	Dead weight tonnes
EUR	euro
kg	Kilogramme
km	Kilometre
toe	Tonnes of oil equivalent
TWh	Terawatt-hours
%	Percentage

OTHER ABBREVIATIONS

ASEAN	Association of south-east Asian nations
ATM	Automatic teller machine
CAP	Common Agricultural Policy
CD	Compact disc
CO_2	Carbon dioxide
CPA	Classification of products by activity
DECT	Digital Enhanced Cordless Telecommunication
DVD	Digital video disc / Digital versatile disc
EDI	Electronic data interchange
FOB	Free on board
FSAP	Financial Services Action Plan
GDP	Gross domestic product
GSM	Global system for mobile communication
HORECA	Hotels, restaurants and cafés
HRST	Human resources in science and technology
ICT	Information and communication technologies
IT	Information technology
LCD	Liquid crystal display
LFS	Labour Force Survey
LPG	Liquefied petroleum gas
NACE	Statistical classification of economic activities in the European Community
n.e.c.	Not elsewhere classified
PC	Personal computer
PWS	Public water supply
REACH	Registration, Evaluation and Authorisation of CHemicals
R&D	Research and development
RON	Research octane number
SARS	Severe acute respiratory syndrome
SBS	Structural business statistics
SME	Small and medium-sized enterprise (employing from 1 to 249 persons)
STS	Short-term business statistics
UCITS	Undertakings for collective investment in transferable securities
USP	Universal service provider
VAT	Value added tax

European Commission

European business – Facts and figures

Luxembourg: Office for Official Publications of the European Communities

2007 — 431 pp. — 21 x 29.7 cm

ISBN 978-92-79-07024-2
ISSN 1830-8147

Price (excluding VAT) in Luxembourg: EUR 25